Jeremy Bentham and Australia

To Ian,

The second part of the Bentham and Australia 1-2!

all the best,

Tim

Jeremy Bentham and Australia

Convicts, utility and empire

Edited by

Tim Causer, Margot Finn and Philip Schofield

First published in 2022 by
UCL Press
University College London
Gower Street
London WC1E 6BT

Available to download free: www.uclpress.co.uk

Text © Contributors, 2022
Collection © Editors, 2022

The authors have asserted their rights under the Copyright, Designs and Patents Act
1988 to be identified as the authors of this work.

A CIP catalogue record for this book is available from The British Library.

ISBN: 978-1-78735-820-1 (Hbk)
ISBN: 978-1-78735-819-5 (Pbk)
ISBN: 978-1-78735-818-8 (PDF)
ISBN: 978-1-78735-821-8 (epub)
ISBN: 978-1-78735-822-5 (mobi)
DOI: https://doi.org/10.14324/111.9781787358188

Contents

List of contributors

Matthew Allen is a Senior Lecturer in Historical Criminology at the University of New England, Australia. His diverse research is focused on understanding the unique and extraordinary transition of New South Wales from penal colony to responsible democracy, and the way that this process was shaped by the conflict between liberal ideals and authoritarian controls within the British world. His work on the history of alcohol, policing, summary justice and surveillance has been published in *Australian Historical Studies, History Australia,* the *Journal of Religious History,* and the *ANZ Journal of Criminology.* He is currently writing a monograph for McGill-Queens University Press, entitled *Drink and Democracy: Alcohol, Politics and Government in Colonial Australia, 1788–1856.*

Anne Brunon-Ernst is Professor in Legal English at Panthéon-Assas University (Paris, France), researcher at the Cersa (Panthéon-Assas) and at the Centre Bentham (ScPo, Paris). Her research interests focus on the British legal philosopher Jeremy Bentham. She edits the *Revue d'études benthamiennes.* Lately, her research has been centred around (i) Bentham's Panopticon schemes (Brunon-Ernst (ed.) *Beyond Foucault,* 2012), (ii) utilitarianism in Foucault's thought (Brunon-Ernst, *Utilitarian Biopolitics,* 2012) and (iii) the concept of indirect legislation both in Bentham and in its contemporary reappropriations (special issue of *History of European Ideas,* 43/1 (2017) with M. Bozzo-Rey and M. Quinn). Thanks to a fellowship at the Australian National University, she is currently working on surveillance models and Bentham's writings on Australia.

Hilary M. Carey is Professor of Imperial and Religious History at the University of Bristol. She is a religious historian with a special interest in missions and colonialism in the settler British Empire. Her books include *God's Empire* (2011) and *Empire of Hell* (2019). She is a Fellow of the Royal Historical Society, an elected Fellow of the Australian Academy of the Humanities, and a Life Fellow of Clare Hall, University of Cambridge. She is currently researching the history of missions to mariners.

Tim Causer is a Senior Research Fellow at the Bentham Project, Faculty of Laws, University College London. He is the former co-ordinator of the award-winning *Transcribe Bentham* initiative and the author of *Memorandoms by James Martin* (2017).

Edward Cavanagh was until recently an advisor to the Chancellor of the Duchy of Lancaster, in the Cabinet Office, on constitutionally significant policy proposals. Prior to this, he sought but ultimately failed to attain a meaningful academic career at the University of Edinburgh, the University of Oxford, and the University of Cambridge, after toiling – in hindsight, perhaps, too hard – with his studies at the Australian National University (2007–9), Swinburne University (2010), the University of the Witwatersrand (2011), and the University of Ottawa (2012–15). His chapter here, which was originally presented in 2019, will be his final published academic output.

Honey Dower completed her PhD at the University of Tasmania in 2021. After finishing a BA in History (Hons) in 2015, she completed an MA (History) at the Australian National University in 2017. Complementing an interest in crime, prisons, and punishments, her research focuses on the health effects of separate treatment at Pentonville Prison in the nineteenth century. She is relocating to the UK in 2022 to continue a career as a historian.

Margot Finn is Professor of Modern History at UCL and is the author of *After Chartism* (1993) and *The Character of Credit* (2003). She has published extensively on the families and material culture of the East India Company and co-edited, with Kate Smith, *The East India Company at Home* (2018). Her current monograph project is entitled *Imperial Family Formations: Domestic Strategies and Colonial Power in British India, c. 1757–1857*. From 2016–20 Margot was President of the Royal Historical Society.

Barry Godfrey is Professor of Social Justice at the University of Liverpool, beginning his career at Keele University in 1995 and leaving as Professor of Criminology in 2011. He has experience in researching comparative and historical criminology. He has published 20 sole- and co-authored books, edited collections of essays and edited special issues of several journals. He has held visiting and honorary appointments at the universities of Tasmania, Western Australia, New England, and Xi'an Jiaotong Liverpool University, is Inaugural Research Fellow of the Howard League for Penal Reform, and now works with researchers in North America, Australia, New Zealand, China and the Netherlands.

Zoë Laidlaw is Professor of History at the University of Melbourne; she previously worked at Royal Holloway University of London. A historian of British imperialism and colonialism in the nineteenth century, Zoë's publications include *Protecting the Empire's Humanity: Thomas Hodgkin and British Colonial Activism* (2021); *Colonial Connections 1815–45: Patronage, the Information Revolution and Colonial Government* (2005); and, as co-editor with Alan Lester, *Indigenous Communities and Settler Colonialism: Land Holding, Loss and Survival in an Interconnected World* (2015). Her current research projects focus on the legacies of British slave ownership in Australia and nineteenth-century imperial commissions of inquiry.

Emily Lanman is a PhD candidate at the University of Notre Dame Australia. Her broad research interest is in the institutions used in the nineteenth century to control and maintain social order in Britain and across the empire. Emily's PhD research focuses on the prisoner experience in Western Australia's prisons through the colonial period. Her Master of Philosophy thesis explored Fremantle Gaol as an example form of Jeremy Bentham's panopticon prison.

Hamish Maxwell-Stewart is a Professor of Heritage and Digital History at the University of New England, Australia. He has written many books and articles on the history of crime and health including *Unfree Workers: Insubordination and Resistance in Convict Australia 1788–1860* (Palgrave 2021) and *Closing Hell's Gates: The Death of a Penal Station* (Allen and Unwin, 2008).

Kirsten McKenzie is Professor of History at the University of Sydney. She is a Fellow of the Australian Academy of the Humanities and the Royal Historical Society. Her major publications include *Scandal in the Colonies: Sydney and Cape Town 1820–1850* (2004), *A Swindler's*

Progress: Nobles and Convicts in the Age of Liberty (2009), and *Imperial Underworld: An Escaped Convict and the Transformation of the British Colonial Order* (2016). As part of a research project led by Professor Lisa Ford (University of New South Wales) she is currently completing the manuscript for *Inquiring into Empire: Remaking the British World, 1819–1831*.

Deborah Oxley was until recently Professor of Social Science History at the University of Oxford. At College – All Souls – she was overlooked by a statue of the first Vinerian Professor of English Law, William Blackstone. Famously, Blackstone's lectures were *not* appreciated by a young student from the adjacent Queen's College, one Jeremy Bentham. Deborah's research draws on social science and biomedical methods, typically underpinned by large archival datasets. She works on health, welfare and nutrition in Britain and the Empire, the microeconomics of the household, child growth, women and economic development, migration, human capital, coercive and free labour markets, colonial economies, crime and punishment.

David Andrew Roberts is an Associate Professor of History at the University of New England, Australia, where he teaches Australian history and edits the *Journal of Australian Colonial History*. His research is funded by an Australian Research Council Discovery Project Grant titled *Inquiring into Empire* (DP18).

Katherine Roscoe is a historical criminologist at the University of Liverpool. Her Leverhulme Early Career Research Fellowship examines the role of convict labour in enabling British maritime power. She received her PhD in history from the University of Leicester in 2018. Her thesis exploring the role of carceral island in the colonization of Australia won the Boydell & Brewer doctoral dissertation prize. She has held research fellowships at the Institute of Historical Research, University of London, and the National Maritime Museum, Greenwich. From 2016, she spent two years as a transcription assistant for the Bentham Project, UCL.

Philip Schofield is Director of the Bentham Project, Faculty of Laws, University College London, and General Editor of the new authoritative edition of *The Collected Works of Jeremy Bentham*.

List of figures and tables

Figures

Tables

Acknowledgements

The editors would like to thank the Arts and Humanities Research Council, whose generous funding made possible not only this collection of essays, but also the new edition of Bentham's writings on Australia. The collection originated in a conference held at University College London's Faculty of Laws on 11–12 April 2019. We are grateful to UCL Laws for hosting the event, to Lisa Penfold and Philip Baker for advice and support in its organization, and to the conference attendees for making it such a stimulating and enjoyable event.

We would like to thank our anonymous referee for generously giving their time to review the collection for UCL Press, and for such positive, helpful, and encouraging feedback and suggestions. We would like to thank Chris Penfold, Commissioning Editor at UCL Press, for his advice and support in bringing this collection to fruition. Thanks are due to University College London Library Services's Special Collections and the National Library of Australia for permission to reproduce images held in their respective collections. Special thanks are owed to Dr Chris Riley of the Bentham Project for his sterling work on formatting the text and references.

Finally, we are incredibly grateful to the scholars who contributed to this collection, amidst all the challenges and difficulties posed by the pandemic. They have produced a body of scholarship which thoughtfully and critically engages with Bentham's writings on Australia, and which makes exciting interventions across a number of fields. Their work makes an impressive contribution to current debates and will set the agenda for future ones.

Introduction

Tim Causer

Jeremy Bentham's writings on Australia, new authoritative editions of which are now published in a volume entitled *Panopticon versus New South Wales and other writings on Australia*[1] in *The Collected Works of Jeremy Bentham*, have had a profound and enduring influence across a number of fields. For instance, according to the historian John Gascoigne, so authoritative during the nineteenth century was Bentham's critique of criminal transportation to New South Wales that 'advocates and critics of transportation ... inevitably tended to couch their arguments against a Benthamite background'.[2] Those advocates included George Arthur, Lieutenant-Governor of Van Diemen's Land 1824–36, who contended in 1833, in defence of the assignment of convicts to private masters, that 'Bentham's notion, that gaolers should possess a personal interest in the reform of the convicts under their charge, is beautifully realized in Van Diemen's Land'.[3] Critics of transportation who took the Benthamite line included Henry Grey Bennet MP, whose *Letter to Viscount Sidmouth* of 1819[4] was avowedly inspired by Bentham's work down to its title, and the philosophical radical Sir William Molesworth MP,[5] chair of the Select Committee on Transportation of 1837–8 and author of its remarkably Benthamite report.[6] The political scientist Hugh Collins, in his study of political ideology in Australia, concluded that 'the mental universe of Australian politics is essentially Benthamite',[7] while in 2019 the political historian Judith Brett, in her examination of the distinctiveness of Australian democracy, argued that if 'John Locke was the foundational thinker for the United States, for Australia it was the philosopher and political reformer, Jeremy Bentham'.[8] In a 2021 study the historian David Llewellyn contended that Bentham's influence in Australia extends to fields 'such as the construction of local government, education, electoral laws, women's empowerment, and, arguably, the character of Australian liberalism', and noted that it 'becomes apparent that Bentham's ideas have been influential in the development of Australia for almost the entire period since the arrival of the first fleet' in 1788.[9] Bentham's wide-ranging influence has thus been recognized despite scholars, at least until 2018 when the preliminary versions of the texts constituting *Panopticon versus New South Wales and other writings on Australia* appeared online,[10] having had to rely on incomplete and inadequate versions.

To give context to the chapters in this collection[11] it will be helpful here to provide a summary of the texts under discussion.[12] *Panopticon versus New South Wales and other writings on Australia* consists of the following seven works: a series of fragmentary comments headed 'New Wales', which date from 1791; a compilation of correspondence and marginal contents which Bentham had sent to the abolitionist and supporter of the panopticon, William Wilberforce, in August 1802; three 'Letters to Lord Pelham' and 'A Plea for the Constitution', which were written in 1802–3; and 'Colonization Company Proposal', written in August 1831. All but 'Colonization Company Proposal' are intimately connected with the genesis and failure of Bentham's panopticon penitentiary scheme.

Bentham was in Russia, visiting his younger brother Samuel, when he first learned of the British government's plan to establish a penal colony at Botany Bay, after his friend Richard Clark had written on 31 August 1786 informing him of the decision 'to send off seven hundred convicts to New Wales, under convoy of a man-of-war, where a fort is to be built, and a colony established, and that a man has been found who will take upon him the command of this rabble'.[13] A matter of weeks later George Wilson, another friend of Bentham's, wrote with further information that 'Government are going at last to send the convicts to Botany Bay in New Holland; the Hulks being found, by sad experience, to be academies for housebreaking, and solitary confinement to any extent, impracticable from the expense of building'.[14] In 'A View of the Hard-Labour Bill' of 1778, around a decade before the decision had been made to send convicts to Botany Bay, Bentham had already established the basis of his opposition to transportation as a criminal punishment, having found transportation to North America – which had been halted by the American War of Independence – ill-conceived on five key grounds. First, he argued that nothing could be 'more unequal than the effect which the change of country has upon men of different habits, attachments, talents, and propensities'; while some individuals were 'glad to go by choice; others would sooner die'. Second, it was an '*unexemplary*' punishment because the pain inflicted upon transportees, so far out of sight, 'was unknown to the people for whose benefit it was designed'. Third, transportation was '*unfrugal*' since it caused 'a great waste of lives ... and a great waste of money'. Fourth, transportation might result in the '*disabling* [of] the offender from doing further mischief to the community', but could not do so 'in so great a degree as the confinement incident to servitude'. Besides, Bentham thought it was 'easier for a man to return from transportation, than to escape from prison'. Fifth, it was only by chance that a convict might be reformed by being transported, since that convict was given over to 'the uncertain and variable direction of a private master, whose object was his own profit'.[15] In short, Bentham had in 1778 come to the view that the only form of punishment which could be calibrated most strictly to adhere to the principle of utility was imprisonment accompanied by hard labour.

The first work contained in *Panopticon versus New South Wales and other writings on Australia* is the hitherto unpublished 'New Wales' material. This was almost certainly written in May or June 1791 as it draws upon some House of Commons papers which Bentham had seen, and the arguments in 'New Wales' correspond with those advanced in the second panopticon 'Postscript', which was being printed at that time.[16] Bentham had, on 23 January 1791, first offered the panopticon penitentiary scheme to the Pitt administration and thereby delivered the national penitentiary for male prisoners provided for by the Penitentiary Act of 1779;[17] thus began a long, torturous, demoralizing, and ultimately unsuccessful attempt to bring his scheme to fruition. The 'New Wales' fragments appear to have been written in response to disturbing reports about the state of New South Wales, a colony which Bentham argued was a 'truly curious scene of imbecility, improvidence, and extravagance'. In Bentham's view, New South Wales was expensive, morally deleterious to the convicts sent there and, as a colony established to increase the national wealth through trade, 'the most hopeless' colony that could ever have been devised. Bentham told his friend and stoic supporter of the panopticon, Charles Bunbury MP, that he was 'strongly tempted to attempt before the public a slight picture of [New South Wales] as soon as I have a little leisure'.[18] The 'New Wales' material may have constituted Bentham's attempt to provide such a sketch, though he seems to have abandoned it fairly quickly – perhaps he had not yet understood that

New South Wales would prove to be a major obstacle to the realization of the panopticon scheme.

In 'New Wales' Bentham questioned whether New South Wales had been established primarily as a 'mode of disposing of convicted criminals' or as a 'business of colonization at large'.[19] As a punishment he found transportation useless, with a major issue being the fate of the transportees once their sentences had expired. If they were allowed to return to the British Isles, then it would undermine the security supposedly afforded by having deported them in the first place, but if they were made to remain in New South Wales, they would be, as he put it in the second panopticon 'Postscript', the victims of *false-banishment for life*'.[20] Bentham thought transportation to New South Wales posed an almost insurmountable conundrum: 'Take away the injustice & you take away the security'.[21] As a scheme of colonization, Bentham expressed his doubts about the economic advantages of colonies and colony-holding, which he subsequently expanded upon in December 1792 and January 1793 in 'Jeremy Bentham to the National Convention of France' (which he later published in 1830 as *Emancipate Your Colonies!*).[22] Bentham contended in particular that the low number of women transported doomed New South Wales to demographic failure, and if his panopticon penitentiary scheme were adopted and built, the colony would not be needed for its penal purpose either, and so a fleet might be sent to Sydney 'to re-import the whole colony at once'.[23] In addition, Bentham drafted two resolutions which neatly summarize the major themes of the 'New Wales' material: first, that no colony would ever return a profit to the colonizing power on the capital it had invested in founding, maintaining, and defending it; and second, that no colony where women were so greatly outnumbered by men could ever 'be of any use in respect to population'.[24] Bentham had perhaps drafted these resolutions with a view to asking Charles Bunbury to introduce them into the House of Commons, but there is no evidence that he showed them – or the 'New Wales' material more generally – to anyone. Though by far the least developed of all of his writings on Australia, the sketches in 'New Wales' are important for understanding the genesis of his thinking on transportation and foreshadow his later, more developed arguments.

The second work in the volume is 'Correspondence, sent to William Wilberforce, of Jeremy Bentham with Sir Charles Bunbury'. Though the construction of the panopticon had been authorized by the Penitentiary Act of 1794 and the Appropriation Act of 1799, public money had been spent on acquiring land on which to build it, and a contract between the government and Bentham to run it had been drawn up, it had become abundantly clear to Bentham by early 1802 that the government was seeking to abandon the scheme. In the course of composing 'A Picture of the Treasury' during 1801–2, in which he gave a detailed account of his dealings with the Home Office and Treasury in relation to the panopticon between 1798 and 1802, Bentham discussed what he called the 'four grounds of relinquishment' of the panopticon scheme that had been put forward in a Treasury Minute of 13 August 1800. One of these grounds was 'the improved State of the Colony of New South Wales', which he discussed with the other three in a section of 'A Picture of the Treasury'. Bentham's interest in transportation to New South Wales grew and, emerging from this section of 'A Picture of the Treasury', were three 'Letters to Lord Pelham' and 'A Plea for the Constitution', on which he spent much of his time from early 1802 to early 1803.

During late August 1802, in order to explain to Wilberforce how Charles Bunbury had been interceding with Pelham, the Home Secretary, Bentham prepared a collection of documents consisting of his correspondence with Bunbury, a note from Bentham to Pelham, and the marginal contents of a draft of 'Letter to Lord Pelham'.[25] On 11 August 1802 Bentham asked Bunbury to pass to Pelham a two-page outline of the first 'Letter to Lord Pelham', but with a warning that if Pelham failed to reply by 18 August 1802 then Bentham would publish the work, thereby revealing the government's shabby conduct towards himself as well as exposing the reality of conditions in New South Wales to the public.[26] Pelham had not replied by 17 August 1802 but, after a reminder from Bunbury, did so on 19 August 1802 with a promise that he would investigate 'what steps have been taken by the Treasury' in relation to the panopticon, and 'endeavour to get something settled before the meeting of Parliament'.[27] Bentham believed that Pelham was merely continuing the administration's policy of manufactured delay in regard to the panopticon and, when Bunbury met Pelham on 30 September 1802 to discuss what steps the Home Secretary would take 'in the Business of the Panopticon Prison', Pelham replied that he would do so once he had 'read through [Bentham's] Books, and conversed with the chancellor, and the Judges on the Subject'.[28] It was this exchange that prompted Bentham to organize the printing of 'Letter to Lord Pelham', the private distribution of which he hoped would rescue the panopticon.

'Letter to Lord Pelham', the third work in the volume, which Bentham had completed the printing of in November 1802, is a superb work of rhetoric and constitutes the first detailed philosophical critique of criminal transportation to Australia – though, as will be discussed below by Matthew Allen and David Andrew Roberts, Bentham's use of evidence in making his case against New South Wales requires thorough interrogation. Though it had little impact during Bentham's own lifetime, 'Letter to Lord Pelham' proved to be a major influence upon the anti-transportation campaigns of the 1830s and 1840s. Building upon and refining the arguments against transportation which he had first set out in 'A View of the Hard-Labour Bill' and 'New Wales', and mining the first volume of David Collins's *Account of the English Colony in New South Wales* as source material, Bentham arranged the text of 'Letter to Lord Pelham' around 'five ends of penal justice', namely (i) example; (ii) reformation; (iii) incapacitation; (iv) compensation; and (v) economy. Unsurprisingly, Bentham found that New South Wales fell far short of meeting each end, whereas the panopticon would achieve, and indeed exceed, each one.

In the first instance, Bentham argued that transportation to New South Wales provided no exemplary punishment since it removed criminals 'as far as possible out of the view of the aggregate mass of individuals' upon whom the deterrent effect was supposed to operate, unlike the panopticon which would be built in the imperial metropolis. Second, Bentham was of the view that reformation was impossible without systematic inspection, which in the panopticon would be 'carried to such a degree of perfection, as till then had never been reached even by imagination, much less by practice'. In New South Wales, meanwhile, convicts had been dispersed across the colony and worked 'altogether out of the habitual reach of every *inspecting eye*'. Third, the incapacitation of convicts from reoffending in Britain was imperfect because significant numbers had returned home, either by absconding or after the expiry of their sentences. Fourth, transporting a criminal to New South Wales provided no compensation or restitution to injured parties, whereas convict labour in a panopticon might be arranged for that purpose. Fifth, Bentham argued that transportation would always be more expensive than a regime of imprisonment and surveillance and that, as a colony, New South Wales would never return the capital expended upon it. New South Wales was, he concluded, doomed to fail.[29]

In the fourth work in the volume, 'Second Letter to Lord Pelham', which Bentham had printed in December 1802, he used the second volume of Collins's *Account of the English Colony in New South Wales* to provide further evidence of the ongoing and profound failure of the penal colony to meet the five ends of penal justice. Bentham contrasted

Collins's reports of drunkenness, arson, murder, and violence in New South Wales, as well as warfare with its Indigenous peoples, with reports of sobriety, order, and industry in the penitentiaries of Pennsylvania and New York which, being run according to regimes of hard labour and close inspection, were in these respects perhaps the closest existing approximation of the panopticon penitentiary. In the fifth work in the volume, 'Third Letter to Lord Pelham', which Bentham wrote in late 1802 and early 1803, but of which only the first few pages were printed, he turned his attention to the hulks, the other major punishment available to the British criminal justice system. Bentham focused upon conditions aboard the hulks at Portsmouth and Langstone harbours, and especially the fearsome mortality rate there, for which he blamed ministers and their underlings at the Home Office and Treasury for having conspired to have the panopticon scheme set aside. Bentham's point was that prisoners who should have been sent to a panopticon penitentiary were instead crowded into already unsuitable local gaols and hulks, with disastrous results for their health and morality. In addition, Bentham claimed that the office of Inspector of the Hulks had been created both as a sinecure for a friend of a Home Office official and, rather than to expose and reform the evils of the south coast hulks created by the setting aside of the panopticon scheme, to cover them up.

Though Bentham had in September 1802 stated that the 'Letters to Lord Pelham' dealt with New South Wales 'on the question of policy',[30] he had concluded the first 'Letter to Lord Pelham' with a broad and serious claim that '*military despotism*' had been planted in New South Wales, and that the colony was a 'vast conservatory of military law', odious 'to the sense of every Briton'.[31] Bentham expanded upon this theme in the sixth work in the volume, 'A Plea for the Constitution', which he printed in 1803 and in which he brought arguments about the illegality of the colonial regime to the fore. He found that, having not been sanctioned by Parliament, New South Wales had been illegally founded, and that certain of the powers assumed and ordinances issued by the colony's governors had no legal basis, and so neither did any punishments inflicted upon individuals in the colony for having violated them. Bentham thought that his findings concerning the illegality of the government of New South Wales were not only shocking, but potentially very dangerous: he initially did not make them widely known, as he told his brother Samuel in July 1802, for fear that the 'natural consequence' of doing so would be the 'setting of the whole colony in a flame' by its resentful convict population.[32] The subversive nature of 'A

Plea for the Constitution' was also recognized by Charles Bunbury, one of the very few to whom Bentham showed the work, who warned him that publishing it would 'bring upon you Enemies irreconcileable, and procure you Friends only amongst the Malefactors of new South Wales'. Bunbury suggested to Bentham that if he were to fail to 'write down the Colony of Thieves at Port Jackson, and annihilate it by Argument' then he should not 'crush it by Rebellion'.[33]

Though Bentham followed Bunbury's advice and did not publish the 'Letters to Lord Pelham' and 'A Plea for the Constitution' in 1802 and 1803, he believed that, being armed with them, he had sufficient ammunition not only to pressure the government into proceeding with the panopticon scheme, but perhaps even to cause the abandonment of New South Wales. (Bentham had suggested, with some bravado, to his brother Samuel in August 1802 at the outset of his campaign against the colony that he might even effect 'the evacuation of that scene of wickedness and wretchedness'.[34]) Bentham was ultimately to be disappointed in both instances: in June 1803 he was informed that the government would not proceed with the panopticon, while the transportation of convicts continued to New South Wales until 1840, to Van Diemen's Land until 1853, and to Western Australia from 1850 until 1868.[35] The panopticon scheme's failure meant that Bentham had no further use for these works until revived interest in building a national penitentiary led to the appointment of a Select Committee of the House of Commons in 1811, chaired by George Holford. Encouraged in particular by Wilberforce that the panopticon scheme might now be favourably received, Bentham finally published 'Letter to Lord Pelham', 'Second Letter to Lord Pelham', and 'A Plea for the Constitution' in a single volume, with the self-explanatory title of *Panopticon versus New South Wales*. The Holford Committee, however, decisively rejected both the panopticon and Bentham's principles of convict management, and its recommendations led to the construction of Millbank Penitentiary, which opened in 1817 having been built upon the land that had been purchased for the panopticon.

Subsequently Bentham did not exhibit much interest in Australian matters until towards the end of his life. In 'Colonization Company Proposal', the seventh and final work in the volume, of which Bentham produced an incomplete draft in August 1831, he commented supportively on the National Colonization Society's proposal to establish a free colony on the southern coast of the Australian continent. Bentham appears to have been prompted to consider the proposal by Edward Gibbon Wakefield, the originator of 'systematic colonization' – that is, colonization by means of the sale of appropriated land to free emigrants, who would settle in a colony of concentrated settlements which would be granted self-government as soon as was practicable. Bentham suggested that any new colony should be arranged on what he called the 'vicinity-maximizing principle', whereby land would be sold to potential emigrants in lots which radiated in an orderly pattern from the main settlement, rather than being allowed to proceed in a disorderly manner as had been the case with New South Wales. The colony would be founded and initially overseen by a joint-stock company, though it would make the transition to representative democracy within a few years – a representative democracy ideally arranged around the principles of Bentham's *Constitutional Code*.

The contributors to this volume were asked to reflect on these seven texts, though they have in many instances ranged more widely across Bentham's corpus – shedding further contextual light on his writings on Australia.

The chapters in this volume are arranged into four thematic parts, which deal broadly with the following topics: first, the historical context in which Bentham wrote on Australia; second, Bentham's views and their intersection with the theory and practice of criminal transportation to and in the Australian penal colonies; third, the constitutional implications of Bentham's writings on Australia; and fourth, the intersection of Bentham's writings with penal institutions and practices in Britain and Australia.

Part I, 'The historical context of Bentham's writings on Australia', begins with Deborah Oxley's chapter entitled 'Bentham and the criminal fiscal state'. Oxley sites Bentham's writings on criminal transportation, and criminal justice more generally, in the context of long-term economic growth in Britain and its empire. Concomitant to this growth was the rise of a powerful fiscal state which was required to manage it, as well as that state's desire to punish, and punish systematically, apparently increasing numbers of criminal offenders. Oxley notes the mercantilism inherent in the Transportation Act of 1718, which provided for the private shipping of offenders to North America and, indeed, the dominance of private provision in the criminal justice system more generally until the end of the eighteenth century, when the loss of the American colonies prompted thought about what might replace transportation and the ramshackle local gaol system. The drive for a national penitentiary, the establishment of the hulks, and perhaps most of all the settlement of New South Wales, all demonstrated a profound shift from the 'outsourcing' of criminal justice to greater state involvement and control. Oxley suggests that Bentham's panopticon penitentiary scheme could never have been seriously considered without the growth in the state's fiscal capital – some of which Bentham sought to capture through his entrepreneurial prison scheme – and the state's willingness to spend more of that capital on the criminal justice system.

In the second chapter, 'Bentham, convict transportation, and the Great Confinement Thesis', Hamish Maxwell-Stewart discusses what has become the standard account of the development of forms of criminal justice in Britain. According to the 'great confinement thesis', a narrative dominated by the history of prisons and penitentiaries, there is a more or less uninterrupted line of progress in criminal punishment, from the judicial violence inflicted by early modern states to the development in the eighteenth century of state bureaucracies incorporating systems of surveillance. Considerable attention in this transition is paid to Bentham's panopticon penitentiary scheme and, perhaps more especially, Michel Foucault's mediation of it. Maxwell-Stewart notes that on the one hand Bentham's abortive scheme became associated with the development of 'modern' penal institutions, while on the other his opposition to convict transportation 'helped to associate the overseas deployment of convict labour with the use of the whip and other outmoded forms of punishment', thereby rendering transportation a 'historical curiosity' that somehow persisted into the nineteenth century 'by accident rather than design'. In response to the 'great confinement thesis', Maxwell-Stewart examines Bentham's critique of criminal transportation against the data to illustrate the ways in which his arguments have shaped subsequent discussions. Particular attention is paid to Bentham's claims about inequalities in the sentencing of convicts and their treatment in New South Wales, and his contention that the panopticon would have been considerably cheaper, and more effectual in meeting the ends of punishment, than the penal colony.

Maxwell-Stewart builds on this discussion to undermine two key planks of the 'great confinement thesis', namely that, first, 'a direct developmental pathway can be traced between the establishment of the bridewell in the late sixteenth century and the rise of the penitentiary', and second, that criminal transportation overseas was 'decisively rejected in the first half of the nineteenth century in favour of the penitentiary'. In fact, he argues, 'the notion that penal transportation operated in opposition to the aims of the panopticon' is 'a fiction', finding instead that the 'carceral archipelago in its colonial guise' contained 'a system of overlapping panoptic devices' to be found in the convict ship, in the paperwork which accompanied each convict to the penal colonies, and in the detailed surveilling documentation generated in Van Diemen's Land in particular to afford strict control over convicts. 'This colonial panopticon', Maxwell-Stewart argues, 'had the power to peer into smoke-filled taverns and under beds in private households' and was used both to maximize convict labour, while also policing convict sexual behaviour – particularly that of women convicts – and family formation, extending 'far beyond anything that Bentham had in mind'.

The third chapter '"Confinement", "banishment", and "bondage": contesting practices of exile in the British Empire', by Kirsten McKenzie, begins Part II on 'Bentham and the theory and practice of transportation to Australia'. McKenzie discusses the conflation identified by Bentham, in the practice of transportation to New South Wales, of three distinct forms of punishment, the use of each of which had a long history in the British Isles. By 'confinement' Bentham meant the convict's inability to leave a penal colony once transported there; by 'banishment' he meant a convict's forced exile from their place of residence; and by 'bondage' he meant a convict being put to forced labour while under a sentence of transportation. These distinctions, McKenzie argues, can be taken 'as a starting point to discuss a wider set of controversies over the legal foundations of forced removal at the turn of the nineteenth century and beyond', which had consequences 'for both the British imperial state and those subjected to its disciplinary practices'. While recent scholarship has explored the functional illegality of aspects of Australian transportation prior to the 1820s, McKenzie finds that 'Bentham's early identification of the problem has not received sustained attention', especially in regard to the British government's use in New South Wales of transportation legislation that had been formulated to provide for the shipping of convicts by merchants to North America. McKenzie then applies Bentham's critique to several case studies, most especially that of the 'Scottish Martyrs', five men transported to New South Wales in 1794 and 1795 – in questionable legal circumstances – for sedition. That the Martyrs were convicted in Scotland, where the crime of sedition was largely unknown in Scots law, only further complicated the meanings of confinement, banishment, and bondage, and led to hesitation among colonial and metropolitan officials concerning the Martyrs' precise status in the colony and how they should be treated. McKenzie concludes that, though Bentham's arguments about the competing meanings of confinement, banishment, and bondage never gained widespread notice in his lifetime, he had nevertheless identified distinctions that 'would lie at the basis for the battles over how transportation worked for the entire period of its operation', and that his ideas found 'quotidian expression in a law-infused world in which even ordinary people could, and did, draw on the gap between metropolitan legal theory and colonial practice to push their own agendas'.

In the fourth chapter, 'Would Western Australia have met Bentham's five measures of penal justice?', Katherine Roscoe and Barry Godfrey turn to Western Australia, the final Australian penal colony to be established, which received almost 10,000 convicts between 1850 and 1868. First, Roscoe and Godfrey apply Bentham's 'five ends of penal justice' – the critical standard by which he had judged New South Wales – to Western Australia to ask whether Bentham's objections still held true about transportation when operating in a different temporal and geographical context. Second, they examine the system of surveillance embedded in the Western Australian convict system, which held echoes of a '"panoptic eye" that was capable of monitoring behaviour (and inculcating self-governmentality)'. They find that Bentham's five 'ends of penal justice' were more applicable not to the system designed for transported convicts, but rather to the imprisonment of Indigenous Australians – who barely feature in his writings on Australia (a topic examined in detail by Zoë Laidlaw below). Through the prism of Bentham's five ends Roscoe and Godfrey examine the treatment of Whadjuk Noongar people imprisoned upon Wadjemup – named Rottnest Island by colonists – for resisting settler encroachment upon their lands. (Wadjemup is also discussed in Emily Lanman's chapter below). Roscoe and Godfrey conclude that transportation to Western Australia did not meet Bentham's standards for a utilitarian system of criminal punishment, but nor would the panopticon, and nor has any subsequent system of incarceration put into place. Nevertheless, they find that criminal transportation made Western Australia an economically viable British colony, but with deleterious effects upon the traditional owners of the land on which the colony was founded.

In the fifth chapter, '"Inspection, the only effective instrument of reformative management": Bentham, surveillance, and convict recidivism in early New South Wales', Matthew Allen and David Andrew Roberts note the centrality of surveillance in Bentham's thinking on punishment, without which criminals could neither be reformed nor prevented from reoffending. In the case of New South Wales, they argue, Bentham's 'theorising rested on weak foundations because [he] had not visited and did not understand the penal colony'. Moreover,

Bentham's picture of New South Wales as beset by drunkenness, violence, and corruption was contradicted by contemporary accounts – not least David Collins's *Account of the English Colony in New South Wales*, on which Bentham chiefly relied – which presented a 'much more nuanced view of the challenge of reforming convicts'. Allen and Roberts examine Bentham's work on criminal justice to establish how he conceptualized reformation and recidivism, and how he applied that standard to New South Wales in the 'Letters to Lord Pelham' and 'A Plea for the Constitution'. They then turn to examine Bentham's use of Collins's *Account* in drawing up his critique of reformation and recidivism in the penal colony, finding that his 'flawed approach to his evidence fatally undermines his claims'. According to Allen and Roberts, Bentham 'lacked insight into Collins's position and the actual operation of the colony' and the circumstances of the fledgling settlement, while his choice of evidence was selective and tendentious. For instance, 'it is unsurprising' Allen and Roberts suggest, given Collins's role as judge advocate, 'that crime and its consequences feature heavily in the *Account*'. These reports were grist to Bentham's mill, yet Bentham ignored instances of reformation, as well as colonial surveillance measures such as the institution of a night watch of sorts in Sydney, regular musters, and a system of certificates and passes; Allen and Roberts note that Bentham 'tellingly ignored' Collins's questioning whether 'many streets in the metropolis of London were not so well guarded and watched' as those of Sydney. They conclude that when Bentham was writing, New South Wales was in fact 'a remarkably effective reformatory, with relatively low rates of recidivism, precisely because the convicts were not under surveillance', and were allowed a measure of independence 'that allowed them to reintegrate into society, or at least integrate into a new one'.

In the sixth chapter, 'Jeremy Bentham and the imperial constitution at the meridian, 1763–1815: legislature, judicature, and office in the administration of England and the British Empire', which begins Part III on 'The constitutional implications of Bentham's writings on Australia', Edward Cavanagh discusses the imperial constitutional ramifications of Bentham's writings on Australia, siting the works amid a revolution in the organization of the British administrative state. Cavanagh's particular focus is upon 'A Plea for the Constitution', which, he argues, goes beyond questioning the legality of the foundation of New South Wales and contends with significant issues at the very heart of the imperial constitution, with Bentham making important criticisms of the law of conquest and acquisition of colonies, and of the crown's presumption to legislate for colonies without Parliament. Moreover, Cavanagh places Bentham's writings in their domestic British context, building upon the work of L.J. Hume and Philip Schofield, on Bentham's ideas about bureaucracy and politics respectively, thereby emphasizing 'the importance of the imperial constitution, and the place of New South Wales within it, for providing a language to facilitate the furtherance of Bentham's thinking on legislature, on judicature – and, above all, on office'. Cavanagh ties Bentham's writings on Australia and the failure of the panopticon penitentiary scheme to his later project of reform of the British establishment, with 'A Plea for the Constitution' emerging as a particularly important work in the evolution of his thinking. As Cavanagh concludes, while 'it is accurate to say that empire was no longer at the forefront of [Bentham's] mind in the period between 1804 and 1819', when he turned his attention to the reformation of the British state 'it is inaccurate to say that empire had entirely left his mind'.

Chapter seven, '"The British Constitution Conquered in New South Wales": Bentham and constitutional reform in early Australia, 1803–24' by Anne Brunon-Ernst, examines the impact of 'A Plea for the Constitution' in the shaping of early European Australian politics up to the passage of the New South Wales Act of 1823. A key theme is the text's subversive and potentially politically dangerous nature, as illustrated by its apparent intellectual inspiration for some of the participants in the coup of 1808 in which Governor William Bligh was deposed by the New South Wales Corps. Bentham contended, Brunon-Ernst notes, that in the absence of the necessary legislation or of a representative assembly, New South Wales had been illegally and unconstitutionally founded, and that these arguments of Bentham's are evident in the constitutional making of the Australian colonies. Crucially, however, Brunon-Ernst argues that Bentham's ideas were not transmitted to New South Wales directly, but mediated by the lawyer and politician, and Bentham's close friend, Samuel Romilly, who chaired the Select Committee on Transportation of 1812. Brunon-Ernst concludes that Bentham's influence, channelled by Romilly, is subsequently exhibited in the reports of 1822–3 of John Thomas Bigge, who had been commissioned by the Colonial Office to examine the transportation system and arrangements for the government of New South Wales, and many of whose recommendations were enshrined in the New South Wales Act.

In the eighth chapter, 'Jeremy Bentham on South Australia, colonial government, and representative democracy', Philip Schofield focuses on 'Colonization Company Proposal', Bentham's commentary on the National Colonization Society's plan to establish a free colony on the south coast of Australia. Schofield summarizes both the Society's prospectus as well as Bentham's commentary, which sought to ensure that any such colony would be based on utilitarian principles – and that control of it should move as soon as practicable from the joint-stock company that funded it to the establishment of representative institutions (and, ideally, institutions arranged around his own democratic blueprint in *Constitutional Code*). Schofield notes that there is seemingly a 'puzzle' posed by 'Colonization Company Proposal': how could Bentham advocate the establishment of a colony in South Australia, when he has acquired a reputation for holding generally anti-colonial views? In his two main works on the topic, *Emancipate Your Colonies!* (written 1792–3) and 'Rid Yourselves of Ultramaria' (written 1822), Bentham had argued that the colonizing power always lost out economically by gaining, holding, and defending colonies, while also recognizing that they were a cause of military conflict, despotism, unfair taxation, and political corruption in both the colonial and imperial spheres. Schofield finds, however, that 'Colonization Company Proposal' is in fact consistent with Bentham's early writings on colonies, noting that he 'does not seem ever to have opposed colonization and colony-holding outright'. Schofield assesses the contention by Edward Gibbon Wakefield that he had 'converted' Bentham to seeing utility in colonization, and identifies and contextualizes instances where, in Bentham's view, establishing and holding colonies 'would be beneficial on the whole', though such benefits were generally felt by those living in the colonies, rather than in the mother country. Schofield suggests that such instances would be where, to relieve population pressures in the colonizing power, supposedly 'vacant lands' elsewhere might be appropriated, or where, in Bentham's opinion, the happiness of the people in a colonized land would be better served by being ruled by Europeans than by ruling themselves. 'Even when Bentham had turned to political radicalism', Schofield argues, Bentham 'did not condemn either colonization or colony-holding outright', and concludes by noting that almost entirely absent in 'Colonization Company Proposal' is 'any consideration of the Indigenous people whose interests might be affected by the establishment of the proposed colony', despite being well aware of their existence. Since it was a 'fundamental principle of Bentham's utilitarianism that each person was to count for one and no one for more than one', Schofield argues, it was 'not only inconsistent but also morally wrong' of Bentham to have failed to 'give due weight to the welfare of indigenous people' – a topic taken up in the next chapter.

In the ninth chapter, '"Peopling the country by unpeopling it': Jeremy Bentham's silences on Indigenous Australia', Zoë Laidlaw examines the long debate on Bentham's views on colonies and colonization, which has generally tended to enhance Bentham's reputation as a major critic of colonies and colony-holding. Laidlaw takes the new edition of *Panopticon versus New South Wales and other writings on Australia* in order to address a key, but hitherto largely unaddressed, issue in this debate: the absence of the Indigenous peoples of Australia, the Americas, and Africa both from Bentham's works on colonization as well as in the debate around his views on the topic. First, Laidlaw addresses the historiographical debate, arguing 'that scholars' preoccupation with delineating Bentham's "authentic" views on colonization from those better known to his nineteenth-century audience, has insulated their analysis from profound shifts affecting the historians of colonialism more broadly'. Second, Laidlaw examines Bentham's writings on Australia for the presence and absence of Indigenous Australian peoples and reveals Bentham's 'enduring – and unacknowledged – support for British *settler* colonialism and explores how and why he denied Indigenous sovereignty'. By so doing, Laidlaw argues, the opportunity is created 'to reassess Bentham's contributions to international law, the intellectual foundations of settler colonialism, and colonialism's political, historical, and historiographical legacies'.

In chapter ten, 'Inverting the panopticon: Van Diemen's Land and the invention of a colonial Pentonville Prison', which begins Part IV on 'Bentham, the panopticon penitentiary scheme, and penal institutions and practices in Australia and Britain', Honey Dower discusses the implementation, at the Port Arthur Separate Prison in 1851, of a colonial adaptation of the metropolitan model penitentiary at Pentonville. The system of prison discipline known as 'separate treatment', which had been developed at Pentonville, was a regime based upon isolating, silencing, and controlling prisoners who had been sentenced to transportation, as means to their reformation. 'Rightly or wrongly', Dower notes, Pentonville has been 'conceptually linked' to Bentham's panopticon scheme, and she argues that any discussion of systems of imprisonment must 'test the disparity between genuflection to penal reform philosophies in comparison to its harsh lived reality'. Dower seeks to 'invert' the panopticon, focusing not on the experiences of the Separate Prison's inmates, but on the policies implemented by the architects of the colonial model prison, John Stephen Hampton (1810–69), Comptroller-General of Convicts in Van Diemen's Land from 1847–55, and his protégé James Boyd (1815–1900), Commandant of the Port Arthur penal station. Dower discusses the architecture of the Separate Prison, its system of management, and how and why 'separate treatment' gained a foothold in Van Diemen's Land, siting it in the context of a decline in the use of corporal punishment in the colony. Perhaps more important is that the use of separate treatment in the 'colonial Pentonville' is inextricably linked with the rising influence of the anti-transportation campaign of the 1840s and 1850s, where colonial anxieties about convict sexual behaviour were manifested alongside the apparent need to control those who committed or were suspected of having committed 'unnatural crime'. Dower finds that Boyd and Hampton persisted with separate treatment in spite of its ill effects on the Separate Prison's inmates, and that the 'experimental colonial milieu could be readily exploited by those in power' for their own material gain.

In the eleventh chapter, 'The panopticon archetype and the Swan River Colony: establishing Fremantle Gaol, 1831–41', Emily Lanman discusses another Australian penal landmark, the Fremantle Gaol at the Swan River Colony. Lanman examines the gaol in its local context, while also suggesting that it represents a colonial reinterpretation of Bentham's penitentiary scheme. The links between the panopticon and Fremantle Gaol are, however, stronger than other apparently panopticon-inspired institutions, being flesh and blood as well as brick and mortar – the building having been designed by Henry Reveley, the son of Willey Reveley, who had worked with Jeremy and Samuel Bentham to produce plans and sketches of a panopticon penitentiary. Lanman makes the case that Fremantle Gaol, like the panopticon, was intended to fulfil multiple institutional roles – asylum, hospital, poor house, and prison – and indeed had to, being Swan River's first permanent structure and therefore having a crucial role in the colony's development. Lanman describes the similarities and divergences between Fremantle Gaol and Bentham's original design, in terms of its construction, management, treatment of prisoners, and labour regimes, with the greatest divergence being in the use of 'auxiliary punishments' within the prison. Bentham had expected that these would have been rendered essentially unnecessary in the panopticon, whereas they were vital to the disciplining of convicts in Fremantle Gaol, and in the colony more generally. Lanman looks in particular at the use of transportation at Swan River, where Europeans convicted and sentenced at Swan River were transported to Van Diemen's Land or New South Wales, whereas the Whadjuk Noongar people, the traditional owners of the land, caught up in the British criminal justice system for acts of resistance, were exiled to Wadjemup (Rottnest Island), where they were subjected to a system of discipline which in principle was similar to that enacted at Fremantle Gaol, but was in practice rather different. Lanman concludes that though Fremantle Gaol does, in many respects, conform to 'the core principles of Bentham's panopticon', the deviations are due to its 'being a colonial response to the archetype'.

In the twelfth chapter, 'Religion and penal reform in the Australian writings of Jeremy Bentham', Hilary M. Carey discusses Bentham's writings on Australia and the panopticon penitentiary in relation to the reform of criminals where, pragmatically, he 'seems to have assumed institutional religion had a part to play'. First, Carey examines Bentham's wider religious scepticism in both his published and unpublished writings, where he was concerned with two key questions: was religion useful, and was it true? In regard to the panopticon penitentiary scheme, Carey finds that, in his detailed 1791 plan, Bentham 'never suggested that penal institutions should be entirely secular and appeared comfortable with conceding the moral regulation of the panopticon to a Christian chaplain', having incorporated a chapel into the design to appeal to religiously minded government ministers. Carey then reflects on Bentham's discussion of religion in his writings on Australia, finding that Bentham's criticism of the colony's first clergymen is somewhat unjustified, largely owing to his reliance on David Collins's *Account*, whose own view of their efforts was indifferent at best. Second, Carey turns to the topic of 'Bentham and Christian Utilitarianism', noting that though Bentham's writings give 'little reason to question his uncompromising scepticism about the function of religion in society', his position – at least in respect to penal reform – is in fact more nuanced. Carey points out, first 'Bentham's unwavering respect for Christian penal reformers, above all John Howard', and second his long-term collaboration over the panopticon, and warm friendship, with William Wilberforce. Carey argues that though it had a distinct 'anti-clerical edge, Bentham's secular vision was not incompatible with that of the Quakers, Unitarians and Congregationalists who adhered to Rational Dissent', with agreement on matters such as classification of prisoners, healthy prison conditions, opportunities for profitable labour within prisons, and opposition to solitary confinement. Carey concludes, however, that the direction taken from the 1830s by secular and Christian utilitarians in relation to penal reform, as embodied in the separation of prisoners in Millbank and Pentonville and the probation system implemented in Van Diemen's Land, would ultimately have disappointed

Bentham for having 'attempted to legislate for morality and education' as the price to be paid for 'reformatory sentencing'.

In the thirteenth chapter, 'The panopticon penitentiary, the convict hulks, and political corruption: Jeremy Bentham's "Third Letter to Lord Pelham"', Tim Causer turns to a hitherto unpublished and little-known work in which Bentham examines the convict hulks, the third major plank – alongside transportation and domestic imprisonment – of the British criminal justice system. (Though established on a temporary basis in 1776, the hulks endured in Britain until 1857.) Causer examines Bentham's views on the hulks as a system of punishment, and demonstrates that they played a significant, though underappreciated, role in the origins and failure of the panopticon penitentiary scheme. First, Causer explores Bentham's written remarks on the hulks, including his visit to the Woolwich hulks in January 1778 and his attempt in 1798 to secure, as compensation for the ongoing delay by the British government in bringing the panopticon to fruition, the hulk contract for himself and build a wooden, temporary panopticon on the Thames. Second, Causer addresses the allegations Bentham makes in 'Third Letter to Lord Pelham' about conditions aboard the hulks, which he argues were caused by the decision of ministers and their underlings in the Home Office and Treasury to kill off the panopticon scheme, despite its construction having twice been authorized by statute and large amounts of public money having been spent in preparing for its construction. Bentham pays particular attention to the appointment in 1802 of the London magistrate Aaron Graham as Inspector of the Hulks. Bentham believed that Graham was a tool of the Home Office, corruptly appointed in order to keep conditions aboard the hulks hidden from the public. Finally, Causer puts Bentham's allegations about Graham and the circumstances of his appointment to the test against the archival record finding that, contrary to Bentham's claims that Graham was but a 'sleepy guardian' of the hulks, he had carried out police work for the Home Office for some time, and had overseen the reorganization of the south coast hulks prior to his appointment as Inspector in 1802. Causer concludes that 'Third Letter to Lord Pelham' reveals Bentham as an important early critic of the hulks, contributes to the understanding of the history of the panopticon scheme, and contains the seeds of Bentham's later critique of office-holding and patronage.

The essays in this collection thus range across topics including, but not limited to, the histories of criminal transportation, settler colonialism, and Indigenous history – a testament to the ongoing relevance of Bentham's writings on Australia and his work more generally. It is hoped that this collection of essays, as the first collective body of scholarship based upon the new edition of *Panopticon versus New South Wales and other writings on Australia*, will further stimulate work on these writings.

NOTE TO THE READER

In the following chapters, all emphases are in the original unless otherwise stated. Where the title of a work of Bentham's is given in quotation marks, this indicates one of three possibilities: first, that the work exists only in manuscript; second, that the work was printed by Bentham, but not published; and third, that the work is a constituent text in either the Bowring edition of *The Works of Jeremy Bentham* or the new authoritative edition of *The Collected Works of Jeremy Bentham*.

Notes

1   Bentham, ed. Causer and Schofield 2022. The title follows that of Bentham 1812, the compilation he published containing 'Letter to Lord Pelham', 'Second Letter to Lord Pelham', and 'A Plea for the Constitution'.
2   Gascoigne with Curthoys 2002, 125–6.
3   *Commons Sessional Papers* (1837), vol. xix, 375.
4   Bennet 1819. Bennet was MP for Shrewsbury 1806–7, 1811–26.
5   Molesworth was MP for East Cornwall 1832–7, Leeds 1837–41, and Southwark 1845–55, and Secretary of State for the Colonies 1855.
6   *Commons Sessional Papers* (1837), vol. xix; *Commons Sessional Papers* (1837–8), vol. xxii.
7   Collins 1985, 148.
8   Brett 2019, 6.
9   Llewellyn 2021.
10 Causer 2018.
11 This collection of essays arises from a conference organized by the Bentham Project and held at University College London's Faculty of Laws on 11–12 April 2019. The conference, as well as the wider project which allowed for the preparation and editing of these foundational texts, was funded by the Arts and Humanities Research Council, grant agreement AH/M009548/1. Professor Philip Schofield was the principal investigator, Professor Margot Finn the co-investigator, and Dr Tim Causer the researcher.
12 For further detail on these, see the Editorial Introduction to Bentham, ed. Causer and Schofield 2022.
13 Clark to Bentham, 31 August 1786, in Bentham, ed. Christie 1971, 488.
14 Wilson to Bentham, 24 September 1786, in Bentham, ed. Christie 1971, 491.
15 Bentham 1778, 2–4, 108–9 (reproduced in Bentham, ed. Bowring 1838–43, iv. 1–35, at 6–7, 31–2).
16 Bentham 1791, iii. 224–7 (reproduced in Bentham, ed. Bowring 1838–43, iv. 169–70).
17 Bentham to Pitt, 23 January 1791, in Bentham, ed. Milne 1981, 223–4.
18 Bentham to Bunbury, 6 May 1793, in Bentham, ed. Milne 1981, 279.
19 'New Wales' in Bentham, ed. Causer and Schofield 2022, 14.
20 Bentham 1791, iii. 226 n. (reproduced in Bentham, ed. Bowring 1838–43, iv. 170 n).
21 'New Wales' in Bentham, ed. Causer and Schofield 2022, 20 & n.

22 Bentham 1793; Bentham 1830 (reproduced in Bentham, ed. Schofield, Pease-Watkin, and Blamires 2002, 289–315).
23 Bentham 1791, iii. 228 n. (reproduced in Bentham, ed. Bowring 1838–43, iv. 228 n).
24 'New Wales' in Bentham, ed. Causer and Schofield 2022, 22.
25 Bentham's correspondence with Bunbury was published in Bentham, ed. Dinwiddy 1988, but appears for the first time in the format in which Bentham had compiled it in Bentham, ed. Causer and Schofield 2022, 25–55.
26 Bentham to Bunbury, 11 August 1802, in Bentham, ed. Causer and Schofield 2022, 33–4.
27 Pelham to Bunbury, 19 August 1802, in Bentham, ed. Causer and Schofield 2022, 36–7.
28 Bunbury to Bentham, 30 September 1802, in Bentham, ed. Dinwiddy 1988, 137.
29 'Letter to Lord Pelham' in Bentham, ed. Causer and Schofield 2022, 75–7.
30 Bentham to Charles Abbot, 3 September 1802, in Bentham, ed. Dinwiddy 1988, 105.
31 'Letter to Lord Pelham' in Bentham, ed. Causer and Schofield 2022, 163.
32 Bentham to Samuel Bentham, c. 21 August 1802, in Bentham, ed. Dinwiddy 1988, 90.
33 Bunbury to Bentham, 6 June 1803, in Bentham, ed. Dinwiddy 1988, 236.
34 Bentham to Samuel Bentham, c. 21 August 1802, in Bentham, ed. Dinwiddy 1988, 90.
35 For an account of Bentham's unsuccessful attempt to use the 'Letters to Lord Pelham' and 'A Plea for the Constitution' to force the administration to proceed with the panopticon scheme, see Causer 2019.

Bibliography

Primary Sources

Parliamentary papers

Commons Sessional Papers (1837), vol. xix. 1–755: 'Report from the Select Committee on Transportation; Together with the Minutes of Evidence, Appendix, and Index', 14 July 1837.
Commons Sessional Papers (1837–8), vol. xxii. 1–424: 'Report from the Select Committee on Transportation; together with the Minutes of Evidence, Appendix, and Index', 3 August 1838.

Printed sources

Bennet, H.G. Letter to Viscount Sidmouth, Secretary of State for the Home Department, on the Transportation Laws, The State of the Hulks, and of the Colonies in New South Wales. London: J. Ridgway, 1819.
Bentham, J. 'A View of the Hard-Labour Bill'. London: n.p., 1778.
Bentham, J. 'Panopticon; or, The Inspection-House: Containing the Idea of a New Principle of Construction Applicable to Any Sort of Establishment, in Which Persons of Any Description Are to be Kept Under Inspection; and in Particular to Penitentiary Houses', 3 vols. London: n.p., 1791.
Bentham, J. 'Jeremy Bentham to the National Convention of France'. London: n.p., 1793.
Bentham, J. Panopticon versus New South Wales: or, The Panopticon Penitentiary System, and Penal Colonization system, Compared. London: Robert Baldwin, 1812.
Bentham, J. Emancipate Your Colonies! Addressed to the National Convention of France A° 1793, Shewing the Uselessness and Mischievousness of Distant Dependencies to an European State. London: Robert Heward, 1830.
Bentham, J. The Works of Jeremy Bentham, published under the superintendence of ... John Bowring, 11 vols. Edinburgh: William Tait, 1838–43.
Bentham, J. The Correspondence of Jeremy Bentham (CW), vol. iii, ed. I.R. Christie. London: The Athlone Press, 1971.
Bentham, J. The Correspondence of Jeremy Bentham (CW), vol. iv, ed. A.T. Milne. London: The Athlone Press, 1981.
Bentham, J. The Correspondence of Jeremy Bentham (CW), vol. vii, ed. J.R. Dinwiddy. Oxford: Clarendon Press, 1988.

Bentham, J. *Rights, Representation and Reform: Nonsense Upon Stilts and other writings on the French Revolution*, ed. P. Schofield, C. Pease-Watkin, and C. Blamires. Oxford: Clarendon Press, 2002.

Bentham, J. *Panopticon versus New South Wales and other writings on Australia*, ed. T. Causer and P. Schofield. London: UCL Press, 2022.

Secondary Sources

Brett, J. *From Secret Ballot to Democracy Sausage: How Australia Got Compulsory Voting*. Melbourne: Text Publishing, 2019.

Causer, T. 'Bentham's "Writings on Australia" – Pre-Publication Texts Now Online' (2018). https://blogs.ucl.ac.uk/bentham-project/2018/09/05/benthams-writings-on-australia-pre-publication-versions-now-online/ [accessed 10 October 2021].

Causer, T. '"The Evacuation of That Scene of Wickedness and Wretchedness": Jeremy Bentham, the Panopticon, and New South Wales, 1802–3', *Journal of Australian Colonial History* 21 (2019): 1–24.

Collins, H. 'Political Ideology in Australia: The Distinctiveness of a Benthamite Society', *Daedalus* 114: 1 (1985): 147–69.

Gascoigne, J. with Curthoys, P. *The Enlightenment and the Origins of European Australia*. Cambridge: Cambridge University Press, 2002.

Llewellyn, D. 'Bentham and Australia', *Revue d'études benthamiennes* 19 (2021). https://doi.org/10.4000/etudes-benthamiennes.8517.

Part I

The historical context of Bentham's writings on Australia

1

Bentham and the criminal fiscal state

Deborah Oxley

Introduction: England's criminal fiscal state

Jeremy Bentham (1748–1832) lived across 85 of the most important years in world history. Much of Bentham's thought engaged with the problems and potential solutions thrown up by the world newly forming around him, when Britain became the first nation to enter what the economist Simon Kuznets would later term 'modern economic growth' (MEG).[1] This is a state of continuous economic gains (typically measured as real Gross Domestic Product per capita), generation after generation, accompanied by rising population. Pre-modern growth was considered Malthusian, restricted to a balance between inputs and outputs, with gains easily gobbled up by induced population growth. Modern economic growth was different: it was powered by technology-driven productivity gains that sustained increased output even with growing population. It now accounts for improving living standards for many, as well as vast increases in the rate at which resources are consumed, with the resultant impact on the environment and climate. So, when did it begin?

Figure 1.1 is based on recent research by Broadberry et al. that estimates a number of important long-run series, in this case real output per head, and the size of the population.[2] An otherwise flat line in output per capita jumped appreciably in the mid-fourteenth century, but it was far from a cause for celebration. Here it is the denominator (population) not the numerator (GDP) that accounts for the increase. When the Black Death hit England in 1348, it certainly earned its name. The population dropped from 4.8 million to just 2.6 million

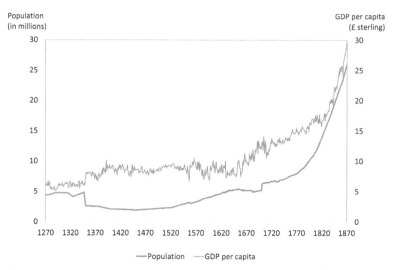

Population
(in millions)

GDP per capita
(£ sterling)

——Population ——GDP per capita

Figure 1.1: Real gross domestic product per capita in England (1270–1700) and Great Britain (1700–1870). It shows a trade-off between per capita economic growth and population size that was not broken until sometime after 1725, signalling the start of modern economic growth. Drawn by the author; data from Broadberry, Campbell, Klein, Overton, and van Leeuwen 2015, 226–44.

three years later. Three centuries were needed to recover. With fewer people, the economy shrank. Retrenching the least productive lands, however, induced growth in output per capita. Output gains after the Civil War, in the latter half of the seventeenth century, were likewise associated with declining numbers of people. The elusive goal was gains with population growth. MEG appears to have arrived sometime after 1725, and at more compelling rates a century later.

The future is always inscrutable. Understanding the time you live through is a challenge, and one that Bentham rose to. Contemporaries of any era can, with some greater modicum of certainty, gaze backwards. Not surprising, then, considering the static long-run historical relationships encapsulated in Figure 1.1, that a belief emerged of the global economy as a fixed cake.[3] The Black Death had delivered a fatal blow to feudalism in England, unleashing forces that would alter the social hierarchy and structure of land usage and the economy, but these were a long time in the making and were not reflected in sustained growth of per capita output or population. Mercantile philosophy emerged. Resources were finite. Wealth and power entwined, alive less in land and more in labour, and much more in capital and specie (i.e.

precious metals). Outflows of labour or specie were a threat (unless serving national interests), whereas inflows enriched. Mercantilism thus justified the use of military and naval power to support private commercial interests abroad. Through favourable trade balances and imperial ambition, Britain could secure a larger slice of the global cake.

With the delightful benefit of hindsight, and with reference to Figure 1.1, it is possible to observe that Bentham was born at a cusp. Something was happening. The economy was no longer flatlining, fixed. Could it be growing bigger? And just how many people were there, in London, in England? No one knew until the census of 1801. But there were more towns, and the towns and the Great Metropolis seemed busier, Greater, and wealthier than before.

Triangular trade was an engine of growth.[4] Africa provided Europe with gold, ivory, spices and hardwoods, and most infamously, European traders kidnapped African people, stripped them of their humanity, and turned them into property, things to be owned. Sourced in England, a currency of guns, cloth, iron and beer incentivized the local capture of Africans, supplying a new, lucrative and increasingly British slave trade. Put to labour where others would not, below the cost of their own reproduction, coerced Africans made unpleasant and otherwise uneconomic crops profitable for their masters. In the Caribbean, enslaved workers produced large quantities of cheap sugar, molasses and their children enslaved for the North American market, which in return traded fish, flour, livestock and lumber. Both regions fed a global market with drugs of prestige and addiction – sugar and tobacco – and eventually with cotton and raw materials for input into British manufacture. The North Americans sold Britain whale oil, lumber, furs, rice, silk, indigo and wood; meanwhile they bought British-traded enslaved people, and British-made luxuries and manufactures. Not a virtuous circle, but a profitable and unpalatable one that exposes deep divisions among historians. Much ink has been spilled contesting Africa's role in England's industrial revolution.[5]

Indeed, there is not much about the industrial revolution that is not contentious: its timing, causes, even its very existence.[6] What is less controversial is that Bentham was born into an era of change. The British Empire was expanding, into Madras, India, but would shortly be failing spectacularly in 1776–83 when it lost all 13 of its American colonies, perhaps prompting incursions into more southern seas. Meanwhile, the Scottish Enlightenment was in full swing. While Bentham was in his cot, David Hume was philosophizing and the young Adam Smith was expounding his ideas on the economy he observed around him. He noted that work was being done differently: labour processes were being fragmented, and in consequence output increased.

The eighteenth was the century of technological invention, and production was changing. Already the Darbys had developed smelting with coke to produce iron, Jethro Tull had designed the seed drill, Newcomen the steam engine, and John Kay the flying shuttle that would revolutionize weaving. Then, in Bentham's lifetime, the pace of change accelerated. James Watt refined the steam engine, making it more powerful, more reliable. There came threshing machines, critical innovations in spinning (jenny, fame and mule), power looms, cotton gins and carding machines; steel rollers and gas turbines. The sextant and the marine chronometer transformed seafaring, navigation and stargazing. In 1769–70 Cook observed the Transit of Venus and 'discovered' Australia. There were hot air balloons, parachutes, bicycles, a steamship, a submarine; gas lighting, flushing toilets and bifocal spectacles; vaccination against smallpox; the telegraph; a precision lathe for cutting metal; in France, the guillotine. The years 1789–99 saw the French Revolution. Political agitation would have its middle-class expression in the Great Reform Act of 1832, which gained royal assent the day after Bentham's death. The world would never be the same again.[7]

Another development of great significance and considerable magnitude, only partially underpinned by sustained economic growth, was the changing capacity of the State.[8] The rise of fiscal states in Europe has been well documented.[9] In England, it was specifically tied to war, both Civil and foreign.[10] By the end of the Interregnum, the fiscal regime had been reconstructed and prepared for growth.[11] Subsequently, revenue increased markedly based on indirect taxation – excise and tariffs – especially on luxury goods. The costs of global conflicts became so great that they gave rise to financial innovation in the form of a permanent public debt – the issue of government bonds – paying off interest in the present and capital in a distant future. A navy and military serving the interests of a merchant elite built a new distri-butional alliance between 'Big Land and Big Commerce' that, according to Mokyr and Nye, changed political possibilities.[12] More commerce, more taxation – not on land or income but on consumption – and a shift in rent-seeking from private monopolies to the state, allowed the eighteenth-century Parliament to emerge as a 'meta-institution' with power, wealth, stability, and a more national focus that further stimulated the economy. Figure 1.2, from O'Brien and Hunt, is a graphic illustration of how government revenue fundamentally shifted compared with

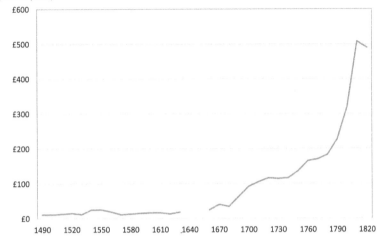

£ million
(1451-75 prices)

Figure 1.2: Nine-year moving averages of total revenue (excluding loan income) in England, 1490–1820 (in constant prices of 1451–75). It shows the marked rise in government revenue from the end of the 17th century, based on taxes, several categories of crown income, net receipts from the sale of assets and net profits from the royal mint. The upward trend further enhanced fiscal capacity as it supported borrowing by the state which rose from a nominal value of £2 million in the reign of James II (1685–8) to in excess of £834 million in the reign of George III (1760–1820), a more than twenty-times increase in annual borrowing. Drawn by the author; data from O'Brien and Hunt 1999, 57–6.

earlier centuries. Britain was exceptional, with tax revenue growing at five times the rate of increase in the economy.[13] The ramifications can be seen in the distribution of expenditure. Figure 1.3 presents an example from later in the century.[14] Everything was dwarfed by the debt charges. Major elements were the Navy and Army, and the ordnance to keep them going. Civil Government commanded less than one-tenth of the total. Of that, the Civil List (the Royals *et al.*) commanded twice the expenditure on government. However, because those debt charges were fuelling an inflated pie, this meant expenditure was on the rise.

What a cocktail! Agricultural improvements freed labour to move to towns and cities without compromising food supply (at least, to begin with), while enclosure of the lands and privatization of the commons impoverished families, marginalized women's contributions, and criminalized traditional wage supplements.[15] Rural dwellers were pushed out of the countryside and pulled into towns to work in services and

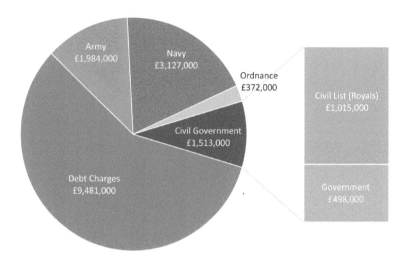

Figure 1.3: Great Britain's public expenditure, 1786 = £16.978 million, showing its distribution across major sectors, including a subdivision for civil government. Drawn by the author; data from Mitchell 2011, 580.

craft manufacture.[16] Urbanization increased dependency on markets while reducing access to informal networks of support and formalized welfare entitlements which were linked to parish of birth.[17] By the late seventeenth century, the balance tipped between food production and population growth, and a long-run decline in food supply increased prices and hunger.[18] Economic growth increased wealth and income, and increasingly uneven distribution meant growing inequality.[19] Cities and towns placed poor and rich cheek-by-jowl: growing supplies of valuable moveable objects found ready pawnbrokers and second-hand markets in a heaving 'economy of makeshifts'.[20] The Glorious Revolution further empowered an elite of owners to craft a Bloody Code to defend their handkerchiefs from nimble fingers. Cashed up, Britain could now expand its reach and become a criminal fiscal state.[21] What a time to be a thinker.

Punishing serious offenders

Much has been written about Bentham's brilliant yet chilling engine of surveillance, the panopticon; of his desire to profit from it, running the institution along with his brother Samuel; of Bentham's shenanigans at manipulating government statistics in pursuit of his dream; of his derision at the operations of the Treasury and Home Office; and of his blistering attack on the punitive failings and illegality of the panopticon's great rival, the New South Wales penal colony. What is offered here is context, of where all this fits in the big picture. The panopticon placed Bentham at the centre of an enormous battle over how to punish the British people found guilty of serious crime.

Punishment in England had for centuries been very cheap to administer. This was a defining characteristic: not its justice, nor its effectiveness, just its low cost. Budget Britain. Compared with today, central government expenditure on the institutions that comprise criminal justice had for centuries been miniscule, largely because many of the institutions we rely on – police, public prosecutors, lawyers, courts, a large network of prisons, a probation system – simply did not exist, either on an equivalent scale, or at all. The criminal justice system that evolved relied on extreme punishment mixed with discretion, to discipline society through example and to deter. And it cost next to nothing.

The process of creating criminals commences with law. The range of offences was comparatively constrained before the eighteenth century, which witnessed a multitude of pieces of legislation which burgeoned into what is now known as the Bloody Code. Roughly speaking, criminal offences fell into two categories: misdemeanours and felonies. The former were those considered minor crimes, for example, drunkenness, breaking the peace, fraud, assault, attempted rape, petty larceny.[22] Shame and pain were key to punishment embodied in the stocks, pillory, and whipping post or cart's tail.[23] Public humiliation had a long genesis in community-based discipline: a drunk might be made to wear a barrel, a 'scold' – a gossip – subjected to a bridle pinning down her tongue. As with the modern concept, this was a form of 'restorative justice' after which (most) offenders were reintegrated into the community.[24]

Reform and reintegration do not appear to be the hallmarks of punishment for *felonies*, the second category of offence, which were serious crimes. Murder, rape, arson; also robbery, burglary, forgery, stealing horses, picking pockets, and grand larceny (being theft above the value of one shilling), to name but a few. This demonstrates the considerable breadth of activities encompassed. Until the eighteenth century, there was just one punishment for guilty felons: death. The aim was elimination, amputating the festering limb to save the body politic.[25] Not surprising then, that one dreadful act had many labels: hanging was 'dancing the Newgate jig', 'doing the Paddington frisk', 'going to Triple Tree', 'being switched off'. Sometimes 'hangers on' sped the process of suffocating death. This was exemplary punishment: high theatre commanding a crowd that they might learn right from wrong. Blending drink and cheer with terror and fear, public execution was a community event to reinforce the consequences of breaking law.[26] Death was a blunt instrument, leading to the adage that one 'might as well be hung for a sheep as a lamb'. Nonetheless, grading forms of death was attempted in *An Act for better preventing the horrid Crime of Murder* in 1752 (25 Geo. II c. 37).[27] This Act sought to add 'further Terror and peculiar Mark of Infamy' to the sentence, inflicting a diet of bread and water, speeding the delivery of justice (execution within two days of sentencing), and arranging for the criminal's cadaver to be dissected and anatomized by a surgeon or hung in chains on the public highway ('gibbeting'). Anyone rescuing such a prisoner would be guilty of felony and sentenced to death without 'Benefit of Clergy', while rescuing the body from the surgeons, also a felony, made use of the latest punishment, incurring seven years' transportation to America.

There is a critical concept here: Benefit of Clergy, which according to William Blackstone operated 'as a kind of statute pardon'.[28] *Privilegium Clericale* is first recorded in the Charter of Liberties of Stephen in 1136: 'I allow and confirm that jurisdiction and authority over ecclesiastical persons ... will be in the hands of the bishops', said King Stephen, recognizing a practice 'observed from antiquity' – which persisted until 1827.[29] Clerks and monks accused of serious crimes were to be processed by church courts, not secular ones. This was challenged in a battle over authority between Church and State in 1164, when Henry II promulgated the Constitutions of Clarendon, creating a new court system which ousted Bishops from their judicial role and brought clergy under secular jurisdiction. This was not well received by the Church. The contest between Henry II and Archbishop of Canterbury Thomas Becket ended in the latter's murder, but the resulting upheaval forced Henry II into the Compromise of Avranches and into accepting the privilege.[30] With only certain exceptions (basically treason plus some obscure forest laws and matters of feudal tenure), clergy accused of serious crime would benefit from trial under canon law in an ecclesiastical court where, 'in the rare event of his failing to clear himself', possible punishments were restricted to being defrocked, relegated to a monastery to do penance, or to be whipped or branded, thereby saving him from a potential death sentence.[31] This right could be claimed *ad infinitum* for those sporting a tonsure (coronal shaved scalp).

The really significant development came following grievous complaints that secular courts were executing 'secular Clerks as well Chaplains, as other Monks, and other People of Religion'. By the Benefit of Clergy Act of 1351, and in return for the Archbishop's promise to punish,

> it is accorded and granted by the said King [i.e. Edward III] in his Parliament, That all Manner of Clerks, as well secular as religious, which shall be from henceforth convict before the secular Justices aforesaid, for any Treasons or Felonies touching other Persons than the King himself, of his Royal Majesty, shall from henceforth freely have and enjoy the Privilege of holy Church, and shall be, without any Impeachment or Delay, delivered to the Ordinaries demanding them.[32]

How was a court to identify a clerk? Through a literacy test. While courts had a choice over which part of the (originally Latin) Bible to examine the subject on, the test typically resolved into reading aloud, 'O God, have mercy upon me, according to thine heartfelt mercifulness'. Not surprisingly, this, the third verse of the 51st Psalm, became known as the 'neck verse'.

Thus are loopholes made. Courts now possessed discretion. They decided who was clergy, *and who was not*, and – over time, and in practice – it had little to do with who the Church ordained. The right to Benefit of Clergy was regularized. In line with its origins, Benefit of Clergy did not apply to misdemeanours but was available for all capital felonies and petty treason.[33] It became practice for benefit to be claimed *after* trial in a secular court.[34] According to Blackstone, a clergied felon – a 'Clerk convict' – might lose their property, but not their legal identity (law of attaint), nor their life.[35] Even a generous court could not pass off a woman as clergy, however, so the liberty afforded men was not shared by female offenders until formalized through legislation in 1691.[36] By 1706 even the reading test was abandoned and Benefit automatically applied.[37] Bentham's law lecturer and later adversary, Vinerian Professor of Law at Oxford, William Blackstone, wrote,

> the wisdom of the English legislature having, in the course of a long and laborious process, extracted, by a noble alchemy, rich medicines out of poisonous ingredients, and converted, by gradual mutations, what was at first an unreasonable exemption

of particular popish ecclesiastics into a merciful mitigation of the general law with respect to capital punishment.[38]

For historian John Beattie, Benefit of Clergy was 'a massive fiction that tempered in practice the harshness of the common law rule that virtually all felonies were capital offenses.'[39]

In the first instance, Benefit of Clergy led to immediate discharge to the Ordinary and thence liberty (providing the gaoler was paid his costs). Recidivism raised its ugly head. The 'presumptuous Boldness' of repeat offenders making serial claims of Benefit of Clergy provoked a revision. Following the passage of the Benefit of Clergy Act of 1488, offenders awarded Benefit of Clergy who could not provide certification of their holy orders would be branded on the braun of the left thumb, M for murder, T for all other felonies.[40] Once branded, an offender could not claim Benefit of Clergy again. The Act had some efficacy, though again opened up avenues for discretion: if lucky, the iron might be cold. A further statutory toughening of Benefit of Clergy in 1575 provided that 'The Justices may retain Offenders in Prison for a Time' not exceeding one year, but this important move did not open the sluice gates on incarceration, possibly owing to the shortage of prison capacity which was only designed for pre-trial custody.[41] Interestingly, the Act of 1575 also excised the role of the Ordinary, with Justices directly releasing clergied offenders from their detention. Thus a system evolved in which most guilty felons were punished in milder form than execution, with branding followed by freedom and restoration to society. This latter ambition was recognized at the time: a brief flirtation with branding criminals on their left cheek, introduced in 1699, was abandoned in 1706 precisely because the stigma disrupted reintegration, 'such Offenders being rendered thereby unfit to be intrusted in any Service or Employment to get their Livelihood in any honest and lawful Way, become the more desperate'.[42] Years later branding still rankled, as 'often disregarded, and ineffectual; and sometimes may fix a lasting Mark of Disgrace and Infamy on Offenders, who might otherwise become good Subjects, and profitable Members of the Commonwealth'. This legislation, in 1779, offered the alternative of a moderate fine or whipping.[43]

The converse of selecting who was freed was deciding who would swing. Juries decided innocence and guilt, and judges selected which individuals could successfully plea for Benefit: in instances where death was deemed desirable, an alternative verse would be selected to test literacy. In so doing, this allowed the selection of certain individuals for exemplary punishment in the Theatre of Death, their last hope a Royal Pardon.[44] Upon that public act of execution hung the entire basis of British justice. When there is little chance of detection and apprehension, prosecution, a guilty verdict, or exacting punishment, then justice has to lever some other instrument to deter offending, and the authorities favoured generating fear of being 'launched into eternity'. This was probabilistic reasoning: the chances of punishment versus its intensity.[45] It instilled fear and dread through an unpredictable but incomparable threat to life that was intended to punish but, most of all, to *deter* other possible offenders. Hence the need to be public, attended, dramatic, threatening, awe-inspiring, and symbolic. And that symbolism was worth an extra bob.

Maximum general deterrence was the order of the day, and such a policy was cheap. Either outcome – freedom or death – kept the costs down. Calum Foster has calculated the cost of hanging from the Sheriffs Cravings.[46] Sheriffs bore the expense of administering justice in their area (organizing Assize and Quarter Sessions, housing visiting judges, effecting judicial punishments, etc.), and then applied annually for reimbursement paid by the Exchequer in London.[47] This generates two sets of valuable figures: costs incurred locally and reimbursed centrally. Invoices ranged from £1.0s.9d to £73.9s.9d for a single execution. Foster cites a similarly large bill for the hanging of wife-murderer John Massey in 1801, a total of some £61.12s.9d.[48] Its composition is informative.

> Erecting a Temporary Gallows for the Execution of
> John Massey – £2.12.6
> Hanging said John Massey – £2.0.0
> Gibbetting John Massey at Congeston 17 miles from Leicester:
> Carpenter's Bill – £29.0.3
> Whitesmith's Bill – £23.0.0
> Expenses at Congeston – £5.0.0[49]

It was the gibbeting, that 'peculiar Mark of Infamy', that cost so much. Where hangings were rare, expertise had to be bought in and a major expense was when sourcing the hangman from a distant location. Despite some very large bills, the average cost per execution was £2 which was, in practice, all the central government would reimburse. As in the case of John Massey, this left Sheriffs well out of pocket. Reimbursements only started creeping up marginally from 1823, when Sealer and Under Secretary to the Chancellor of the Exchequer,

Richard Boyle Adderley, acknowledged the greater expenses incurred beyond the economies of scale seen in London and its surrounding counties.

Limited local policing and detection, private prosecution, a mobile rather than permanent court system, two pounds per hanging, and a negligible sum for branding Clerk convicts, all saved the central government from shelling out large sums of money on criminal justice. This system, based on a creative mix of freedom, death and terror, looks pretty cheap.

Bleeding criminals

Cost, however, is not everything, and people getting away with murder was not always popular. Running contiguously with the developments outlined above, another process pushed the law in an altogether more brutal direction. Certain offences – those considered especially dire, or prevalent and difficult to deter – were *excluded* from Benefit of Clergy. This recreated a genuinely capital code. The first such Act rescinded Benefit of Clergy for petty treason in 1496, and was professedly prompted by the 'abominable and wilful' behaviour of those who 'eschew the Peril and Execution of the Law by the Benefit of their Clergy':

> That the said *James Grame*, for the Murder of the said *Richard Tracy* his late Master, be attainted of the said Murder as a Felon that hath offended in Pety Treason; that the same *James*, for the same Murder, shall be drawn, and hanged in such Manner and Form, as by the Law of this Land hath been used in such Cases, as Persons being no Clerks, doing like Murder, have or ought to be punished, any Privilege of his Clergy, or his Demand of the same notwithstanding. (5) Also be it ordained by the said Authority, That if any Lay Person hereafter prepensedly murder their Lord, Master, or Sovereign immediate, that they hereafter be not admitted to their Clergy; (6) and after Conviction or Attainder of any such Person so hereafter offending had after the Course of the Law, that the same Person be put in Execution as though he were no Clerk.[50]

Murder, rape, buggery (committed with mankind or beast), burglary (night-time), housebreaking (daytime), highway robbery, robbery, man robbery, horse stealing, theft from churches, picking pockets, etc., were removed from Benefit of Clergy – sometimes repeatedly – over the course of the sixteenth century.[51] After a lull – the nation being otherwise occupied – in 1670 the process of legislative refinement of Benefit of Clergy resumed. Stealing cloth from the rack, receiving stolen goods, and embezzling from rented lodgings, were examples of further offences denied Benefit of Clergy. Remaining mute (not pleading) also became grounds for exclusion from the privilege; another was challenging more than 20 persons called for the jury.[52] While cut-purses and those frequenting churches, lodgings and tenter-fields would in theory swing, grand larceny remained clergyable and most thieves were not hanged. This was not to last.

The Glorious Revolution empowered a Parliament of vested private interests.[53] After 1689, a series of statutes removed different types of theft from Benefit of Clergy. Thence followed a process of net widening, both reducing the claim to Benefit of Clergy and creating entirely new offences. The Riot Act of 1714 restricted unlawful public assembly with a threshold of 12, making it a felony without Benefit of Clergy.[54] Private property was redefined by the Criminal Law Act of 1722 (commonly known as the Black Act) which itself created 50 capital offences: it outlawed popular wage supplements such as collecting firewood or gleanings and sweepings from the fields; game laws were strengthened and widened; items of a 'base' nature (hares, dogs, fish, etc.) were now property to be owned, so taking them was theft: poaching.[55] As the ditty went:

> The law locks up the man or woman
> Who steals the goose from off the Common
> But leaves the greater villain loose
> Who steals the common from the goose!

And the laws kept coming. There were so many because they were often so specific, reflecting very private concerns.[56] By the early nineteenth century, a Bloody Code of somewhere between 160 and as many as 223 capital statutes had been constructed – at a time when France had just six.[57]

This was not the deliberate creation of a new penal order or a modern justice system. This was not a considered bureaucratic response to changes in crime patterns. As Blackstone observed, the reshaping of the criminal law was left as 'a matter of indifference to the passions or interests of a few, who upon temporary motives may prefer or support such a bill'.[58] John Beattie elaborates:

> eighteenth-century restrictions on clergy tended to be aimed at essentially trivial offenses that appeared (to someone) to be increasing. They proceeded from a habit of mind that thought of the gallows as the only real deterrent, and they proliferated in part because momentary and sudden anxieties could be much more easily translated into legislation now that parliament was meeting regularly for the first time.[59]

Mostly, the Bloody Code was a reflection of private interest groups having influenced Parliament. Some were motivated by the fact that property was now worth privatizing, as a changing economy recalibrated the value of wood needed for industry, land for output, agricultural produce for market. At the same time rural households in particular were being squeezed by the decline of the cottage industry and the contraction of the commons, and urban centres struggled to cope with growing populations, immature food markets, inadequate infrastructure, and under- and unemployment. One process created more crimes, the other potentially more criminals. Both were happening at a time of unrecognized and unprecedented population growth that induced the sense of a crime wave.

All this increased the demand for punishment. All states face a question of legitimacy. Had this state come anywhere near executing as many offenders as the laws sanctioned, it is hard to image that the people would have simply tutted and got on with their day. It has been argued by J.S. Cockburn that the desecration of the criminal body authorized by the Murder Act of 1752 was one such step too far.[60] It angered a public already questioning the legitimacy of a state whose ballooning and Bloody legal code clearly served the interest of property-owning Parliamentarians and a few others, at the expense of the many. That so much had to be legislated, repeatedly, attempting to compel courts to greater severity, itself indicates a lack of consensus. Recent work has highlighted how regions contested this push from Westminster.[61] And, of course, in 1780 the Gordon Riots symbolically liberated London's own Bastille: Newgate.

Secondary punishment

The authorities did not, however, execute everyone they now could. Instead, they innovated. Indeed, it looks suspiciously like this burgeoning of capital statutes was partly unleashed by structural change in punishment. The hunt was on for secondary punishments.

It has already been noted that in 1699 an attempt was made to stiffen the costs of being awarded Benefit of Clergy, by branding the face not the hand. While this policy was reversed by the Burglary Act of 1706, the Act did so much more. Removal of the literacy test automated the application of Benefit of Clergy. Most significantly, it broadened the penal menu by casting imprisonment with hard labour as an alternative to immediate release for Clerk convicts. Since it pertained to theft and larceny, it had the potential to affect large numbers of people. In addition to burning, judges were granted discretion to commit offenders

> to some House of Correction or publick Work-house within the County, City, Town, or Place where such conviction shall be, there to be, remain, and be kept, without Bail or Mainprize, for such Time as such Judge or Justices shall then judge and award, not less than six Months, and not exceeding two Years ... shall be there set at Work, and kept at hard Labour.[62]

The Burglary Act was important. It was one of two Acts made in 1706 which enabled felons to be committed to a term of hard labour in a House of Correction.[63] Hitherto, custody had only been part of the process, detaining the accused for examination, awaiting trial, awaiting the delivery of punishment, or holding for want of sureties or inability to pay the Gaoler the debt incurred for services rendered, or as a debtor.[64] Now, incarceration became punishment for the felony of larceny. To herald forth capacity, welfare institutions (Elizabethan workhouses and houses of correction) were co-opted. This was an easy elision, considering their relative functions. But the problem was too big for this to work. Another solution was needed.

A (nearly) new weapon was launched: penal transportation. The Transportation Act of 1718 introduced three key innovations.[65] Transportation to work in his Majesty's colonies and plantations in America became (i) an alternative to death for capital felonies (death commuted to 14 years transportation); (ii) a substitute for branding/

imprisonment/freedom for those entitled to Benefit of Clergy (converted to seven years transportation for theft, larceny, stealing from the person, house or other; and 14 years for the receivers of stolen goods); and (iii) a sentence in its own right, as petty larceny – a misdemeanour – was reclassified as a transportable offence (replacing whipping with seven years' transportation). This latter point is particularly intriguing. Theft could now be punished as a misdemeanour or a felony, offering judges the full repertoire of punishments up to and including death. Clearly, the monetary value of the theft, which distinguished grand from petty larceny, was going to be an important area of negotiation. Unauthorized return from America would lead to execution.

The preamble to the Transportation Act sat well with mercantilist thought:

> in many of his Majesty's Colonies and Plantations in *America*, there is great Want of Servants, who by their Labour and Industry might be the Means of improving and making the said Colonies and Plantations more useful to this Nation.[66]

Previously, Royal Mercy had been granted to convicts 'upon Condition of transporting themselves to the *West-Indies*': not surprisingly, DIY transportation was limited by non-compliance.[67] This time round, private shippers would be responsible, incentivized by selling convict labour to American colonists. So advantageous was this option for Britain that the Act even facilitated the emigration of non-criminal males and females aged 15–21 years, who were too young to contract to be indentured, devising a process for their legal indenture and conveyancing to America.[68] In the first instance, the practice of penal transportation seems to have cost the Government more than anticipated,

> until it was generally discovered that the adjudged services of felons became a saleable article in Maryland, and were extremely profitable to the Contractors; hence arose a competition which (if I am rightly informed) enabled Government, some years previous to the American war, to make Contracts for transporting felons without any expense whatsoever.[69]

As Bruce Kercher observes, American transportation effected through the private sector 'suited Britain's self-perception as a place of liberty as much as it did its treasury'.[70] The system worked, until the American

War of Independence closed the borders in 1776. London judges rapidly shifted their sentencing patterns to favour incarceration, and those sentenced to transportation were placed in prison hulks.

Reformers seized the opportunity. Imprisonment was back on the agenda. William Eden, William Blackstone, John Howard, and other collaborators actively began drafting legislation. Various Bills pertaining to imprisonment, hulks and hard labour were devised, discussed, demurred and some passed. A grandiose vision aspired to replace transportation as the principal punishment for felonies with imprisonment at hard labour in a national network of institutions. Bentham's 'A View of the Hard-Labour Bill' (1778) is now recognized as a seminal work in the development of his ideas, if somewhat 'scrappy and inconclusive' and not influential on the final Penitentiary Act.[71] Pragmatically, he was enthusiastic that both Bill and Act embedded his duty and interest junction principle, that 'it may become the *interest* as well as the *duty* of each governor to see that all persons under his custody be regularly and profitably employed', which he later leveraged in his panopticon scheme. Semple notes Bentham was perhaps 'motivated by worldly ambition'.[72] The Penitentiary Act as passed in 1779 was tempered, envisaging just two national penitentiaries.[73] While these were never built, the values and principles enunciated both reflected and shaped local prison reform and were influential in the prison building boom of the 1790s.[74] The Act also gave a statutory basis for Bentham to leverage in his subsequent bid to create his panopticon.

The full title of this famous piece of legislation is not the Penitentiary Act, but 'An Act to explain and amend the Laws, relating to the Transportation, Imprisonment, and other Punishment, of certain Offenders'. The Act in fact sanctioned two secondary punishments: the building of two penitentiaries and the revival of transportation.[75] It made transportation lawful 'to any Parts beyond the Seas, whether the same be situated in *America,* or elsewhere'.[76] The choice was made a few years later, in 1785: it was to be New South Wales. What was novel about Transportation Version 2.0 was that the state was funding punishment on an entirely new scale, and was very hands on in its management.

New South Wales was fundamentally different to America. There was no pre-existing colony, no planters hungry for workers, *ipso facto* no market for shippers selling indentured labour. Establishing a penal colony in Australia would necessarily be a costly government endeavour. The First Fleet set out in 1787 and was a successful naval enterprise, though one which Bentham targets in the preface to 'A Plea for the Constitution'.[77] Thence the government contracted and paid shippers but neglected to tightly specify the terms. The next ship to sail, full of convict women, was the *Lady Juliana*: it set the record for longest journey, perhaps because the private Master was paid by the day. The Second Fleet was utterly disastrous, with a mortality rate more than ten times that of the First Fleet. Four ships carrying 1,042 mainly male convicts managed to land just 750 alive. While five fatalities resulted from the *Guardian* being wrecked on an iceberg, the other 287 deaths were caused through neglect, mistreatment, hunger and disease, especially on the biggest ship, *Neptune*, which lost more than one-third of its men. Most survivors were in desperate need of medical attention on arrival and a further 80 perished within three weeks of landing.[78] Thenceforth masters would be paid a fee per convict landed (as opposed to embarked), and surgeon superintendents would monitor convict welfare onboard. The outcome of this added expense was an astonishingly low mortality rate. Such effort affirms that transportation was not intended as a *de facto* death sentence.

Managing convicts pre-transportation, coping with the half who were never actually sent, and conveying the others half-way round the world, was a serious undertaking. The government did not add in the cost of repatriation, an issue Bentham would later criticize. Then there was setting up and running a distant colony which required bureaucracy, guards, and provisioning a Commissariat. None of this came cheap – except the land for which no recompense was given to its Indigenous owners. Attempt was made to compute the cost of the colony a decade on. In 1798, with opaque contributions from a vested party, a report by a Select Committee estimated the government had spent £1,011,440.6s.7¾d on the colony.[79] Such 'luxury in punishment' was, as seen above, equivalent to funding the Royals for a year or to two years of total government expenditure.[80] Penal transportation to Australia stands out as a turning point. Even if this figure was hopelessly inflated, the central government in England was now funding punishment for serious crime at a hitherto unimaginable level. This was a piece of the state worth capturing.

Bentham's panopticon versus penal transportation

Bentham was shocked to find that in 1787 penal transportation had been resurrected and a fleet sent to New South Wales. Between 1785 and 1788, Bentham was out of the country, spending most of 1786 and

1787 visiting his brother Samuel in Russia, where ideas about labour management cross-fertilized with his interest in prison, giving birth to the panopticon.[81] This meant Bentham missed the 1785 Beauchamp Committee that took the decision to commence transportation to NSW. Bentham's return to England unleashed an almighty fight. He approached the Irish government about a penitentiary (1790), printed his writings on the panopticon (1791), outlined the failure of the very new colony in 'New Wales' (1791), and told the National Convention of France to *Emancipate Your Colonies!* with an address 'shewing the uselessness and mischievousness of distant dependencies to an European state'.[82] A two-pronged attack on British systems of criminal punishment was to follow. Bentham was to promote prison, and denigrate penal transportation.

In 1791 Bentham approached the British government with a view to a new career, contracting to run a panopticon penitentiary. In 1794 he proffered a revised proposal 'for a new and less expensive Mode of employing and reforming Convicts', outlining 'a system of superintendence, universal, unchargeable, and uninterrupted, the most effectual and indestructible of all securities against abuse'.[83] His proposal was impressive and innovative, including – but going further than – John Howard's invocations.[84]

1. Unlimited quantity of wholesome food

2. Superior neat clothing

3. Clean, separate beds and bedding

4. Artificial warmth and light

5. No alcohol

6. Seclusion in assorted companies

7. Share in the proceeds of work

8. Convert Prison into a School

9. Penalty payment for every escape

10. Spiritual and medical assistance

11. Penalty payment for every excess death in custody (age-sex adjusted)

12. Annuity payment for old age pension

13. Post-release factory employment

14. Penalty payment for reconviction

15. Pay for and produce Annual report

16. Fee-paying amusement for the public

This was a comprehensive package, designed to overcome the criticisms of incarceration, especially that the end of sentence released the offender back into society, and the threat of escape. Private contractors paying a fine for subsequent recidivism was one such tantalizing notion proposed in order to allay fears of reoffending. Better still, Bentham could deliver this impressive service for some 25 per cent less than the annual net cost of keeping a convict on a hulk, then estimated at £13 to £15 each.

The deal was undoubtedly entrepreneurial, a joint venture with Samuel. Private provision of public justice was normal. For centuries the local prison system had been run privately, with gaolers making their income through fees and the sale of services, especially the provision of alcohol (creating very perverse incentives). As Hume notes, contracts were a familiar feature of American transportation.[85] Magistrates and the Bow Street Runners represented a private service. Sinecures had also been a way of life. But Bentham's vision of farming convict labour to work his brother Samuel's inventions under his own direct control was quite at odds with management by central government as conceived in the Penitentiary Act.[86] An integrity revolution was underway in Britain. Recent reforms endeavoured to regularize administration of local prisons, creating salaried positions and constraining fees and costs imposed before releasing detainees.[87] That costs might be defrayed through the labour of prisoners was, however, an established – but usually unrealized – ambition.[88]

Bentham's proposal was initially met with enthusiasm: £36,000 was allocated by Government, and £2,000 was advanced 'To Jeremy Bentham, Esquire, on Account of the Convicts proposed to be confined in Penitentiary Houses'.[89] As his plans ran up against objections, Bentham became more vociferous in attacking penal transportation, and the conduct of government, with the Treasury and Home Office particularly in his sights. Secretly, Bentham was a 'principal author' of the section on New South Wales of the 1798 Select Committee on Finance, chaired by his step-brother, Charles Abbot, computing the heinous costs of the convict colony made in the Committee's report.[90]

He had also drafted a shadow report.[91] Bentham penned key contributions in the conflict between his panopticon versus New South Wales. A volume of this name was published in 1812, comprising the first two 'Letters to Lord Pelham' and 'A Plea for the Constitution', which were written in 1802–3.

Tim Causer offers a compelling account of these and other of Bentham's excoriating attacks on penal transportation and the young convict colony.[92] In sum, for Bentham there were five 'ends of penal justice': example, reformation, incapacitation, compensation and economy.[93] How transportation failed in Bentham's eyes! Its effect was not exemplary, but invisible to those in the British Isles, and for some offenders, transportation was desirable. That it reformed was 'make-believe'. For incapacitation – a weak point for those advocating incarceration at home – Bentham made the grand claim that it was easier to return from transportation than escape prison, while relying on private masters made both surveillance and punishment uncertain in a system akin to slavery. There was no compensation to victims. It was 'a great waste of lives … and great waste of money'.[94]

There was even more wrong with its practice in New South Wales. Additional failings included its even greater expense, a luxury in punishment footed by the poor British taxpayer. Colonies were never a good thing, but one with so few women precluded adequate population growth and fostered debauchery. Then there was the illegal use of naval ships for conveying convicts.

Bentham identified six shocking discoveries about the illegality of the government in New South Wales, which if known would, he surmised, lead to insurrection.[95] Bentham's friend, and long-time supporter of the panopticon, Charles Bunbury warned Bentham not to publish 'A Plea for the Constitution', his postscript reading 'If you can't write down the Colony of Thieves at Port Jackson, and annihilate it by Argument, don't crush it by Rebellion.'[96] While demurring to set the colony ablaze, Bentham nonetheless shared a copy of the 'Plea' with David Collins, who took it with him on his return to New South Wales to head a new settlement at Port Phillip. Collins selectively shared Bentham's findings among the colony's elite. News circulated. Taxation without consent reared its head.[97]

What was so incendiary was broadcast in the title, *A Plea for the Constitution: shewing the enormities committed to the oppression of British Subjects, innocent as well as Guilty, in breach of Magna Carta, the Habeas Corpus Act, the Petition of Rights; as Likewise of the several Transportation Acts; in and by the design, foundation, and government of the*

penal colony of New South Wales: including an inquiry into the right of
the Crown to legislate without Parliament in Trinidad, and other British
colonies. Here were Bentham's powerful arguments on the illegality
of the convict colony. Failure to repatriate time-expired convicts
amounted to indefinite detention.[98] Extending convict sentences as
colonial punishment was illegal and therefore false imprisonment.
Transporting those already on the brink of freedom added insult
to illegal injury. Presumption of liberty was replaced by presuming
servitude in cases where convict indents failed to record duration of
sentence. At their core, the existing Acts of Parliament were insufficient to grant the Governor legitimate power to legislate, exposing all
colonial office holders to potential legal action and ruin should convicts
choose to litigate.[99]

Section 6 of 'A Plea for the Constitution', entitled *'Nullity of*
Legislation in New South Wales, for want of an Assembly to consent', is
pivotal, regarding the legal basis of the convict colony. Considering the
British colonization of America, Bentham identifies two 'indispensable'
features: *'Consent* on the part of the colonists' through an Assembly
and *'irrevocability* of the privileges granted by such charters' (secure
property rights).[100] New South Wales fell foul on both counts.

There is a problem here with Bentham's analysis. The Crown
used charters to convey property rights over colonized territories in
America, but these rights were held by the recipients of this largesse
– the proprietors, the Trading Companies – not the ordinary colonists
who included locally born whites, free migrants, indentured workers,
and certainly not enslaved or indigenous peoples. Similarly, political
power in the form of a constitution or assembly resided with the
proprietors, not ordinary men and women who could no more vote in
America than they could in England.

Bentham found that there was no one in New South Wales to
accept a charter. What he did not recognize was that in New South
Wales, charters were not needed. There were no private enterprises, no
pre-existing businesses on the hunt for cheap and indentured labour.[101]
This was a government endeavour. Bentham likewise finds there is no
one in New South Wales to accept a political assembly. Contemptu-
ously, he asks, 'Who is there, or who ever can there be, to accept it in
New South Wales? A charter to impower a free man to lead a life of
slavery, and to be flogged as often as he endeavours to escape from it!'[102]
Who can there ever be? Clearly he did not consider the Indigenous
owners as contenders. If not convicts, what of their spouses, their
children when grown, emancipated convicts, the officers, bureaucrats

and guards who inhabited the colony? Clearly, the free man Bentham was envisaging was akin to an American plantation owner, so not very likely to be flogged even if venturing to New South Wales.

Essentially, Bentham accepted the legal validity of colonialism based on private trade, but not as a direct government enterprise. He had legitimate grounds for criticizing it. That he reached for some less-convincing arguments, and that he walked away from the contest when his private interests in the panopticon ran out of hope, suggests a less ideological position. But perhaps the most important lines in 'A Plea for the Constitution' remain, to this day, unresolved.

To Bentham's 'No charter, no colony', we might now add 'No treaty, no conquest'.[103] From no conquest, no legitimacy. In *Truth-Telling: History, Sovereignty and The Uluru Statement*, Henry Reynolds notes Bentham's observation that the colonizing of New South Wales involved no treaty.[104] Bentham's concern with the 'Inhabitants' of New South Wales refers in the main to Europeans, but there is a valuable paragraph where he writes of Bennelong and Yemmerrawanne visiting England 'in the character of private gentlemen, travelling for their amusement, or at least for our's: they signed no *treaty* with his Majesty, or brought with them any diplomatic powers'.[105]

However, Bentham actually appears to commend the failure to write a treaty. The text is vivid, the point central. The sentence quoted above was prefaced:

> To the host of follies included in the circumstances of distant *possession*, this colony at least, with all its peculiarities and all its faults, has not added that vulgar and crowning folly of distant *conquest*. It is needless to enquire, what on this occasion might have been the virtue of a string of *wampum*; no wampum, nor any substitute for wampum, has either been received or given in New South Wales.[106]

But enquiry is needed. Herein lies the comment with most reverberation ringing down to today. On what legal basis did Britain acquire property rights over the Great Southern Land or any part of it, for whatever purpose? Without conquest and treaty exchange, that land has never been ceded.

Conclusion

Bentham was an astute observer, having mused in 1791 on whether the underlying ambition of the New South Wales colony was a 'mode of disposing of convicted criminals' or a 'scheme of colonisation at large'.[107] Britain had just lost 13 colonies, so may not have been averse to replacing them.[108] That colony-holding would 'never be an object of national benefit' did not deter Bentham from his support of the private venture for colonizing South Australia by (convicted felon) Edward Gibbon Wakefield.[109] Bentham advised Wakefield on the naming of his plan:

> More, [as] will be immediately perceived, will be found the convenience from the having for the designation and communication of a state of things on which every thing depends *a locution composed of no more than three words* [emphasis added].[110]

Here, those three words might be: criminal fiscal state. Neither New South Wales nor the panopticon would have been on the agenda without the growing fiscal capacity and willingness of the British state to spend on criminal justice. In the early eighteenth century, the state commenced experimenting with both forms of secondary punishments. It was much later in the century that it countenanced paying for them. When it did, the costs of criminal justice ballooned, and this created opportunities for entrepreneurial thinkers.

With his all-seeing eye, Jeremy Bentham was engaged in perhaps the greatest battle in the history of criminal justice: how to punish serious offenders. For a very long time the answer, in theory, was death. In practice what operated was a literally judicious blend of exemplary executions for the few, mixed with branding and then freedom for the many. Or – as noted by Peter King – the process *was* the punishment, often lengthy, always uncertain, of being detected, arrested, examined, a bill found, court, judgment, and detention while awaiting the final outcome.[111] For many, this was ultimately freedom. Many, many lives were saved by 'that queer old exemption, benefit of clergy, so strangely distorted from its original purpose'.[112] Freedom mixed with death cemented authority through discretion, while keeping costs – and deaths – down. It substituted the remote chance of execution for a fully functioning justice system. This reached its limits. Particularly so in the wake of an expanding capital code. What followed was a three-way fight between capital punishment and the two secondaries:

transportation versus imprisonment. The resolution would shape the future of punishment for centuries to come. How many centuries, we do not yet know, as we remain amid a time when incarceration dominates.

The limitations of relying on the death penalty/freedom dichotomy were legion. Bentham's friend Samuel Romilly later observed 'the law is nominally too severe, practically not severe enough'.[113] Harsh laws were 'too cruel for application' and 'where some punishment was deserved, no punishment was at all inflicted, and the offender escaped altogether with impunity'.[114] In 1811, Sir John Anstruther told Parliament,

> The great evil of making the laws too severe was, that judges became *astute* and *cunning* in evading the laws, and the juries hesitated to convict. The sympathies of the multitude were generally turned in favour of the accused, which is a great moral evil. When sentences of death were pronounced, which every one knew would not be executed, that solemnity which would otherwise be impressive, was considered a mere legal form and mockery.[115]

Such extreme punishment as death made Grand Juries reluctant to find a 'true bill'. It deterred prosecutors, some because they did not want offenders to swing, others because of the low likelihood of conviction. It deterred juries from convicting, and they engaged in 'pious perjury', meaning they could acquit, find guilty as charged, or issue a partial verdict whereby a capital crime could be made a non-capital felony and a clergiable felony could be deemed a misdemeanour, both of which reduced the penalty. (The value of those stolen candlesticks might easily be deflated.) The lower likelihood of conviction for a felony potentially incentivized the commission of more serious crime. Behaviour was distorted every step of the way.

In 1819 Fowell Buxton declared to the House of Commons that the chances of being convicted of a crime and punished for it were a thousand to one against.[116] The systems the reformers brought in moved towards Beccaria's call for celerity and changed the odds. A modern matrix of criminal justice institutions and practices was put in place, but not until later in the nineteenth century. The advent of modern policing improved detection, public subsidy increased the likelihood of prosecution, as did a system of graduated punishments designed to fit the crime. Belief in the courts and their practitioners further encouraged juries to find offenders guilty as charged rather than piously perjuring themselves. Soon, the great edifice of criminal justice needed to relinquish terror would be erected. Until then, imprisonment would have to wait its turn.

Bentham's timing was just wrong. The Penitentiary Acts of 1779 and 1794 and the panopticon scheme came around a half-century too soon.[117] England could not yet embrace the prison until supported by a comprehensive justice system, especially policing. At least, not with its expansive criminal code. This is why transportation persisted and was a necessary step in the process of relinquishing the death penalty. Bentham conjured transportation as an attack on English liberty, a violation of the British constitution.[118] Romilly concurred.[119] Bentham's withering criticism had, he believed, posed an existential threat to the colony. Yet, when in 1803 his panopticon project had clearly failed, Bentham's interest in New South Wales fizzled out.[120] Later, he either disowned or forgot this great endeavour.[121] In 1803, less than one-third of the 160,000 or so convicts sent to Australia from the British Isles had been transported: the golden age of transportation was yet to come. Until those wider – and very expensive – institutions were in place, English punishment needed to terrify. Fear filled the gaps. The prison was not an effective option, not simply because of lack of capacity, but because it failed to pack sufficient dread. Transportation could. Symbiotically, each retrenchment of the death penalty in England was bought by ramping up the severity of punishment in Australia, in New South Wales in 1820, and in Van Diemen's Land in 1840 when a sentence of transportation incorporated a period of colonial imprisonment. Transportation offered a useful alternative to death and freedom because it could be graded yet had the characteristic of being dreaded, without actually terminating life, and it could be applied more readily because of this. That was the direction of travel – *more* punishment – and imprisonment would eventually be its apotheosis. Bentham believed 'all punishment in itself is evil', only justified by excluding a greater evil and thereby acting as a deterrent.[122] Ironically, the evolution of the modern system, with imprisonment at its core, would deliver far more punishment to the British and the people of its empire.

Notes

1   Kuznets 1966.
2   Broadberry *et al.* 2015.
3   Winch 1966.

4   Zahedieh 2013.
5   Most famously, Williams 1944; more recently Inikori 2002. Arguments for and against are canvassed in Solow and Engerman 1987.
6   Allen 2009b.
7   There are long and contentious debates over the role of technology, invention and innovation in economic growth. For some key literature, see: Landes 1969; Mokyr 2002; Allen 2009b; Mokyr 2009; Jacob 2014.
8   For Bentham's thinking, influenced by the imperial constitution, on legislature, judicature, and office during this period, see Cavanagh's chapter in this volume.
9   For example, see Bonney ed. 1999.
10 O'Brien and Hunt 1999.
11 O'Brien 2002.
12 Mokyr and Nye 2007, 54. It is popular among New Institutional Economists to argue for the 1688–9 Glorious Revolution as a turning point: see also North and Weingast 1989. Other scholars argue for different causation, for example O'Brien 2009.
13 O'Brien 2002.
14 There may be faults with Mitchell's figures, but they are indicative of share. Note Figures 1.2 and 1.3 are expressed in a different currency baseline and are not directly comparable.
15 Humphries 1990; Jones 1982.
16 Wallis, Colson, and Chilosi 2018; Shaw-Taylor and Wrigley 2014.
17 Snell 1985. For a fascinating new account of the Elizabethan Poor Law, see Szreter, Cooper, and Szreter 2019.
18 Meredith and Oxley 2014.
19 Lindert 1986; Milanovic 2018; Allen 2009a; Allen 2018; Humphries and Weisdorf 2019.
20 The phrase 'economy of makeshifts' belongs to Olwen Hufton writing on the diverse strategies deployed by the French poor to make ends meet. See essays collected in King and Tomkins eds. 2015.
21 Part of what Innes 2009 calls 'The Domestic Face of the Military-Fiscal State'.
22 Value below one shilling (1 shilling = 12 pence), about a day's wages for a male labourer in the late eighteenth century.
23 Germany had its gender-inverting 'laughing stocks'.
24 Providing they survived the objects lobbed at them while in the stocks or pillory.
25 McGowen 1987, 661–2.
26 Cockburn 1994.
27 King 2017.
28 Blackstone 1765–70 [1893], iv. 373.
29 An Act for farther improving the Administration of Justice in Criminal Cases in England (7 & 8 Geo. IV, c. 28).
30 Cross 1917, 551.
31 Cross 1917, 552.
32 25 Edw. III, Stat. 6, c. 4. The Ordinary was the Bishop's representative. These sentiments were reiterated when the issue came up again in the Indictments, etc. Act of 1402 (4 Hen. IV, c. 2).
33 Blackstone 1765–70, iv. 373.
34 Cross 1917, 552.
35 Blackstone 1765–70 [1893], iv. 373–4.
36 Benefit of Clergy, etc. Act of 1691 (3 Will. & Mar., c. 9, § 6).
37 Burglaries, etc. Act of 1706 (6 Ann., c. 6, § 4).
38 Blackstone 1765–70 [1893], iv. 364 (373).
39 Beattie 1986, 141.
40 4 Hen. VII, c. 13. There was no limit on the claim to Benefit for ordained clerics.
41 Benefit of Clergy Act of 1575 (18 Eliz. I, c. 7).
42 Preamble to the Burglaries etc. Act of 1706. Branding on the cheek was introduced by the Clerks of Assize (Fees) Act of 1698 (10 Will. III, c. 23, § 12).
43 See the Penitentiary Act of 1779 (19 Geo. III, c. 74, § 3).
44 Devereaux 2007.
45 Bentham sought to work out these calculations in great detail in Bentham, ed. Burns and Hart 1970.

46 Foster 2019. The following is based on some 27,349 individuals appearing in these records from 1800 to 1845, covering almost all death sentences imposed and those actually carried out.
47 Hurren 2016, 175, quoted in Foster 2019.
48 John Massey was an agricultural worker, wrestler and drunkard who murdered his wife. Massey was executed at Red Hill, Birstall, and his body was gibbeted where the crime had been committed, 'Congeston' being Congerstone, adjacent to Bilstone. The Bilstone Gibbet Post still stands, a testament to the carpenter and the powerful symbolism.
49 'Leicestershire Sheriff's Craving 1801', The National Archives, Kew (hereafter TNA), E 197/34.
50 Benefit of Clergy Act of 1496 (12 Hen. VII, c. 7).
51 Benefit of Clergy Act of 1531 (23 Hen. VIII, c. 1); Abjuration, Benefit of Clergy Act of 1536 (28 Hen. VIII, c. 1); Benefit of Clergy Act of 1566 (8 Eliz. I, c. 4); Benefit of Clergy Act (18 Eliz. I, c. 7).
52 Benefit of Clergy Act of 1670 (22 Cha. II, c. 5); Benefit of Clergy Act of 1691.
53 More broadly, Innes 2009, 12 argues that, in the eighteenth century, 'In order to meet local needs, people turned (increasingly often) to a national body'.
54 Riot Act of 1714 (1 Geo. I, Stat. 2, c. 5).
55 Criminal Law Act of 1722 (9 Geo. I, c. 22).
56 For example, that iron railings were under threat: Theft Act of 1730 (4 Geo. II, c. 32).
57 Blackstone identified 160 different felonies excluded from Benefit of Clergy: see Blackstone 1765–70 [1893], iv.
58 Blackstone 1765–70 [1893], iv. 4.
59 Beattie 1986, 144–5.
60 Cockburn 1994: 170–1, 175, 178–9.
61 King and Ward 2015; Innes 1999.
62 Burglaries, etc. Act of 1706, § 2.
63 The other being the Game Act of 1706 (6 Ann., c. 14).
64 Also used to hold debtors but they were not criminally convicted.
65 The Transportation Act of 1718 (4 Geo. I, c. 11).
66 See the Transportation Act of 1718.
67 There had been earlier attempts at transportation. For example, seditious Sectaries could be transported according to the Conventicle Act of 1664 (16 Cha. II, c. 4), and transportation was used as a substitute for death in the cases of stealing cloth and woollen manufactures from tenterfields or stealing stores from the Navy, by the Benefit of Clergy Act of 1670.
68 Transportation Act of 1718, § 5. Curiously, the Act also punished a particular type of fraud: prisoners guilty of unlawfully exporting wool or woollens, detained for want of Bail, could also be transported for seven years.
69 '4th May 1798.—Further Examination of Patrick Colquhoun, Esq.', Appendix D. in 'Twenty-Eighth Report from the Select Committee on Finance, &c. Police, including Convict Establishments', 26 June 1798, in ed. Lambert 1975, cxii. 63.
70 Kercher 2003, 532.
71 Hume 1973, 705; Semple 1993, 62.
72 Semple 1993, 45.
73 Devereaux 1999.
74 Mehta 2021, ch. 3 argues these reforms were already being anticipated at the local level.
75 See also Hume 1973, 704.
76 Penitentiary Act of 1779, preamble. As noted earlier, the Act also introduced the options of fines and whipping for offenders claiming Benefit of Clergy: see § 3.
77 'A Plea for the Constitution' in Bentham, ed. Causer and Schofield 2022, 317–20.
78 For an account see Flynn 1993.
79 'An Account of the Annual Number of Convicts transported to New South Wales, and Norfolk Island, since the Establishment of those Settlements respectively; and of the Annual Expence of such Transportation, and of the Annual Establishments of such Support, and of such Settlements, as far as the same can be made out to the End of the Year 1797', Appendix O in 'Twenty-Eighth Report', in ed. Lambert 1975, cxii. 122–3.
80 The phrase 'luxury in punishment' is Bentham's, quoted in Jackson 1988, 55.
81 Hume 1973, 607 gives the dates 1786–7 while Jackson gives 1785–8.

82 Bentham had published *Emancipate Your Colonies!* in 1830, though he had written the work in late 1792 and early 1793, and had it printed in 1793 as 'Jeremy Bentham to the National Convention of France': see Bentham, ed. Schofield, Pease-Watkin, and Blamires, 2002.

83 Bentham, 'Proposal for a new and less expensive Mode of Employing and Reforming Convicts' [1794] TNA, HO 42/29, fos. 257–60, which also appears in Appendix E, 'Twenty-Eighth Report', in ed. Lambert 1975, cxii. 63–6.

84 Howard 1777.

85 Hume 1973, 706–7.

86 Hume 1973, 706.

87 Mehta 2021, 13, 34, 60, 134, 151–2, 210–15.

88 Mehta 2021, 102–11.

89 'An Account of the Money paid by His Majesty or the Public, for or in respect of the Convicts, Confinement, Employment, and Maintenance of Persons convicted of Felonies or Misdemeanors, from the 7th March 1786 to the 31st December 1797; specifying the Totals of the Sums expended in each Year', Appendix L.2, in 'Twenty-Eighth Report', in ed. Lambert 1975, cxii. 106–7.

90 For a riveting account, see Jackson 1988.

91 Semple 1993, 207–8.

92 Causer 2019.

93 Causer 2019, 8.

94 Causer 2019, 8.

95 Bentham to Charles Abbot, 3 September 1802, in Bentham, ed. Dinwiddy 1988, 102–15.

96 Charles Bunbury to Bentham, 6 June 1803, in Bentham, ed. Dinwiddy 1988, 236.

97 Atkinson 1994, 262–3.

98 Bentham had highlighted the paradox, either 'false banishment for life' or destroy British security by their return. Quoted in Causer 2019, 5.

99 Although Bentham makes no mention of it, convicts did litigate, as recognized by his editors: see 'A Plea for the Constitution' in Bentham, ed. Causer and Schofield 2022, 349 n. The first civil case was heard in 1788, when convict couple Henry Cable and Susannah Holmes successfully sued their ship's Master, Duncan Sinclair, for losing their possessions on the journey out, securing £15 damages. What is particularly interesting is that both Cable and Holmes had been convicted of burglary and transported in lieu of the death penalty (Cable for seven years, Holmes for fourteen), yet were not treated in the colony as attainted (see Kercher 1995). That Governor Arthur Phillip, Judge Advocate David Collins and Reverend Richard Johnson – the Judicial Group of the Colony – facilitated this prosecution perhaps speaks to a more sympathetic attitude on the ground. Indeed, Alan Atkinson postulates Phillip's 'up-to-date notions, on penal discipline' may have derived from encounters with Bentham through Lord Lansdowne's coterie of advanced thinkers. See Atkinson 1994, 62.

100 'A Plea for the Constitution' in Bentham, ed. Causer and Schofield 2022, 342.

101 This might have been different, if James Matra had had his way and New South Wales had homed 10,000 American Loyalists.

102 'A Plea for the Constitution' in Bentham, ed. Causer and Schofield 2022, 345.

103 'A Plea for the Constitution' in Bentham, ed. Causer and Schofield 2022, 344.

104 Reynolds 2021, 134. Reynolds attributes Bentham's sentence 'The flaw is an incurable one' (see 'A Plea for the Constitution' in Bentham, ed. Causer and Schofield 2022, 345) to the absence of a treaty, but Bentham appears to be referring to charters.

105 'A Plea for the Constitution' in Bentham, ed. Causer and Schofield 2022, 345.

106 'A Plea for the Constitution' in Bentham, ed. Causer and Schofield 2022, 345. Wampum beads held, among several characteristics, ceremonial value as a record of an important agreement, and were exchanged as part of Treaty negotiations in British North America. See also Zoë Laidlaw's chapter in this volume.

107 'New Wales' in Bentham, ed. Causer and Schofield 2022, 4.

108 There is an extensive debate over whether convicts or empire drove this agenda. Both forces worked together.

109 'New Wales' in Bentham, ed. Causer and Schofield 2022, 22.

110 'Colonization Company Proposal' in Bentham, ed. Causer and Schofield 2022, 408.

111 King 2000, 356.

112 Cross 1917, 565.

113 Romilly was thus paraphrased by his opponent Colonel Frankland during debate over the 'Dwelling House Robbery Bill'. Frankland continued, sarcastically: 'The criminal looks to practical results. In his meditations he reflects, that prosecutors decline prosecuting, juries acquit, judges mitigate, kings pardon, nobody is ever hanged.' See *House of Commons Debates*, 29 March 1811, vol. xix. 637.

114 Sir Samuel Romilly, *House of Commons Debates*, 17 February 1813, vol xxiv. 563.

115 See *The Parliamentary Register*, 29 March 1811, 493.

116 T.F. Buxton, maiden speech, Commons sitting of Tuesday, 2 March 1819. *Hansard*, First Series, vol. xxxix. 819.

117 For a discussion of the dominant place of the penitentiary in the history of criminal justice, see Maxwell-Stewart's chapter in this volume.

118 For related arguments see Atkinson 1994. In North America, convicts, like the enslaved, were involuntary migrants set apart from 'political society', becoming the 'independent republic of vice' against which, in part, the new 'republic of virtue sought to define itself': Atkinson 1994, 113–14.

119 Samuel Romilly to Bentham, 28 August 1802, in Bentham, ed. Dinwiddy 1988, 92. It is somewhat surprising how his letter rapidly moved on to the mundane. See also Romilly to Bentham, 15 February 1803, ibid, 201–2.

120 Causer 2019, 19, 23.

121 In March 1830, acting on behalf of the Home Secretary Robert Peel, the bookseller Thomas Egerton approached Bentham as to 'whether he has published any work on Transportation', Bentham replied, directly to Peel, that 'no work written directly and by its title on the subject of that mode of punishment was ever published or written by me'. See Causer 2019, 23.

122 Bentham, ed. Burns and Hart 1996, 158, quoted in Causer 2019, 3.

Bibliography

Primary Sources

Archival sources

National Archives UK, HO 42, Home Office: Domestic Correspondence, 1782–1820.
E 197/34, Bills of Sheriff's Cravings, 1800–6.

Parliamentary papers

House of Commons Sessional Papers of the Eighteenth Century, ed. S. Lambert, 145 vols. Wilmington, DE: Scholarly Resources Inc., 1975.

Printed sources

Bentham, J. *An Introduction to the Principles of Morals and Legislation*, ed. J.H. Burns and H.L.A. Hart. Oxford: Clarendon Press, 1970.

Bentham, J. *The Correspondence of Jeremy Bentham* (*CW*), vol. vii, ed. J.R. Dinwiddy. Oxford: Clarendon Press, 1988.

Bentham, J. *Rights, Representation, and Reform: Nonsense Upon Stilts and other writings on the French Revolution*, ed. P. Schofield, C. Pease-Watkin, and C. Blamires. Oxford: Clarendon Press, 2002.

Bentham, J. *Panopticon versus New South Wales and other writings on Australia*, ed. T. Causer and P. Schofield. London: UCL Press, 2022.

Blackstone, W. *Commentaries on the Laws of England*, 4 vols. Oxford: Clarendon Press, 1765–9.

Hansard, first series.

House of Commons Debates.

The Parliamentary Register.

Secondary Sources

Allen, R.C. 'Engels' Pause: Technical Change, Capital Accumulation, and Inequality in the British Industrial Revolution', *Explorations in Economic History* 46: 4 (2009a): 418–35.

Allen, R.C. *The British Industrial Revolution in Global Perspective*. Cambridge: Cambridge University Press, 2009b.

Allen, R.C. 'Class Structure and Inequality during the Industrial Revolution: Lessons from England's Social Tables, 1688–1867', *Economic History Review* 72: 1 (2018): 88–125.

Atkinson, A. 'The Free-Born Englishman Transported: Convict Rights as a Measure of Eighteenth-Century Empire', *Past and Present* 144: 1 (1994): 88–115.

Atkinson, A. *The Europeans in Australia: A History, Volume I*. Melbourne: Oxford University Press, 1997.

Beattie, J. *Crime and the Courts in England, 1660–1800*. Oxford: Clarendon Press, 1986.

Bonney, R., ed. *The Rise of the Fiscal State in Europe c.1200–1815*. Oxford: Oxford University Press, 1999.

Broadberry, S., Campbell, B.M.S., Klein, A., Overton, M., and van Leeuwen, B. *British Economic Growth 1270–1870*. Cambridge: Cambridge University Press, 2015.

Causer, T. '"The Evacuation of That Scene of Wickedness and Wretchedness": Jeremy Bentham, the Panopticon and New South Wales, 1802–1803', *Journal of Colonial History* 21 (2019): 1–24.

Cockburn, J.S. 'Punishment and Brutalization in the English Enlightenment', *Law and History Review* 12: 1 (1994): 155–79.

Cross, A.L. 'The English Criminal Law and Benefit of Clergy during the Eighteenth and Early Nineteenth Century', *American Historical Review* 22: 3 (1917): 544–65.

Devereaux, S. 'The Making of the Penitentiary Act, 1775–1779', *The Historical Journal* 42: 2 (1999): 405–33.

Devereaux, S. 'Imposing the Royal Pardon: Execution, Transportation, and Convict Resistance in London, 1789', *Law and History Review* 25: 1 (2007): 101–38.

Flynn, M. *The Second Fleet: Britain's Grim Convict Armada of 1790*. Sydney: Library of Australian History, 1993.

Hitchcock, T. and Shoemaker, R. *London Lives: Poverty, Crime and the Making of a Modern City, 1690–1800*. Cambridge: Cambridge University Press, 2015.

Hufton, O. *The Poor of Eighteenth Century France 1750–1789*. Oxford: Clarendon Press, 1974.

Hume, L.J. 'Bentham's Panopticon: An Administrative History – I', *[Australian] Historical Studies* 15 (1973): 703–21.

Humphries, J. 'Enclosures, Common Rights, and Women: The Proletarianization of Families in the Late Eighteenth and Early Nineteenth Centuries', *Journal of Economic History* 5: 3 (1990): 17–42.

Humphries, J. and Weisdorf, J. 'Unreal Wages? A New Empirical Foundation for the Study of Living Standards and Economic Growth in England, 1260–1860', *The Economic Journal* 129 (2019): 2867–87.

Hurren, E.T. *Dissecting the Criminal Corpse: Staging Post-Execution Punishment in Early Modern England*. London: Palgrave Macmillan, 2016.

Inikori, J.E. *Africans and the Industrial Revolution in England*. Cambridge: Cambridge University Press, 2002.

Innes, J. 'What Would a "Four Nations" Approach to the Study of Eighteenth-Century British Social Policy Entail?'. In *Kingdoms United? Great Britain and Ireland since 1500: Integration and Diversity*, ed. J.S. Connolly, 181–99. Dublin: Four Courts Press, 1999.

Innes, J. *Inferior Politics: Social Problems and Social Policies in Eighteenth-Century Britain*. Oxford: Oxford University Press, 2009.

Jackson, R.V. 'Luxury in Punishment: Jeremy Bentham on the Cost of the Convict Colony in New South Wales', *Australian Historical Studies* 23 (1988): 42–59.

Jacob, M.C. *The First Knowledge Economy: Human Capital and the European Economy, 1750–1850*. Cambridge: Cambridge University Press, 2014.

Jones, D. *Crime, Protest, Community, and Police in Nineteenth-Century Britain*. London: Routledge, 1982.

Kercher, B. *Unruly Child: A History of Law in Australia*. St. Leonards: Allen & Unwin, 1995.

Kercher, B. 'Perish or Prosper: The Law and Convict Transportation in the British Empire, 1700–1850', *Law and History Review* 21: 3 (2003): 527–84.

King, P. *Crime, Justice, and Discretion in England 1740–1820.* Oxford: Oxford University Press, 2000.

King, P. *Punishing the Criminal Corpse, 1700–1840: Aggravated Forms of the Death Penalty in England.* London: Palgrave, 2017.

King, P. and Ward, R. 'Rethinking the Bloody Code in Eighteenth-Century Britain: Capital Punishment at the Centre and on the Periphery', *Past and Present* 228 (2015): 159–205.

King, S. and Tomkins, A., eds. *The Poor in England 1700–1850: An Economy of Makeshifts.* Manchester: Manchester University Press, 2003.

Kuznets, S. *Modern Economic Growth: Rate, Structure and Spread.* New Haven: Yale University Press, 1966.

Landes, D.S. *The Unbound Prometheus: Technological Change and Industrial Development in Western Europe from 1750 to the Present.* Cambridge: Cambridge University Press, 1969.

Lindert, P.H. 'Unequal English Wealth since 1670', *Journal of Political Economy* 94: 6 (1986): 1127–62.

McGowen, R. 'The Body and Punishment in Eighteenth-Century England', *Journal of Modern History* 59: 4 (1987): 651–79.

Meredith, D. and Oxley, D. 'Food and Fodder: Feeding England, 1700–1900', *Past and Present* 222: 1 (2014): 163–214.

Milanovic, B. 'Towards an Explanation of Inequality in Premodern Societies: The Role of Colonies, Urbanization, and High Population Density', *Economic History Review* 71: 4 (2018): 1029–47.

Mitchell, B.R. *British Historical Statistics.* Cambridge: Cambridge University Press, 2011.

Mokyr, J. *The Gifts of Athena: Historical Origins of the Knowledge Economy.* Princeton: Princeton University Press, 2002.

Mokyr, J. *The Enlightened Economy: An Economic History of Britain 1700–1850.* New Haven: Yale University Press, 2009.

Mokyr, J. and Nye, J.V.C. 'Distributional Coalitions, the Industrial Revolution, and the Origins of Economic Growth in Britain', *Southern Economic Journal* 74: 1 (2007): 50–70.

North, D.C. and Weingast, B.R. 'Constitutions and Commitment: The Evolution of Institutions Governing Public Choice in Seventeenth-Century England', *Journal of Economic History* 49: 4 (1989): 803–32.

O'Brien, P.K. 'Fiscal Exceptionalism: Great Britain and its European Rivals from Civil War to Triumph at Trafalgar and Waterloo'. In *The Political Economy of British Historical Experience, 1688–1914,* ed. D. Winch and P.K. O'Brien, 245–66. Oxford: Oxford University Press, 2002.

O'Brien, P.K. and Hunt, P.A. 'England, 1485–1815'. In *The Rise of the Fiscal State in Europe c.1200–1815,* ed. R. Bonney, 54–100. Oxford: Clarendon Press, 1999.

Reynolds, H. *Truth Telling: History, Sovereignty and the Uluru Statement.* Sydney: NewSouth Publishing, 2021.

Semple, J. *Bentham's Prison: A Study of the Panopticon Penitentiary.* Oxford: Clarendon Press, 1993.

Shaw-Taylor, L. and Wrigley, E.A. 'Occupational Structure and Population Change'. In *The Cambridge Economic History of Modern Britain,* ed. R. Floud, J. Humphries, and P. Johnson, 53–88. Cambridge: Cambridge University Press, 2014.

Snell, K.D.M. *Annals of the Labouring Poor.* Cambridge: Cambridge University Press, 1985.

Solow, B.L. and Engerman, S.L., eds. *British Capitalism and Caribbean Slavery: The Legacy of Eric Williams.* Cambridge: Cambridge University Press, 1987.

Szreter, S., Cooper, H., and Szreter, B. *Incentivising an Ethical Economics: A Radical Plan to Force a Step Change in the Quality and Quantity of the UK's Economic Growth.* London: Institute for Public Policy Research Economics Prize, 2019.

Wallis, P., Colson, J., and Chilosi, D. 'Structural Change and Economic Growth in the British Economy before the Industrial Revolution, 1500–1800', *Journal of Economic History* 78: 3 (2018): 862–903.

Williams, E. *Capitalism and Slavery.* Chapel Hill: University of North Carolina Press, 1944.

Winch, D. *Classical Political Economy and the Colonies.* Cambridge, MA: Harvard University Press, 1965.

Zahedieh, N. 'Regulation, Rent-Seeking, and the Glorious Revolution in the English Atlantic Economy', *Economic History Review* 63: 4 (2009): 865–90.

Zahedieh, N. 'Copper, Colonies and the Market for Inventive Activity, 1680–1730', *Economic History Review* 66: 3 (2013): 805–25.

Unpublished theses

Foster, C. 'The Demise of Death: Capital Punishment in England and Wales during the First Half of the Nineteenth Century'. M.Phil. in Economic and Social History: University of Oxford, 2019.

Mehta, K. 'Courts and Prisons: Criminal Imprisonment in the London Metropolis, 1750–1845'. D.Phil. in History: University of Oxford, 2021.

2

Bentham, convict transportation, and the Great Confinement Thesis

Hamish Maxwell-Stewart

Since the 1970s the literature on the evolution of British criminal justice systems has been dominated by the history of prisons and penitentiaries.[1] The 'great confinement thesis' – a narrative that seeks to explain the history of judicial sanctions as a function of state power – has shaped much of that literature. According to its proponents, where central authority was weak, systems of kin-based restorative justice dominated. As early modern states evolved, monarchs imposed their authority through the use of judicially sanctioned violence. The development of more effective institutions of government was accompanied by a rise in professional police forces and other systems of surveillance. Bentham's proposal for a panopticon is often seen as a pivotal moment in this transformation. In Michel Foucault's words, it formed a blueprint – not just for a new form of prison – 'but also for a hospital, for a school, for a workshop'. It was in short a template 'for all institutions'.[2]

The great confinement thesis refocused attention on Bentham's work, particularly his plan for a panopticon. As Peter Renfield put it, the scrutiny of Foucault and his followers assured the emergence of 'Bentham's architectural ode to surveillance' from 'the dusty closet of history'.[3] While Bentham's proposal for a system of colour-coded national penitentiaries became associated with a forward-looking concept (rather than a design failure), his opposition to penal transportation helped to associate the overseas deployment of convict labour with the use of the whip and other outmoded forms of punishment. As a result, transportation has often been regarded as something of an historical curiosity – an 'archaic and unscientific punishment' that survived into the nineteenth century by accident rather than design.[4]

The first half of this chapter will revisit Bentham's opposition to transportation, in order to illustrate the ways in which his arguments have helped to shape the subsequent literature. The second will critically examine two assumptions that underpin the 'great confinement thesis'. The first of these is the notion that a direct developmental pathway can be traced between the establishment of the bridewell in the late sixteenth century and the rise of the penitentiary in the nineteenth century. The second assumption is that the transportation of offenders to overseas colonial possessions was decisively rejected in the first half of the nineteenth century in favour of the penitentiary. As the chapter will show, both of these arguments are flawed.

Bentham and transportation

Bentham's opposition to penal transportation was first laid out in 'A View of the Hard-Labour Bill' in 1778, and then expanded upon in his two 'Letters to Lord Pelham' and 'A Plea for the Constitution' in 1802–3.[5] His main concerns were that transportation was an unequal and disproportionate punishment which had the additional disadvantage of being anachronistic and costly. Its only benefit in his eyes was that it put the labour of convicts to productive use, although he argued that this could be better achieved in a domestic penitentiary system. Bentham also shared Cesare Beccaria's principal objection to transportation. Both thought it was an inappropriate punishment because it extracted labour from the body of the condemned at a place that was far distant from the location of the original crime, and thus failed to act as a sufficient deterrent to other would-be offenders.[6] As Bentham noted in 'A View of the Hard-Labour Bill', transportation had 'at all Times been found insufficient, both for the Reformation of Criminals, and also for the deterring others by Their Example'.[7] Finally, Bentham argued that the colony was bound to fail because of the disproportionate number, and poor quality, of women dispatched to Botany Bay.[8] It was thus doomed to demographic extinction.

Bentham was on solid ground in terms of his first objection. There was indeed a large discrepancy in the terms served by prisoners sentenced to be transported and those imprisoned in the first half of the nineteenth century. As convicts were questioned about their previous encounters with the courts on arrival in the Australian penal colonies, it is possible to use this confessional data to compare the variation in transportation and imprisonment sentence lengths imposed upon this cohort (Table 2.1). Counting life as 21 years, the mean length of a transportation sentence was 13 years compared to just 0.39 years for all previous convictions that resulted in a sentence to imprisonment. Even prosecutions for forgery and other offences against the currency, an offence which Georgian and early Victorian courts tended to treat with some severity, resulted in mean prison terms of under a year compared to nearly 14 years' transportation. Some of the discrepancies in sentence tariffs in Table 2.1 can be explained by differences in sentencing court. Thus, many of the former convictions reported by transported convicts are likely to have been awarded by magistrates' benches or petty sessions. While such summary courts were empowered to sentence an offender to a term of imprisonment in a house of correction, periods of confinement in these institutions were usually short – a matter of weeks or even days. The data nevertheless highlights the issue that concerned Bentham, namely the huge increase in tariff between sentences to imprisonment and transportation.

Table 2.1: Male convicts, sentence length comparisons.

	Sentenced to imprisonment		Sentenced to transportation	
	Number	Mean sentence length (years)	Number	Mean sentence length (years)
Offences against the person	2,987	0.22	1,490	15.41
Offences against property	29,327	0.51	40,456	11.12
Forgery and offences against currency	326	0.90	947	13.82
Offences against good order	4,467	0.15	215	10.54
Other civil offences	1,317	0.24	1,127	13.77
Offences against military discipline	1,450	0.32	856	13.00
All	39,874	0.39	45,091	12.94

Note: a sentence for Life was calculated at 21 years.
Sources: Tasmanian Archives and Heritage Office (TAHO), CON 31, 33, 40 and 41.

This difference in sentencing patterns was driven by economics. As imprisonment was costly, terms were deliberately kept short. This was true of both houses of correction and county gaols. By contrast, the minimum sentence to transportation in the seventeenth century was fixed at seven years, that is, much longer than any custodially-based form of punishment.[9] This was designed to ensure that convicts remained saleable in the transatlantic market in unfree labour. A seven-year sentence was considerably longer than the mean length of contract signed by an indentured servant. There were pragmatic reasons for this, as the prior criminal record of convicts made them less attractive to colonial buyers.[10] Such disadvantages could be offset by increasing the term that each prisoner was bound to serve – a longer sentence effectively discounted the services of prisoners, making them more attractive to colonial masters.

Unlike in the Atlantic economies of the seventeenth and eighteenth centuries, the labour of convicts was not sold to private sector buyers in the Australian colonies. Nevertheless, sentence length continued to be an important driver of the colonial economy. While the work performed by prisoners built the infrastructure upon which an expanding colonial economy depended, settlers further benefited from the labour of prisoners assigned to the private sector for free prior to 1840 and lent out at minimal rates thereafter. Although masters had to house, clothe and feed their convict servants, in the 1830s these costs amounted to an estimated 59 per cent of a free wage. While the amount of saving to the private sector fluctuated over time, the foregone earnings of convicts effectively subsidized the income of their masters.[11] It is thus no surprise that in most years the demand for convict labour outstripped supply. Available labour depended, not just upon the number of convicts landed in the Australian colonies, but on the length of time they were bound to serve without wages. Thus, although the property rights the state acquired in the body of a convict were no longer sold as in the seventeenth- and eighteenth-century Atlantic, the scale of profits that accrued from their exploitation still depended upon the length of time they were unfree. The upshot of this was that a recidivist's first encounters with the court system were likely to result in very short custodial terms, followed by a 3,318 per cent increase in tariff severity when the court decided on a transportation sentence rather than another term of imprisonment. That increase in time enabled the British to use the labour of thieves to steal a continent.

In Bentham's view the problem was even greater than this, since each sentence to transportation was in effect two sentences – a fixed term to be spent in bondage and the balance of the convict's life in exile.[12] It mattered little in his eyes if each prisoner was technically free to return to Britain and Ireland once their sentence had expired, if he or she was not provided with the material means to accomplish this act.[13] If Australia was a gaol, it was a place from which the vast majority of those condemned to serve would never leave. This was a point that was certainly not lost on the British government. By the mid-1820s it had established a system of gradated transportation experiences. Convicts sentenced to hard labour overseas might serve their time out in the hulks, never actually leaving the confines of a metropolitan port, be sentenced to Bermuda where they would be returned to the British-based hulk system after serving a proportion of their sentence, or be dispatched to New South Wales or Van Diemen's Land.

An examination of 9,398 convict men discharged from the hulks in the Thames and Solent estuaries in the decade 1835–45 reveals that age, sentence, marital status, literacy and occupation all influenced convict outcomes (see Appendix 1 for a detailed breakdown of these results). Those who were aged between 17 and 25 were at greater risk of being transported compared to younger and older convicts who were disproportionately pardoned or transferred to other domestic institu-tions without setting foot on a transport vessel. Sentence length also played a powerful role in the decision to transport a convict. Convicts with seven-year sentences (the shortest period a convict could be transported for) were less likely to be sent into exile. Social capital also influenced the probability of a convict leaving domestic shores. Those who could read and write, or claimed white-collar occupations, were at significantly less risk of being shipped to a penal colony.

Selection also played a part in determining which colony a convict was sent to. Construction workers were statistically more likely to end up in Bermuda or Gibraltar where their services could be put to good use in naval dock construction and maintenance. Conversely, those with a record of military service were disproportionately sent to Australia to be deployed as constables, overseers and flagellators. Bermuda and Gibraltar men differed in other ways too. As with their former hulk mates who remained in Britain, they were more likely to be sentenced to seven years. Importantly, they were also more likely to be married. This suggests that consideration of a convict's familial relations played a role in the state's decision whether to condemn them into permanent exile or not. As Bermuda and Gibraltar men were returned to Britain to be released back into metropolitan populations post-sentence, married convicts dispatched to those colonies could be expected to be reunited with their families should they survive the experience. Thus, the operation of the trans-imperial transportation system in action provides de facto evidence that the fault lines predicted by Bentham eventuated in ways that were sufficiently problematic to necessitate intervention to ameliorate their impact.

There were other ways in which it might be argued that a sentence to transportation was unequal and disproportionate. Bentham was particularly concerned about the degree to which it placed convicts in a state of servitude, subjecting them to the 'uncertain and variable direction of a private master'.[14] Transportation's dependence on the vagaries of colonial labour markets ensured that prisoners were punished, not according to the perceived severity of the offence for which they were transported, but their colonial utility. Thus, textile workers were much more likely to be flogged compared to clerks, ploughmen and carpenters because there was no colonial demand for their skills.[15] There were other pernicious effects too. The prosecution risk, and hence the chances of being punished, were higher for convicts assigned to urban areas than for those engaged in agricultural work.[16] This was in part a product of more intensive policing – a feature of colonial towns – which in turn increased surveillance rates. Masters based in urban conurbations also had easier access to courts as well as labour depots and other sites where convicts waiting to be assigned were housed. By contrast, those in rural locations were likely to incur greater costs in bringing a convict servant to trial and greater delays in receiving a replacement, consideration of which is likely to have impacted upon the decision to prosecute.[17]

While Bentham had good reason to question the degree to which the punishment of transportation fitted the crime, his other objections appear to have been based on less solid reasoning. He was incorrect in his assumption that the poor quality and small number of women transported would doom the convict settlement to demographic failure.[18] While he was correct in predicting that fertility rates amongst transported women would be lower than those in the general British and Irish population, this turned out to be due to the impacts of punishments on female bodies rather than the alleged vices of the transported (see below). He also failed to appreciate the extent to which cheap labour and handouts of former First Nation land for minimal rents would attract British and Irish settlers with capital. Fertility rates amongst this group were much higher than for convicts and former convicts (Figure 2.1 below). While the number of European women in Van Diemen's Land lagged behind men, a product of the smaller

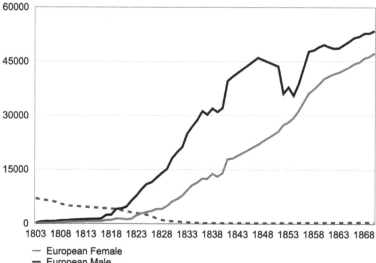

Figure 2.1: Population of Van Diemen's Land/Tasmania, 1803–70.
Source: Australian Bureau Statistics, 2014.

number transported relative to male convicts, the European population nevertheless rose sharply. Notoriously, this was in sharp contrast to the fall in the Indigenous population.

The crux of Bentham's opposition to transportation, however, was founded on a belief that transportation could not meet the proper ends of punishment, while a system of national penitentiaries could, and would prove a cheaper alternative to operate. He was convinced that savings would result from the installation of more efficient surveillance systems, which would lead to a reduction in the costs of employing warders and other staff. He also argued that effective monitoring would lead to an increase in the profits derived from the employment of prisoners.[19] A reduction in the rate of recidivism might also result in further savings to the state. He gambled that, collectively, these factors would outweigh the costs of building and maintaining a series of panopticons.

In this Bentham was almost certainly wrong. His 1787 plan for a panopticon would have housed about 224 inmates.[20] The 1791 revised plan expanded the number of floors from four to six but reduced the number of cells on each floor to just 24. This version could accommodate only 144 prisoners if solitary confinement was employed. In the course of rethinking his redesign, however, Bentham abandoned his previous enthusiasm for the principles of solitary. This was an inevitable concession. As subsequent penal architects would discover, solitary was a costly experiment. Yet, even if four prisoners were put in each cell, the maximum capacity of the second version of the panopticon was 664 – less than the 775 convicts transported on the First Fleet.[21] Although the government at one stage toyed with constructing a panopticon that would house a thousand convicts, it is difficult to see how this number could have been accommodated within any of Bentham's designs, unless more than one panopticon was incorporated into a single institution. Bentham himself appears to have never fully grasped these logistical constraints. As Tim Causer points out, he even suggested that upon the completion of his panopticon a fleet might be dispatched to Botany Bay to reimport the inhabitants of Britain's far-flung thief colony.[22] Even allowing for deaths at sea, the number of returned exiles is likely to have swamped his surveillance machine.

The rise in convictions following the end of the Napoleonic Wars would have presented even greater logistical challenges. A penitentiary on the scale envisaged by Bentham would have been woefully insufficient to house the 3,056 convicts landed in the Australian colonies in 1820, for example. Yet, this considerably understates the problem as it assumes that each prisoner would only serve a year in custody. By 1828 the number of serving convicts in Australia had mushroomed to 23,574. Even accounting for a reduction in the amount of time served by each prisoner, panopticon construction would have surely struggled to keep pace with the British Empire's capacity and desire to dispatch convicts to its penal colonies. The initial plan to set the minimum sentence of confinement in a national penitentiary to five years would have necessitated the rapid construction of multiple institutions as each previous design became clogged with serving prisoners. Populating the panopticon was an altogether different proposition to populating a continent.

Bentham used the authority of the 1798 Finance Committee's Report on police and convict establishments to support his case for the panopticon, despite the fact this Committee had used his own inflated estimates of transportation costs.[23] Yet, even these figures fail to support Bentham's argument. Frank Lewis's detailed reconstruction of the costs and return to the British government suggest that, although transportation was initially expensive, by 1805 the net costs were about the same as warehousing convicts in hulks moored in British estuaries. By 1810 the equation had tilted decisively in favour of transportation. Lewis estimates that, on average, a male convict aged 20 or more transported to the Australian colonies yielded a small net profit to the government of £2 per year, while a similar convict housed in a hulk accumulated a loss of £10.7s.[24] Hulks, however, were relatively cheap to operate compared to a penitentiary. Millbank Penitentiary, constructed on the site originally purchased in 1799 for Bentham's panopticon, though managed according to considerably different principles, had cost £500 per cell by the time of its completion in 1821. At full capacity its annual running costs were £16 per inmate, but its many design failures meant that for most of its operational life it was half empty.[25] Even discounting its considerable establishment costs, the first attempt at a national penitentiary proved much more expensive than transportation.

As had been recognized as early as 1779, the expense of building and maintaining a system of penitentiaries was unlikely to be met by the profits extracted from the labour of prisoners.[26] The problem was exacerbated by adherence to the principles of solitary confinement, which limited the nature of work that could be performed by inmates to tasks such as weaving, picking oakum, laundry and sewing. It soon became obvious that the labour of prisoners would do little to defray maintenance costs – a marked contrast to penal transportation.[27]

Other early attempts to construct penitentiaries on the Bentham model proved equally problematic. The institution that adhered most closely to Bentham's design – Pittsburgh's Western Penitentiary – was such an utter failure that it was razed to the ground in 1826, just seven years after its completion.[28] Richmond Gaol in Dublin fared little better. The sister project to Millbank Penitentiary, this establishment opened its doors in 1820 but discharged its last prisoner 11 years later in 1831.[29] The new penitentiaries failed in other ways too. Millbank, an attempt to stitch seven panopticon-inspired buildings together within the confines of one structure, was widely regarded as a design failure. Its many miles of corridors were punctuated by angled corners and circular staircases that were notoriously difficult to navigate. Worse still, its elaborate internal ventilation system allowed prisoners to communicate with each other. Not only did Millbank fail to provide an efficient means of observing prisoners, but it failed in its objective of establishing total segregation. By 1835 the state conceded the need to establish a prison inspectorate to oversee the operation of penitentiaries – surely an admission of failure.[30] Given the unpromising nature of these early penitentiary experiments, it is perhaps not surprising that as late as 1867, the year before the final convict vessel arrived in Western Australia, there were still only nine national penitentiaries in England and Wales.

Transportation and the birth of the prison

As John Braithwaite has argued, the rise of the prison has been 'read as the enduring central question' by many historians interested in the evolution of European criminal justice systems.[31] Yet, the slow development of the penitentiary presents a problem for the great confinement thesis, at least in its conventional form. While there were many county gaols, until the mid-nineteenth century these were primarily used to house those awaiting trial or inmates on very short sentences. As can be seen from Table 2.2, prior to 1780 less than 5 per cent of Old Bailey verdicts resulted in a sentence to imprisonment. Five times as many prisoners were sentenced to be branded and whipped as those ordered to be confined. Accounting for capital felons reprieved on condition of transportation, ten times more prisoners were condemned to colonial servitude than the number domestically incarcerated. Even after 1780 the rise of the prison was a protracted affair. In the years from 1781 to 1816, when the first cohort of prisoners entered through the forbidding gates of Millbank, the proportion sentenced to transportation and imprisonment was about the same. While the cessation of transportation to the American colonies precipitated a sentencing crisis, the courts resorted to a variety of options to address this, including non-custodial alternatives such as corporal punishment and fines. From 1817 to 1842, the year Pentonville opened, the share of sentences to imprisonment increased to 46 per cent. At 37 per cent, however, transportation was the second most common sentencing option. It was only after the establishment of a national penitentiary system in the years following 1842 that the share of sentences to transportation started to markedly decline. Between the years 1843 and the arrival of the last transport vessel in Western Australia in 1868, penal servitude accounted for just 13 per cent of Old Bailey verdicts compared to 83 per cent of cases resulting in a prison sentence.

While both Foucault and J.H. Langbein traced the origins of confinement in Britain to the development of bridewells in the sixteenth century, it is difficult to see how this worked in practice.[32] There was never a straight line of development between these two institutions. For the most part, houses of correction and county gaols and lock-ups remained small-scale institutions consisting of little more than a few rooms until at least the Howard reforms of the late eighteenth century. In part this was because of political opposition, as many argued that subjecting prisoners to hard labour was a continental

Table 2.2: Sentences recorded in Old Bailey Proceedings, January 1674–December 1780, by percentage.

Sentence	1674–1780	1781–1816	1817–42	1843–68
Death	19.31	12.82	6.58	0.41
Transportation	47.28	26.77	37.38	12.60
Imprisonment	4.85	27.09	46.29	81.98
Branding	12.59	0.07	0.00	0.00
Corporal punishment	11.08	11.78	4.83	1.01
Military duties	0.47	0.30	0.00	0.00
Fines, sureties etc.	2.99	18.05	2.62	1.12
Pardoned or sentence respited	1.44	3.12	2.29	2.87
	100.00	100.00	100.00	100.00

Source: Tim Hitchcock, Robert Shoemaker, Clive Emsley, Sharon Howard and Jamie McLaughlin *et al.*, *The Old Bailey Proceedings Online, 1674–1913* (www.oldbaileyonline.org, version 7.0, 24 March 2012).

practice the adoption of which 'would draw too great an Odium on the Government'.[33] Yet, without the extraction of labour from the bodies of inmates, incarceration remained a prohibitively expensive option. As late as 1776 the total number of convicted prisoners incarcerated in England and Wales was estimated to be just 1,647, little more than the 1,147 transported annually to the American colonies.[34] The majority of gaol inmates were either debtors or prisoners awaiting trial. The only exceptions to this were those sentenced to transportation who were awaiting sale to a contractor.[35]

Yet, these numbers only tell part of the story. As most seventeenth- and eighteenth-century carceral institutions were poorly funded, gaolers relied on fees levied upon inmates to supplement meagre or non-existent salaries. Prisoners regularly had to pay for the use of their cell, bedding, food and even their release (although the latter was made illegal in 1774).[36] Thus, while prisoners were invariably sentenced to short terms in custody, many were incarcerated beyond the expiration of their sentence because they had become indebted to their gaoler. This rendered them liable to quasi-transportation. Gaolers redeemed debts in the same manner as crimps profited from the labour of indebted sailors. The only means that many prisoners had of regaining their freedom was to sign an indenture – in effect condemning themselves to further years of unfreedom by selling their labour to a colonial shipping merchant who would in turn sell on the indenture for a profit in the colonial market for bonded servants.[37] Interestingly, Bentham's suggested release mechanism from a penitentiary bore many similarities. Once a sentence had been served, the prisoner either had to find a householder willing to pay a £50 good behaviour bond, or join the military; if unable or unwilling to do either, they would enter the 'subsidiary panopticon', a much more relaxed regime, but still a form of confinement.

The governors of bridewells and city and town corporations utilized a similar system to offset their costs. Between 1617 and 1648 the Bridewell court books contain orders for the transportation of 1,106 individuals condemned to service in Barbados, Virginia, Bermuda and 'the sea'.[38] While it is unlikely that all of these were actually contracted to shipping merchants, the court books contain details for only a third of those committed to Bridewell.[39] In the first half of the sixteenth century this institution alone may have condemned several thousand to transportation. Nor was it a practice confined to London. Scottish and other English towns and cities also organized for the transportation of vagrants and petty criminals, effectively apprenticing the convicted poor into colonial labour.[40] Transportation was thus neither a small-scale practice, nor a process that operated independently of the workhouse and prison. Instead, the bridewell, gaol and the overseas plantation were formally and informally connected through economics. The cost of incarceration was effectively offset, either through the direct sale of the convict's labour, or by turning a blind eye to practices that allowed poorly paid officials to profit through informal sales. Thus, the operation of bridewells and county gaols was always entangled with the evolution of transportation. The two systems needed each other. Without the sale of inmate labour into transatlantic markets, it would have been impossible to operate a parsimonious domestic system of confinement. In short, there were never two competing policies, a nascent shore-based apparatus of confinement aimed at fashioning docile bodies, and a more archaic alternative strategy that pitched transported labour into the bloody world of the Atlantic plantation. In reality these two criminal justice systems were always attached at the hip.

Thus, the operation of penal transportation was critical in driving many of the outcomes hitherto credited to domestic systems of incarceration. This was particularly the case with the reduction in the execution rate, which was inversely correlated with the number of prisoners shipped overseas.[41] As the numbers show, the shift in the public exercise of judicial violence – a central feature of the 'great confinement thesis' – was driven, not by the rise of the prison, but by the off-shoring of Britain's and Ireland's system of criminal correction. That off-shoring process, however, had other deeper connections to the rise of criminal justice surveillance systems.

There has always been a tendency to see transportation as a judicial sanction that operated externally from any institution – a form of criminal justice on the loose. Yet, this is only because the institutions critical to the operation of transportation, the plantation and the ship, have not been traditionally conceived as sites of surveillance. This is to some extent puzzling as both fit neatly into Foucault's carceral archipelago argument. As we have seen, for him the significance of Bentham's design for a panopticon was that it operated as a blueprint for all manner of other institutions. Yet, in similar fashion, the ship and the plantation were regimented places of labour where time was strictly regulated. Both have been claimed as important early forms of industrialization that informed later management practices. As Du Bois put it, the plantation 'corresponds' to the modern factory in its 'worst conceivable form'. For him, the connection between the two systems was the way in which work was organized so that it could be constantly surveyed. This was the role performed by drivers and overseers who were the equivalent of factory line managers.[42]

On board a ship it was the petty officers who were charged with maintaining a watchful eye on the other members of the crew. Yet, it was the industrial management of ship-board time that distinguished maritime work from other early modern forms of labour.[43] The ship's bell beat out the divisions into which the day was divided, which itself was separated into watches, each watch being further divided into eight half-hour increments. At sea, a bell rang every half-hour ensuring that all worked, ate and slept to the same rhythm. This was factory discipline at work – a form of regimentation experienced by tens of thousands of workers at sea before factory walls sprung up in significant numbers on land.[44]

Both of these panoptic devices were critical to the management of convict labour in Australia. Indeed, far from being a form of transoceanic paddy wagon whose sole task was to convey the body of the condemned to the site of colonial labour extraction, the ship was a floating system of prison management. While every transportation vessel operated as a place of confinement, they also contained a schoolroom and a hospital. It is also easy to forget the extent to which they also functioned as a workspace. Divided into watches, decks or divisions, convicts were put to work scrubbing deck, washing clothes, airing bedding and sewing, as well as performing that most prison-like of tasks – picking oakum. The transport vessel was in effect multiple institutions wrapped up in one. As such it played a crucial role as an umbilical cord that linked metropolitan and colonial places of incarceration. Its key task was to discipline convict bodies while on the move. In short it was a machine designed to convert the 'idle poor' into penal labourers. While Bentham saw the transport ship as merely a cost that could be used to highlight the virtues of a more sophisticated shore-based form of management, there is an argument that this remarkably flexible device constituted a floating panopticon in its own right.

Transportation to Australia was panoptic in other ways too. As well as its human cargo, the transport vessel conveyed much in the way of paperwork to Australia. This included the indent, the legal document that transferred labour rights in the sentence of convicts to the colonial administration, and British and Irish hulk and gaol reports. These documents formed the nucleus of an archive designed to manage the operation of an increasingly complex colonial penal system. After 1816, all convicts were interrogated on arrival. As part of this 'rite of passage' each was informed that the colonial administration already knew much about their circumstances and that any lies detected as part of the interrogation process would result in punishment.[45] Colonial officials credited such checks and balances with ensuring that the information elicited from convict charges was broadly correct. Subsequent cross-tabulations of the details coughed up by convicts support this assessment.[46] As well as a record of next of kin, place of birth, literacy, age, conviction history and workplace skills, a detailed physical description of each convict was also committed to file.

As the Antipodean penal system evolved, it developed ever more elaborate record-keeping practices. By the mid-1820s colonial surveillance and documentation techniques were already in advance of their metropolitan counterparts.[47] This included the use of identifiers to ease the task of tracking information that referenced the same convict across multiple record series. It also included the conduct records, a precursor to the prison licence system introduced in Britain in 1857.[48] This elaborate series of registers summarized successive court encounters, enabling colonial officials to appraise the extent to which an individual convict might merit an indulgence as a reward for meritorious conduct or alternatively greater levels of punishment. Many other legal structures created to regulate Antipodean convict lives were subsequently adopted by British and Irish penal managers. The ticket of leave, for example, pre-empted parole, and the mark system was incorporated into British prisons from 1861 following what was seen as its successful Australian implementation.[49]

A good case could be made, however, that the operation of convict management in Australia outstripped anything implemented in pre-twentieth-century Britain. Importantly, it was the lack of walls that drove Antipodean record-keeping innovation, a point not lost on one of the chief architects of the Australian penal system, George Arthur, Lieutenant-Governor of Van Diemen's Land from 1824–36, who claimed that 'Bentham's notion that gaolers should possess a personal interest in the reform of convicts is beautifully realised in Van Diemen's Land'.[50] Arthur understood that what Bentham meant by reform was the transformation of the dissolute and idle into compliant workers. This after all was the central aim of the panopticon – a mill designed to grind rogues honest.[51] The aim of Britain's trans-imperial carceral archipelago was the manufacture of 'docile bodies'.[52] Convict management in Britain's far-flung penal colonies took this one stage further by lessening the dependency of any social engineering process on a single institution, or even a series of institutions operating in parallel. What was unique about the exercise of criminal justice in Australia was that it was threaded across hundreds of private and public sector enterprises. This was an open institution enabled by record-keeping that penetrated so many aspects of everyday life routines that it anticipated the closed-circuit television camera. What was particularly remarkable about this criminal justice record-keeping triumph was the manner in which it facilitated the turning of urban spaces into open gaols.

Ever since Russel Ward popularized the idea in the 1950s, there has been a tendency to view convict labour as a largely non-urban phenomenon, primarily linked with the development of Australia's pastoral and agricultural industries.[53] Historically, however, significant numbers of convicts were stationed in towns and cities. At any one point in time, for example, one-third of all male convicts deployed in Van Diemen's Land and two-thirds of all women were located in Hobart Town and Launceston.[54] They worked in both the private and public sector and occupied all levels of the convict system. Many were undergoing punishment in the female house of correction or public-works chain gangs, while others were assigned to a wide variety of urban-based businesses or worked as domestic servants. Significant numbers held tickets-of-leave that enabled them to seek waged labour.

Thus, while there was no single institutional wall enclosing this penal population, the carceral convict town or city was composed of a host of institutional environments whose collective disciplinary practices enabled the distribution of power throughout the social body. Curfews, high levels of policing and personal identification systems including passes, and an associated paperwork bureaucracy, made it possible to operate a form of panoptic surveillance that went far beyond anything envisaged by Bentham. This was sufficiently complex to affect the selection of convicts for transportation. Those with military skills were disproportionately sent to Australia so that they could assist with the task of placing the eyes of a gaoler on street corners, roads, public houses and other nodes of communication, rather than constraining the gaze of the state to fixed points at the centre of expensive and restrictive buildings (see Appendix 1).

While convict Australia was administratively in advance of the British and Irish penal systems, it had gained a reputation for being inhumane. It is certainly true that, compared to the metropolitan use of judicially sanctioned violence, penal colonies remained brutal places. The crude execution rate in pre-1830 colonial Australia was, for example, 110 times higher than that in England and Wales. Even taking into account differences in population structure – there were fewer children and aged persons in Australia, as well as a sex imbalance that was skewed toward men – this is a striking difference. Yet, as in Britain, there was a marked shift in the use of judicially sanctioned violence in the Australian colonies that started in the late 1820s. This included a pronounced fall in the rate at which colonial felons were executed post-1830. This coincided with the completion of an elaborate system of penal stations and female factories. Thus, convict Australia relied on the public exercise of violence when it lacked institutional structures, but this changed as the colonial state acquired the means to subject an ever-greater proportion of the convict population to secondary transportation.[55]

There were other marked shifts in the way in which the bodies of convicts were subjected to punishment. The pain inflicted on convict bodies was far from trivial (Table 2.3). Close to 1.5 million strokes of the lash were administered in Van Diemen's Land alone, and convict men and women in that colony spent nearly 20 million days engaged in hard labour. Measured in terms of lashes per male convict on strength, the peak flogging year occurred relatively early in 1823, the same year that the Bigge Report was delivered.[56] Thereafter flogging rates declined sharply (Figure 2.2). A particular surprise was that the decline was especially marked within the confines of penal stations – although traditionally these have been seen as sites of ultra-violence.[57] This is an important detail. Just as the rate of execution reduced in line with the capacity to condemn offenders to an expanded system of penal stations, female factories and other punishment locations, so did other legally sanctioned public displays of violence. The temporary rise in flogging in the early 1830s in Van Diemen's Land coincided with the winding down of Macquarie Harbour and Maria Island, and the development of the much larger penal station at Port Arthur on the Tasman Peninsula. Once Port Arthur had expanded to the point where it could accommodate 1,000 convicts, the downward trajectory in the rate of flogging quickened pace.

Table 2.3: Distribution of punishments for male and female convicts arriving in Van Diemen's Land, 1803–53.

	Female (total)	Mean per convict	Male (total)	Mean per convict
Strokes of the lash	25	0.0	1,435,775	24.3
Days solitary	278,237	20.9	548,881	9.3
Days hard labour	3,606,776	270.4	16,045,600	272.0

Sources: TAHO, CON 31, 32, 33, 40 and 41.

There were other changes in the way that punishment was administered in the Australian colonies that underscore the extent to which Britain's far-flung penal colonies experienced a transition in punishments from the body to the mind on a similar scale to metropolitan institutions. As well as declining in frequency, flogging became an increasingly private spectacle – retreating behind the walls of regional lock-ups rather than being conducted in public. Hangings also disappeared behind closed walls in line with British practice, and the gibbeting of the remains of executed prisoners became rare in Eastern Australia after the end of the Napoleonic Wars.[58]

These changes were even more perceptible in relation to the treatment of female prisoners. The only woman ever to be flogged in Van Diemen's Land was Elizabeth Murphy. She was sentenced on 15 March 1806 'to be tied by her Hands to the Cart drawn by the G[aol]. Gang, stripped & receive 25 Lashes'.[59] By contrast, women were flogged in public in England until 1817 and in private within the walls of an institution until 1820.[60] Other public punishments were also used in the colonies. On 86 occasions women in Van Diemen's

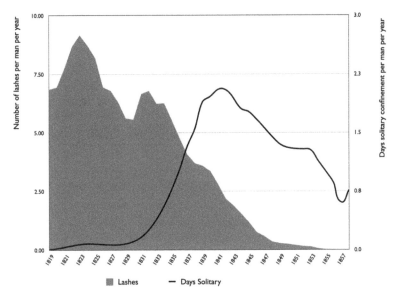

Figure 2.2: The shift from the lash to solitary confinement in Van Diemen's Land (moving five year average).
Sources: TAHO, four per cent systematic sample of every entry in the male convict conduct registers, CON 31, 32, 40, 37.

Land were sentenced to wear an iron collar, and on 111 to have their head shaved. Most of these humiliating spectacles were administered before the opening of the Launceston Female Factory in 1834. As with reliance on the lash and executions, the rate at which female convict bodies were used as public markers of state power diminished after public institutions were erected in major urban centres that possessed sufficient capacity to encompass significant numbers of refractory women.

While the completion of the Launceston Female Factory was a significant marker of this process, this building was important for other reasons too. It was one of a number of colonial correctional institutions that borrowed important design features from Bentham's panopticon. A circular structure at the heart of the institution housed the superintendent and his family. Four accommodation wings for the inmates radiated out from this central inspection facility. This ensured that, as the women in each class worked and exercised in the enclosed yards between each wing, they were under the constant gaze of the middle-class moral entrepreneur charged with regulating their institutional lives.

Such colonial architectural borrowing was far from accidental. Following Bentham, there has been a tendency to see the evolution of metropolitan criminal justice institutions as a process that occurred in opposition to a more free-track, anarchic Australian alternative. Yet the British penitentiary evolved in lock-step with the Australian system. Millbank and Pentonville were designed as holding depots for convicts awaiting transportation. This was similar to the role the Duke of Portland envisaged for the panopticon, much to Bentham's chagrin.[61] As transportation evolved, convicts were liable to spend more time confined within the walls of these institutions before they stepped on board a transport ship. By the mid-1840s nearly all transported convicts had completed part of their sentence in a British and Irish institution where they were subjected to separate treatment – a form of solitary confinement where inmates were worked in their cell in isolation but not deprived of light. From there they were socialized into divisions on board the transport vessel to be schooled and worked in teams.[62] This regimentation was preserved on disembarkation. Convicts from each arriving transport vessel were sent to particular probation stations to be worked in gangs. From there they could rise to the first class or sink to the third, each movement between classes being noted on individual conduct records and the printed pages of the government gazette. Promotion to the first class enabled the convict to sign a passholder contract with a private sector business. Thereafter continued good behaviour might earn a ticket-of-leave, while further encounters with the magistrates' bench were likely to place the convict back in the clutches of the probation station superintendent or, worse still, a chain gang, penal station or the crime class in the female house of correction. In short this was not two systems in operation, but one integrated experience that started with the penitentiary and ended with that ultimate panoptic experience, work in the carceral colony.

Panopticon versus the penitentiary

While the notion that penal transportation operated in opposition to the aims of the panopticon can be exposed as a fiction, it is also false to argue that the metropolitan penitentiary that emerged post-transportation was Bentham's architectural design in action. As others have pointed out, Bentham's utilitarian supporters were shocked by the lack of emphasis Britain's evolving national penitentiary system placed on productive labour.[63] John Stuart Mill, for example, argued that for the prison 'to instill a *desire* to work in shiftless and lazy inmates it would need to function as a miniature model of the free-track economy'.[64] Here the organization of the metropolitan penitentiary contrasted strongly with the colonial deployment of convict penal labour. A good illustration of this is the contrasting domestic and colonial use of treadwheels.

Treadwheels became popular in the early nineteenth century following the installation of William Cubitt's improved device in the Suffolk county gaol in 1819 – a design that enabled 56 prisoners to be simultaneously punished.[65] While they were more efficient than solitary cells in that they had the capacity to punish multiple prisoners in shifts, treadwheels were costly and needed to be housed in substantial institutions. Nevertheless, their use was championed by many early nineteenth-century penal reformers on the grounds that they subjected the prisoner to a species of 'severe, tedious and irksome' punishment where even 'the most artful' could not shirk their share.[66]

By 1842 over half the gaols and houses of correction in operation in England, Wales and Scotland had treadwheels in place. Initially these were used to grind grain, crush beans, cut cork, beat hemp, power looms, break rocks and pump water. Quickly, however, the treadwheel became a machine designed to regulate toil, rather than to put the labour of prisoners to productive use. Many were disconnected from the millstones or other mechanisms to which they had once been attached. Like the hand cranks which were increasingly installed in cells, prisoners were charged with making a certain number of revolutions each day, but the effort they expended was otherwise wasted.[67] This reflected administrative desires to ensure that the domestic spectacle of punishment was not associated with the exercise of 'executive tyranny'. As the mounting opposition to transportation to Australia demonstrated, forced public labour was associated in the popular imagination with slavery. The danger was that an increase in central administrative control of the criminal justice system would be interpreted as a threat to liberty more generally.[68] Yet, this was not the carceral institution at work as envisaged by Bentham.

The post-transportation prison has evolved as an exclusionary device. Rather than preparing prisoners for a life of toil, it has separated them from the workplace, making it difficult to secure work post-release. As Braithwaite argues, this is in stark contrast to the operation of penal transportation.[69] The irony of course is that if Bentham's panopticon was ever constructed anywhere, it was in Australia. A way of illustrating the power of the Australian surveillance machine is to explore its impacts on convict fecundity.

As we have seen, Bentham argued that Australia was doomed to demographic failure. He based this assertion on the impact that transportation was likely to have on indigenous populations and his confidence that loose morals and high levels of sexually transmitted disease were likely to inhibit the rate at which the transported convict population would reproduce. While his prediction proved incorrect, this was largely because Bentham failed to appreciate the manner in which the infrastructure developed as a result of penal transportation, and how the prospect of cheap labour and handouts of First Nation land would attract settler capitalists. He was right, however, that birth rates for transported convict women would be low. This does not appear to have been a product of previous exposure to sexually transmitted disease, however. One of the questions female convicts disembarked in Van Diemen's Land were asked was whether they had been 'on the town' – a nineteenth-century euphemism for sex work.[70] While every month a convict woman confessed to having been engaged in sex work was indeed associated with a reduced likelihood that they would give birth to a child in the colonies, the impact was far less than that associated with a month spent in solitary confinement (see Appendix 2).

The colonial state had particularly pernicious attitudes when it came to convict families. Most female convicts were forced to abandon their children when they were sentenced to transportation, although about 2,000 accompanied their mothers to Van Diemen's Land. On arrival in Australia these children were sent to the orphan school.[71] The measure was designed to maximize the number of convict women who could be assigned as domestic servants to 'respectable' settlers unencumbered by dependents. Convict women were also prevented from marrying without the permission of the state. In most years this was only forthcoming late in a woman's sentence and where inspection of her conduct record revealed that she had gone more than a year without a colonial charge being entered against her name.[72]

Disciplinary devices were also created to criminalize convict attempts to form de facto unions. Between 1822 and 1860 a total of 838 charges were laid against convict women for having sex with men or being found secreted in a private place with a man.[73] Examples include Emma Holdsworth who was sentenced to six months' hard labour after she was found 'locked up in a bed room in her master's house with a young man'; Mary Smith who was sent to the Female Factory for three months for allowing her master's overseer into her bedroom; and Mary Woodcock who was sentenced to three months in the factory, fourteen days of which was to be spent in solitary confinement on bread and water, for 'having a man secreted under a bed in the kitchen'.[74]

Convict servants who fell pregnant were sent to the house of correction as a matter of course. Thus, Ann Boys was deprived of her ticket-of-leave and sent to the Cascades Female Factory in Hobart Town when she was discovered to be pregnant.[75] Mary MacDonald, an assigned servant working for Mrs Midwood who ran a seminary for young ladies in Elizabeth Street, Hobart Town, was sent to the female factory with instruction that she was to be transferred to the crime class as soon as she was delivered of her child.[76] Isabella McMaster was sent to the 'house of correction for females' for 12 months as she was 'far advanced in pregnancy' and 'consequently useless'.[77] Concealing a birth was also an offence. Ann Lawrie was given nine months' hard labour for 'refusing to acknowledge that she was pregnant half an hour before she gave birth to a still born child'.[78]

After giving birth, convict mothers who had been committed to a female factory were permitted to wean their children. Thereafter they were separated – the convict being shifted to a separate yard to undergo a period of six months' punishment under watchful eye of the superintendent and his family.[79] This mostly consisted of labour at the washtubs servicing the laundry requirements of the state and nearby private households. Suitably chastized female convicts were redeployed into assigned service, whereas their children were sent to what were euphemistically known as orphan schools where, after the age of 12, they too could be apprenticed out as cheap labour.[80] The factory was thus much more than a disciplinary institution – it was an ancillary device designed to facilitate the servicing of colonial middle-class households. In order to work, however, it needed to operate as a part of a wider system of surveillance that extended far beyond the walls of any single institution. The inverse relationship between the number of children born to convict mothers and their documented history of solitary confinement provides a stark illustration of the extent to which state control extended in the penal colonies.

The carceral archipelago in its colonial guise was a sophisticated machine – a system of overlapping panoptic devices that was sufficiently powerful to tailor the birth rate in order to suit colonial labour demands. This was a surveillance system that was not restricted to the view from a central tower anchored at the heart of a single correctional building. This colonial panopticon had the power to peer into smoke-filled taverns and under beds in private households, effectively curtailing both convict sexual proclivities and desires for family formation. In short, it was a system designed to maximize production at the expense of reproduction. What makes this exercise in biological engineering particularly chilling is the way in which the supposed lax morals of female convicts were used to justify both the exploitation of their labour and their biological rights. This extended far beyond anything that Bentham had in mind, although – as Foucault pointed out – it aligns closely with the logical trajectory of panoptic thought. Contrary to the 'great confinement thesis', however, the way that trajectory played out in Australia had little to do with the penitentiary, which developed into an exclusionary and costly blind alley.

Appendix 1: Probability of being transported

These three logistic regression models explore the probability that male convicts would be transported to particular destinations. The models use records for 9,398 convicts housed in British hulks in the period 1835–45. The first panel shows the probability that convicts of different ages, marital status, sentence lengths, literacy levels and occupation in British hulks would be embarked on a transport vessel. If the result is negative, convicts with that attribute were less likely to be transported and more likely to serve out their sentence in the hulk without ever departing overseas. The second panel explores the probability that a convict would be transported to the Royal Navy dockyards in Gibraltar and Bermuda; the third panel shows the probability to New South Wales and Van Diemen's Land. The stars indicate the probability that each result could occur by chance: *** = 1% probability that this is the case; ** = 5% probability and * = 10% probability.

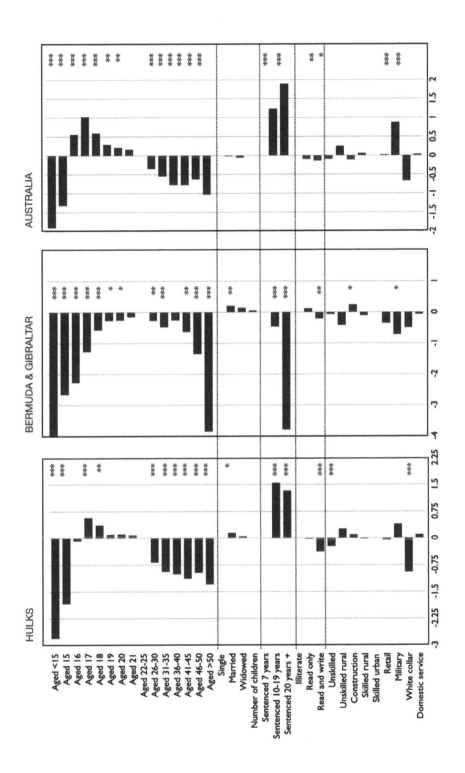

Appendix 2: Factors influencing colonial birth rates for convict women

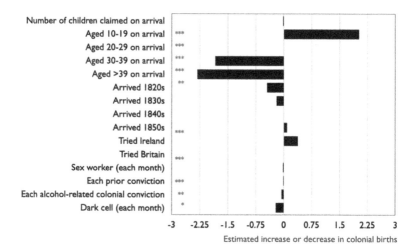

Estimated increase or decrease in colonial births

*** = significant at 1 per cent level
** = significant at 5 per cent level
* = significant at 10 per cent level

Note: This Ordinary Least Squares regression estimates that the average number of colonial births for a woman born in Britain (as opposed to Ireland) who arrived in Van Diemen's Land aged in her twenties in the 1840s was 2.8. The model plots the estimated variation for a series of independent variables. As expected, convict women who were aged 19 or less had a greater probability of giving birth in the colony while those aged over 30 were substantially less likely to raise a colonial family. The decade of arrival also made a difference, reflecting the ways in which the rules regarding convict marriage were relaxed in the post-1840 period. Irish women had a greater probability of conceiving in the colony than their English, Welsh and Scottish counterparts. While a record of sex work, prior convictions and alcohol-related offences were all associated with decreased fertility, the negative penalty was not as great as a month in solitary.

Notes

1   Foucault 1977; Ignatieff 1978, 102.
2   Foucault 1977, 75.
3   Renfield 2000, 52.
4   Willis 2005, 174; Causer 2019, 4.
5   Causer 2019, 1.
6   McConville 1981, 83.
7   Devereaux 1999, 428.
8   'New Wales' in Bentham, ed. Causer and Schofield 2022, 4.
9   Balak and Lave 2002, 911.
10 Grubb 2001, 297.
11 Panza and Williamson 2019, 582–3.
12 'Letter to Lord Pelham' in Bentham, ed. Causer and Schofield 2022, 112.
13 Jackson 1989, 236.
14 Causer 2019, 4.
15 Maxwell-Stewart 2015, 182–93.
16 Read 2020, 210.
17 Dillon 2008, 188; Hindmarsh 2002, 164.
18 'New Wales' in Bentham, ed. Causer and Schofield 2022, 4.
19 Dobson and Fisher 2007, 312.
20 1787 design for the Panopticon. Plate 1 in Bentham 1796.
21 Steadman 2007, 10–11.
22 Causer 2019, 5.
23 Jackson 1988, 48–55; Causer 2019, 7.
24 Lewis 1988, 507–24.
25 McConville 1981, 137; Willis 2005, 189.
26 Devereaux 1999, 422–3, 430.
27 McConville 1981, 141.
28 Dobson and Fisher 2007, 308.
29 Heany 2003.
30 Willis 2005, 190.
31 Braithwaite 2001, 11–14.
32 Foucault 1989, 40–1; Langbein 1976, 39.
33 Ekirch 1990, 230.
34 Roth 2006, 253.
35 Willis 2005, 177.
36 McConville 1981, 66–73; Devereaux 1999, 409; Willis 2005, 186.
37 Baine 1993, 1–19.
38 Beier 1978, 219; Waring 2017, 33.
39 Dabhoiwala 2006, 805–6.
40 Morgan and Rushton 2013, 9, 15–17; Newman 2015, 73.
41 Maxwell-Stewart 2020, 10.
42 Quoted in Sell 2015, 55.
43 Rediker 2007, 9.
44 For a wider discussion of these issues see Thompson 1967, 56–97.
45 Maxwell-Stewart 2016, 48–9.
46 Oxley 1996, 98–128; Maxwell-Stewart and Bradley 1997, 81–4.
47 Maxwell-Stewart 2016, 414–17; Roberts 2017, 588–606.
48 Forsythe 1978, 73.
49 Winter 2016, 6; Millett 2007, 51.
50 *Commons Sessional Papers* (1837) xix. 375.
51 'Postscript—II' in Bentham, ed. Bowring 1838–43, iv. 226.
52 See Foucault 1995, 293–308.
53 Ward 1958.
54 Ewing 1824–48.
55 Maxwell-Stewart 2020.

56 This three-volume report written by the former Chief Justice of Trinidad, John Thomas Bigge, recommended sweeping changes to the administration of convict discipline and management in Australia. See also Evans 2009.

57 Edmonds and Maxwell-Stewart 2016.

58 Anderson 2020.

59 Tasmanian Archives and Heritage Office (hereafter TAHO), CON 40/1/7, 5.

60 McConville 1981, 143.

61 'Editorial Introduction' in Bentham, ed. Causer and Schofield 2022, xxix, and relatedly at lxii.

62 Gibbs 2001, 61.

63 Pratt 1993, 384–6.

64 As quoted in Evans 1982, 297.

65 Shayt 1989, 910–11.

66 C.C. Western as quoted in McConville 1981, 241.

67 Shayt 1989, 910–11.

68 Willis 2005, 199.

69 Braithwaite 2001, 45–6.

70 Leppard-Quinn 2013.

71 Frost 2012, 98–142.

72 Reid 2007, 138.

73 TAHO, CON 40 and 41 series. A huge debt of thanks is due to the Female Convicts Research Centre who transcribed the 84,344 bench encounters summarized in these two series. These were coded by Kelsey Priestman for the *Founders and Survivors* project. Charges against the rules and regulations governing sex account for 1 per cent of all court appearances by female convicts.

74 TAHO, Emma Holdsworth, 3 August 1853, CON 41/1/32, 85; Mary Smith, 21 December 1831, Con 40/1/9, 99; Mary Woodcock, 15 August 1837, Con 40/1/9, 325.

75 TAHO, Ann Boys, 11 May 1843, CON 40/1/2, 56.

76 TAHO, Mary MacDonald, 13 April 1830, CON 40/1/7, 46.

77 TAHO, Isabella McMaster, 13 April 1832, CON 40/1/7, 48.

78 TAHO, Ann Lawrie, 21 September 1853, CON 41/1/35, 128.

79 Kippen 2005.

80 Frost 2012, 80–121.

Bibliography

Primary Sources

Tasmanian Archives and Heritage Office, Hobart

CON 31, Conduct Registers of male convicts arriving the period of the Assignment System, 1803–43.

CON 32, Supplementary Conduct Registers, 1828–53.

CON 33, Conduct Registers of male convicts arriving in the period of the Probation System, 1844–53.

CON 37, Conduct Registers of male convicts arriving on non-convict ships or locally convicted, 1840–93.

CON 40, Conduct Registers of female convicts arriving in the period of the Assignment System, 1803–43.

CON 41, Conduct Registers of female convicts arriving in the period of the Probation System, 1844–53.

Parliamentary papers

Commons Sessional Papers (1837), vol. xix. 1–755: 'Report from the Select Committee on Transportation; Together with the Minutes of Evidence, Appendix, and Index', 14 July 1837.

Printed sources

Bentham, J. *Management of the Poor.* Dublin: James Moore, 1796.

Bentham, J. *The Works of Jeremy Bentham, published under the superintendence of … John Bowring,* 11 vols. Edinburgh: William Tait, 1838–43.

Bentham, J. *Panopticon versus New South Wales and other writings on Australia,* ed. T. Causer and P. Schofield. London: UCL Press, 2022.

Ewing, T.J. *Statistics of Van Diemen's Land, 1824–48.* Hobart Town: Government Printer, 1824–48.

Secondary Sources

Anderson, S. *A History of Capital Punishment in the Australian Colonies, 1788 to 1900.* London: Palgrave, 2020.

Baine, R.M. 'New Perspectives on Debtors in Colonial Georgia', *Georgia Historical Quarterly* 77: 1 (1993): 1–19.

Beier, A.L. 'Social Problems in Elizabethan London', *Journal of Interdisciplinary History* 9: 2 (1978): 203–21.

Braithwaite, J. 'Crime in a Convict Republic', *Modern Law Review* 64: 1 (2001): 11–50.

Causer, T. '"The Evacuation of That Scene of Wickedness and Wretchedness": Jeremy Bentham, the Panopticon and New South Wales, 1802–1803', *Journal of Australian Colonial History* 21 (2019): 1–24.

Dabhoiwala, F. 'Justice in Early Modern London', *English Historical Review* 121: 492 (2006): 796–822.

Devereaux, S. 'The Making of the Penitentiary Act, 1775–1779', *The Historical Journal* 42: 2 (1999): 405–33.

Dobson, J.E. and Fisher, P.F. 'The Panopticon's Changing Geography', *Geographical Review* 97: 3 (2007): 307–23.

Edmonds, P. and Maxwell-Stewart, H. '"The Whip is a Very Contagious Kind of Thing": Flogging and Humanitarian Reform in Penal Australia', *Journal of Colonialism and Colonial History* 17 (2016). https://doi.org/10.1353/cch.2016.0006.

Ekirch, A.R. *Bound for America: The Transportation of British Convicts to the Colonies, 1718–1775.* Oxford: Clarendon Press, 1990.

Evans, R. *The Fabrication of Virtue.* Cambridge: Cambridge University Press, 1982.

Evans, R. '19 June 1822, Creating an "Object of Real Terror": The Tabling of the First Bigge Report'. In *Turning Points in Australian History,* ed. M. Crotty and D.A. Roberts, 48–61. Sydney: University of New South Wales Press, 2009.

Forsythe, W.J. *The Reform of Prisoners 1830–1900.* London: Croom Helm, 1987.

Foucault, M. *Discipline and Punish: The Birth of the Prison.* London: Penguin, 1977.

Foucault, M. *Madness and Civilization: A History of Insanity in the Age of Reason.* London: Routledge, 1989.

Frost, L. *Abandoned Women: Scottish Convicts Exiled beyond the Seas.* Sydney: Allen and Unwin, 2012.

Gibbs, M. 'The Archaeology of the Convict System in Western Australia', *Australasian Historical Archaeology* 19 (2001): 60–72.

Heany, H. 'Ireland's Penitentiary 1820–31: An Experiment that Failed'. In *Criminal Justice History: Themes and Controversies from Pre-Independence Ireland,* ed. I. O'Donnell and F. McCauley, 175–84. Dublin: Four Courts Press, 2003.

Ignatieff, M. *A Just Measure of Pain: The Penitentiary in the Industrial Revolution 1705–1850.* New York: Pantheon, 1978.

Jackson, R.V. 'Luxury in Punishment', *Australian Historical Studies* 23: 90 (1988): 42–59.

Kippen, R. '"And the Mortality Frightful": Infant and Child Mortality in the Convict Nurseries of Van Diemen's Land', 2006. https://www.femaleconvicts.org.au/docs/seminars/RebeccaKippen_InfantMortality.pdf [accessed 20 February 2018].

Langbein, J.H. 'The Historical Origins of the Sanction of Imprisonment for Serious Crime', *Journal of Legal Studies* 5: 1 (1976): 35–60.

Leppard-Quinn, C. 'Labelling the Transported Prostitute: An Exercise in Textual Archaeology', *Tasmanian Historical Studies* 18 (2013): 35–59.

Lewis, F. 'The Cost of Convict Transportation from Britain to Australia, 1796–1810', *Economic History Review* 2nd series, 41: 4 (1988): 507–24.

Maxwell-Stewart, H. and Bradley, J. '"Behold the Man": Power, Observation and the Tattooed Convict', *Australian Studies* 12: 1 (1997): 71–97.

Maxwell-Stewart, H. 'The State, Convicts and Longitudinal Analysis', *Australian Historical Studies* 47: 3 (2016): 414–29.

Maxwell-Stewart, H. 'Western Australia and Transportation in the British Empire 1615–1939', *Studies in Western Australian History* 34 (2020): 5–21.

McConville, S. *A History of English Prison Administration: Volume I, 1750–1877.* London: Routledge, 1981.

Millett, P. 'The Distribution of an Offensive Population: Classification and Convicts in Fremantle Prison, 1850–1865', *Studies in Western Australian History* 25 (2007): 40–56.

Morgan, G. and Rushton, P. *Banishment in the Early Atlantic World: Convicts, Rebels and Slaves.* London: Bloomsbury, 2013.

Newman, S. '"In Great Slavery and Bondage": White Labour and the Development of Plantation Slavery in British America'. In *Anglicizing America: Empire, Revolution, Republic*, ed. I. Gallup-Diaz, A. Shankman, and D.J. Silverman, 59–82. Philadelphia: University of Pennsylvania Press, 2015.

Oxley, D. *Convict Maids: The Forced Migration of Women to Australia.* Cambridge: Cambridge University Press, 1996.

Panza, L. and Williamson, J.G. 'Australian Squatters, Convicts and Capitalists: Dividing-Up a Fast-Growing Frontier Pie, 1821–71', *Economic History Review* 72: 2 (2019): 568–94.

Pratt, J. '"This is Not a Prison": Foucault, the Panopticon and Pentonville', *Social and Legal Studies* 2: 4 (1993): 373–95.

Rediker, M. *The Slave Ship: A Human History.* New York: Viking, 2007.

Reid, K. *Gender, Crime and Empire: Convicts, Settlers and the State in Early Colonial Australia.* Manchester: Manchester University Press, 2007.

Renfield, P. *Space in the Tropics: From Convicts to Rockets in French Guiana.* Berkeley: University of California Press, 2000.

Roberts, D.A. 'Colonial Gulag: The Populating of the Port Macquarie Penal Settlement, 1821–1832', *History Australia* 14: 4 (2017): 588–606.

Roth, M.P. *Prisons and Prison Systems: A Global Encyclopedia.* Westport, CT: Greenwood Press, 2006.

Sell, Z. 'Worst Conceivable Form: Race, Global Capital, and "The Making of the English Working Class"', *Historical Reflections* 14: 1 (2015): 54–69.

Shayt, D.H. 'Stairway to Redemption: America's Encounter with the British Prison Treadmill', *Technology and Culture* 30: 4 (1989): 908–38.

Steadman, P. 'The Contradictions of Jeremy Bentham's Panopticon Penitentiary', *Journal of Bentham Studies* 9 (2007): 10–11.

Thompson, E.P. 'Time, Work-Discipline and Industrial Capitalism', *Past and Present* 38 (1967): 56–97.

Ward, R. *The Australian Legend.* Oxford: Oxford University Press, 1958.

Waring, J. *Indentured Migration and the Servant Trade from London to America, 1618–1718.* Oxford: Oxford University Press, 2017.

Willis, J.J. 'Transportation versus Imprisonment in Eighteenth- and Nineteenth-Century Britain: Penal Power, Liberty, and the State', *Law & Society Review* 39: 1 (2005): 171–210.

Winter, S. 'Coerced Labour in Western Australia during the Nineteenth Century', *Australasian Historical Archaeology* 34 (2016): 3–12.

Part II

Bentham and the theory and practice of transportation to Australia

3

'Confinement', 'banishment', and 'bondage'

contesting practices of exile in the British Empire

Kirsten McKenzie

As the contributions to this volume attest, Bentham's war on convict transportation to the Australian continent was fought on many fronts. This chapter considers one cache of his ammunition: the distinction he drew between the three 'constituent elements' of the punishment – *'confinement'*, *'banishment'* and *'bondage'*.[1] Put simply, Bentham used these terms to refer to inability to leave the penal colony once transported ('confinement'), forcible exile ('banishment'), and enforced labour while there ('bondage'). Bentham argued that these three punishments were legally distinct but had become entangled in the practice of transportation to New South Wales. The result, in his view, was yet another illegality in a system that affronted the British constitution.

It has become well established in recent scholarship that penal transportation systems are bound up in global labour and colonization practices.[2] The triumvirate that Bentham considered an illegal combination – confinement to a required locality, exile from home, and enforced labour – was necessary to achieve these related goals. This prompts us to question whether exploring these particular Benthamite objections has any significance beyond reminding us yet again of the difference between theory and practice in penal transportation.[3] Were such arguments about illegality simply a form of lawyerly hair-splitting by means of which Bentham promoted his panopticon scheme? Bruce Kercher's foundational work on the New South Wales legal systems rightly warns us that it is 'rather arid to focus on the formal legality of actions' in the preliminary years of a colony where systems of government in general were so expedient, and where justice was administered at all levels by men with limited legal training.[4] If transportation practice simply disregarded constitutional niceties, do Bentham's theoretical objections have any relevance in the real world of forced removal in general and convict transportation to Australia in particular? My contention in this chapter is that Bentham's critiques can be used as a starting point to discuss a wider set of controversies over the legal foundations of forced removal at the turn of the nineteenth century and beyond, controversies that had real-world consequences for both the British imperial state and those subjected to its disciplinary practices. While the functional illegality of aspects of Australian convict transportation before the 1820s is an increasing focus of scholarly interest, Bentham's early identification of the problem has not received sustained attention.[5] The difficulties of establishing a solid legal foundation for convict transportation to Australia occupied administrators in both colony and metropole for decades. Those difficulties also opened up a significant weakness against which those subjected to forced removal could push in asserting their rights.

Bentham's bugbears: defining practices of exile

Terms such as 'exile', 'banishment' and 'transportation' were frequently used interchangeably in the eighteenth and early nineteenth centuries, sometimes to the annoyance of contemporary commentators.[6] Bentham, as we shall see, was not alone in voicing his irritation on this score. Recent studies have highlighted both the overlapping categories and methods of punitive relocation in imperial systems, and the problematic marginalization of such practices from the scholarship on punishment.[7] The punitive regimes of European empires had long incorporated a whole range of practices for forcible relocation, drawing on military and administrative techniques as well as those of the criminal justice system. British transportation in the Atlantic world was eroded by the rise of slavery as a preferred source of labour across the eighteenth century, and finally ended by the loss of the American colonies in 1783. It would re-emerge and, despite Bentham's objections, expand rapidly in the nineteenth century, now focused primarily on its Australian, Indian Ocean and Asian colonies. Yet other practices of removal did not disappear with British transportation's reinvigoration.

Exile was frequently used against indigenous rulers in colonial wars of expansion, as well as against wider communities, including rebellious Maroons, slaves and indigenous people fighting European settler incursions. Such tactics were used both within colonial possessions and across them, binding imperial localities together by means of punitive forced migration.[8] Extra-judicial practices of banishment survived in the British empire by the exercise of royal prerogative, allowing the state to sidestep prohibitions against banishment without trial in both Magna Carta and the Habeas Corpus Act.[9] These methods overlapped with practices of transportation both to and within the Australian colonies.[10] In the expansion of their imperial reach during the French revolutionary and Napoleonic Wars, the British also grafted the practices of conquered territories onto their own evolving systems, creating pluralistic legal responses to the challenge of protecting state security through what Dutch colonial law evocatively called 'political removal'.[11] If Bentham's legal precision belies how entangled these histories were and remain, his criticism also underscores the fact that this entanglement was always a potential pressure point for both critics and subjects of punitive regimes.

In the arsenal of forcible removal deployed by the British state, then, the relationships between 'confinement', 'banishment' and 'bondage' (to use Bentham's own definitions) were both complex and in flux. In particular times and circumstances there were heated debates over their legal applicability and the precise distinctions that existed between them. At other moments they could exist in a conveniently loose alignment. Bentham was determined they should be kept separate, as he argued in 1802–3, first in his two letters to Lord Pelham (which Bentham described as approaching the topic of the new colony through questions of policy) and secondly, in more detail, in 'A Plea for the Constitution' (in which he took a self-consciously legal perspective).[12]

'Exile, confinement, and bondage – inflictions perfectly distinct', Bentham complained in 'A Plea for the Constitution', 'are the ingredients of which ... the complex punishment styled *transportation* is composed'.[13] There were two main thrusts to his criticism of this definitional fuzziness. The first related to the duration of a convict's exile and their confinement to the boundaries of New South Wales. The isolation of the penal colony and the inability of most to return meant that, in effect, both 'exile' and 'confinement' were perpetual, lasting long after many convicts had served the years of their sentences. The 'mere change of local situation – I mean by the substitution of the superlatively distant, and comparatively inaccessible, territory of New South Wales, to the so much nearer and more accessible coasts of British America' had completely changed the punishment of transportation without any commensurate shift in its legal foundations.[14] This, Bentham went on, violated the provisions of both Magna Carta and the Habeas Corpus Act, since these laid down that 'no man can be exiled, or banished out of his native country' outside the provisions of the law.[15] 'Confinement', to use Bentham's term, was a function of the new geography of transportation after 1788, when return from exile became much more costly and difficult.

Bentham's second accusation of illegality concerned the relationship between 'banishment' (exile according to his definitional categories) and 'bondage' (enforced labour). The roots of this problem lay in the fact that the shape of modern British penal transportation had emerged from the mechanisms of the Atlantic labour market itself.[16] By the middle of the seventeenth century, the connection between exile and forced labour had been firmly established. Yet as Bentham himself pointed out in his first 'Letter to Lord Pelham', English statute law did not explicitly require that convicts be put to labour as punishment – only that they be removed for the period of their sentences.[17] It was in relation to operational provisions that labour was first specified by the Transportation Act of 1718[18] – its sale was to defray the costs of transporting convicts, and wealthy felons could pay for their voyage and purchase their freedom upon arrival.[19] As Bentham put it succinctly: 'When transportation was to America, the bondage might be bought off or begged off'.[20]

This aspect of what Bentham called 'the *old* transportation system' was iniquitous in his view. The punishment 'upon the face of the letter of the law', as he argued in his first 'Letter to Lord Pelham', was '*banishment*'. For the poor, however, a separate and 'perfectly distinct punishment of *bondage*' (forced labour) was added to it: 'banishment from the mother country, bondage to be endured in the country to which the convict was to be expelled'.[21] For those with financial means transported to the Americas, 'a very moderate sum of money was sufficient to enable a man to exempt himself from this most afflictive part of the punishment: for wherever it happened that, through the medium of a friend or otherwise, he could bid more for himself than would be bidden for him by a stranger, liberty thereupon of course took place of bondage'.[22] 'Poverty therefore,' wrote Bentham, 'rather than the crime of which a man was convicted, was the offence of which the bondage was the punishment'.[23]

Under the new system of transportation to Australia, Bentham went on, the distinction between those who must labour and those who must not was even more arbitrary. It now rested on the whim of the Governor, 'the fluctuating decision of the local despot', as he put it in 'A Plea for the Constitution'.[24] Such men were likely to exercise 'a proportionate degree of indulgence' towards anyone 'whose education and mode of life had habitually exempted him from ordinary labour'.[25] Thus, while 'Transportation' was the word used in all the relevant Acts of Parliament, complained Bentham, the effects were highly inconsistent. As he wrote in his first 'Letter to Lord Pelham':

> *Transportation* is the word used alike for all transportable Convicts in the Acts of Parliament. *Transportation* is therefore (I take for granted) the word that has been used for all alike in the judicial sentence or order, in virtue of which, in execution of these Acts, the Convicts have been sent abroad. Yet, somehow or other, so it has been in practice, that under the same provision in the Act, and under a judicial sentence or order couched in the same terms, *transportation* has been (as your Lordship has seen) to one man simple banishment, to another banishment aggravated by bondage: as if to men in general, and in particular to men of British blood, the difference between bondage and liberty were a matter not worth speaking about.[26]

As Bentham pointed out, there was a mismatch between the legislative framework, devised for circumstances in the Atlantic world, and the new Antipodean context. The 'only apology that could ever have been made' for this abuse, claimed Bentham, was that it 'was an antient one'.[27] Transportation to New South Wales was provided for by the Transportation Act of 1784,[28] yet the new legislation was marked by an extraordinary degree (in modern parlance) of cutting and pasting. It largely replicated the language of the 1718 statute that had regulated transportation to the Americas without taking the new circumstances into account. As Bentham pointed out in the critique mounted in 'Letter to Lord Pelham', the contractor taking a convict over to the Americas was deemed to have 'property in his [or her] service', property which could be sold upon arrival. It was for the sake of this profit that contractors were 'ready and willing to take upon themselves the charge of the transportation, without further recompense. 'Under the modern transportation laws', Bentham continued, 'the same form of words is still copied, the practice under them being (as already stated) as far as the condition of the convict at least is concerned, as different as possible'.[29] Thus, as Bentham pointed out, the 'modern' transportation laws of 1784 largely replicated their precursors, and yet transport of convicts was now paid for by the state. There was no one to whom property in the service of the convict could be sold upon arrival in the Antipodes. 'By what law', then argued Bentham, 'does the Governor exercise the power he takes upon himself to exercise in New South Wales over the Convicts during their terms? Is the property of the service of each convict assigned over to him by the Merchant transporter under his contract?'[30] Secondly, 'By what law does the Commander of a King's ship (the Glatton for instance) take upon himself to transport Convicts? Is he made to sign a contract for the transportation of these his passengers, as an independent Merchant would be for the performance of the same service? If the formality of a contract is employed, where is the legality, if not, where is the honesty of the practice?'[31] In short, who now had rights over the property in service of the convict, and how could it be legally deployed? The labour practices of Antipodean transportation, he concluded, were a violation of British law.

Once Bentham finally accepted that his lobbying for the panopticon had been in vain, he largely lost interest in transportation and the Australian colonies. He had little further use for the arguments he had advanced in the 'Letters to Lord Pelham' and 'A Plea for the Constitution', beyond publishing them in a compilation entitled *Panopticon versus New South Wales* in 1812 when the government showed another brief glimmer of interest in his scheme.[32] The definitional objections he had outlined with regard to 'confinement', 'banishment' and 'bondage' were, however, to cast a long shadow over the subsequent effective reorganization of convict transportation to the Antipodes.

The Scottish Martyrs: contesting practices of exile

In the rest of this chapter, I will take up Bentham's theoretical objections in relation to a series of controversies that arose respecting British practices of forced removal to Australia and beyond. To begin, I consider one of the most famous examples, that of the so-called 'Scottish Martyrs', in some detail. Their case has long been a focus for the public commemoration of democratic activism and of Scottish identity.[33] Historians of convict transportation, both popular and scholarly, have been drawn to their story in part because of its dramatic narrative possibilities as a tale of brave rebels, tyrannical authorities and daring escapees.[34] For the purposes of this discussion, it is particularly illuminating on questions of convict legal status, and has served as the opening vignette in two recent studies of that topic.[35] The Scottish Martyrs have a parallel, and equally significant genealogy in Scottish legal and political historiography,[36] though (perhaps predictably) these metropolitan and Antipodean strands do not always meet. Here I confine myself to the applicability of Bentham's definitional objections to their case.

The five men known as the Scottish Martyrs arrived in Sydney under sentences of transportation in 1794 and 1795.[37] They had been convicted for their attempts to mobilize organizations pushing for reform of the British constitution and were part of an internationally connected group of reformers and revolutionaries that reached from the United States, across the Atlantic World to Ireland and France. The shaky legal foundations of much of the evidence accepted against them, the pressure put on jurors to convict and the unusually harsh sentences handed down – four of the men were sentenced to transportation for fourteen years, the fifth to seven – were a function of the wider political crisis in Britain and state repression of reform and popular radicalism in the 1790s.[38] The trials became an international sensation. A transcript of Thomas Muir's trial, for example, went into three editions, two of them published in New York, and his three-hour defence speech became a best-selling pamphlet.[39] Of Thomas Muir, Thomas Fyshe Palmer, William Skirving, Joseph Gerrald and Maurice Margarot only two (Muir and Skirving) were Scots. Their trials, however, all took place in Scotland. This added several layers of legal complexity to their case, layers that highlight wider problems of defining transportation under the law. The first was specific to their alleged crimes. The second has wider implications for the question of labour appropriation practices as a whole.

There was much confusion during the trials themselves over both the crimes and the sentences given to the five men. Questions of legality and process were raised at the highest levels of government.[40] Official protests were made to the Home Secretary (Secretary of State for War from July 1794), Henry Dundas, and opposition Members of Parliament took up the case of the Scottish Martyrs in a series of debates across March and April 1794. Amongst the most informed voices was that of MP William Adam, a Scottish lawyer well versed in the technicalities at issue, whose lengthy speech laid out in great detail the problematic legal foundations of the cases. One point of contention was the importation of the English legal concept of sedition, with which the men were charged, on which there was 'little or no statute law, and hardly any case law' in Scotland.[41] At issue was sedition's supposed correlation with 'leasing-making' – on which Scottish statute law did exist and which was defined as 'speaking words tending to excite discord between the King and his people'.[42] Recent historiography on the trials' place in British political history suggests that, rather than being characterized by judicial incompetence, as one nineteenth-century commentator suggested, the legal foundations of the prosecution's case were in fact a tactical political choice. Since sedition (unlike leasing-making) required intent to be proved, it allowed the prosecution to assert to the jury (and by implication to the public) that the Scottish Martyrs and by extension a larger body of radicals sought to overthrow the government. Furthermore, the discourse of sedition trials could be shot through with allusions to treason, making sedition appear an even more sinister crime than it was under the law.[43]

As a Whig statement of objections delivered to the Secretary of State pointed out, the Scottish Act anent [about] leesing makers and slanderers of 1703 provided that leasing-making was punishable by a fine, imprisonment, or banishment.[44] Sedition in England, by contrast, could be punished by means of transportation. In Scotland, banishment survived as a judicial procedure well into the nineteenth century, something to which Bentham alluded, though he never commented on the case of the Scottish Martyrs in his writings on transportation.[45] In this form it was effectively a practice of deportation with removal from the boundaries of the polity more important than the destination or fate of the offender. English customs of transportation to the Americas (with forced labour at the destination) were absorbed into Scottish procedures in the seventeenth and early eighteenth centuries, even if there was no legal framework to support them. Indeed the Transportation Act of 1718 specifically excluded Scotland.[46] It was only in 1766 that formal legislation authorizing the same processes in Scotland was introduced.[47] In their study of Scottish exile practices in the eighteenth century, Gwenda Morgan and Peter Rushton argue that it was a 'kind of synthesis of old and new practices – one that left banishment and transportation side by side in an uncertain framework where the distinction was not obvious'.[48] The case of the Scottish Martyrs in the 1790s brought the uneasy relationship between the two legal systems to a head.

In arguing for a mistrial, the Whig opposition laid great emphasis not only on the distinction between leasing-making and sedition, but on the distinction between their punishments – Scottish banishment as opposed to English transportation. In making this criticism, they anticipated several of the arguments that Bentham would employ in his writings on New South Wales. On the floor of the House of Commons on 10 March 1794, William Adam acknowledged that while the *words* were frequently used with 'great inaccuracy and want of precision', an essential distinction existed between the *concepts* of banishment and transportation. Banishment was the 'mere expulsion from the society, country, or realm, to which the expelled person belongs; leaving every other country open to his approach, without restraint'. Transportation had two crucial elements that distinguished it from banishment in his eyes – the confinement to a specified locale ('being sent to another place, which he cannot quit') and enforced labour 'in a situation of servitude'. Quoting Governor Phillip's instructions to the commandant of Norfolk Island, Adam reiterated a central tenet of transportation: 'the convicts being the servants of the crown, till the time for which they are sentenced is expired, their labour is to be for the public'.[49]

The statement of objections delivered, in support of the Martyrs, to Henry Dundas by prominent Whigs cited the 1703 Scottish law on leasing-making, and complained that translating banishment into transportation, as the sentences effectually did, was 'extremely unreasonable when we consider how wide is the difference between banishment and transportation both in the nature of things and in the laws and practice of nations'. 'Punishments so distinct', they continued, 'have not been confounded in the laws of any civilized nation'.[50] The Judges of Scotland's High Court of Justiciary, citing the wording of sentences from the late seventeenth to early eighteenth century, retorted in a justificatory report to the Secretary of State that 'BANISHMENT, is a generic term, importing a punishment, more or less severe, according as the sentence may direct, and Transportation, is not a different kind of punishment, but one of the modes of banishment in the discretion of the court'.[51] Whig opposition only galvanized the government to back the Scottish sentences by dividing the response to the case along party political lines. The Scottish Martyrs were duly transported to New South Wales, but they would continue to use the uncertainty over their sentencing to push back against their detention in the colony.

In negotiating and protesting the terms of their exile, the Scottish Martyrs drew heavily on the same legal distinctions that Bentham would outline. Before departure, for example, Margarot wrote a defiant letter to Henry Dundas, demanding clarification on 'a constitutional point' – whether he would be 'a slave' at Botany Bay, 'the transferable property of the King of Great Britain, and be forced to labour under the goad of a task-master' or 'restored to liberty' upon arrival. Was he authorized to remove himself from New South Wales to 'any other part of the world not belonging to Great Britain'?[52] Tellingly, on the voyage itself, Muir, Skirving, Palmer and Margarot (Gerrard travelled separately) were kept separate from the other convicts. They were extremely pointed about paying their own transport costs and were effectively allowed the privileges of free passengers, much to the chagrin of some genuinely free on board. Reporting on the bickering about shipboard accommodation, the captain noted the 'instructions I received from my employer by desire of high authority of Government to make those people's situation as comfortable as possible'.[53] Accompanying them on their voyage to the penal colony were specific instructions to the Lieutenant-Governor from the Home Office Under Secretary John King about their labour. Still couched in the language of Atlantic transportation, it noted 'you are to observe in the Orders in Council for the transportation of the Scotch convicts, that in those cases where their sentences do not transfer their services to the contractor for their transportation, you are not at liberty to compel their services. On the other hand, they are not entitled to any provision from the Crown without doing such service as you shall think proper to enjoin them'.[54]

When John Hunter arrived in the colony as Governor in 1795, he was greeted by a petition from Muir, Palmer and Skirving (they had fallen out with Margarot, who on the voyage out had allegedly informed the ship's captain that his fellow Martyrs had planned to incite a mutiny) asking to clarify their legal position.[55] The men argued that

> the extent of our punishment is banishment. The mode of carrying the punishment into effect is transportation. The penalty imposed upon breach of the sentence is death. Already the terms of the sentence are completed. We have been banished by transportation, and there can be no higher security against our returning to Britain than the forfeiture of our lives. To all the rights of free men we are entitled, with the single exception of interdiction from one portion of the dominions of the Empire.[56]

To back up their claim they cited the legal opinions aired within the debates on their case subsequent to their trials. Hunter conveyed the petition to the Duke of Portland, the Home Secretary, with a sympathetic covering letter laying out what he considered to be their ambiguous legal status as well as the problems that ambiguity caused in the colony, and asking for instructions. Perhaps, as a Scot himself, he may even have had some familiarity with the legal distinctions at issue.[57] Just as Bentham objected to 'confinement' being part of the sentence of transportation, Hunter had felt obliged to agree with the men that he could not forcibly detain them in New South Wales against their will. While acknowledging that they could not return to 'any part of Great Britain but at risk of life, they probably might have a desire to pass their time in Ireland'. Hunter noted that it was 'customary to have the servitude of other convicts assigned over to the Governor of the settlements for the time being, in order to their being disposed of for the benefit of the public; but this has not been the case with respect to these men'. The Scottish Martyrs had also been very careful to keep off the public stores, reported Hunter, thus negating any claim the state might have made to their labour.[58]

Hunter was put right as speedily as the lengthy process of communication between Sydney and London allowed. Portland replied in two stages – in the first instance he put paid to the idea that Ireland might be exempted from the prohibition against their return, but he clearly felt he needed further legal advice on the other aspects of the claim.[59] On request from Portland, Robert Dundas, the Lord Advocate of Scotland (who had acted as prosecutor in the cases) laid down in no uncertain terms that Hunter would be 'guilty of a breach of duty if he permits them to leave that settlement' and that it 'makes no difference, as Governor Hunter seems to suppose, that the service of these convicts has not been assigned by their sentences during the respective periods of their transportation. There are innumerable instances of the same kind, and there must be convicts at present undergoing their sentences in New South Wales who are precisely in the same situation'. The High Court of Justiciary, he argued, had seen many instances of transportation in which the adjudication of servitude was dropped, or restricted to a portion of the term of transportation. The only difference between these men and the wider group of convicts was that they had paid their own way to the settlement. While their labour could not be compelled by the state, their transportation specified a period of 14 years (a wording judiciously left out of the petition), argued Dundas, and for 14 years they were obliged to remain.[60]

By the time Hunter had received these legal opinions, the matter was a moot point for three of the men at issue. Gerrald and Skirving were both in ill-health and died within days of one another in March 1796. Muir had escaped from Sydney earlier that year – embarking on an improbably dramatic series of global adventures involving imprisonment in Cuba, severe injury in a naval battle with the British off Cadiz, and ultimately rescue by the French. In Paris he was fêted as a revolutionary hero. His renewed political career (seeking French support for revolution in Scotland) was cut short when he died of his injuries in January 1799. Palmer was pardoned in 1801, but faced the challenge of making his own way home. Having bought and renovated a second-hand vessel, he died in a Spanish prison in 1802 after his ship sank off Guam. Only Margarot survived to return to Britain a free man in 1810, where he would mount extensive criticisms of the convict system as a witness before the 1812 Select Committee on Transportation.

The Scottish Martyrs may have failed in asserting their right to leave the colony, but the authorities in both colony and metropole showed significant uncertainty over their claims. In using their case to analyze the legal foundations of convict transportation to the Australian colonies, there is admittedly much that is distinctive about their circumstances. The debate over the entanglement of Scottish banishment and English transportation in their specific indictments (sedition versus leasing-making) certainly played a role in stirring up controversy. So too did the status of the men at issue, who were both personally articulate and had powerful political friends. Nevertheless, the definitional problems Bentham would flag in his attacks on transportation to New South Wales were also pivotal. Moreover, they were much wider and deeper than the specifics of this high-profile case.

From informality to illegality: reforming practices of exile

Building on the pioneering work of Alan Atkinson and Bruce Kercher, Alan Brooks has traced the legal complexities of assigning property in the services of Britain's transported offenders between 1717 and 1853, and has shed new light on the confusion caused by administering Antipodean transportation under a legal framework designed for the Atlantic context. Incorporating Scottish law into the practicalities of transportation to the Antipodes, argues Brooks, proved an especially vexing problem. This was not only a result of the overlapping systems of banishment and transportation that I have described above, but also because Scottish law, unlike that of England, gave judges a discretionary power to adjudge the services of the transported offender. By implication, therefore, they also had the power to withhold those services, thus disaggregating 'banishment' from 'bondage', as Bentham would have termed it.[61] Brooks's research into Scottish convicts transported to New South Wales and Van Diemen's Land up to 1812 reveals that only a very small proportion – 10 per cent – were explicitly subject to adjudgment of service when sentenced. Despite the claims of Robert Dundas, Lord Advocate of Scotland, that there must be 'innumerable' convicts in New South Wales in the same position as the Scottish Martyrs, this distinction in regard to adjudgment of service was routinely ignored by colonial administrators on the ground. Muir and his comrades were in fact exceptions to the reality that, once in New South Wales, Scottish convicts were routinely subject to forced labour for the duration of their sentences of transportation.[62] Nevertheless, at least one Scottish convict, in the second decade of the nineteenth century, successfully protested to the Home Department that while he had been transported for life, his labour was under constraint for only seven years.[63] In 1816 a second Scottish Governor, Lachlan Macquarie, sought clarification on the problem of Scottish sentences. Directed to investigate the matter, the Law Officers of the Crown implicitly supported colonial officials on the ground over the sentences handed down by Scottish judges, when they responded to Macquarie's enquiry and confirmed, in their view, that transportation legislation conferred servitude. In this the Law Officers of the Crown ignored the mismatch between the legislation and the circumstances of the new colony, and backed up what was already being worked out on the ground, pragmatics that had far wider application than Scottish convicts alone.[64] As Lisa Ford and David Andrew Roberts have argued, 'in New South Wales hard labour and transportation were conflated earlier and more decisively than they were in the metropole'. Legislation followed colonial practice, rather than the reverse.[65]

It was only with the passing of the New South Wales Act of 1823[66] and the Transportation Act of 1824[67] that imperial transportation law was brought into line with *ad hoc* colonial practice, officially placing property in the service of the transported convict in the governor's hands, and legislating his power to assign it to private masters. The Transportation Act of 1824 finally repealed those parts of the 1718 Act that referred to private contractors being reimbursed for the transportation of offenders, and declared that 'property interest in service is vested in the governor for the entire term'. Even when he assigned convicts to private individuals, property in that convict's service continued to be held by the governor.[68] These developments were part of a raft of legislation that followed an exhaustive British parliamentary investigation into New South Wales by Commissioner John Thomas Bigge.[69]

Bigge arrived in 1819 with instructions from Earl Bathurst, Secretary of State for War and the Colonies, to make transportation an 'object of real Terror',[70] in the midst of the social upheaval and apparently increasing crime rates that followed the end of the Napoleonic Wars. This much-quoted directive to Bigge, contained in the first of three letters of instruction, is well-known. Yet the rest of Bathurst's meditation on the situation in New South Wales – part history lesson, part criminological treatise, part justification for state intervention – is equally illuminating. Bathurst's letter is noteworthy for the way it wrestles with the same problems flagged by Bentham almost 20 years earlier. Unlike Bentham, however, Bathurst was less concerned with transportation's legality than with ensuring it was fit for purpose. As Bathurst explained, the original idea was that forcible removal to the far side of the world under 'a system of just discipline' would 'render Transportation an Object of serious Apprehension'.[71] In the earliest decades of the settlement, he went on, this had worked to some effect. Disregarding its real severity, the spectre of Botany Bay fulfilled its requirements because of the 'peculiar Apprehension' it exercised on the minds of those in Britain.[72] In the earliest decades of the settlement, he went on, this had worked to some effect. Disregarding its real severity, the spectre of Botany Bay fulfilled its requirements because of the 'peculiar Apprehension' it exercised on the minds of those in Britain.[73] By the late 1810s, however, New South Wales's rapidly evolving economy made it look dangerously akin to a land of economic opportunity. If, as Bathurst argued, the 'Great End of Punishment is the Prevention of Crime', then he lamented that 'mere Expatriation ['banishment' in Bentham's language] is not in these days an Object of considerable Terror'. Transportation had to be reformed so as to ensure a convict's 'sad Estrangement from the sweets and comforts of Life, which their Guilt has forfeited'. Without such measures it 'cannot operate as an effectual example on the Community at large', as a proper expression of the law, or as a 'proper punishment' for crimes against which the community had the 'right to claim protection'.[74]

The wide-ranging reforms that followed Bigge's investigation were designed to regulate a rapidly expanding system, as the number of both transported convicts and free emigrants to the colonies of eastern Australia increased exponentially. The privileges granted to convicts such as the Scottish Martyrs largely became a thing of the past. Now the costs of supporting transported convicts would be reduced by assigning them to free emigrants with capital who would be given preferential access to land grants. The numerous subsequent parliamentary investigations into convict transportation to the Australian colonies exemplified a process of constant negotiation and recalibration. Such colonial adjustments, argues a recent collection on transportation, deportation and exile, underscore the vulnerability of systems of forcible relocation and 'the making of empires as an ongoing process'.[75]

Debates over the legal parameters of British forced removal were being waged well beyond the Australian colonies during this period. At the same time that the New South Wales Act of 1823 and the Transportation Act of 1824 were being passed, three scandals related to this question erupted into lengthy controversy before the British parliament. In 1823 two free men of colour, Louis Lecesne and John Escoffery, were deported from Jamaica by executive order under the auspices of that colony's alien legislation. In the same year James Silk Buckingham, editor of the *Calcutta Journal*, was deported for his criticism of the East India Company under the practice of 'transmission' which revoked his licence to reside in Bengal. Finally, in 1824, another newspaper editor, George Greig, was threatened with expulsion from the Cape colony by means of the Dutch colonial practice of 'political removal' (*politieke uitzetting*). All three cases, while invoking different techniques, effectually involved extra-judicial banishment by executive order. All three cases would provoke extensive controversy as to their legality, invite lengthy investigations (lasting at least a decade in the case of Buckingham[76]), and end in compensation or redress by the British home government.[77] Bentham's objections to the legalities of punishment by forced removal can therefore be placed within a much longer history that would open up at the beginning of the nineteenth century over matters of forced removal, the definition of British subjecthood, the rights of the individual, and the protection of the state.

The new penal structure that emerged from the Bigge reforms, and the legislation that followed, might have sought greater legal uniformity and regularity, but it did not end lawyerly and definitional debates.[78] Nor did it temper the willingness of those transported to push back against the convict system with the strategic use of arguments about their legal rights. In the words of Ford and Roberts, some post-Bigge legislation designed to bring colonial practice under the sway of proper legal procedure merely 'turned local informality into illegality'.[79] As Ford and Roberts also point out, it may indeed have provided greater ammunition by illuminating the gaps between metropolitan theory and colonial practice, especially for the better educated and more legally astute transportees. Bentham's definitional critiques of transportation never found widespread readership in their published form in the early nineteenth century, for all that they circulated in elite circles in both metropole and colony.[80] But the problems he described were perfectly evident to those suffering at the coalface of convict-era Australia. Such distinctions would remain the basis of the battles over how transportation worked for the entire period of its operation. Amongst the most common forms of resistance by convicts were absconding (resisting 'confinement') and arguments over what right the state, and their representatives, had over labour (the distinction between 'banishment' and 'bondage').[81] Jeremy Bentham's critiques of convict transportation to New South Wales were written on the eve of several decades of heated debate on the legal foundations of various methods of state-sanctioned exile. His ideas found quotidian expression in a law-infused world in which even ordinary people could, and did, draw on the gap between metropolitan legal theory and colonial practice to push their own agendas.

Notes

1   'A Plea for the Constitution' in Bentham, ed. Causer and Schofield 2022, 375.
2   This is a vast literature that I can only touch on here. As well as the citations on issues specific to this essay included in the notes below, see pioneering work from the 1980s that emphasized the question of labour in Australian transportation such as Nicholas ed. 1988, and Duffield and Bradley eds. 1997. Wider area studies examples include Anderson 2000 and Ward 2008. Recent scholarly interpretations are increasingly global in reach, such as Anderson and Maxwell-Stewart 2013, 102–17; De Vito and Lichtenstein eds. 2015; and Anderson ed. 2018.
3   A difference of which Bentham himself, of course, was entirely aware. Jackson 1989, 232.
4   Kercher 1996, 9. See also Neal 1991; Kercher 1995; and Kercher 2003. On the gap between transportation practice in the Atlantic and the legal niceties of the English constitution, see Atkinson 1994, 88–115.
5   Exceptions include Rice 1984, 44–7; Brooks 2016.
6   This remains characteristic of popular discourse on convict transportation today. When not explicitly analyzing varieties of forced removal, scholarly works can also use such terms very loosely.
7   De Vito, Anderson, and Bosma eds. 2018.
8   Chopra 2018; Harman 2012.
9   31 Car. II, c. 2.
10 See Bleichmar 1999, 115–63; Ford and Roberts 2014, 1–13; Powell 2016, 352–71; and Roscoe 2018.
11 For an example of such tactics of forced removal in the Cape Colony see McKenzie 2015, 787–806, and McKenzie 2016.
12 Causer 2019, 8.
13 'A Plea for the Constitution' in Bentham, ed. Causer and Schofield 2022, 376.
14 'A Plea for the Constitution' in Bentham, ed. Causer and Schofield 2022, 376.
15 'A Plea for the Constitution' in Bentham, ed. Causer and Schofield 2022, 380.
16 A good summary of the place of transportation within the Atlantic labour market can be found in Maxwell-Stewart 2010, 1221–42. See also Morgan and Rushton 2004. For a study which emphasizes legal parameters see Atkinson 1994, 88–115.

17 'Letter to Lord Pelham' in Bentham, ed. Causer and Schofield 2022, 112.
18 4 Geo. I, c. 11.
19 Kercher 2003, 533.
20 'A Plea for the Constitution' in Bentham, ed. Causer and Schofield 2022, 376.
21 'Letter to Lord Pelham' in Bentham, ed. Causer and Schofield 2022, 99.
22 'Letter to Lord Pelham' in Bentham, ed. Causer and Schofield 2022, 99.
23 'Letter to Lord Pelham' in Bentham, ed. Causer and Schofield 2022, 99.
24 'A Plea for the Constitution' in Bentham, ed. Causer and Schofield 2022, 376.
25 'Letter to Lord Pelham' in Bentham, ed. Causer and Schofield 2022, 100.
26 'Letter to Lord Pelham' in Bentham, ed. Causer and Schofield 2022, 111–12.
27 'Letter to Lord Pelham' in Bentham, ed. Causer and Schofield 2022, 111.
28 24 Geo. III, Sess. 2, c. 56.
29 'Letter to Lord Pelham' in Bentham, ed. Causer and Schofield 2022, 113.
30 'Letter to Lord Pelham' in Bentham, ed. Causer and Schofield 2022, 113.
31 'Letter to Lord Pelham' in Bentham, ed. Causer and Schofield 2022, 113. The Transpor-
    tation Act of 1802 (43 Geo III, c. 15) was passed to allow Royal Navy vessels to be used
    as convict transports. On attempts to redress the illegality of shipments of convicts from
    Britain, Bentham's critiques and the problem posed by the *Glatton* see Brooks 2016, 223–6.
32 Causer 2019, 23.
33 The relative emphasis on these two elements has waxed and waned over time. The
    Political Martyrs Monument in Edinburgh was erected to the men in 1844 'by the Friends
    of Parliamentary Reform in England and Scotland', as the monument's inscription attests.
    More recently, Muir (in particular) has been claimed by the movement for Scottish
    independence with former First Minister Alex Salmond calling for his posthumous pardon
    at the inaugural Thomas Muir Lecture in 2015. *The National*, 25 August 2015, https://
    www.thenational.scot/news/14899191.salmond-demands-full-pardon-for-radical-muir/
    [accessed 9 May 2021].
34 The men known as the Scottish Martyrs were early contributors to their own legend,
    publishing accounts of their trials and of their transportation: see, for instance, Palmer
    and Skirving 1797. Their tale has attracted popular history writers including Clune 1969
    and Armstrong 2014. Selected scholarly literature includes Bewley 1981; Parsons 1985,
    163–76; Leask 2007, 48–69; and Moore 2010.
35 Ford and Roberts 2014; Brooks 2016.
36 McFarland 1994. Legal analysis of the political trials of the 1790s, both in Scotland and
    England, began shortly after the trials themselves and continued across the nineteenth
    century: see Hume 1797; Cobbett 1809–26; Cockburn 1888. See Wold 2016. In his
    reinterpretation of the trials, Wold argued that the traditional view that the trials were
    a miscarriage of justice has obscured understandings of the legal and political questions
    surrounding the cases, particularly with regard to definitions of treason and sedition. Wold
    2015, 58. See also Barrell 2000.
37 For all their fame they were not the only transportees from their movement. George
    Mealmaker (1768–1808), for example, arrived in Sydney under sentence of transportation
    in November 1800.
38 See Emsley 1981, 155–84.
39 Anon. 1793 and 1794.
40 Wold 2015, 53.
41 Wold 2015, 48–9.
42 *House of Commons Parliamentary Debates* (1794), vol. xxxviii, 493. The question of sedition
    and leasing-making was taken up at length by David Hume, nephew of the famous philos-
    opher and professor of Scots law at the University of Edinburgh at the time of the trials in
    1794, in his foundational work *Commentaries on the Law of Scotland* (1797). Wold 2016,
    170.
43 Cockburn 1888, i. 245–6, quoted in Wold 2015, 58; Barrell 2000, 167.
44 *Records of the Parliaments of Scotland to 1707*, https://www.rps.ac.uk/trans/1703/5/191
    [accessed 9 May 2021]. 'Statement of objections to the sentence passed on Messrs Muir
    and Palmer – delivered to the Secretary of State [Henry Dundas] by Lord Lauderdale, Mr
    Grey and Mr Sheridan', Windham Papers, vol. xxxii, British Library, Add. MS 37,873, fos.
    245–67. The response of the High Court of Justiciary was that Muir and Palmer had been
    charged with sedition, not leasing-making, and that this charge had ample precedent in

Scottish law. 'Report of the Judges of the High Court of Justiciary, relative to the cases of Thomas Muir, and Thomas Fisch Palmer', British Library (hereafter BL), Add. MS 37,873, f. 245.

45 'A Plea for the Constitution' in Bentham, ed. Causer and Schofield 2022, 378; Morgan and Rushton 2013, ch. 2. Bentham was aware of the Scottish Martyrs' case and received a first-hand account of Muir's trial from Samuel Romilly (Bentham, ed. Milne 1981, 469–71), but his only reference to them in his publications on transportation is to note Muir's escape ('Letter to Lord Pelham' Bentham, ed. Causer and Schofield 2022, 117). I am grateful to Tim Causer for bringing this reference from Bentham's correspondence to my attention.

46 Atkinson 1994, 88–115.

47 The Transportation (Scotland) Act of 1766 (6 Geo. III, c. 32).

48 Morgan and Rushton 2013, 42. Scottish practices of banishment attracted increasing criticism in the early nineteenth century since forced migration to England, in the context of industrialization and an expanding southern economy, became regarded as a reward rather than a punishment. It was eventually abandoned as a result: Morgan and Rushton 2013, 44–5.

49 *House of Commons Parliamentary Debates* (1794), vol. xxxviii, 497.

50 'Statement of objections to the sentence passed on Messrs Muir and Palmer – delivered to the Secretary of State [Dundas] by Lord Lauderdale, Mr Grey and Mr Sheridan', BL Add. MS 37,873.

51 'Report of the High Court of Justiciary relative to the cases of Thomas Muir and Thomas Fisch Palmer 1793', BL Add. MS 37,873 fos. 250–62. The wording of the sentence indicates 'banishment' as the punishment and 'transportation' as the mode of carrying it out. There is no explicit mention of forced labour although this is implied through the destination – frequently listed as the 'plantations' of the East or West Indies.

52 Britton and Bladen eds. 1892–1901, vol. ii. 853.

53 Patrick Campbell to Under Secretary King, 22 April 1794 in Britton and Bladen eds. 1892–1901, vol. ii. 856.

54 King to Grose, 26 April 1794 in Britton and Bladen eds. 1892–1901, vol. ii. 856.

55 Hunter already had experience serving in the penal colony, having first arrived with the First Fleet under Governor Phillip.

56 Muir, Palmer, and Skirving to Governor Hunter, 14 October 1795 in Britton and Bladen eds. 1892–1901, vol. ii. 883–4.

57 Brooks 2016, 292.

58 John Hunter to Duke of Portland, 25 October 1795 in Britton and Bladen eds. 1892–1901, vol. ii. 883.

59 Portland to Hunter, undated except 'August 1796' in Britton and Bladen eds. 1892–1901, vol. iii. 98.

60 Robert Dundas to Duke of Portland, 5 September 1796 in Britton and Bladen eds. 1892–1901, vol. iii. 111–15. An undated and unsigned legal opinion headed 'Powers of the Justiciary Court' reiterates these points and was apparently penned by one of the legal advisors to the Home Office to whom the petition and Hunter's covering letter had been submitted: see ibid., vol. ii. 886.

61 Brooks 2016, 274.

62 Brooks 2016, 313.

63 Brooks 2016, 299.

64 Brooks 2016, 303.

65 Ford and Roberts argued that internal relocation to peripheral penal settlements such as Newcastle (from 1804) was fundamental to this: Ford and Roberts 2014, 2. See also Roberts 2017, 470–85.

66 4 Geo. IV, c. 96.

67 5 Geo. IV, c. 84.

68 Kercher 2003, 568; Ford and Roberts 2015, 174–91.

69 For a wider discussion of Bigge's views on property in the service of the offender, see Brooks 2016, 353–4.

70 Earl Bathurst to Commissioner Bigge, 6 Jan. 1819 in Watson ed. 1914–25, vol. x. 7. See also Evans 2009, and Spigelman 2009.

71 Bathurst to Bigge, 6 January 1819 in Watson ed. 1914–25, vol. x. 4.

72 Bathurst to Bigge, 6 January 1819 in Watson ed. 1914–25, vol. x. 5.

73 Bathurst to Bigge, 6 January 1819 in Watson ed. 1914–25, vol. x. 5.
74 Bathurst to Bigge, 6 January 1819 in Watson ed. 1914–25, vol. x. 7, 8.
75 De Vito, Anderson, and Bosma 2018, 8.
76 During which Bentham would offer both financial and moral support to Buckingham. See for example Bentham to Robert Peel, 8 May 1826 in support of Buckingham's petition to the House of Commons protesting the 'blind and relentless tyranny' (Bentham's words) of the authorities in forcing Buckingham's removal from India for his efforts to secure freedom of the press. Bentham, ed. O'Sullivan and Fuller 2006, 213–16, at 214. My thanks to Tim Causer for bringing this reference to my attention.
77 These cases are the subject of ongoing research and forthcoming publications by Jan Jansen (in the case of Lecesne and Escoffery) and myself. On Lecesne and Escoffery see Heuman 1981. On Buckingham see Turner 1930; Zastoupil 2010; and Bayly 2012. On Greig see McKenzie 2016.
78 New South Wales Chief Justice Francis Forbes was still raising the question of the technical differences between banishment, enforced labour and convict transportation to the House of Commons Select Committee on Transportation in 1837. Brooks 2016, 227.
79 Ford and Roberts 2015.
80 Atkinson 1978, 1–13.
81 See Roberts 2005, 97–122. My thanks to Hamish Maxwell-Stewart for making this connection between Benthamite theory and everyday colonial practice.

Bibliography

Primary Sources

Archival sources
British Library, Add. MS 37,842, Windham Papers 1660–1845, vol. xxxii. 1782–1810.

Newspapers
The National.

Parliamentary papers
House of Commons Parliamentary Debates (1794), vol. xxxviii.
Records of the Parliaments of Scotland to 1707, https://www.rps.ac.uk/.

Printed sources
[Anon.] *The Trial of Thomas Muir, Younger of Huntershill, before the High Court of Justiciary, at Edinburgh: on Friday, the 30th of August, 1793: on a charge of Sedition. From the records of the court, and notes of the evidence taken during the trial* (Edinburgh, 1793; London, 1793; New York, 1794).
Bentham, J. *The Correspondence of Jeremy Bentham, Volume 4: October 1788 to December 1793 (CW)*, ed. A.T. Milne. London: The Athlone Press, 1981.
Bentham, J. *The Correspondence of Jeremy Bentham, Volume 12: July 1824 to June 1828*, ed. L. O'Sullivan and C. Fuller. Oxford: Clarendon Press, 2006.
Bentham, J. *Panopticon versus New South Wales and other writings on Australia*, ed. T. Causer and P. Schofield. London: UCL Press, 2022.
Cobbett, W. *A Complete Collection of State Trials and Proceedings for High Treason and other Crimes and Misdemeanours from the Earliest Period to the Present Time*. London: T.C. Hansard, 1809.
Historical Records of Australia, Series I. ed. F. Watson, 26 vols. Sydney: Government Printer, 1914–25.
Historical Records of New South Wales, ed. A. Britton and F.M. Bladen, 7 vols. Sydney: Government Printer, 1892–1901.

Hume, Baron D. *Commentaries on the Law of Scotland, respecting the Description and Punishment of Crimes*, 2 vols. London: Bell and Bradfute, 1797.

[Palmer, T. and Skirving, W.] *A Narrative of the Sufferings of T.F. Palmer and W. Skirving During a Voyage to New South Wales, 1794 on board the Surprise Transport*. London: Benjamin Flower, 1797.

Secondary Sources

Anderson, C. *Convicts in the Indian Ocean: Transportation from South Asia to Mauritius, 1815–53*. Basingstoke: Palgrave, 2000.

Anderson, C., ed. *A Global History of Convicts and Penal Colonies*. London: Bloomsbury, 2018.

Anderson, C. and Maxwell-Stewart, H. 'Convict Labour and the Western Empires, 1415–1954'. In *The Routledge History of Western Empires*, ed. R. Aldrich and K. McKenzie, 102–17. London: Routledge, 2013.

Armstrong, M. *The Liberty Tree: The Stirring Story of Thomas Muir and Scotland's First Fight for Democracy*. Edinburgh: World Power Books, 2014.

Atkinson, A. 'Jeremy Bentham and the Rum Rebellion', *Journal of the Royal Australian Historical Society* 64 (1978): 1–13.

Atkinson, A. 'The Free-Born Englishman Transported: Convict Rights as a Measure of Eighteenth-century Empire', *Past and Present* 44 (1994): 88–115.

Barrell, J. *Imagining the King's Death: Figurative Treason, Fantasies of Regicide, 1793–1796*. Oxford: Oxford University Press, 2000.

Bayly, C.A. *Recovering Liberties: Indian Thought in the Age of Liberalism and Empire*. Cambridge: Cambridge University Press, 2012.

Bewley, C. *Muir of Huntershill*. Oxford: Oxford University Press, 1981.

Bleichmar, J. 'Deportation as Punishment: A Historical Analysis of the British Practice of Banishment and Its Impact on Modern Constitutional Law', *Georgetown Immigration Law Journal* 14: 115 (1999): 115–63.

Brooks, A. 'Prisoners or Servants? A History of the Legal Status of Britain's Transported Convicts'. PhD thesis: University of Tasmania, 2016.

Causer, T. '"The Evacuation of That Scene of Wickedness and Wretchedness": Jeremy Bentham, the Panopticon, and New South Wales, 1802–1803', *Journal of Australian Colonial History* 21 (2019): 1–24.

Chopra, R. *Almost Home: Maroons between Slavery and Freedom in Jamaica, Nova Scotia, and Sierra Leone*. New Haven: Yale University Press, 2018.

Clune, F. *The Scottish Martyrs*. Sydney: Angus and Robertson, 1969.

Cockburn, Lord. *An Examination of the Trials for Sedition Which Have Hitherto Occurred in Scotland*, 2 vols. Edinburgh: David Douglas, 1888.

De Vito, C.G. and Lichtenstein, A., eds. *Global Convict Labour*. Leiden and Boston: Brill, 2015.

De Vito, C.G., Anderson, C., and Bosma, U., eds. 'Transportation, Deportation and Exile: Perspectives from the Colonies in the Nineteenth and Twentieth Centuries', special issue of the *International Review of Social History* 63: 26 (2018): 1–24.

Duffield, I. and Bradley, J., eds. *Representing Convicts: New Perspectives on Convict Forced Labour Migration*. London: Leicester University Press, 1997.

Emsley, C. 'An Aspect of Pitt's "Terror": Prosecutions for Sedition during the 1790s', *Social History* 6: 2 (May 1981): 155–84.

Evans, R. '19 June 1822: Creating "An Object of Real Terror" – the Tabling of the First Bigge Report'. In *Turning Points in Australian History*, ed. M. Crotty and D.A. Roberts, 48–61. Sydney: UNSW Press, 2009.

Ford, L. and Roberts, D.A. 'New South Wales Penal Settlements and the Transformation of Secondary Punishment in the Nineteenth-Century British Empire', *Journal of Colonialism and Colonial History* 15: 3 (2014): 1–13.

Ford, L. and Roberts, D.A. 'Legal Change, Convict Activism and the Reform of Penal Relocation in Colonial New South Wales: The Port Macquarie Penal Settlement 1822–1826', *Australian Historical Studies* 46: 2 (2015): 174–91.

Harman, K. *Aboriginal Convicts: Australian, Khoisan and Māori Exiles*. Sydney: UNSW Press, 2012.

Heuman, G.J. *Between Black and White: Race, Politics and the Free Colored in Jamaica, 1792–1865*. Oxford: Praeger, 1981.

Jackson, R.V. 'Bentham's Penal Theory in Action: The Case Against New South Wales', *Utilitas* 1: 2 (1989): 226–41.

Kercher, B. *An Unruly Child: A History of Law in Australia*. Sydney: Allen and Unwin, 1995.

Kercher, B. *Debt, Seduction and Other Disasters: The Birth of Civil Law in Convict New South Wales*. Sydney: Federation Press, 1996.

Kercher, B. 'Perish or Prosper: The Law and Convict Transportation in the British Empire, 1700–1850', *Law and History Review* 21: 3 (2003): 527–54.

Leask, N. 'Thomas Muir and The Telegraph: Radical Cosmopolitanism in 1790s Scotland', *History Workshop Journal* 63 (2007): 48–69.

Maxwell-Stewart, H. 'Convict Transportation from Britain and Ireland, 1615–1870', *History Compass* 8: 11 (2010): 1221–42.

McFarland, E.W. *Ireland and Scotland in the Age of Revolution: Planting the Green Bough*. Edinburgh: Edinburgh University Press, 1994.

McKenzie, K. '"The Laws of His Own Country": Defamation, Banishment and the Problem of Legal Pluralism in the 1820s Cape Colony', *Journal of Imperial and Commonwealth History* 43: 5 (2015): 787–806.

McKenzie, K. *Imperial Underworld: An Escaped Convict and the Transformation of the British Colonial Order*. Cambridge: Cambridge University Press, 2016.

Moore, T. *Death or Liberty: Rebels and Radicals Transported to Australia, 1788–1868*. Sydney: Murdoch Books, 2010.

Morgan, G. and Rushton, P. *Eighteenth-Century Criminal Transportation: The Formation of the Criminal Atlantic*. Basingstoke: Palgrave Macmillan, 2004.

Morgan, G. and Rushton, P. *Banishment in the Early Atlantic World: Convicts, Rebels and Slaves*. London and New York: Bloomsbury, 2013.

Neal, D. *The Rule of Law in a Penal Colony: Law and Power in Early New South Wales*. Cambridge: Cambridge University Press, 1991.

Nicholas, S. ed. *Convict Workers: Reinterpreting Australia's Past*. Cambridge: Cambridge University Press, 1988.

Parsons, T.G. 'Was John Boston's Pig a Political Martyr? The Reaction to Popular Radicalism in Early New South Wales', *Journal of Royal Australian Historical Society* 71 (1985): 163–76.

Powell, M. 'The Clanking of Medieval Chains: Extra-Judicial Banishment in the British Empire', *Journal of Imperial and Commonwealth History* 44: 2 (2016): 352–71.

Rice, B. 'Were the First Fleet Convicts Bond or Free?', *Journal of the Royal Historical Society of Victoria* 55 (1984): 44–7.

Roberts, D.A. 'A "Change of Place": Illegal Movement on the Bathurst Frontier, 1822–1825', *Journal of Australian Colonial History* 7 (2005): 97–122.

Roberts, D.A. 'Exile in a Land of Exiles: The Early History of Criminal Transportation Law in New South Wales, 1788–1809', *Australian Historical Studies* 48: 4 (2017): 470–85.

Roscoe, K. 'A Natural Hulk: Australia's Carceral Islands in the Colonial Period, 1788–1901', *International Review of Social History* 63 (2018): 45–63.

Spigelman, J.J. 'The Macquarie Bicentennial: A Reappraisal of the Bigge Reports', *History Council of New South Wales Annual History Lecture*. Sydney: History Council of New South Wales, 2009.

Turner, R.E. *The Relations of James Silk Buckingham with the East India Company, 1818–1836*. Pittsburgh, PA: Ralph Turner, 1930.

Ward, K. *Networks of Empire: Forced Migration in the Dutch East India Company*. Cambridge: Cambridge University Press, 2008.

Wold, A.L. *Scotland and the French Revolutionary War, 1792–1802*. Edinburgh: Edinburgh University Press, 2015.

Wold, A.L. 'Was There a Law of Sedition in Scotland? Baron David Hume's Analysis of the Scottish Sedition Trials of 1794'. In *Liberty, Property and Popular Politics: England and Scotland, 1688–1815. Essays in Honour of H.T. Dickinson*, ed. Gordon Pentland and Michael T. Davis, 163–75. Edinburgh: Edinburgh University Press, 2016.

Zastoupil, L. *Rammohun Roy and the Making of Victorian Britain*. New York: Palgrave, 2010.

4
Would Western Australia have met Bentham's five measures of penal justice?
Katherine Roscoe and Barry Godfrey

Western Australia was the last Australian colony to receive convicts, with nearly 10,000 convicts transported there between 1850 and 1868. It was the endpoint of an Antipodean convict system that Jeremy Bentham had thoroughly criticized much closer to its inception, having produced in 1802 and 1803 three works setting out to Lord Pelham his objections to transportation, whilst smarting under the administration's failure to further advance his proposal for an ideal prison. The first two 'Letters to Lord Pelham' and 'A Plea for the Constitution' – which later appeared together in the *Panopticon versus New South Wales* compilation in 1812 – laid out what Bentham saw as the major failings of transportation to Australia compared to his proposed panopticon penitentiary. At the time of writing these works, New South Wales was the only part of Australia that had been colonized, with 7,430 convicts transported there from Britain and Ireland between 1788–1801.[1] Bentham's critique of convict transportation had little impact on government penal policy. By the time Bentham had finished penning his third letter to Lord Pelham in early 1803, Van Diemen's Land (Tasmania) was soon to be colonized, with convicts arriving the following year aboard the *Calcutta* (by way of Port Phillip), and thousands more followed thereafter to the Australian penal colonies.

To his 1793 critique of colonization, Bentham added a postscript in June 1829 for its publication as *Emancipate Your Colonies!* (1830), exempting British India and the Swan River Colony (as Western Australia was then known) from much of his criticism. He noted that a positive account of the new colony's prospects, settled in 1829, had appeared in the *Morning Chronicle*.[2] Considering Bentham's prediction that all Australian colonies would have 'emancipated themselves' from British rule as representative democracies 'long before this century is it an end', Western Australia was the last to become self-governing in 1890, three decades after its neighbours.[3] In August 1831, Bentham wrote 'Colonization Company Proposal' about establishing a colony of free settlers in Australia and its subsequent transition into a representative democracy. This work was Bentham's response to Edward Gibbon Wakefield's plan of 'systematic colonization' where crown land would be sold at a sufficiently high price to fund the passage of selected free immigrants.[4] Wakefield's plan presented an alternative to government either having to finance free emigration directly or rely on convict labour, as it had done in colonizing eastern Australia.

To the west of the continent, the situation in Swan River exemplified the obstructions to colonization, as Wakefield and Bentham saw them, namely relying on land grants of vast and dispersed territories to raise funds, with a dearth of capital and labour to generate profit. The National Colonization Society subsequently turned its attention to the south coast of the Australian continent, and it was only when the Society's successor organization, the South Australia Association, agreed after considerable negotiation to seek a Charter for a crown colony, to be administered by commissioners, that the British government supported their scheme. Bentham passed away before the Wakefieldian experiment of South Australia began in 1836, and did not live to see penal transportation end; in fact he died in 1832 just as it was peaking in New South Wales. But why was Bentham so opposed to transportation?

In Bentham's first 'Letter to Lord Pelham' (1802), he measured New South Wales against five 'ends of penal justice' – namely, example, reformation, incapacitation, compensation and economy – standards that transportation and colonization through the creation of penal colonies should be judged against.[5] In this chapter, after exploring the transformation of the Swan River Colony into the last Australian penal colony between 1829 and 1850, we analyse whether Bentham's objections to transportation to New South Wales also held true for Western Australia. How effective were the systems put into place in Western Australia, tested against Bentham's five measures? How would the contextual factors evident in Western Australia condition the success of the penal system, and was it a system that was fit for purpose? Would Bentham have approved of Australia's last penal colony, or would he have concluded that it shared the same failings as its first?

The first four of Bentham's five measures of successful punishment were in tune with other commentators and notably chimed with the views of English jurist William Blackstone in his *Commentaries on the Laws of England* (which were themselves much influenced by Cesare Beccaria, the Italian penal theorist). The first, 'example', Bentham defined as the 'prevention of similar offences … at large'.[6] He posited that transportation was not an effective deterrent because the convicted were punished remotely, out of sight and mind of the home population. The fate of transported convicts was uncertain and irregular, he argued, rendering it even more ineffective as a deterrent.[7] The imposition of a few set periods of transportation – seven years, fourteen years, life – meant that British judges could not easily calibrate sentences to each offence (let alone each offender).

The second, 'reformation' of the convicted, Bentham defined as the 'prevention of similar offences … by *curing him* [our emphasis] of the will to the like in the future'.[8] According to Bentham, the central 'inspection principle' of the panopticon would rehabilitate convicts, because prisoners' behaviour could be inspected at any time from the central tower, though the prisoners could not see the inspector and so had to assume that they were under constant surveillance.[9] To avoid punishment, inmates would conduct themselves well, building habits of good behaviour. Bentham contrasted this with New South Wales, where convicts were assigned to work in 'field husbandry', beyond any 'inspecting eye' that would check their 'vicious habits', under which heading he included 'sloth, drunkenness, gaming, venereal irregularities, profaneness, quarrelsomeness, mischievousness, rapacity'.[10]

Bentham's third measure was the incapacitation of convicts, or the 'prevention of similar offences … by *depriving them* [our emphasis] of the power to do the like'.[11] He was critical of the government's view that 'distance the supposed mother of security, was the virtue which … was regarded as making up the absence of every other'.[12] Since prisoners were not being reformed by being transported abroad, Bentham argued, they were likely to continue offending in the colonies. Since transportation was a binary sentence – you were either sent abroad or not – it could not be gradated in order to provide the required calibration of a just measure of punishment to outweigh the benefits of committing the crime. Moreover, although terms of transportation were fixed at seven or fourteen years, all convicts were effectively banished for life as it was almost impossible to return home. This was, Bentham argued, an additional illegal extrajudicial punishment. Furthermore, the 'bondage' of forced labour convicts faced on arrival was not properly regulated since the severity of their punishment was dependent on which master they were assigned to. Bentham contrasted this with American penitentiaries which used 'chronical punishment' as prisoners progressed through the system.[13]

Fourth, the 'compensation or satisfaction … of victims'[14] was an issue for Bentham because convicts were removed to a remote location as their punishment, which provided no compensation for the victim through payment of a fine or restitution for the wider community. In New South Wales, private entrepreneurs and colonists were the only ones to gain from labour extracted from convicts, not the victims of the original offence who effectively paid, via taxation, for a convict system whose labour benefited colonists at the other end of the world. A benefit of the panopticon scheme, Bentham argued, was that it would generate sufficient profit to 'offer at least some portion of indemnity to the parties injured'.[15] Victims were tasked with the costly business of bringing and prosecuting the case, and though a 1778 statute allowed prosecutors to seek expenses regardless of the outcome of the case, these were not always reimbursed in full, or at all.[16] Therefore the criminal justice system did not provide adequate or equal access to justice for women, the young, and the poor, something which would have undermined Bentham's notions of utilitarianism by means of equal access to justice. Moreover, the growth in numbers of trials (and victims), as well as the increasing willingness of the state to take over the costs of the judicial system, in return for control over the way it worked, meant that victims gradually disappeared from the nation's courtrooms as the nineteenth century progressed in any case. Nevertheless, until the prosecution of offenders was taken over by a professional police and Public Prosecutor as a duty of state in the later nineteenth century, Bentham was right to reason that victims would need some (financial or other) incentive to bring people to justice.

Finally, Bentham argued that colonization offered no additional benefit to international trade, and entailed additional expenses of 'founding, maintaining, and protecting a colony'.[17] The extreme remoteness of Australia from Britain, and the need to import food due to poor harvests, made New South Wales a particularly expensive colony. In comparison to the cost of transportation, estimated by Bentham to stand at between £33.9s.5d and £47.7s.¼d. per convict per annum, the per inmate expense of the panopticon proposal was considerably less, at £12 per head (excluding the expense of buying land and building the penitentiary, which raised the total cost to £13.10s).[18] Bentham concluded 'Letter to Lord Pelham' by questioning what 'real advantage' (if any) was to be 'derived from the plan of colonizing the antipodes – colonizing them with the settlers selected for their unfitness for colonization'.[19]

From free colony to the last Australian penal colony, 1829–68

Bentham's criticism was aimed at New South Wales, but may also apply to Swan River, a colony he barely lived to see established, and which he did not live long enough to see whether it would meet his five measures of penal justice.

Despite calls to action in the 1820s, the British government was unmoved by the assertion that it would need to move quickly to prevent French or American expansion into the vast territory of Western Australia. Instead, private sector entrepreneurism provided the original thrust and impetus from 1827 for British intrusion into the Swan River (Derbal Yaragan) region, country of the Whadjuk Noongar people. Only later would expansion become a governmental project when an initial speculative foray was attempted by a few hundred European colonists in 1829. When Captain Charles Fremantle of the Royal Navy arrived, new colonists followed, with Perth (Borloo) chosen as the main place for a European settlement.

The colonists had arrived at Swan River with meagre resources, and a paucity of money to buy resources from merchants in eastern Australia. According to the British historian of policing, Arthur Haydon, 'The settlements which quickly sprang up around new townships like Fremantle (Wallyalup) were of the nature of an experiment, a utopian scheme in fact, and like others of its kind, it contained many defects'.[20] Not least of these 'defects' was opposition from the traditional owners of the land directed towards the colonists, as more and more of their homeland was appropriated. As early as 1830, diarist and barrister George Moore wrote that he feared violent conflict unless the Noongar community were 'removed wholesale to some island'.[21] Tensions rose as Noongar people continued to seek access to land and water on territory newly occupied by settlers. In June 1832 resistance leaders Yagan, Donmera and Ningina were tricked into a boat, placed in chains and marched to the courthouse to stand trial for attacking colonists in retaliation for one of their countrymen being killed while taking potatoes from the settlers' garden.[22] They were exiled to Carnac Island (Ngooloomayup) rather than executed, after colonist Robert

Lyon pleaded that they be treated as de facto prisoners of war, instead of common criminals.[23] The European colonists were concerned about the prospect both of continued violent conflict and poor harvests due to poor-quality land and drought. Moore wrote in his diary in 1834 that 'the colonists are a cheerless, dissatisfied people with gloomy looks, who plod through the sand from hut to hut, to drink grog and grumble out their discontent to each other'.[24]

Since grog and discontent could easily lead to fighting, drunkenness, and disorder, an inchoate criminal justice system took shape in the colony's early decades. The Round House in Fremantle, built in 1831, was part of an early penal complex formed of a police station, a courthouse, and the formidable circular prison itself which acted as common gaol and also a House of Correction.[25] The Round House's architect, Henry Reveley, was the son of Willey Reveley, the architect who drew up Bentham's panopticon designs, and scholars have speculated that the Round House's design was partly modelled on Bentham's panopticon.[26] However, it lacked a central observation post, and was more reminiscent of a round military blockhouse with a handful of cells around the circular perimeter which could together hold tens, but not hundreds, of prisoners. Not that it would need to hold more, since the population of the colony was small at this time: in 1829 there were just 769 men and 234 women in the colony, and 20 years later there were still fewer than 6,000 colonists.[27]

The majority of prisoners kept in the Round House during the 1830s were young, poorly educated European men who had previous convictions in the colony. Most were imprisoned for minor violence and low-level public order offences. Imprisonment was part of a melange of responses to their offending, as can be seen in the reports of one day's business in Fremantle Quarter Sessions. On New Year's Day 1836 William Fraser pleaded not guilty to a charge of assault. He provided an alibi, supported by two witnesses, who stated that he was in a public house at the time of the offence. The case against him was dismissed. John Woods was then charged with coining and found guilty. The court recommended him to mercy, on the grounds that the offence had not been carried on to any great extent, and that he was so bad at coining that his offences were easily detectable. Woods was sentenced to be transported to Van Diemen's Land for seven years. Joseph Walford would join him after being convicted of stealing tea, a box of sauces, and a keg of peas. Next the servant of a hat-shop owner was convicted of obtaining goods by false pretences, and the theft of a hat. Rather than being transported, he was sent to the Round House for two months, with hard labour. The last defendant of the day, Nassip, described as a 'man of color' by *The Perth Gazette and Western Australian Journal*, was charged with stealing three pocket handkerchiefs. In his defence he stated that he was too drunk to account for his actions, which did not prevent him from receiving a public flogging and six months inside the Round House.[28] The mentally ill were also confined in the Round House.[29] The mixing together of convicted criminals and those in need of psychiatric treatment, free settlers and Aboriginal people, is reminiscent of many colonial makeshifts that belied contemporary British penal theory, but suited the somewhat chaotic state of colonial law and order.

In the early years of settlement, Aboriginal people were flogged, imprisoned and transported for 'crimes' against settlers, without trial.[30] Extra-judicial punishment operated alongside massacres (known as 'punitive expeditions') to quell uprisings. In 1834, at Pinjarra, a detachment of 24 soldiers and colonists attacked around 80 Binjareb Noongar civilians, killing at least 15.[31] Throughout the 1830s, Britain's treatment of Indigenous people in its imperial possessions was under scrutiny. In 1835 a parliamentary Select Committee, chaired by abolitionist Thomas Fowell Buxton, was formed to investigate the treatment of Aboriginal people in Britain's settler colonies. Fowell Buxton's report modelled a new mode of colonization, whereby Indigenous peoples' welfare would be ensured through appointed 'protectors', and their 'civilisation' encouraged through religious education.[32] The imposition of institutions of law and order was part of the British government's attempt to avoid the genocidal violence that had marked the colonization of Van Diemen's Land, causing an 'indelible stain upon the character of the British government'.[33] Likewise, in 'Colonization Company Proposal' (1831), Bentham noted in the margin that the dispersed and haphazard settlement of Van Diemen's Land, which brought more colonists and Aboriginal people into conflict than a smaller colony founded on principles of 'vicinity-maximisation', had 'determined to absolutely extirpate the natives'.[34]

Bentham had proposed that centralized land grant allocation on the principle of 'vicinity maximisation' would best prevent the dispersed settlement that escalated tensions between larger numbers of Aboriginal and European people. [35] However, he did not account for a limited amount of good quality land. In Western Australia, Governor Stirling split the allocated acreages between small strips of fertile land along the Swan and Canning Rivers, near the main settlements at Perth, and plots across the Darling Range. Since settlers had to 'improve' their land to retain control over it, this led to conflict between Aboriginal and European prisoners over access to a dispersed set of territories.[36]

The Western Australian authorities were well aware of the growing 'humanitarian' ethos in London, as conflict escalated in the colony itself. In 1835, Governor James Stirling wrote to the Colonial Office, urging the need to create a 'sufficient establishment' for 'protecting, controlling, managing and gradually civilizing the aboriginal race' to prevent the outbreak of war and 'extermination' of the Indigenous population.[37] Stirling's successor, Governor John Hutt, proposed a new judicial system built around the principle of 'protection through punishment'.[38] Protectors, appointed in London, would act as mediators between the Indigenous and European communities. To operate effectively, he argued, new legislation would have to be passed to extend the sentencing powers of magistrates over Aboriginal people in pastoral districts. Hutt claimed that these new powers were intended not as 'an act of coercion', but to 'extend ... the protecting hand of government', as otherwise settlers would enact vigilante justice.[39] As part of the same colonial 'civilising' project, Indigenous peoples were brought under government surveillance and into institutions. In 1837, the first criminal trial of Noongar defendants under the new system took place at Perth's Quarter Sessions, where several Aboriginal people were convicted for repeated theft from settlers.[40] From then on, Aboriginal defendants could receive sentences of up to seven years' transportation to Garden Island (Meeandip) and, from 1838, to Rottnest Island (Wadjemup), both off the coast near Fremantle.[41] Prisoners were held at the Round House before being shipped across to the island. By 1842, the prisoners had built a main prison building on Rottnest with a large dormitory and several small cells where they were locked in at night.[42] Rottnest subsequently housed approximately 25 Aboriginal prisoners on a daily basis until 1850.

At the same time, on the other side of Australia, transportation was falling out of favour in the eastern colonies. When New South Wales and Van Diemen's Land began to grow from penal colony to civil society, agitation to end transportation in the east increased.[43] In the west, however, enthusiasm for unfree labour grew. A range of coerced labourers had been imported since the colony's inception – including indentured European, Indian and Chinese labourers, and emigrant and convicted juveniles – but never at a scale to overcome labour shortages.[44] The use of Aboriginal people as forced labour to build roads and bridges had already proved to the colonists that a more consistent and regular flow of such labour could be used and was vital to sustain and improve the colony's infrastructure.[45] In 1847 the influential pastoralists of the York Agricultural Society petitioned the colony's Legislative Council to consider the introduction of convict labour so that they could reap a similar economic benefit as New South Wales and Van Diemen's Land had. Historian A.G.L. Shaw suggested that the colonists and the British government were 'willing to risk moral corruption for the economic advantages of transportation', although it would be fairer to say that they sought to exchange the immoral exploitation of Aboriginal labour for the large-scale exploitation of convict labour.[46]

Initially, the British government were unconvinced by the request. They believed that Western Australia lacked the natural advantages of the penal colony of Van Diemen's Land. Whereas that colony was essentially a prison without walls because of its natural geography, Western Australia looked porous. The Pentonville Commissioners believed that men could 'lose themselves in a larger colony', or more accurately, they worried that they would be lost to the authorities.[47] However, the decline of transportation in the east was causing the British authorities considerable difficulty as it risked removing transportation as a sentencing option, and, due to the lack of enthusiasm from other colonies to accept transported convicts, the government eventually came to gratefully accept the offer from Western Australia. Not everyone was enthusiastic. Some free settlers lamented the introduction of a 'convict stain' to their community, while some in the eastern states feared that freed and escaped Western Australian convicts would 'prey' on their colonies. Their concerns were legitimate.[48] Nevertheless, the *Scindian* arrived in Fremantle in 1850 with a shipment of 76 convict men (no women were sent to the Western Australian penal colony during its 18 years of operation). In 1853, transportation to Van Diemen's Land ended, and Swan River became the sole Australian destination for convicts transported from Great Britain.[49]

Criminal justice capacity increased alongside the new convict intake, with the formation of the Western Australia mounted police in 1848. In 1850 police constables were appointed to various districts funded from convict establishment budgets, and two years later there were 87 police officers who channelled defendants through the courts, and ultimately into prison. The Round House continued to be used for both local European and Aboriginal prisoners until 1886 (and as a police lock-up until 1900). In 1850, as white convicts arrived, Rottnest was disbanded as a prison and all Aboriginal prisoners transferred to the mainland to work on the Perth–Albany road. Perth Gaol was built in 1855, with a total capacity of 100 inmates, which was sufficient whilst both the colonial and the convict populations remained fairly small.[50] However, the population of the colony grew significantly after it became a penal colony, and so did penal capacity to deal with the influx of convicts. From 1855 Fremantle Convict Depot started to take in newly arrived convicts, and by 1859 it had the capacity to hold 1,000 men.[51]

A relatively small number of the approximately 168,000 or so convicts transported to Australia were sent to Western Australia, less than 5 per cent of the total, though their numbers were significant in comparison to the colonial population. In 1851, one year after becoming a penal colony, the European population stood at 7,186. It more than doubled by 1861.[52] After only three years of transportation to Western Australia, the Penal Servitude Act of 1853 stipulated that shorter terms of 'penal servitude' would be served in Britain, which reduced the number of men eligible to be transported to the colony.[53] Fewer than 300 men were transported between 1854 and 1856; just 224 in 1859.[54] Thereafter, there was an increase in convict traffic from 1861 to 1868, when the British government suspended the regulations. By the time that the last convict ship, the *Hougoumont*, had docked in Fremantle, altogether nearly 10,000 convicts had passed through the port of Fremantle between 1850 and 1868 (see Figure 4.1). By this time the colony had been established for over 40 years. The considerable amount of extant data generated by the convict bureaucracy, as well as contemporary court and prison records, permits us to analyse whether the Western Australian penal system achieved or failed to meet Bentham's five measures of success.

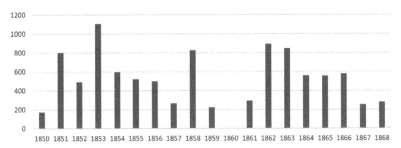

Figure 4.1: Numbers of men transported to Western Australia, 1850–68
Source: Blue Books for the Colony of Western Australia (Microfilm Reproduction), 1837–1905, State Library of Western Australia.

Bentham versus Western Australia

Bentham based his critique on the transportation system that operated in New South Wales during his lifetime, and unsurprisingly, by the time transportation to Western Australia had begun in 1850 the management of convicts had changed. In every Australian penal colony, convicts had first been put to work on government projects, building the colonial infrastructure, and then later assigned to work as servants and labourers for individual private employers (who were often ex-convicts themselves). Sending convicts out on assignment had ended in the 1830s in the eastern Australian colonies as it was considered a failure.[55] Nevertheless, it was a useful system for distributing convict labour to geographically dispersed settlements where free labour would not venture, and so was used extensively in Western Australia. During the period when they were under sentence, convicts experienced a progressive system, journeying through each stage until they had either earned early release, or when the sentence imposed upon them by a British court had expired (hence the term 'expirees' being used for ex-convicts no longer serving a sentence). The first stage commenced when a convict was awarded a ticket-of-leave, which allowed them to contract for work, travel within prescribed areas and spend time on their own pursuits as long as they obeyed a ten o'clock curfew, kept out of trouble, and did not consort with people the state considered undesirable. For a time, convicts who had already served a portion of their sentence in British prisons or prison hulks (about a quarter of those arriving in Fremantle) were immediately issued with tickets-of-leave and were assigned at the start of their life in the colony.[56] By December 1852, over half of the transported men were working for private employers.[57] However, this policy was reversed when the British government removed the stipulation that convicts had to spend half their sentence in British prisons before being transported. Newly transported convicts were then instead forced to spend more time on road gangs and in government work before becoming eligible for tickets-of-leave and assignment to private employers.[58] Having completed that stage, they were given a conditional, and finally, a full pardon. They were then, aside from a prohibition on murderers returning to England, essentially 'free'.[59] Few made the trip home, however, as it was self-funded and expensive, and prospects for most were better in their new country.

The progressive stage system and the strong systems of surveillance that were embedded in Western Australia had echoes of Bentham's ideas about the panoptic 'Inspector's eye' monitoring behaviour and inculcating self-governmentality among the inmates.[60] The Western Australian systems of surveillance were all designed to watch over behaviour – if not as closely as a centrally-positioned prison warder could, then as much as was possible in a colonial system which had to deal with thousands of convicts (rather than the thousand that might have been housed in Bentham's panopticon).[61] As Barry Godfrey notes,

> Even when in receipt of their ticket – which they were required to carry around with them for inspection by police constables – convicts were confined to a geographical area, were required to make regular reports to the local resident magistrate, had restrictions on their drinking of alcohol, could not apply for civil service posts, or serve on juries (although they were permitted to prosecute cases and act as witnesses in court). They were subject to curfew at 10pm … and they remained under the supervision of the police (in a similar way to the British convicts who were subject to habitual offender legislation passed in the 1860s and 70s).[62]

Once free, however, neither the experience of transportation nor the possibility of the detection of wrongdoing by a strong system of surveillance appeared to deter offenders (in other words, the system did not provide the 'example' that Bentham favoured). In fact, the high level of surveillance designed to prevent reoffending meant that convicts who failed to reform were much more likely to have their offences noticed and therefore punished. The rate of recidivism was accordingly very high in the penal colony. Between 1861 and 1891, nearly one in ten transported men were convicted in the Western Australian Supreme Court (mostly of property crimes), between 1858 and 1868 just under three-quarters of Fremantle Prison's inmates were transported convicts, and from 1862 to 1868 two-thirds of defendants appearing at Fremantle and Perth magistrates' courts were transported convicts (see Figure 4.2).[63]

No more convicts were landed in Western Australia after 1868, but many transported men remained on 'tickets', and a significant proportion of the population were expirees. These men continued to commit disproportionate amounts of crime. In Perth, in 1870, two years after transportation had ended, they were responsible for about one-third of all crimes, and they still figured disproportionately highly in court proceedings during the 1880s. In Perth, in 1880, nearly one in ten men who had originally been transported between 1861 and 1868

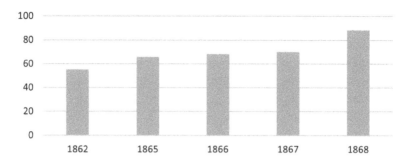

100
80
60
40
20
0

1862   1865   1866   1867   1868

Figure 4.2: Convicts on ticket-of-leave or conditional pardon who were reconvicted at petty sessions (%) 1862–8.[64]
Source: Blue Books of Western Australia, 1862–8. National Archives (UK), CO 22/40–22/46 inclusive.

appeared before either the colony's Supreme or magistrates' court, despite being members of an aging population. Take, for example, two Yorkshiremen who both arrived on the *Nile* in 1858. Thomas Shaw was an unmarried miner from Northallerton who was transported for committing larceny, having already previously committed a felony. Receiving his ticket-of-leave in 1860, he travelled around various parts of Western Australia until he was convicted of two separate thefts in 1867, receiving 21 days and six months respectively, in Fremantle Prison as punishment. In 1869, he was then charged with feloniously breaking and entering the dwelling house of a shepherd's hut and stealing clothing. He was committed for trial at the Supreme Court, where he was convicted and sentenced to six years' penal servitude. He received his second ticket-of-leave in 1874, when he was 40 years old, and his certificate of freedom the year after. He lived in York, then Fremantle, where he died in 1877.

His fellow shipmate on the *Nile*, Robert Briggs, was convicted of shop-breaking at Bradford in 1856. He received a ticket in 1864 and his freedom a year later. By 1868, he was employed as a blacksmith and was married with three children. He was subsequently imprisoned in Fremantle Prison for larceny, serving six months. This was a short sentence compared to the six years' penal servitude that was imposed upon him in 1872 for the theft of an iron chest from a house in Fremantle. The newspaper report was damning:

> Burglary, or house breaking, described by our Trans-Atlantic cousins as one of the fine arts, appears to have revived, and nothing

seems to be impossible to professed hands. In this instance the prisoners improved the occasion while Mr. Oakley, on a Sunday evening, was at Church; and the 'operation' is unmatched for cool deliberate daring. The thieves were, however, tracked by the police and caught red handed with their booty. The house, it appears, was left in charge of a female servant, who, as soon as her master had gone to church, stepped into the veranda to have a chat with her sweet heart, one of the guardians of the public safety. Mr. Oakley returning about nine o'clock, found the sash of his office window open, and the 'safe' missing.[65]

The police tracked Briggs and fellow burglars to his house where they found an opened safe next to a blacksmith's hammer. The evidence was convincing to the jury, and the judge sentenced him accordingly. He was released in 1877 on his second ticket and given his freedom in 1880. Over the next few years, he was subject to several charges of drunkenness at Fremantle Magistrates' Court.[66] The costs of policing and imprisoning men like Briggs were significant. Indeed, the financial costs of establishing a new colony in Western Australia were high, for the British government at least, even if private sector employers gained from a supply of cheap labour. The convict establishment formed a significant component of colonial expenditure. In 1858, one-third of the government's budget was spent on convicts, at £12 per convict per year.[67] This was still cheap, however, compared to the £33 per convict per year cost for imprisonment in Britain. In criticizing New South Wales, Bentham calculated that his panopticon would be cheaper, but, in fact, his estimates of the costs of maintenance per convict per year matched the Western Australian transportation costs of £12 per head.[68]

Bentham's panopticon (or, more realistically, system of panopticons) might have been built more cheaply, run more efficiently than Victorian prisons, and may have, as Bentham intended, at least covered its costs, but it seems unlikely that it would have financially undercut the Western Australia transportation system. Neither would the panopticon have contributed to a cheap supply of labour for governmental or private enterprise, conveniently kept in line for years by the criminal code. Unfree labour and the modest financial gains from prison labour would have lightened the colony's financial burden. However, the personal costs of the Western Australian system to its convicts, as well as the families they left behind, were also considerable, although mainly unacknowledged by the authorities. As Barry Godfrey and David Cox conclude, 'Transportation hit many men so hard that all they were left with was a washed-up life, alcoholism, drifting through life and through the colony as vagrants and occasional inmates of the prison and the asylum'.[69]

Whilst transportation and the prison estate are usually treated as separate systems by researchers, in Australia they were inextricably linked. Transportation was midwife to the prison because the removal of people from their country of birth, their families, and their relationships was almost bound to encourage a dissolute life.[70] Transportation as a system held little reformative power, and reoffending was rife. In New South Wales, Van Diemen's Land, and Western Australia, prison-building projects trailed in the wake of the convict ships. This penal nexus was a trait of transportation Bentham identified at the outset, decrying in his first 'Letter to Lord Pelham' (1802) that the imperfect penal measures transportation was supposed to replace – gaols and hulks – were being replicated in the colony.[71] What he did not explicitly account for is the rise of a separate carceral apparatus for Indigenous Australians.

The colonial authorities believed that Aboriginal people feared being sent to Rottnest Island prison far more than being worked in chains on the mainland. William Cowan, Guardian of Aborigines for York, reported that 'confinement on the mainland does not fill their minds with same indefinite terrors that have operated so powerfully in deterring them from crime' as being sent to Rottnest.[72] For Noongar people, the island was wanniatch (forbidden) to visit, and the prospect of being sent there induced a particular dread.[73] The colonial government knew this, as Governor Hutt reported to London in 1841 'there is nothing which alarms them more than the threat of sending them to Rottnest'.[74]

The continued use of Rottnest Prison was driven by a desire to satisfy victims, primarily European settlers at the frontier (Bentham's fourth measure). Prominent pastoralists were influential within their community, and lobbied for measures to protect their livestock holdings and themselves from harm. They were vocal in their demands to introduce more policemen, and to grant additional summary powers to both the police and magistrates to protect them from 'tribes of savages hostile in every instance'.[75] In 1883, the colonial secretary Malcolm Fraser wryly observed that 'the wholesale deportation of the natives is one way of protecting the settlers from sheep stealing'.[76] In 1831 in 'Colonization Company Proposal', Bentham recognized that settlers' incursions over Indigenous people's territory would result in violence, as being at a great distance from the seat of colonial government would result in 'insecurity against damage to person and property from the hostility of the uncivilised aborigines'.[77] The government met that 'insecurity' by extending devolved powers of sentencing to dispersed rural magistrates. The representatives of these northern districts complained that transporting prisoners over hundreds of kilometres to Rottnest was too expensive, suggesting instead that Aboriginal prisoners build roads locally as a form of compensation.[78] Though the prisoners on Rottnest performed work in different industries, they never generated a profit sufficient to cover their running costs, and so did not meet a monetary standard of 'compensation' Bentham deemed necessary under a utilitarian system.

As well as providing for general deterrence, Rottnest seemed to fit Bentham's bill as being a prison designed for the 'reformation' of prisoners (Bentham's second measure). The government did not perceive Indigenous people as inherently criminal (or morally at fault), but rather 'uncivilised'. Being taught to farm and to live in settled ways on Rottnest was viewed as a 'civilising' mechanism that would encourage Aboriginal people to work for European settlers upon release. According to an editorial in the *Perth Inquirer* in 1855, on Rottnest 'natives were taught habits of regular and useful labour' and 'cut off from all their former associations' which would inculcate permanent 'moral effect'.[79] This focus on learning 'habits of civilized life', rather than converting them through scripture, reflects Bentham's theories that criminals were reformed by being forced to change their exterior behaviours through surveillance.[80]

The re-establishment of Rottnest Prison in 1855 was motivated by repeated escapes from the road gangs into the bush (which Aboriginal people were far more adept at navigating than their captors).[81] Yet they were not easily held in prisons either, escaping more often than their European counterparts.[82] In 1856, seven Aboriginal prisoners managed to abscond into the scrub on Rottnest Island. To try and force them out of hiding, superintendent Henry Vincent set fire to the bush which spread rapidly and damaged the prison accommodation. To replace it, the government proposed a village of huts, but Vincent insisted that a more secure prison was needed. An octagonal prison, with both cells and association wards, was designed to hold 106 men.[83] This embodied a shift away from 'humanitarian' punishment towards European carceral norms of cellular segregation, closer surveillance, greater security, and a higher level of incapacitation.[84]

Following its re-establishment, the government hoped that Rottnest Prison would become 'self-sustaining' within one year. The costs of road-gang labour were quite high, estimated at one shilling per head per day in rations, amounting to £730 per annum (excluding costs of accommodation and recapturing escapees).[85] On Rottnest, where prisoners could grow their own food to defray the prison running costs, supplementing their diet by fishing and hunting, that could be reduced to £40 per annum.[86]

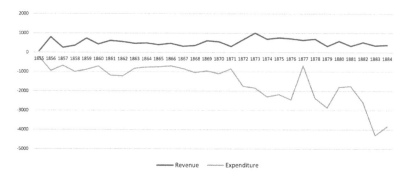

Figure 4.3: Revenue and expenditure for Rottnest Penal Establishment, 1855–70.[87]
Source: *Inquirer and Commercial News* 1856; *Perth Gazette and Western Australian Times* 1856, 1866; *Fremantle Herald* 1871; *Western Australian Times* 1870; *Lords Sessional Papers* 1859, 1861–4, 1866–9, 1871, 1878, 1881, 1884–5, 1888.

However, expenditure was far greater than anticipated, reaching £234 in 1855, and averaging £15 per head per year over the period 1855–70 (see Figure 4.3). Some revenue was generated through sale of excess agricultural produce and salt produced on the island (which is excluded from these figures). In 1847, 150 tonnes of Rottnest salt were valued at £3 per tonne.[88] In the 1870s, as more prisoners arrived from remote northern districts, prison costs rocketed to over £2000 per annum, mainly owing to the cost of transportation over hundreds of kilometres, and feeding a large prison population from limited, over-cultivated land. However, it is impossible to put a price on the natural resources that were 'freed' up for colonization by incarcerating men at Rottnest, disrupting Indigenous communities and limiting their capacity for resistance.

To some extent, the system of punishment for Aboriginal Australians met Bentham's criteria to a greater degree than the European transportation system did, or the prison estate that followed it. However, it scarcely seemed to result from any rational or systematic utilitarian planning. The treatment meted out by colonists to the traditional owners of the land was as irrational as it was immoral.

Along with other Enlightenment thinkers, Bentham's utilitarianism relied on rationality.[89] It was not unreasonable to conclude that statutes legislated by a democratic parliament would be enforced by a defined and regulated system of policing, sentencing, and punishment. Imprecision and the difficulties of calibrating a just measure of punishment, as well as the vagaries and variability of experiences by those subjected to it, had no place in Bentham's world. His panopticon scheme promoted self-governmentality in 'mitigated seclusion', with prisoners incarcerated in cells with two or three others. On Rottnest, necessity – rather than design – led to three or even five prisoners being squeezed into small cells.[90] Though prison officials claimed Aboriginal prisoners preferred to be in company, Aboriginal prisoner Bob Thomas testified to the 1882 commission of inquiry that 'There are two others besides myself in my cell; it is close and the smell is bad in the morning'.[91] An 1882–3 outbreak of influenza and measles led to the death of between 63 and 80 prisoners.[92] Overall, of the 3,676 Aboriginal prisoners sent to Rottnest between 1838–1931, around 400 died in custody.[93]

The exponential growth in inmates during the 1880s (see Figure 4.4) was due to the frontier expanding rapidly northwards, bringing new Indigenous communities under the purview of colonial magistracy, who convicted them primarily for theft of livestock.[94] The mass-sentencing of Aboriginal people – upwards of 20 at a time – became increasingly commonplace. Aboriginal prisoners were also being sentenced for longer periods. In 1849, a resident magistrate could sentence Indigenous people to up to six months in prison and 24 lashes. A decade later, in 1859, this had risen to three years.[95] Highly variable sentencing emerged as a result. In the Upper Murchison, itinerant magistrate Charles Foss sent 23 Aboriginal prisoners to Rottnest, three were remanded for trial on a murder charge, and the rest sentenced to imprisonment from three to nine years for theft (Superintendent William Henry Timperley recommended they be released earlier).[96]

To reduce prison overcrowding and costs of maintenance, in the 1880s Rottnest's prisoners were 'loaned' out to other government departments, including the postal service, surveying and telegraph departments, and as 'native assistants' to the police. The latter helped track Aboriginal suspects and interpret for European constables.[97] In theory they operated under strict European supervision to bring Aboriginal suspects into custody. In practice, being armed and on horseback, they led raids on Aboriginal camps at the frontier, sometimes using lethal force.[98] Unlike in colonies like New South Wales and Queensland where the native police acted as a paramilitary force,

Western Australia's native assistants and their European constables at least retained the fiction of operating within the law, bringing many Aboriginal people into custody for trial by magistrates. This prevailed largely because Western Australia still remained under direct rule of the British government until 1890, contrary to Bentham's expectations and hopes for the colony in *Emancipate Your Colonies!*[99] Summary jurisdiction proved far more effective at curbing 'offences against the persons or against property' committed by Aboriginal people in Western Australia, than it had – from Bentham's perspective – against convicts in New South Wales. Unlike in the Eastern colonies where police forces aimed to 'disperse' Aboriginal people from the frontier, in Western Australia police brought Indigenous 'offenders' under the remit of settler colonial state, through conviction, incarceration and redeployment working for government departments at the frontier. Bentham was not likely to have approved of Aboriginal prisoners being selected for government service based primarily on where they were from, rather than their good behaviour. The punishment did not fit the crime when there was such volatility in both sentencing and in selection of those who were effectively 'released' during custody – a situation which echoed Bentham's argument that the fate of those transported to NSW was essentially down to luck, rather than correlating to their sentence or offence.

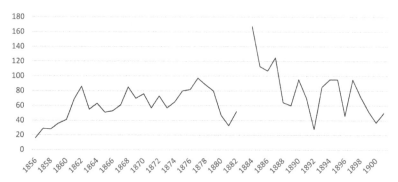

Figure 4.4: Rottnest prison population, 1855–1900.
Source: Blue Books for the Colony of Western Australia (Microfilm Reproduction), 1837–1905, State Library of Western Australia.

If Bentham wanted the 'greatest happiness for the greatest number', under the Western Australian convict system Aboriginal people would always come out short. Their population, estimated in tens of thousands prior to colonization, was decimated through disease, violence and lack of access to hunting and fishing grounds.[100] In 1881, a settler population of 29,708 employed 2,346 Aboriginal people (with an uncounted number living independently).[101] To be included in Bentham's utilitarian equation, they would at least need to be accounted for. The colonial administration fictively removed Aboriginal people by claiming their land was *terra nullius* (empty land) to deny Indigenous sovereignty, and the colonial and then commonwealth administration continued not to 'count' Aboriginal people in censuses or as citizens until 1967.[102] This was rooted in Enlightenment thinking which codified Aboriginal people as 'sub-human', scientifically inferior to Europeans. The colonial government only counted white settlers fully as citizens, and Aboriginal people were secondary as 'subjects' of British rule. As a result, Indigenous people were caught up in a criminal justice system designed for colonial uses, which they did not want or fully understand, and which had, even on its own terms, manifestly failed.

Conclusion

Transportation did not deter future offending, either through close and regular supervision or through harsh punishment. Instead, transportation necessitated the need for a large and expensive prison system which continued to grow in Australia and which Indigenous people still disproportionately suffer under to this day. Neither penal transportation, nor any alternative to transportation has been successful in reforming prisoners, although one might argue that probation, introduced in Britain progressively from the 1890s, and the introduction of semi-carceral institutions, and divergence schemes for young people, have been most successful. Whilst it remains highly improbable that Bentham's panopticon would itself have successfully met his own objectives, it has been demonstrated that no nineteenth-century or even twenty-first-century system of imprisonment has met them either.[103]

Bentham was equally concerned about the utilitarian benefits of colonization as he was about the creation of an ideal prison. In regard to Western Australia, the creation of a penal colony was not the impetus for colonization. Rather, it became a working solution only once the free Swan River Colony had been founded and was starting to fail. The colonists needed to bring in cheap labour quickly, which it could not attract by way of free settlers. Had it not been for the option of welcoming in convicts, the colony may well have disappeared, though it may have re-emerged at another point or in another place in Western Australia (perhaps becoming a French or American settlement). Colonization was a powerful philosophy for Europeans in the eighteenth and nineteenth centuries. It supposedly offered material benefits craved and demanded by the governments in the northern hemisphere (and of course, by colonial administrations in the southern hemisphere once they had established their foothold).

Two years before transportation ended, an editorial in the *Perth Inquirer* in 1866 remarked that by welcoming convicts to their shores 16 years earlier the colonists had strengthened their economy, but had 'bid farewell to anything like Jeremy Bentham's ideal of social life'.[104] The colony had life breathed into it by penal transportation and the labour it brought, but it continued to grow away from anything that Bentham would have recognized or approved of when the convict period had ended. It proved to be economically viable – indeed the state became a powerful economic motor for Australia once the mining industry was established. The colony of Western Australia flourished into a successful venture for the descendants of European colonists and new white settlers, though not for the traditional owners of Swan River and surrounding lands, the Noongar people.

Notes

1   Oxley 1996, 253–4.
2   'Editorial Introduction' in Bentham, ed. Causer and Schofield 2022, xcvi.
3   'Editorial Introduction' in Bentham, ed. Causer and Schofield 2022, xcvi.
4   'Editorial Introduction' in Bentham, ed. Causer and Schofield 2022, xcvii.
5   'Letter to Lord Pelham' in Bentham, ed. Causer and Schofield 2022, 74.
6   'Letter to Lord Pelham' in Bentham, ed. Causer and Schofield 2022, 74.
7   Hirst 1983, 10.
8   'Letter to Lord Pelham' in Bentham, ed. Causer and Schofield 2022, 74.
9   Bentham 1791, vol. 1, 181, 223.
10 'Letter to Lord Pelham' in Bentham, ed. Causer and Schofield 2022, 77.
11 'Letter to Lord Pelham' in Bentham, ed. Causer and Schofield 2022, 74.
12 'Letter to Lord Pelham' in Bentham, ed. Causer and Schofield 2022, 103.
13 'Letter to Lord Pelham' in Bentham, ed. Causer and Schofield 2022, 98.
14 'Letter to Lord Pelham' in Bentham, ed. Causer and Schofield 2022, 74.
15 'Principles of Penal Law' in Bentham, ed. Bowring 1843, 501.
16 Friedman, 1995, 477.
17 'Letter to Lord Pelham' in Bentham, ed. Causer and Schofield 2022, 151.
18 'Letter to Lord Pelham' in Bentham, ed. Causer and Schofield 2022, 139.
19 'Letter to Lord Pelham' in Bentham, ed. Causer and Schofield 2022, 161.
20 Haydon 1912, 30.
21 Moore 1884, 215.
22 Green 1997, 80.
23 Green and Moon 1997, 80.
24 Quoted in Bennett and Grono 1979, 48.
25 O'Brien 1960, 43. There was another very small gaol in Albany (Kingarling, Minang Noongar country) which was also under the jurisdiction of the Justices of the Peace.
26 Hudson-Rodd and Farrell 1998, 152–62; Maude 2013, 398.

27 Steadman 2007, 1; Colebatch 1929, 465.
28 *The Perth Gazette and Western Australian Journal*, 9 January 1836, 683.
29 Thomas Dent died whilst incarcerated. His demise was noted in the 1848 *Census and Statistics of Western Australia*, which stated that 'humanity revolts at the necessity of thus dealing with the insane'. See also Hudson-Rodd and Farrell 1998; Bavin 1993, 121–48.
30 Hunter 2012, 171.
31 'Colonial Frontier Massacres in Australia, 1788–1930', 'Pinjarra', https://c21ch.newcastle.edu.au/colonialmassacres/detail.php?r=887.
32 Lester and Dussart 2014.
33 Murray to Arthur, 5 November 1830, quoted in Lawson 2014, 56.
34 Bentham 1831, 155.
35 Stirling to Earl of Aberdeen, 10 July 1835, in *Commons Sessional Papers* (1837–8), vol. lx. 191–2.
36 Statham 1981b, 17–18.
37 Stirling to Earl of Aberdeen, 10 July 1835, in *Commons Sessional Papers* (1837–8), vol. lx. 191–2.
38 Nettelbeck 2012.
39 Hutt to Glenelg, 3 May 1839, in *Commons Sessional Papers* (1844), vol. xxxiv. 365.
40 Hunter 2012, 172.
41 Hunter 2006, 220. For punishments inflicted on Indigenous prisoners at Wadjemup/Rottnest Island, see Lanman's chapter in this volume.
42 Green 1997, 19.
43 Kingston 1988, 161–2; Statham, 1981; Calvert 1894, 17.
44 Moss 2020.
45 Roscoe 2018, 44; Roscoe 2020.
46 Shaw 1966, 353–4.
47 Shaw 1966, 353.
48 Whilst on gang or road work convicts were guarded by warders, 'trusted' prisoners who were deputized to act as special constables, and also by the Mounted Police, but 'At times the temptation to escape was too strong to be resisted, and convict after convict made a vain attempt to gain freedom in the bush' (Haydon 1912, 312). Haydon asserted that very few made their way to South Australia on foot, but did admit that 'prisoners broke gaol, committed robberies and worse crimes, even took to the Bush for what time they could prey on their neighbours' (Haydon 1912, 311). Many journeyed further than just into the Bush, especially after gold was discovered in Victoria.
49 Kingston 1988, 161–2; Statham 1981; Calvert 1894, 17.
50 Nicolls 2019, 99.
51 Cullity 2016; Millett 2007; Taylor 1981.
52 Van Den Berg 2002, 112.
53 16 & 17 Vic., c. 99.
54 Shaw 1966, 355.
55 Winter 2013.
56 Crowley 1960, 33; Kercher 1995, 41.
57 Shaw 1966, 355.
58 Kercher 2003, 548.
59 Finnane 1997, 6–8; Braithwaite 2001; Kerr 1984.
60 Bentham 1791, 67.
61 Bentham 1791, 344.
62 Godfrey 2019, 1143.
63 Godfrey 2019.
64 Figures taken from Blue Books of Western Australia, 1862–8. National Archives (UK), CO 22/40–22/46 inclusive.
65 *Inquirer and Commercial News*, 11 December 1872, 2.
66 *Daily News,* 26 May 1890.
67 Durlacher 1859.
68 Durlacher 1859.
69 Godfrey and Cox, 2008.
70 This was especially the case in Australian penal colonies since return home was very difficult. People transported to the American colonies between 1650 and 1784 would have

found it much easier to journey back across the Atlantic, and indeed many did. This may have delayed the development of an American penal estate, which indeed did only develop much later in the nineteenth century.

71 Bentham 1802, 29.
72 *Perth Gazette*, 1 February 1850, 3.
73 Stasiuk 2015, 27–8.
74 Hutt to Russell, 15 May 1841, in *Commons Sessional Papers* (1844), vol. xxxiv. 384.
75 Fitzgerald to Earl Grey, 9 October 1850, in *Commons Sessional Papers* (1852–3), vol. lxiii. 75.
76 Fraser to Robinson, 28 April 1883, The National Archives, Kew, War and Colonial Department and Colonial Office: Western Australia, Original Correspondence 1883, CO 18/199, 456.
77 'Colonization Company Proposal' in Bentham, ed. Causer and Schofield 2022, 155. For the general absence of Indigenous peoples in Bentham's works, see Laidlaw's chapter in this volume.
78 Padbury, 9 August 1876, 29; Padbury, 5 September 1876, 150; Padbury, 13 August 1877, 133–4; Marmion, 2 August 1883, 13–14, in *Western Australia Parliamentary Debates Hansard Archive*. https://www.parliament.wa.gov.au/hansard/hansard.nsf/NewAdvanced Search.
79 *Perth Gazette*, 12 October 1855, 3.
80 Symmons to Hutt, 31 December 1840, in *Commons Sessional Papers* 1844, vol. xxxiv. 390.
81 Harman and Grant, 2016.
82 Harman and Grant, 2016.
83 Green and Moon 1997, 24.
84 Green and Moon 1997, 24.
85 Kennedy to Russell, 18 October 1855, in *Commons Sessional Papers* (1856), vol. xliii. 113.
86 Kennedy to Russell, 18 October 1855, in *Commons Sessional Papers* (1856), vol. xliii. 113.
87 These figures have been collated from the following newspapers:
Inquirer and Commercial News, 11 June 1856, 2; 28 October 1857, 2; 21 October 1868, 2. *Perth Gazette and Western Australian Times*, 26 June 1856, 3; 26 October 1866, 3. *Fremantle Herald*, 29 April 1871, 3; 2 February 1871, 3. *Western Australian Times*, 30 December 1870, 3. Figures are also derived from the following volumes of *Lords Sessional Papers*: 1859 session II, vi. 238; 1861, x. 306; 1862, xiv. 347; 1863, xix. 315; 1864, xi. 336; 1866, xi. 382; 1867, xii. 434; 1867–8, xiv. 393; 1868–9, lxiii. 208; 1871, xlviii. 181; 1878, xiii. 182; 1881, xvii. 165; 1884–5, xxiii. 202; and 1888, xxxii. 861.
88 Lt.-Col. Frederick Irwin, *Minutes of the Proceedings of the Legislative Council*, 3 June 1847, 460.
89 Beccaria 1764.
90 Green and Moon 1997, 24–7.
91 Forrest 1884, 16.
92 Green and Moon 1997, 59–61; Roscoe 2016.
93 Green and Moon 1997, 59.
94 Green 2011, 79.
95 'An Ordinance to provide for the Summary Trial and Punishment of Aboriginal Native Offenders in certain cases' of 1849, 12 Vict. 18 (WA); 'An Act to amend "An Ordinance to provide for the Summary Trial and Punishment of Aboriginal Native Offenders in certain cases' of 1859, 23 Vict. 10 (WA).
96 *The Fremantle Herald*, 30 December 1882, 3; Green and Moon 1997, 47.
97 Nettelbeck and Ryan 2018, 60.
98 Owen 2016, 169.
99 Nettelbeck and Ryan 2018, 59; 'Editorial Introduction' in Bentham, ed. Causer and Schofield 2022, xcvi.
100 Green 1984, 183–8.
101 Fraser 1901, 203–7.
102 Briscoe 2003, 6–7.
103 Godfrey *et al.* 2007; Godfrey *et al.* 2010.
104 *Inquirer and Commercial News*, 5 September 1866.

Bibliography

Primary Sources

Archival sources

National Archives UK, CO 18/199, War and Colonial Department and Colonial Office: Western Australia, Original Correspondence, January–March 1883.

National Archives UK, CO 22/40–22/46, Blue Books of Western Australia, 1862–8.

Newspapers

Daily News.
Fremantle Herald.
Inquirer and Commercial News.
Perth Gazette.
Perth Gazette and Western Australian Journal.
Western Australian Times.

Parliamentary papers

Commons Sessional Papers of the Nineteenth Century (1837–8), vol. lx, 188: 'Return of the Expenses defrayed by this Country in the Colony of Western Australia during the last Three Years, ending 5 April 1838, in each Year respectively', 18 June 1838.

Commons Sessional Papers of the Nineteenth Century (1844), vol. xxxiv, 315–415: 'Copies or Extracts from the Despatches of the Governors of the Australian Colonies, with Reports of the Protectors of Aborigines, and any other Correspondence to illustrate the Condition of the Aboriginal Population of the Said Colonies', 9 August 1844.

Commons Sessional Papers of the Nineteenth Century (1852–3), vol. lxiii, 285–384: 'Papers relative to Crown Lands in the Australian Colonies. Part II. (South and Western Australia and Van Diemen's Land)', 16 August 1853.

Commons Sessional Papers of the Nineteenth Century (1856), vol. xliii, 566–7: 'Return, as complete as can be furnished, of the Quantity of Gold Exported from the several Ports in Australia in each Year, from the Commencement of the Gold Discoveries to the End of the Year 1855, and specifying to what Countries such Exports have been made', 23 June 1856.

Commons Sessional Papers of the Nineteenth Century (1868–9), vol. lxiii, 135–658: 'Statistical Tables relating to the Colonial and Other Possessions of the United Kingdom. Part XIII. 1867', 1869.

Commons Sessional Papers of the Nineteenth Century (1871), vol. xlviii, 701–941: 'Return of the Rates of Taxes and Imposts from which the Revenues of the several Colonies of the British Empire were raised, together with the Gross Amount yielded by each Tax or Impost, showing the Total Gross Revenue of each Colony in the Year 1868', 17 August 1871.

Lords Sessional Papers of the Nineteenth Century (1859, session II), vol. vi, 1–267: 'The Reports Made for the Year 1857 to the Secretary of State having the Department of the Colonies; in continuation of the Reports annually made by the Governors of the British Colonies, with a view to exhibit generally The Past and Present State of Her Majesty's Colonial Possessions. Transmitted with the Blue Books For the Year 1857', 9 August 1859.

Lords Sessional Papers of the Nineteenth Century (1860), vol. xii, 1–486: 'Statistical Tables relating to the Colonial and Other Possessions of the United Kingdom. Part V. (1858)', 1860.

Lords Sessional Papers of the Nineteenth Century (1861), vol. x, 1–580: 'Statistical Tables relating to the Colonial and Other Possessions of the United Kingdom. Part VI. (1859)', 1861.

Lords Sessional Papers of the Nineteenth Century (1862), vol. xiv, 1–494: 'Statistical Tables relating to the Colonial and Other Possessions of the United Kingdom. Part VII. (1860)', 1862.

Lords Sessional Papers of the Nineteenth Century (1863), vol. xix, 1–501: 'Statistical Tables relating to the Colonial and Other Possessions of the United Kingdom. Part VIII. (1861)', 1863.

Lords Sessional Papers of the Nineteenth Century (1864), vol. xi, 1–524: 'Statistical Tables relating to the Colonial and Other Possessions of the United Kingdom. Part IX. (1862)', 1864.

Lords Sessional Papers of the Nineteenth Century (1866), vol. xi, 1–534: 'Statistical Tables relating to Colonial and Other Possessions of the United Kingdom. Part X. (1863)', 1866.

Lords Sessional Papers of the Nineteenth Century (1867), vol. xii, 1–634: 'Statistical Tables relating to the Colonial and Other Possessions of the United Kingdom. Part XI. (For Two Years 1864 and 1865)', June 1867.

Lords Sessional Papers of the Nineteenth Century (1867–8), vol. xiv, 1–554: 'Statistical Tables relating to the Colonial and Other Possessions of the United Kingdom. Part XII. (1866)', August 1868.

Lords Sessional Papers of the Nineteenth Century (1878), vol. xiii, 1–629: 'Statistical Tables relating to the Colonial and Other Possessions of the United Kingdom. Part XV. 1871-2-3-4-5', 1878.

Lords Sessional Papers of the Nineteenth Century (1881), vol. xvii, 1–566: 'Statistical Tables relating to the Colonial and Other Possessions of the United Kingdom. Part XVI. (1876–7-8)', April 1881.

Lords Sessional Papers of the Nineteenth Century (1884–5), vol. xxiii, 115–754: 'Statistical Tables relating to the Colonial and Other Possessions of the United Kingdom. Part XVII. 1879–80–81', 83, C.4519 (1884–5).

Lords Sessional Papers of the Nineteenth Century (1888), vol. xxxii, 666–1304: 'Statistical Tables relating to the Colonial and Other Possessions of the United Kingdom. Part XVIII. 1882–83–84'.

Western Australian Legislative Council, Minutes of the Proceedings. Perth, 1847.

Western Australia Parliamentary Debates Hansard Archive. https://www.parliament.wa.gov.au/hansard/hansard.nsf/NewAdvancedSearch.

Western Australia Registrar General's Office, Census and General statistics of the Colony, 1848. Perth, 1849.

Printed sources

Beccaria, C. Dei delitti e delle pene (1764), ed. and trans. R. Bellamy. In On Crimes and Punishments and Other Writings. Cambridge: Cambridge University Press, 2013.

Bentham, J. 'Panopticon or the Inspection-House, containing the idea of a new principle of construction applicable to any sort of Establishment, in which persons of any description are to be kept under inspection', 3 vols. London: n.p., 1791.

Bentham, J. 'Principles of Penal Law'. In The Works of Jeremy Bentham, published under the superintendence of … John Bowring, vol. 1, 365–580. Edinburgh: William Tait, 1838.

Bentham, J. 'Emancipate Your Colonies!' (1830). In Rights, Representation, and Reform: Nonsense Upon Stilts and other writings on the French Revolution, ed. P. Schofield, C. Pease-Watkin, and C. Blamires, 289–316. Oxford: Clarendon Press, 2002.

Bentham, J. Panopticon versus New South Wales and other writings on Australia, ed. T. Causer and P. Schofield. London: UCL Press, 2022.

Colebatch, H. A Story of 100 Years. Western Australia 1829–1929. Perth: Fred Simpson, 1829.

Durlacher, A. Report on the General Statistics of the Colony as Shewn by the Census taken for the Year 1859. Western Australia: Government Press, 1859.

Haydon, A.L. The Trooper Police of Australia: A record of Mounted Police Work in the Commonwealth from the Earliest Days of Settlement to the Present Time. London: A.C. McLurg, 1911.

Moore, G.F. Diary of Ten Years Eventful Life of an Early Settler in Western Australia: And Also A Descriptive Vocabulary of the Language of the Aborigines. London: M. Walbrook, 1884.

Secondary Sources

Bavin, L. 'Punishment, Prisons and Reform: incarceration in Western Australia in the 19th century', Studies in Western Australian History 14 (1993): 121–48.

Bennett, B. and Grono, W. Wide Domain: Western Australian Themes and Images. London: Angus and Robertson Publishers, 1979.

Braithwaite, J. 'Crime in a Convict Republic', Modern Law Review 64: 1 (2001): 11–50.

Briscoe, G. Counting, Health and Identity: A History of Aboriginal Health and Demography in Western Australia and Queensland, 1900–1940. Canberra: Aboriginal Studies Press, 2003.

Calvert, A.F. *Western Australia, Its History and Progress*. London: Simpkin, Marshall, Hamilton, Kent & Company, 1894.

Cox, P. and Godfrey, B. 'The "Great Decarceration": Historical Trends and Future Possibilities', *Howard Journal of Criminal Justice* 59: 3 (2020): 261–85.

Crowley, F.K. *Australia's Western Third: A History of Western Australia from the First Settlements to Modern Times*. London: Macmillan, 1960.

Cullity, O. 'Reform and Punishment: Fremantle Prison 1850 to 1890', *Studies in Western Australian History* 31 (2016): 63–79.

Cuneen, C. *Conflict, Politics and Crime: Aboriginal Communities and the Police*. Canberra: Allen and Unwin, 2001.

Finnane, M. *Punishment in Australian Society*. Melbourne: Oxford University Press, 1997.

Finnane, M. 'Settler Justice and Aboriginal Homicide in Late Colonial Australia', *Australian Historical Studies* 42: 2 (2011): 244–59.

Fraser, M.A.C. 'Aboriginals', in *Seventh Census of Western Australia: Taken for the night of 31st March 1901*, vol. 1: *Superintendent's Report*, 203–7. Perth: W.A. Watson, government printer, 1904.

Friedman, D.D. 'Making Sense of English Law Enforcement in the Eighteenth Century', *University of Chicago Law School Roundtable* (1995): 475–505.

Gill, A. *Convict Assignment in Western Australia, 1842–1851*. Carlisle: Hesperan Press, 2016.

Godfrey, B. 'PRISON versus WESTERN AUSTRALIA: Which Worked Best, the Australian Penal Colony or the English Convict Prison System', *British Journal of Criminology* 59: 5 (2019): 1139–60.

Godfrey, B. and Cox, D. 'The "Last Fleet": Crime, Reformation, and Punishment in Western Australia after 1868', *Australian and New Zealand Journal of Criminology* 41: 2 (2008): 236–58.

Godfrey, B., Cox, D., and Farrall, S. *Criminal Lives: Family, Employment and Offending*. Oxford: Oxford University Press, 2007.

Godfrey, B., Cox, D., and Farrall, S. *Serious Offenders: A Historical Study of Habitual Criminals*. Oxford: Oxford University Press, 2010.

Green, N. *Broken Spears: Aborigines and Europeans in the Southwest of Australia*. Perth: Focus Education Services, 1984.

Green, N. 'Aboriginal Sentencing in Western Australia in the Late 19th Century with Reference to Rottnest Island Prison', *Records of the Western Australian Museum* 79 (2011): 77–85.

Green, N. and Moon, S. *Far from Home: Aboriginal Prisoners of Rottnest Island, 1838–1931*. Nedlands: UWA Publishing, 1997.

Harman, K. and Grant, E. '"Impossible to Detain … without Chains?": The Use of Restraints on Aboriginal People in Policing and Prisons', *History Australia* 11: 2 (2014): 157–76.

Hirst, J.B. *Convict Society and Its Enemies: A History of Early New South Wales*. Sydney: George Allen & Unwin, 1983.

Hudson-Rodd, N. and Farrell, G.A. 'The Round House Gaol: Western Australia's First Lunatic Asylum', *Australian and New Zealand Journal of Mental Health Nursing* 7: 4 (1998): 152–62.

Hunter, A. *A Different Kind of Subject: Colonial Law in Aboriginal–European Relations in Nineteenth Century Western Australia 1829–61*. North Melbourne: Australian Scholarly Publishing, 2012.

Kercher, B. *An Unruly Child: A History of Law in Australia*. St Leonards, NSW: Allen & Unwin, 1995.

Kercher, B. 'Perish or Prosper: The Law and Convict Transportation in the British Empire, 1700–1850', *Law and History Review* 21: 3 (2003): 427–574.

Kerr, J.S. *Design for Convicts: An Account of Design for Convict Establishments in the Australian Colonies during the Transportation Era*. Sydney: Library of Australian History, 1984.

Kingston, B. *The Oxford History of Australia, Volume 3: 1860–1900, Glad, Confident Morning*. Oxford: Oxford University Press, 1989.

Langton, M., Mazel, O., Palmer, L., Shain, K., and Tehan, M. *Settling with Indigenous People: Modern Treaty and Agreement-Making*. Annandale: Federation Press, 2006.

Lawson, T. *The Last Man: A British Genocide in Tasmania*. London: I. B. Tauris, 2014.

Lester, A. and Dussart, F. *Colonization and the Origins of Humanitarian Governance: Protecting Aborigines across the Nineteenth-Century British Empire*. Cambridge: Cambridge University Press, 2014.

Maude, Phil. 'Treatment of Western Australia's Mentally Ill during the Early Colonial Period, 1826–1865', *Australasian Psychiatry* 21: 4 (2013): 397–401.

McPherson, M. 'A Class of Utterly Useless Men: Convict Lunatics in Western Australia', *Studies in Western Australian History* 24 (2006): 62–70.

Millett, P. 'The Distribution of an Offensive Population: Classification and Convicts in Fremantle Prison, 1850–1865', *Studies in Western Australian History* 25 (2007): 40–56.

Moss, K. 'The Swan River Experiment: Coerced Labour in Western Australia 1829–1868', *Studies in Western Australian History* 34 (2020): 23–39.

Nettelbeck, A. '"A Halo of Protection": Colonial Protectors and the Principle of Aboriginal Protection through Punishment', *Australian Historical Studies* 43: 3 (2012): 396–411.

Nettelbeck, A. and Ryan, L. 'Salutary Lessons: Native Police and the "Civilising" Role of Legalised Violence in Colonial Australia', *Journal of Imperial and Commonwealth History* 46: 1 (2018): 47–68.

O'Brien, G.M. *The Australian Police Forces*. Melbourne: Oxford University Press, 1960.

Owen, C. *'Every Mother's Son is Guilty': Policing the Kimberley Frontier of Western Australia 1882–1905*. Nedlands: University of Western Australia Press, 2016.

Oxley, D. *Convict Maids: The Forced Migration of Women in Australia*. Melbourne: Cambridge University Press, 1996.

Pike, D.H. *Australia: The Quiet Continent*. London: Cambridge University Press, 1962.

Roscoe, K. '"Too Many Kill 'em. Too Many Make 'em Ill": The Commission into Rottnest Prison as the Context for Section 70', *Studies in Western Australian History* 30 (2016): 43–57.

Roscoe, K. 'Work on Wadjemup: Entanglements between Aboriginal Prison Labour and the Imperial Convict System in Western Australia', *Studies in Western Australian History* 34 (2020): 79–95.

Ryan, L., Debenham, J., Pascoe, B., Smith, R., Owen, C., Richards, J., Gilbert, S., Anders, R.J., Usher, K., Price, D., Newley, J., Brown, M., Le, L.H., and Fairbairn, H. *Colonial Frontier Massacres in Australia, 1788–1930*. https://c21ch.newcastle.edu.au/colonialmassacres/.

Shaw, A.G.L. *Convicts and the Colonies: A Study of Penal Transportation from Great Britain and Ireland to Australia and Other Parts of the British Empire*. London: Faber and Faber, 1966.

Statham, P. 'Why Convicts? [Series of two parts]: Part 1: An Economic Analysis of Colonial Attitudes to the Introduction of Convicts. Part 2: The Decision to Introduce Convicts to Swan River', *Studies in Western Australian History* 4 (1981a): 1.

Statham, P. 'Swan River Colony, 1829–50'. In *A New History of Western Australia*, ed. C.T. Stannage, 181–210. Nedlands: University of Western Australia Press, 1981b.

Steadman, P. 'The Contradictions of Jeremy Bentham's Panopticon Penitentiary', *Journal of Bentham Studies* 9 (2007): 1–31.

Taylor, S. 'Who Were the Convicts? A Statistical Analysis of the Convicts Arriving in Western Australia in 1850/51, 1861/62 and 1866/68', *Studies in Western Australian History* 4 (1981): 19–45.

Van den Berg, R. *Nyoongar People of Australia: Perspectives on Racism and Multiculturalism*. Leiden: Brill, 2002.

Winter, S. 'Legislation, Ideology and Personal Agency in the Western Australian Penal Colony', *World Archaelogy* 45 (2013): 797–815.

Unpublished theses

Edgar, W. 'The Convict Era in Western Australia: Its Economic, Social and Political Consequences', PhD thesis, Murdoch University, 2014.

Hunter, A. 'A Different Kind of "Subject": Aboriginal Legal Status and Colonial Law in Western Australia, 1829–1861', PhD thesis, Murduch University, 2006.

Nicholls, T. 'Perth Gaol and Colonial Penality 1875 to 1888', PhD thesis, University of Western Australia, 2019.

Roscoe, K. 'Island Chains: Carceral Islands and the Colonisation of Australia', PhD thesis, University of Leicester, 2018.

Stasiuk, G. 'Wadjemup: Rottnest Island as Black Prison and White Playground', PhD thesis, Murdoch University, 2015.

5

'Inspection, the only effective instrument of reformative management'

Bentham, surveillance, and convict recidivism in early New South Wales

Matthew Allen and David Andrew Roberts

In 1802–3, Jeremy Bentham produced an extended critique of penal transportation in general, and of the colony of New South Wales in particular, in a series of public letters to the Home Secretary, Lord Pelham.[1] By that date Bentham had been advocating for the construction of panopticon penitentiaries under his management for over a decade. On this occasion his tirade was inspired by a Home Office review which found that the 'improved state' of the colony made his proposals unnecessary.[2] Dissenting strongly from the Home Office's position, Bentham argued that New South Wales was inferior to imprisonment, especially in a panopticon, in relation to five 'ends of penal justice'. These were: setting an 'Example' to others, 'Reformation' of the offender, preventing recidivism through 'Incapacitation', providing 'Compensation' to the victim, and ensuring 'Economy' for the state.[3] In particular he stressed that 'Inspection' was 'the only effective instrument of reformative management', and he contrasted the 'frequent and regular inspection' of penitentiaries in general, perfected in his ideal panopticon, with the penal colony's 'radical incapacity of being combined with any efficient system of inspection'.[4] In his view, the nature of convict life and labour in the distant colony made systematic surveillance impossible, not least because it depended on the rigour of private masters who were not subject to meaningful oversight.[5] Drawing on David Collins's published accounts of the colony, Bentham found abundant evidence that '*reformation* [was] replaced in New South Wales by *corruption*' and that this explained the persistent viciousness and criminality of the convicts.[6] Concern about reform and recidivism was thus essential to his attack on the penal colony.[7]

These were not new arguments. Through three prior decades of writing about criminal justice, transportation and the panopticon Bentham had developed his theory that genuine reformation depended upon close surveillance of deviants who, through certainty of both punishment and reward, would reform themselves. In his view, a remote penal colony could not provide the intricate systems required to ensure that convicts were reformed by their punishment and prevented from reoffending on their release. But this careful theorizing rested on weak foundations because Bentham had not visited and did not understand the penal colony. Contemporary observers, including Bentham's chief source of evidence, David Collins, had a much more nuanced view of the challenge of reforming convicts. Drawing on this evidence, we argue that during the period Bentham was writing, the penal colony was more often perceived as an effective reformatory, with relatively low rates of recidivism, in part because the convicts were not always under surveillance.

This argument draws on recent literature on convict reform and recidivism, centred on John Braithwaite's 2001 article, 'Crime in a Convict Republic'.[8] Braithwaite identifies a broad five stage model of the historical development of state regulation commonly adopted by sociologists and criminologists: (i) pre-state restorative justice; (ii) weak state corporal and capital punishment; (iii) strong state professional policing and penitentiaries; (iv) welfare state discipline and reform; and (v) contemporary regulatory state. He argues that convict transportation usefully troubles this schema and can help to 'de-centre the penitentiary, and indeed punishment, in the history of regulation'.[9] He rejects Michel Foucault's emphasis on discipline as the distinctive feature of modern social control, a theory he sees as grounded in Foucault's unawareness and neglect of transportation.[10] For Braithwaite, transportation was evidence of a sixth stage of regulatory development, located between the 'Bloody Code' and the penitentiary, focussed on exile as both a form of imperialism and a means of restorative justice that reintegrated convicts into a new colonial society.[11]

A central element of Braithwaite's theoretical interpretation is the argument that the Australian colonies were effective reformatories where the 'convicts and their children turned away from a life of crime'.[12] In contrast to American slavery, the convict system was 'more procedurally fair' and Australia (largely) avoided rebellion and revolution 'because ... convicts had hope, a stake in the future' and in general 'worked shorter hours, were better housed, better clothed, and had better access to medical care than both American slaves and free English workers'. Convicts were largely 'repeat offenders [and] probably serious recidivists' but not 'dangerous people, [nor] members of a criminal class'. Colonial conditions, especially labour shortages, caused the authorities to treat most convicts as workers, not prisoners, and incentivized them accordingly. Combined with 'high levels of reintegration [and] high levels of procedural justice', these conditions led to rapid and striking declines in crime rates in the second half of the nineteenth century. Although a significant minority of transported criminals were brutalized into greater defiance, most were sufficiently reformed to live out their lives as free citizens.[13]

Braithwaite's argument is, deliberately, a general theory of convict reform that emerged from his larger project of advocating reintegrative shaming as a means to shift contemporary criminology away from punitive punishment and towards restorative justice.[14] As such it has come in for criticism from a number of historians specializing in crime and convictism who point to significant exceptions to the broad thesis, and who in some cases argue that the overall theory is wrong. Barry Godfrey and David J. Cox have compared court data from Hobart, Freemantle and Perth, rates of imprisonment in New Zealand, Australia and England, and a detailed cohort study of the convicts on the 'Last Fleet' – the *Hougoumont*, the final ship to bring convicts to Australia in 1868 – to draw a more nuanced picture of convict reform. They found that 'processes of integration had supported a general desistence from [serious] crime among the convict population' but that 'convicts did ... contribute significantly to the high levels of crimes of minor violence, minor property offences and public disorder'.[15] In a recent update to this work, Godfrey explored the 'natural experiment in punishment' between 1850 and 1868 when men convicted of similar crimes could be either sent to prison in Britain or transported to Western Australia. He shows that the two cohorts were broadly comparable in severity of offences and were each subject to a progressive system of stages of punishment, culminating in the Ticket-of-Leave, which was theoretically designed to incentivize reform. He finds that '[r]e-offending was rife in both Western Australia and Britain' and suggests that 'numerous, but statistically quite small, individual examples of Australian convicts "making good" may have blinded historians and criminologists to the reality of life for the majority of transported convicts'.[16]

Godfrey explicitly frames this natural experiment as a test of Bentham's views in *Panopticon versus New South Wales*. But Bentham, had he lived to see it, would have been highly unlikely to accept that the system of imprisonment in question lived up to his panoptical ideal. More importantly for our purposes, Godfrey contrasts a radically different system of transportation to that which Bentham critiqued. The half-century between them made a great deal of difference. As Godfrey shows, convicts under assignment in Western Australia were subjected to a strict regime of surveillance by a professional police force and an efficient and practiced bureaucracy. But the penal colony Bentham attacked was of a very different time and place. Early New South Wales, in its first two decades, was a new experiment, uncertain and undeveloped, struggling to effectively monitor its residents – both free and bond – in large part due to an inability to control movement and to develop a nascent convict-information state.[17] Furthermore, while Godfrey may be correct that English governments 'paid very little attention to recidivism' until after 1850, it is certainly not true of 'penal theorists and proto-criminologists', since Bentham's panopticon was explicitly designed (in part) as a solution to that problem.[18] We now turn to Bentham's criminal justice corpus, to show how he understood the questions of recidivism and convict reform and how he applied these ideas to New South Wales.

Bentham, inspection, and reformatory punishment

Bentham had been concerned about the problems of punishment and reform for three decades before he wrote his pamphlets attacking New South Wales.[19] In manuscripts from the 1770s and 1780s he laid out a utilitarian theory of punishment, starting from the premise that all punishment 'is an evil'.[20] On this basis he sought to outline the legitimate justifications for this evil, and argued that the 'chief end' of punishment ought to be the 'general prevention' of offences, but that it should also aim at the 'incapacitation, reformation, and intimidation' of the 'particular delinquent' and at 'compensation to the party injured'.[21] Importantly, with reference to prevention, Bentham stressed a distinction between superficial and genuine reform, criticizing punishments that 'render those who undergo them still more vicious':

> All punishment has a certain tendency to deter from the commission of offences; but if the delinquent, after he has been punished, is only deterred by fear from the repetition of his offence, he is not reformed. Reformation implies a change of character and moral dispositions.[22]

This distinction between apparent and actual reform would prove essential to his attack on New South Wales as a failed reformatory.

Genuine reform, in Bentham's analysis, was best achieved through a careful focus on the motive of the original offence, operating from the core utilitarian principle that '[p]ain and pleasure are the great springs of human action'.[23] Property crime was chiefly motivated by 'rapacity' – the 'pecuniary interest' turned to bad ends – and 'indolence' – the 'love of ease' likewise. The best means of reforming these bad motives, he said, was through 'penal labour'.[24] On this basis he identified only two forms of punishment capable of achieving genuine reform: imprisonment and hard labour. Prisons could only reform offenders when they successfully inspired 'penitent reflections' by combining moral and religious instruction with the use of motivating hardships, specifically 'solitude, darkness, and hard diet' which produced a 'gradual and protracted scene of suffering'.[25] But the general practice of imprisonment employed in England was 'directly opposed to reformation' since the 'promiscuous association of prisoners' strengthened their 'rapacious' motives, diminished moral and religious restraints, and improved their criminal skills, functioning as 'schools of vice'.[26] Labour was the other effective form of reformative punishment since 'force of habit' would 'reconcile and accommodate' criminals to industriousness that they would retain when they were 'left to work at liberty and by choice'.[27]

Even before the colony was founded or the panopticon proposed, Bentham applied this critique to transportation. In 1778 he produced a pamphlet on the recent hard labour bill (drafted in response to the suspension of convict transportation to the American colonies), arguing that the former system of transportation to America was inadequate 'for the purposes of example and reformation', and offering qualified praise and suggestions for improving the proposed system of imprisonment in penitentiaries.[28] Importantly, in this work he also demonstrated his earliest concern with the problem of recidivism. Praising the plan to grant convicts a certificate of good conduct (where appropriate) and a supply of clothing and money, on their release from the prison, Bentham noted that it was very difficult for released convicts to find honest work, and that the system of certificates would, perversely, exacerbate this problem since 'the denial of such a certificate ... amounts in fact to a certificate of the contrary'.[29] He thus suggested that either convicts be detained until their conduct was certified, or that those without a certificate be compulsorily enlisted into the military. In manuscript writings from 1782 for 'Indirect Legislation' he expanded on these ideas, noting that many convicts 'were bred up in thieving and have no other trade' and so should be classed with other 'dishonest or suspicious' indigents and confined to institutions where they would be made to work for their keep.[30]

These ideas about reform and recidivism were also central to his panopticon writings. Bentham argued that his 'simple idea in Architecture' and the 'inspection principle' it facilitated were applicable to 'all establishments whatsoever in which ... persons are meant to be kept under inspection', but stressed its value as a means of reforming convicts.[31] In particular, he emphasized the provisions for ensuring solitude and promoting industriousness. In contrast to most contemporary penologists who advocated monotonous labour to encourage repentance, he proposed that prisoners be free to choose their trade and meaningfully remunerated for their work, since this would incentivize them to reform and provide them with useful skills that would discourage recidivism.[32] He also expanded on his suggestions for monitoring convicts on their release. To 'ensure ... at the least expense, their good behaviour and subsistence', convicts should only be discharged into the military, or bound into service to either a 'responsible householder' or a private contractor who paid a recognizance for their good behaviour.[33] This would ensure that even if convicts were not genuinely reformed, they could not reoffend: 'be [they] ever so incorrigible, the public will have nothing to fear from [them], since, till [they have] given satisfactory proof to the contrary, [they] will not be let loose'.[34]

Bentham's ideas continued to develop in his writings over the next decade, during which he vainly sought a government contract to build and run a panoptical penitentiary.[35] In drafts towards a penitentiary bill in 1794 he further elaborated his proposals for an institution to house discharged prisoners, which he now termed a metasylum. This was to be a privately run, panoptical workhouse into which released convicts, who declined to go into the military and could not find a private employer (willing to pay a bond for their good behaviour), would be discharged. The metasylum was governed by a complex (and typically Benthamite) system of bureaucratic rules designed to prevent the possibility of recidivism. Convicts would be given an identifying tattoo on their upper arm, their records would be scrupulously maintained and circulated to relevant county and parish authorities, they would only be entitled to leave after three consecutive years of certified good behaviour, and would subsequently be required to carry a discharge certificate to avoid re-arrest as a suspected escapee.[36] These extreme provisions reflected the fact that the contractor of the metasylum – Bentham proposed himself – would be responsible to the government for the conduct of prisoners under his charge and bound to pay compensation for any further crimes they committed on release.

Similar ideas were reflected in Bentham's contribution to the 1798 Select Committee on Finance, which was largely concerned with the growing expenditure on criminal justice. The two key witnesses to the Committee were Bentham himself and the police reformer, Patrick Colquhoun, a magistrate and active supporter of Bentham's panopticon plans (he also collaborated quietly with Bentham on legislation for the Thames River Police in the late 1790s).[37] Bentham stressed the advantages of panopticons over transportation, noting that he would 'make himself personally responsible for the reformatory Efficacy of his Management'.[38] The Committee suggested that this concern for the problem of recidivism was the source of the 'great and important Advantages' of the plan over transportation and recommended proceeding with the construction of panopticon penitentiaries as 'a new and less expensive mode for employing and reforming convicts'.[39] This view was informed by Colquhoun's observations of the persistence of recidivism in London and his fulsome endorsement of Bentham's plans.[40] Colquhoun even went so far as to claim that all the convicts who had returned from New South Wales had resumed a life of crime. If he and Bentham were to be believed, there was nothing about transportation or the convict colony that could serve any of the core ends of penal justice.

From its earliest origins, Bentham's critique of New South Wales was framed in terms of inspection and reform. In his published proposal for the panopticon, he noted that the early evidence of immorality in the colony demonstrated that convicts were not genuinely reforming:

> 2000 convicts of both sexes, and 160 soldiers … jumbled together in one mass, and mingling like beasts: in two years, from fourteen marriages, eighty-seven births; the morals of Otaheite introduced into New Holland by the medium of Old England.[41]

The connection between this apparent sexual dissipation and criminal recidivism was not detailed, but Bentham proposed that the chances of reforming convicts in New South Wales were undermined by a number of factors unique to the colony.[42] His 'Letters to Lord Pelham' expanded on this, arguing that '[d]elinquents, especially of the more criminal descriptions ... may be considered as persons of unsound mind ... [or] a sort of grown children' necessitating 'particularly close inspection ... [and] preventive coercion'.[43] However, convicts in New South Wales, employed in forms of agricultural labour and accommodated in private huts, were only under 'imperfect, interrupted, and accidental' inspection. Subsequently, there was 'no preventive check to [their delinquent] propensities', leading to 'those vicious habits which are regarded as the immediate sources of crimes'.[44] In particular, he noted the lack of adequate religious instruction, and the 'sinister fidelity' and 'antipathy to Government' harboured by the convicts, which corrupted even honest men.[45]

According to Bentham, the evidence of this failure to reform was abundant. He cited numerous examples of convict immorality and criminality, largely drawn from the recently published work of David Collins, now returned to England after serving eight years as the colony's chief law officer. Bentham read Collins's *Account of the English Colony in New South Wales* as an eye-witness chronicle of the 'promiscuous and unbounded association [of convicts], joined to much opportunity of sloth and to unbounded drunkenness'.[46] It appeared to him to demonstrate that New South Wales was a comprehensive failure as a reformatory, since 'the longer [convicts] stay in that scene of intended reformation, and the more they are left to themselves ... the worse they are'.[47] For Bentham, Collins's *Account* definitively proved that the colony was overwhelmed by the crimes of recidivist convicts, thus proving his theories about the necessity for close inspection to ensure reform.

Bentham and recidivism in Collins's New South Wales

However, Bentham's flawed approach to his evidence fatally undermines his claims about New South Wales. His use of Collins was selective, and his interpretation often depended on reading the *Account* against the grain. As R.V. Jackson has observed, Bentham wrote as 'an "enemy" of the convict colony ... [and his] interpretation of the evidence ... was often strained and sometimes in error'.[48] In particular, he lacked insight into Collins's position and the actual operation of the colony.

Collins was a career soldier who had travelled on the 'First Fleet' as Deputy Judge Advocate to take charge of a nascent Court of Criminal Jurisdiction and to act as a magistrate, despite the fact he had no judicial training. He was thus central to the administration of justice and discipline, in its various forms, throughout the early period of the colony's existence.[49] The first volume of the *Account* was written after his arrival home in 1797, amid a series of financial and career setbacks, and his stated aim was to document the formative 'transactions' of a bold and eclectic colonial experiment, 'penned as they occurred'.[50] It was a reputable and popular work of travel and imperial literature, marketed as an eyewitness account of the unprecedented and macabre challenges of colonizing with criminals. Following its success, a second volume, published in 1802, covered a period from September 1796 to October 1800. Collins was not a witness to the events he related in the second volume, though he claimed to have privileged access to authentic materials, principally from Governor John Hunter.[51] While Bentham's first letter to Lord Pelham largely depended on Collins's eyewitness accounts in volume one, the examples relied on in the second letter were drawn from the second-hand material of volume two.[52]

Given Collins's role in the colony, it is unsurprising that crime and its consequences feature heavily in the *Account*. He recorded the Governors' orders and reported on almost every major crime, its investigation and punishment; indeed, the term 'punish' and its variations appear almost 200 times in volume one alone. It is however the minutiae that are most impactful and that Bentham relied upon – the continuous flow of minor details about convicts not doing their work, getting drunk, showing insolence, thieving and fighting, and the number of lashes awarded on each and every occasion. The latter Collins related assiduously, if not obsessively. The detail reflected his role in the settlement and his own particular vantage point, although not everyone was impressed by the tone of the work. Later, an abridged edition of the *Account*, edited by Collins's wife, omitted much of that detail for being too 'distressing and tedious'. These changes pleased one reviewer who thought the abridgements 'relieve[d] the History of the Colony from that striking resemblance, which … [it previously] bore to the form of a Newgate Calendar'.[53]

Nonetheless, in the preface to the first volume, Collins recorded his intention to give 'some account of the gradual reformation of such flagitious characters' who had been written off by his countrymen as 'being past the probability of amendment'.[54] To that end, he cited

Dr Samuel Johnson's essay on the 'Different Degrees of Virtue' ('Let none too hastily conclude that all goodness is lost, though it may for a time be clouded and overwhelmed'). Collins intended to defy those bigots who could not countenance criminal reformation as a genuine phenomenon, and he reported that the colony was 'in some instances *reforming* [convict] dispositions, and in all cases rendering their *labour* and talents *conducive* to the public good'. Though he began the second volume with regrets 'that a soil of so much promise has not produced better fruit', he called for patience, prophesying that 'much may yet be effected'.[55] However, Bentham dismissed Collins's claims as the wishful thinking of a 'professed panegyrist', claiming that 'as to any evidence of [convict] reformation … it is all of it in his [Collins's] wishes, there is none of it in his book'. Bentham was adamant that there were hundreds of recidivists for every individual who reformed.[56]

There certainly is some basis for Bentham's assessment. At times Collins was quite unequivocal in his disdain for convicts and in his disbelief that any change in character was at all possible. Frequently, such sentiments grew out of moments of sheer frustration and fatigue since at times the state of affairs in early New South Wales appeared as mayhem, descending into the types of disorder and profligacy that many contemporary readers expected of a congregation of criminals in exile. On almost every page of the *Account*, convicts went missing. Stock was stolen, huts were broken into, gardens were plundered, and public stores were purloined. When the Criminal Court was convened to 'check these enormities', the combination of severe punishment and strategic mitigation did little good.[57] Characteristically, Collins was quick to blame the criminals themselves, there being 'among us some minds so habitually vicious' that no threat or incentive 'was of any weight'. No matter how severe the penalties, there seemed to be those who 'committed thefts as if they stole from principle'.[58] Attempts to shame the offenders – such as having a woman's crime painted across her frock – had little effect, for these people had 'too long been acquainted with each other in scenes of disgrace, for this kind of punishment to work much reformation among them'.[59] After one busy Criminal Court session, which was distinguished by a punishment of 800 lashes for an attempt to commit bestiality, he opined:

> How unpleasing were the reflections that arose from this catalogue of criminals and their offences! No punishment however exemplary, no reward however great, could operate on the minds of these unthinking people. Equally indifferent to the pain which

the former might occasion, and the gratification that the other might afford, they blindly pursued the dictates of their vicious inclinations, to whatever they prompted; and when stopped by the arm of justice, which sometimes reached them, they endured the consequences with an hardened obstinacy and indifference that effectually checked the sensations of pity which are naturally excited by the view of human sufferings.[60]

But Collins's *Account* also presents much of this recidivism – if that is what it was – as a product of the extraordinarily harsh conditions and exigencies of the fledgling settlements. Crime and ill-discipline thrived in a 'season of general distress'. Hunger served to aggravate and revive old criminal propensities, for 'while there was a vegetable to steal, there were those who would steal it'.[61] And Collins was not alone in making such observations. As fellow marine officer Watkin Tench noted, 'the first step in every community, which wishes to preserve honesty, should be to set the people above want. The throes of hunger will ever prove too powerful for integrity to withstand'. The result, in early New South Wales, was 'a repetition of petty delinquencies, which no vigilance could detect, and no justice reach'.[62] Governor Arthur Phillip summarized the situation in much the same way. There were 'very few crimes' in his colony 'but what have been committed to procure the necessaries of life'.[63] These eyewitnesses agreed that the travails of founding a remote colony were simply not conducive to moral regeneration. But their explanation was significantly different from the motives of 'rapacity', 'pecuniary interest' and 'indolence' which Bentham believed turned men and women into thieves.

In passages that undoubtedly piqued Bentham's interest, Collins also frequently blamed lawlessness on a lack of surveillance, notably 'the want of proper overseers' and the reliance on 'people selected among themselves' to act as figures of oversight and authority.[64] The problem of monitoring movement – what Collins called 'the impracticability of keeping the convicts within the limits prescribed for them' – was the colony's quintessential weakness and significant difference from a panopticon.[65] On this count, Collins's narrative provided Bentham ample scope for comparison and scorn. In New South Wales there were mass abscondings and attempts to exist in what historian Grace Karskens describes as the 'nefarious geographies' outside the limits of the settlements.[66] The ruthless bush and its Indigenous owners provided imperfect prison walls. But the more consistent and niggling problem lay in preventing convicts from taking small, daily liberties unobserved. 'Frequent and regular inspection', such as Bentham demanded, was impossible.

However, the colonial authorities crafted their own solutions, including extensive (though often failed) efforts to monitor convicts through a system of certificates and passes, weekly musters and dissemination of orders through the *Sydney Gazette*.[67] The particular problem of convicts leaving their huts at night led to the first establishment of a 'night-watch' in Sydney, staffed by select convicts after the military refused to serve, and the division of the settlement into discrete patrolling districts.[68] Collins, in considerable detail, explained this expedient as a means of rehabilitating convicts, for though they might suffer the 'scorn of their fellow-prisoners', convict constables could experience 'a pride in being distinguished from their fellows, and a pride that might give birth to a returning principle of honesty'.[69] The impact of the night-watch, in both deterring crime and detecting it, was quick and pronounced, and was noted by numerous observers.[70] Indeed, Collins suggested that 'many streets in the metropolis of London were not so well guarded and watched', a comment Bentham tellingly ignored.[71]

Bentham's treatment of colonial policing and surveillance perfectly illustrates his selectivity and bias. Rather than evidence of efficiency, he argued that Collins's persistent references to crime demonstrated 'either extreme negligence, or complicity with the malefactors' on the part of the constables, and claimed that Collins had reported that constables 'had been *tampered with ... to neglect their duty*'.[72] In fact, Collins simply quoted from an order issued by Governor Hunter, in which the concern was not with the constables in general but the specific negligence which had resulted in 'frequent escapes' from the Sydney gaol.[73] In general, Hunter shared Collins's enthusiasm for the effectiveness of his police. He reported that they had saved the colony from being 'plung'd' into a 'dreadful state of wickedness and profligacy' and that in consequence of their watchfulness 'every inhabitant can now sleep in security'.[74] The Colonial Office was also impressed, urging that Hunter standardize the collection of police reports to ensure 'the establishment of future order and regularity'.[75] Similarly, Bentham misrepresented Collins's concerns about the pass system.[76] Writing about a spate of robberies in the colony in mid-1799 and the ongoing problem of 'wandering pests', Collins opined that 'the regulations which had long since been established as a check to such an evil' were being 'wholly disregarded', a remark Bentham cited with glee.[77] But Bentham ignored Collins's previous sentence which reported that in response to Hunter's orders, 'several idle people ... were apprehended ... [and]

ordered to labour in the gaol gang'.[78] Collins's regular reporting of crimes and punishments probably owed much to the high detection and apprehension rates effected by the new constabulary.

Bentham certainly mischaracterizes Collins's assessment of colonial policing and surveillance. Collins constantly cited the constables' work in detecting and preventing crime, and described the election of constables as 'introducing something like a system of regularity' to the colony.[79] In a particularly clear example, ignored by Bentham, Collins reported concerns in February 1800 about increasing numbers of 'idle and suspicious persons' committing robberies in Sydney at night, which prompted orders for the military 'centinels on duty' to require a 'counter-sign' from those out after ten o'clock, and 'very strict' patrols by the constables, leading to the arrest of a group of 'Irish prisoners'.[80] In Collins's view, no doubt echoing his own source, there was a great 'improvement' in the organization of the 'civil police' during Governor Hunter's term which 'considerably checked the commission of robberies of every kind'.[81] In contrast to Bentham, Collins had a measured and pragmatic view of colonial policing. He was well aware of the problems posed by the reliance on convicts and ex-convicts, and the difficulty of monitoring convict movements, but he also understood how effective these measures were in creating a more orderly society and reducing recidivism.[82]

Overall, although he was neither primarily interested in the colony as a reformatory, nor easily capable of transcending the prejudices of his time and class, Collins was inclined to moments of generosity and optimism. His observations featured a certain authenticity and matter-of-factness that sets his account apart from Bentham's ideological and self-serving take on the convict colony. Although the general picture Collins painted seemed messy, at times even ugly, yet he could concede that convicts 'conducted themselves with more propriety than could have been expected from people of their description'.[83] Reading his *Account* gives a very different picture of the colony, and of convict recidivism, than Bentham's polemical interpretation.

New South Wales as an effective reformatory

Bentham did not solely rely on Collins in painting his censorious picture of the colony, but he employed a similarly selective and partial approach with his other sources. For example, he cited a private letter written by Governor John Hunter to Samuel Bentham (Jeremy's younger brother) in May 1799, in which Hunter described the colony as 'a good country [that] will do well'. Bentham, however, focussed instead on the Governor's caveat that progress would be swifter if the British government were 'prevailed upon not to overstock us with the worst description of characters'.[84] This was hardly a definitive statement of Hunter's views on transportation and the colony. He used roughly the same language in a communication to the Home Secretary at around the same time, when deriding the colonial workforce as a means of undermining the money-making schemes of local capitalists.[85] In fact, he was less troubled by the numbers of convicts arriving than by the fact that he was not always receiving records of their sentences.[86] He was loudly scathing and resentful of Irish 'transports'.[87] But Hunter's greater concern was not the character of the convicts who were arriving, but the 'turbulent conduct' of the emancipists who were boasting that they were now 'free men and wou'd do as they pleas'd'.[88] Otherwise, his official communications blamed the colony's woes on a severe drought, rampaging bushfires and a small clique of elite opponents who were thwarting him at every opportunity. Nevertheless, Bentham took Hunter as a key witness to the failure of the convict colony. In a flight of rhetorical exuberance, Bentham claimed that the colony's current state was the work of the devil and that Hunter's testimony indicated that the colony's only 'chance of improvement' was for transportation to cease.[89]

Bentham's characterization hardly represented Hunter's views, which were formed on the ground. As with all the early governors, Hunter began his tenure in 1795 critical of his predecessors' mistakes and confident in his own capacity to make the colony serve as an effective reformatory. Hunter in fact went to some lengths to publicize his achievements, having a number of leading citizens testify that his reforms had rescued the colony from a state of 'riot and dissipation, and licentiousness and immorality'.[90] In a pair of despatches written a little over a year into his term, he lamented that the 'original discipline of the colony is sadly relax'd', due to 'private speculation and traffic', but hoped to restore good order through his vigorous reforms.[91] By the time of his letter to Samuel Bentham in 1799, he was defending himself from anonymous charges of corruption and maladministration, and it is in this context that he privately and publicly complained about the growing numbers of 'idle and worthless' former convicts who refused to work and were responsible for a spate of property crimes.[92] But reflecting on the colony with the benefit of hindsight, to the Select Committee on Transportation of 1812, he claimed that in general the convicts 'conducted themselves very quietly and decently', and that the behaviour of former convict settlers was 'generally … very correct', many of them being 'as respectable as any people who have gone from this country … living in a handsome decent manner … very exemplary people … fit to serve on juries'.[93] Clearly Hunter's recollections were shaped by their context. Like Collins, he had concerns about a class of former convicts who he perceived as idle and inclined to crime. But his overall view of the colony was positive and at least by 1812 he was convinced that most former convicts had been successfully converted into industrious settlers.

Moving beyond the sources Bentham relied upon, there is considerable contemporary evidence for the colony as an effective reformatory. During Collins's time in New South Wales, Watkin Tench reported 'that [the convicts] behaved better than had been predicted of them – To have expected sudden and complete reformation of conduct, [was] romantic and chimerical'.[94] Similarly, Governor Arthur Phillip, who thought the best spur to reformation was the prospect of being allowed to settle on some land, opined shortly before he departed that 'the convicts in general behave better than ever could be expected'.[95] These were strained compliments, obviously, but they came close to a begrudging concession that, all things considered, the first few thousand convicts unloaded in the colony gave a reasonably good account of themselves.

Philip Gidley King, who succeeded Hunter as governor in September 1800, and was thus in charge when Bentham wrote his 'Letters to Lord Pelham', expressed a similar ambivalence about the prospects of former convicts. Reporting from Sydney on the character of the convicts, he cited a list of the punishments inflicted in 1803, not as evidence of immorality, but rather as proof that 'the morals of the inhabitants and punishment of vice is not neglected', stressing that '[the convicts] certainly are not so generally depraved as may be imagined' and emphasizing that there were 'some very good characters among them'.[96] In an overall report on the state of the colony, written at the end of 1801, he focussed more explicitly on former convicts and their reform. He noted that many 'do not quit their bad habits on resuming the condition of free men', claiming that the 'utmost licentiousness' of this class was 'notorious', although he conceded that they 'have used the most laborious exertions in clearing land'.[97] But King's main explanation for this problem was not a lack of inspection, but rather the way such ex-convict farmers had been 'hitherto oppressed' by the monopolistic practices of the spirit-trading elite. He claimed that due to his stricter regulation of this trade '[i]ndustry appears to be returning'.[98] A final report written on his departure in 1806 bore out these hopes.

King reported that the 'greater part' of the ex-convict settlers were thriving in the colony, and that their 'progress is more rapid than the free settlers', though he continued to lament a minority who 'caring but little for the morrow, content themselves with earning sufficient to procure the means of intoxication'.[99] Clearly King, like Collins, was aware of the problems of idleness and drunkenness among ex-convicts. But his overall view was a nuanced and optimistic one, and he certainly did not see the challenge of providing close inspection as a fundamental threat to convict reform.

Writing some years later in 1811, the transported forger and emancipist, David Mann, offered a similarly balanced and optimistic picture. Mann arrived in Sydney in 1800, received an absolute pardon in 1802, and sailed for London in 1809 where he published *The Present Picture of New South Wales*, both a history of the early colony and a reflection on its prospects.[100] He argued that by the time of Hunter's arrival crime had declined significantly because 'many of the convicts had reformed their lives, and, instead of being examples of depravity, had turned to habits of industry, and endeavoured to benefit that society on which they had formerly preyed'.[101] Reflecting on colonial morals, he claimed that tales of convict vice were often exaggerated. In fact, Mann suggested that the reality of the new society was similar to Britain, where recidivism was discouraged by the threat of 'severe punishment', and that many former convicts had become 'striking examples of probity, industry, temperance, and virtue'.[102] Arguing for the introduction of jury-trial to New South Wales, he suggested that there were 'a great many' former convicts 'whose conduct during the term of their punishment has been such as to give general satisfaction, and who have proved by their conduct that they have reformed their dispositions, corrected their principles, and are likely to become useful, and consequently valuable, members of society' who were suitable to sit on juries.[103]

Like Hunter, the other witnesses to the Select Committee on Transportation of 1812 were also asked about the degree to which convicts were reformed by transportation. William Bligh, Governor of New South Wales from 1806–8, was more critical of convict conduct, claiming most convicts were 'extremely idle' and 'should be kept fully at their labour', but he also reported that some emancipists were 'equally good [as] the free settlers with respect to industry'.[104] William Palmer, the commissary, reported that 'the people behaved ... much better than could be expected' and that in general the colony was an effective reformatory, while Robert Campbell, a merchant and magistrate, agreed in general that the convicts 'are reforming'.[105] Two convict clerks reported contradictory impressions on the effectiveness of the system. Thomas Robson, who had been transported for seven years for stealing paper from the Crown, claimed that transportation was not effective at reforming convicts, although he had spent only four years in New South Wales. On the other hand, William Richardson, who stole shoes and was transported for seven years on the 'First Fleet' (he was initially intended for Africa), claimed that convicts were 'treated with respect, according to their situations; and a great reformation took place among them; those who were the most notorious villains in this country became in that country very good members of society'.[106]

The Committee on Transportation was seemingly convinced by this positive testimony. They argued for an extension of the assignment system, noting that when convicts were 'removed from their former companions, and forced into habits of industry and regularity, the chance of reformation must be infinitely greater'.[107] They also approved of the practice of encouraging marriages and especially of granting land at the expiry of the sentence, suggesting a clear pathway to reform:

> if from convicts, they became well-behaved and industrious servants, a farther possibility is opened to them of becoming prosperous and respectable settlers … they have an opportunity of establishing themselves in independence, and by proper conduct to regain a respectable place in society.[108]

They cited approvingly Governor Macquarie's principle that 'long-tried good conduct should lead a man back to that rank in society which he had forfeited' and that this prospect of reintegration was 'the greatest inducement … towards the reformation of … manners'.[109] In a telling analysis, directly contrary to Bentham's theory, they concluded that:

> [the colony's] improvement in wealth, and the means of properly employing and reforming the convicts, are essential to the progress of each other; if the prosperity of the Colony be checked by unwholesome restrictions, the exertions and industry of the convicts cannot be advantageously called into action during their servitude, and but little inducement will be held out to them to become settlers after their emancipation.[110]

Bentham had argued that the economic growth of the colony was directly opposed to the reformation of convicts because such progress relied on the spread of settlement, preventing efficient inspection.[111] But informed by a wider range of evidence than Bentham had access to, and not reading it through the lens of the inspection principle, the Committee on Transportation saw the opportunities provided by a growing colony as key to reforming convicts. Ironically, they concluded that what Bentham deemed genuine reform was possible in New South Wales, but precisely because it was incentivized by prosperity in the absence of inspection.

Conclusion

As we have shown, Bentham's analysis of inspection and reform in New South Wales relied on manipulated evidence. Contemporary observers of the colony, including Collins himself, were often critical of convict morals and concerned about recidivist crime, but they were also aware that many convicts were successfully transformed into settlers. They lamented the failure of inspection and the disorder it permitted, but they also believed that New South Wales was at least capable of being an effective reformatory. Bentham's polemic fitted the apparent evidence to his predetermined theory and so he found in Collins and others precisely the apparent marks of a failed system of punishment that would justify building panopticons. In fact, contemporary accounts largely support Braithwaite's view that New South Wales effectively reintegrated convicts.

Interestingly, many of Collins's critical observations about recidivism – especially those which Bentham cited – were made in relation to the ex-convict settlers who increasingly farmed the flood-plain of the Hawkesbury River. In Bentham's eyes, convicts and emancipists were pretty much one and the same. Collins repeatedly drew attention to the conduct of these Hawkesbury settlers, and while he noted that some were 'industrious and thriving', others were reported to be 'idle, vicious, given to drinking, gaming, and other such disorders as lead to poverty and ruin … oftener employed in carousing in the fronts of their houses, than in labouring themselves, or superintending the labour of their servants in their grounds'.[112] Reading between the lines, what concerned Collins was the way that the relative isolation and rich soils of the Hawkesbury allowed ex-convicts independence, and self-determination; in Bentham's terms, freedom from inspection.[113] As Grace Karskens observes in her study of the *People of the River*, the abundance of the soils on the flood-plain made farming easy and in consequence, 'according to the authorities in Sydney ... the ex-convict settlers were enjoying themselves too much ... [which] defied the notion that the lot of workers was unceasing labour, time discipline and meek obeisance'.[114] At its core, Bentham's concern about inspection was about precisely this problem. But it is here that he most tellingly misunderstands reform: it was precisely this independence permitted to ex-convicts in early New South Wales that allowed them to reintegrate into society, or at least integrate into a new one.

Notes

1 These letters were written, printed and privately circulated in 1802 but only published in 1812 as Bentham 1812. We rely on the new and comprehensive editions produced by the Bentham Project, namely the three 'Letters to Lord Pelham' and 'A Plea for the Constitution' in Bentham, ed. Causer and Schofield 2022. The Editorial Introduction to that edition provides important details of their publication history.

2 'Letter to Lord Pelham' in Bentham, ed. Causer and Schofield 2022, 73. For more on the context of this work see Semple 1993, 230–41; Causer 2019.

3 'Letter to Lord Pelham' in Bentham, ed. Causer and Schofield 2022, 74.

4 'Letter to Lord Pelham' in Bentham, ed. Causer and Schofield 2022, 77.

5 'Letter to Lord Pelham' in Bentham, ed. Causer and Schofield 2022, 76–7, 101.

6 'Second Letter to Lord Pelham' in Bentham, ed. Causer and Schofield 2022, 169–70; Collins 1798–1802. For more on Bentham's reliance on Collins, see Jackson 1993.

7 We use the term recidivism advisedly since it only gained currency in the late nineteenth century. However, it is the widely accepted term in modern criminology and a similar concept, usually gathered under the label reformation, is at stake in Bentham's writings. For the etymology see: 'recidivist, n. and adj.', in *OED Online* (Oxford University Press), accessed 10 July 2020, http://www.oed.com/view/Entry/159515. For more on the history of concern about recidivism see: Cox *et al.* 2014. For current theories of recidivism see Zara and Farrington 2016, ch. 1. For Bentham's use of the concept (if not the term) see below.

8 Braithwaite 2001.

9 Braithwaite 2001, 12.

10 Braithwaite 2001, 45.

11 Braithwaite 2001, 47–50.

12 Braithwaite 2001, 19. This is not an original claim, though Braithwaite has made the argument most explicitly and has influentially framed recent debate. For earlier versions see Hughes 1988, 356–7, 587–8; Hirst 2008, 194–7; Reynolds 1969. Such claims perhaps reflect a much older concern for the reputation of Australia's convict settlers. Earlier historians, for example, debated whether the convicts were victims of inequality and harsh justice in their homelands, or whether they were professional criminals and 'ne'er-do-wells'. See Roberts 2007; Roberts 2008.

13 Braithwaite 2001, 20–5, 29, 33.

14 See for example: Braithwaite 1989; Braithwaite 2000; Braithwaite 2002.

15 Godfrey and Cox 2008.

16 According to Godfrey 2019, 1145, the ideological aims of the system were meaningfully different since '[t]he Australian system was driven by labour-need, but the British system was focused on controlling surplus labour'.

17 Higgs 2003.

18 Godfrey 2019, 1146. We would suggest that Godfrey's claim is only really true of English governments (and only once transportation to Australia was well established) since recidivism was a regular concern in colonial New South Wales. See for example the Report of the 1835 Police Committee of the New South Wales Legislative Council which suggested

that 'many convicts who become free by servitude or hold the indulgence of tickets of leave take possession of Crown Lands in remote Districts, and thus screened from general observation … raise a property by committing depredations on their neighbouring flocks and herds; or by selling spirits and providing other inducements for thieving, gaming, and every species of debauchery' (437). For the emergence of English government concern about recidivism see: Cox *et al*. 2014. For Bentham see below.

19 Semple 1993, ch. 2. For more on the theoretical and practical context of Bentham's work on punishment see, for example: Ignatieff 1978; McGowen 2003. For Bentham's position in these debates see: Rodman 1968; Bedau 2004.

20 Bentham 1830, 1. This work was mostly drawn from Bentham's manuscripts of the 1770s and 1780s but was originally published as a recension in French as Dumont 1811 and then retranslated by Richard Smith into English. For more detail on this publication history see Semple 1993, 2. We will use both works to illustrate Bentham's theory of punishment prior to the proposal of the panopticon.

21 Bentham 1830, 20–1.

22 Bentham 1830, 48–9.

23 Bentham 1830, 19. For a more extensive discussion of motives see Bentham 1789, ch. 10. There, Bentham defined motives as things which 'by influencing the will … serve as a means of determining [action]' (95) and stressed that motives were not bad in themselves but could become bad 'on account of their tendency to produce pain, or avert pleasure' (99).

24 Bentham 1789, 104, 114–15, 192–3. Bentham also stressed 'confinement to a spare diet' as the best means of reforming crimes motivated by 'ill-will' and especially by 'an obstinate refusal … to do something … lawfully required' (193).

25 Bentham 1830, 115–18. He specifically contrasted the 'protracted' suffering of these hardships with 'acute' suffering caused by whipping which was accordingly less reformatory. It is important to note that Bentham's views on these auxiliary punishments changed over time: see note 31, below.

26 Bentham 1830, 122–8.

27 Bentham 1830, 163–4.

28 Bentham 1778, 2–4. For more on the context of this debate see: Devereaux 1999, 405–33. Bentham repeated this criticism of transportation to America in his letters to Pelham: 'Letter to Lord Pelham' in Bentham, ed. Causer and Schofield 2022, 99–101.

29 Bentham 1778, 66–7.

30 Bentham Papers, Special Collections, University College London Library, lxxxvii. 79, 83, 86 (hereafter UC. Roman numerals refer to the boxes in which the papers are placed, Arabic to the leaves within each box). For more on this unpublished manuscript see: Bozzo-Rey, Brunon-Ernst, and Quinn 2017.

31 Bentham 1791, 1–2, 35–6. In the initial panopticon 'Letters' of 1787 Bentham stressed the constant 'solitude' of prisoners in the panopticon as a reformatory advantage of his plan. But by the time he wrote the postscripts (which he had printed, along with the 'Letters' in 1791) he called for 'mitigated seclusion', arguing that isolation was only useful as a temporary measure for 'breaking the spirit' (141–2).

32 Bentham 1791, 48–9, 67–8. On the importance of industriousness to reformation see Semple 1993, 153–6.

33 Bentham 1791, 526–33, at 526.

34 Bentham 1791, 534.

35 For the details of Bentham's campaign for a government contract to build a panopticon see Semple 1993, chs. 6–11.

36 Semple 1993, 177–87. On tattooing cf. Bentham's earlier proposal for a universal system of identifying marks in 'Indirect Legislation' at UC lxxxvii. 135–6, 182–91, 193–6.

37 For more on Colquhoun and his ideas about police reform see Colquhoun 1797; Dodsworth, 2008; Barrie 2008.

38 House of Commons 1799, 82–3.

39 House of Commons 1799, 23–4, 27–8.

40 House of Commons 1799, 22–4. For Colquhoun's evidence on recidivism see 67–9.

41 Bentham 1791, 424. These comments probably originated in an unpublished manuscript of 1791: see 'New Wales' in Bentham, ed. Causer and Schofield 2022, 3–22; Causer 2019.

42 Bentham 1791, 534–9. On Bentham's understanding of the balance between liberty and

43 'Letter to Lord Pelham' in Bentham, ed. Causer and Schofield 2022, 76.

44 'Letter to Lord Pelham' in Bentham, ed. Causer and Schofield 2022, 76–7.

45 'Second Letter to Lord Pelham' in Bentham, ed. Causer and Schofield 2022, 193, 199, 207. Original emphasis. Bentham was especially concerned about the lack of Catholic priests given the increasing numbers of 'malcontents from Ireland' sent to New South Wales. He noted that Collins's second volume reported the transportation of Father James Harold and regretted that 'instead of this seditionist, a loyalist [Catholic] clergyman' had not been sent. This reflected his view that religion was a 'useful defence against the … spirit of tumultuary violence' ('Letter to Lord Pelham' in Bentham, ed. Causer and Schofield 2022, 79–80).

46 'Third Letter to Lord Pelham' in Bentham, ed. Causer and Schofield 2022, 253. For his evidence, drawn from Collins, see: 'Letter to Lord Pelham' in ibid., 85–8; 'Second Letter to Lord Pelham' in ibid., 170–7, 179–87, 209–17. In relation to colonial drunkenness and its significance for Bentham's critique see Allen 2012.

47 'Letter to Lord Pelham' in Bentham, ed. Causer and Schofield 2022, 85.

48 Jackson 1993, 326. Jackson cites a series of examples where Bentham manipulates Collins in the service of his argument (324–6).

49 'Collins, David (1756–1810)' in *Australian Dictionary of Biography* (hereafter *ADB*) 1966; Currey 2000.

50 Collins 1798–1802, vol. i. vii.

51 Collins 1798–1802, vol. ii. advertisement; Currey 2000, ch. 10. Barton 1889, 256–7, claimed that the second volume was effectively written by Hunter, although his view has not prevailed.

52 'Editorial Introduction' in Bentham, ed. Causer and Schofield 2022, xix.

53 'Editor's Introduction' in Collins, ed. Fletcher 1975, vol. i. xiv.

54 Collins 1798–1802, vol. i. vii–x.

55 Collins 1798–1802, vol. ii. advertisement.

56 'Letter to Lord Pelham' in Bentham, ed. Causer and Schofield 2022, 83–4.

57 Collins 1798–1802, vol. i. 9.

58 Collins 1798–1802, vol. i. 10, 146.

59 Collins 1798–1802, vol. i. 47–8.

60 Collins 1798–1802, vol. i. 473.

61 Collins 1798–1802, vol. i. 108, 111.

62 Tench 1793, 110.

63 Phillip to Dundas, 2 October 1792 in Watson ed. 1914–25, vol. i. 373.

64 Collins 1798–1802, vol. i. 9, 57.

65 Collins 1798–1802, vol. i. 57. For context, see Karskens 2005.

66 Karskens 2009, 280–309.

67 For more on the ambition and limitations of this convict information state see Allen 2021.

68 Allen 2020.

69 Collins 1798–1802, vol. i. 78–9.

70 Tench 1793, 33, said of 'this patrol' that 'nightly depredations became less frequent and alarming'.

71 Collins 1798–1802, vol. i. 85.

72 'Second Letter to Lord Pelham' in Bentham, ed. Causer and Schofield 2022, 83–4. Original emphasis; Collins 1798–1802, vol. ii. 139. In the same section of his letter, Bentham also drew attention to a betrayal of trust by Reverend Johnson's convict servant, ignoring the fact that this attempted theft was detected by the diligence of a constable who concealed himself during divine service to catch the offender in the act ('Second Letter to Lord Pelham' in Bentham, ed. Causer and Schofield 2022, 201; Collins 1798–1802, vol. ii, 60–1).

73 For more on Hunter's concerns see General Order, 5 December 1798 in Britton and Bladen eds. 1892–1901, vol. iii. 513.

74 Hunter to Portland, 1 November 1798 in Watson ed. 1914–25, vol. ii. 236; Hunter to Portland, 25 July 1798 in ibid. 170. See also: Hunter to Portland, 10 June 1797 in ibid. 15–16.

75 Portland to Hunter, 18 September 1798 in Watson ed. 1914–25, vol. ii. 226.

76 For the system see Government Order, 30 November 1796 in Watson ed. 1914–25, vol. ii. 69. That was an extension of an earlier order allowing constables and watchmen to 'examine

all male and female convicts and all suspicious persons' who appeared to be at large. Government Order, 2 October 1795 in ibid., vol. i. 678. It was further extended and penalties increased a few months later: Government Order, 20 March 1797, in ibid., vol. ii. 76–7.

77 Collins 1798–1802, vol. ii. 219. 'Second Letter to Lord Pelham' in Bentham, ed. Causer and Schofield 2022, 204.

78 Collins 1798–1802, vol. ii. 219.

79 Collins 1798–1802, vol. ii. 64.

80 Collins 1798–1802, vol. ii. 286.

81 Collins 1798–1802, vol. ii. 110.

82 For more on the challenges of early policing see Allen 2020.

83 Collins 1798–1802, vol. i. 25.

84 Hunter to Samuel Bentham, 20 May 1799 in Britton and Bladen eds. 1892–1901, vol. iii. 713 n., cited in 'Letter to Lord Pelham' in Bentham, ed. Causer and Schofield 2022, 89.

85 Hunter to Portland, 25 July 1798 in Watson ed. 1914–25, vol. ii. 166.

86 Hunter to Portland, 25 June 1797 in Watson ed. 1914–25, vol. ii. 31.

87 Hunter to Portland, 15 February 1798 in Watson ed. 1914–25, ii. 129–30.

88 Hunter to Portland, 20 June 1797 in Watson ed. 1914–25, vol. ii. 23.

89 'Letter to Lord Pelham' in Bentham, ed. Causer and Schofield 2022, 90.

90 Marsden to Hunter, 11 August 1798 in Watson ed. 1914–25, vol. ii. 185–8.

91 Hunter to Portland, 12 Nov. 1796 in Britton and Bladen eds. 1892–1901, vol. iii. 168–9, 175.

92 Hunter to Portland, 1 May 1799 in Britton and Bladen eds. 1892–1901, vol. iii. 666.

93 *Commons Sessional Papers* (1812), vol. ii. 592–4. Hunter was by this date an early advocate for introducing jury trial to the colony. In many ways, this longstanding campaign is an index of its proponents' faith in the colony's capacity for reform. For more on this issue see: Neal, *Rule of Law* 1991, ch. 7.

94 Tench 1793, 3.

95 Phillip to Grenville, 5 November 1791 in Watson ed. 1914–25, vol. i. 273.

96 King to Hobart, 1 March 1804 in Watson ed. 1914–25, vol. iv. 471.

97 'State of His Majesty's Settlements in New South Wales', 31 December 1801 in Britton and Bladen eds. 1892–1901, vol. iv. 655–6.

98 'State of His Majesty's Settlements in New South Wales', 31 December 1801 in Britton and Bladen eds. 1892–1901, vol. iv. 655–6.

99 'Present State of His Majesty's Settlements on the East Coast of New Holland, called New South Wales', Britton and Bladen eds., 1892–1901, vol. vi. 241.

100 Parsons, 'Mann, David Dickenson (1775–1811)', *ADB* 1967. https://adb.anu.edu.au/biography/mann-david-dickenson-2426/text3225 [accessed 20 July 2021].

101 Mann 2003, 9.

102 Mann 2003, 51–2.

103 Mann 2003, 81–2.

104 *Commons Sessional Papers* (1812), vol. ii. 602, 618.

105 *Commons Sessional Papers* (1812), vol. ii. 632, 643. Two other civil officers were more ambivalent. Rev. Johnson used the question to argue for an improved Church establishment, claiming that if a clergyman with a 'proper salary' were sent out ' a great deal of good might be done' (67); Major Johnston, fresh from his court-martial, would only speak to his own servants but claimed they 'behave very well' as a result of his diligent overseer (645) but was generally sceptical about the respectability and orderliness of the colony (646).

106 *Commons Sessional Papers* (1812), vol. ii. 624, 628.

107 *Commons Sessional Papers* (1812), vol. ii. 583.

108 *Commons Sessional Papers* (1812), vol. ii. 584–5.

109 *Commons Sessional Papers* (1812), vol. ii. 585, and 685 citing: Macquarie to Castlereagh, 30 April 1810. Notably the Committee disagreed with Bligh's position that former convicts should never be permitted to 'hold places of trust and confidence' or become part of society (608).

110 *Commons Sessional Papers* (1812), vol. ii. 581.

111 'Second Letter to Lord Pelham' in Bentham, ed. Causer and Schofield 2022, 72; cf. 'Letter to Lord Pelham' in ibid., 41.

112 Collins 1798–1802, vol. i. 393. For more examples see ibid., 376, 382, 385, 387, 388, 393; vol. ii. 6, 133, 289.

113 For more on this trope of the 'lazy and feckless' Hawkesbury settlers see Karskens 2009, 220–1.
114 Karksens 2020, 396–7.

Bibliography

Primary Sources

Archival sources
UCL Library Special Collections, Bentham Papers, box lxxxvii.

Parliamentary papers
Commons Sessional Papers (1812), vol. ii, 573–689: 'Report from the Select Committee on Transportation', 10 July 1812.

Printed sources

Bentham, J. 'A View of the Hard-Labour Bill'. London: T. Payne and Son, 1778.
Bentham, J. An Introduction to the Principles of Morals and Legislation. London: T. Payne, 1789.
Bentham, J. 'Panopticon; or, The Inspection–House: Containing the Idea of a New Principle of Construction Applicable to Any Sort of Establishment, in Which Persons of Any description Are to be Kept Under Inspection; and in Particular to Penitentiary-Houses', 3 vols. London: n.p., 1791.
Bentham, J. Rationale of Punishment, ed. and trans. R. Smith. London: Robert Heward, 1830.
Bentham, J. Panopticon versus New South Wales and other writings on Australia, ed. T. Causer and P. Schofield. London: UCL Press, 2022.
Collins, D. An Account of the English Colony in New South Wales, 2 vols. London: T. Cadell Jun. and W. Davies, 1798–1802.
Collins, D. An Account of the English Colony in New South Wales, ed. B. Fletcher, 2 vols. Sydney: Reed, 1975.
Colquhoun, P. A Treatise on the Police of the Metropolis. London: C. Dilly, 1797.
Dumont, É. Théorie des peines et des récompenses, 2 vols. London: Vogel and Schulze, and B. Dulau and Co., 1811.
Historical Records of Australia, Series I, ed. F. Watson, 26 vols. Sydney: Government Printer, 1914–25.
Historical Records of New South Wales, ed. A. Britton and F.M. Bladen, 7 vols. Sydney: Government Printer, 1892–1901.
House of Commons, Report of the Select Committee ... Relative to the Establishment of a New Police in the Metropolis, &c and the Convict Establishment. London: R. Shaw, 1799.
Mann, D.D. The Present Picture of New South Wales [1811]. Sydney: University of Sydney Library, Scholarly Electronic Text and Image Service, 2003. http://purl.library.usyd.edu.au/setis/id/manpres [accessed 20 July 2021].
New South Wales Legislative Council. First report from the Committee on Police and Gaols. Sydney: NSW Legislative Council, 1835.
Tench, W. A Complete Account of the Settlement at Port Jackson. London: G. Nicol and J. Sewell, 1793.

Secondary Sources

Allen, M. 'Alcohol and Authority in Early New South Wales: The Symbolic Significance of the Spirit Trade, 1788–1808', History Australia 9: 3 (2012): 7–26.
Allen, M. 'Convict Police and the Enforcement of British Order: Policing the Rum Economy in Early New South Wales', Australian & New Zealand Journal of Criminology 53: 2 (2020): 248–64.

Allen, M. 'Convict Surveillance and Reform in Theory and Practice: Jeremy Bentham vs New South Wales'. In *Histories of Surveillance from Antiquity to the Digital Era: The Eyes and Ears of Power*, ed. A. Marklund and L. Skouvig, 70–86. Abingdon: Routledge, 2021.

Barrie, D.G. 'Patrick Colquhoun, the Scottish Enlightenment and Police Reform in Glasgow in the Late Eighteenth Century', *Crime, Histoire & Sociétés / Crime, History & Societies* 12: 2 (2008): 59–79.

Barton, G.B. *History of New South Wales from the Records*, vol. 1: *Governor Phillip, 1783–1789*. Sydney: Charles Potter, 1889.

Bedau, H. 'Bentham's Theory of Punishment: Origin and Content', *Journal of Bentham Studies* 7 (2004): 1–15.

Bozzo-Rey, M., Brunon-Ernst, A., and Quinn, M. 'Editors' Introduction' to special issue, 'Indirect Legislation: Jeremy Bentham's Regulatory Revolution', *History of European Ideas* 43: 1 (2017): 1–10.

Braithwaite, J. *Crime, Shame and Reintegration*. Cambridge and Sydney: Cambridge University Press, 1989.

Braithwaite, J. 'The New Regulatory State and the Transformation of Criminology', *British Journal of Criminology* 40: 2 (2000): 222–38.

Braithwaite, J. 'Crime in a Convict Republic', *Modern Law Review* 64: 1 (2001): 11–50.

Braithwaite, J. *Restorative Justice and Responsive Regulation*. New York and Oxford: Oxford University Press, 2002.

Causer, T. '"The Evacuation of That Scene of Wickedness and Wretchedness": Jeremy Bentham, the Panopticon, and New South Wales, 1802–3', *Journal of Australian Colonial History* 21 (2019): 1–24.

Cox, D.J., Godfrey, B., Johnston, H., and Turner, J. 'On Licence: Understanding Punishment, Recidivism and Desistance in Penal Policy'. In *Transnational Penal Cultures: New Perspectives on Discipline, Punishment and Desistance*, ed. V. Miller and J. Campbell, 184–201. Abingdon: Routledge, 2014.

Currey, J. *David Collins: A Colonial Life*. Carlton South, Vic: Melbourne University Press, 2000.

Devereaux, S. 'The Making of the Penitentiary Act, 1775–1779', *The Historical Journal* 42: 2 (1999): 405–33.

Dodsworth, F.M. 'The Idea of Police in Eighteenth-Century England: Discipline, Reformation, Superintendence, c. 1780–1800', *Journal of the History of Ideas* 69: 4 (2008): 583–604.

Engelmann, S.G. '"Indirect Legislation": Bentham's Liberal Government', *Polity* 35: 3 (2003): 369–88.

Godfrey, B. and Cox, D.J. '"The Last Fleet": Crime, Reformation, and Punishment in Western Australia after 1868', *Australian & New Zealand Journal of Criminology* 41: 2 (2008): 236–58.

Godfrey, B. 'Prison versus Western Australia: Which Worked Best, the Australian Penal Colony or the English Convict Prison System?', *British Journal of Criminology* 59 (2019): 1139–60.

Higgs, E. *The Information State in England: The Central Collection of Information on Citizens since 1500*. Basingstoke: Palgrave, 2003.

Hirst, J.B. *Freedom on the Fatal Shore: Australia's First Colony*. Melbourne: Black Inc., 2008.

Hughes, R. *The Fatal Shore: A History of the Transportation of Convicts to Australia 1787–1868*. London: Pan Books, 1988.

Ignatieff, M. *A Just Measure of Pain: The Penitentiary in the Industrial Revolution, 1750–1850*. London: Pantheon Books, 1978.

Jackson, R.V. 'Theory and Evidence: Bentham, Collins, and the New South Wales Penal Settlement', *Australian Journal of Politics and History* 39: 3 (1993): 318–29.

Karskens, G. '"This Spirit of Emigration": The Nature and Meanings of Escape in Early New South Wales', *Journal of Australian Colonial History* 7 (2005): 1–34.

Karskens, G. *The Colony: A History of Early Sydney*. Crows Nest, NSW: Allen and Unwin, 2009.

Karskens, G. *People of the River: Lost Worlds of Early Australia*. Crows Nest, NSW: Allen and Unwin, 2020.

McGowen, R. 'The Problem of Punishment in Eighteenth-Century England'. In *Penal Practice and Culture, 1500–1900: Punishing the English*, ed. P. Griffiths and S. Devereaux, 210–31. New York: Palgrave Macmillan, 2003.

National Centre for Biography. *Australian Dictionary of Biography*. Canberra: Australian National University, 1966. https://adb.anu.edu.au/biography [accessed 20 July 2021].

Neal, D. *The Rule of Law in a Penal Colony*. Melbourne: Cambridge University Press, 1991.

Reynolds, H. '"That Hated Stain": The Aftermath of Transportation in Tasmania', [*Australian*] *Historical Studies* 14: 53 (1969): 19–31.

Roberts, D.A. '"More Sinned against than Sinning": George Arnold Wood and the Noble Convict'. In *Making Australian History: Perspectives on the Past since 1788*, ed. D. Gare and D. Ritter, 122–7. Melbourne: Thomson, 2007.

Roberts, D.A. 'Russel Ward and the Convict Legend', *Journal of Australian Colonial History* 10: 2 (2008): 37–58.

Rodman, B.-S. 'Bentham and the Paradox of Penal Reform', *Journal of the History of Ideas* 29: 2 (1968): 197–210.

Semple, J. *Bentham's Prison: A Study of the Panopticon Penitentiary*. Oxford: Clarendon Press, 1993.

Zara, G. and Farrington, D.P. *Criminal Recidivism: Explanation, Prediction and Prevention*. London and New York: Routledge, 2016.

Part III

The constitutional implications of Bentham's writings on Australia

6

Jeremy Bentham and the imperial constitution at the meridian, 1763–1815

legislature, judicature, and office in the administration of England and the British Empire

Edward Cavanagh

The British (and still very *English*) administrative system looked very different at the end of the Seven Years War in 1763 when compared to how it would look at the end of the Napoleonic Wars in 1815. It looked more different still when compared to how it would look upon the outbreak of the Crimean War in 1853. The imperial constitution that took shape in tandem with these developments was one in which allocations of official, judicial, and legislative power came to be monitored with greater sensitivity, and under different conditions, than before. Some appreciation of this landscape must be attained before admiring any portrait.

Like many objects of government, the direction and operation of war and colonies, allocated to an array of offices on crown commissions for military and colonial service, began to be coordinated into an expanding state bureaucracy that was increasingly beholden to parliament. Hence there came into existence, at the outset of the nineteenth century, a 'war and colonial office' (with 'office' meaning, in this new iteration, *government department* instead of *individual role*). If these were some of the first steps towards a modern bureaucratic civil service, the destination is unlikely to have been arrived at without the imposition of new expectations upon individuals who, whether home or abroad, held some *office* from the crown (with 'office' here meaning *a role or station* held with some honour and obligation). Starting with a series of enquiries into public accounts in the 1780s, through to the select committees on income and expenditure in 1828 and 1831 (and the reorganization of the civil list in the midst of those enquiries), a number of key offices were stripped back of the perks they had picked up over centuries as their holders were turned into dignified employees of state. At home and across the British Empire, a salaried class of officials across a wide spectrum – judges, governors, commanders, captains, collectors, secretaries, and more – became subject to conventions written down in more constrictive commissions. And they could be made to show obedience to fresh statutory law, with some of this legislation carrying an extraordinary territorial reach, as officeholders stationed abroad became liable (after 1802) to face prosecution for any 'crime, offence, misdemeanour' short of treason in the Court of King's Bench (and, subsequently, the Court of Queen's Bench).[1]

The judicature itself remained fixed in an awkward state of suspension between feudalism and modernity over the same period. Spiritually and intellectually, the common law still ran and never looked like it would stop running from the monarch, even if it was still thought to be unacceptable for a king or queen to establish new courts by his or her prerogative alone: there were to be no more Star Chambers under the Hanoverians.[2] The King's Bench did start playing host to some novel criminal trials, as courts generally were made to show greater receptivity towards an increasingly prolific parliament in the criminal domain of the public law, but this has more to do with the swelling mandate of the legislature than with the wider court system, which was resistant to noteworthy structural change throughout an age of revolution.[3] The King's Bench remained a forum in which it was still possible to hear the (albeit increasingly strained) suggestion that negligent or irresponsible official behaviour could be insulated from rebuke owing to a degree of authority once delegated from a king who could do no wrong. Of course, very few lawyers in the late eighteenth century would have failed to grasp the importance of seventeenth-century constitutional milestones which seemed to confirm, and on more than one occasion, that whenever the king apparently *did* undertake to perform a public wrong, the High Court of Parliament might convene and pass judgment. But such happenings were exceptional and, besides, occurred *away* from the court system itself and the lawyers who worked in it. In that world, over the law and its guardians, the king's influence was not yet insignificant at the end of the eighteenth century. Chief Justices, Chancellors, and sundry other holders of the high judicial offices in England and Wales, though fearless of the prospect of royal dismissal during the reigns of Anne, George I, George II, and George III, still continued to go about their jobs after 1760, like the law officers of the crown who waited in turn to replace them, with an undiminished sense of deference to the crown and the common law enterprise upon which all their livelihoods depended.

Bigger changes were afoot in the legislature over the same period. Parliament, as the supreme legislature of the kingdom and empire, underwent two profound transformations. These are more precisely located between the divestment of George III's kingship into regency administration in 1811 and the crisis of Victoria's bedchamber in 1839. When Tory ministers of the crown shook off the lame king's influence to become de facto caretakers of the prerogative – first for the prince regent and then for subsequent monarchs – they took to governing with a sense of remove from the wider House of Commons. This eventually became unpalatable to a number of prominent MPs. This disquiet in turn inspired the adoption of a new standard of accountability: namely, that while the ministry enjoyed the *confidence* of the monarch, the same ministry was more importantly *responsible* to the Commons. Crucially, this was a standard of executive-legislature relations that became suitable for export.[4] The other standout development of the period in relation to the imperial legislature came with the passage of the electoral reforms of 1832. Long championed by the Whigs, here resounded the clearest statutory statement yet, in British constitutional history, of the principle that elected members should appear to represent the people of the country.

In summary, these years were marked by several key developments. Government departments, however imperfectly organized, were solidifying and their ambits were becoming more expansive. Holding office from the crown was on its way to becoming a more rule-bound profession. The executive was becoming responsible to parliament. The Commons was beginning to look more democratic. And yet, both the structural organization of the king's courts, and the procedural and substantive aspects of the common law, remained stubbornly unchanged in the face of wider changes in thinking about crime and commerce stemming from the social, moral, and economic upheavals of the period.

To read Jeremy Bentham's writings cursorily, or fixated upon one specific subject among the many that caught his attention, or confined to look through one specific window of a long and prolific life, is to face up to the possibility of overlooking a series of often unpredictable continuities and discontinuities in the operation of the institutional centrepieces of the administrative system: office, judicature, and legislature. Such a possibility undoubtedly attaches to any attempt to discuss Bentham's *British Constitution Conquered*, which is a rather more apt title for his critique of New South Wales in relation to (among other things) the common law of conquest and its apparent provision for prerogative legislative power, before the tract was renamed 'A Plea for the Constitution: ... including an Inquiry into the Right of the Crown to Legislate Without Parliament' (1803).[5] This is a work optimally read in relation to office, judicature, and legislature, to be sure; but it is also a work that cannot be divorced from an understanding of the changes being made to the imperial constitution in an age that has been likened to a 'meridian' by C.A. Bayly, and with good reason.[6] For not only would these alterations to the governance of the British Empire affect both hemispheres of the globe, but they would also witness all the storms and tempests normally attending the rise of 'a new moon with the old moon in her arms' (to invoke a maritime folk ballad in vogue during the period under examination): the rising of a new system, operationalized, through a bureaucratic civil service bound to parliament, with an air of *accountability*, eclipsing an old system, operationalized, by personal and corporate agencies, through the manipulation of *influence*.[7] Such was the new empire compared to the old empire, resulting from a transformation that had only just begun when Bentham was attending Blackstone's lectures in his youth, and which was only just finishing as Bentham devoted what remained of his life to the *Constitutional Code*.

On a superficial reading, Bentham's legal and political writings can appear chaotic. He commanded a surprising variety of interests. Coupled with that was a propensity of his, which is more pronounced in his hot-tempered and hurried constitutional writings, to become distracted in the middle of a passage and introduce peripheral elements to a particular topic that are not always consistent with his thinking in previous writings. These traits do little to discourage reiterations of the caricature of Bentham as a thinker of thoughts in disarray. But an appraisal of this kind is too simple in view of the complexities thrown up in his own lifetime, as this chapter will reveal by attending to the context of the Westminsterian administrative state and the wider imperial constitution fastened to it. To perceive Bentham as a wayward shooter is to show insufficient regard for the quickness and unpredictability with which so many of his targets were moving around him as he wrote. Official powers, judicial powers, and legislative powers were never fixed in his lifetime. Questions over their locus, allocability, accountability, performance, and limitation – in short, questions concerning the constitutionality of such powers alone and in connection with each other – were many and often unanswered in this half-century of British political history (1780–1830), a period sitting on the brink of a more reformist half-century (1830–80) of which Bentham only ever got the briefest glimpse.

The ambitions of this chapter are not particularly radical from a historiographical point of view. My analysis follows from the appraisals of L.J. Hume and Philip Schofield. Hume seems right to have highlighted the rise and fall of the panopticon scheme as a key determinant behind Bentham's developing ideas about bureaucracy between 1791 and 1802.[8] Schofield has further refined our understanding of Bentham's politics by pointing out that it was 'the emergence of sinister interest, a product of Bentham's own disappointing experiences as a "projector" of reform, rather than the events of the French Revolution, which would ultimately be responsible for pushing him into a novel form of radical politics' – and Schofield locates these developments to between 1804 and 1809.[9] This chapter builds upon these observations by emphasizing the importance of the imperial constitution, and the place of New South Wales within it, for providing a language to facilitate the furtherance of Bentham's thinking on legislature, on judicature, and, above all, on office.

Bentham and the imperial constitution before 1801

Each of Great Britain's North American colonies to emerge from the Seven Years' War was a constitutionally distinctive entity. Integrating characteristics of corporate, proprietary and royal government into their own administrative formats, these (with the exception of Quebec and Florida) were systems of government modelled upon, and mutated from, the institutions and ideas of England. Great variations were to be found among them in 1763 when it came to the allocation of supreme official (that is, gubernatorial) legislative and judicial powers. And no colony was perfect when it came to the *balance* of these powers, at least in the minds of influential settlers, and occasionally a rogue officeholder or two, in the colonies themselves. But for the immediate time being, the grievances felt by settlers from place to place were so seldom comparable to allow for their airing together. This circumstance changed after a series of enactments of the imperial parliament between 1764 and 1770, which were designed to generate more lucrative local revenues and install new commissioners to collect them, among other things. It was the uniformity of these provisions that encouraged delegates from up and down the Atlantic coast to meet in order to determine what principles of government they shared in common. All of this inspired a new spirit of shared grievance, which ultimately led to the Declaration of Independence of July 1776 – an event that triggered Jeremy Bentham into penning his first serious comments, albeit anonymously, upon the imperial constitution.

While his 'Short Review of the Declaration', which features at the end of John Lind's *Answer to the Declaration* (1776), is perhaps best known for its forensic analysis of the language of natural law (ridiculing the distinction between 'the laws of Nature, and of Nature's God'), and also of the categories of 'life, liberty, happiness, and government' (identifying the definitional incompatibility of the fourth of these rights with the first three), there is an extended passage towards the end of this essay that is relevant to what Bentham would later argue in respect of New South Wales.[10] This concerns the charge that '[The King of Great Britain] has obstructed the administration of justice, by refusing his assent to laws for establishing judiciary powers'. The complaint here was substantially a North Carolinian one. In 1759, 1762, and again in the early 1770s, the legislature there had been prevented by the crown, through the governor, from erecting courts and removing gubernatorial discretion over the enjoyments of judicial office.[11] Bentham sensed that what had lain behind this controversy was more of a political need than a judicial one. As he reminded his American readers, the king-in-parliament had been going out of his way to provide judicial forums for his subjects across the Atlantic. 'Strange indeed', he wrote, that the efforts of 'Parliaments [in Westminster], under the present reign, for the *convenience* of the Colonists, and to obviate *their own objections* of delays arising from appeals to England, to establish a Board of Customs, and an Admiralty Court of Appeal', had been so ungratefully forgotten. But that was beside the main point. Bentham's principal concern in connection to this episode was about the allocation, to subordinate entities, of any mandate to reform the judiciary: for the 'establishment of new Courts of Judicature', by a colonial legislature, would amount to 'an exertion of power, which might be dangerous', as he put it.[12]

Anxieties in Quebec were of a slightly different character after the Royal Proclamation of 1763 had advertised it to be the 'will' and 'pleasure' of the king to see the crown's new colonial acquisitions arranged into bounded new formats. In keeping with the genre – proclamations were prerogative instruments used to signpost the administrative preferences of the crown – this one gave guidelines for the granting of land, largely for the benefit of a smattering of officials now despatched on new commissions, who took their commands from complementary sealed instructions drawn up in London.[13] Administratively, Quebec became an especially vexing mandate following its capitulation in 1759, which was followed by a series of official instructions issued both before and after the Royal Proclamation of 1763 along with a treaty drawn up and signed by European powers in Paris. All of this combined to produce a number of conflicted visions for the province by 1764. Contentions began to surface in that year over the composition of the legislature, the extent of gubernatorial power, the coexistence of French civil law and English criminal law, the practicality of harmonizing the laws of real property, and the provision of religious liberty to Roman Catholic subjects (among other matters).[14]

For all the differences of opinion about these challenges, there was never much controversy, in the North ministry anyway, about the optimal instrument for overcoming them: namely, an Act of Parliament. From late in 1772 through to the first part of 1774, a variety of potential bills were drafted and amended by the attorney general, the solicitor general, the advocate general, the colonial secretary, and the Chief Justice of King's Bench (Lord Mansfield), before a bill was presented to parliament on 2 May 1774, which finally proceeded into law on 22 June 1774.[15] The resultant Quebec Act of 1774 introduced a mixed legal system, installed a legislative council, and provided for the religious liberty of Catholics.[16]

This law, 'by which', Bentham confided to Bowring in 1827, 'a constitution in the true Tory style, and under the auspices, if not by the pen, of Lord Mansfield, was given to Canada', was one of a handful of statutes singled out for criticism by Lind in his *Remarks on the Principal Acts of the Thirteenth Parliament of Great Britain* (1775).[17] Published anonymously, this tract was one from which Bentham thereafter struggled to escape his association, despite only authoring (as he admitted) the framing essay of the book.[18] It is probable that Bentham shared a number of Lind's views on the Quebec Act ('he wrote as he thought, which was as I thought').[19] Exception should probably be granted for one particular aspect: namely, Lind's argument for the retention of ambiguity in the language of the statute's provision for an established church, which culminated in his denunciation of the pedantry of literalistic interpretations of the provision.[20] It is far easier to imagine Bentham sharing Lind's criticism of the Act's provision, not for a legislative assembly, but for a legislative *council*, constituted to enjoy 'absolute power'. This was a measure, wrote Lind, 'impossible to defend'.[21] And in that assessment, he was proven correct some years later when the Clergy Endowments Act (1791) replaced the Quebec Act (1774), separating common-law Upper Canada from civil-law Lower Canada, and providing each with its own representative assembly, appointed council, and governor.[22]

Similar kinds of constitutional frictions were felt, and often with greater sensitivity, in the Caribbean. Grenada fell somewhat into the same category as Quebec in 1763 upon its conquest and cession to Great Britain as a colony identifiably Christian (and therefore exempt from the wholesale legal reorganization imposable upon communities of 'infidels', according to the common law).[23] Like Quebec, the guidelines of the Royal Proclamation of 1763 were complemented by additional measures of administrative guidance issued separately. But whereas Quebec would eventually take heed of the unambiguously superior authority of an Act of Parliament in respect of its constitution, Grenada was made to wade through a number of instruments of a prerogative kind. The order in which these instruments were offered, along with the measures they purported to implement, were called into question when the planter Alexander Campbell brought an action into the City of London court at Guildhall in 1773, to recover the amount he paid to a crown customs officer, William Hall. Alleging the deficiency of Hall's authority, Campbell's suit ultimately led to a special verdict of the King's Bench, and delivered by Lord Mansfield, that comprehensively exposed the kind of legislative power that ought to have grafted to the royal prerogative upon the act of conquest. To Bentham's displeasure, Mansfield's precedents and authorities were prioritized unusually in places (nowhere more so than with regards to the deference he showed throughout his ruling to a hesitant and noncommittal report about the legal receptivity of Jamaica in relation to its local legislative authority, which had been drawn up in 1722 by Attorney General Philip Yorke and Solicitor General Clement Wearg).[24] Mansfield construed this material carefully enough not to appear as though he was departing too far from the jurisprudence of Edward Coke (1552–1634), John Holt (1642–1710), and other leading jurists before him. In the end, Mansfield's judgment for the plaintiff – delivered in November 1774 and printed in Cowper's Reports in 1784 – boiled down to a consideration not of the *deficiencies inherent* in the instruments but of the *incorrect order* of their promulgation. Letters patent passing the seal on 20 July 1764, imposing the duties in question, had been disqualified by an earlier commission issued on 9 April 1764, instructing the governor to convene a *legislative assembly* (which was the only mechanism, by implication if not by convention, capable of imposing duties of the kind collected from Campbell by Hall). In other words, on Mansfield's reading, the king's endorsement (expressed in the commission) of the installation of a legislative assembly for Grenada had divested the king of his power to create laws by his prerogative alone (expressed in the letters patent), and thereupon only such laws passed by the imperial parliament, or passed subordinately 'by the assembly with the governor and council', were valid in conquered and ceded colonies like Grenada.[25] And many more Caribbean colonies were soon to follow and be made to square with this determination, starting with Trinidad and Tobago from 1802, and then Berbice, Demerara, Essequibo, Guiana, and St Lucia from 1815.

The constitutional politics of South Asia had developed a markedly differently character to the Atlantic world of planters and settlers. Persistently after 1767, the House of Commons had been making overtures (with subtle variations) in order to assume greater control over the East India Company, starting first with its 'territorial revenues', before turning to its administrative machinery. Important in this respect was Lord North's regulating bill, which was enacted on 21 June 1773. This statute established new official appointments for India, including a chief justice and three judges (as 'the Supreme Court of Calcutta') along with a governor-general and a council of four to advise him (as the 'Supreme Council of Bengal').[26] Even before the first cohort of these officeholders could complete their five-year terms, scandals about their misdeeds in India were capturing the attention of the Commons, and these would carry on well into the 1780s and call into question, once again, the administrative system of company India.[27] Rejecting the more extensive reforms proposed by Charles Fox and Edmund Burke in 1783, the Commons instead passed William Pitt the Younger's Regulating Act (1784) and a few other measures. A compromise of sorts, this legislation was designed 'to take from the Company the entire management of the territorial possessions, and the political government of the country', leaving the corporation only with 'commercial concerns and arrangements'. Establishing a royal 'board of control', it placed stricter controls upon the central governance of the corporation, which entailed greater official and (if only indirectly) parliamentary oversight.[28]

Parliament did not identify, in the population of India, a nation of subjects of the crown and proceed from there to impose English law upon those subjects uniformly. For a number of reasons, these steps would have been unimaginable in 1784. Disencumbered, by this stage, of a series of old prejudices in the common law about the receptivity of non-Christian societies to English merchants and laws, Great Britain was beginning to throw its lot in with the ideals of 'commercial society'. This entailed more of an embrace of 'common humanity' and some distancing from any 'jealousy of trade'.[29] Sentiment like this could not and never would develop into an overarching policy of installing pluralistic legal systems in the colonies so long as intellectuals, administrators, and philanthropists in Great Britain remained happy to distinguish between what they perceived to be the beliefs, customs, characters, and propensities to 'civilisation' of various indigenous populations, south Asian communities just a few of many across the globe. Sentiment like this *did* lead, on the other hand, to the beginning of a new conversation among British jurists and philologists about the comparability of European and Indian legal ideas and institutions – a conversation into which Jeremy Bentham intruded with his essay on 'The Influence of Time and Place on Legislation' (1782).[30]

Similar in certain key respects to Montesquieu's *Spirit of the Laws* (insofar as it rehearsed similar calls for legislators to take '[c]limate, face of the country, natural productions, present laws, manners, customs, [and] religion of the inhabitants' into consideration), Bentham turned to Bengal in order to illustrate that '[t]he people of every country are attached to their own laws'.[31] It followed for Bentham, in the fifth and most absorbing chapter of that essay, that the transplantation of any body of laws could only detract from its coherence and usefulness. This was especially true of those laws he knew best: as 'English law is, a great part of it, of such a nature as to be bad every where', Bentham explained, '… it would not only be, but appear, worse in Bengal than in England'.[32] The example he gave for this was the imposition of a law of forfeiture in 'a country where there is no king'. In making this observation, Bentham could not help but draw attention to the recent treatment of Maharajah Nandakumar, a collector of taxes, who had been ordered to hang by the Chief Justice of the Supreme Court of Bengal, Elijah Impey, in 1775.[33] This was one of many obvious signs throughout the essay that Bentham had been taking an interest in the administrative politics of India after 1773; this interest he signalled again by concluding the fifth chapter with a fictitious account of an argument between the Chief Justice of the Supreme Court and the Governor-General of the Supreme Council. As he imagined their disagreement playing out, these officeholders quarrelled over the distinction between interpreting law and making law and which of those powers, the judicial and the legislative, ought to be superior and which of those inferior.[34]

In the years following 1787, Bentham turned his attention to New South Wales as a critic of convict transportation.[35] While undoubtedly intrigued by the colony's potential to facilitate social experimentation on a grand and exotic scale, Bentham became whole-heartedly convinced that it would represent better policy to reform the penitentiaries at home than to continue transportation with all its uncertainties and imperfections. This did not prevent him from dabbling in the field of 'colonisation at large', against the backdrop of the French Revolution and, what is less appreciated, renewed efforts to harmonize the constitution of Canada. Between May and June of 1791, in the same period that a bill replacing the defective Quebec Act (1774) was drafted, debated, and passed, Bentham appears to have written 'New Wales' (1791), an eccentric and hastily organized paper on the penal colony.[36]

There is little in this work of any constitutional profundity, making possible exception for a passage on the crown under the heading of 'Influence', although it is a struggle to make it coherent.[37] Concerned in this passage not with convict society but instead with settler society, Bentham professed to feel 'no fanatic terrors of the influence of the Crown' in the transposed administration. Influence was virtually certain to be exercised through stationed officeholders in the colony (presumably those who Bentham identified as 'the pampered sons of opulence and its inseparable attendants, indolence and ignorance'). But Bentham felt that the more that this influence were to be permitted in the colony, the greater would be the 'expence' to the government at home. This was about as safe a way as any to incline him towards the reduction of influence 'to nothing' in New South Wales. But there was another benefit to such a reduction. If the regime for the settlers were to be left deliberately in a state of neglect, then a principle of self-government would naturally be fostered among the population. As Bentham predicted, this would lead 'the people' to throw off their 'aristocratical representation' and 'think of insisting on a real Deputation'. It is of some interest here that the only hindrance Bentham is able to imagine standing in the way of such a progression is the imposition of constraints to 'the liberty of the press' (and for this, he blames only 'the endeavours of lawyers').[38] Sneering contempt for 'the lawyers' and disgust at the scope of libel laws is more character-istic of later Bentham (i.e. 1804–10) than it is of this period, so these comments stand out somewhat here.

What makes these remarks even harder to interpret is their inclusion, within the wider appraisal in which they appear, alongside a wild recommendation for a British prince to follow a handful of precedents in Europe and go out to India to accede and reign in the place of the East India Company:

> I could behold with pleasure the crown of Hindostan fished out of the filth of Leadenhall Street and added to the regalia in the tower: but it is with transport I should see the precedent of Spain and Naples, the precedent of France and Spain, the precedent of Austria and Tuscany, pursued in the British empire, and behold the diadem of Hindostan bound upon the brow of one of his Majesty's sons, emancipated, forisfamiliated [i.e. severed from patrilineal claimancy], and sent to live among his people. He would not want for followers, nor the golden harvests of India want for English reapers.[39]

Supportive only of the symbolic presence rather than the political power of monarchy across the British Empire, Bentham here offered a peculiar digression that he might not otherwise have offered had it not been for the recent developments in France inspiring a brief commitment to constitutional conservatism on Bentham's part ('No change in the Constitution—no Reform in Parliament').[40] Of course, it is certainly hard to square these remarks with Bentham's feelings towards the king during the regency decade (i.e. the 1810s), but that would be to put the cart before the horse.

Unlike 'New Wales', Bentham's pitch for a panopticon was far more considered. It took a number of different forms, and these went across the desks of many individuals connected in various ways to the long Pitt ministry (and the many different formats that ministry took on). Time and again, however, Bentham's ardent efforts were to be frustrated by a handful of men holding offices of the crown, some of them showing him indifference or dismissiveness, others sending him mixed or inconsistent messages. Bentham was resolute, if occasionally tactless. He was able to get around some of these antagonists and even came to enjoy, if briefly, the support of parliament (which was expressed in no lesser form than statute). But for all his resolution, there were some offices in high government that proved insurmountable as their holders repeatedly quashed his efforts to introduce and implement his system of penitentiary design and penal management. He encountered resistance from the Treasury (chief secretary, junior secretary, and counsel), the Home Office (successive Home Secretaries, under secretary, and counsel), and the Law Officers of the Crown (attorney general and solicitor general). In the process, Bentham saw first-hand the individual obsequiousness and benediction to government that characterized this world of office, and he did not like what he saw.[41] Worse still, despite his obstinacy and intellect, Bentham would prove no match for them. After over a decade of having his proposals and budgets queried and audited by the Treasury, and his contracts and bills criticized and contorted by the Law Officers, the panopticon was bureaucratically put out of its misery in a treasury minute of March 1801, a cause of death confirmed in the autopsy undertaken by the new attorney general of the Addington government the following year.[42]

Bentham and the imperial constitution after 1801

When, at the outset of the nineteenth century, in a state of exhaustion and feeling no small sense of victimhood, Bentham reflected on his repeated misadventures with the panopticon, he was able to make out, in crisper outline, the many flaws he had seen bedevilling the administrative system of the Georgian state. In this crucial period – and more specifically between the middle of 1802 and the end of 1803 – Bentham began to transform the grudge he felt towards certain officeholders into a more sophisticated critique of officeholding itself.

This observation should not be taken to suggest that Bentham had been ignorant of office as a field of intellectual enquiry until the formation of the Addington ministry. As early as 1789, if at that stage only with a French audience in mind (with a readership, that is, of anti-aristocratic revolutionaries moving towards codification in view), Bentham had experimented with a set of criteria for the assessment of offices in a reformed political system: 'their functions – numbers – subordination to the Assembly – dependence upon the Assembly – the powers they ought to have – by whom they should be appointed – who they should be – and how chosen'.[43] Not for another decade, however, would Bentham begin to consider seriously the problem of holding office unaccountably of the crown within the British administration, which he did with greater perceptivity towards the undue influence of the monarch over all officeholders and 'functionaries' attached to the executive (which for Bentham included the judiciary). This is evident in the several hundred pages of his 'Picture of the Treasury with a Sketch of the Secretary of State's Office', and, if one looks closely enough, it is detectable in the 'Plea for the Constitution'. Fobbed off by the Duke of Portland with a questionable admission that conditions for convicts were good and getting better in New South Wales,[44] and now faced with the Transportation Act (1802), which represented the clearest statutory announcement since 1787 that the penal colony had become an entrenched part of government policy,[45] Bentham turned again to the imperial constitution.

'A Plea for the Constitution' opens with the observation that some kind of legislative power was necessary for the maintenance of government in a colony like New South Wales. Judicial power alone, without legislative power, was never going to suffice in a colony of such 'novelty', as the demand for 'fresh obligations' was likely to be 'urgent'. Even if, as Bentham reasons, 'the whole mass of law existing in the Mother Country [was] to be transplanted in one lot into the Colony', the power of making new law, as superior to the judicial power, needed to extend over all resident subjects.[46] Such a power, however, had not yet been positively or lawfully established, Bentham protested. He admitted that a 'court of criminal judicature' had been established in the New South Wales Courts Act (1787), which carried the provision for 'a civil government', but neither institution had been empowered to make law. On the contrary, all the Act appeared to provide for was the authority to punish 'outrages and misbehaviours', which for Bentham was too vague and implied the expediency of adjudging such transgressions by different standards to those applicable 'in this realm'.[47] During the first decade of the colony's foundation, Bentham complained, governors (as 'agents of the crown') had assumed the authority of passing ordinances upon the authority of instructions issued by 'superiors here at home'.[48] Tracing the lines of authority from office to office, from the crown through its delegates to the governor, Bentham found that no such 'right to confer on the Governor this power was actually existing in the authority thus assuming and exercising the power' in the first place.[49] For Bentham it was inconceivable that such a power could reside in the crown as a reserve to be exercised in certain conditions; a power of this kind could only come from parliament. 'I take for granted', and he was true to his word, for this was a point more stated than proven,

> that whatever power of legislation could be given by the crown, to any body, to be exercised in this colony, has all along been given by the crown to the several successive Governors. All this notwithstanding – all this being admitted – what I maintain is

that, no such authority having been given to the crown, in the [New South Wales Courts Act of 1787], by the legislature, it was no more in the power of the crown, to confer any such power of legislation (except the limited, and not so denominated, but only virtual powers of legislation above excepted) on the Governor, or any other person or persons, than in mine.[50]

Of that extent of legislative power Bentham was prepared to concede might lawfully reside in the office of governor without an Act of Parliament first empowering the crown to delegate such a power to governors,[51] it could only ever extend to certain classes of inhabitant. This included officers and privates in the army and navy, commanders and crews of British and foreign vessels, and convicts in bondage, if however over none of whom could such a right be exercised untrammelled. Over civil officers in the king's service ('chaplains, surgeons, superintendants, &c.'), the governor only harboured a right of dismissal, and by extension enjoyed some 'influence' over these appointments, but this amounted to no 'legal power'. Likewise over wives and children of convicts in bondage, emancipated convicts and their families, along with free settlers and their families, the governor was also powerless (being 'without fresh authority from Parliament').[52]

Here Bentham's view was contradicted by almost two centuries of imperial practice, which he himself acknowledged. Charters, and not statutes, had been at the royal foundation of colonial enterprise in America and the West Indies, with parliament having very little to say on the matter before the reign of George III. For Bentham, 'this practice of organizing governments for British dependencies, in territories out of Great Britain, by the sole power of the Crown, may, I think, be said to have been relinquished, and virtually acknowledged to be indefensible ... by the precedent set, by the Act commonly called the *Quebec Act*, in which, whatever was done in the way of establishing subordinate powers of *legislation*, was in *that* case, as well as in the case of *judicature*, done either by Parliament itself, or by authority therein given to the Crown by Parliament'.[53] This was to talk of a statute as though it were a precedent of common law: inferring that the same principles underpinning a specific piece of legislation, for the particular circumstances of a colony, conquered from and ceded by the French, and housing a predominately Catholic settler population, were applicable in general to New South Wales and its peculiar place in the imperial constitution for the sole reason that its statutory foundation (in 1787) came after the Quebec Act of 1774.[54]

Less conventional still was the common law reasoning that followed Bentham's next assertion, namely that the crown had never enjoyed a right to legislate for colonies without parliament – starting inevitably, if unsophisticatedly, with Magna Carta (a 'statute', he said) but proceeding quickly therefrom to 'Lord Coke's time'. Instead of beginning at the most logical point of entry into the debate, with *Calvin's Case* (1608) – the report of which carried well-known dicta in support of the king's power to alter and replace laws of colonies taken by conquest – Bentham took to construing the lesser-known *Clark's Case* (1596), or what he called *St Alban's Case*, to his own ends. This was a shaky authority, scanty in details, and perfect for using out of context. It concerned the false imprisonment of a burgess (i.e. Clark) in the town of St Albans, a corporation whose charter carried an unexceptional power to issue ordinances for local effect. Making use of this delegated legislative authority, as many a town did, the burgesses in assembly (which included Clark) enacted an ordinance authorizing the collection of revenues from residents of the town for the establishment of local courts on sufferance of imprisonment for anyone refusing to pay. When later Clark refused to pay, his imprisonment was ordered by the mayor, John Gape, an order that was subsequently disputed. Judgment held for Clark not because the legislative authority to establish the judicature was unlawful, but because the provision of the ordinance carrying the penalty of imprisonment was contrary to the principle of *nullus liber homo imprisonetur*[55] (as carried in the 29th chapter of Magna Carta), regardless of Clark's support for the ordinance in quorum ('lassent le pl[aintife] ne poit alter le ley in tiel case').[56] 'Against *colonization charters*', Bentham declared, was this 'direct *judgment* grounded on it', even if, as Bentham himself noted, James I/VI and Charles I had issued charters without showing any hint of regard for it. And there was more still for St Albans to do: on Bentham's unique reading of a case that had nothing to do with parliamentary legislation – and more importantly had done nothing by way of discrediting the allocation of legislative powers to towns in charters of a standard kind that were issued and reissued all throughout the Tudor period – 'the decision disaffirm[ed] the King's right to legislate over Englishmen without Parliament'.[57] On this wobbly case all others should rest; 'And who is there that will deny, that, in the scale of common law, a thousand unjudicial precedents are not equal to one judicial one?' This was a most pointed question indeed, and one that bears raising again in the context of what Bentham would write on *Campbell v Hall* (1774) and the common law of conquest.[58]

Before he could address Mansfield, however, Bentham first had to establish that New South Wales, being a 'purely royal' and 'daringly anti-parliamentary' colony, did not qualify as a 'conquest' by such criteria as had been developed by common lawyers during the seventeenth century (what Bentham with a sneer would deride as 'the Natural History of the Law of Colonies').[59] Founded without a charter, and surviving only upon the terms of two insufficiently worded and error-strewn statutes, New South Wales ought to have received the laws of England alongside a local legislature, but instead received only such provisions as the 'advisers of the Crown' deemed fit to impose and all without the consent of British subjects there. Therefore, as Bentham acknowledged, the colony was being treated as though it had been obtained by conquest and cession when neither event had in fact taken place: no European power was ever strong-armed into surrendering a claim to New South Wales in post-war negotiations because none had developed an effective claim to surrender, while the Aboriginal polity had been insufficiently possessed of a recognizable legal personality (its representatives were 'private gentlemen') to cede the land in any public capacity ('they signed no *treaty* with his Majesty').[60]

In the context of a legal argument about the receptivity of the colony to '*English-made law*' and institutions, it should not be too surprising that Bentham had no more to say about Indigenous Australians aside from this remark (however interesting it may be to speculate upon what, in light of his earlier writings on India, he might have made of the influence of time and place on Aboriginal law). Bentham had no need to advance an argument about the continuity or discontinuity of Aboriginal law because an argument of this kind was only relevant in connection to colonies acquired by conquest, in the scope of which the common law was most resourceful when it came to the abrogation of laws followed by 'infidels' (being 'against the law of God and of nature'), laws *malum in se* (inherently bad), and laws 'contrary to fundamental principles'.[61] Pointing out, correctly, that New South Wales had not been (recognizably) conquered or ceded allowed Bentham to bypass this line of argument, and moreover, what was more important in the frame of his argument, it allowed him to reiterate the inconceivability of governing an unconquered colony by prerogative alone, which was, after all, one of the main objectives of the 'Plea'.[62]

When Bentham turned to the question of judicial power, he distanced himself from the common law in order to confront more robustly the constitutional division of powers. Gubernatorial ordinances could only accomplish so much without the establishment of a dedicated court to interpret and enforce such obligations, Bentham argued. To this assertion was added a clever observation about the propriety of providing a stronger statutory footing to the government of New South Wales. Why, asked Bentham, had there been, in 1787, a need to 'apply to Parliament for powers, for the organization of a judicial establishment', when there had not been considered any need to do the same for legislative powers? 'Judicial power is in its nature inferior, subordinate to legislative', as he put it: 'If the Crown had an original right to create the superior power', it could not 'have been without the right of creating the subordinate'.[63] This was not the case in New South Wales. There, legislative power flowed from the crown to the governor who might, with such power, create a specific offence, 'but neither he nor any body else has any power to punish or try the offender for it, when committed'. That condition left the governor with little option but to establish a court for himself – 'a court thus arbitrary' and very much, as Bentham envisaged, in the Tudor style:

> to be composed of the Governor alone, for the trying of offences created by the Governor alone? – If so, here then we have the very quintessence of despotism; too rank one should have thought, even for the meridian of New South Wales. It is Star-Chamber out-Star-chamberized: legislature and judicature confounded and lodged together, both in one and the same hand.[64]

This was a jurisdictional shortcoming left unaddressed by the New South Wales Courts Act of 1787, which instead provided for the establishment of a criminal court, 'for the trial and punishment of all such outrages and misbehaviours as if committed within *this realm*'.[65] The expression 'this realm' gave Bentham a chance to show off his famous fussiness towards unconsidered statutory language in an entertaining little footnote revealing how 'these two words [offered] a proof [of] how little of the mind of the legislature was bestowed upon this business'.[66]

With more criticism still to be levelled at the common law of conquest, Bentham returned to *Campbell v Hall* (1774), or what he called 'the Granada Case'. This he did in a fashion characteristic of his long-felt suspicion towards the interpretative discretion enjoyed by judges to prioritize certain precedents over others, a clear example of which is also to be seen in the dismay he felt about Coke's views in *Calvin's Case* (1608) being prioritized within imperial constitutional thought over Coke's views in *Clark's Case* (1596).[67] At the same time,

Bentham's observations on this head were also illustrative of a newly found apprehensiveness towards the place of officeholders in the administrative system and the instrumentality, more specifically, of judicial officers of the crown in giving shape to the imperial constitution.[68] Bentham took particular delight in Mansfield's appraisal of the 'inattention of the *King's Servants*' (which was the terminology reported by Cowper) with a sense of satisfaction that ran far deeper than plain agreement with the Chief Justice about the specific mistakes made in relation to disorderly promulgation of instruments for Grenada in 1764 by Attorney General Fletcher Norton and Solicitor General William de Grey. '[H]is Majesty's Law-advisers in this behalf have not been altogether masters of this part of their business', Bentham maligned, while freely citing from Mansfield's judgment:

> The power of legislation, as exercised in that Colony, in the way of taxation … by the King alone, without the concurrence of any other authority – either that of Parliament here, or that of an assembly of the Colony *there* – exercised on the ground of its being a CONQUERED Colony – is there supposed … to have been in itself indisputable. But … these his Majesty's careless servants, not knowing or not minding what they were about, had so managed as to divest him of it: and it was after having so done, that, forgetting what they had done, they picked it up again, and in the name of their Royal Masters, exercised it as above: 'inverting' (says Lord Mansfield) 'the order in which the instruments should have passed, *and been notoriously published*, the last act' was under their management 'contradictory to, and in violation of the first:' and this is the 'inattention' spoken of.[69]

Inasmuch as Mansfield's judgment appeared to confirm a view that the law officers of the crown were 'not infallible' in 1764, Bentham supposed that similar errors might just as easily have characterized the advice offered by Attorney General Richard Arden and Solicitor General Archibald MacDonald around which the policy for New South Wales was shaped in 1787.[70] And Bentham did not stop there. Similar misgivings were also expressed about the 'non-judicial opinion' proffered by holders of the same office in 1724 about the power of the crown to levy taxes upon English residents of Jamaica without the endorsement of the imperial parliament or a local legislature: a power, it had been reckoned by Attorney General Philip Yorke and Solicitor General Clement Wearg, which applied only to conquered countries.[71] Bentham may have approved of this principle only insofar as it appeared to imply that colonies not conquered should receive legislative institutions, but he was unprepared to give the opinion any more weight than that. That is because it appeared to rely too much upon the 'extrajudicial ravings' of Edward Coke in his *obiter dictum* upon *Calvin's Case,* and more specifically because it had taken for gospel Coke's suggestions that the crown enjoyed a blanket power to legislate in colonies coming to it by conquest.

Indeed, were it not for Coke's opinion, Bentham hypothesized, there would never have been any need over the last two centuries to distinguish so strictly and unreasonably between the administrative attributes of colonies founded by *conquest and cession* and colonies founded by *occupation or settlement without conquest.* However unplanned and illogical such a distinction was – and it was – there was still far more by way of seventeenth- and eighteenth-century jurisprudence in favour of it than against it, and not all of it was a direct transmission from *Calvin's Case,* but this was not a worry to Bentham.[72] Wiping away all the inventions of common law was great play for him; and looking justifiably with suspicion upon the means by which an array of juristic conceptions, together with the briefs and opinions of law officers of the crown, were being treated as though they represented a positive kind of law, Bentham was able to call into question the whole imperial constitution and the role played by the fiction of conquest within it (all in a surprisingly cautious, if not sarcastic, tone):

> If, in humble imitation of such high and sincerely respected authority, and in precisely the same view, viz. that of seeing important constitutional questions settled on the broadest and most solid grounds, it may be allowable for an obscure ex-lawyer, on this same ground, *to travel,* as the phrase is, *a little way out of the record,* I will venture to state it as a question, which notwithstanding the opinion so distinctly given by that great lawyer in the affirmative, remains still quite open, whether, even in the case of *conquest,* in any colony acquired since the Revolution, *Trinidad* for example, the right of the King to legislate without Parliament – I mean without express authority from Parliament – would, *in case of dispute,* be found maintainable in law.[73]

Now considering *how* the king's powers had momentarily come to be amplified in Grenada (this 'vacant territory remote from the eye of Parliament'), a conspiracy began to take shape in his mind. The king had only been allowed to arrogate such powers to himself because 'it was in the power of his law-servants, by any such management, to oust Parliament of its rights: I mean its exclusive right of legislation, as established in *St. Alban's Case*'. The very same devotion to the crown at the expense of the constitution was to be seen in the wording of the charters too. So many of them emulating the 'manor of East Greenwich', authorizing summary trials and punishments, and doing more that was *ultra vires* besides, had been 'exercises of regal power' entirely conceived by 'Crown lawyers audacious enough to make their king grant ... privileges which had already been declared illegal'.[74] The declaration of martial law at Norfolk Island by the lieutenant-governor in 1790, and subsequently approved of and endorsed by the governor of New South Wales, fell into the same category as a transgression for which 'his Majesty's "officers and ministers" here at home' were responsible, for as Bentham guessed (and correctly) a provision of theirs in some commission or instruction must have permitted such a course of action or else the rebuke or recall of the governor should have followed (but did not).[75] Holders of high judicial office, and the law officers of the crown in particular, were single-handedly to blame for the encouragement of despotism abroad – despotism of a style that could never have prospered at home, in other words.

Bentham's solution would have come as no surprise to readers who knew him. If all such defects, inconsistencies and mischiefs thus embedded into the imperial constitution from the Stuart period onwards had originated in non-judicial musings, unwarranted dicta, and official sleights of hand, then for Bentham it appeared all the more obvious that positive law, in the form of statute, was the only appropriate means of addressing such problems: 'that rights of such importance should be fixed upon the rock of *legislation*, instead of being left to totter upon the quick-sands of expected judicature ... for the chance of saving a little longer the stump of a rotten prerogative, and perhaps the pride of a few lawyers'.[76]

The rest of the 'Plea for the Constitution' amounts to a stocktaking of the grounds upon which gubernatorial legislation in New South Wales was bad. For Bentham, the most egregious transgressions were evident in specific ordinances promulgated for the prevention of famine and drunkenness and for the detention of 'expirees' and others without trial. On a more general level, Bentham repeated his concerns with the allocation of legislative and judicial power to the governor for his 'anti-constitutional purposes' and without any authority from parliament. All such conduct was shown to be 'illegal' against a number of well-known authoritative standards with which Bentham permitted himself the liberty of amplifying by way of analogy or inference: Magna Carta, of course, but also the Petition of Right of 1628, the Habeas Corpus Act of 1679, the Declaration of Rights of 1689, and the Transportation Acts of 1718, 1784, 1788 and 1803.[77]

Conclusion: Bentham and the constitution in the imperial meridian

That Bentham should have put 'Trinidad' in the long published title for 'A Plea for the Constitution' in 1812, and that he should have preserved in that essay two passing references to the island (as conforming to an example of a colony where gubernatorial despotism flowed from the crown as a result of conquest), is intriguing. This may suggest that Bentham was preparing to expand his critique of office, judicature, and legislature in the imperial constitution. Trinidad would have been ideal for consideration in such a context, if for reasons that Bentham is unlikely to have grasped in 1803, when he completed the essay, but which would eventually become much clearer in 1812, when the essay appeared in *Panopticon versus New South Wales*.

After the island of Trinidad fell under the military occupation of the forces of Ralph Abercromby in 1797, the new British administration coalesced around an autocratic governor, who was given amplified judicial powers and a small council to advise him. It was decided that the common law should not supersede the mutated Spanish law already in existence, thereby allowing the gubernatorial regime of Thomas Picton to become one of the most notorious in the history of the British Empire. Ordering dozens of executions and hundreds of corporal punishments, Picton moved to introduce a stricter disciplinary regime across the slaveholding colony before his resignation in disgrace in 1803.[78] What demanded the most thorough judicial investigation was the torture, ordered by Picton in 1801, of Luisa Calderon, a young girl professedly innocent for her involvement in a theft. The procedural history of the case is not straightforward; but then few state trials concerning matters of importance to imperial jurisprudence in the meridian were. Picton was the first overseas officeholder ever to fall foul of the terms of the Criminal Jurisdictions Act that had been passed in June of 1802 (a statute which provided that any officeholder accused of committing a 'crime, offence, or misdemeanour' abroad, by the standards of English law, was to be investigated and, if necessary, tried in the King's Bench), and he was accordingly indicted in 1804.[79] By the terms set out in this statute, *mandamus* had to be issued (which, for all its Latin appearance, was a writ of early modernity allowing the judiciary, on behalf of the crown, to compel inferior officers and entities to perform public duties requested of them). This triggered an enquiry into Picton's administration at a special court in Government House at Port of Spain, which returned information to the Court of King's Bench in early 1806 whereupon the case was tried in two parts: one leading to an ordinary verdict, and the other requiring new writs of *mandamus* and more information late in 1807, which returned to court a year later for the delivery of a special verdict in early 1808. This was contested in 1810, before finally the whole matter fizzled out in 1812.[80]

Lord Chief Justice Ellenborough presided over the entire affair and his influence throughout was not inconsiderable: special juries were assembled in 1806 and 1808 and the blunt questions put to them were narrow and sometimes technical (and for both reasons, therefore, unconventional); he adjudicated with a sense of impatience (distracted, as he confessed on more than one occasion, by the more pressing trials at Guildhall requiring his attention), which often inspired his own interjections to hurry arguments along; and when he interjected into the arguments of counsel sympathetic to Calderon, he did so with a diminished sense of charity that was evident in his goading and bullying of them into considering questions of law that were in no way advantageous to their arguments (for example, in 1810, when it came to the nature of powers reserved to the prerogative).[81] Then, of course, came the remarkable denouement of the whole affair. Upon the adjournment of the court in the second trial, it was allowed to slip through the gaps and never come back. Picton had become a war hero by this time, having received a number of commissions to lead major campaigns in the Napoleonic Wars. Giving up his life for the crown at Waterloo in 1815, he would face no judgment in this world for his Caribbean misconduct.

Trinidad revealed all too starkly how the efforts of British legal thinkers to generate some order from the consequences of war in the imperial meridian could be reducible to minimal practical importance owing to the outstanding bellicosity of the wider world that surrounded them. This might explain Bentham's failure to follow up on any of his passing references to Trinidad, despite both Picton's governorship in Trinidad and the subsequent judicial investigation in England containing a number of those very same ingredients for which Bentham was fast losing tolerance in the first decade of the nineteenth century: starting with the abuse, in the peripheries, of delegated legislative and judicial powers originating without authority from parliament, and ending with an elongated and disjointed trial in England, throughout which *Calvin's Case*, and not *Clark's Case*, was examined in arguments rehearsed before special juries and an interventionist judge, and which resulted in a shrug of indifference to the authority of the crown being used to support despotic and autocratic regimes abroad. There was assuredly much about all of this that Bentham would have disliked. But if his failure to reform the penal colony of New South Wales had taught him anything, it was how elements of the imperial constitution could be insulated from criticism owing to the large doses of pragmatism and expediency that were needed in the shaping of colonial policy, along with the discretionary opinions of law officers of the crown that were mobilized, often behind the scenes, in the process of *formulating* such policy. In London, commentary upon colonial constitutional controversies could be dismissed more easily than criticism of the executive itself (which was a term, it bears repeating, that Bentham used flexibly to include judicial officeholders alongside ministers of the crown).

Justifiably, then, Bentham returned to the domestic front where his efforts were most likely to be rewarded – or at least this is how we are accustomed to reading his writings between 1803 and 1812.[82] A succession of libel cases heard in the King's Bench between 1806 and 1808 prompted him to sharpen his critique of high judicial offices and their holders, targeting in particular Attorney General Vicary Gibbs and Chief Justice Ellenborough, and the 'sinister interests' animating them, in his *Elements of the Art of Packing* (1809).[83] Around the same time, Commons select committees on public expenditure and sinecures, which Bentham appears to have followed with some interest, published their findings in a flurry of reports, accounts, and papers, which indicted the huge expense, and sometimes outright wastefulness, of so many offices held of the crown.[84] With law reports and ledger books of the period both seeming to point to the same pressing need to reform the system of office in the administrative system, Bentham spent the next two decades perfecting his notion of 'official aptitude'. With his focus fixed at first upon the conduct of members of parliament, who for Bentham were most likely to fall under the influence of the king and his ministers (whom he called the 'Corruptor-General & Co.' in partial mimicry, perhaps, of the title of the law officers of the crown), he eventually broadened and rendered more sophisticated his models of probity into a suite of new standards for officeholding generally.[85]

It was in these spheres that Bentham, as a constitutional thinker, was at his most original and erudite. But if it is accurate to say that empire was no longer at the forefront of his mind in the period between 1804 and 1819, it is inaccurate to say that empire had entirely left his mind. For example, it is surely significant that, at the outset of the 'Catechism of Parliamentary Reform' (written in 1809 but not published until 1817), when explaining the concept of 'appropriate probity' (a foundation stone for his developing theory of official conduct), Bentham explicitly juxtaposed the interests 'of the whole of the British Empire' against those of the king and his ministers.[86] And for all that his letters to Pelham and his 'Picture of the Treasury' had become, by this time, the remnants of an intellectual project long given up on, it was his failure to succeed with the panopticon scheme and his critique of New South Wales that remained, for some time in his mind, the source of inspiration behind extraordinary outbursts of a kind that went far beyond office – outbursts of a kind that went deeply and profoundly into the officeholding mentality of the bureaucratic state itself.[87] None of this should come as any surprise for, as this chapter has shown, Bentham had been reflecting upon office, legislature, and judicature in the imperial constitution since his early days as a critic of Blackstone and a comrade of Lind, before spending the better part of an entire decade thinking about penal reform in connection to New South Wales. It was only when, after his misfortunes with the panopticon, Bentham turned to prepare a critique of delegations of legislative power unauthorized by parliament in the colony that a new perspective began to take shape in his mind. 'A Plea for the Constitution' prepared the way for Bentham's synthesis of a number of hitherto disparate strands in his thinking: namely, what became his critique of 'sinister influence', a factor extending to all common lawyers, to all officeholders, to both law officers of the crown, to all ministers of state, and to the monarch (the 'Corruptor-General') atop them all. Without New South Wales – or, without any constitutional register permitting an appraisal of its place as a penal colony within the wider British Empire – it is unlikely that his thinking on office, legislature, and judicature (and office in particular) would have taken the shape it did.

Notes

1   i.e. by the Criminal Jurisdiction Act of 1802 (42 Geo. III, c. 85).
2   See Cavanagh 2022.

3   An appellate court for the British Empire, the Judicial Committee of the Privy Council was statutorily erected in 1833, but even that, which was little more than a prerogative advisory board afforded its own branch in the existing judicature, entailed only minor structural recalibration of the wider system. See Howell 1979.
4   It remains underappreciated by British political historians that both Upper and Lower Canada had been trying to introduce the model that eventually became known as 'responsible self-government' at least a decade before it was tried and tested in Westminster, even if their endeavours were not rewarded until the end of the 1840s. Australasian colonial legislatures followed in staggered progression after the Canadas, but Caribbean legislatures became derailed from the same trajectory. For this, see Ward 1976.
5   To understand the draft title of the work, one must first consult the draft preface, where Bentham declares that a 'political conquest' of the constitution had taken place for 40 days in 1766, following the authorization by Lord Chancellor Camden and the Earl of Chatham ('Pitt the Elder') of the suspension of certain Acts of Parliament without the consent of Lords or Commons. This was an extraordinary principle of government that Bentham argued would later be rolled out to New South Wales. See the 'Appendix' to 'A Plea for the Constitution' in Bentham, ed. Causer and Schofield 2022, 395–400.
6   Bayly 1989.
7   The 'Ballad of Sir Patrick Spens' was first published in Percy 1765, 1: 72–3, and later popularized by Coleridge 1802.
8   Hume 1974, 51–4; Hume 1981.
9   Schofield 2006, 107.
10 See Hart 1976.
11 Gerber 2011, 179–98.
12 Lind 1776, 126–7.
13 Recent interpretations of this technique of colonial government include McHugh 2020 and Siddique 2020.
14 See Lawson 1989.
15 Cavanagh 2019a.
16 14 Geo III, c. 83.
17 Lind 1775.
18 Bentham to John Bowring, 30 January 1827, in Bentham, ed. O'Sullivan and Fuller 2006, 292–3: 'Before I had any knowledge of this project of my friend's, I put together in a few pages, my thoughts relative to the ground, on which it appeared to me that the question between the mother-country and the colony ought to be determined. Upon his communicating his design to me, I put the paper into his hand, and when the first sheet or two had come out of the press, not small was my surprise at finding this paper of mine placed at the commencement of his work, and constituting the foundation of it. Of this work I have preserved a copy, and shall say more of it by and by. He wrote with rapidity and carelessness; without looking at it, he would have signed with eagerness any thing that I wrote; his style was rather loose and negligent ... I touched it up a little in several places. But before it was brought to the length of the Quebec-Act, I lost sight of it'.
19 Bentham to Bowring, 30 January 1827, in Bentham, ed. O'Sullivan and Fuller 2006, 293.
20 Lind 1775, 449–68.
21 Lind 1775, 479–82.
22 31 Geo III, c. 31. For a recent appraisal, see Girard 2020.
23 Cavanagh 2019b.
24 Cavanagh 2019a, 623–5, 637–9.
25 *Campbell v Hall* (1774), 239–354.
26 13 Geo III, c. 63.
27 21 Geo III, c. 65; 33 Geo. III, c. 52; 53 Geo III, c. 155, which collectively became known as the 'Charter Acts'.
28 24 Geo. III, s. 2, c. 25, seeing also 24 Geo. III, s. 2, c. 2, and s. 2, c. 34; *Cobbett's Parliamentary History* (hereafter *PH*), 1806–20, 27: 93.
29 Cavanagh 2019b, 392–402, 406–9.
30 Kanalu 2020.
31 Bentham, ed. Schofield and Engelmann 2011, 179.
32 Bentham, ed. Schofield and Engelmann 2011, 181.
33 Bentham, ed. Schofield and Engelmann 2011, 186: 'What became of the spoils of the

Bramin Nindocomar, whom the English Judges hanged on pretence that a set of men in London had made forgery a felony without the benefit of English Braminship?' (ibid. 187). For the classic treatment of Impey's impeachment, which is equally revealing of the case in question and the viewpoints of an author peculiarly experienced with the workings of the imperial constitution, see Stephen 1885.

34 Bentham, ed. Schofield and Engelmann 2011, 192–3. Bentham never again returned to consider the place of India in the imperial constitution with the same fullness of consideration, notwithstanding his offer to Sir Henry Dundas in 1793 to help with the preparation of 'legislation … for Hindostan', after so much unsatisfactory 'penmanship of the Statutes'. See Bentham to Henry Dundas (20 May 1793), in Bentham, ed. Milne 2017, 429–30. For this and Bentham's influence on James and John Stuart Mill, see Pitts 2003.

35 This was a topic that received consideration in Bentham 1778.

36 'New Wales' in Bentham, ed. Causer and Schofield 2022, 1–22.

37 'New Wales' in Bentham, ed. Causer and Schofield 2022, 12–13, comparing UC cxix. 92.

38 'New Wales' in Bentham, ed. Causer and Schofield 2022, 13.

39 'New Wales' in Bentham, ed. Causer and Schofield 2022, 12.

40 Bentham Papers, Special Collections, University College London Library clxx. 173 (hereafter UC. Roman numerals refer to the boxes in which the papers are placed, Arabic to the leaves within each box). See also Schofield 2006, 94–106.

41 Of this there is an astonishing account provided in the 'Appendix' to 'Correspondence, sent to William Wilberforce, of Jeremy Bentham with Sir Charles Bunbury', in Bentham, ed. Causer and Schofield 2022, 64, particularly when he turns to the roles of Chief Secretary John Hiley Addington and Junior Secretary Charles Long in their response to his own repeated insistence upon the support shown to his plans in parliament: 'The doctrines were laid down principally, if not exclusively, by Mr Long. Informant of the oracles, rather than invention, was the task of his new-entered successor [i.e. Hiley Addington]. Being, from what judgment I could make in so short an interview, a good-natured man – his tone and manner were adapted to the more lenient part: the part of soothing and smoothing away, by a mixture of reproof and kindness, such obstinacy as mine … All the axioms, whether of politics or ethics, that had been laid down by this Anti-Fortiscue, about the nullity of parliaments – about the futility of the fancied distinction between absolute and limited monarchies – about the exemption belonging to gentlemen in such high offices as touching moral obligations, were so many truisms to Mr Hiley Addington: but the notions seemed rather adopted in deference to such high authority, than brought out as the fruit of his own reflections and experience'. For office, see generally Condren 2006; Condren 2009, 15–28; McHugh 2018, 892–8; McHugh 2020.

42 Hume 1973; Hume 1974. The burial was finally arranged in mid-June 1803 by Pelham, the Home Secretary. For this, and a discussion of the Treasury Minute of 1801, see Bentham, ed. Causer and Schofield 2022, lxxxviii–lxxxix, xxviii.

43 Bentham to Andrew Morellet (1789), UC clxix. 164.

44 See 'Copy of Treasury Minute, of the 13th August 1800', in 'Further Proceedings of the Lords Commissioners of His Majesty's Treasury, &c. respecting the matters stated in The Reports of the Committee of Finance, so far as they relate to The Several Offices concerned in the Receipt and Expenditure of the Public Money', 12 June 1801, in ed. Lambert 1975, vi. 585. This is where the 'four grounds of relinquishment' originated, of which the 'improved state' of NSW was one, and which Bentham was so aggravated by. Interested readers should also consult the 'Third Letter to Lord Pelham' in Bentham, ed. Causer and Schofield 2022, 249–302, and which is covered by Causer's chapter in this volume.

45 43 Geo III, c. 15.

46 'A Plea for the Constitution' in Bentham, ed. Causer and Schofield 2022, 325–6.

47 'A Plea for the Constitution' in Bentham, ed. Causer and Schofield 2022, 326–7.

48 'A Plea for the Constitution' in Bentham, ed. Causer and Schofield 2022, 327, seeing also 345–6: 'Instructions and counter instructions – insinuations and counter insinuations – instructions in form, and instructions not in form; – despotism acting there by instructions, and without instructions, and against instructions; – all these things there may be, and will be, in abundance. But of charters – unless such instructions be called charters – of constitutions – that any body that can help it will be governed by; – of any lawful warrants, unless from Parliament; – from the present day to the day of judgment there will be none'.

49 'A Plea for the Constitution' in Bentham, ed. Causer and Schofield 2022, 328, seeing also 359: 'The displaceable instruments of the Crown – the successive Governors of New South Wales – have, for these fourteen years past, been exercising legislative power, without any authority from Parliament: and either without any authority at all from any body, or at most without any authority but from the King: and all along they have been, as it was most fit they should be, placed and displaced at his Majesty's pleasure'.

50 'A Plea for the Constitution' in Bentham, ed. Causer and Schofield 2022, 332.

51 'A Plea for the Constitution' in Bentham, ed. Causer and Schofield 2022, 328–9, seeing also ibid.: 'Legislative power exercised by an officer of the crown, for such a course of years, without authority from Parliament! On what possible ground could any conception of the legality of such a system be seriously entertained?'

52 'A Plea for the Constitution' in Bentham, ed. Causer and Schofield 2022, 329–32.

53 'A Plea for the Constitution' in Bentham, ed. Causer and Schofield 2022, 333–4.

54 See also Bentham's reading of the Naval Prize Act of 1740 (13 Geo. II, c. 4) at 'A Plea for the Constitution' in Bentham, ed. Causer and Schofield 2022, 334–5.

55 i.e. 'No free man shall be imprisoned'.

56 i.e. 'The assent of the plaintiff cannot alter the law in this case'. See *Clark's Case* (1596).

57 'A Plea for the Constitution' in Bentham, ed. Causer and Schofield 2022, 341, 353. For the means by which royal charters were interpreted for distinct colonial applications, see Cavanagh, 2017.

58 'A Plea for the Constitution' in Bentham, ed. Causer and Schofield 2022, 341.

59 'A Plea for the Constitution' in Bentham, ed. Causer and Schofield 2022, 344–5: 'To the host of follies included in the circumstance of distant possession, this colony at least, with all its peculiarities and all its faults, has not added that vulgar and crowning folly of distant conquest'.

60 'A Plea for the Constitution' in Bentham, ed. Causer and Schofield, 2022, 345.

61 The notion that infidelity conferred a defective legal personality onto non-Christian individuals may have fallen sharply out of fashion in the last quarter of the eighteenth century, as Bentham recognized, but these other means of assessing substantive repugnance (contrariness to nature and 'fundamental principles') were still very much alive into the nineteenth century, as the rehearsal of *Calvin's Case* (1608), *Blankard v Galdy* (1693), *Anonymous* (1722), and *Campbell v Hall* (1774) together often showed. See, for example, *King v Thomas Picton* (1804–12). Coke had been largely to blame for this trend, according to 'A Plea for the Constitution' in Bentham, ed. Causer and Schofield 2022, 354: 'Pronouncing the laws of every infidel (i.e. non-christian) country void in the lump, and so forth: Turkey, Hindostan, and China, for example. – Whenever the Khan of the Tartars sounded his trumpet after eating his dinner, it was to allow other princes to eat theirs. When this christian barbarian thus sounded his trumpet, it was to prohibit other potentates from eating their dinners: at least from eating them in peace and quietness: – All infidels (he says) are perpetual enemies'. Now emulating Bentham's own propensity to place a footnote within a footnote, it bears noting that his ecumenism, if not agnosticism towards the religious convictions of individuals taking heed from the common law, should be contrasted with his cynicism in a later speech written for the Pasha of Tripoli, in which a direct message from the Prophet Muhammad is fabricated for the purposes of encouraging devoted Muslims to embrace modern forms of judicature and legislature. See Bentham, ed. Schofield 1990, 74–8.

62 Had Bentham allotted to himself the task of considering what form a settler constitution might take in the event of a rebellion against British rule in Australia, it is improbable he would have viewed the outcome any differently to that of the United States of America after 1783: with 'America having since taken itself into its own hands, and conquered itself within itself, much remains not of the prior conquest, unless it be the honour and glory—in which, however, was contained all the value of it'. Although the British crown was no conqueror in New South Wales, in other words, that did nothing to stop the convicts from turning into settlers and arrogating to themselves the same kind of absolute power, albeit without a monarch. If this hypothetical digression should be of any interest, readers might profitably reconsider his view on dictatorships in 'Colonization Company Proposal' in Bentham, ed. Causer and Schofield 2022 (1831), 424, alongside Schofield's chapter in this volume.

63 'A Plea for the Constitution' in Bentham, ed. Causer and Schofield 2022, 346.

64 'A Plea for the Constitution' in Bentham, ed. Causer and Schofield 2022, 347–50.

65 27 Geo III, c. 2.

66 This attack constitutes the most entertaining footnote of the tract: see 'A Plea for the Constitution' in Bentham, ed. Causer and Schofield 2022, 347–8.

67 'A Plea for the Constitution' in Bentham, ed. Causer and Schofield 2022, 357–8: 'How much better for this country, as well as so many other countries, would it have been, if instead of fishing for drops of sense out of the extrajudicial ravings of Lord Coke, men of law had attended ... to the direct decision of the judicial authority, as reported, in sober though very energetic language, by the *same* God of their idolatry, in the *St. Alban's* case'. This appears alongside a similar criticism about the ignorance shown to a provision of the Bill of Rights negativing the king's power to keep a standing army which appears, in Bentham's imaginative mind, to disqualify any attempt to govern by conquest.

68 'A Plea for the Constitution' in Bentham, ed. Causer and Schofield 2022, 350: 'It is not the minister alone, and *his* subordinates, that are implicated. This is not mere *Treasury* business. The acts have not only the *King's* name and signature to them, but the sanction of the whole *Council-Board*, with the opinions of this and that and t'other *great dignitary of the law* included in it'.

69 'A Plea for the Constitution' in Bentham, ed. Causer and Schofield 2022, 351–2.

70 It appears both relevant to this chapter, and revealing of the progression and careerism of law officers, that Macdonald had appeared (for Campbell) against the Attorney General Thurlow (who appeared for Hall) in 1774; that Thurlow had become Lord Chancellor as a supporter of George III and a strategic ally of Pitt in 1786; and that Macdonald had been appointed into the office of Baron of the Exchequer in 1793.

71 Opinion of Yorke and Wearg (18 May 1724), in Chalmers 1858, 230–1. For the origins and applications of this opinion, see Cavanagh 2019a, 622–5, 637–41.

72 The most obvious omission from consideration in this context was Chief Justice John Holt (1642–1710), to whose jurisprudence this distinction between two types of colonies must partially at least be attributed. Other English authorities contributing in some way or other to an understanding of the operation of the prerogative in relation to conquests included Sir John Davies (1569–1626), Sir John Selden (1584–1654), and Sir Matthew Hale (1609–76), all of whom Bentham overlooked. Continentals like Gentili, Grotius, Bynkershoek, Pufendorf, and Vattel each had their own things to say on war and government in early modern empires too, of course, but not even a mind so assiduous as Bentham's could have synthesized their ideas with those of English legal thought to generate any coherent 'doctrine of conquest'.

73 'A Plea for the Constitution' in Bentham, ed. Causer and Schofield 2022, 355–6.

74 'A Plea for the Constitution' in Bentham, ed. Causer and Schofield 2022, 357–8.

75 'A Plea for the Constitution' in Bentham, ed. Causer and Schofield 2022, 383–4: 'On this, as on all other occasions of *necessity*, real or apparent, I impute not any moral blame to the *Governor*: moral blame might, for aught I know, have been imputable to him, had he acted otherwise. *Elsewhere* however – I mean to his Majesty's 'officers and ministers' here at home – I see not how it can be that moral blame should not be imputable: I mean, if, under *constitutional* blame, *moral* be included; – if a regard for the constitution of their country – for the '*laws and statutes according to which*' they are thus pledged '*to serve*' their royal master – have any sort of place among the articles of their moral code. Amongst the documents which composed the legal armature of the Governor, was any such power as that of declaring martial law, in that nursery of despotism, included? If so, then has there been, in that behalf, on their part, an open and point-blank breach made in this constitutional and hard-earned bulwark of the constitution. Again, be this as it may, when with or without precedent authority, from these his Majesty's 'officers and ministers', martial law had *actually* been proclaimed, was information of such proceeding officially transmitted to them in consequence? That, in one way or other, at one time or other, information of this fact has come to their cognizance, is beyond dispute: if not by the next conveyance, and in the way of official correspondence (an omission not naturally to be presumed), at any rate it was received by them in 1798, through the medium of the press'.

76 'A Plea for the Constitution' in Bentham, ed. Causer and Schofield 2022, 359.

77 'A Plea for the Constitution' in Bentham, ed. Causer and Schofield 2022, 360–95. Through his combination of analogy, principle, and authority, Bentham's method was exemplary of imperial legal thought, even if his own intellectual style was particularly frenetic in places. See Cavanagh 2020, esp. 1–35.

78 Epstein 2007; Epstein 2012; Benton and Ford 2018.

79 42 Geo III, c. 85. That Bentham appears not to have commented upon this statute is intriguing, given his displeasure both with the New South Wales Act and with certain gubernatorial instructions issued after it.

80 *King v Thomas Picton* (1804–12).

81 For example, *King v Thomas Picton* (1804–12), 536–40, 803–4, 898.

82 Dinwiddy 1975; Hume 1981, 165–208; Schofield 2006, 78–170.

83 *Draper v Sullivan* (1806–7); *Draper v Fullarton* (1808–9); *Attorney General v Hart and White* (1808); *Carr v Hood* (1808); Bentham 1821 (1809), esp. 5–10.

84 See the reports at *Commons Sessional Papers* (1806), vols. vii. 1–905, xiii. 1029–1153, (1807), vol. ii. 313–78, 423–34, (1808), vol. iii. 257–400, (1809), vol. iii. 61–90, (1810), vol. ii. 381–506, 591–646, and (1810–11), vol. iii. 961–99. For some context, see Chester 1981, 123–68, and generally Parris 1969, but we are all still wanting a definitive study of the officeholding aspect of 'constitutional bureaucracy'.

85 Bentham, ed. Schofield 1993.

86 Bentham 1818 (1817), 126–7: 'appropriate probity consists in [a Representative of the People] pursuing that line of conduct, which, in his own sincere opinion, being not inconsistent with the rules of morality or the law of the land, is most conducive to the general good of the whole community for which he serves; that is to say, of the whole of the British empire: forbearing, on each occasion, at the expense either of such general good, or of his duty in any shape, either to accept, or to seek to obtain, or preserve, in any shape whatsoever, for himself, or for any person or persons particularly connected with him, any advantage whatsoever, from whatsoever hands obtainable; and in particular from those hands, in which, by the very frame of the constitution, the greatest quantity of temptation is necessarily and unavoidably lodged, viz. those of the King, and the other members of the executive branch of the government, the King's Ministers.'

87 Few better examples of this will be found than his letter to Viscount Sidmouth (17 September 1812), carrying his mockery of the official mentality of 'Gentlemen', who were so imaginatively constrained as to believe that the creation of more offices was the solution to any administrative problem conceivable, in Bentham, ed. Conway 1988, 279–80: 'Now, my Lord, what is the panacea? Oh, my Lord, considering who the Physicians are, an answer is almost a superfluity – Offices! offices! Yes my Lord: the nests of offices promised, with the expences attached to them, innumerable. To begin with, a few thousands a year in offices. Reformation is it still tardy? a few thousands a year more to quicken it; and so on till the cure is perfected. Yes, my Lord: it is among the maxims of Honourable Gentlemen, that if in an establishment of this sort any thing is amiss, it is for want of offices. It is among their *postulates*, that every man who is paid for doing duty will do it in perfection, provided the reality of patronage, and shew of superintendance, is in the hands of Honourable Gentlemen, whose whole time is demanded for higher duties, and who have neither interest in, nor affection, other than contempt, for this *low* business ... Such is the *purity* of Honourable Gentlemen, such is even their *simplicity – the* species of interest constituted by patronage, coupled or not coupled with irresponsible power, is among the species of sinister interest they have no conception of'. For this letter in the context of the panopticon, see Causer's chapter in this volume.

Bibliography

Primary Sources

Archival sources

UCL Library Special Collections, Bentham Papers.

Legal decisions

Anonymous (1722), 24 Eng. Rep. 646.
Attorney General v Hart and White (1808), ST 30: 1193–1344.
Blankard v Galdy (1693), 90 Eng. Rep., 1089, and 91 Eng. Rep. 357.

Calvin's Case (1608), 7 Co[ke's] Rep[orts], 1a, at *ST* 2: 559–697.
Campbell v Hall (1774), at *ST* 20: 239–354.
Carr v Hood (1808), included within *Tabart v Tipper* (1808), 170 Eng. Rep. 983.
Clark's (or Clarkes) Case (1596), 5 Co[ke's] Rep[orts], 64a, at *Quinta Pars Relationum Edwardi Coke aurati, Regij Attornati Generalis.* London: Company of Stationers, 1605.
Draper v Fullarton (1808–9), *ST* 1063–1130.
Draper v Sullivan (1806–7), *ST* 30: 959–1062.
King v Thomas Picton (1804–12), *ST* 30: 225–959.

Parliamentary Papers

Commons Sessional Papers (1801), vol. vi. 507–89: 'Further Proceedings of the Lords Commissioners of His Majesty's Treasury, &c. respecting the matters stated in The Reports of the Committee of Finance, so far as they relate to The Several Offices concerned in the Receipt and Expenditure of the Public Money', 12 June 1801.
Commons Sessional Papers (1806), vol. vii. 1–905: 'Reports of the Commissioners Appointed by Act 25 Geo. III. Cap. 19. To enquire into the Fees, Gratuities, Perquisites, and Emoluments, which are or have been lately received in the several Public Offices therein mentioned', 11 April and 20 June 1786, 27 December 1787, 10 January, 14 February, 10 March, 20 March, 17 April, 1 May, and 30 June 1788.
Commons Sessional Papers (1806), vol. xiii. 1029–153: 'Accounts and Papers presented to the House of Commons, relating to The Increase and Diminution of Salaries, &c. In the public offices of Great Britain', 18 July 1806.
Commons Sessional Papers (1807), vol. ii. 313–78: 'Report from The Committee on the Public Expenditure, &c. Of the United Kingdom', 22 July 1807.
Commons Sessional Papers (1807), vol. ii. 423–34: 'Third Report from The Committee on the Public Expenditure &c. Offices, Places, Sinecures, & Pensions', 10 August 1807.
Commons Sessional Papers (1808), vol. iii. 257–400: 'Third Report from the Committee on the Public Expenditure, &c. Of the United Kingdom. Pensions, Sinecures, Reversions, &c.', 29 June 1808.
Commons Sessional Papers (1809), vol. iii. 61–90: 'Supplementary Report to the Third Report from the Committee on The Public Expenditure, &c. of the United Kingdom. Pensions, sinecures, reversions, &c.', 31 May 1809.
Commons Sessional Papers (1810), vol. ii. 381–506: 'Fifth Report (Second Part) from the Committee on the Public Expenditure, &c. of The United Kingdom. Audit of Public Accounts', 20 June 1810.
Commons Sessional Papers (1810), vol. ii. 591–646: 'The First Report from the Select Committee Appointed to consider, – What Offices in the United Kingdom, and in the Foreign Dominions of His Majesty, come within the Purview of the 2d, 3d, and 4th Resolutions of the House, on the Third Report from the Committee on the Public Expenditure of The United Kingdom', 20 June 1810.
Commons Sessional Papers (1810–11), vl. iii. 961–99: 'Second Report from the Select Committee on Sinecure Offices', 18 June 1811.
House of Commons Sessional Papers of the Eighteenth Century, ed. S. Lambert, 145 vols. Wilmington, DE: Scholarly Resources Inc., 1975.

Printed sources

Bentham, J. 'A View of the Hard-Labour Bill'. London: T. Payne and Son, T. Cadell and P. Elmsley, and E. Brooke, 1778.
Bentham, J. *Plan of Parliamentary Reform, in the Form of a Catechism* (1817). London: T. J. Wooler, 1818.
Bentham, J. *The Elements of the Art of Packing, as Applied to Special Juries, Particularly in Cases of Libel Law.* London: Effingham Wilson, 1821.
Bentham, J. *The Correspondence of Jeremy Bentham, Volume 8: January 1809 to December 1816*, ed. S. Conway. Oxford: Clarendon Press, 1988.
Bentham, J. *Securities against Misrule and Other Constitution Writings for Tripoli and Greece*, ed. P. Schofield. Oxford: Clarendon Press, 1990.

Bentham, J. *Official Aptitude Maximized; Expense Minimized* (1810–30), ed. P. Schofield. Oxford: Clarendon Press, 1993.

Bentham, J. *The Correspondence of Jeremy Bentham, Volume 12: July 1824 to June 1828*, ed. L. O'Sullivan and C. Fuller. Oxford: Clarendon Press, 2006.

Bentham, J. 'Place and Time' (1782). In *Jeremy Bentham: Selected Writings*, ed. P. Schofield and S. Engelmann, 152–219. New Haven: Yale University Press, 2011.

Bentham, J. *The Correspondence of Jeremy Bentham, Volume 4: October 1788 to December 1793*, ed. A.T. Milne. London: UCL Press, 2017.

Bentham, J. *Panopticon versus New South Wales and other writings on Australia*, ed. T. Causer and P. Schofield. London: UCL Press, 2022.

Chalmers, G. ed. *Opinions of Eminent Lawyers on Various Points of English Jurisprudence*. Burlington: G. Goodrich and Co., 1858.

Cobbett's Complete Collection of State Trials (*ST*), 34 vols. London: various, 1809–28.

Cobbett's Parliamentary History (*PH*), 32 vols. London: Hansard, 1806–20.

Coleridge, S.T. 'Dejection: An Ode', *Morning Post*, 4 October 1802.

Lind, J. *Remarks on the Principal Acts of the Thirteenth Parliament of Great Britain*. London: T. Payne, 1775.

Lind, J. *An Answer to the Declaration of the American Congress*. London: T. Cadell, J. Walter, and T. Sewell, 1776.

Percy, T. *Reliques of Ancient English Poetry*, 3 vols. London: J. Dodsley, 1765.

Secondary Sources

Bayly, C.A. *Imperial Meridian: The British Empire and the World, 1780–1830*. London: Longman, 1989.

Benton, L. and Ford, L. 'Island Despotism: Trinidad, the British Imperial Constitution and Global Legal Order', *Journal of Imperial and Commonwealth History* 46: 1 (2018): 21–46.

Cavanagh, E. 'Charters in the Longue Durée: The Mobility and Applicability of Donative Documents in Europe and America from Edward I to Chief Justice John Marshall', *Comparative Legal History* 5: 2 (2017): 262–95.

Cavanagh, E. 'The Imperial Constitution of the Law Officers of the Crown: Legal Thought on War and Colonial Government, 1719–1774', *Journal of Imperial and Commonwealth History* 47: 4 (2019a): 619–51.

Cavanagh, E. 'Infidels in English Legal Thought: Conquest, Commerce and Slavery in the Common Law from Coke to Mansfield, 1603–1793', *Modern Intellectual History* 16: 2 (2019b): 375–409.

Cavanagh, E., ed. *Empire and Legal Thought: Ideas and Institutions from Antiquity to Modernity*. Leiden: Brill, 2020.

Cavanagh, E. 'Monarchy'. In *The Cambridge Constitutional History of the United Kingdom*, eds. P. Cane and H. Kumarasingham. Cambridge: Cambridge University Press, 2022.

Chester, N. *The English Administrative System, 1780–1870*. Oxford: Clarendon Press, 1981.

Condren, C. *Argument and Authority in Early Modern England: The Presupposition of Oaths and Offices*. Cambridge: Cambridge University Press, 2006.

Condren, C. 'Public, Private and the Idea of the "Public Sphere" in Early Modern England', *Intellectual History Review* 19: 1 (2009): 15–28.

Dinwiddy, J.R. 'Bentham's Transition to Political Radicalism, 1809–10', *Journal of the History of Ideas* 36: 4 (1975): 683–700.

Epstein, J. 'Politics of Colonial Sensation: The Trial of Thomas Picton and the Cause of Louisa Calderon', *American Historical Review* 112: 3 (2007): 712–41.

Epstein, J. *Scandal of Colonial Rule: Power and Subversion in the British Atlantic during the Age of Revolution*. Cambridge: Cambridge University Press, 2012.

Gerber, S.D. *A Distinct Judicial Power: The Origins of an Independent Judiciary, 1606–1787*. Oxford: Oxford University Press, 2011.

Girard, P. '"Rearguard or Vanguard?": A New Look at Canada's Constitutional Act of 1791', *Journal of Imperial and Commonwealth History*, forthcoming, https://doi.org/10.1080/03086534.2021.1985215.

Hart, H.L.A. 'Bentham and the United States of America', *Journal of Law and Economics* 19: 3 (1976): 547–67.

Howell, P.A. *The Judicial Committee of the Privy Council, 1833–1876: Its Origins, Structure and Development*. Cambridge: Cambridge University Press, 1979.

Hume, L.J. 'Bentham's Panopticon: An Administrative History, Part I', *[Australian] Historical Studies* 15: 61 (1973): 703–21.

Hume, L.J. 'Bentham's Panopticon: An Administrative History, Part II', *[Australian] Historical Studies* 16: 62 (1974): 36–54.

Hume, L.J. *Bentham and Bureaucracy*. Cambridge: Cambridge University Press, 1981.

Kanalu, N. 'The Pure Reason of Lex Scripta: Jurisprudential Philology and the Domain of Instituted Laws during Early British Colonial Rule in India (1770s–1820s)', in Cavanagh ed. (2020): 462–91.

Lawson, P. *The Imperial Challenge: Quebec and Britain in the Age of American Revolution*. Montreal and Kingston: McGill-Queen's University Press, 1989.

McHugh, P.G. 'Imperial Law: The Legal Historian and the Trials and Tribulations of an Imperial Past'. In *Oxford Handbook of Legal History*, ed. M. Dubber and C. Tomlins, 883–900. Oxford: Oxford University Press, 2018.

McHugh, P.G. 'Prerogative and Office in Pre-Revolutionary New York: Feudal Legalism, Land Patenting, and Sir William Johnson, Indian Superintendent (1756–1774)', in Cavanagh (2020): 425–61.

Parris, H. *Constitutional Bureaucracy: The Development of British Central Administration since the Eighteenth Century*. London: George Allen & Unwin, 1969.

Pitts, J. 'Legislator of the World? A Rereading of Bentham on Colonies', *Political Theory* 31: 2 (2003): 200–34.

Schofield, P. *Utility and Democracy: The Political Thought of Jeremy Bentham*. Oxford: Oxford University Press, 2006.

Siddique, A.K. 'Governance through Documents: The Board of Trade, Its Archive, and the Imperial Constitution of the Eighteenth-Century British Atlantic World', *Journal of British Studies* 59: 2 (2020): 264–90.

Stephen, J.F. *The Story of Nuncomar and the Impeachment of Sir Elijah Impey*, 2 vols. London: Macmillan and Co., 1885.

Ward, J.M. *Colonial Self-Government: The British Experience, 1759–1856*. London: Macmillan, 1976.

7

'The British Constitution Conquered in New South Wales'

Bentham and constitutional reform in early Australia, 1803–24

Anne Brunon-Ernst

On 26 January 1808, Governor William Bligh of New South Wales was arrested and the colony placed under military rule. The Rum Rebellion – as it came to be known – was, and is, Australia's first and only military coup. The starting point of the present chapter is historian Alan Atkinson's contention that Jeremy Bentham's ideas could have been instrumental in bringing about the uprising. Atkinson states: 'Bentham, the great radical philosopher, can be held responsible for the only *coup d'état* in our early history, the Rum Rebellion of 26 January 1808'.[1] Indeed, Bentham's own correspondence teems with hints of the potentially subversive nature of his writings on transportation, such as when his friend and supporter, Charles Bunbury MP, warned him: 'If you can't write down the Colony of Thieves, … don't crush it by Rebellion'.[2] There are thus striking connections to be made between Bentham's premonitory warnings and the turn of events in the colony. Atkinson delves in detail into the relationships between Bentham and the rebel leaders and makes a very convincing argument.[3]

Most of the existing literature deals with the causes of the Rebellion,[4] trying to answer the question asked in 1810 by one the officers on the bench at the court martial of Colonel George Johnston, who was commander of the New South Wales Corps, rebel leader and interim governor: 'It would be a satisfaction to know what was the cause of so great a revolution'.[5] This is not, however, the purpose of the present study. Instead, it considers Bentham's influence on the constitutional development of Australia before and beyond the 1808 coup. It does not disclaim the importance of the coup, but contends that Bentham's arguments in favour of applying the English Constitution to Australia, thus requiring a more representative government, were influential in bringing about constitutional change in the colony far beyond the Rum Rebellion, and at least up to the passage of the New South Wales Act of 1823.[6] In making this contention, it implies that Atkinson did not go far enough in identifying the use made of Bentham's arguments in the settlers' calls for more democratic institutions. It seeks to prove that Bentham's early assessment of the constitutional quicksand on which the colony was built informed the way in which subsequent claims for greater representative government were put forward until at least 1824. In support of this contention, the chapter examines the 1812 Report of the Select Committee on Transportation, on which sat some members close to Bentham, including Samuel Romilly who, a decade earlier, had provided legal advice to Bentham pertaining to New South Wales. The chapter further studies the questions put to witnesses to show that the questions were framed from the perspective of Bentham's writings on the colony. It also looks at how the points raised in the 1812 Report were channelled in the 1822–3 publication of Commissioner John Bigge's Reports on the state of New South Wales and Van Diemen's Land,[7] which paved the way for the first colonial advisory council in 1824.[8]

Bentham's influence on the making of early Australia extends beyond the coup to embrace a wider and more sustained platform to establish representative institutions in the colony.[9] In support of this contention, the first part of this chapter presents the constitutional framework of early Australian history, while the second studies the circulation of Bentham's ideas in the colony, thus setting Atkinson's study in the wider context of different players involved in issues of transportation. More importantly, the third part looks at the report of the Select Committee on Transportation of 1812, before finally turning to its influence on the constitutional challenge posed by the subsequent Bigge Reports, and on the constitutional changes in the colony during the 1820s. The present chapter seeks to establish that Bentham's arguments played a prominent role in the constitutional making of early Australia.

The early Australian constitutional conundrum

This first part deals with the constitutional conundrum of the making of early Australia. Indeed, the Australian colonies were founded on uncertain legal grounds. It is a telling example that 22 years after settlement in 1788, one of the members of the Johnston Court Martial asked witness John Macarthur, the mastermind of the Rebellion, 'by what law is the colony governed; is it by military or civil law?'[10] Atkinson, in another seminal paper, explains in great detail the legal differences between Governor Phillip's two commissions, and between other examples of similar systems of government existing across the British Empire.[11] Indeed, while Governor Phillip's first commission established a military government,[12] the categories were not as clear cut in his second commission.[13] There, the powers of the governor were wide-ranging, but the existence of criminal[14] and civil[15] courts points to the mixed nature of government in New South Wales.

The equivocal constitutional nature of the new colony was part of wider concerns about the absolute powers granted to the governors of New South Wales, and Bentham was not the first writer to point out that they held excessively broad powers. Watkin Tench, who was present when Phillip's Commission was read at Port Jackson on 7 February 1788, commented on the shortcomings of governance in the new colony.[16] He was surprised at the Governor's 'plenitude of power',[17] noting the absence of any form of assembly as '[no] mention is made of a council to be appointed, so that [the Governor] is left to act entirely from his own judgment'.[18] In other words, calls for some balance and limitations to the governor's executive, legislative and judicial powers were not exclusive to Bentham. Indeed, Englishmen in Australia were disappointed to be deprived of their English rights, and rather expected, at the very least, to be granted similar rights as those of their fellow Englishmen in other British colonies. In order to trace as accurately as possible Bentham's input in the constitutional debate at home and in the colony, the specificities of Bentham's legal arguments need to be identified.

On account of the known, though limited, circulation of Bentham's 'A Plea for the Constitution' among circles in Australia and in Britain, this chapter focuses on this document exclusively. In it, Bentham's main claim is that the Governor had some power to make laws and regulations, but only over certain groups of the colonial population.[19] Thanks to a careful study of judicial precedents[20] and legal provisions (Habeas Corpus,[21] Magna Carta,[22] Bill of Rights[23] and the Transportation Acts[24]),

Bentham demonstrates how the power of the Governor could be legally enforced only on certain categories of inhabitants (convicts, officers and soldiers in the navy and the army, crews of British and foreign vessels) but not on others (civil servants, former convicts, free settlers, and relatives of convicts and former convicts).[25] The crux of his argument is that English rights and liberties apply to all Englishmen irrespective of where they are located,[26] and thus Bentham's first contention flows from this statement: the principle that the concurrence of the three estates (King in Parliament with the Lords Temporal and Ecclesiastical, and the Commons) is mandatory for valid legislation.[27] Any power exercised by the governor on the second category of inhabitants was therefore illegal in the absence of an assembly or of the individual's consent:[28]

> The successive governors of New South Wales have for these fourteen years past been exercising legislative power without any authority from Parliament: and either without any authority at all from anybody, or at most without any authority but from the King.[29]

Bentham makes repeated claims that either an Act of Parliament or a legislative assembly was required in New South Wales to remedy these violations[30], before taking his arguments a step further.

From a study of the regulations passed in the colony up to 1797,[31] Bentham derives a second important contention relative to judicial operations in New South Wales: he shows that the governor, on account of the specific circumstances in the colony,[32] had to establish new rules to regulate matters which were not considered as offences in English law, thus he wonders how such offences can be legally heard, as the courts in the colony were explicitly set up to try English offences.[33] In doing so, he undercuts the legitimacy of both the legislative power of the governor, as well as of the judicial institutions in Botany Bay.

Demands for the institution of jury trials, and challenges to the authority of the courts to hear cases, occurred regularly in early Australian colonial history.[34] They originate in the English consciousness of individual rights, and therefore cannot be traced alone to 'A Plea for the Constitution'. However, Bentham's specific arguments about the legal power of the courts and applicable law are reported as being relied upon by Macarthur in 1805 (as communicated by Governor Philip King in 1806 and the West India merchant Thomas William

Plummer in 1809), by Romilly in the report of the Select Committee on Transportation of 1812, and subsequently in providing the foundation for Henry Grey Bennet's avowedly Benthamite challenge to the British government's penal policy in Parliament in 1819. Thus, most of the discussion which follows focuses on questions about the legality of acts of the governor, as it is this legal challenge that distinguishes Bentham's analysis from that of other commentators.

This first section has described the uncertain legal grounds for the government of the colony, and their assessment by Bentham in 'A Plea for the Constitution' more specifically. The point is now to establish to what extent Bentham's argument that New South Wales had been founded illegally, central to the text, was circulated and embraced in the colony. As explained below, Bentham's influence was not direct, but mediated by Romilly. This influence is to be seen most clearly at two different periods: first as a trigger to the 1808 coup; and second as a driving force for constitutional change in the report of the Select Committee on Transportation of 1812. The next section will deal with the former, and the section after that with the latter.

The circulation of Bentham's ideas in New South Wales, 1803–10

While Atkinson does trace convincingly the possible circulation of ideas from Bentham to Macarthur,[35] the role played by Romilly is overlooked in his study.[36] There is evidence in Bentham's correspondence that Bentham met former Judge-Advocate of New South Wales, David Collins, three times in London,[37] that they discussed transportation and the panopticon,[38] and that he gave Collins a copy of 'A Plea for the Constitution'.[39] Bentham's argument that actions of the governor were illegal then materializes unexpectedly in the colony in an 1806 memorandum of a conversation Governor King had with Macarthur in 1805:

> [Macarthur] introduced the subject of some counsel's opinion of the illegality of all local Regulations, and that no Order or Regulation given by a Governor could be binding or legal unless sanctioned by an Act of Parliament.[40]

In this quotation, we can discern Bentham's main argument in regard to the illegality of the governor's legislative acts. Atkinson explained this striking coincidence by the acquaintance of Collins and Macarthur, as well as the fact that they were in London at the same time[41] and could quite possibly have met prior to Collins's departure to Van Diemen's Land in 1803. Demands for a council or assembly – thus pointing to the unsatisfactory constitutional arrangements which prevailed up to the time of Governor Lachlan Macquarie, as the Bigge Reports show – also appears in Thomas William Plummer's presentation of Macarthur's claims to Macquarie in 1809.[42] Atkinson therefore rests his hypothesis of Bentham's role in the Rum Rebellion on one indirect reference from 1805, and one indirect challenge to the authority of the governor in 1809. This is very thin evidence. Atkinson explains why these arguments could not be found elsewhere, neither in Johnston's declaration after the coup (27 January 1808),[43] nor in his letter justifying the coup to the Secretary of State Viscount Castlereagh (10 April 1808),[44] nor again as a line of defence at the court martial.[45] Indeed, the illegality argument could be used against the interests of the military, free settlers and expirees who had become rich under the authority of the governor and the courts. In other words, disclaiming the acts of the governor as *ultra vires* could endanger the validity of any title to assets on Australian soil.[46]

The claim that governors had illegally made ordinances seems to have been made for the first time in Australia by Macarthur, according to Governor King. This idea is at the heart of Bentham's line of reasoning in 'A Plea for the Constitution' as seen above. However, ideas do not circulate in an unadulterated manner. There is no evidence that Macarthur had read Bentham's pamphlet himself, but he might have been informed by Collins, who presumably had read the copy of the pamphlet given to him by Bentham, of the legal limbo in which the colony operated. Macarthur then repeated the arguments, stating that the Governor's rules were only illegal for certain categories of inhabitants (to which Macarthur then incidentally belonged).

Atkinson's argument that Macarthur was aware of Bentham's opinion is plausible, with the caveat that Bentham's ideas arrived and circulated in New South Wales having been vetted by Romilly. The use of the term 'counsel' in the correspondence and in the memorandum points towards this interpretation. Indeed, Governor King refers repeatedly to a 'counsel' Macarthur would have referred to, without giving his name:

As Mr Macarthur was not possessed of that authority, or chose to mention the name of the *counsel* who gave the opinion, I could only observe that this was the first time I ever heard of such an objection, as all the local Regulations were regularly sent the Minister for the colonies.[47]

Bentham's own correspondence also extensively refers to a 'counsel' in relation to 'A Plea for the Constitution', and this 'counsel' is Romilly.[48]

There is evidence that Bentham sent 'A Plea for the Constitution' to Romilly to have his legal opinion.[49] Romilly took some time to answer, and although the advice is short, it is said by Bentham to have been carefully discussed, argued and pondered.[50] 'What you state respecting Botany Bay', writes Romilly, 'has very much astonished me. It has the more astonished me because I take the law upon the subject to be exactly as you have stated it'.[51] Moreover, in his correspondence with others[52] on topics related to this opinion Bentham referred to Romilly as a 'Counsel of the first eminence'.[53] It is quite probable that Bentham used this authoritative argument in the same terms to Collins, in order to lend more credence to the ideas he set out in 'A Plea for the Constitution' – Romilly was a barrister and would become Solicitor General and Member of Parliament later in 1806. For the same reasons, if Collins then shared the idea with Macarthur, the former might have pointed out that the ideas had been vetted by the authority of established counsel in London,[54] rather than having originated with some obscure and quaint penal reformer.

My argument here rests on similar mentions of a 'counsel' in Bentham's reference to Romilly in his correspondence, and in Macarthur's reference to an authority in his conversation with Governor King. It is a tenuous argument, but its significance goes beyond merely accurately pinning down Macarthur's source of information. What is at stake here is the pivotal place of Romilly in the circulation of Bentham's ideas in the colony, which will be further developed in the next section.

This second section has explained Atkinson's argument in regard to the circulation of Bentham's views in the colony and made an additional assumption on the role Romilly played in lending credential to Bentham's ideas to a limited and select audience. As will be seen in the next section, Romilly had also a decisive role in publicizing Bentham's ideas to a wider audience in London as well as in the colony.[55]

Informing the debate for constitutional change: the 1812 Report of the Select Committee on Transportation

This section looks into the heart of the argument of the present research: the critical importance of the Report of the Select Committee on Transportation of 1812. In trying to connect the dots between Bentham, Collins, Macarthur, the Rum Rebellion and the 1812 Report, explicit references to Bentham were sought for fruitlessly. The reason lies most certainly in the way ideas circulate. Indeed, Macarthur himself might not have even been able to trace the origins of the ideas he communicated to Governor King, other than in stating that it was an authoritative legal opinion. However, the key to the present research was the realization that, as in the 1810 court martial of Colonel Johnston,[56] one could not expect truth from the witnesses but rather a *line of argument* to which the parties adhered. In the same way, it was not in the *answers* of the expert witnesses summoned before the Select Committee that Bentham's influence would be shown, but in the *questions* asked by the members of the Committee.

The members of the Select Committee were Whigs, radicals or people very much aware of the penal theories at the time, and among their number were at least two reformers: Romilly and George Eden – son of William Eden, author of the *Principles of Penal Law* and architect of what eventually would become the Penitentiary Act of 1779. Romilly's influence on the Committee extended beyond his mere membership. Indeed, the Committee itself had been set up on account of comments made by Romilly in the House of Commons. On 5 June 1810, Romilly made a very critical speech about the colony:

> An experiment more unpromising or bolder than that of founding a Colony, which was to consist altogether of thieves and convicts, of the very refuse of society, of men habituated to idleness, and having no motive for wishing success to the Colony they were founding, never was tried in any former age or by any other nation ... Thieves and their Keepers, Prisoners and their Jailors, these were to be the whole population.[57]

In particular, he stressed the uncertain hardships of transportation, referring in particular to the unknown hardships of the voyage, and that no one in Britain could know with any certainty the sort of treatment a convict would undergo in New South Wales. In the debate that followed, a suggestion was made that the issue be referred to a committee.

The second section had provided evidence that Romilly had carefully read Bentham's 'A Plea for the Constitution', discussed its legal points with him, might have revised it for him and given his opinion, which – albeit short – was understood to be that of a legal counsel to be used and advertised as such. The chapter now intends to show that Romilly's writings were informed by Bentham's arguments, before turning to the events that led to the setting up of the Committee and the questions raised there.

In Romilly's speeches in Parliament, as well as in his writings,[58] the influence of Bentham's ideas is very obvious. For instance, Table 7.1 provides a comparative view of arguments used by Bentham in 'A Plea for the Constitution' and by Romilly in his speeches.

As can be inferred from Table 7.1, Romilly shared Bentham's views about the evils of transportation as a criminal punishment. It is, however, important to point out that the key arguments contained in Bentham's 'A Plea for the Constitution' were not raised by Romilly in his speeches in Parliament. As in the case of Johnston's court martial, Romilly must have concluded that these arguments would be antagonizing and thus counterproductive in the context of seeking to amend and reform trans-portation legislation, and could also be potentially subversive to public order in the colony. This is to be seen two years later when Romilly became a leading member of the Select Committee on Transportation, which he was instrumental in establishing, as his questions to witnesses do not directly challenge the legitimacy of gubernatorial power in the colony. However, the present study aims to prove that the nullity of legis-lation in New South Wales, on grounds of the absence of an assembly to give consent, as well as the nullity of the governors' ordinances for want of a court to try offences against them, both of which are specifically Benthamite arguments, inform the Committee's line of questioning.

It is important to understand that Romilly's attacks upon the penal colony in New South Wales were made in the broader context of debates relating to the reform of criminal law,[59] and of new and competing penal options such as penitentiary houses including revived interest in the panopticon scheme.[60] At the time when these issues were being debated in Parliament, Bentham's panopticon was also being scrutinized by a Select Committee on Penitentiaries.[61] There is ample evidence from the questioning that Romilly himself set the *scope* of inquiry, as he stated: 'the latter subject … had originated with himself'.[62] The similarities between the questions raised by the members and

Table 7.1: Comparative table of Bentham's and Romilly's criticism of transportation to New South Wales.

Argument	Bentham, 1802–3	Romilly, 1810[1]
Principles of punishment	X	X
Comparison with the American transportation experience	X	X
Nullity of legislation in NSW	X	
Nullity of Governor's ordinances for want of a court to try offences against them	X	
Transportation being a state of perpetual slavery or bondage	X	X
Disregard for length of convict's conviction	X	X
No selection of convicts with required skills	X	X
No consistent system of pardon or promotion, i.e. convicts with most-needed skills or with money will be granted early pardon	X	X
No provision for expirees' return	X	X
Hardships of transportation	X	X
Expense of the colony[2]	X	X
Population of NSW consisting of prisoners and their keepers, which does not bode well for achieving the end of reformation, as well as the success of the colony[3]	X	X

Notes to Table 7.1:
1   'Penitentiary Houses, 9 May 1810', in Romilly 1820, vol. i. 247–54 and Romilly, 'Penitentiary Houses, 5 June 1810', ibid., 262–84.
2   This contention is also made by Smith 1802.
3   Smith 1802.

Bentham's arguments points to the fact that Romilly also set the *agenda* of the Committee.

The Committee itself sat for 13 days over a period of four months and heard 14 witnesses. Unfortunately, most of these witnesses gave evidence unrelated to the inquiry at hand.[63] The Committee also heard from four former convicts, and three former Governors (Hunter and Bligh were physically present, while Macquarie's reports were considered), and two witnesses who spoke in favour of Governor Bligh, as well as Captain Johnston, then promoted to the rank of Lieutenant-Colonel, who led the Rum Rebellion. The present study relies mainly on questions put to Governors Hunter and Bligh as can be seen in Table 7.2 below.

Table 7.2: Types of questions asked of former governors of New South Wales by the Select Committee on Transportation of 1812.

Questions of members of the Committee	Implication	Bentham in 'Plea' and 'Letters to Lord Pelham'
Assessing the number of classes of inhabitants in the colony.[1]	That the colony is composed of different categories of persons, requiring differentiated treatment.	• Ten classes of colonial inhabitant.[2] • Legality of regulations depends upon which class the regulation was addressed to.[3]
Determining whether there was an official or social differential treatment of people according to the class they belonged to.[4]	• Are the aims of reformation met? • Is government adapted to the class of person concerned?	Mode of government in NSW defeats the purpose of reformation.[5]
Whether the colonial government kept track of convict's convictions, and time left to serve until expiration of sentence.[6]	Former convicts had their sentence extended without any due process or reason, in contravention of English laws.	On account of lack of evidence of commencement and duration of sentence, Englishmen were kept in confinement and bondage.[7]
Whether a legislative assembly should be created.[8]	Absolute law-making power of the governor was not satisfactory.	Legislative power of governor was illegal.[9]
In regard to the extent of the judicial power of the governor.[10]	That the governor acted *ultra-vires* in punishing or pardoning.	The governor inconsistently and capriciously awarded pardons and privileges.[11]
Whether punishment was meted out by a magistrate.[12]	That the power of the governor was absolute, as punishment was ordered by the governor rather than by a magistrate.	Punishment can be applied without being ordered in court.[13]
In regard to the ease with which ex-convicts could return to England at the end of their sentence.[14]	That convicts were banished for life, whatever their court-awarded sentence of transportation.	Convicts were forcibly detained in the colony.[15]

In regard to the composition, as well as the punishment and law applied in criminal courts.[16]	That the New South Wales criminal courts applied non-English law.	That the New South Wales courts functioned differently from England's,[17] and tried offences not considered as such in England.[18]
In regard to the composition of the civil court, and appeals heard by it.[19]	That Englishmen were deprived of access to an impartial civil court.	That a court, known as a 'civil court', had been instituted without authority from Parliament.[20] 'For the trying of offences created by the Governor alone?—If so, here then we have the very quintessence of despotism'.[21]

Notes to Table 7.2

1   *Commons Sessional Papers* (1812), vol. ii, 591–2, 608.
2   'A Plea for the Constitution' in Bentham, ed. Causer and Schofield 2022, 329–30.
3   'A Plea for the Constitution' in Bentham, ed. Causer and Schofield 2022, 330–1, 360–1.
4   *Commons Sessional Papers* (1812), vol. ii, 594, 601–2, 620.
5   '[S]tate of radical and incurable repugnancy to every one of the points that were or ought to have been the *objects* of such an establishment: to every one of the *ends* of penal justice; *example* — *reformation* — *incapacitation* for fresh offences — compensation for injury by past offences — and *economy*': see Bentham to Charles Abbot, 3 September 1802, in Bentham, ed. Dinwiddy 1988, 102–15, at 104.
6   *Commons Sessional Papers* (1812), vol. ii, 595–6, 605.
7   'A Plea for the Constitution' in Bentham, ed. Causer and Schofield 2022, 366–7. See also Bentham to Etienne Dumont, 29 August 1802, in Bentham, ed. Dinwiddy 1988, 93–101.
8   *Commons Sessional Papers* (1812), vol. ii, 616, 621.
9   'A Plea for the Constitution' in Bentham, ed. Causer and Schofield 2022, 341–6, 351–2, 353, 386, 389. See also Bentham to Abbot, 3 September 1802, in Bentham, ed. Dinwiddy 1988, 103–4 and Bentham to Dumont, 29 August 1802, ibid., 93–101.
10 Commons Sessional Papers (1812), vol. ii, 606–7, 620. See in particular 616–17 on the subject of pardons.
11 'A Plea for the Constitution' in Bentham, ed. Causer and Schofield 2022, 375.
12 *Commons Sessional Papers* (1812), vol. ii, 592–3, 602, 604–6, 620–1.
13 'A Plea for the Constitution' in Bentham, ed. Causer and Schofield 2022, 331–2.
14 *Commons Sessional Papers* (1812), vol. ii, 617–18, 621.
15 'A Plea for the Constitution' in Bentham, ed. Causer and Schofield 2022, 366–72. See also Bentham to Abbot, 3 September 1802, in Bentham, ed. Dinwiddy 1988, 103–4 and Bentham to Dumont, 29 August 1802, ibid., 93–101.
16 'Do the same laws of evidence and the same criminal law, prevail in the colony as prevail in England? – Just the same; I always did and should guide myself by the laws of this country as near as possible': see *Commons Sessional Papers* (1812), vol. ii, 613, 41. See also 614–15 and 616.
17 'A Plea for the Constitution' in Bentham, ed. Causer and Schofield 2022, 327.
18 'A Plea for the Constitution' in Bentham, ed. Causer and Schofield 2022, 347.
19 *Commons Sessional Papers* (1812), vol. ii, 597, 613–14, 620.
20 'A Plea for the Constitution' in Bentham, ed. Causer and Schofield 2022, 385.
21 'A Plea for the Constitution' in Bentham, ed. Causer and Schofield 2022, 349.

The report made a number of recommendations. The first related to the control of alcohol in the colony, an item which had injured the health and the social stability of New South Wales,[64] and the second asked for a change in the court system:

> The permission of distillation within the Colony, and the reform of the Courts of Justice, are two measures which Your Committee, above all others, recommend as most necessary to stimulate agricultural industry, and to give the inhabitants that confidence and legal security which can alone render them contented with the Government under which they are placed.[65]

The report also hinted that an assembly would be an effective means to control the Governor's

> ... most enlarged powers, uncontrolled by any Council ... The manner in which these extensive powers have been used, has not always been such as to give satisfaction to the Colony; nor can it be expected that where so much authority and responsibility are thrown into the hands of one man, that his will however just, and his administration however wise, will not at times create opposition and discontent amongst men unused, in their own country, to see so great a monopoly of power.[66]

These two last reforms had been proposed by Bentham, as well as other writers, as noted above. However, the questions asked to the witnesses, especially to former Governors Hunter and Bligh, allow a line of inquiry similar to the critical framework set by Bentham in 'A Plea for the Constitution'. Table 7.2 presents my summary of these questions and implications that can be drawn from them, with a comparison of Bentham's arguments in 'A Plea for the Constitution', as described in two letters, one to Etienne Dumont and the other to Charles Bunbury, as he might have discussed his ideas with Romilly in the same terms.

The issues covered in the Committee's report have a wider scope than the limited constitutional points raised in 'A Plea for the Constitution', as listed above. Indeed, the Report deals with geography, economy (currency and trade), the cost of the colony, land grants, education, morals (including marriage, prostitution and religion), and the conditions of convicts during transportation and detention.[67] However, one cannot fail to note the congruence of ideas raised in both documents, especially as the report contains the first hint regarding official condemnation of unsatisfactory constitutional arrangements in New South Wales.

The influence of the 1812 Report on constitutional reform up to 1824

The importance of the report of the Select Committee of 1812 is often underrated. While the recommendations made in the report were not followed by any immediate change of law,[68] its impact must be assessed by the long-term effects it produced. It clearly raised awareness about the abuse of power in the colony and about the shortcomings of the convict system, to the extent that in 1815 the transportation laws were renewed for only a year, in the face of the growing opposition to the system.[69] In the long term, it also contributed to the abolition of transportation to New South Wales. Closer to the issue at hand, its critical stand on the constitutional organization of New South Wales emboldened demands for responsible institutions in the colony, as can be seen in petitions presented to Parliament, such as the Vale-Moore petition of 1817 against the laws of New South Wales, the unjust and oppressive power of the governor, and the absence of jury trials.[70] In addition, such demands raised interest in the conditions of convicts and settlers in New South Wales in reformist circles in London, thus leading to further official investigations, such as the Bigge Commission of Inquiry in 1819–21.

Assumptions about the proper governance of a colony were implicit in the questions raised by the Select Committee. Although not reported in the *Sydney Gazette,* there is no doubt that the report was read, circulated and commented on officially and unofficially by the Colony's influential elite.[71] Macarthur was in London at the time (although not asked to testify), while Johnston was called as a witness and later returned to live on his property in Australia, and, in seeking to understand how secure their status and possessions would be in New South Wales, they must have regarded the findings as of the highest interest. Macarthur would also be one of the five appointed members of the Legislative Council of New South Wales, which was established in 1824. The recommendation made in the report that such a council be established was channelled through books, too, such as Wentworth's influential *A Statistical, Historical and Political Description* of 1819.[72] The establishment of the Legislative Council was but one of the constitutional changes made by the New South Wales

Act of 1823,[73] which gave birth to more democratic institutions on Australian soil.

While the report of 1812 cannot have failed to attract long-lasting interest in the colony, in London it became part of the wider debate on the future of transportation. In 1817, the Secretary of State for the Colonies, Henry Bathurst, set the ball rolling again on the reform of transportation, when he asked for an inquiry to determine whether the settlement should be reorganized to fulfil its purpose of deterrence and reformation, or if transportation should be abandoned.[74] Rather than trying to assess the direct influence of the 1812 Report, it is more relevant to view it as a stepping stone on the long road to responsible government, contributing to the dissemination of Bentham's ideas on the illegality of the power of the governor, and on the questionable jurisdiction of courts over offences not known to English law. Another such stepping-stone was the much-publicized Bigge Reports, published a decade after the 1812 Select Committee,[75] which cover some of the constitutional issues raised in the 1812 report.[76] Moreover, Bigge had read the report of 1812, as it was the only precedent for the inquiry he was commissioned to carry out into New South Wales.[77]

At the time Bigge was commissioned to conduct his inquiry in New South Wales and Van Diemen's Land, the innuendoes about constitutional mismanagement in the Australian colonies, hinted at in 1812, had been explicitly voiced in Parliament, following the Vale-Moore petition mentioned above, and a petition of 1819 against the infliction of punishment for offences unknown to English law.[78] Henry Grey Bennet, for instance, pointed to the absence of the sanction of an Act of Parliament for several powers which had been exercised by the governor, and suggested the establishment of a council to remedy these shortcomings.[79] While any decision about the constitutional future of the colony, especially in relation to juries and a council, needed to be delayed till Bigge's report be completed, certain quarters of British political life were becoming more receptive to the complaints of colonists in Australia in regard to the illegal power of the governor.[80] Those claims had originated with Bentham but had been channeled by Romilly in the Select Committee of 1812, before finding their way into mainstream political debate in the form of Bennet's motions in Parliament[81] and Bigge's highly influential reports.

Policy change in the colony must be understood as a series of concurrent demands raised over several decades, leading ultimately to new constitutional arrangements in New South Wales. The report of the Select Committee of 1812 was the first official statement made by a body of MPs appointed by the home legislature, which came, after a close investigation, to the conclusion that reforms were needed in areas of colonial government and administration of justice. These demands had been made repeatedly by governors to secretaries of state,[82] and continued to be made by high-ranking civil servants in the colony,[83] by the subsequent Bigge Reports,[84] by court cases,[85] and by petitions.[86] These demands were partly acceded to in the New South Wales Act of 1823, with the establishment of Courts of Appeal, and a procedure to assess the validity of rules and regulations passed in Australia.

A whole range of events made reform necessary. The 1808 Rum Rebellion acted as an opportunity for advocating change. Indeed, whether or not the rebellion originated in the constitutional issues raised by Bentham, as Atkinson argues, it did create expectations among settlers and expirees for constitutional reform, which were not fulfilled with the arrival of Governor Macquarie, following the deposition of Governor Bligh.[87] In 1819, in the first edition of his influential *Statistical, Historical and Political Description*, Wentworth voiced these concerns: 'The colony of New South Wales, is the only one of our possessions exclusively inhabited by Englishmen, in which there is not at least the shadow of a free government, as it possesses neither a council, a house of assembly, nor even the privilege of trial by jury'.[88] Both demands – for representative institutions and for trial by jury – were not unique to Bentham, but awareness of the illegality of the constitutional framework of the colony might have given increased weight to the calls for a representative body which would make legislation valid.

The long-awaited reforms of the New South Wales Act of 1823 were not unanimously approved of as they were considered not radical enough to solve the constitutional issues that had plagued the colony since its foundation. Indeed, while the constitution of a legislative council was hailed by the colonial elite as a long-awaited vindication of the rights of free, English inhabitants of the colony, it was not deemed effective enough, as it established an appointed council rather than provided for an elected assembly. These criticisms were framed around the illegality argument, which has echoes of 'A Plea for the Constitution', that is:

> By an act passed in the last session of Parliament ... much of the power with which the Governors of this colony and its

dependencies had been theretofore armed; or rather, which they had till then *illegally* exercised, – has been wisely restrained and impliedly reprobated.[89]

Commentators in Australia were disappointed that reform did not go further, with Wentworth noting that 'a Legislative Council has been created by way of substitute for a Legislative Assembly; and a wretched mongrel substitute it is',[90] later referring to it as a 'legislative junta'.[91] Settlers called for a petition of the Crown and Westminster for an elected House of Assembly:

> to concede to them in the fullest extent a privilege, or, to speak more accurately, a right, which they have derived from the valour and wisdom of their ancestors; – a right without which there can be no security of person or property; – no certain inviolability at least of either, consequently no public confidence; – a right in fine which is part of the natural inheritance of Britons, or the descendants of Britons, in whatever quarter of the empire they may reside, and of which … nothing in short but a clear and indubitable incapacity to exercise it, – can justify the suspension.[92]

Such a demand for a deliberative legislature and for a judicial body was not new. Indeed, as early as 1788 Tench had noted its absence and, after the Rum Rebellion, Plummer's memorandum, acting as a mouth-piece for Macarthur's proposals, and presented to the newly appointed Governor Macquarie, had in 1809 also called for an assembly. What is of interest though in 1824 again, is that the calls for more democratic institutions use the arguments of illegality put forward by Bentham in 1802. These arguments were channelled to the colony thanks to Romilly's authoritative opinion, as well as to his careful management of the agenda of the Transportation Committee in 1812.

Conclusion

This chapter has established that Bentham's 1802 discussion in 'A Plea for the Constitution' informed the constitutional debate in, and about, New South Wales, during the following 20 years, up to the creation of the first legislative council in the colony in 1824. If historians were aware of the extent to which Collins and Macarthur were instrumental in spreading Bentham's ideas and his subsequent influence on the Rum

Rebellion, the present chapter further contends that Romilly played a pivotal role in giving actual leverage to Bentham's ideas, on account of Romilly's standing in the legal and political world. Bentham's influence on the creation of more representative institutions was effectively mediated by Romilly's work against transportation in the Commons and at the Select Committee of 1812.

Notes

1   Atkinson 1978, 1.
2   Bunbury to Bentham, 6 June 1803, in Jeremy Bentham, ed. Dinwiddy 1988, 236. See also Bentham's comments in Bentham to Collins, 5 April 1803, ibid., 220–3 and Bentham to Charles Bunbury, 10 June 1803, ibid., 237–8.
3   Atkinson 1978. Atkinson's arguments are taken up by Dunk 2019, in particular ch. 7.
4   Ritchie ed. 1988; Atkinson 1990; Clark 1962; Dando-Collins 2007; Duffy 2003; Ellis 1955; Evatt 1938; Fitzgerald Hearn 1988; Karskens and Waterhouse 2010; McMahon 2006; Spigelman 2008.
5   Ritchie ed. 1988, 90.
6   An Act to provide for the better Administration of Justice in New South Wales … and for the more effectual Government thereof (4 Geo IV. c. 96).
7   Bigge 1822; Bigge 1823a; Bigge 1823b.
8   New South Wales Act of 1823.
9   This is well documented in Brett 2019.
10 Ritchie ed. 1988, 215.
11 Atkinson 2003.
12 Atkinson 2003; 'Governor Phillip's First Commission, 12 October 1786', in Watson ed. 1914–25, vol. i. 1–2.
13 'Governor Phillip's Second Commission, 2 April 1787', in Watson ed. 1914–25, vol. i. 3–8.
14 New South Wales Courts Act of 1787 (27 Geo III c 2).
15 Charter of Justice, 2 April 1787 (Letter of Patent).
16 The Commission was read as per 'Governor Phillip's Instructions, 25 April 1787', in Watson ed. 1914–25, vol. i. 9–16.
17 Tench 1996, 47.
18 Tench 1996, 47.
19 'A Plea for the Constitution' in Bentham, ed. Causer and Schofield 2022, 322.
20 'A Plea for the Constitution' in Bentham, ed. Causer and Schofield 2022, 337.
21 'A Plea for the Constitution' in Bentham, ed. Causer and Schofield 2022, 377–9.
22 'A Plea for the Constitution' in Bentham, ed. Causer and Schofield 2022, 379–81.
23 'A Plea for the Constitution' in Bentham, ed. Causer and Schofield 2022, 381–4.
24 'A Plea for the Constitution' in Bentham, ed. Causer and Schofield 2022, 389–92.
25 'A Plea for the Constitution' in Bentham, ed. Causer and Schofield 2022, 329–32.
26 'A Plea for the Constitution' in Bentham, ed. Causer and Schofield 2022, 338–9.
27 'A Plea for the Constitution' in Bentham, ed. Causer and Schofield 2022, 339–40, 389.
28 'A Plea for the Constitution' in Bentham, ed. Causer and Schofield 2022, 341–6, 351–2, 353, 386, 389.
29 'A Plea for the Constitution' in Bentham, ed. Causer and Schofield 2022, 359.
30 'Legislation, exercised by the Governor alone, without authority from parliament at home, or the concurrence of any assembly, standing in the place of parliament, in New South Wales': 'A Plea for the Constitution' in Bentham, ed. Causer and Schofield 2022, 386.
31 Bentham relies almost exclusively on one source: Collins 1798 and 1802.
32 For famine see 'A Plea for the Constitution' in Bentham, ed. Causer and Schofield 2022, 360–4; for drunkenness see ibid., 364–6; and for detention of former convicts see ibid., 366–72.

33 'A Plea for the Constitution' in Bentham, ed. Causer and Schofield 2022, 347.
34 See notes 79 to 83 below.
35 Atkinson 1978.
36 Atkinson mentions Romilly neither in his seminal paper (Atkinson 1978) nor in his history of Australia (Atkinson [1997] 2016).
37 Bentham to Samuel, 22 February 1803, in Bentham, ed. Dinwiddy 1988, 205.
38 Collins to Bentham, 4 April 1803, in Bentham, ed. Dinwiddy 1988, 219–20.
39 Collins to Bentham, 11 January 1803, in Bentham, ed. Dinwiddy 1988, 188. Collins thanked Bentham for his Pamphlets in Bentham to Collins, 5 April 1803, ibid., 220–3, and mentioned giving Collins another pamphlet, which happens to be referred as 'Plea' in Bentham to Charles Bunbury, 10 June 1803, in ibid. 237–8.
40 'Memorandum by Governor King on the Legality of Government and General Orders, 2 January 1806', in Watson ed. 1914–25, vol. A.i. 43.
41 Macarthur having arrived in London in 1801 and departed in late 1804.
42 T.W. Plummer to Colonel Macquarie, 4 May 1809, Watson ed. 1914–25, vol. vii. 198–210. See Karskens, and Waterhouse 2010, 20 and Atkinson 1978, 6. T.W. Plummer was a merchant, as well as an MP for Yarmouth (Isle of Wight) 1806–7, and spokesman for the anti-abolition interest. His career might thus have contributed to his views on property. For more biographical information, see https://www.historyofparliamentonline.org/volume/1790-1820/member/plummer-thomas-william-1817, and he also appears in the *Legacies of British Slave-ownership* database at https://www.ucl.ac.uk/lbs/person/view/2146645169. I am indebted to Tim Causer for this reference.
43 Johnston 1808.
44 Watson ed. 1914–25, vol. i. 208–40.
45 Ritchie ed. 1988.
46 Atkinson 1978.
47 'Memorandum by Governor King, 2 January 1806', in Watson ed. 1914–25, A.i. 44. Emphasis added. See also other mention of counsel in note 54 below.
48 Bentham signs himself at the end of 'A Plea for the Constitution' as a 'Bencher of Lincoln's Inn', which could also be interpreted as being a 'counsel'. However, considering that Bentham was not well known until after 1802 following the success of Bentham, ed. Dumont 1802, it would be reasonable to state that any reference to 'counsel' would be to a more prominent legal authority at the time, namely Romilly.
49 See Bentham to Bunbury, 9 August 1802, in Bentham, ed. Dinwiddy 1988, 71–3; Bentham to Charles Abbot, 3 September 1802, in Bentham, ed. Dinwiddy 1988, 102–15, at 112.
50 Bentham to Charles Abbot, 3 September 1802, in Bentham, ed. Dinwiddy 1988, 112. See also Bentham to Dumont, 29 August 1802, in Bentham, ed. Dinwiddy 1988, 93–101, where Bentham suggests that Romilly had revised the 'Plea' – though it is not clear to what extent. See also 'Editorial Introduction' in Bentham, ed. Causer and Schofield 2022, lxxxv, in relation to Bentham's revision of the 'Preface' to 'A Plea for the Constitution' in light of Romilly's criticism.
51 Samuel Romilly to Bentham, 28 August 1802, in Bentham, ed. Dinwiddy 1988, 92–3.
52 '[M]y eminently learned friend, to whom … I have applied as Counsel': see Bentham to Charles Abbot, 3 September 1802, in Bentham, ed. Dinwiddy 1988, 102.
53 Bentham to Charles Bunbury, 9 August 1802, in Bentham, ed. Dinwiddy 1988, 72.
54 Medd 1968.
55 The joint intellectual assault of Bentham and Romilly against transportation is implied in Ernest Scott's statement that the transportation committee was appointed as a result of their joint efforts: see Scott ed. 1933 [1989] 108.
56 George Johnston (1764–1823) was a Scottish-born colonial soldier and an Australian landowner. He arrested Governor Bligh in 1808 and assumed the lieutenant-governorship, allegedly to protect the colony against Bligh's tyrannical rule. He was court-martialled in London for his role in the coup and received the relatively mild sentence of being cashiered. He subsequently returned to Sydney as a landowner. See *Australian Dictionary of Biography,* vol. 2, 1967.
57 'Penitentiary Houses, 5 June 1810', in Romilly 1820, vol. i. 262–84, at 269.
58 Romilly 1813.
59 The debate on the modern reform of criminal law in Europe is generally assumed to have begun in the eighteenth century with Beccaria [1764] 1995, followed by Eden 1772 and by

John Howard's thorough inquiries of prisons in Europe (see, for instance, Howard 1777). Alongside Bentham, Romilly was a great advocate of criminal reform (see Romilly 1813) and of the abolition of transportation. These efforts culminated in a series of consolidated Acts of Parliament more than a decade later in the field of criminal law: the Criminal Law Act of 1826 (consolidation of acts related to criminal procedure), the Larceny Act of 1827 (consolidating 92 statutes), the Malicious Injuries to Property Act of 1827 (consolidating 48 statutes), the Offences against the Person Act of 1828 (consolidating 56 statutes), and the Forgery Act of 1830 (consolidating 120 statutes), as well as in the abolition of transportation to New South Wales in 1840 (Hirst 1983, 9–27). See also Davie 2017 and Ignatieff 1978.

60 For further insight into the relationship between the panopticon penitentiary scheme and Bentham's strategic criticism of transportation, see Causer 2019.

61 *Commons Sessional Papers* (1810–11), vol. iii. 569–691.

62 *Parliamentary Debates*, House of Commons (1812), vol. 21, 604.

63 Two witnesses were officers then based in England: Captain Matthew Flinders gave evidence on the Australian coastline he had explored, and a Lieutenant Edwards, who had been posted in Van Diemen's Land, and thus did not have first-hand knowledge of the situation in New South Wales.

64 The politics of the sale and consumption of alcohol in New South Wales has been extensively mapped. Revisionist studies which challenged the supposed importance of access to alcohol in instigating what was seen as the misnamed 'Rum Rebellion' include, among others, Hainsworth 1972 and Butlin 1983. However, more recent research by Allen 2012, 2015 and 2019 has highlighted that traditional rural drinking culture, brought to the colony by convicts, intertwined with calls for freedom to distill spirits, were of importance in the 1808 mutiny.

65 *Commons Sessional Papers* (1812), vol. ii, 586.

66 *Commons Sessional Papers* (1812), vol. ii, 580.

67 While 'Letter to Lord Pelham' in Bentham, ed. Causer and Schofield 2022 deals extensively with transportation, discussions of trade, costs, currency, land grants, education, morals and so on can also be found in this work (on the issue of costs, ibid., 82; currency, ibid., 155; and morals, ibid., 160), as well as in 'Second Letter to Lord Pelham' in Bentham, ed. Causer and Schofield 2022, on the subject of trade at 173 and 246–7 n.

68 The recommendations of the report were not implemented as Bathurst refused to act under pretenses of 'differences of opinion': see Bathurst to Macquarie, 23 November 1812 in Watson ed. 1914–25, vol. i. 669–76.

69 Phillips 1909, chapter 10.

70 Ritchie 1969, 130–1.

71 There is ample evidence of the report being in the colony. Indeed, a letter from Bathurst to Macquarie, 23 November 1812 in Watson ed. 1914–25, vii. 669–76, encloses the report and Bathurst's comments upon it, including on the distillation of spirits, reform of the legal administration, establishment of a Supreme Court (criminal side) and Governor's Court (civil side) and how they were to be constituted. But Bathurst did not impose changes to the convict administration at this stage, and instead asked for a report from Macquarie as to what changes he recommended. Macquarie's response to Bathurst's request seems to be in a letter dated 28 June 1813 at ibid., 771–82. I am indebted to Tim Causer for this reference.

72 Wentworth 1819, 231.

73 4 Geo. IV, c. 96.

74 Ritchie 1969, vol 1, 2–4.

75 Bigge 1822; Bigge 1823a; Bigge 1823b.

76 See the Commission of the reports which grants authority 'to examine into all the Laws Regulations and Usages of the Settlements in the said Territory and its Dependencies, and into every other Matter or Thing in any way connected with the Administration of the Civil Government, the Superintendence and Reform of the Convicts, the State of the Judicial, Civil and Ecclesiastical Establishments, Revenues, Trade and internal Resources thereof' in Lord Bathurst, Enclosure No 1: Commission of John Thomas Bigge, in 'Addendum A', 1819, in Bigge 1822.

77 See mentions of the 1812 Report in Bigge 1823a, 36, 64; and Ritchie 1916, vol. 1, 113.

78 Petition by Colonists for Redress of Grievances, 22 March 1819, in Watson ed. 1914–25, vol. x. 57.

79 Ritchie 1969, vol. 1, 155–7. Bennet was MP for Shrewsbury 1811–26.
80 Ritchie 1969, vol. 1, 173. An instance of this are the reviews in the *Edinburgh Review*, of works such as Slater 1819, Bennet 1819, and Wentworth 1819. While the oddities of the fauna and the flora in New South Wales were underlined, the reviews criticized transportation, the power of the governor and the lack of reform in the colony.
81 Ritchie 1969, vol. 1, 137–45.
82 Hunter to the Duke of Portland, 26 August 1796, in Watson ed. 1914–25, vol. i. 602–3; King to Under Secretary King, 21 August 1801, in ibid., iii. 245; Bligh to Right Hon. William Windham, 31 October 1807, in ibid., vi. 151; and Macquarie to the Earl of Liverpool, 18 October 1811, in ibid., vii. 393.
83 See the anonymous 'Letter from Sydney' of 29 October 1791, purporting to be from a settler, in Britton and Bladen eds. 1892–1901, vol. ii. 787; and Judge-Advocate Bent to Under Secretary Cooke, and Bent to the Earl of Liverpool, 19 October 811, in Watson ed. 1914–25, vol. A.i. 49–50, 64.
84 Bigge 1822; Bigge 1823a; Bigge 1823b.
85 The cases of *R. v. Marshall* (1801), *Macarthur v. Campbell Junior* (1807), and *R. v. Macarthur* (1808) respectively raised concerns about the incompetence of the court to hear Marshall's case, of Campbell to sit as a Magistrate, and of Atkins to sit in judgment of Macarthur, and thus point to the shortcomings of the administration of justice. *Bullock v Dodds* (1819), a case decided in an English court, was also certainly very influential in alerting the British government to the need for change in the rules of administration in the colony. It found that, in English law, convicts were deprived of the right to sue. Bullock had been pardoned by Governor Macquarie, and the pardon had been notified, but not granted under Great Seal, thus not signed by Minister and Sovereign. Thus, Bullock had not been restored in his full civil rights and could not sue Dodds in court. The case highlighted the illegality of the acts of the Governor. The problem was resolved with the passing of the New South Wales Act in 1823 which retrospectively pardoned all convicts who had been granted a pardon previously, and established a system of general pardons: see Woods 2002.
86 'Petition by Colonists for Redress of Grievances', 22 March 1819, in Watson ed. 1914–25, vol. x. 57.
87 'Never was there a period since the foundation of the colony, when the impolicy of its present form of government was so strikingly manifest; and never, perhaps, will there be an occasion, when the establishment of a house of assembly, and of trial by jury, would have been hailed with such enthusiastic joy and gratitude: and accordingly the disappointment of the colonists was extreme, when on the arrival of Governor Macquarie, it was found that the same unwise and unconstitutional power, which had been the cause of the late confusion and anarchy was continued in all its pristine vigor; and that he was uncontrolled even by the creation of a council': see Wentworth 1819, 174–5.
88 Wentworth 1819, 164.
89 Wentworth 1824, 322. Emphasis added.
90 Wentworth 1824, 323.
91 Wentworth 1824, 326.
92 Wentworth 1824, 324.

Bibliography

Primary Sources

Acts of Parliament, orders, regulations and legal instruments and documents

Charter of Justice, 2 April 1787 (Letter of Patent).

Commons Sessional Papers of the Nineteenth Century (1810–11), vol. iii, 567–689: 'Report from the Committee on the Laws relating to Penitentiary Houses', 31 May 1811.

Commons Sessional Papers of the Nineteenth Century (1810–11), vol. iii, 691–9: 'Second Report from the Committee on the Laws relating to Penitentiary Houses', 10 June 1811.

Commons Sessional Papers of the Nineteenth Century (1812), vol. ii, 363–421: 'Third Report from the Committee on the Laws relating to Penitentiary Houses', 27 June 1812.

Commons Sessional Papers of the Nineteenth Century (1812), vol. ii, 573–689: 'Report from the Select Committee on Transportation', 10 July 1812.

Historical Records of Australia, Series I, ed. F. Watson, 26 vols. Sydney: Library Committee of the Commonwealth Parliament, 1914–25.

Historical Records of New South Wales, ed. A. Britton and F.M. Bladen, 7 vols. Sydney: Charles Potter, Government Printer, 1892–1901.

Johnston, G. 'Proclamation', Sydney, 27 January 1808. http://nla.gov.au/nla.obj-39357294/ view?partId=nla.obj-82861568 [accessed 30 June 2020].

'King's speech, 23 January 1787', Parliamentary Debates, House of Lords. London, 1787, vol. 26, 211.

New South Wales Act of 1823, An Act to provide for the better Administration of Justice in New South Wales … and for the more effectual Government thereof (4 Geo IV. c. 96).

New South Wales Courts Act of 1787 (27 Geo III. c. 2).

Parliamentary Debates, House of Commons. London, 1811, vol. 19.

Parliamentary Debates, House of Commons. London, 1812, vol. 21.

Transportation Act of 1802, 43 Geo III. c. 15, 29 December 1802. An Act to facilitate, and render more easy the Transportation of Offenders.

Legal cases

Bullock v. Dodds (1819) 2 B. and Ald. 358.
Marsden v. Mason [1806] NSWKR 1; [1806] NSWSupC 1.
Macarthur v. Campbell Junior, 24.10.1807, HRNSW, vol. 6, 335.
R. v. Macarthur [1808] NSWKR 1; [1808] NSWSupC 1.
R. v. Marshall [1801] NSWKR 1; [1801] NSWSupC 1.
R. v. Nicholls [1799] NSWKR 3; [1799] NSWSupC 3.

Printed sources

Bathurst (Lord). 'Enclosure No 1: Commission of John Thomas Bigge', in 'Addendum A', 1819. The State of the Colony of New South Wales. London: House of Commons, 1822.

Beccaria, C. On Crime and Punishment, and Other Writings [1764], ed. R. Bellamy. Cambridge: Cambridge University Press, 1995.

Bennet, H.G. Letter to Viscount Sidmouth, Secretary of State for the Home Department, on the Transportation Laws, the State of the Hulks, and of the Colonies in New South Wales. London: J. Ridgway, 1819.

Bentham, J. Traités de législation civile et pénale, ed. É. Dumont, 3 vols. Paris: Bossange, Masson et Besson, 1802.

Bentham, J. The Correspondence of Jeremy Bentham, Volume 7: January 1802 to December 1808, ed. J.R. Dinwiddy. Oxford: Clarendon Press, 1988; repr. 2006.

Bentham, J. The Correspondence of Jeremy Bentham, Volume 8: January 1809 to December 1816, ed. S. Conway. Oxford: Clarendon Press, 1988; repr. 2007.

Bentham, J. Panopticon versus New South Wales and other writings on Australia, ed. T. Causer and P. Schofield. London: UCL Press, 2022.

Bigge, J.T. The State of the Colony of New South Wales. London: House of Commons, 1822. Project Gutenberg.

Bigge, J.T. The Judicial Establishments of New South Wales and of Van Diemen's Land. London: House of Commons, 1823a.

Bigge, J.T. The State of Agriculture and Trade in the Colony of New South Wales. London: House of Commons, 1823b.

Blackstone, W. Commentaries on the Laws of England, vol. i. Oxford: Clarendon Press, 1765.

Clark, C.M.H., ed. Select Documents in Australian History, 1788–1850. Sydney: Angus & Roberson, 1950.

Collins, D. An Account of the English Colony in New South Wales, vol. i. London: T. Cadell Jun. and W. Davies, 1798.

Eden, W. Principles of Penal Law. Dublin: John Milliken, 1772.

Howard, J. *The State of the Prisons in England and Wales: With Preliminary Observations, and an Account of some Foreign Prisons*. Warrington: William Eyres, 1777.

Locke, J. *Second Treatise of Government* (1690), ed. and intro. C.B. Macpherson. Indianapolis: Hackett Publishing Company, 1980.

Mudie, J. *The Felonry of New South Wales* (1837). Melbourne: Lansdowne Press, 1964.

Ritchie, J., ed. *The Evidence of the Bigge Reports: New South Wales under Governor Macquarie*. Melbourne: Heinemann, 1971.

Ritchie, J., ed. A *Charge of Mutiny: The Court Martial of Lieutenant Colonel George Johnston for Deposing Governor William Bligh in the Rebellion of 26 January 1808*. Canberra: National Library of Australia, 1988.

Romilly, S. *Observations on the Criminal Law of England, as it Related to Capital Punishments: and on the Modes in which it is Administered*, 3rd ed. London: T. Cadell and W. Davies, 1813.

Romilly, S. *Speeches of Sir Samuel Romilly in the House of Commons*, 2 vols. London: J. Ridgway and Sons, 1820.

Romilly, S. *Memoirs of the Life of Sir Romilly*, 2 vols. London: Murray, 1840.

Slater, J. *A Description of Sydney, Parramatta, Newcastle, &c. Settlements in New South Wales, with some Account of the Manners and Employment of The Convicts, In a Letter from John Slater, To His Wife in Nottingham, Published for the Benefit of his Wife and Four Children*. Bridlesmith-Gate: Sutton and Son, 1819.

Tench, W. *1788, Comprising A Narrative of the Expedition to Botany Bay (1789) and A Complete Account of the Settlement at Port Jackson (1793)*, ed. T. Flannery. Melbourne: Text Publishing Company, 1996.

Wentworth, W.C. *A Statistical, Historical and Political Description of the Colonies of New South Wales and its Dependent Settlements in Van Diemen's Land*, 1st ed., 2 vols. London: G. and W.B. Whittaker, 1819.

Wentworth, W.C. *A Statistical, Historical and Political Description of the Colonies of New South Wales and its Dependent Settlements in Van Diemen's Land*, 3rd ed., 2 vols. London: G. and W.B. Whittaker, 1824.

Secondary Sources

Allen, M. 'Alcohol and Authority in Early New South Wales: The Symbolic Significance of the Spirit Trade, 1788–1808', *History Australia* 9: 3 (2012): 7–26.

Allen, M. 'Policing a Free Society: Drunkenness and Liberty in Colonial New South Wales', *History Australia* 12: 2 (2015): 143–64.

Allen, M. 'Distilling Liberty: Reconsidering the Politics of Alcohol in Early New South Wales', *Australian Historical Studies* 50: 3 (2019): 339–53.

Atkinson, A. 'Jeremy Bentham and the Rum Rebellion', *Journal of the Royal Australian Historical Society* 64 (June 1978): 82–5.

Atkinson, A. 'Taking Possession: Sydney's First Householders'. In *A Difficult Infant: Sydney before Macquarie*, ed. G. Aplin, 72–90. Sydney: UNSW Press, 1988.

Atkinson, A. 'The Little Revolution in New South Wales, 1808', *International History Review* 12 (February 1990): 65–75.

Atkinson, A. 'The Free-Born Englishman Transported: Convict Rights as a Measure of Eighteenth Century Empire', *Past and Present* 144 (August 1994): 94–8.

Atkinson, A. *The Europeans in Australia: A History, Volume 1*. Sydney: UNSW Press, 1997.

Atkinson, A. 'The First Plans for Governing New South Wales, 1786–87', in *British Imperial Strategies in the Pacific, 1750–1900*, ed. J. Samson, 163–81. Aldershot: Ashgate, 2003.

Bennett, J.M. 'The Establishment of Jury Trial in New South Wales', *Sydney Law Review* 3: 3 (1961): 463.

Bonyhady, T. *The Colonial Earth*. Melbourne: Miegunyah Press, 2000.

Brett, J. *From Secret Ballot to Democracy Sausage: How Australia Got Compulsory Voting*. Melbourne: Text Publishing, 2019.

Butlin, N.G. 'Yo, Ho, and How Many Bottles of Rum?', *Australian Economic History Review* 23 (March 1983): 1–27.

Causer, T. '"The Evacuation of That Scene of Wickedness and Wretchedness": Jeremy Bentham and the Panopticon Prison versus New South Wales, 1802–3', *Journal of Australian Colonial History* 21 (2019): 1–24.

Clark, C.M.H. *A History of Australia, Volume 1: From the Earliest Times to the Age of Macquarie*. Melbourne: Melbourne University Press, 1962.

Dando-Collins, S. *Captain Bligh's Other Mutiny: The True Story of the Military Coup that Turned Australia into a Two-Year Rebel Republic*. Sydney: UNSW Press, 2007.

Davidson, A. *The Invisible State: The Formation of the Australian State 1788–1901*. Cambridge: Cambridge University Press, 1991.

Davie, N. *The Penitentiary Ten: The Transformation of the English Prison, 1770–1850*. Oxford: Bardwell Press, 2017.

Duffy, M. *Man of Honour: John Macarthur, Duellist, Rebel, Founding Father*. Sydney: Pan Macmillan, 2003.

Dunk, J. *Bedlam at Botany Bay*. Sydney: NewSouth, 2019.

Ellis, M.H. *John Macarthur*. Sydney: Angus and Robertson, 1955.

Ellis, M.H. 'Rum Rebellion Reviewed', *Quadrant* 2 (Summer 1957–8): 13–24.

Evatt, H.V. *Rum Rebellion: A Study of the Overthrow of Governor Bligh by John Macarthur and the New South Wales Corps*. Sydney: Angus & Roberson, 1938.

Fitzgerald, R. and Hearn, M. *Bligh, Macarthur and the Rum Rebellion*. Kenthurst, New South Wales: Kangaroo Press, 1988.

Fitzpatrick, B. *British Imperialism and Australia, 1783–1833*. London: George Allen and Unwin, 1939.

Haines, R. '"The Idle and the Drunken Won't Do There": Poverty, the New Poor Law and Nineteenth-Century Government-Assisted Emigration to Australia from the UK', in *British Imperial Strategies in the Pacific, 1750–1900*, ed. J. Samson, 183–203. Aldershot: Ashgate, 2003.

Hainsworth, D.R. *The Sydney Traders: Simeon Lord and His Contemporaries*. Melbourne: Cassell Australia, 1972.

Hirst, J.B. *Convict Society and Its Enemies: A History of Early New South Wales*. Sydney: Allen and Unwin, 1983.

Hughes, R. *The Fatal Shore: A History of the Transportation of Convicts to Australia, 1787–1868*. London: Macmillan, 1988.

Ignatieff, M. *A Just Measure of Pain: The Penitentiary in the Industrial Revolution*. London: Macmillan, 1978.

Karskens, G. *The Colony: A History of Early Sydney*. Crows Nest: Allen & Unwin, 2010.

Karskens, G. and Waterhouse, R. '"Too Sacred to be Taken Away": Property, Liberty, Tyranny, and the "Rum Rebellion"', *Journal of Australian Colonial History* 12 (2010): 1–22.

Kociumbas, J. *The Oxford History of Australia, Volume 2: 1770–1860*. Melbourne: Oxford University Press, 1992.

McMahon, J. 'Not a Rum Rebellion but a Military Insurrection', *Journal of the Royal Australian Historical Society* 92 (June 2006): 125–44.

Medd, P. *Romilly: A Life of Sir Samuel Romilly, Lawyer and Reformer*. London: Collins, 1968.

Nagle, J.F. *Collins, the Courts, the Colony: Law and Society in Colonial New South Wales, 1788–1796*. Sydney: UNSW Press, 1996.

National Library of Australia. *Cook's Endeavour Journal: The Inside Story*. Canberra: National Library of Australia, 2008.

Neal, D. *The Rule of Law in a Penal Colony*. Melbourne: Cambridge University Press, 1991.

Phillips, M. *A Colonial Autocracy: New South Wales under Governor Macquarie, 1810–1821*. London: King, 1909.

Ritchie, J. *The Wentworths: Father and Son*. Melbourne: Melbourne University Press, 1997.

Robson, L.L. *History of Tasmania: Van Diemen's Land from the Earliest Times to 1855*, vol. 1. Melbourne: Oxford University Press, 1983.

Scott, E., ed. 'Part 1: Australia', in *Cambridge History of the British Empire*, vol. 7. Cambridge: Cambridge University Press, 1989.

Shaw, A.G.L. 'Some Aspects of New South Wales, 1788–1810', *Journal of the Royal Australian Historical Society* 57 (June 1971): 93–112.

Smith, S. 'Article II. *Account of the English Colony in New South Wales*. By Lieutenant-Colonel Collins of the Royal Marines. Vol. 2, 410. Cadell & Davies, London', *Edinburgh Review* 2 (2 April 1802): 30–42.

Spigelman, J.J. 'Bicentenary of the Coup of 1808 (January 22, 2008)', *Australian Bar Review* 30: 2 (2008): 129–43.

Thomas, N. 'Licensed Curiosity: Cook's Pacific Voyages', in *British Imperial Strategies in the Pacific, 1750–1900*, ed. J. Samson, 77–97. Aldershot: Ashgate, 2003.

Walsh, R., ed. *In Her Own Words: The Writings of Elizabeth Macquarie*. Wollombi: Exisle Publishing, 2011.

Whitaker, A.-M. *Joseph Foveaux: Power and Patronage in Early New South Wales*. Sydney: UNSW Press, 2000.

Woods, G.D. *A History of Criminal Law in New South Wales: The Colonial Period, 1788–1900*. Sydney: The Federation Press, 2002.

Unpublished theses

Ritchie, J. 'Punishment and Profit: The Reports of Commissioner Bigge on the Colonies of New South Wales and Van Diemen's Land, 1822–23; Their Origins, Nature and Significance'. PhD Thesis, Australian National University, 1969.

8

Jeremy Bentham on South Australia, colonial government, and representative democracy

Philip Schofield

In 'Colonization Company Proposal: being a Proposal for the formation of a Joint-Stock Company on an entirely new principle intituled the Vicinity-maximizing or Dispersion-preventing principle', a short and incomplete essay written between 4 and 11 August 1831, Bentham outlined a scheme for the establishment of a colony on the south coast of Australia.[1] In view of Bentham's reputation as an anti-colonial writer,[2] this essay presents a puzzle. Taking his career as a whole, Bentham may have been simply inconsistent in his approach to colonies, as Donald Winch suggests,[3] or he may have had a late change of mind – a change for which Edward Gibbon Wakefield, the promoter of colonization, claimed credit. Bentham wrote 'Colonization Company Proposal' in response to a scheme put forward by the National Colonization Society, which had first met in London in February 1830 in order to promote Wakefield's plan of 'systematic colonization'.[4] The scheme, expounded in a prospectus issued by the Society, aimed to settle young married pauper couples and persons of marriageable age in a concentrated settlement in South Australia and thereby both relieve poverty in Britain and expand the market for British manufactures. The basic idea was to secure an adequate supply of labour for maintaining the long-term productivity and profitability of the newly settled land. It was important to avoid what the Society considered to be the bane of other British colonies in Canada, South Africa, and Australia, namely the rapid exhaustion of the soil and subsequent dispersion of population to hitherto uncultivated land, which removed all possibility of the division of employment, the creation of a surplus, and the maintenance of a civilized society among the settlers.[5]

Following negotiations with the Colonial Office, a revised proposal was drafted and approved for circulation at a meeting of the Society on 3 August 1831. The fundamental principle that 'every appropriation of land must be accompanied by a correspondent increase of the supply of labour and the colonial population' was reiterated. In return for the sanction of a Royal Charter, it was proposed that the whole cost of the scheme would be borne by a joint-stock Company established in London. The new Company would be established with a capital of £500,000, divided into shares of £50 each. A quarter of the capital would be paid to the British government for a grant of land, some of which would be retained by the Company, but the remainder sold in lots of not less than 80 acres each to capitalists in exchange for their paying for the passage of young emigrant labourers. A further quarter of the Company's capital would be made available in the form of loans to small capitalists, while the remaining half would be used to add value to the Company's land, through, for instance, the building of roads and bridges. The point was that the scheme would give employment to capital for which there was no profitable employment at home.

The revised proposal contained plans for the government of the colony, a topic that had not been considered in the prospectus of 1830. The cost of governing the colony would initially be met by the Company, which would have a claim on the colony for repayment when the colony became self-governing. The supreme power would be vested in a Governor, commissioned by the Crown, on the nomination of the Company and removable by the Company, though any nomination would be subject to a veto by the Crown. A set of regulations would be proposed by the Company, with certain provisions which could not be altered by the Governor, who would otherwise enjoy unlimited legislative power. Magistrates would be elected by the inhabitants of the districts over which they had jurisdiction. A permanent government would be established once the colony had 10,000 adult males, who would annually elect a Legislative Assembly, while a Governor would be appointed by the Crown, with the power of suspending any new law and referring it to the Crown, which would have a veto. In the meantime, the Company would establish educational institutions, but avoid any interference in religion, while no restrictions would be placed on trade.[6] It was this scheme to which Bentham, apparently prompted by Wakefield, responded in 'Colonization Company Proposal'.[7]

Colonization Company Proposal

The first known contact between Bentham and Wakefield appears to have taken place in July 1829 when Wakefield, serving a prison sentence in Newgate for abduction, anonymously sent Bentham his 'Sketch of a Proposal for Colonizing Australasia'.[8] They had met by 4 August 1831, when Bentham, who on that day began work on 'Colonization Company Proposal', informed Joseph Hume that he had recently read Wakefield's *Facts relating to the Punishment of Death in the Metropolis*,[9] had found it 'a most valuable work' and Wakefield himself 'a most valuable man', adding: 'I have thrown my mantle over him and shall turn him to good account'.[10]

In the full title of 'Colonization Company Proposal', Bentham emphasized the novelty of 'the Vicinity-maximizing or Dispersion-preventing principle' which the scheme incorporated, a principle that he had presumably borrowed from Wakefield.[11] He defined the principle as 'that according to which maximization of *vicinity* will be made as between the spot granted to and occupied by each Colonist or say *Settler*; relation had to the aggregate of spots, granted to and occupied by the Colonists which the grant finds already in existence'.[12] Hence, the new colony would be established around a port, which would constitute the main settlement, and expand to contiguous land as and when sufficient numbers of emigrants had been recruited in order to work that land productively. In line with the National Colonization Society's 'Proposal' of August 1831, Bentham explained that the scheme would be administered by a chartered Company, which would sell plots of land in the colony to those able to afford it, or hire the labour of those unable to buy a plot outright until they had earned enough money to do so. A number of benefits would accrue from the establishment of the colony: the emigrants would be transferred 'from a state of indigence to a state of affluence' and receive an education that would ensure their future well-being; the remaining inhabitants of the mother country would be relieved from the taxes that they would otherwise have been required to pay because of the increase in the numbers of indigent; the market for the produce of the mother country would be increased; and stockholders in the Company would receive an increasing rate of return on the capital advanced.[13] In terms of its government, the colony would be governed in the first instance by a Dictator (understood in the ancient Roman sense of a person with extensive but time-limited powers) who would be appointed by the Company. Bentham envisaged that, after a few years, perhaps as few as four, the colony would become an independent state. The colonial legislature and people of the colony would pay compensation to the Company in London, with the British government guaranteeing the debt, thereby not discouraging potential shareholders who might otherwise fear the loss of their capital. Where Bentham differed from the 'Proposal' of August 1831 was in relation to the government of the colony following the end of the Dictatorship. There would be no Crown-appointed Governor, nor any British veto – the colony would be an independent republic.[14]

Bentham was adamant that the government of the colony should not be modelled on the British constitution. The colony should have neither King nor House of Lords. It simply would not have the resources to maintain a monarchy and an aristocracy. A monarch would need to have a crown and, Bentham asked, 'what is a Crown, without its dignity? What is such dignity made of, but the matter of wealth – say in one word *money*?' An 'unlimited' number of years would pass before the whole surplus labour of the colony, beyond what was necessary for bare subsistence, would be sufficient for supporting a monarch. For the same reason – the lack of sufficient resources – there could be no House of Lords, but not even the most ardent supporter of Britain's balanced constitution would think it made sense to have a House of Lords without a monarch: 'House of Lords without King would be moon without sun, wherewith should she be illuminated'.[15]

There was really no choice about the matter. The only feasible government for the new colony, claimed Bentham, was a common-wealth – in other words, a representative democracy. One possibility was to adopt the constitution of the United States of America. A second possibility was to adopt Bentham's own constitutional code, which would need some adaptations to the circumstances of the colony, but that would not pose a difficulty since, he noted, he had already laid down the principles on which such adaptations might be made. In comparing these alternatives, Bentham, as might be expected, preferred his own constitutional code. In general, he was a great admirer of the United States as a large-scale functioning democracy,[16] but, as he explained in 'Colonization Company Proposal', the problem with the United States constitution lay in the existence of a second legislative chamber, the Senate. The American founders had unthinkingly copied the English constitution. While they had rejected an aristocracy, they had not objected to a second chamber and had associated the idea of a Senate, 'by etymology and Roman history', with 'the idea of wisdom'. The share that the Senate held in the legislative power, however, was itself 'pure evil', and the evil was doubled by its share in the administrative power and trebled by its share in the judicial power. The single good effect of the United States Senate was to give some additional influence to the smaller states, but this was irrelevant in the context of the proposed South Australian colony, since there would be no federal union to complicate matters.[17] As he explained elsewhere, Bentham's second major objection to the United States system of government was its adoption of the English Common Law, a result of the baneful influence of the lawyers who dominated the various legislative assemblies.[18] What was not made explicit in the National Colonization Society's *Statement* was whether or not the Common Law would be transplanted into the new colony, but Bentham would no doubt have offered his penal and civil codes as well as his constitutional code as a far better alternative.[19]

Representative democracy

In the course of his discussion of the proposed colonial government for the South Australian colony, Bentham cited three of his own published works. He referred to *Jeremy Bentham to his fellow-citizens of France, on Houses of Peers and Senates*[20] for his objections to systems of government that incorporated more than one legislative assembly and to *Plan of Parliamentary Reform*[21] and the first volume of *Constitutional Code*[22] for the 'fundamental principles and substance' of the scheme that he was recommending. When he began to write on parliamentary reform in 1809, he had advocated 'democratic ascendancy', whereby effective power would be placed in a House of Commons annually elected by universal manhood suffrage through the secret ballot, but in late 1817 or early 1818 had committed himself to republicanism. The constitutional structure he thereafter advocated contained no monarchy, no aristocracy – titles of honour would be abolished – and no established church. Bentham had always been sceptical about the virtues of a mixed constitution, with its notions of the division and balance of powers. His basic objection – and this was his essential objection to multi-chamber legislatures – was that if an institution of government was established which was motivated to promote the greatest happiness, then any other institution that had the same motivation was redundant, and any that had a different motivation was mischievous.[23]

The scheme of government that Bentham envisaged for the new colony, therefore, was that put forward in his writings on the constitutional code, his blueprint for representative democracy, on which he began work in 1822. The great problem in all systems of government, Bentham explained, was corruption. He had a broad understanding of corruption, in that a corrupt act was any that was detrimental to the general interest or the happiness of the community as a whole. An official in government, for instance, acted corruptly when he performed an act that benefited himself or a small group and at the same time had a detrimental effect overall on the happiness of all the persons affected by the act. An official who had an interest – in other words expected some benefit – from performing a corrupt act had a 'sinister interest', as opposed to an official who had an interest in promoting the welfare of the community as a whole, who had a 'right and proper interest'. To act corruptly was to perform a 'sinister sacrifice'. All these notions – such as interest, benefit, and happiness – only made sense when they were related to the sensations of pain and pleasure. Hence, to act corruptly was to increase the balance of pain over pleasure in the world.

The point about a representative democracy was not that it was necessarily free from corruption, but that it was the only form of government in which effective 'securities against misrule' could be established and thereby ensure, as far as possible, that officials acted to promote the general interest. As Bentham explained in 'Constitutional Code Rationale', written in 1822, the actual end of government had always been, and always would be – or rather should always be assumed to be – the greatest happiness of the rulers themselves. This was because each individual was predominantly self-interested and, if he had the power to do so, would promote his own interest, no matter what the effect might be on the interests of other persons. Rulers were no different from anyone else in being predominantly self-interested, but because they were endowed with power, they had both the desire and the means to promote their own interest. The right and proper end of government was ideally the greatest happiness of all, but since there would inevitably be clashes of interest between the individuals in any community, the best that could be achieved was the greatest happiness of the greatest number. In general, then, there existed an opposition between the actual end of government, that is the greatest happiness of rulers, and the right and proper end, that is the greatest happiness of the greatest number – in other words, between the interests of the ruling few and those of the subject many. The purpose of constitutional law was to replace this opposition of interests with an identification of interests, thereby bringing the actual end into coincidence with the right and proper end of government. The aim was to put rulers in a situation whereby the only way that they could promote their own interest was through the promotion of the general interest. This was possible because everyone, including rulers, had a share in the general interest. Rulers would only be able to increase their own happiness by increasing that of the community as a whole. The means of achieving the identification of interests was to make rulers – that is legislators and other government officials – subject to the persons whose interest constituted the general interest itself, namely the people.[24]

Hence, in *Constitutional Code*, Bentham announced: 'The sovereignty is in *the people*.'[25] The code itself consists of a series of detailed administrative provisions based on the principles of good government that Bentham had been developing throughout his career, but especially since 1809 when he began writing on parliamentary reform. There would not be any balance or separation of powers, but rather a chain of subordination, whereby the sovereign people would elect a single-chamber legislative body, which would in turn appoint an executive consisting of an administrative department (headed by a prime minister) and a judicial department (headed by a justice minister). The electorate would consist of all males over the age of 21 who had passed a literacy test. Similar voting rights should be extended to females when (male) public opinion had become sufficiently enlightened not simply to dismiss the proposal with a sneer. The electorate would be divided into equal electoral districts, vote annually by means of the secret ballot, and enjoy the power to remove their deputy to the legislature at any time by means of a petition signed by a quarter of the electorate and subsequent majority vote. Deputies to the legislature would be paid only when they attended, and their attendance, along with their votes, would be publicly recorded, as would the proceedings and debates in the chamber. The prime minister and ministers in the administrative department would in effect be expert civil servants. Ministers, like more minor officials, would be required to pass relevant examinations in order to qualify for their offices, which they would hold for life, subject to removal by the legislature, prime minister, or petition and majority vote of the electorate. Neither prime minister nor ministers would have a vote in the legislature, and the prime minister would not have a seat there, though he might be summoned to answer questions and to provide information. Ministers would have a seat, since their role was to advise the legislature on matters pertaining to their respective sub-departments.[26]

There still remained a significant danger that, even in the structure of a representative democracy, officials in general, and the prime minister in particular, would have enough inducements at their disposal to corrupt a majority of members of the legislative assembly and thereby turn the government into a virtual monarchy or aristocracy. However, unlike other regimes, it was possible under a representative democracy to introduce what Bentham termed 'securities against misrule' in order to obviate the danger of corruption. The point of these securities was to 'maximize official aptitude' and to minimize the expense of government – in other words, to get government to do the best possible job at the least possible cost. Bentham divided aptitude into three branches: first, an official (or functionary, in Bentham's terminology) possessed moral aptitude when he was motivated to pursue the greatest happiness and not to promote a sinister interest; second, the functionary possessed intellectual aptitude when he had the relevant knowledge and judgement for his tasks; and third, the functionary possessed active aptitude when he actually performed the tasks in question. The securities for moral aptitude included publicity and hence open government, the subjection of functionaries to legal punishment in case of misbehaviour, the minimization of the power and money at their disposal, and the abolition of titles of honour; those for intellectual aptitude included public examination and the 'economical auction', whereby potential candidates for an office made bids for the associated pay; while that for active aptitude was payment in return for attendance.[27] Such was the scheme that Bentham recommended for adoption in the proposed South Australian colony once it was deemed capable of ruling itself.

Bentham's anti-colonial arguments

The puzzle concerning 'Colonization Company Proposal' is not that it remained an unfinished sketch, but that Bentham wrote it at all, given the fact that he is more often noted for his anti-colonial views. Bentham had a long history of writing in opposition to colony-holding. Pertinent here is an insight provided by unpublished material written for 'Letters to Lord Pelham'. In a manuscript dated 4 June 1802,[28] in relation to his anti-colonial principles, and in answer to the charge that he had adopted them merely in order to support his arguments against New South Wales as 'an instrument in the hand of penal Justice', he noted: 'I can trace the birth of them to the publication of a pamphlet of Dr Anderson's of 1777 or thereabouts intituled, The Interests of Great Britain with regard to her Colonies considered'. The work in question was James Anderson, 'The Interest of Great-Britain with regard to her American Colonies considered', printed at London in 1782. Anderson's basic principle was that the strength of a country consisted in the number of its inhabitants, while its wealth was proportional to their industry.[29] Just as Spain had been ruined by the emigration of vast numbers of her people to her colonies, Britain had been weakened by the dispersal of its population to America, with the expense of government increased and heavier taxation imposed, resulting in discouragement to manufactures.[30] Anderson also argued that, from a political point of view, extended empire led to corruption and despotism and, moreover, made war more likely.[31] Neither trade nor manufactures, argued Anderson, were insepa- rably connected with colonies, and the probability was that Britain's foreign trade, as well as its internal commerce, would have increased to a much greater degree than it had done, had it not been for the American colonies.[32] Anderson recommended that the monopoly on American trade should be renounced[33] and other nations allowed a free participation in Britain's trade with a view to encouraging them to remove any 'destructive regulations' on Britain's trade with them.[34]

While Anderson's arguments were directly concerned with America and the War of Independence, many of his substantive views were echoed in Bentham's writings on colonies: that the economic advantages of free trade were most efficiently reaped when trading with independent states; that colonies were a source of war; and that colonies increased the patronage at the disposal of rulers in the mother country and hence were a source of corruption. These themes were developed, for instance, in a series of essays written shortly after the outbreak of the French Revolution with a view to persuading the new regime in France to relinquish its colonies. In 'Short Views of Economy for the use of the French Nation but not unapplicable to the English', written in or around September 1789,[35] Bentham offered advice to the National Assembly on the measures that might be taken to alleviate the fiscal crisis threatening France. He pointed out that colonies were a source of wasteful expense. Not only had France to bear the cost of governing, garrisoning, and providing naval protection to its colonies, they were also a potential cause of war, with all the expense that entailed. Moreover, the French colonies did not produce any clear revenue to offset the expense. The only profit that France derived from its colonies was the produce of the taxes imposed on its trade with them, but such taxation did not depend upon their status as colonies: 'The profit to be derived from Colonies as *markets* has nothing to do with the profit derivable from them as *possessions*'.[36] The persons who benefited were ministers, since colonies added to the means of corruption at their disposal.[37] Colonies were also 'a source of complication', in that their affairs distracted the attention of the French government from more pressing concerns.[38] Hence, the emancipation of the French colonies was a potential source of retrenchment in itself, and it would also help to lessen military expenditure and reduce the possibility of war.[39] If colonies were not at issue, Bentham noted, Britain and France would have no cause of quarrel.[40]

In 'Colonies and Navy', probably written in late 1790, Bentham reiterated his view that, if France and Britain agreed to relinquish their colonies, 'the principal difficulty would be removed to the establishment of a plan of general and permanent pacification for all Europe'. He went on to elaborate his economic arguments against colony-holding, founded on the 'so plainly and obviously true' proposition that the trade of a nation was limited by the quantity of its capital. It was for this reason that prohibitions placed on foreign trade were simply pointless, while attempts at encouragement, such as bounties or non-importation agreements, were positively harmful, since they 'force money from one man in order to pay another man for carrying on a trade which, if it were not a losing one, there would be no need of paying him for'.[41] Bentham noted that the main argument put forward for maintaining colonies was that they benefited trade, and if Britain gave up its colonies, another country would take control of them and they would no longer trade with Britain. Even if this were the case, retorted Bentham, it would not result in any loss since the capital employed in trading with colonies would be shifted to some other trade. Moreover, it was assumed that all trade with colonies was unalloyed profit, but goods produced by colonies had to be paid for in the same way as goods produced elsewhere. The proper question to ask concerned the degree of profit that might be made from different 'modes of productive industry', and even then, there was a tendency towards equilibrium, since more profitable trades would attract more capital, and thence, through competition, reduce the rate of profit.[42]

Similar arguments were rehearsed in 'New Wales', a series of fragments written in the late spring and early summer of 1791 and which appear to constitute Bentham's earliest response to the establishment of the first Australian penal colony. He complained, though failed to elaborate in most instances, that the advantages ascribed to colonies – including 'extension of empire', increase in national wealth, augmentation of the army and navy, propagation of 'the true religion', the extension and diversification of trade, new discoveries of animals, plants, and minerals – were either illusory or not worth the cost.[43] He admitted that there might be some advantage to the mother country were a colony a source of diamonds or precious metals, but otherwise colonies were 'drains to the mother country: until the mutually happy and every where too long protracted æra of independence'. The mother country might try to profit from the taxation of trade, but only if the colonists themselves were weak and foolish enough to pay duties on imports from the mother country, while the rate of taxation obtainable on colonial imports into the mother country would be limited by smuggling. Moreover, imposing a monopoly on trade would bring no advantage, since the home market was large enough to ensure that competition drove down prices to their lowest level, and even produced disadvantages by increasing the cost of freight.[44]

Bentham presented his arguments in more systematic form in 'Jeremy Bentham to the National Convention of France', printed in late 1792 or early 1793. He repeated his economic arguments against colony-holding, but also drew attention to the political corruption that colonies engendered. France had never and never would gain any surplus revenue from its colonies. The revenue which France received was unlikely to meet the cost of defending them in time of peace, and certainly would not in time of war, particularly if Britain were the enemy. The colonies were an enormous drain on the French finances; they were a potential source of conflict with other nations, especially Britain; and they were a source of political corruption.[45] The French had chosen their own government, and for the sake of consistency they should permit the colonies to enjoy the same right. It was no answer to say that the colonists would be allowed to send deputies to the National Assembly: 'To govern a million or two of people you don't care about, you admit half a dozen people who don't care about you. To govern a set of people whose business you know nothing about, you encumber yourselves with half a dozen [strangers] who know nothing about yours'. Open domination would be preferable to such masked tyranny. It was to the advantage neither of the French themselves nor the colonists that the colonies be governed from France. The time required for communication between France and the colonies made effective government impossible: orders or instructions would not arrive in time to meet the emergency for which they were designed, while any infor-mation on which they were based would be incomplete and defective.[46] Emancipation was not only a matter of justice, but would lead in turn to a reduction in the navy, in taxes, in offices, and in corruption.[47]

In 1802–3 Bentham opposed the settlement of New South Wales as a penal colony because it could not accomplish any of the objectives of punishment, namely example, reformation, incapacitation, compensation, and economy, that would be achieved by the panopticon penitentiary. He also argued that the settlement could not be defended on the grounds that, as a colony, it constituted a valuable possession. There was no real advantage, noted Bentham, to the mother country from any colony. Goods obtained from a colony might be obtained either from the home market or from foreign countries without the expense of maintaining and protecting the colony. Statesmen seemed to assume that the goods obtained from a colony were obtained for nothing, but something had to be given in return for the produce of the colony. In the case of New South Wales, there was no produce to sell to the mother country. The settlers in New South Wales bought but did not sell, and what they bought was bought by money received in the form of pay, derived from taxation imposed on the mother country. Britain, therefore, was transferring wealth to New South Wales, and receiving nothing or at most just a fraction of its value in return. As for the prospect, advanced by David Collins,[48] that New South Wales would prove valuable as a nursery for soldiers and seamen for the East India possessions, Bentham retorted that it would be better to send soldiers directly to the East Indies rather than involving them in a further two-months' voyage to New South Wales, while seamen might as well be sent on a voyage to some other destination as to New South Wales. Collins's argument was circular – colonies were good for nursing a large navy; a large navy was good for keeping and conquering colonies. The only advantage that Bentham could see from colonizing the antipodes with settlers who were unfit for colonization was the discovery (as he had been informed) of 250 new plants, but colonization was not necessary for the gathering of seeds. The one thing that had in fact been planted in Botany Bay, he concluded, was a military despotism.[49]

Many of these arguments resurfaced when Bentham came to think about the economic and constitutional implications of colony-holding in his writings on Spain and her overseas possessions 20 years later in 1820–2. The main difference was that the emergence of sinister interest in Bentham's thought between 1804 and 1809, which had led him to embrace democracy,[50] gave him an enhanced understanding of the dangers of the corruption engendered by colony-holding. In a series of essays addressed to the new liberal regime in Spain which had been established following the restoration of the Constitution of Cadiz in 1820,[51] Bentham argued that the Spanish Constitution was essentially sound in that it recognized the greatest happiness of the greatest number as the proper end of government, but that many of its detailed provisions, and especially those concerning the colonies, were ill-conceived in that they tended to facilitate the return of royal despotism. The fundamental principles of the Constitution, announced in Articles 4 and 13, were, in Bentham's view, based on the principle of utility in that 'the *felicity* of all the individuals of which the nation or political society in question is considered as being composed' was recognized as 'the *right and proper* end of government: object of pursuit to all measures of government'.[52] In contrast, Article 1, which proclaimed 'The Spanish Nation consists of all Spaniards of both hemispheres', was a source of great danger, since it enshrined the determination to maintain the Empire.[53] Referring to those elements amongst Spain's ruling classes who saw their advantage in maintaining the claim over Ultramaria, Bentham remarked:

> Spain is *one*! such will be their *arithmetic*. It has its *Peninsular* part and its *Ultramarian* part! such will be their *geography*. As well might it be said – Spain and the Moon are *one*! it has its *earthly* part: it has its *lunar* part ... But, a body of human law, how well soever arranged in other respects, does not suffice for converting *impossibilities* into *facts*.[54]

Since the existence of the overseas colonies was the main threat to its liberal regime, Spain should grant independence to the colonies, and in doing so would be financially stronger and militarily more secure, while a great deal of the corruption that would otherwise impel the country towards royal despotism would be removed. There would be danger from corruptive influence even if Spain had no overseas colonies, but from their existence the danger received 'a boundless encrease'.[55]

The retention of, or even the attempt to retain, the colonies, would add to the amount of corruptive influence that could be directed towards the people's representatives in the Cortes. The King and his ministers had money and other 'sweets of government' to distribute to the representatives. In return, the representatives would promote the sinister interest of the King and his ministers. Unless the people intervened in some way, warned Bentham, their representatives would be converted into the tools of 'a virtual despotism – of a government in which, not less compleatly than under a despotism governing by force, the universal interest will be made a compleat sacrifice of to that knot of particular and sinister interests'. The people would be left with nothing beyond what was necessary for bare subsistence.[56]

Wakefield and Bentham

Given his anti-colonial views, expressed in his writings for France in 1789–93, for New South Wales in 1791 and 1802–3, and for Spain in 1820–2, Bentham's advocacy of the colonization of South Australia in 1831 appears to represent an extraordinary turnaround in his thinking. That it was a turnaround, and that he was responsible for it, was a point insisted on by Wakefield. Writing after Bentham's death, Wakefield, in *England and America*, published in 1833, credited himself with persuading Bentham that his opposition to colonization on the grounds that his fundamental principle, namely that the quantity of trade was limited by the quantity of capital, and that the expense of emigration would, therefore, 'diminish the amount of employment for labour at home', was misconceived. Bentham had been misled by 'a *non-sequitur* which had got possession of his mind'. Even though it were true that 'the quantity of labour applicable to any object, is limited by the quantity of capital that can be employed in it', as Bentham had stated,[57] it did not follow that 'capital always finds a field in which to employ labour'. Wakefield continued:

> During the summer of 1831, Mr. Bentham's attention was called to this subject. At first he urged the objection to colonization which has been here examined, but finally abandoned it. Then, immediately, notwithstanding his great age and bodily infirmities, he proceeded to study the whole subject of colonization, and even to write upon it at some length. His written remarks upon the subject, now in my possession,[58] show that he lived to consider colonization, not 'an agreeable folly,'[59] but a work of the greatest utility. I am proud to add, that the form of the present treatise [i.e. *England and America*] was suggested by one of the wisest and best of mankind.[60]

A similar account appears in the first of two letters signed 'A Benthamite', most likely Wakefield himself, addressed to the Editor of the *Westminster Review*, dated 23 October 1834, and published in *The Spectator*, 8 November 1834. The author argued that a recent article in the *Westminster Review* had misrepresented Bentham's views by claiming that he had been opposed to the establishment of a colony in South Australia.[61] On the contrary, Bentham had 'warmly approved' of the scheme:

The project of founding a colony at that place, and upon that plan, having been submitted to him not long before his death, he at first urged many objections to it; but, after examining it with great care, he declared his unqualified approbation of it, wrote in favour of it at some length, mentioned it frequently to his friends in terms of admiration, advised its author to publish a treatise on the subject, and actually made a sketch of what he considered the best form for such a treatise. In compliance with that advice, and in strict conformity with that sketch, the author of the plan did write a treatise on the subject ... published ... about this time last year, in two volumes, under the title of *England and America;* and what is more, the second volume contains a statement of the fact, that the form of the work was suggested by Bentham.[62]

Wakefield repeated his claim in a private letter to Leigh Hunt (1784–1859), probably written in late 1835, when sending a copy of a new edition of the first volume of Smith's *Wealth of Nations* containing a commentary of his own.[63] He noted that the work

contains the best statement of that principle of *Combination* of Labour which forms the base of the System of colonization. You will also find in that vol., under the head of profits & wages, a fuller explanation than is given elsewhere of the grounds on which, as is told in 'England & America', Bentham altered his opinion as to the utility of colonization – I allude to the new doctrine of *superabundance* of *capital* as well as population, which calls for the creation of new fields of employment for both capital & labour.[64]

To what extent, then, did 'Colonization Company Proposal' represent a decisive shift in Bentham's attitude towards colonization and colony-holding?

Bentham's pro-colonial arguments

Bentham does not seem ever to have opposed colonization and colony-holding outright. In material written for 'Institute of Political Economy' in 1801, he recognized that, given certain circumstances, the establishment and holding of colonies would be beneficial upon the whole. In the first place, he supported the colonization of what he considered to be vacant lands in response to the pressure of population growth in the mother country, and in the second place, he supported colonial rule in countries where the native rulers were unfit to govern,[65] and went so far as to say that, 'taking futurity into the scale, the well-being of mankind appears to have been promoted upon the whole by the establishment of colonies'.[66] The point was that while colony-holding was a burden to the mother country, it was outweighed by the benefit to the colonists themselves. In overall terms, the establishment of colonies resulted in an increase in wealth. Land, as well as labour, was necessary to the increase of wealth, and the land acquired by colonization was 'generally of a superior kind; rich even in raw materials which require nothing but extraction and conveyance to give them a value'. The benefit, however, accrued to the colonists, 'the individual occupiers of the fresh land', and not to the mother country. At first the colonists could not pay taxes to the mother country, and afterwards would not. On the other hand, the colonists required civil, military and naval establishments, the expense of which had to be borne by the mother country. As far as the mother country was concerned, the capital employed in establishing and maintaining colonies would have been more profitably employed at home. The only compensation to offset the loss of increase to national wealth was the diversification of produce through the introduction of novel commodities such as sugar, tea, coffee and chocolate: 'in so far as novelty and variety are sources of enjoyment, as these encrease, so does wealth, if not in *quantity*, yet (what is as good) in *value*'.[67]

As far as Britain was concerned, Bentham was worried that if the population continued to grow rapidly, it would lead to a 'great diminution of relative opulence, a severe sense of general poverty and distress', and eventually to the outstripping of the means of subsistence. Colonization of vacant lands would provide a solution.[68] Furthermore, colonization from Britain would have peculiar advantages:

> It is desirable for mankind that offsets should be taken from the most flourishing and soundest root: that the races propagated every where in parts of the earth as yet vacant, should be races whose habits of thinking in matters of government should be taken from that constitution from which the greatest measure of security has been seen to flow, and whose habits of acting in the sphere of domestic economy and morals should be taken from

that society which, in those respects, is in the most improved as well as improving state.

It was for the advantage of the colonies that they should continue under the government of the mother country, since their rulers, both in terms of law and moral conduct, would be 'men whose education has been derived from that most pure and elevated source':

> men among whom are to be found some whom hereditary opulence has exempted from the necessity of binding down their minds to the exclusive pursuit of pecuniary gain: to whom it is possible at least to think chiefly for the public instead of acting and thinking exclusively for themselves: men who have leisure as well as money to bestow upon those more elevated pursuits by which the heart is softened and the understanding expanded and adorned.

In a nutshell, British aristocrats would make better rulers than the colonists' own representatives. It would, for instance, have been to the advantage of the United States to have remained in a state of subjection to Britain and 'to have sent their children, such whose circumstances could have admitted of it, to that school of moral and intellectual virtue, and to have received from thence all their governors with a large proportion of their clergy, their military and naval officers, their professional men and artists'. They might then have 'escaped the exhibiting that unvaried scene of sordid selfishness, of political altercation, of discomfort, of ignorance, of drunkenness, which by the concurrent testimony of all travellers it presents at present'. The subjection, however, would not have been advantageous to Britain: '[h]ad wisdom prevailed over passion, the object of contention' in the American War of Independence 'would have been reversed', the Americans wishing to retain their subjection, Britain to renounce it. It was not just that colonists who had emigrated to vacant lands were better off under the government of the mother country, but also Indigenous peoples whose own rulers lacked the education, and whose system of laws did not provide the security, of those of Britain or even of those of France.[69]

Bentham advanced a similar argument in 'Defence of a Maximum', also written in 1801. Two domestic conditions had to be fulfilled before colonization was desirable: first, the threat of scarcity caused by the growth of population; and second, an over-supply of capital. In these circumstances, the 'efflux' of population would mitigate the scarcity, and the 'efflux' of capital would mitigate the depreciation of capital. It was not that colonies did not continue to be 'a drain', but that, for that very reason, they constituted 'a relief'. If people and capital did have to emigrate, it was better that they emigrated 'to our own colonies', so long as the expense of governing and defending them did not increase. While no additional income would be extracted from the colonies, either from trade or from duties on trade, the future 'retribution' for the past expense would be 'a scene from *Paradise Lost* – a prospect such as the angel shewed to Adam:[70] men spreading in distant climes, through distant ages, from the best stock, the earth covered with British population, rich with British wealth, tranquil with British security, the fruit of British law'.[71]

Bentham's sporadic pro-colonial arguments need to be placed in context. In the wake of the French Revolution, Bentham had come to look favourably on the security provided by the British constitution and at the same time was suspicious of the emerging democratic governments in the United States. In his writings on the poor laws in 1797–8, for instance, he had objected to the notion of popular participation in politics.[72] Hence, he expressed admiration for British political and legal institutions and recommended their adoption in British colonies. These sentiments were not aberrant, but a reflection of the fact that events in France had turned him, in line with most of his countrymen, against the desirability of political reform in Britain.[73] It is impossible, however, to conceive of Bentham writing in praise of British rulers following his commitment to democracy in 1809, or even after he had been informed in 1803 that the government had decided that the panopticon penitentiary would not be built – a decision that he attributed to the unconstitutional machinations of successive ministries. In this context, Bentham's writings on New South Wales in 1802–3, produced in an attempt to save the panopticon prison scheme, take on an additional importance as a departure point in his journey from conservative supporter to fierce critic of the British establishment.

Bentham did maintain that colony-holding was, except in the particular circumstances of an over-supply of capital, economically disadvantageous to the mother country. Yet from the perspective of 'a citizen of the world', as Bentham liked to regard himself,[74] he considered it desirable that the mother country maintain its dominion insofar as its rulers were more likely to promote the welfare of the colonized peoples than rulers drawn from the colonies themselves. In the writings he addressed to France and Spain, Bentham argued that, in the instance of their established colonies, this was not the case and hence their colonies should be emancipated. As he came to think the worse of the British government (following his discovery that sinister interest permeated the whole British establishment), and to think the better of the United States government, his view changed about the merits of American independence and perhaps about the merits of independence more generally. He came to the view that the Americans had been right to throw off British rule because of the impossibility of being ruled well at such a distance.[75] Furthermore, in 1827 he drafted a petition for the emancipation of Canada from British rule. He suggested that the grievances suffered by Canada were attributable to its distance from the mother country and recommended that the colony join the United States. He added, however, that emancipation for British India was inappropriate, since the inhabitants were unable to provide themselves with security for their property and could only receive such security from the slow and gradual influence of European civilization.[76]

Yet very soon afterwards in 1829, Bentham expressed both anti-colonial and pro-colonial views when he published 'Jeremy Bentham to the National Convention of France' under the title of *Emancipate Your Colonies!* While the original pamphlet itself was one of Bentham's strongest anti-colonial statements, in a 'Postscript', dated 24 June 1829 and added for the published version, he stated that, as a 'citizen of *Great Britain and Ireland*', he wished for the emancipation of the British colonies:

> But, as a citizen of the British Empire, including the sixty millions already under its government in British India, and the forty millions likely to be under its government in the vicinity of British India, not to speak of the one hundred and fifty millions, as some say ... of the contiguous Empire of China, – his opinions and consequent wishes are the *reverse*. So likewise, regard being had to the colonization of Australia ...

This was because he regarded it as

> preponderantly probable that, long before this century is at an end, the settlements in that vast and distant country will, all of them, have emancipated themselves, changing the government from a dependency on the English monarchy, into a represent-ative democracy.[77]

Even when Bentham had turned to political radicalism, he did not condemn either colonization or colony-holding outright. Under his Constitutional Code, moreover, it would have been the duty of the Education Minister and Indigence Relief Minister to consider whether an excess of population might be relieved by sending orphans or the children of the indigent to colonize 'land unappropriated or unemployed, in this state or any friendly foreign State, near, adjacent, or in any degree remote'.[78]

Conclusion

Bentham, as we have seen, had at various points suggested that there were circumstances in which colonization and colony-holding might be beneficial. He had approved of the colonization of vacant lands in response to the pressure of population growth in the mother country and of colonial rule in countries where the native rulers were unfit to govern. In relation specifically to the proposed South Australian colony, there were two points that distinguished it from the colony-holding that Bentham had criticized elsewhere. First, the proposed scheme of government would not be a source of corruption, neither immediately following its establishment, nor when it had been transformed into a representative democracy. Second, economic benefits would arise to the mother country. Although he had earlier insisted that the amount of trade depended solely upon the amount of capital, he had also recognized the problem of an over-supply of capital, and so Wakefield's claim that he had persuaded Bentham significantly to change his views from anti- to pro-colonization should be treated with some scepticism, especially as Bentham did not rely simply on economic factors when considering colonization and colony-holding. A more plausible scenario might be that Wakefield had persuaded Bentham that the circumstances were such, namely that there did exist a superabundance of capital and that a colony founded in South Australia would produce an increase in the extent of market and hence promote an increase in trade. In any case, Bentham might have seen the scheme as a straightforward means of relieving over-population and hence poverty. Rather than 'Colonization Company Proposal' being inconsistent with Bentham's general thinking on colonies, it represented a very particular form of colonization that avoided the general political and economic objections to colonialism that Bentham had advanced elsewhere. Bentham's South Australian scheme was, moreover, consistent with the views expressed in the 'Postscript' to *Emancipate Your Colonies!* The establishment of the colony made economic sense in the circumstances in question; corruptive influence would be excluded; the colony would be emancipated as soon as was practicable; and a representative government would be established. In short, what appear to be inconsistent accounts of colony-holding – namely the anti-colonial writings for France, New South Wales, and Spain on the one hand, and the pro-colonial writings of 1801 on the other – were here reconciled. The key was Bentham's ability to propose an acceptable form of government for the new colony, and a process by which it might be established, which avoided the creation of patronage in the hands of the executive government. Bentham had not abandoned his general opposition to colonization and colony-holding, nor his support for it in particular circumstances. It is only if consistency is regarded as consisting in either an absolute opposition or an absolute support for colonies that Bentham's position appears muddled.

What is missing, however, from Bentham's 'Colonization Company Proposal' is any consideration of the Indigenous people whose interests might be affected by the establishment of the proposed colony. It was not that there was any lack of awareness of their existence. In the 'Proposal' of August 1831, reports made by explorers of the presence of 'natives' along the coast was presented as evidence that the land was suitable for habitation.[79] In 'Colonization Company Proposal' itself, Bentham referred to 'Insecurity against damage to person and property from the hostility of the uncivilized aborigines' as a problem with the dispersion of settlement, and in a marginal note added, 'In Van Dieman's land it has been determined absolutely to extirpate the natives', a reference to the so-called Black War of 1824–31, but made no further comment.[80] Given that it was a fundamental principle of Bentham's utilitarianism that each person was to count for one and no one for more than one,[81] it was, by his own standard, not only inconsistent but also morally wrong of him not to give due weight to the welfare of Indigenous people.[82]

Notes

1   Bentham drafted around 50 sheets of manuscript for the work which he initially entitled 'Colonization Society Proposal'. It is published for the first time in Bentham, ed. Causer and Schofield 2022, 401–32.
2   See Boralevi 1984, 120–41; Pitts 2005, 103–22; Cain 2011, 1–24.
3   Winch 1965, 25–38, 128–9.
4   See [Wakefield] 1829a; [Wakefield] 1829b, reproduced in Wakefield, ed. Lloyd Pritchard 1968, 93–186. For the standard account of the various initiatives and protracted

negotiations with the Colonial Office that eventually led to the passing of the South Australia Act of 1834 see Pike 1967, 52–73.

5   See [National Colonization Society] 1830.
6   See [National Colonization Society] 1831.
7   Pike 1967, 57, mistakenly assumes that Bentham was responding to the prospectus of 1830.
8   Bentham's copy, which he has inscribed 'Jeremy Bentham. 13 July 1829. Received from the Unknown Author without accompanying note', is at British Library (hereafter BL) shelfmark C.T. 77. (10).
9   See Wakefield, ed. Lloyd Pritchard 1968, 187–267.
10 Bentham to Hume, 4 August 1831, BL Add. MS 89,039/1/1.
11 In 1802 Bentham did, however, criticize the New South Wales colony because the dispersal and scattering of its settlements constituted an impediment to inspection: see 'Second Letter to Lord Pelham' in Bentham, ed. Causer and Schofield 2022, 215–16.
12 'Colonization Company Proposal' in Bentham, ed. Causer and Schofield 2022, 408.
13 'Colonization Company Proposal' in Bentham, ed. Causer and Schofield 2022, 407–8, 421, 424–32.
14 In the negotiations between the promoters of the colony and the Colonial Office, the question of the future government of the colony proved to be a difficult one to resolve. The promoters wished to avoid any form of Crown patronage, while the British government would not endorse the prospect of an independent democratic republic. The suspicion is that Bentham must have had some influence, either direct or indirect, on the proposed form of government outlined in [National Colonization Society] 1831.
15 'Colonization Company Proposal' in Bentham, ed. Causer and Schofield 2022, 428.
16 See Hart 1982, 53–78, for an account of Bentham's attitude towards the United States.
17 'Colonization Company Proposal' in Bentham, ed. Causer and Schofield 2022, 429–32. For a critique of second legislative chambers see Bentham, ed. Schofield 1989, 101–12.
18 See Bentham, ed. Schofield and Harris 1998, 325–30.
19 See 'Codification Proposal, addressed to all nations professing liberal opinions', in Bentham, ed. Schofield and Harris 1998, 243–384.
20 Bentham 1830a.
21 Bentham 1817.
22 Bentham 1830b, republished as Bentham, ed. Rosen 1983.
23 See the ironic description of the mixed constitution in Bentham, ed. Burns and Hart 1977, 461–73, and the critique of the division of powers in Bentham, ed. Schofield, Pease-Watkin, and Blamires 2002, 405–18.
24 Bentham, ed. Schofield 1989, 229–43.
25 Bentham, ed. Rosen 1983, 25.
26 The institutional structure of the Constitutional Code is described in Rosen 1983, 130–67.
27 For a detailed account of the securities for the various branches of aptitude see Bentham, ed. Schofield 1989, 3–95.
28 Bentham Papers, Special Collections, University College London Library cxvi. 229 (hereafter UC. Roman numerals refer to the boxes in which the papers are placed, Arabic to the leaves within each box).
29 Anderson 1782, 24–5.
30 Anderson 1782, 34–7, 56–9.
31 Anderson 1782, 100–5.
32 Anderson 1782, 121–3.
33 Anderson 1782, Appendix, 15.
34 Anderson 1782, 35–6.
35 See Bentham, ed. Schofield, Pease-Watkin, and Blamires 2002, 193–203.
36 Bentham, ed. Schofield, Pease-Watkin, and Blamires 2002, 199.
37 Bentham, ed. Schofield, Pease-Watkin, and Blamires 2002, 201.
38 Bentham, ed. Schofield, Pease-Watkin, and Blamires 2002, 199–200.
39 Bentham, ed. Schofield, Pease-Watkin, and Blamires 2002, 195.
40 Bentham, ed. Schofield, Pease-Watkin, and Blamires 2002, 200, 201.
41 Bentham, ed. Quinn 2016, 155–8.
42 Bentham, ed. Quinn 2016, 160–1.
43 'New Wales', in Bentham, ed. Causer and Schofield 2022, 3.

44 'New Wales', in Bentham, ed. Causer and Schofield 2022, 8–10.
45 Bentham, ed. Schofield, Pease-Watkin, and Blamires 2002, 291.
46 Bentham, ed. Schofield, Pease-Watkin, and Blamires 2002, 291–5.
47 Bentham, ed. Schofield, Pease-Watkin, and Blamires 2002, 310.
48 Collins 1798, Preface, pp. ix–x.
49 'Letter to Lord Pelham' in Bentham, ed. Causer and Schofield 2022, 157–8, 161.
50 Schofield 2006, 109–36.
51 Bentham began to draft his most sustained essay under the title of 'Emancipation Spanish' in the summer of 1820 and virtually completed it by April 1822 under the revised title of 'Rid Yourselves of Ultramaria'. Ultramaria was the term that he coined for Spain's overseas possessions.
52 Bentham, ed. Schofield 1995, 31.
53 For the lack of any significant opposition to the retention of the colonies on the part of both *liberales* and *serviles* in Spain see Costeloe 1986.
54 Bentham, ed. Schofield 1995, 52–3.
55 Bentham, ed. Schofield 1995, 23–4.
56 Bentham, ed. Schofield 1995, 85–6. For a more detailed account of Bentham's critique of the Spanish Constitution see Schofield 2019, 40–58.
57 Wakefield was quoting Bentham 1825, 241, a work edited by Richard Smith and consisting of an English translation of the second volume of Bentham 1811.
58 Wakefield may have meant a version of 'Colonization Company Proposal', but it is possible he had been given some other material by Bentham.
59 This phrase appears in Bentham 1825, 288: 'If colonization is a folly when employed as a means of enrichment, it is at least an agreeable folly.'
60 [Wakefield] 1833, ii. 98–102, reproduced in Wakefield, ed. Lloyd Pritchard 1968, 517 & n.
61 'New South Australian Colony', *Westminster Review* 21: 42 (1 October 1834), 441–76, reviewing works on Australia, including [Wakefield] 1834.
62 'Mr Bentham and the Westminster Review', *The Spectator* 7: 331 (1 November 1834), 1038–9. The 'sketch' has not been identified.
63 Smith 1835–9.
64 See Wakefield to Leigh Hunt, 30 November [n.d.], BL Add. MS 38,523, fo. 149.
65 See the passage entitled 'Non-faciendum the fourth: Encreasing the quantity of land, viz. by colonization', in 'Institute of Political Economy', in Bentham, ed. Stark 1952–4, iii. 301–80, at 352–7. Stark has conflated several sequences of manuscript to produce the text of this passage. The bulk of the material, including that quoted here, dates from August and October 1801.
66 Bentham, ed. Stark 1952–4, iii. 355.
67 Bentham, ed. Stark 1952–4, iii. 353–4.
68 The introduction of a demographic argument in 'Institute of Political Economy' (missing from the earlier writings on colonies, and not utilized in the writings for Spain of the early 1820s where the problem was generally acknowledged to be depopulation) may indicate the influence on Bentham of T.R. Malthus's pessimistic forecasts concerning the consequences of population growth outlined in [Malthus] 1798.
69 Bentham, ed. Stark 1952–4, iii. 355–7.
70 See Milton 1667, xi–xii, where the Angel Michael takes Adam to the top of a high hill and reveals visions of the future, from Cain's murder of Abel through to the second coming of Christ.
71 Bentham, ed. Stark 1952–4, iii. 301–2.
72 Bentham, ed. Quinn 2010, 193–6.
73 Schofield 2013.
74 See, for instance, Bentham, ed. Stark 1952–4, i. 27, and Bentham, ed. Schofield 1995, 204.
75 Bentham, ed. Bowring 1838–43, x. 63.
76 UC viii. 137–8 (11, 14 September 1827).
77 See Bentham, ed. Schofield, Pease-Watkin, and Blamires 2002, 314.
78 Bentham, ed. Bowring 1838–43, ix. 443.
79 See [National Colonization Society] 1831, 22–3, 25, 32.
80 'Colonization Company Proposal' in Bentham, ed. Causer and Schofield 2022, 409.
81 See Bentham, ed. Bowring 1838–43, vii. 334.

82 The criticism, while valid, has less force in relation to his writings on New South Wales in 1802–3, since his aim there was the abandonment of the colony. Furthermore, any consideration given to the welfare of the Indigenous people would not have had any traction with the British political establishment, to whom his arguments were addressed. In that context, it suited his polemical purpose to present the Indigenous people both as savage and, as such, a threat to the settlers.

Bibliography

Primary Sources

Archival sources

British Library Add. MS 38,523. Correspondence of Leigh Hunt, 1807–44.
British Library Add. MS 89,039/2/1. Joseph Hume Correspondence, 1818–54.

Periodicals

Spectator.
Westminster Review.

Printed sources

Anderson, J. *The Interest of Great-Britain with regard to her American Colonies considered. To which is added an Appendix, containing the outlines of a plan for a general pacification.* London: T. Cadell, 1782.

Bentham, J. *Théorie des peines et des récompenses*, ed. E. Dumont, 2 vols. London: Merie de Vogel et Schulze, 1811.

Bentham, J. *Plan of Parliamentary Reform*. London: R. Hunter, 1817.

Bentham, J. *Constitutional Code; for the use of all nations and all governments professing liberal opinions. Vol I*. London: Robert Heward, 1830a.

Bentham, J. *Jeremy Bentham to his fellow-citizens of France, on Houses of Peers and Senates.* London: Robert Heward, 1830b.

Bentham, J. *The Works of Jeremy Bentham*, ed. J. Bowring, 11 vols. Edinburgh: William Tait, 1838–43.

Bentham, J. 'Institute of Political Economy'. In *Jeremy Bentham's Economic Writings*, ed. W. Stark, 3 vols, iii. 301–80. London: George Allen and Unwin, 1952–4.

Bentham, J. *A Comment on the Commentaries and A Fragment on Government*, ed. J.H. Burns and H.L.A. Hart. London: Athlone Press, 1977.

Bentham, J. *Constitutional Code: Volume I*, ed. F. Rosen and J.H. Burns. Oxford: Clarendon Press, 1983.

Bentham, J. *First Principles Preparatory to Constitutional Code*, ed. P. Schofield. Oxford: Clarendon Press, 1989.

Bentham, J. *Colonies, Commerce, and Constitutional Law: Rid Yourselves of Ultramaria and other writings on Spain and Spanish America*, ed. P. Schofield. Oxford: Clarendon Press, 1995.

Bentham, J. *'Legislator of the World': Writings on Codification, Law, and Education*, ed. P. Schofield and J. Harris. Oxford: Clarendon Press, 1998.

Bentham, J. *Rights, Representation, and Reform: Nonsense Upon Stilts and other writings on the French Revolution*, ed. P. Schofield, C. Pease-Watkin, and C. Blamires. Oxford: Clarendon Press, 2002.

Bentham, J. *Writings on the Poor Laws: Volume II*, ed. M. Quinn. Oxford: Clarendon Press, 2010.

Bentham, J. *Writings on Political Economy Volume I*, ed. M. Quinn. Oxford: Clarendon Press, 2016.

Bentham, J. *Panopticon versus New South Wales and other writings on Australia*, ed. T. Causer and P. Schofield. London: UCL Press, 2022.

Collins, D. *An Account of the English Colony in New South Wales*, vol. i. London: T. Cadell Jun. and W. Davies, 1798.

[Malthus, T.] *An Essay on the Principle of Population, as it affects the future improvement of society, with remarks on the speculations of Mr. Godwin, M. Condorcet, and other writers.* London: J. Johnson, 1798.

Milton, J. *Paradise Lost. A Poem Written in Ten Books.* London: Peter Parker, Robert Boulter, and Matthias Walker, 1667.

[National Colonization Society]. *A Statement of the Principles and Objects of a proposed National Society for the cure and prevention of pauperism, by means of Systematic Colonization.* London: James Ridgway, 1830.

[National Colonization Society]. 'Proposal to His Majesty's Government for Founding a Colony on the Southern Coast of Australia'. London, 1831.

Smith, A. *An Inquiry into the Nature and Causes of the Wealth of Nations. With a Commentary by the Author of 'England and America',* 4 vols. London: Charles Knight, 1835–9.

[Wakefield, E.G.]. 'Sketch of a Proposal for Colonizing Australasia, &c. &c. &c.' [London, 1829a].

[Wakefield, E.G.]. *Letter from Sydney, the Principal Town of Australasia. Ed. Robert Gouger. Together with the Outline of a System of Colonization.* London: Joseph Cross, Simpkin and Marshall, and Effingham Wilson, 1829b.

[Wakefield, E.G.]. *England and America. A Comparison of the Social and Political State of Both Nations,* 2 vols. London: Richard Bentley, 1833.

[Wakefield, E.G.]. *The New British Province of Australia; or a Description of the Country, Illustrated by Charts and Views; with an Account of the Principles, Objects, Plan, and Prospects of the Colony.* London: C. Knight, 1834.

Wakefield, E.G. *The Collected Works of Edward Gibbon Wakefield,* ed. M.F. Lloyd Pritchard. Glasgow and London: Collins, 1968.

Secondary Sources

Boralevi, L.C. *Bentham and the Oppressed.* Berlin and New York: Walter de Gruyter, 1984.

Cain, P.J. 'Bentham and the Development of the British Critique of Colonialism', *Utilitas* 23 (2011): 1–24.

Costeloe, M.P. *Response to Revolution: Imperial Spain and the Spanish American Revolutions, 1810–1840.* Cambridge: Cambridge University Press, 1986.

Hart, H.L.A. *Essays on Bentham: Jurisprudence and Political Theory.* Oxford: Clarendon Press, 1982.

Pike, D. *Paradise of Dissent: South Australia 1829–1857,* 2nd ed. Melbourne: Melbourne University Press, 1967.

Pitts, J. *A Turn to Empire: The Rise of Imperial Liberalism in Britain and France.* Princeton and Oxford: Princeton University Press, 2005.

Rosen, F. *Jeremy Bentham and Representative Democracy: A Study of the Constitutional Code.* Oxford: Clarendon Press, 1983.

Schofield, P. *Utility and Democracy: The Political Thought of Jeremy Bentham.* Oxford: Oxford University Press, 2006.

Schofield, P. 'Jeremy Bentham and the British Intellectual Response to the French Revolution', *Journal of Bentham Studies* 23 (2013), https://doi.org/10.14324/111.2045-757X.040.

Schofield, P. 'Jeremy Bentham and Spanish Constitution of 1812'. In *Happiness and Utility: essays presented to Frederick Rosen,* ed. G. Varouxakis and M. Philp, 40–58. London: UCL Press, 2019.

Stark, W. 'Introduction'. In *Jeremy Bentham's Economic Writings,* ed. W. Stark, 3 vols, i. 11–78. London: George Allen and Unwin, 1952–4.

Winch, D. *Classical Political Economy and Colonies.* London: G. Bell and Sons, 1965.

9

'Peopling the country by unpeopling it'

Jeremy Bentham's silences on Indigenous Australia*

Zoë Laidlaw

For over 50 years, historians have debated Jeremy Bentham's views on colonization. From Donald Winch in the 1960s and Lea Campos Boralevi in the 1980s, through to twenty-first century contributions by Philip Schofield, Jennifer Pitts and Peter Cain, scholars have interrogated each freshly published or newly discovered morsel of Bentham's writings to argue about when, why, and to what degree his attitude to colonization changed between the 1760s and the 1830s. As a body, this scholarship has tended to enhance Bentham's reputation as a critic of colonization, distinguishing him from those near contemporaries, like James Mill and his son, John Stuart Mill, who invoked Bentham in their own defences of empire. Not atypically, this reassessment led Peter Cain in 2011 to describe Jeremy Bentham as making 'one of the greatest contributions to anti-colonial literature anywhere in the Western world'.[1] This chapter takes up a question that the debate on Bentham and colonization has left unaddressed, but which the Bentham Project's new edition of *Panopticon versus New South Wales and other writings on Australia* gives us new scope to examine. Informed by recent scholarship, in the fields of settler colonial studies,

* I am especially grateful to Tim Causer, Justin Champion, Penelope Edmonds, Julie Evans, Kirsten McKenzie, and Philip Schofield for their comments on earlier versions of this chapter, as well as those who provided feedback at the 'Bentham and Australia: Convicts, Utility and Empire' Conference at UCL of April 2019, and the Monash University History Programme Research Seminar of 30 August 2019.

Critical Indigenous Studies, and the critical history of international law, which foregrounds the experiences and dispossession of Indigenous peoples as a result of colonization, the chapter asks what happens when we view Bentham's writings on colonies through the lens of settler colonialism? And, specifically, what do Bentham's writings on Australia reveal if our analysis prioritizes the continent's Indigenous peoples and their unceded sovereignty?

The absence of the Indigenous peoples of Australia, the Americas, and Africa both from Bentham's writings on colonization and from the scholarly debate about those writings is startling. While as early as 1795 Bentham claimed boldly that the 'way of living' adopted by Aboriginal peoples in Australia was 'well known', from 1791 onwards his writings on the legitimacy and prospects of the Australian colonies either invoked Aboriginal peoples rhetorically or erased them entirely from spaces given over to 'settlers'.[2] In his Australian – as in his other – colonial writings, Bentham focused instead on different parties to colonization: metropolitan elites; convicts; settler colonizers and their descendants; or Britain's colonized subjects in India. Scholarly interpretations of Bentham's views of colonization have analysed his evolving attitudes to these groups, with the analytical waters muddied, on the one hand, by his sometimes ambiguous description of settlers as 'natives', and, on the other, by historians' tendency to accept too readily Bentham's offhand characterization of lands subjected to settler colonization as previously 'unsettled' or 'vacant'. Such erasures neither began nor ended with Bentham, but their significance in his work is important, not least because of Bentham's status as a positivist, a critic of natural rights, and a theorist of international law. By reinserting Aboriginal peoples into this debate, and interrogating not only Bentham's silences and omissions, but also those who have analysed Bentham's views on colonization, this chapter reveals Bentham's enduring – and unacknowledged – support for British *settler* colonialism and explores how and why he denied Indigenous sovereignty. In so doing, it creates the opportunity to reassess Bentham's contributions to international law, the intellectual foundations of settler colonialism, and colonialism's political, historical and historiographical legacies.

The chapter begins by outlining the debate on Bentham and colonies, suggesting that scholars' preoccupation with delineating Bentham's 'authentic' views on colonization from those better known to his nineteenth-century audience has insulated their analysis from profound shifts affecting the historians of colonialism more broadly. In particular, the advent of the 'new imperial history' (focussing attention on the co-constitution of metropolitan and colonial thought, society and politics) and settler colonial studies (centring analysis of the relationship between settler colonizers and Indigenous peoples) demand that we explore the place of Indigenous peoples in Bentham's writings on settler colonies. The chapter concludes by reflecting more closely on where the Aboriginal peoples of Australia are, or are not, in Bentham's writings, and, in the light of recent scholarship, explores the impact of their erasure.

Bentham and colonies: the debate

At issue in the debate on Bentham and colonization are the nature and dimensions of Bentham's hostility to European colony-holding, an animus particularly evident in his two best-known works on colonies. The first, 'Jeremy Bentham to the National Convention of France', was distributed privately to members of France's National Convention in 1793 but published only in 1830 as *Emancipate Your Colonies!* Bentham's other well-known essay on colonization, 'Rid Yourselves of Ultramaria', addressed slightly more nuanced, but no less trenchant, views to liberal Spaniards in 1822. The scholarly debate arose because Bentham's criticisms of colonialism were much less clear cut in a series of his other writings dating from the 1770s through to 1831. He was, for example, mostly dismissive of the colonists' claims during the American Revolution, though recanting on this point in 1827.[3] Equally, while at times stridently critical of the East India Company, Bentham defended British rule as the *best available* option for Indian governance, despite the political harms it risked in Britain.[4] Moreover, although scathing about the establishment of a penal colony in New South Wales, Bentham intervened in favour of South Australia in 1831 and similarly promoted emigration to British colonies to reduce damaging domestic over-population.[5]

At his death in 1832, some of these writings about colonialism remained in Bentham's vast collection of unpublished, and often incomplete, manuscripts. Versions of others appeared in the digests prepared from 1802 by Bentham's French translator. As Étienne Dumont translated Bentham's writings into French, he shortened, altered, and sometimes added to them; these abstractions were in turn translated into Spanish, Russian, German and other languages. Between 1838 and 1843, Bentham's friend and literary executor John Bowring oversaw the production of 11 volumes of Bentham's writings: alongside most of the already published texts, this series also incorporated English translations of Dumont's digests, and some previously unpublished texts from manuscript. Recognizing both the deficiencies and the very significant omissions of the Bowring volumes, in 1959 UCL established the Bentham Committee to oversee the production of the new *Collected Works of Jeremy Bentham* by researchers affiliated to the Bentham Project.[6] Each new, authoritative volume published by the Bentham Project has furthered the divide between what David Lieberman characterized as the 'historical Bentham' – the Bentham known to his nineteenth-century audience – and the 'authenticity Bentham', that is, the Bentham emerging from his manuscripts via the *Collected Works*.[7] While the scholarship of Philip Schofield, in particular, has largely pinned down the 'historical Bentham', the large scale and slow pace of the Bentham Project make identifying the 'authenticity Bentham' more troublesome. Editorial decisions from now long-distant decades have had unintended consequences, not least as new fields of scholarship and changing questions within existing fields suggest quite different thematic groupings, juxtapositions and priorities to those originally agreed upon. The so-called 'authenticity Bentham' remains highly malleable.

Donald Winch, in his 1965 *Classical Political Economy and Colonies*, and then Lea Campos Boralevi, in her 1984 *Bentham and the Oppressed*, used both these published works and some of Bentham's manuscripts to explain his apparently contradictory views about colonialism. Whilst disagreeing with one another, they made considerable headway in excavating and accounting for Bentham's views on topics including the American Revolution and slavery. It is worth noting, in particular, Boralevi's acute observation that Bentham approached each colonial situation afresh; he did not develop a theory of colonialism that could effectively explain European imperial policy, but rather applied his theory of utility to individual instances of colonization. Thus, in some cases, Bentham argued that the benefits of colonies outweighed their very considerable costs.

In the early twenty-first century, editions published by the Bentham Project allowed historians to portray the 'authenticity Bentham' as, for the most part, a critic of colonialism. Schofield, for example, demonstrated how Bentham's growing political radicalism informed his critique of colonies in the early nineteenth century.[8] In an important series of interventions Jennifer Pitts improved understandings of Bentham's position on British India, doing most to differentiate Bentham's views from those of James and John Stuart Mill.

Moreover, when in 2011 Schofield and Stephen Engelmann published an important new edition of Bentham's 1782 essay, 'Place and Time', Pitts and Engelmann used it to reveal Bentham as considerably more tolerant of non-European cultures than nineteenth-century versions of the same piece suggested.[9]

While Bentham's attitude to Indians living under British rule has been explored carefully, his views on other colonized subjects have featured less prominently, whether in the debate between historians, or indeed in Bentham's writings themselves. For example, although Donald Winch focused on what he termed the 'white dominions' and the 'colonies of settlement' in his *Classical Political Economy and Colonies*, he did not comment on either those colonies' Indigenous peoples or Bentham's indifference to them. Even when reflecting on the strengths and limitations of his 1965 analysis three decades later, Winch dealt with 'native peoples' in one sentence.[10] In 1984, by contrast, Lea Campos Boralevi devoted a chapter of her *Bentham and the Oppressed* to 'Native People of the Colonies'. This analysis explored Bentham's attitude to India and its inhabitants, but other Indigenous peoples made only the most fleeting of appearances.[11] Confusingly, Boralevi also used the term 'native people' to describe *settler colonizers*, those who came from, or whose ancestors came from, metropolitan societies.[12] Her book divided the colonized world in two: first, the 'advanced societies', which were populated by 'colonists of European descent and civilization'; and second, the 'underdeveloped countries', with small European and majority Indigenous populations.[13] In this way, Boralevi's analysis ignored the Indigenous peoples of settler colonies.

Although in overlooking Indigenous peoples who endured settler colonialism, Boralevi and Winch mimicked Bentham, such historical and contemporary silences have both shaped our understanding of colonialism and contributed to its ongoing impact. Questions about how such silences should be conceptualized have helped shape fields including critical indigenous studies and settler colonial studies, which in turn have influenced historians of both colonialism and international law. When Patrick Wolfe reinvigorated the concept of 'settler colonialism' in the late 1990s, he identified its most salient features as the mass transfer of 'settlers' from Europe to overseas colonies, and the focused efforts of those settlers not only to acquire Indigenous land, but also to claim sovereignty over it.[14] As historians including Lisa Ford, Paul McHugh and Bain Attwood have subsequently shown, at the time of Australian colonization, European conceptualizations of sovereignty were in transition, prompted not least by the need to legitimize settler colonialism and settler colonizers' land tenure. Increasingly, Europeans defined sovereignty in terms of jurisdiction over territory, rather than jurisdiction over individuals.[15] Settler colonizers' interest in land often, though certainly not always, outweighed their claims to Indigenous labour; this, argued Wolfe, differentiated settler colonialism from other forms of colonialism (such as, for example, plantation slavery). Settler colonialism is also now recognized as enduring: it entails the ongoing dispossession, and the attempted erasure, of Indigenous peoples through an array of physical, cultural and intellectual means.[16]

The scholars debating Jeremy Bentham's views on colonies have emphasized only the first of these features: they understand settler colonialism as a story about mass European migration. But, of course, the effort to replace Indigenous peoples with European immigrants relied, and continues to rely, on intellectual erasures and silences, as well as on physical force, violence, legal instruments, and government endorsement. When Boralevi dissected Bentham's view of the benefits of future 'colonization', for example, she wrote about 'almost uninhabited or uncultivated land, such as in Australia', where colonization 'need not entail the oppression of any long-established community of people'.[17] Like Bentham himself, Bentham scholars have characterized settler colonies by an absence of people – 'vacant', 'unpopulated', 'unoccupied' – or stressed prior inhabitants' failure to 'use' or to 'improve' land, via terms like 'uncultivated' and 'waste'. Such language reinscribes a European discourse about 'waste lands' that extends back beyond John Locke. In this discourse, lawful possession of land depended upon usage that accorded with specific European practices. Other scholars have followed Winch and Boralevi by side-stepping the implications of settler colonialism for Indigenous peoples in Bentham's work. When Peter Cain, for example, characterized Bentham as making 'one of the greatest contributions to anti-colonial literature anywhere in the Western world', he went on to suggest that this contribution was 'one which in some ways was never improved upon in Britain'.[18] Clearly this accolade is highly dependent on what colonies are assumed to be. Like Boralevi, Cain divided them into 'offshoots of Britain', with (white) settler populations occupying 'much empty land', or, alternatively, 'dependencies with large native populations'.[19] Philip Schofield has made the same distinction.[20]

Such binary divisions into, essentially, 'white' and 'non-white' colonies obscure the dynamics of settler colonialism. The problem is illuminated by critical approaches to race and indigeneity. Critical

Race Theory, for example, demonstrates how hegemonic structures and ideas in society – including not only the courts, or the common law, but also scholarly disciplines – are constructed in a way that obscures white normativity. In consequence, as Cheryl Harris argues, to praise a law or a policy for being ostensibly 'colour-blind', may be to ignore its profoundly different impact on white and black citizens; impacts that are determined by structural inequalities. Critical Race Theory reminds us that while 'race' is a construction, 'racism' has powerful manifestations.[21] Meanwhile, Critical Indigenous Studies warns against conflating 'race' and 'indigeneity'. In this vein, Aileen Moreton-Robinson highlights how Indigenous sovereignty is first erased, and then that erasure rationalized, by what she terms 'white possessive logics'. These refer to structures of thinking, legislating, and knowing, all of which deny the possibility of Indigenous sovereignty, unless that sovereignty takes a form that accords with (incommensurable) Western criteria.[22] This shows how European notions of 'waste lands' and 'possession' helped disavow Aboriginal sovereignty twice over. First, ignorantly, Europeans failed to acknowledge that Aboriginal Australians did indeed occupy, inhabit and cultivate their sovereign territory.[23] Second, self-servingly, they refused to recognize that their own constructions of sovereignty were not universal, but specific to Europe, and incommensurable with Indigenous sovereignty.[24] Antony Anghie, in laying out a framework for a critical history of international law, reminds scholars to focus on how hegemonic European notions of sovereignty have been 'constituted through colonialism' and underpinned by the 'persistently hierarchical structure of the global order'.[25]

Jennifer Pitts' work points to a different way that Indigenous peoples might be silenced or erased from historical scholarship. Her work implicitly posits settler colonies and their Indigenous peoples as less central to Britain's imperial project and history than British India, the West Indies, or tropical Africa. Pitts has argued, particularly in relation to Bentham's 1782 essay 'Place and Time', that he offered 'something of an antidote to liberal imperialism and to the interventionist universalism that is its heir'. Bentham, she claims, 'almost ostentatiously' declined 'to typecast societies as savage or civilized' and should not be read 'as a participant in the imperial liberalism of the nineteenth century but as a counterpoint to it'.[26] Pitts' analysis effectively disentangles Bentham's views from those of the 'Benthamites', who sought to harness his name and reputation to their own projects. Especially in her co-authored article with Stephen Engelmann, Pitts demonstrates how the 'authenticity' Bentham diverged from the 'historical' Bentham. The 2011 Schofield-Engelmann edition of 'Place and Time' reveals Bentham as more tolerant and open-minded than suggested by either Dumont's 1802 or Richard Smith's 1830s version of the same essay.[27] But to stress Bentham's relatively more tolerant views on India risks obscuring his denigration and dismissal of colonized subjects elsewhere. In fact, in the decades after 1782, when Bentham did consider the Indigenous peoples of North America, Southern Africa and Australasia, he typically resorted to exactly the dichotomy of 'civilized' and 'savage'. If, like Pitts, we risk allowing India's inhabitants to represent all those who were colonized, we miss Bentham's denial of the existence, humanity and rights of the Indigenous peoples who stood in the way of settler colonialism.[28]

One work that does directly, if briefly, consider Bentham's attitude to Indigenous people in settler colonies (whilst also distinguishing him from the Benthamites), is Gunhild Hoogensen's 2005 *International Relations, Security and Jeremy Bentham*.[29] Hoogensen argued that Bentham thought that while white and creole colonists in the Americas 'deserved' emancipation from imperial rule, subjects of the East India Company rule would 'benefit' from further guidance. According to Hoogensen, Bentham struggled when these two classes of colonial subjects – resident colonizers and colonized – occupied 'the same area'. This was a problem Bentham could not resolve; he was 'not comfortable with emancipation for all people'.[30] Hoogensen did not use the terminology of 'settler colonialism', but her focus on the space occupied by colonialism and the uncomfortable juxtaposition of colonizers and Indigenous peoples suggests this would be a useful lens to apply.

As this discussion has demonstrated, previous scholarship has overlooked the implications of settler colonialism for our understanding of Bentham.[31] Historians must be conscious that rendering Indigenous peoples invisible in their scholarship helps legitimize settler claims to sovereignty. As Adam Barker remarked, 'Understanding settler colonialism by definition requires piercing this invisibility, revealing that which colonial power would obscure for its own interests'.[32] Turning now to Bentham's newly edited writings on Australia, I seek the Indigenous presence in those writings and question Indigenous absences in order to reveal the mindset that created, enabled, and still fuels, settler colonialism.

Bentham and Australia

The Bentham Project's *Panopticon versus New South Wales* provokes three questions with respect to the Indigenous peoples of Australia. The first relates to Indigenous invisibility. The legal fiction of *terra nullius* – where sovereignty over the Australian continent was claimed on the basis that no one occupied the land – was bolstered by textual and visual erasures of Indigenous peoples from the time of James Cook's 1770 visit to eastern Australia.[33] Certainly, in Bentham's renderings, Australia appears almost as if literally uninhabited prior to European colonization. *Almost*, but not absolutely, uninhabited. So what do the faint traces – the shadows – of the Indigenous peoples of Australia in Bentham's writings reveal?[34] The second question is provoked particularly by Bentham's 1831 intervention on South Australia, but has roots in the early 1800s. This relates to land, and to Bentham's conceptualization of possession, property and sovereignty. Did the ways in which Indigenous sovereignty was 'unthinkable' for Bentham shift over time? Both these concerns highlight the central logic of settler colonialism as a phenomenon: erase the natives – or at least their sovereignty – and seize their land; seize the land and erase the natives. Finally, did Bentham particularly distinguish 'Australia' and its Indigenous peoples from other Indigenous peoples and settler colonies, and if so, how should this backhanded recognition be read?

'New Wales': silencing the 'very dregs even of savage life'

Written in mid-1791, Bentham's 'New Wales' slightly predated his better-known attack on French colonialism, *Emancipate Your Colonies!* Neither *Emancipate*, nor its 1822 counterpart criticizing Spanish colonialism, 'Rid Yourselves of Ultramaria', attended to the mechanics of establishing a colony: rather they focused on the political and economic costs of maintaining existing colonies. By contrast, 'New Wales' also addressed the practical obstacles to founding a sustainable colony, and especially a penal colony. It reveals that Bentham found little to recommend the New South Wales venture.[35] He saw penal transportation as a poor way to effect colonization, with its unwilling vectors and probable imbalance between men and women.[36] In fact, Bentham's sole, oblique, reference to the Indigenous peoples of Australia in 'New Wales' addressed the demographic problem that having too few white women posed for the colony. In response, Bentham raised – but then dismissed – what might be called 'the Sabine solution'. That is, he invoked the Romans' eighth-century BCE attempt to populate Rome via the abduction and rape of the Sabine women. Bentham was not explicit about which population Australia's colonizers might so raid, but did suggest 'peopling the country by unpeopling it after the manner of Mexico and Peru'. This aside evokes the widespread abuse of Aboriginal women by British colonists, and suggests both that Bentham had Indigenous women in mind, and that he was cognisant of the likely consequences of colonialism for them.[37]

As well as the new penal colony, 'New Wales' also condemned colonialism in general. In this context, Bentham considered the rights and prospects of non-European indigenous populations, although not specifically the Aboriginal peoples of Australia.[38] By convention, European powers in the eighteenth century laid claim to sovereignty via one of three methods: conquest, cession or discovery. Bentham did not adopt these categories exactly, and his divergence from them suggests how problematic their distinctions were in practice. In 'New Wales', Bentham differentiated between *conquests* and *colonies*.[39] *Conquests* he defined as entailing the subjugation of one people by an invading nation, as in Britain's growing empire in the 'East Indies'; or what Bentham described as the Incas' 'more civilised' rule over the ancient Peruvians. In these cases, Bentham accepted the potential benefits of colonial – or 'civilised' – rule. For India, he wrote, 'the quiet and secure and steady government of European masters' constituted 'a less evil than the least bad of their own bloody and fluctuating and unsecure and barbarous ones'.[40]

Bentham's deployment of the term *colonies* was more ambiguous. In 'New Wales', he described colonies as 'wild' and 'at a distance': it was clear that this distance had both geographical and cultural dimensions.[41] Bentham's colonies were inhabited – exclusively, it seems – by 'colonists': these settlers, like their ancient Greek predecessors, came from, or were descended from, the mother country, and did not include the local Indigenous population. Unlike in some of his later works, Bentham did not discuss treaties as devices for ceding sovereignty in colonies in 1791. Tellingly, he placed Spain and Portugal's contemporary possessions in the Americas in the category of colony, but categorized the Incas' earlier rule over the ancient Peruvians as a conquest.[42] In this way, he treated European settler colonies as being without prior or Indigenous inhabitants, or at least without prior inhabitants who were worthy of consideration.[43] Similarly, when addressing the legitimacy of James Cook's possessive claim over Australia, Australia's Aboriginal peoples and their sovereignty did not affect Bentham's analysis; he conceptualized those Aboriginal peoples as 'outside' colonial society. Rather, he dwelt on whether earlier visits by the Dutch might upset Britain's claims, and whether the short duration of the *Endeavour's* visit to the eastern coast was sufficient to transform 'discovery' into 'possession'.[44] In sum, the Indigenous peoples of Australia featured either rhetorically, or not at all, in Bentham's 1791 analysis of New South Wales.

A decade later, Bentham's 1803 essay, *A Plea for the Constitution*, mounted an exploration of the legal basis of colonial power, in order to argue that New South Wales had been illegally founded.[45] Bentham did not, though, invoke the Aboriginal peoples of Australia, or their unceded sovereignty, as evidence of this illegal foundation. As in 'New Wales', his definition of 'colony' remained focused on British jurisdiction over British people, rather than territory. Bentham's taxonomy of New South Wales, for example, divided the population into ten groups – none of which included Aborigines. His analysis of the Ordinances issued to secure the colony 'against injuries from the *native savages*' further emphasized this exclusion of Aboriginal peoples from colonial society: Bentham categorized such Ordinances as 'security against mischiefs from without'.[46] As this awkward formulation suggests, the exclusion of Indigenous peoples from his conceptualization of New South Wales required some effort on Bentham's part. His 'Letter to Lord Pelham', written and printed in 1802, drew on the journal of New South Wales' Judge Advocate David Collins to demonstrate the threat Aborigines posed to the colony. The Indigenous peoples of Australia, concluded Bentham, were 'a set of brutes in human shape, the very dregs even of savage life'.[47] This exclusion from the colony, and even from humanity, was underlined in 'A Plea for the Constitution' by a rare, and possibly unique, passage in Bentham's writing that identified individual Indigenous people.[48] Almost as unusually, Bentham here not only acknowledged the Indigenous peoples of Australia, but sought to differentiate them from their counterparts in North America.

The discussion in question addressed the legal instruments deployed when founding colonies. In North America, companies of settlers had been issued with legal charters; but this had not been the case for the penal colony in New South Wales. Bentham also highlighted a difference in how the British engaged with the Indigenous peoples of America and Australia respectively. European colonization in North America (which in this instance Bentham characterized as conquest) had been accompanied by treaty-making with

First Nations. By contrast, he wrote, '[N]o wampum, nor any substitute for wampum, has either been received or given in New South Wales'.[49] According to Bentham, New South Wales was not a *conquest*: rather, it had been *colonized* or *acquired*.[50] The basis of British sovereignty in both America and Australia would continue to be debated, particularly in the 1820s and 1830s, but Bentham's discussion of the apparently casual 'acquisition' of New South Wales shows how he construed Indigenous incapacity when it came to sovereignty. Bentham referred to the Eora kinsmen, Bennelong and Yemmerrawanne, who had travelled to England in 1793 with former Governor Arthur Phillip. 'When', wrote Bentham,

> from their immense continental island, *Benillong* and *Yem-mer-ra-wannie* did us the honour to bestow a glance upon this our little one, it was in the character of private gentlemen, travelling for their amusement, or at least for our's: they signed no *treaty* with his Majesty, nor brought with them any diplomatic powers.[51]

In denying the Eora visitors diplomatic powers, Bentham was arguing that Australia's Indigenous peoples lacked any recognizable government and any claim to sovereignty; their alleged 'savagery' placed them outside the colony.

Bentham had laid the groundwork for this denial in 'Nonsense Upon Stilts', his 1795 critique of the French Declaration of Rights, in which he identified the Indigenous peoples of Australia as exemplifying 'savage nations or rather races of mankind'. Arrogantly, Bentham dismissed 'the savages of New South Wales, *whose way of living is so well known to us*', as 'below the level' of beasts in happiness. Bentham's inability to recognize Aboriginal government or sovereignty had significant consequences, as he went on to outline: 'No government, consequently no rights: no rights, consequently no property: no legal security, no liberty'.[52] To be without government was to be incapable of civilization; yet civilization could only flourish with the security that flowed from government. Bentham thus permanently excluded Australian Aborigines from both. The speed with which Bentham moved to disavow Indigenous sovereignty – indeed to deny Indigenous peoples' capacity for sovereignty – suggests at least tacit acknowledgment of the inconsistencies in Britain's claims to its colonies. As Antony Anghie has argued, the discourses of disqualification applied by Europeans to Indigenous sovereignty shift constantly, driven by the always incomplete task of shoring up settler claims to legitimacy.[53]

'Vacant Lands' in the 'Institute of Political Economy' (1801)

Jeremy Bentham's writings from the early 1800s set out the tangible benefits of colonialism, and not just its costs. These benefits, according to Bentham, arose when colonies provided a destination for an excess of metropolitan population, or, in certain cases, for excess capital.[54] But, as Philip Schofield has shown, even as Bentham identified the potential benefits of colonies, his critique of colony-holding strengthened in the 1810s and 1820s, when he argued that colonialism served only regressive 'sinister interests' in the metropole.[55] These nineteenth-century writings also illuminate Bentham's evolving attitudes to settler colonialism and to land, and, as a consequence, although he did not acknowledge them as such, to the Indigenous owners of land. While Bentham's 1801 essay 'Institute of Political Economy' was not directly concerned with Australia, it reveals how Bentham discounted the rights of those displaced and dispossessed by burgeoning settler colonialism.

In one fragment of that 1801 work, Bentham argued that an *increase of land* was an *increase of wealth*, land being 'no less indispensable' than labour to wealth's production.[56] He went on to justify what today would be termed settler colonialism. Colonies, argued Bentham, helped avoid ruinous over-population in Britain; they also provided benefits to those who took up their 'fresh' land.[57] In this analysis, Bentham identified colonies that he knew had Indigenous populations: his text specified Egypt and America, while his marginal notes referred to New Holland, tropical and southern Africa, and the West Indies. Despite this cognisance, Bentham in each case presumed what he variously described as 'fresh land', 'unappropriated land', and the parts of the earth 'as yet vacant'.[58] Bentham's dismissal of non-European peoples' use of land, and his equally strong association between the use of land and its lawful possession, shows how hegemonic contemporary discourse on waste land had become.[59] This discourse contributed to the new conception of sovereignty as jurisdiction over territory, and underpinned the land grab that characterized settler colonialism.

Thirty years later Bentham explicitly endorsed this discourse. In June 1829, he wrote a postscript for the otherwise unaltered text of his 1793 address to the National Convention of France, which would be published for the first time the following year as *Emancipate Your Colonies!* This brief postscript has caused historians much consternation, for at a time when Bentham was known also to champion Canadian self-government, it expressed support for British rule in India, and even China. However, if different types of colonialism are disaggregated, the postscript can be read as providing unambiguous support for British *settler colonialism*, or for the right to self-determination of white settler colonizers in British settler colonies. In the postscript, Bentham spoke favourably of Australian colonization and particularly the new settlement at Swan River in what would become Western Australia, predicting that Australia's settlements would emancipate themselves to become representative democracies.[60] In Bentham's view, Australia's white settlers (like those of Canada) deserved emancipation; non-white subjects in India did not. Once again, the postscript rendered Indigenous peoples in the settler colonies invisible and their 'rights' irrelevant. This would be even more apparent in Bentham's final work on colonization, his 1831 endorsement of a proposal for a South Australian colony.

'The greatest happiness of all the inhabitants': Colonization Company Proposal

By the late 1820s, the ideas of Edward Gibbon Wakefield, and those who would become known as the 'systematic colonizers', were starting to circulate in Britain. Promising to establish profitable colonial settlements 'without cost or burden to the mother country', a series of colonies based more or less closely on Wakefield's plans were founded in the 1830s and 1840s, including in South Australia and across New Zealand. In his 1829 *A Letter from Sydney*, Wakefield decried the damage to both economy and society that the wide dispersal of land-hungry settler colonizers caused: in essence, he charged, capital and labour had not been mixed in the right proportions in Britain's settler colonies. Wakefield proposed instead to devolve the establishment of new colonies to colonization companies. These, via the controlled sale of land for a fixed price, would create concentrated settlements served with essential infrastructure and populated by a skilled and socially differentiated (white) population. The 'sufficient price' paid for land would fund the emigration of labourers from Britain, but also preclude those immigrant labourers from rushing into land ownership themselves.[61] Although Wakefield's plans were most substantially implemented in South Australia and New Zealand, they were influential across Britain's expanding mid-century empire of settlement. One of Wakefield's foundational assumptions was that land had little or no value while it remained 'unimproved' by Europeans: systematic colonization was predicated on the acquisition of colonial land by colonizing companies either for nothing, or for very little. During the 1830s, the systematic colonizers would become more responsive to concerns about the impact of settler colonialism on Indigenous peoples, but the attention they paid to their rights or needs remained tokenistic at best.[62]

Against this background, in August 1831 Bentham wrote a response to the National Colonization Society's newly released plan for a South Australian colony. Wakefield subsequently made much of how he had 'converted' Bentham to systematic colonization via the South Australian plan,[63] although historians including Bruce Buchan and John Gascoigne have argued for Bentham's 'influence over' the systematic colonizers.[64] As Tim Causer and Philip Schofield note, no direct correspondence between Wakefield and Bentham remains extant and it is not known when they first met.[65] While the nature of Bentham and Wakefield's relationship remains tantalizingly unclear, Bentham's 1831 engagement with Wakefieldian thinking in his 'Colonization Company Proposal' reveals the place of the Indigenous peoples of Australia in his late envisioning of the continent's future.

The systematic colonizers' plan for South Australia assumed the availability of 'waste land liable to be appropriated' by emigrant Britons and their descendants.[66] Their *Proposal to His Majesty's Government for Founding a Colony on the Southern Coast of Australia* recommended that the British Crown gift this land to the colonizing company; the occupation and industry of immigrants would then transform it according to Wakefield's theories. Adopting Lockean notions of land use, the systematic colonizers' plan connected the value of land to particular European modes of 'occupation', while downplaying the (obvious) value of land to both colonizing company and settlers. This proposal did refer to the Indigenous peoples of South Australia, although not in terms that recognized Indigenous sovereignty or possession of land; no payment to the land's Indigenous owners, for example, was envisaged. Despite making provision for a militia, the systematic colonizers' *Proposal* did not explicitly construe Aborigines as a threat to their endeavour.[67] Thus, when the proposed colony was described as 'a spot now absolutely desert and removed from any settlement', this referred solely to its distance from other British colonies. Indeed, Aborigines made no appearance in the systematic colonizers' 1831 discussions of South Australia's foundation, modes of land disposal, or government.

Instead, Indigenous peoples were only mentioned when the systematic colonizers discussed the colony's 'Situation': here they were invoked, like kangaroos, as a measure of habitability. For example, Port

Lincoln – one possible site for the initial settlement – was described thus: 'On this favoured spot the inhabitants must be numerous, for the whole coast appeared to us to be covered with the fires of the natives'; 'this spot was far more thickly peopled than any other part of the southern coast'.[68] Kangaroo Island, by contrast, where the earliest party of South Australian settlers would actually alight, was described as having 'no native inhabitants'.[69]

Bentham's response to the systematic colonizers' *Proposal* omitted even such fleeting acknowledgement of the Indigenous peoples inhabiting southern Australia. It began by considering the three different parties who would have to co-operate to found the colony.[70] As in Bentham's 1803 taxonomy of New South Wales, none of these parties included Aborigines: his imagined South Australia excluded Indigenous peoples without comment.[71] But those peoples cannot have been utterly absent from Bentham's mind. The analysis mounted in his 'Colonization Company Proposal' identified 14 disadvantages for colonies where the population was dispersed, rather than concentrated, and the very first was 'insecurity against damage to person and property from the hostility of the uncivilized aborigines'. A marginal note recorded – bluntly – the decision in contemporary Van Diemen's Land 'absolutely to extirpate the natives'.[72] Yet Bentham's analysis anticipated no expenditure for defence, nor weapons, nor indeed for any trade goods or presents for South Australia's Indigenous peoples. The costs he calculated did not include funds for land purchases from Indigenous owners. For Bentham, it seems, the systematic colonizers' principle of concentrated European settlement simply obviated any risk from Aborigines.[73]

Bentham's 'Colonization Company Proposal' identified the 'all-comprehensive end' of South Australian government as 'the greatest happiness of all the inhabitants'. Again, however, all the ways he explored to guarantee this outcome ignored Indigenous peoples and the impact of colonization on them. For example, he imagined future colonists becoming dissatisfied with absentee investors, who expatriated profits from land sales while resident settlers shouldered the costs of government. Bentham stressed the foundational, and transformative, role played by such aggrieved settlers. Without them, he observed, 'those same lands would be uninhabited, unoccupied and nothing worth'.[74] Again, Bentham unquestioningly accepted the connection between the 'appropriate' use of land and an individual's, or a society's, capacity to possess that land. Nor did he comment on the two interlocking principles the systematic colonizers' *Proposal* set out for the disposal of so-called 'waste land'. The first was that anyone *'able* and *willing'* to cultivate land should be allowed to do so; the second, by contrast, specified that no one who was *'unwilling or unable'* to cultivate waste land 'should be allowed to appropriate the same under any pretext whatsoever'.[75] Together, the propositions responded to, whilst also working to deny, the possibility of Indigenous possession. This formulation intersected with Bentham's readiness – from a position of profound ignorance – to dismiss Aboriginal society, culture and sovereignty. Bentham did not feel the need to know the Indigenous peoples of Australia; he was already able to classify them as 'savages', and on that basis to disregard their capacity, rights and sovereignty; even to deny their presence. As Brenna Bhandar has argued, the 'discourse of savagery' effectively made 'aboriginal rights to their land a nonquestion'.[76]

Civilization and savagery, or possession and dispossession: law, government and property in a settler colonial context

Causer and Schofield's edition of *Panopticon versus New South Wales* allows us to interrogate the construction of settler colonial societies and their claims to sovereignty. But the collection of four decades' worth of Bentham's reflections on the British colonization of Australia also highlights the too often silenced counterpart to those settler claims and societies: Indigenous dispossession and the denial of Indigenous sovereignty. Until now, the debate on 'Bentham and colonization' has not addressed Bentham's embrace of settler colonialism as such. Instead, Bentham has increasingly been cast as a critic of colonialism, his antipathy inferred from his advocacy of settler self-government in the French, Spanish, and latterly British, Empires. To accept this version of the 'authenticity Bentham', however, is to look away from how Bentham, like many other European political thinkers and philosophers, contributed to colonialism. Bentham deployed and elaborated existing understandings of sovereignty, civilization, and possession to become an advocate of settler colonialism. It serves settler colonialism's ongoing interests if twenty-first century scholarship on political thought is not attentive to its specific forms.

It is worth noting that Bentham found these concepts difficult. As Hoogensen argued, he struggled to envisage a colony inhabited simultaneously by both (so-called) 'civilized' and 'uncivilized' peoples, precisely because such a juxtaposition threatened the future security and representative government that Bentham thought 'civilized' colonizers deserved.[77] Bentham's Australian writings suggest that his solution was to exclude the 'uncivilized' (that is, Indigenous peoples) from the colony, both conceptually and legally. The Indigenous peoples of Australia persisted in Bentham's writings on Australia only as a shadow on the landscape, a feature of space, but not of place; Bentham rendered colonies as settler places. Bhandar points to Bentham's tautological renderings of 'savagery' and civilization. 'Savagery', she writes, 'defined by the lack of respect for property law, is that which property law must guard itself against'. Yet, 'the "beneficent genius" that civilises savagery is security', which stems from government, law, and property.[78] Bentham's writings on Australia and his 1795 essay 'Nonsense Upon Stilts' encapsulate Bhandar's argument almost perfectly. The latter, of course, explicitly posited Australia's Indigenous peoples as the antithesis of civilized France. To be savage, for Jeremy Bentham, was to be *permanently* excluded from government, liberty, property and rights.[79] Bhandar also shows how Bentham's work on 'abstract notions of ownership' would help shore up the new, territorial, conceptions of sovereignty that rose to prominence in tandem with nineteenth-century settler colonialism. Such abstraction helped transform land into a commodity, into 'free and fungible' property, and facilitated Indigenous dispossession.[80]

Jeremy Bentham's career coincided with an era of 'world crisis', set against a conjuncture that included the American, French and Haitian Revolutions, and the massive expansion of British imperial power in Asia and across its settler colonies.[81] From this global canvas, and on the slimmest of evidential bases, Bentham chose the Indigenous peoples of Australia as his archetypal – and also most degraded – 'savages'. Bentham had global pretensions, and although his notion of a 'Universal Jurisprudence' stalled, he was hailed in his lifetime, as Jennifer Pitts and David Armitage both remind us, as the 'legislator of the world'. Armitage, in a characteristically elegant exploration of Bentham's universal vision, warns against 'throwing the universalist baby out with the imperialist bathwater'.[82] But in differentiating Bentham from his successors and acolytes, we should beware perpetuating the damaging myths and silences on which Bentham's 'criticisms' of colonialism rested. Although Indigenous sovereignty would be denied – explicitly or practically – in Britain's settler colonies throughout the nineteenth century, not all of Bentham's British contemporaries accepted the characterization of Indigenous peoples as savage or uncivilized.[83] Thus, asking why Bentham posited Australian Aborigines as his particular antithesis to civilization gives us an opportunity to discuss how the edifice of British sovereignty was constructed, extended and defended. We must continue to explore both his denial of Aboriginal sovereignty, and the enacting of this denial through silences and erasures, and only ever the faintest of traces of Australia's Indigenous peoples.

Notes

1 Cain 2011, 24.
2 Bentham, ed. Schofield, Pease-Watkin, and Blamires. 2002, 329–30; 'New Wales' in Bentham, ed. Causer and Schofield 2022, 3–22.
3 Winch 1997, 147–54, at 149–50; Campos Boralevi 1984, ch. 6; Schofield 2006, 58–9, 217: Bentham thought it would have been advantageous for the American colonists to remain British.
4 Schofield 2006, 201, 218, quoting UC viii. 137–8, 11, 14 September 1827.
5 'Colonization Company Proposal' in Bentham, ed. Causer and Schofield 2022, 401–32. Semmel 1961, 513–25, noted Bentham's 1831 support for Edward Gibbon Wakefield's South Australian project.
6 The construction of the 'historical' Bentham is clearly explained in Schofield 2009, 29–43.
7 Lieberman 2000, 108.
8 Schofield 2006, 202.
9 Bentham, ed. Schofield and Engelmann 2011; Pitts 2007; Pitts 2011; Engelmann and Pitts 2011.
10 Winch 1965. It was only in a 1997 reflection on his and Boralevi's earlier work that Winch noted: 'Neither in Australia nor Latin America did Bentham choose to confront any of the issues raised by the native populations ... presumably because he believed that any solution that suited the European colonists would redound to the benefit of the aboriginals as well.' Winch 1997, 149.
11 Boralevi 1984, ch. 6, 'Native People of the Colonies'. Boralevi's characterization of Bentham's views of Indians is contested by more recent scholarship, including that of Engelmann and Pitts.
12 Boralevi 1984, 126, discusses Bentham's 'passionate defence of the interests of the native people of the French and English colonies in Canada, and in particular, of the Spanish colonies in "Ultramaria", who were in his opinion oppressed by the government of *their* mother country'. Emphasis added.
13 Boralevi 1984, 128, 133.
14 Wolfe 1999; Wolfe 2001.
15 Ford 2010; McHugh 2004; Attwood 2008, 72–82.
16 As Tracey Banivanua Mar and Penelope Edmonds put it: 'settler colonists went ... to new lands to appropriate them and to establish new and improved replicas of the societies they left. As a result Indigenous peoples ... found an ever-decreasing place for themselves in settler colonies as changing demographics enabled ever more extensive dispossession. Settlers, in the end, tended not to emigrate to assimilate into Indigenous societies, but rather emigrated to replace them'. Banivanua Mar and Edmonds 2010, 2.
17 Boralevi 1984, 127, 129.
18 Cain 2011, 24.
19 Cain 2011, 2, 10.
20 Schofield 2006, 215–17, and notes 57–61. Schofield's analysis here is of 'Non-faciendum the fourth: increasing the quantity of land, viz., by colonization', included in Bentham, ed. Quinn 2019, 21–7.
21 Harris 1993.

22 Moreton-Robinson 2015, xii–xiii; Land 2015; Black 2011.
23 Pascoe 2018.
24 Moreton-Robinson 2015, xx–xxiii.
25 Anghie 2005, 38; Pitts 2018, 15–16.
26 Pitts 2011. Pitts argues that Bentham wrote in 'Place and Time' more precisely and impartially of nations that are 'unletter'd, however civilized in other respects'. However, Pitts' argument rests on considerable special pleading, and is coloured by its focus on India, and especially by the new edition of 'Place and Time'. Pitts' recent work is alert to the problems of the 'conventional narrative', which both depicts modern international law as a European product and export, rather than 'partly forged in the course of European imperial expansion and through European interactions with extra-European states and societies', and 'suggests that the (European) blocks of modern international law were truly universalist': Pitts 2018, 14.
27 Engelmann and Pitts 2011; 'De l'influence des temps et des lieux en matière de législation' in Bentham, ed Dumont 1802; Bentham, ed. Schofield and Engelmann 2011.
28 Pitts' conclusions have become hegemonic, e.g. Buchan 2008, 13. Pitts' 2018 *Boundaries of the International* positions itself as a contribution to Anghie's project of critical international law. In this, Pitts charts Bentham's shift from his work of the 1780s to, in his 1827 'International Law' sketch, the restriction of international law to civilized nations. Pitts suggests Bentham's transition may have reflected 'the shift of the centre of gravity of imperial domains from the settler colonies of the Americas ... to India and other non-white populations', but stresses that Bentham had earlier 'insisted on the emancipation of all colonies, India specifically included, and not just colonies whose loudest voices were white settlers'. Pitts 2018, 122, 141–2, 144–5. This explanation does not consider the claims or experience of Indigenous peoples in settler colonies during an era of mass immigration from the British Isles, nor Bentham's apparent obliviousness to them: Middleton 2019, 195–7.
29 Hoogensen 2005, 149–54. Hoogensen graciously linked Boralevi's ambiguity on 'native people' to the imprecise terms Bentham himself deployed for colonial populations.
30 Hoogensen 2005, 149–50, 152–4. She finds further evidence of this in the 1829 postscript to *Emancipate Your Colonies!*
31 A recent and important exception to this is provided by Arneil 2020.
32 Barker 2012.
33 On terra nullius, see Moreton-Robinson 2015, 18, who notes that this legal fiction positioned Indigenous peoples 'as trespassers'. Kercher 2002; Miller *et al.* 2010, 171–87. Sovereignty was claimed on the basis that no one occupied the land; a fiction instantiated in the late nineteenth century, and challenged legally, if not conclusively overturned, only in 1992.
34 Discussing the challenges of colonial archives for historians of Indigenous peoples, Tracey Banivanua Mar spoke of these 'shadows' as 'whisper-thin': quoted in Evans 2017, 155.
35 'New Wales' in Bentham, ed. Causer and Schofield 2022, 14–16.
36 'New Wales' in Bentham, ed. Causer and Schofield 2022, 4–6.
37 'New Wales' in Bentham, ed. Causer and Schofield 2022, 6. On the role played by sexual violence in settler colonization, see, e.g., Atkinson 2002, 57–64; Woollacott 2015, 152–78. On settler colonizers' persistent mischaracterizations of Aboriginal women: Conor 2014.
38 'New Wales' in Bentham, ed. Causer and Schofield 2022, 4.
39 This distinction is more apparent in Bentham's writings (including 'A Plea for the Constitution' of 1803) on New South Wales than in his well-known appeals to France and Spain, where he was more likely – as Boralevi notes – to distinguish between existing colonies and future colonization. Bentham did not invoke contemporaneous discussions of the 'doctrine of discovery'. See Miller *et al.* 2010; Arneil 1996.
40 'New Wales' in Bentham, ed. Causer and Schofield 2022, 9. Note that 'New Wales' was written a decade after 'Place and Time'. Here, and elsewhere, Bentham persistently qualified his opposition to colony-holding by justifying the governance of a less 'civilized' population by a more 'civilized' colonizing power. Bentham deployed this qualification to justify continued governance; later 'liberal imperialists' were to suggest that imperial activity to 'civilize' was in fact a moral responsibility. See Mantena 2007.
41 'New Wales' in Bentham, ed. Causer and Schofield 2022, 8.
42 'New Wales' in Bentham, ed. Causer and Schofield 2022, 9.

43   On how discourses of disqualification have shifted over time, see Anghie 2005.

44   'New Wales' in Bentham, ed. Causer and Schofield 2022, 17–18. Here, Bentham seemed to temper arguments for the relevance of 'discovery'. In the US context, see Marshall's 1823 discussion of how discovery gave title to colonizers, but this title was consummated by possession: Williams 1990, 313.

45   In her examination of 'A Plea for the Constitution', Lauren Benton notes as an aside that Bentham did 'not address many of the legal issues that would become the focus of conflict in the colony in coming decades', including 'the legal status of Aborigines'. Benton 2009, 191–6.

46   'A Plea for the Constitution', in Bentham, ed. Causer and Schofield 2022, 361.

47   'Correspondence, sent to William Wilberforce, of Jeremy Bentham with Sir Charles Bunbury' in Bentham, ed. Causer and Schofield 2022, 31–2; 'Letter to Lord Pelham' in ibid., 94; 'Second Letter to Lord Pelham' in ibid., 185, 241.

48   'A Plea for the Constitution' in Bentham, ed. Causer and Schofield 2022, 344–5, Section 6, on the 'Nullity of Legislation in New South Wales for want of an Assembly to consent'.

49   'Wampum' referred to the material manifestation of treaties favoured by some east coast First Nations, particularly the Iroquois: see Edmonds 2016, 52.

50   In seeming contrast with his 1791 comments, however, which showed how conquered territories could benefit from more civilized government, Bentham thought New South Wales was better off as a colony. Despite 'all its peculiarities and all its faults' it had at least 'not added that vulgar and crowning folly of distant *conquest*'. But see also notes 39 and 44 on contemporary debates in the context of the United States.

51   'A Plea for the Constitution', in Bentham, ed. Causer and Schofield 2022, 345.

52   Bentham, ed Schofield, Pease-Watkin, and Blamires 2002, 329–30. Emphasis added.

53   Anghie 2005, ch. 2.

54   Winch 1965, 31–6.

55   Schofield 2006, 202.

56   Bentham, ed. Quinn 2019, 21.

57   Bentham, ed. Quinn 2019, 21.

58   Bentham, ed. Quinn 2019, 21, 3, 23.

59   On the development of this discourse, see Arneil 1996, ch. 6.

60   Bentham, ed. Schofield, Pease-Watkin, and Blamires 2002, 314–15.

61   [Wakefield] 1829.

62   Attwood 2013, 50–82.

63   Semmel 1968; Winch 1997, 149; Winch 1965, 129; Schofield 2006, 219–20.

64   Buchan and Gascoigne refer more persuasively to 'Benthamite' and 'utilitarian' influence than to Bentham himself, suggesting that it was the 'historical' rather than 'authenticity' Bentham, whose influence they could perceive: Buchan 2008, 124; Gascoigne 2002, ch. 3.

65   'Editorial Introduction' in Bentham, ed. Causer and Schofield 2022, xcviii.

66   [National Colonization Society] 1831, 3–4. See also 'Edward Gibbon Wakefield on the Colonization Society's Plan, 23 Aug. 1831' in Bentham, ed. Causer and Schofield 2022, 435–6.

67   [National Colonization Society] 1831, 18. Note that this is a contrast to Bentham's 1802 'Letters to Lord Pelham', which drew on David Collins's publications to depict Aborigines as a threat.

68   [National Colonization Society] 1831, 25, 26, 29. This evidence was drawn from the expedition of Nicholas Baudin; the *Proposal* also used Matthew Flinders' account of his expedition: [National Colonization Society] 1831, 22.

69   [National Colonization Society] 1831, 28.

70   'Colonization Company Proposal' in Bentham, ed. Causer and Schofield 2022, 403.

71   'Colonization Company Proposal' in Bentham, ed. Causer and Schofield 2022, 413–16.

72   'Colonization Company Proposal' in Bentham, ed. Causer and Schofield 2022, 409.

73   Bentham described this principle as 'dispersion-preventing'.

74   'Colonization Company Proposal' in Bentham, ed. Causer and Schofield 2022, 423.

75   [National Colonization Society] 1831, 4.

76   Bhandar 2018, 96.

77   Hoogensen 2005, 149–50.

78   Bhandar 2018, 101.

79   Bentham, ed. Schofield, Pease-Watkin, and Blamires 2002.

80 Bhandar 2018, 96.
81 Bayly 2004, ch. 3.
82 Pitts 2005; Armitage 2011, 65, 82.
83 Laidlaw 2021.

Bibliography

Primary Sources

Bentham, J. 'De l'influence des tems et des lieux en matière de législation'. In *Traités de législation civile et pénale*, ed. É. Dumont, 3 vols, iii. 323–95. Paris: Bossange, Masson et Besson, 1802.

Bentham, J. 'Of the Influence of Time and Place in Matters of Legislation'. In *The Works of Jeremy Bentham*, ed. J. Bowring, 11 vols, i. 169–94. Edinburgh: William Tait, 1838–43.

Bentham, J. 'Nonsense Upon Stilts'. In *Rights, Representation and Reform: Nonsense Upon Stilts and other writings on the French Revolution*, ed. P. Schofield, C. Pease-Watkin, and C. Blamires, 317–402. Oxford: Clarendon Press, 2002.

Bentham, J. 'Emancipate Your Colonies!'. In *Rights, Representation and Reform: Nonsense Upon Stilts and other writings on the French Revolution*, ed. P. Schofield, C. Pease-Watkin, and C. Blamires, 289–316. Oxford: Clarendon Press, 2002.

Bentham, J. 'Place and Time', ed. P. Schofield and S.G. Engelmann. In *Selected Writings: Jeremy Bentham*, ed. S.G. Engelmann, 152–219. New Haven: Yale University Press, 2011.

Bentham, J. 'Appendix C' to 'Method and Leading Features of an Institute of Political Economy'. In *Writings on Political Economy, Volume V: Wealth, Money, and Prices*, ed. M. Quinn, pre-publication version, The Bentham Project, 2019 [https://rdr.ucl.ac.uk/articles/dataset/Writings_on_Political_Economy_Volume_V_Preliminaries_and_preliminary_text_files_1-2_5-15_/10110860/1].

Bentham, J. *Panopticon versus New South Wales and other writings on Australia*. London: UCL Press, 2022.

[National Colonization Society]. *A Proposal to His Majesty's Government for founding a colony on the South Coast of Australia*. London: W. Nicol, 1831.

[Wakefield, E.G.]. *A Letter from Sydney, the Principal Town of Australasia together with the Outline of A System of Colonization*. London: Joseph Cross, 1829.

Secondary Sources

Anghie, A. *Imperialism, Sovereignty, and the Making of International Law*. Cambridge: Cambridge University Press, 2005.

Armitage, D. 'Globalizing Jeremy Bentham', *History of Political Thought* 32 (2011): 63–82.

Arneil, B. *John Locke and America: The Defence of English Colonialism*. Oxford: Clarendon Press, 1996.

Arneil, B. 'Origins: Colonies and Statistics', *Canadian Journal of Political Science* 53 (2020): 735–54.

Atkinson, J. *Trauma Trails, Recreating Song Lines: The Transgenerational Effects of Trauma in Indigenous Australia*. North Melbourne: Spinifex Press, 2002.

Attwood, B. *Possession: Batman's Treaty and the Matter of History*. Melbourne: Miegunyah Press, 2008.

Attwood, B. 'Returning to the Past: The South Australian Colonisation Commission, the Colonial Office and Aboriginal Title', *Journal of Legal History* 34 (2013): 50–82.

Banivanua Mar, T. and Edmonds, P. 'Introduction'. In *Making Settler Colonial Space: Perspectives on Race, Place and Identity*, ed. T. Banivanua Mar and P. Edmonds, 1–24. Basingstoke: Palgrave Macmillan, 2010.

Barker, A. 'Locating Settler Colonialism', *Journal of Colonialism and Colonial History* 13: 3 (Winter 2012).

Bayly, C.A. *The Birth of the Modern World, 1780–1914*. Oxford: Blackwell, 2004.

Benton, L. *A Search for Sovereignty: Law and Geography in European Empires, 1400–1900*. Cambridge: Cambridge University Press, 2009.

Bhandar, B. *Colonial Lives of Property: Law, Land and Racial Regimes of Ownership*. Durham, NC: Duke University Press, 2018.

Black, C. *The Land is the Source of the Law: A Dialogic Encounter with an Indigenous Jurisprudence*. London: Routledge, 2011.

Boralevi, L.C. *Bentham and the Oppressed*. Berlin and New York: Walter de Gruyter, 1984.

Buchan, B. *The Empire of Political Thought: Indigenous Australians and the Language of Colonial Government*. London: Pickering and Catto, 2008.

Cain, P. 'Bentham and the Development of the British Critique of Colonialism', *Utilitas* 23 (2011): 1–24.

Conor, L. *Skin Deep: Settler Impressions of Aboriginal Women*. Crawley: University of Western Australia Press, 2016.

Edmonds, P. 'Honourable Colonisation? Australia'. In *Honourable Intentions? Violence and Virtue in Australian and Cape Colonies, c. 1750–1850*, ed. P. Russell and N. Worden, 46–62. London: Routledge, 2016.

Engelmann, S.G. and Pitts, J. 'Bentham's "Place and Time"', *The Tocqueville Review/La Review Tocqueville* 32 (2011): 43–66.

Evans, J. 'A Life Unthinking and Undoing Colonialism: Tracey Banivanua Mar (1974–2017)', *Law & History* 4 (2017): 151–7.

Ford, L. *Settler Sovereignty: Jurisdiction and Indigenous People in America and Australia*. Cambridge, MA: Harvard University Press, 2010.

Gascoigne, J. *The Enlightenment and the Origins of European Australia*. Cambridge: Cambridge University Press, 2002.

Harris, C. 'Whiteness as Property', *Harvard Law Review* 106 (1993): 1709–91.

Hoogensen, G. *International Relations, Security and Jeremy Bentham*. Abingdon: Routledge, 2005.

Kercher, B. 'Native Title in the Shadows: The Origins of the Myth of *Terra Nullius* in Early New South Wales Courts'. In *Colonialism and the Modern World*, ed. G. Blue, M. Bunton, and R. Crozier, 100–19. Abingdon: Routledge, 2002.

Land, C. *Decolonizing Solidarity: Dilemmas and Directions for Supporters of Indigenous Struggles*. London: Zed Books, 2015.

Lieberman, D. 'Economy and Polity in Bentham's Science of Legislation'. In *Economy, Polity and Society: British Intellectual History 1750–1850*, ed. S. Collini, R. Whatmore, and B. Young, 107–34. Cambridge: Cambridge University Press, 2000.

Mantena, K. 'The Crisis of Liberal Imperialism'. In *Victorian Visions of Global Order: Empire and International Relations in Nineteenth-Century Political Thought*, ed. D. Bell, 113–35. Cambridge: Cambridge University Press, 2007.

McHugh, P.G. *Aboriginal Societies and the Common Law: A History of Sovereignty, Status, and Self-Determination*. Oxford: Oxford University Press, 2004.

Middleton, A. 'Boundaries of the International: Law and Empire by Jennifer Pitts', *Journal of Imperial and Commonwealth History* 47 (2019): 195–7.

Miller, R.J., Ruru, J., Behrendt, L., and Lindberg, T. *Discovering Indigenous Lands: The Doctrine of Discovery in the English Colonies*. Oxford: Oxford University Press, 2010.

Moreton-Robinson, A. *The White Possessive: Property, Power and Indigenous Sovereignty*. Minneapolis: University of Minnesota Press, 2015.

Pascoe, B. *Dark Emu*. Broome: Magabala Books, 2018.

Pitts, J. 'Jeremy Bentham: Legislator of the World?'. In *Utilitarianism and Empire*, ed. B. Schultz and G. Varouzakis, 57–91. Lanham, MD: Lexington Books, 2005.

Pitts, J. 'Boundaries of Victorian International Law'. In *Victorian Visions of Global Order: Empire and International Relations in Nineteenth-Century Political Thought*, ed. D. Bell, 67–88. Cambridge: Cambridge University Press, 2007.

Pitts, J. '"Great and Distant Crimes": Empire in Bentham's Thought'. In *Selected Writings: Jeremy Bentham*, ed. S.G. Engelmann, 478–99. New Haven: Yale University Press, 2011.

Pitts, J. *Boundaries of the International: Law and Empire*. Cambridge, MA: Harvard University Press, 2018.

Schofield, P. *Utility and Democracy: The Political Thought of Jeremy Bentham*. Oxford: Oxford University Press, 2006.

Schofield, P. *Bentham: A Guide for the Perplexed*. London: Continuum, 2009.

Semmel, B. 'The Philosophic Radicals and Colonialism', *Journal of Economic History* 21 (1961): 513–25.

Williams Jr., R. *The American Indian in Western Legal Thought: The Discourses of Conquest*. New York: Oxford University Press, 1990.

Winch, D. *Classical Political Economy and Colonies*. London: London School of Economics, 1965.

Winch, D. 'Bentham on Colonies and Empire', *Utilitas* 9 (1997): 147–54.

Wolfe, P. *Settler Colonialism and the Transformation of Anthropology: The Politics and Poetics of an Ethnographic Event*. London and New York: Cassell, 1999.

Wolfe, P. 'Land, Labor, and Difference: Elementary Structures of Race', *American Historical Review* 106 (2001): 866–905.

Woollacott, A. *Settler Society in the Australian Colonies: Self-Government and Imperial Culture*. Oxford: Oxford University Press, 2015.

Part IV

Bentham, the panopticon penitentiary scheme, and penal institutions and practices in Australia and Britain

10

Inverting the panopticon

Van Diemen's Land and the invention of a colonial Pentonville Prison

Honey Dower

If Jeremy Bentham had lived to 1842 and witnessed the construction of Pentonville Prison and its many iterations across the nineteenth-century world, he would have been aghast. After all, he had inadvertently become the intellectual forefather of a new type of prison discipline known as 'separate treatment'.[1] First experimented with at London's Pentonville Prison, separate treatment was intended to be a strict reformative regime based on the principles of isolation, silence and control to engender lasting moral and social change in British prisoners sentenced to transportation to the Australian colonies. Under this regime, prisoners were confined in a well-lit yet isolated cell, let out only for private exercise and to attend chapel. Prisoners were required to wear a mask when outside of their cell and were only permitted to speak privately to prison staff – otherwise, they lived in absolute silence. Separate treatment differed from traditional solitary confinement in its execution – these cells were scientific marvels, with a ventilation system and underfloor heating – and its intent, for solitary confinement was a punishment, and separate treatment was a method of reclamation and reformation. Separate treatment was the latest iteration of penitentiary imprisonment prompted by a cross-section of international reformers, having evolved from the American system of 'silent treatment' experimented with at the end of the eighteenth century, and praised for its more humane outlook. However, by 1853, a little under a decade since the Pentonville Prison 'experiment' began, Colonel Joshua

Jebb, Surveyor-General of Prisons, warned that it 'was not the *use* but the *abuse* of separate confinement that is to be guarded against'.[2]

In the context of Van Diemen's Land, the southernmost Australian colony, this warning was especially apt.[3] In 1844, two men directly associated with the Pentonville Prison 'experiment' were tasked with overseeing the transportation of the first prisoners to be exposed to separate treatment.[4] These two men were James Boyd (1815–1900) and Dr John Stephen Hampton (1810–69). In just under five years, Boyd and Hampton had successfully established their own 'model' Pentonville Prison at the Port Arthur penal settlement, where the system of separate treatment was used increasingly against specific types of convicts and persisted with despite reports of mental disturbance among prisoners. Through his association with Hampton, Boyd was appointed the Port Arthur Commandant and held this position from 1853–71. The Separate Prison itself lasted until the breakup of the settlement in 1877. Boyd and Hampton's ventures led historians James Semple-Kerr and Joan Torrance to describe them as 'the earliest Pentonville system disciples in the Australian colonies'.[5] This was in spite of colonial commentators observing that Boyd deserved praise for his perseverance with his Separate Prison, particularly as it was, according to one anonymous critic, 'such a useless and expensive establishment'.[6] The experiment at Port Arthur was condemned for its costliness, its 'utter uselessness, its abuses', and – perhaps most interestingly – 'the petty interested motives for continuing all these in defiance of public opinion'.[7] The Port Arthur Separate Prison was, in Marcus Clarke's words, 'a monument of official stupidity'.[8]

This chapter will explore Semple-Kerr and Torrance's claim that Boyd and Hampton were 'disciples' of Pentonville Prison. While it is simple to describe them as such, this view only works in the abstract. When we view these men in the context of Van Diemen's Land, it becomes evident that their personal ambition was a driving factor in bringing the system of separate treatment to the colony. Rightly or wrongly, Pentonville Prison is conceptually linked to Jeremy Bentham's panopticon.[9] Any survey of prison development must test the disparity between genuflection to penal reform philosophies in comparison to its harsh lived reality. Therefore, I intend to unpack Semple-Kerr's claim in the colonial context by 'inverting' the panopticon: instead of the prisoners, this chapter focuses on individuals, namely James Boyd, who came to be the longest serving Commandant of the Port Arthur penal station (1853–73), and was the driving force behind the Port Arthur Separate Prison (1851–77). If the panopticon was 'of great biographical significance for Bentham', with 'a decade or more' of his life spent on the project, it stands to reason that the enterprise of other penal reformers should be considered in a similar light.[10] In other words: were Boyd and Hampton disciples of Pentonville Prison, and by extension, Jeremy Bentham?

Existing studies of eighteenth- and nineteenth-century prison reformers focus on noted figures, like John Howard (1726–90) and Elizabeth Fry (1780–1845), while the roles of ostensibly minor players are considered collectively and given little individual attention.[11] It is not enough to write about reform without understanding what, or who, is being reformed. Likewise, if we avoid engaging on an intimate level with historical actors, we risk underestimating how much their competing motivations guided their reality and the realities of others. In other words, by finding what Katie Barclay terms the 'self' of historical actors, we can start to untangle the identities held by a man like Boyd: a wealthy Victorian man, a colonial authority, a penal reformer, and a self-styled prison administrator.[12] Similar to Bentham, decades of Boyd's life were tied to the fate of his Separate Prison – though, unlike Bentham, Boyd's ambitions were realized. If a system like separate treatment promised to impart 'moral discipline' into an individual's character, it naturally follows that taming prisoners called for a new and disciplined character management ideal: the professional penal administrator.[13] Indeed, if a facet of the Victorian period was the 'moral training' of prisoners, the same should be said of 'moral training' required of the middle-class men tasked to enact systems of control.[14] In his observations on Bentham, Michael Ignatieff writes: 'What was rational was impersonal, and what was impersonal was humane'.[15] This view may well have been the mantra for men like Boyd and Hampton, particularly in informing and affirming their personal and professional masculine identities. There is a clear tension between their commitment to self-reform, moral and intellectual improvement, and the various regimented gendered pressures of nineteenth-century life.[16] As historical actors nested in a wider political, social, administrative and intellectual context that searched for the 'ideal' prison system, this task required an 'ideal' prison administrator.[17] In this chapter, I suggest that unless the sites of power in which the empowered live are examined, their reality, and that of those they oppress, is obscured. In other words, what can we learn about colonial penal reform by understanding the people charged to enforce it?

Before James Boyd and John Hampton set sail from England to Van Diemen's Land in 1844, several challenges were awaiting them at their destination. This chapter examines these challenges and explains why and how separate treatment gained such a foothold in the colony. The first factor was the decline in the use of corporal punishment. The practice of flogging convicts had been waning since the early part of the decade; however, the subsequent increase of isolation-based confinements did not instil the same level of fear and compliance in recalcitrant convicts it was supposed that corporal punishment could. Informed by contemporary ideas around the reformative qualities promised by sensory-deprivation punishments, the introduction of separate treatment – at first in a modified, then complete, form – with its apparent virtues of religious and social reformation, proved appealing to colonial authorities. Second, the prevalence of 'unnatural' sexual crimes among male and female convicts sparked a moral panic heightened by three factors: the anti-transportation debates and William Molesworth's committee on the subject; colonial-Victorian sensibilities on morality and sexuality; and the tenure of Governor John Eardley Eardley-Wilmot (1783–1847), whose efforts to address charges of unnatural crimes were undermined by salacious allegations about his personal life. These forces are integral to understanding the penal and cultural landscape of Van Diemen's Land and, when read together, clarify how separate treatment was presented as a solution to the deeply embedded moral and disciplinary challenges facing the colony prior to the arrival of Boyd and Hampton.

To prepare for the arguments set out in this chapter, a summary of literature on penal experimentation in colonial transportation will be helpful. The dominant view of Van Diemen's Land and other Australian colonies is that they were often viewed disparagingly, as 'culturally incompetent, morally suspect', and as an imperial project that was 'inherently unstable and anxious'.[18] However, this perspective has been challenged by recent scholarship on colonial transportation. For example, Katherine Foxhall points out that as the convict transportation vessel was the place in which 'convicts became colonists', the ship was a 'uniquely isolated penal space' that demanded adaptation and ingenuity on the part of naval surgeons.[19] These studies support Clare Anderson's argument that this period saw the expansion of Foucault's 'carceral archipelago', suggesting that penal settlements and colonies were 'socially and culturally distinct carceral spaces'.[20] For instance, Amy Kamphuis finds that Van Diemen's Land was not the medical backwater contemporaries believed it was, while Steven Anderson notes that public executions ended in Australia far earlier than in Britain.[21] Rather than cringing in Britain's shadow, Van Diemen's Land could be viewed as a place of local ingenuity. Existing studies have perhaps misinterpreted the degree to which experimental reforms were imposed on the colony by Britain as evidence of an absent colonial imagination. With the system of separate treatment considered the most cutting-edge development in nineteenth-century penal reform, the decision to test it in Van Diemen's Land might suggest that it was a wholly British intervention.[22] However, as this chapter demonstrates, the decision to implement separate treatment in the colony was multifaceted and was an enterprise rapidly adapted by colonial authorities to suit colonial purposes.

The current scholarship on colonial separate treatment does little to unpack how this experimental prison system arrived in the colony. The most significant contribution to the literature is by local historian Ian Brand, whose material survey is unparalleled, despite his failure to scaffold a conceptual framework to contextualize his historical actors.[23] Brand argues that the success of the Pentonville Prison experiment had moved Earl Grey, Secretary of State for War and the Colonies, to suggest that from 1846 the separate system should be established in Van Diemen's Land. Without further explanation, Brand notes that by 1847–8 the decision had been made to model Port Arthur's new prison on Pentonville.[24] Maggie Weidenhofer expands upon this slightly by suggesting that the adoption of separate treatment was influenced by historic issues facing the colony, like the problem of persistent recidivism, and the failure of corporal punishment to reform those convicted of particularly heinous crimes.[25] Alex Graham-Evans and Michael Ross put forward a similar argument, though they go further by contextualizing the cultural and economic problems facing the colony. They conclude that the longevity of the separate system, despite the negative charges brought against it, was due to James Boyd, a prison warder from Pentonville, and subsequently the Port Arthur Commandant from 1853.[26] Moreover, despite the centrality of separate treatment to the pre- and post-transportation convict experience, few studies give sufficient explanation for its importation to Van Diemen's Land. The only in-depth study on separate treatment in the colony is by Phil Hilton, whose thesis argues that the goal of separate treatment at Port Arthur was to criminalize resistance and annihilate 'convict subculture'.[27] His use of 'subculture', however, only relates to convict labour and the resistance to it, and does not take into account the moral context in which separate treatment was imagined, developed and implemented. From this survey, it is evident that several basic questions around colonial separate treatment are left unanswered.

Bodies, sex, and morals: colonial punishment in context

Up to and during the 1840s, tensions mounted in Van Diemen's Land around how properly to punish convicts. With corporal punishment representative of an archaic and punitive system of criminal justice, it is little wonder that the legacy of colonial punishments was viewed as cruel and outdated. Mid-twentieth-century scholarship suggests that in Van Diemen's Land there was an 'agonising tension between enlightened penal ideas and the pitifully slow progress towards judicial humanity'.[28] Yet, flogging convict women was abolished in 1810, and in contrast to the metropole, colonial capital punishment declined steadily in proportion to population.[29] The turn away from corporal punishment in the early part of the century has been partly attributed to the sentiments and efforts of humanitarian reformers, who argued that pain as a disciplinary tool was inappropriate for modern, progressive societies.[30] These notions dovetailed with the rise of the abolitionist movement.[31] Catie Gilchrist further posits that the 'unspeakable nature' of corporal punishment 'imaginatively violated' bourgeois moral sensibilities.[32] Such 'social justifications for bodily pain' competed with evolving ideas of 'decency, respectability, and manliness'.[33] These sensibilities were further influenced by fears associated with a disgruntled convict class.[34] As this section demonstrates, twin anxieties around progressive reform and the constant threat of a convict uprising played different roles in the decline of corporal punishment and the rise of isolation-based confinements.

In the first half of the nineteenth century, humanitarian advocacy for penal reform was theologically grounded yet sought practical solutions. In the context of Van Diemen's Land before the 1840s, this is arguably exemplified by the arrival of Quaker humanitarians and missionaries James Backhouse and George Washington Walker as they journeyed through the colony in 1832–4.[35] When Backhouse reflected on the types of punishment employed in the colony, he divined a difference between coercive discipline and conformity.[36] Punishment had to be weighed against the necessity of suffering, for a punisher's desire to subjugate a prisoner ran contrary to the 'divine prerogative' and rendered retributive punishment 'un-Christian'.[37] As religious figures and social reformers, Backhouse and Walker could navigate spaces traditionally occupied by oppressor and oppressed; in this sense, the eight reports they produced for Lieutenant-Governor Sir George Arthur on matters pertaining to reform and punishment signalled a shift in colonial disciplinary culture. While they did not condemn settler colonialism, they were highly critical of it, and 'outlined its wrongdoings to colonial officials in no uncertain terms'.[38] As religious, and therefore moral, representatives, their view on humane, socially acceptable reform put them in a unique position to observe and prescribe alternatives to coercive punishment. Coercion, Backhouse wrote, excited feelings of resistance and revenge, while engendering conformity sought 'not to injure, much less kill, the body, but to mend the mind'.[39] His opinion was that the more severe the punishment, the more crime increased.[40]

The same view was held by colonial authorities. Penelope Edmonds and Hamish Maxwell-Stewart find that the rate of flogging in the colony was in decline before Backhouse and Walker's critique of corporal punishment, and they argue that where flogging continued to be employed it did so 'in inverse proportion to the capacity' of different spaces in which to punish convicts.[41] Flogging was a cheap punishment – but it also carried the danger of rebellion. This had been the case in the 1846 Norfolk Island riot.[42] With a tension between the flogger and the flogged, the degradation of a convict reflected the brutalization of the punisher. If there was a problem with a convict learning nothing from his punishment, there was also the issue of a flogger deriving 'gratification in inflicting and witnessing human misery'.[43] These were binary problems on the same moral spectrum. As Chartist John Frost declared, the brutal injustice of flogging could only lead to 'the descent of man into a permanent state of immorality and bestiality'.[44] Indeed, as 'hardened, degraded, and dehumanised' male convicts were made by corporal punishment, their suffering was further imagined to induce them to 'indulge in "unspeakable" depravity', meaning 'unnatural crime', because they had nowhere lower to fall.[45]

In this period, 'unnatural' crime encompassed sodomy, bestiality, paedophilia, homosexuality, and unlawful relations, such as adultery or pre-marital sex.[46] The flexibility of this definition afforded contemporary observers much freedom in conceptualizing sites and spaces of sexual transgression. In one instance, an 1846 Launceston newspaper article claimed that a convict's 'guilty connection is not confined to their species and sex but extends even to domestic animals'.[47] This type of public dialogue relied heavily on naming the unnameable, or 'speaking the "unspeakable"', a discourse 'powerful and productive' enough to mobilize change, or at least elicit reactions.[48] Therefore, so-called 'unnatural' crimes were not believed at this time to be exclusive to a type of person: rather, this was an act that, once 'taught' or 'indulged', stained a convict indelibly.[49] In the colonial-Victorian mind, shame and punishment were intimately linked; flogging left a metaphysical scar.[50] As corporal punishment came to be understood as inhumane and partly responsible for perpetuating cycles of vice, the shift away from punishing convict bodies to punishing their minds was a necessary, even crucial, change. While historians have persuasively argued that policing convict sexuality centred on women, colonial administrators had to think about punishing male sexual transgressions as they were constantly confronted by these crimes in their positions of authority.[51] For the first half of the century, a spectrum of punishment emerged, subtly, if not entirely, informed by moral charges brought against convicts. But moral fallibility was subjective and diagnostically complicated by a competing hierarchy of crime, changing disciplinary objectives, and the moral sensibilities of those in power.

In the wake of Backhouse and Walker's visit, weighing the moral dimension of convict discipline fell to the clergy. In the late 1830s, Father William Ullathorne observed: 'Treat a man like a brute and he will become one'.[52] Corporal punishment exacerbated a convict's negative world-view and pushed him away from religious and social reformation into the arms of their criminal companions, whose 'unnatural' sexual intentions produced 'an ultimate state of corruption' – these 'shamefully fallen' men were those he and other clergy were 'strenuously labouring to rise up and reform'.[53] If the object of transportation as a whole was the prevention of crime and this could only be attained by improving 'the prudential, moral, and religious character of convicts', reforming convicts was therefore a form of social normalization.[54] Views similar to Father Ullathorne's were held by other members of the clergy regardless of denomination. For example, in 1837 Reverend Henry Phibbs Fry, chaplain of St George's Hobart, called for an increased effort to reform offenders under the influence and direction of the church.[55] Religious representatives like Father Ullathorne and Reverend Fry were 'symbiotically involved' in the penal reform movement, and like many expatriate groups sought to negotiate their role as clergymen at the fringe of empire.[56] This search for independence often brought them into intimate contact with social causes, thereby placing them at critical junctures of reforming of the colonial regime.[57]

One element that further incited colonial penal reform was the rise of the anti-transportation movement, specifically the reports of the Molesworth Committee. Named after its chair and advocate, Sir William Molesworth, the Molesworth Committee of the British House of Commons met over two sessions in 1837–8, conducting interviews on the state of the Australian colonies with an anti-transportation slant.[58] The Committee's inflammatory reports blamed the system of transportation for the prevalence of sodomy in the colonies. In the nineteenth century and well before, an allegation of sodomy could fracture a man's reputation. The defining factor in sexual allegations was class: the sexuality of convict men was complicated by their identity as criminals; the sexuality of the governing class or colonists was complicated by middle-class standards of morality, propriety, and respectable masculinity. Of the latter, heterosexual masculinity was central to Victorian and colonial society.[59] The development of convict masculinity was tightly woven into a colonial military-penal matrix that 'fostered discipline, inequality, deference, and brutality'.[60] One aspect of the multi-faceted portrayal of convict men was, in Carol Pateman's words, a hegemonic masculine thought that accentuated a 'binary divide between certain, publicly heterosexual men' and a 'range of "others"' that included women, children, and 'sodomites'.[61] Ideological justifications for punishment ranged from the concept of innate criminality, which demanded retributive punishment, to the state's demand for exploited labour as a means of expiating an offence; in other words, transgressive convict behaviour could be portrayed as bestial in a variety of ways. Convict sexual behaviour was 'well placed' as another factor which might undermine a variety of reform efforts across colony and empire.[62]

With this in mind, we should hardly be surprised that sexually charged concerns gained traction in a colony already considered 'a moral wilderness'.[63] Indeed, a central tenet of Sir William Molesworth's anti-transportation argument was to expose how common, and therefore how unpunished, unnatural crimes were in the colonies.[64] However, Molesworth's 'findings' conflict with the data available. From 1839–45 documented charges of unnatural crime were startlingly low in Van Diemen's Land: for instance, only three charges of sodomy were made in 1843.[65] While bringing a sexual charge against a convict was complicated for a variety of reasons, many of them practical – for example, in many cases a witness might choose not to report what they observed out of ignorance or solidarity – it is remarkable how few convictions of unnatural crime were carried through.[66] This is why, even at the simplest level, the allegations cast by the Molesworth committee were powerful not because they were necessarily true, but because the claims spoke to a deeper colonial *anxiety* around criminal sexuality and the punishment of it. By its very nature, measuring the rate of sexual crimes was obfuscated by the moral climate of Van Diemen's Land at the time.

Furthermore, if it was difficult to find a man guilty enough to charge him, it was equally difficult to punish him for it. Before separate treatment, there was no way systematically to punish convicts specifically charged with unnatural offences, although this is not to say colonial authorities did not attempt to find a way. Many of these punishments focused on efforts to emasculate the offender. The Macquarie Harbour surgeon John Barnes remarked that male convicts found whipping 'a most unmanly kind of punishment'.[67] In Van Diemen's Land, a colonial administrator observed in an 1830s sodomy case that: 'Scourging on the breech [is] a disgraceful punishment, and therefore better suited to repress a disgraceful crime'.[68] It is clear that the ways authorities responded to and attempted to control convict sexuality were informed by the masculinities and sexual politics of the governing and the governed; in many ways, regulating the sexual practices of colonizer and colonized was 'fundamental to the colonial order of things'.[69] As Deana Heath argues, colonial efforts to 'regulate the bodies of the colonised were often more effective in regulating those of the colonisers'.[70] If male convicts represented 'a concentrated microcosm' of the larger moral concerns that affected empire, the same argument can be made for the colony's figures of power.[71]

One way to understand how separate treatment became synonymous with the punishment of convict 'immorality' is by taking a top-down approach and framing it with reference to governing masculinities. In 1846, Van Diemen's Land Lieutenant-Governor John Eardley Eardley-Wilmot was dismissed from office. William Gladstone himself resolved that: 'The difficulty with which you had to meet was a *moral* one and this I must add was its chief characteristic'.[72] Eardley-Wilmot had been Lieutenant-Governor for only three years, and that time was occupied by the struggle to combat the colony's image problem as a modern 'Gomorrah'.[73] He first flagged the issue to Secretary of State Lord Stanley in 1843, stating that despite vigilance and superintendence, male convicts in Van Diemen's Land 'commit sodomy to a great extent with one another'.[74] Lord Stanley's response some two years later refuted Eardley-Wilmot's allegations and concluded there was no evidence that the convict system 'afforded peculiar temptations or facilities for the perpetuation of such offences'.[75] When Eardley-Wilmot's requests for further guidance went unheeded, he and the local administration were moved to respond to the problem 'silently and unremittingly', owing to the fiscal and social problems facing the colony.[76] In addition to suffering an economic downturn, an 'avalanche' of convicts from 1840 expanded the colony's prisoner population by

40 per cent.[77] New public houses spilled out over Hobart, and to top the list of abuses suffered by convict children, child prostitution was rampant. Moreover, under Eardley-Wilmot's lax governance the probation system, introduced in 1842 under the directive of his predecessor Sir John Franklin, spiralled out of control, leading to claims of bush-ranging, increased crime, and even cannibalism.[78] The final straw for the settler population came in 1844, when it was revealed that the management of the Norfolk Island penal settlement was to be transferred to Van Diemen's Land, which meant that the colony, rather than New South Wales, would subsequently receive Norfolk Island men who had served their time. A report on the state of Norfolk Island, which was ordered by Eardley-Wilmot and carried out in 1846 by Robert Pringle Stuart, a visiting magistrate, bristled with charges of sexual immorality and disciplinary laxity; this prompted the dismissal of Major Joseph Childs, Norfolk Island Commandant.[79] As such, with Norfolk Island's notorious reputation thrown into the mix, it is little wonder that the prevalence of 'unnatural' crime came to be regarded as the worst of the colony's troubles.[80]

Without direction from Lord Stanley, Eardley-Wilmot hastily attempted to solve the problem. By 1846, changes had been implemented across different sites in the colony. For instance, the superintendent of the Hobart Barracks, William Gunn, employed surveillance tactics such as separation boards in the sleeping quarters, bright lamplight, and random evening patrols to quell 'any irregularity'.[81] For the purposes of this chapter, the initiative taken by William Champ, Commandant of Port Arthur, stands out. After feverish reports emerged from the coal mines at the Tasman Peninsula of convict gang rape and a culture of sexual coercion, Champ ordered the construction of 18 solitary confinement cells and *200* separate apartments.[82] He explained that 'in order to prevent crime, even where remedy does not appear to be called for' separate apartments were 'indispensably necessary' to eliminating unnatural crime.[83] Medical examinations were also ordered, indicating, in the fashion of medico-criminal Victorian thinking, that vice could be embodied and was therefore diagnosable.[84] Champ's decision explicitly confers that separate treatment, albeit in a modified form, was first implemented in the colony as a disciplinary tool against 'immorality'.

While the decision to dismiss Eardley-Wilmot has been largely attributed to his inability to combat convict sexuality, the charges of sexual immorality made against *him* were also a significant contributing factor.[85] If male convict sexuality was characterized by the absence of women, Eardley-Wilmot's sexuality was judged by the abundance of them. For instance, it was suggested Eardley-Wilmot would bring convict women from the Cascades Female Factory to Government House and have them dressed up.[86] A contemporary remarked in 1845 that Eardley-Wilmot 'Had no taste for Science of any kind … his only society was young ladies without their mamas, or young married ladies without their husbands'.[87] Earlier the same year it was printed in a British newspaper that 'No person of any standing will now enter Government House, except on business; no ladies can'.[88] Clearly, these dalliances disrupted the sensibilities of the colonial moral domain.

To reiterate Heath's suggestion that 'efforts to regulate the bodies of the colonised were often more effective in regulating those of the colonisers', we should remember that beneath layers of political discourse the topic of male sexuality lay close to the heart of both British and colonial society.[89] Efforts to control convict sexuality naturally led to the scrutiny of colonial officials. Moreover, the perceived prevalence of 'unnatural' crime was compounded by the lack of appropriate discipline. With Eardley-Wilmot 'polluting the morals of Government House society' in tandem with the 'unnatural' activities of the convicts, it was clear to Britain that every layer of the colonial hierarchy was tainted, from the highest echelons of office to the lowest road gang.[90] The lack of opportunity for convicts to better themselves, and the dangers posed by excessive corporal punishment, meant that a man's sexuality was bound to his moral propriety. Convict men were further damned as they also had to overcome a perceived innate criminality. In other words, with corporal punishment driving convict men to debased depths, and no alternative system of reformative punishment in place to rescue them, an opportunity arose in the colony to divine a more rigorous discipline that could combat such evils.

In his twilight days in office, Eardley-Wilmot resignedly wrote to Lord Stanley, stating that as sodomy 'more or less prevailed' among convicts regardless of efforts to stop it, its recurrence 'might be lessened yet it is impossible wholly to prevent it'.[91] By 1846, it was evident a more responsible government was needed to quell the imagined moral dangers in Van Diemen's Land.[92] As addressed previously, the claims of immorality in the colony were seized upon by the anti-transportation movement, resulting in warnings that unless action (i.e. the cessation of transportation) was taken, Van Diemen's Land would 'exhibit a spectacle of vice and infamy such as the history of the world cannot parallel' – a lurid claim, we must remember, that was intended to evoke a strong response.[93] In an effort to stem anti-transportation rumblings, the new

British Whig government placed a moratorium on the transportation of male convicts from 1846–8.[94] Later that year, the superintendent of the Port Phillip district, Charles La Trobe, was brought forward to govern temporarily until a replacement could be found.[95] La Trobe was advised to observe the situation in Van Diemen's Land, make a report, and improve arrangements wherever possible. His companion in the venture was none other than John Hampton, the new Comptroller-General of Convicts; it was remarked that Hampton's advice would be most useful, namely because of his experience in penal affairs.[96]

The wind was changing direction. In the same year, an excerpt from a report written by Hampton's protégé James Boyd was published in the *Launceston Examiner*. Van Diemen's Land, Boyd wrote, was rife with 'unnatural' crime:

> What a blessing it would be to society, as well as to the convicts themselves, if the thousands of prisoners subjected to the demoralising influence of gang association, were instead brought within the pale of reformatory prisons such as Pentonville.[97]

With Hampton accompanying La Trobe in his survey of Van Diemen's Land, and Boyd publicly affirming the possibilities of separate treatment, the Pentonville Prison model was understood by the colonial newspapers as 'an academy for purification, not as a gaol of oppressive or vengeful punishment'.[98] When news of the cutting-edge London institution reached the colony in December 1842, some colonists remarked that a similar undertaking would be 'extremely useful for a Van Diemen's Land prison'.[99] In the wake of Eardley-Wilmot's dismissal and the lingering issue over convict discipline, the presence of Hampton and, shortly afterwards, Boyd, signalled a daring new era for the colony. As the next section finds, this was a British experiment that rapidly became a colonial one.

Inventing a colonial Pentonville

Back in Britain, preparations were being made. In 1844, the first cohort of British criminals sentenced to transportation had completed their probationary period under the separate treatment regime at London's Pentonville Prison. Hopes were held in Britain that separate treatment would prepare a new generation of convicts for a life in the colonies, where they would leave their old ways and become useful members of colonial society. These first convicts were colloquially known as 'Pentonvillains', a moniker used at home and in the colony. In the larger scheme of penal intervention and innovation, the 1844 voyage of the ship *Sir George Seymour* was a pivotal moment. Onboard the *Sir George Seymour* were 345 convicts who had all experienced separate confinement at Pentonville for periods ranging from 15 to 22 months.[100] Once arrived in Australia, half were disembarked in Hobart, while the remaining men sailed to Port Philip.[101] The charge of these 'Pentonvillains' fell auspiciously to two men who would come to loom over the disciplinary system of Van Diemen's Land in the following decades: Dr John Stephen Hampton and his protégé, James Boyd.

Ten years Boyd's senior and a fellow Scotsman, Hampton had embarked on a career as an assistant naval surgeon. From 1841–5 he served as surgeon-superintendent on three prominent convict transport vessels, notably the *Sir George Seymour*. Hampton was described as a 'somewhat tyrannical and harsh' man, prone to behaving 'like the white overseer of a slave plantation', a serious insult in abolitionist Britain.[102] Boyd held a different reputation. Born in Stevenston, Ayrshire, in July 1815, he was one of three children. Boyd had enlisted in Edinburgh as a bombardier when he was 17, serving for the next 12 years. By then he had married his first wife, Margaret, and together they had three children, though only their eldest, Marion, lived to adulthood.[103] In early 1841 he was appointed as a 'discipline warder' at Millbank Penitentiary, and the following year was promoted to the position of 'warder' at the newly constructed Pentonville Prison. As a warder he was responsible for the daily management of prisoners, acting as a point of contact between a prisoner and prison officials. Only 29 at the time of this promotion, Boyd already had an enviable reputation as a 'trustworthy and intelligent man of much experience and active habits, and a good disciplinarian'. Ian Brand also describes Boyd as 'without doubt, the top officer in the Convict Service at the time of his appointment'.[104] The decision to promote the young, ambitious, and self-composed Boyd as assistant superintendent of the *Sir George Seymour* in 1844 was bolstered by the promise of a permanent post in the colony upon completion of the voyage. At this point, it is probable that Boyd's self-styling as a career prison administrator took a firm hold, particularly given the opportunity to work with and learn from his senior and mentor, Hampton.

Naval surgeons like Hampton were well placed from the outset to use their medical observations to 'carve themselves an important niche as astute and ardent critics of British penal reforms'.[105] In spite of, or perhaps because of a surgeon-superintendent's role as mediator of a voyage, subtle discrepancies arose between the official report of the voyage of the *Sir George Seymour* and the popular recollection of it. These discrepancies betrayed an intent to amplify the benefits of transportation as a criminal punishment in comparison to reformed British penitentiaries. In his government report on the *Sir George Seymour*'s voyage, Hampton noted that 'the sudden change from extreme seclusion to the noise and bustle of a crowded ship' produced convulsions, nausea, vomiting, and fits among the Pentonville convicts – scenarios soon reflected across other ships carrying men exposed to separate treatment.[106] More problems arose around the convicts' social health upon their arrival in the colony. Releasing the men into Hobart risked exposing them to 'contaminating influences' that were potentially destructive to their prospects as remade men.[107] Many of those exiled to Port Philip, for instance, were observed to have abandoned themselves the moment they arrived in the colony to drinking and gambling, thereby once more merrily launching down the road to sin. The same was reported to have occurred with the convicts disembarked at Hobart, where they faced prejudice owing to their reputation. Convict James Johnston wrote to Hampton in March 1845 and complained that to be recognized as a Pentonville man was 'quite condemnatory', while even mentioning the *Sir George Seymour* inspired 'the strongest prejudice'.[108] Soon, colonial authorities understood that the lack of reformative discipline in Van Diemen's Land endangered the 'mental and moral culture' of convicts supposedly reformed by separate treatment.[109] It is little surprise that the 'hopefulness of reformation' was subsequently believed to hinge on a revised trans-imperial disciplinary framework.[110] As James Boyd wrote in 1845 to his former employer Robert Hosking, Governor of Pentonville Prison:

> Thousands of prisoners are at this moment going about idle, polluting the atmosphere in which they move; is it to be wondered at, then, if the Pentonville men should fall when thus exposed to the deteriorating influence of such abominations as they daily see and hear of?[111]

The *Sir George Seymour* was significant to the British authorities because it was the first instance of exposing criminals to the experimental system of separate treatment – and it was significant to colonial authorities because these men represented a new 'type' of convict remade by seclusion and refinement, the antithesis of the thieving and peripatetic figures that had plagued the colony since its inception. Indeed, Hampton wasted little time in impressing upon the British government how critical and long-awaited a colonial enterprise this was: in one communication to the commissioners of Pentonville Prison, he included 19 colonial newspaper clippings that mentioned Pentonville Prison and the *Sir George Seymour* in the same breath.[112] He also alluded to Eardley-Wilmot's 'inattention and neglect' of disciplinary matters in the colony.[113] However, a Mr Holland in Hobart also wrote to the commissioners reporting that Hampton's response to the problems faced by the Pentonville men was 'unjust, uncalled for, and highly impolite', suggesting that the image Hampton carefully presented to Britain was not true to the reality of the colony.[114] Holland's frustration was justified. Accounts continued to mount of the difficulties faced by the Pentonville men in Port Phillip and Hobart. Characteristically, Hampton reinterpreted colonists' reports of the 'lassitude and want of energy' of the Pentonville men, probably evidence of confinement-related health problems, as proof that separate treatment smoothed the 'sharp, deceitful habits so notoriously characteristic of convict servants'.[115] While Port Phillip was challenging, the atmosphere of Van Diemen's Land was purported to be so degrading that it would only be a matter of time before the men's 'former evil habits of thought and action' returned.[116] This rhetoric advanced the idea that a colonial version of Pentonville Prison might be in the colony's best interests so that 'fallen' separate treatment men might be caught once more in the snare of reformative discipline. In August 1845, Hampton boldly announced to the commissioners that in the interests of the Board, the Pentonville men, 'and the ultimate success of the separate system of prison discipline', he would draw on his practical experience to prepare a plan for the colonial management of convicts exposed to reformative discipline in Britain.[117]

Hampton and Boyd often reinforced the ineffectiveness of the existing system of colonial discipline by comparison to that undertaken at Pentonville. In 1845, shortly after the arrival of the *Sir George Seymour*, Boyd was approved as Senior Assistant-Superintendent of the Darlington Probation Station at Maria Island. Upon Boyd's arrival, the station was in an unsatisfactory state: the barracks were crowded with only small partition boards between beds; the 102 separate apartments there were 'extremely ill adapted' for convicts; and the absence of a night watch led Boyd to opine on the extent of 'unnatural' crimes, a subject about which he had heard 'the most disgusting evidence'.[118] Darlington's separate apartments, where it was alleged a modified form of separate treatment took place, were small and narrow, made of wood, and had none of the modern amenities of the Pentonville cells, such as ventilation or warmth, and communication between convicts abounded.[119] Boyd determined these apartments could not be considered as separate, as he understood the term. Rather, the apartments were adapted solitary cells which merely kept select convicts isolated at night.[120] Even solitary confinement at Darlington was a rudimentary punishment, carried out in what amounted to a wooden shed and overseen by lackadaisical convict watchmen, many of whom were charged with misconduct while Boyd was there.[121] Darlington Probation Station represented two dominant problems in the colony: a lack of reformative discipline; and the supposed prevalence of 'unnatural' crime. Under Boyd's control, the station formalized the use of solitary confinement, built proper cells, and cracked down on homosexuality. Within a year he had turned the site around to become what Charles La Trobe described as 'the best suited and best arranged station' in Van Diemen's Land.[122] The results at home and in the colony were self-evident: by employing career penal administrators with experience in cutting-edge reform, long-term problems would be attacked head on.

Accompanied by Hampton, La Trobe toured Van Diemen's Land over four months and concluded that the probation system had been 'a fatal experiment' that needed replacing as soon as possible.[123] Upon the completion of this report, La Trobe was replaced in January 1847 by Lieutenant-Governor Sir William Denison. Hampton had been made Comptroller-General of Convicts the previous year with strict instructions to reinvigorate the Convict Department.[124] With the colony now taken in hand by Hampton and Denison, matters soon began to change. Hampton transferred William Gunn, the long-serving superintendent of Hobart Prisoners' Barracks – who under Eardley-Wilmot implemented a regime of surveillance at the Barracks to combat immorality – and replaced him with none other than James Boyd. Denison wrote to Earl Grey informing him that preparations were being made to introduce the separate treatment system properly to the colony, and he had Hampton's 'most hearty co-operation'.[125] The moratoriums on transportation of 1846–8 permitted the Convict Department to reorganize and refit a huge number of convict establishments.[126] These efforts focused on tightening convict discipline, particularly the modified versions of separate treatment scattered across sites in the colony.

One of these modified versions of separate treatment was that used against female convicts. From the outset it was altered significantly from the original vision of separate treatment. From the 1840s, separate apartments were built at the Cascades Female Factory, a labour depot for convict women in Hobart. These cells were built almost exclusively to restrict the opportunity for 'unnatural' sexual offences and criminal collusion.[127] In 1846, for example, 24 cells were built at the Launceston Female Factory, where it was 'intended to make an experiment of the separate system'.[128] Even before Lieutenant-Governor Denison and Hampton assumed control of the convict system, correspondence on the state of female discipline in the colony between Lady Jane Franklin, wife of then Lieutenant-Governor Sir John Franklin, and the Quaker reformer Elizabeth Fry, illustrated how adjustments to the system were informed by their perspectives on the psychological and physical endurance of women.[129] To reiterate, the ways in which contemporaries perceived the minds and bodies of female convicts changed how separate treatment was carried out. Gendered interpretations of women's behaviour in confinement concentrated upon reports of mental and physical distress. That oft-repeated promise that separation led to reformation appeared instead only to generate 'loneliness, isolation, and madness'.[130] The problems that arose around confining women, in reality very similar to the reports of madness and mental distress among the men of Pentonville Prison at this time, were discounted on the basis of their sex. While separate treatment was tested first on female convicts, it was modified and mediated for their benefit. As reformer Alexander Maconochie reflected: 'The pressure which only bends an oak may crush a willow'.[131] As separate treatment as a formalized system was subsequently designed by men for men, the way women reacted to their imprisonment created 'an unexpected problem of discipline', one complicated by Victorian views of femininity and female criminal reformation.[132] While a form of separate treatment was first used in the colony against female convicts, in practice it deviated significantly from the plan put forward by Lieutenant-Governor Denison and Hampton.

The proposed benefits of the separate system continued to outweigh the negatives as they emerged, especially when the system was framed as a solution to problems that had long plagued the colony. While Lieutenant-Governor Denison admitted that 'there is no doubt but that the discipline is severe', he maintained it was the only system strict enough to temper the convict spirit.[133] For 'unnatural' offences, contemporaries proposed that nothing less than a 'rigid adherence' to the system could suppress 'this horrid crime'.[134] In the midst of the apparent success of the Pentonville Prison experiment (1842–9), in late 1846 Earl Grey recommended to Denison that every new convict to the colony should be subjected to confinement under the separate system for six to 12 months. Above all, he should be 'treated as nearly as possible upon the system adopted at Pentonville'.[135] By April 1847, a prison plan modelled on Pentonville was put forward to Denison by Hampton, and construction began at the Port Arthur penal station shortly afterwards, with 18 cells completed by 1849.[136] In that time, acting on Earl Grey's recommendation, Denison proposed a legislative change to commute sentences of transportation to a period under separate confinement: with this, he would have the means at his disposal to tame 'the most mutinous spirit'.[137]

It is unquestionably a testament of colonial reform ideology that less than three years after Eardley-Wilmot's dismissal, over 950 separate apartments and 2,723 bed partitions in barracks had been constructed across Van Diemen's Land.[138] To illustrate the rapidity of construction at Port Arthur, two cells per month on average were built, totalling 28 complete cells in the 'Model' or 'Separate' Prison by December 1849.[139] By the next year, Hampton reported that the first convicts confined to the Separate Prison had been transformed from 'ungovernable' to 'quiet and orderly'.[140] In every sense, Hampton in his position as Comptroller-General, and Boyd as a local penal adminis-trator, demonstrated that the way to take a runaway colony in hand was to act swiftly and ruthlessly. It is no exaggeration to state that by this time Hampton could be considered the second most powerful individual in the colony after the Lieutenant-Governor.

The Separate Prison at Port Arthur was intended to model Penton-ville Prison in every way.[141] As a site of secondary punishment, the convicts admitted there were subjected to a medical examination, shaved, and dressed in a regulation uniform that mirrored Pentonville's: this included the famous 'hood' that ostensibly shielded a convict's identity, but what London critics John Mayhew and Matthew Binny regarded as a 'piece of wretched frippery'.[142] Convicts were confined to their cell for 22 hours a day: one hour was reserved for private exercise, and one to attend chapel. They laboured, slept, prayed, and received pastoral care in their cell. To heighten their sense of isolation, convicts were referred to by their registration number, not their name. As added disciplinary measure, if a convict broke one of the several rules of the prison, he could be further punished with a period in a 'deaf and dumb', or solitary, cell, thereby compounding an already intense confinement. As Boyd himself remarked: 'Separation, watchfulness, and restraint, are, or ought to be, the grand cardinal objects to be sought for in all good systems of prison discipline'.[143] Boyd's philosophy proved career-making. In 1853, Boyd was appointed as Port Arthur Commandant, a position gained with Hampton's support and bolstered by the numerous positive reports on his reforms enacted at the Prisoners Barracks under his management.[144] Reflecting the prestige attached to this appointment was a salary increase from £400 to £600 per annum, making him the third highest paid man in the colony after his mentor, Hampton, and Lieutenant-Governor Denison.[145]

The Separate Prison was completed in 1852, one year before the cessation of colonial transportation. British reformers understood that exporting separate treatment across empire would necessarily mean deviating from the original model, depending on the judgement and capacity of local administrators, but it is startling how frequently the Port Arthur Separate Prison was adapted and remade to suit colonial interests and to address colonial problems.

Conceptually and in practice, the system of Van Diemonian separate treatment had been associated with sexual transgressions since 1846, when then Commandant William Champ ordered separate apartments to be built at the coal mines for the punishment of sodomy. This association had since festered in the colonial imagination. For instance, commentators on the voyage of the *Sir Robert Seppings* (1852), a vessel carrying convicts from Norfolk Island to Port Arthur, alleged the men whose uniforms were branded 'S.T.' for 'separate treatment' might have been kept separate from the other convicts, but it was alleged they managed to bugger each other during the voyage regardless, with the insinuation being that their degradation knew no bounds.[146] To address insubordination, absconding, and sex – dangers believed to be character-istic of former Norfolk Island convicts, then gradually being evacuated to Van Diemen's Land in advance of the impending closure of the island penal settlement – Hampton suggested a more widespread adoption of separate treatment at Port Arthur.[147] Arguably, Hampton played on the mythology surrounding Norfolk Island to further his regime.[148] From 1852–3, a flurry of construction resulted in the completion of 22 new cells at the Separate Prison. In 1854, Commandant Boyd proposed adding another storey to the original building, bringing it more in line with the Pentonville design.[149] The experiment taking place at Port Arthur was soon revealed as strict enough 'to keep even the most incor-rigible in awe'.[150] The Separate Prison, Boyd observed, was such an efficient, important institution, that only by careful attention could its powerful disciplinary effects be felt: it was to be, in his words, a 'formi-dable place of punishment to the incorrigible'.[151]

The Separate Prison was certainly formidable for the liberties taken with its design. Discrepancies between the Pentonville Plan and the Separate Prison were evident from the outset. In the first place, despite his assurance that the colonial model would be identical to that in London, Hampton intervened in the plan, reducing the cell size by two-thirds and removing the piped water, wash basins, and heating facilities.[152] According to Pentonville architect Colonel Joshua Jebb, Surveyor-General of Prisons, such features were essential to all modern prisons.[153] In the second place, sentences under separate treatment at Port Arthur were sometimes far longer than at Pentonville. From 1842–8, increasing reports around deteriorating prisoner health prompted the commissioners of Pentonville Prison to reduce sentence lengths from 18 to nine months.[154] In contrast, the ordinary period of confinement in the Separate Prison ranged from four to 12 months. In 1853, Boyd determined that the optimal period for producing 'a powerful effect in changing the evil tendencies of convicts' minds' was a sentence from *eight* to 12 months.[155] In the third place, despite the defining characteristic of separate treatment as consisting of a non-corporal punishment, from 1856 convicts confined in the Separate Prison and charged with serious offences could be held in heavy leg irons; in addition, in 1869, Boyd altered the prison regulations so that the institution would only house convicts serving a life sentence, or those charged with 'unnatural' offences.

Instituting smaller, colder cells, increasing the duration of sentences served, and specifying the 'type' of convict to be confined under separate treatment, drastically redefined separate treatment in the colony and distinguished it from the British model. The conflation of 'unnatural' offences with separate treatment carried with it a heavy historic legacy. From at least the early part of the nineteenth century, fears associated with sexual misconduct were harnessed to further the interests of colonial reformers but were further amplified with the advent of separate treatment. Even if this contribution to fearmongering was not the intention, men like Hampton and Boyd were successful in linking separate treatment and immorality in the popular colonial imagination. This is evident in the intra-colonial use of the term 'separate treatment character'.[156] In 1860 a select committee was formed to enquire into the ways ticket-of-leave men were discharged from Port Arthur. The chairman, Sir Robert Officer, observed that sentences of separate treatment were 'too well understood as indicating the commission of a crime of peculiar enormity'.[157] A report by Boyd furnished the committee with several cases where a convict had committed an 'unnatural' sexual offence – usually against or with other men but, in many instances, young children – and for which they were sentenced to separate treatment for up to two years. In the case of one convict: 'He had been sent [to Port Arthur] for some crime not stated on his Police Sheet, with the remark "separate treatment man"'.[158] 'Separate treatment' became colonial shorthand. From 'Pentonvillains' to 'separate treatment men', these convicts were isolated, literally and figuratively, as representatives of the 'worst' class of men.

By 1871, only 77 men remained under separate treatment at Port Arthur, and the Separate Prison limped along, shedding aged convicts, until the settlement's closure in 1877.[159] In describing John Hampton and James Boyd, historians James Semple-Kerr and Joan Torrance christened them 'disciples' of Pentonville Prison. Were they? They were certainly a different *class* of 'separate treatment men'. There can be little doubt they devoted a dominant part of their lives to the enterprise of establishing separate treatment in Van Diemen's Land. Yet, even contemporaries doubted their success. According to one shrewd anonymous commentator writing in 1865, the colonies had 'never had any close approximation' of the 'new system' of punishment; the Port Arthur Separate Prison was merely a 'pretty resemblance' of its British cousin.[160] Moreover, the type of separate treatment established in Van Diemen's Land was developed in response to the 'moral problem' of the colony, a problem heightened by the fall into disfavour of corporal punishment and the rise of reformative discipline theory, and exacerbated by factors such as the report of the Molesworth Committee and other lurid accounts of convict sexuality. The design and disciplinary changes made to the Separate Prison also distinguished it from the Pentonville model, just as Pentonville was distinguished from the panopticon. Bentham, who had condemned the use of solitary confinement in the panopticon, surely would have been dismayed to see the principle of isolation carried to such extravagant lengths by future penal reformers.[161] Boyd and Hampton might, therefore, be 'disciples' in the sense that they formalized the use of separate treatment in the colony, but this chapter demonstrates they are better seen as inventing a 'colonial Pentonville'. Above all, Hampton and Boyd's 'petty interested motives' in pursuing separate treatment, in spite of evidence it detrimentally affected prisoners, demonstrates that the experimental colonial milieu could be readily exploited by those in power, especially those self-styled men whose business it was to redeem the irredeemable.

Notes

1   Ignatieff 1978, 110–13.
2   Emphasis mine. *Commons Sessional Papers* (1854), vol. xxxiii. 17.
3   Van Diemen's Land was renamed 'Tasmania' in 1856. This chapter uses 'Van Diemen's Land' before that year and 'Tasmania' after it.
4   The Pentonville Prison 'experiment' lasted from 1842–9.
5   Semple-Kerr and Torrance 1988, 160.
6   Bobbin 1868, IV.
7   *The Tasmanian*, 31 May 1873, 8.
8   *The Argus*, 12 July 1873, 1.
9   Evans 1982, 230.
10   Schofield 2013, 51–70, at 61.
11   A recent and comprehensive survey of the suite of penal reformers is Davie 2016.
12   Barclay 2018, 459–73, at 468–9.
13   Wiener 1994, 103–4.
14   Letter from Sir William Denison to Earl Grey, 12 September 1850, Tasmanian Archives and Heritage Office (hereafter TA), GO 33/1/69, 1151.
15   Ignatieff 1978, 76.
16   Castieau and Finnane 2004, 2.
17   Ogborn 1995, 295–311, at 296.
18   Epstein 2012, 271; McKenzie 2013, 5.
19   Foxhall 2011, 13–14.
20   Anderson 2021, 22; Anderson 1997, 164–82, at 164–6; Foucault 1977, 293; and on carceral geographies, see Morin and Moran 2015, 2.
21   Kamphuis 2012; Cave 2012; Anderson 2021.
22   The first attempt at implementing separate treatment in the southern colonies was in New Zealand. There, a model of Pentonville Prison was built in 1843, though the venture was never completed. Pratt 2013, 38.
23   See Brand 1980; Brand 1988; Brand 1990a; Brand 1990b; Brand and Staniforth 1994, 23–42; Brand 1998.
24   Brand, 1990a, 8; Brand 1980, 55.
25   Weidenhofer 1981, 75.
26   Graeme-Evans and Ross 1993, 41–53.
27   Hilton 1999, 38–9.
28   Davis 1974, 38.
29   Gatrell 1994, 589.
30   Abruzzo 2011, 1–2.
31   Baldry *et al.* 2015, 168–89.
32   Gilchrist 2004, 18.
33   McLaren and McLaren 1997, 19; Dwyer and Nettelbeck 2017, 112, 14.
34   Braithwaite 2001, 11–50.
35   Edmonds 2012, 769–88, 779.
36   Backhouse 1843, xlix.
37   Edmonds and Maxwell-Stewart 2016, 5.
38   Edmonds 1973, 776.
39   Backhouse 1843, xlix; Bevan and Forster 1821, 213.
40   Backhouse 1843, xlviii.
41   Edmonds and Maxwell-Stewart 2016, 12–13.
42   Causer 2012, 4.
43   Frost 1856, 30.
44   Frost quoted in Reid 2008, 481–95, at 482.
45   Gilchrist 2007, 1–28, at 16.
46   Taylor 2020, 2–3.
47   Quoted in Gilchrist 2005, 151–61, at 151.
48   Gilchrist 2005, 157.
49   'Horrible scenes of suffering and iniquity took place in the convict ships among the

prisoners locked up in crowded berths, and little that was impious, unnatural, and corrupt in act or word was *left untaught and unpractised among them'*. Emphasis mine. See Fry 1850, 151.

50 Bonwick 1856, 89.
51 Ludwig 2013, 2.
52 Ullathorne 1837, 25.
53 Ullathorne 1837, 32.
54 Gladstone to Eardley Wilmot, 20 February 1846, in *Commons Sessional Papers* (1846), vol. xxix. 368; Gibson 2011, 1040–63, at 1043.
55 Fry 1847, 23; Carey 2019, 202.
56 Scharff Smith 2004, 195–220, at 199; Milton, Gregory, Strong, Morris, and Sachs 2017, 241.
57 Milton *et al.* 2017, 241.
58 Peart 2019, 263–96, at 273.
59 Gilchrist 2004, 49.
60 Evans and Thorpe 1998, 17–34, at 19.
61 Pateman 1988, 78.
62 See *Commons Sessional Papers* (1837–8), vol. xxii. 81; McKenzie 2003, 3.
63 Nicholls 1973, 160; and let us not forget Frost's inciting image of Van Diemen's Land as 'the modern Gomorrah' in Frost 1856, 25–8.
64 McKenzie 2003, 2.
65 Number compiled from 'A Return showing the number of Convictions, and the Offences; the number of Acquittals, and the number discharged by Proclamation; also the Number sentenced to Death, against whom sentence of Death was ordered to be recorded, and the Number pardoned, during the years 1839, 1840, 1841, 1842, 1843, 1844, and 1845' in *Commons Sessional Papers* (1847), vol. xlviii. 137.
66 For a contemporary account of the 'duty' of witnesses to report homosexuality, see Syme 1848, 199–200.
67 *Commons Sessional Papers* (1837–8), vol. xxii. 88.
68 Quoted in Davis 1974, 32.
69 Stoler 1995, 4.
70 Heath 2010, 14.
71 Gilchrist 2005, 26–7.
72 Gladstone to Eardley-Wilmot, 30 April 1846, in *Commons Sessional Papers* (1847), vol. xxxviii. 515. Original emphasis.
73 Hughes 1987, 530.
74 Quoted in Coad 2002, 27.
75 Reid 2017, 206.
76 Upward 1974, 73.
77 Foxhall 2018, 34.
78 Petrow 2001, 176–99, at 177.
79 Peart 2019, 263–96, at 264.
80 Eardley-Wilmot to Lord Stanley, 21 September 1844, in *Commons Sessional Papers* (1846), vol. xxix. 380.
81 Gilchrist 2004, 108.
82 Champ to Eardley-Wilmot, 14 March 1846, in *Commons Sessional Papers* (1847), vol. xlviii. 143. Emphasis added.
83 Champ to Eardley Wilmot, 14 March 1846, in *Commons Sessional Papers* (1847), vol. xlviii. 130.
84 Out of 1,200 men examined only one was found 'diseased' and he had recently come from the coal mines. See Eardley-Wilmot to Lord Stanley, 6 February 1846, in *Commons Sessional Papers* (1847), vol. xlviii. 130.
85 Reid 2017, 247; Mickleborough 2011, 279–80; Upward 1974, 170–94; Clark 1999, 324.
86 See Enclosure No. 2, in Eardley-Wilmot to Gladstone, 5 October 1846, in *Commons Sessional Papers* (1847), vol. xxxviii. 533.
87 Mickleborough 2011, 279–80.
88 Gilchrist 2005, 160–1.
89 Heath 2010, 14; Gilchrist 2007, 25.
90 Clark 1999, 324.

91 Eardley-Wilmot to Stanley, 17 March 1846, in *Commons Sessional Papers* (1847), vol. xlviii. 142.
92 Causer 2012, 230–40.
93 'The Humble Petition of the undersigned Free Colonists of Van Diemen's Land, Enclosure, in Eardley Wilmot to Stanley, 1 August 1845, *Commons Sessional Papers* (1846), vol. xxix. 330; Causer 2012, 4.
94 Harling 2014, 80–110, at 81, 85; Foxhall 2018, 36.
95 Ritchie 1976, 21.
96 Ritchie 1976, 22.
97 *Launceston Examiner*, 30 December 1846, 7.
98 *The True Colonist*, 8 March 1844, 4.
99 *The Austral-Asiatic Review, Tasmanian and Australian Advertiser*, 10 March 1843, 3.
100 Foxhall 2011, 1–19, at 11.
101 Foxhall 2011, 11; and for an account of the Port Philip exiles, see Wood 2014, 147–89.
102 Battye 1985, 294.
103 Both of Boyd's male children died while the family lived at Pentonville Prison (*The Mercury*, 23 March 1876, 3).
104 Brand 1998, 109.
105 Foxhall 2011, 2.
106 Foxhall 2011, 11–12.
107 Boyd to the Reverend Whitworth Russell and Robert Hosking, 29 April 1845, *Commons Sessional Papers* (1846), vol. xxix, 429–30. Hosking was governor of Pentonville Prison.
108 James Johnston to Hampton, 29 March 1845, in *Commons Sessional Papers* (1846), vol. xxix. 431.
109 *Launceston Examiner*, 30 December 1846, 7.
110 Burt 1852, 36.
111 Boyd to Robert Hosking, 29 April 1845, *Commons Sessional Papers* (1846), vol. xxix. 430.
112 Hampton to the Commissioners for the Government of Pentonville Prison, 30 April 1845, *Commons Sessional Papers* (1846), vol. xxix. 428.
113 No. 1549, The National Archives of the United Kingdom, Kew (hereafter TNA), PCOM 2/86/AJCP Reel No 5978, 260.
114 No. 1589, TNA, PCOM 2/86/AJCP Reel No 5978, 280.
115 Hampton to the Commissioners of Pentonville Prison, 9 August 1845, *Commons Sessional Papers* (1846), vol. xxix. 434.
116 Hampton to the Commissioners of Pentonville Prison, 9 August 1845, *Commons Sessional Papers* (1846), vol. xxix. 434.
117 Hampton to the Commissioners of Pentonville Prison, 9 August 1845, *Commons Sessional Papers* (1846), vol. xxix. 434.
118 Boyd to Hampton, 31 December 1845, *Commons Sessional Papers* (1846), vol. xxix. 437.
119 Boyd to Hampton, 31 December 1845 *Commons Sessional Papers* (1846), vol. xxix. 438.
120 Boyd to Hampton, 31 December 1845, *Commons Sessional Papers* (1846), vol. xxix. 438.
121 Boyd to Hampton, 31 December 1845, *Commons Sessional Papers* (1846), vol. xxix. 441–2.
122 Semple-Kerr and Torrance 1988, 55.
123 Barnes 2007, 65–75, 21–2.
124 Preston 2013, 89.
125 Denison to Grey, 4 December 1847, *Commons Sessional Papers* (1849), vol. xliii. 146.
126 Tuffin 2007, 75–6.
127 This topic has an extensive historiography. Some of the recent scholarship includes Nolan 2013, 291–304, at 299; Casella 2005, 143–168, at 143–59.
128 *Launceston Examiner*, 15 August 1846, 3.
129 Letter from Elizabeth Fry to Jane Franklin, 29 April 1842, University of Tasmania Library Special and Rare Materials Collection, RS 16/1, 2–3.
130 Menis 2019, 68.
131 Maconochie 1839, 128–9.
132 Bennett 2020, 2.
133 Denison to Grey, 15 May 1848, *Commons Sessional Papers* (1849), vol. xliii. 263.
134 Enclosure 24 (William Baylie to Dr Roberton, 9 March 1846), in Eardley Wilmot to Stanley, 17 March 1846, *Commons Sessional Papers* (1847), vol. lxviii. 152.
135 Grey to Denison, 30 September 1846, *Commons Sessional Papers* (1847), vol. lxviii. 157.

136 Brand 1990a, 8.

137 Denison to Grey, 5 December 1847, *Commons Sessional Papers* (1849), vol. xliii. 185.

138 Hampton to Denison, 15 November 1847, *Commons Sessional Papers* (1849), vol. xliii. 186.

139 'No. 11, Return showing the Number of Wards of Huts, Separate Apartments and Solitary Cells finished and in progress at Stations, &c., on 31st December 1849, the Number of Men who can be accommodated in the Wards or Huts in Bed-places completely separated by Battens, and the Number in Bed-places separated by Side-boards', *Commons Sessional Papers* (1850), vol. xlv. 269.

140 Hampton to Denison, 30 January 1850, *Commons Sessional Papers* (1850), vol. xlv. 262.

141 A contemporary account of a convict's experience in the Port Arthur Separate Prison is that by Mark Jeffrey, which, while complicated for several reasons, remains powerful testimony by a man also imprisoned at both Millbank and Pentonville prisons under separate treatment. See Jeffrey 1968, 81.

142 Mayhew and Binny 2011, 141.

143 Boyd quoted in Syme 1848, 361.

144 For a 'small' selection of these character reports, see 'Copy of all Entries made in Strangers' Visiting Book during the Half Year ending 31st December 1852', *Commons Sessional Papers* (1854), vol. liv. 334–40.

145 Enclosure 1 (Hampton to Denison, 11 August 1853), in Denison to the Duke of Newcastle, 13 September 1853, *Commons Sessional Papers* (1854), vol. liv. 385.

146 Causer 2009, 285.

147 Enclosure 2 (Memorandum from Sir William Denison, 27 May 1852) in Denison to Grey, 12 June 1852, *Commons Sessional Papers* (1852–3), vol. lxxxii. 93–4, 98.

148 See, for instance, Enclosure 1 (Hampton to Sir Denison, 25 June 1853), in Denison to Newcastle, 2 July 1853, *Commons Sessional Papers* (1854), vol. xliv. 371–2.

149 The second storey was never completed.

150 Denison to Newcastle, 13 February 1854, *Commons Sessional Papers* (1854–5), vol. xxxix. 284–5.

151 'Report of the Civil Commandant and Superintendent, Port Arthur', 19 January 1854, *Commons Sessional Papers* (1854–5), vol. xxxix. 132–3.

152 Semple-Kerr and Torrance 1988, 65.

153 *Commons Sessional Papers* (1844), vol. xxviii. 132–3.

154 Mayhew and Binny 2011, 105.

155 Brand 1990a, 62. Emphasis added.

156 28 January 1867, 'Civil Commandant's Office: Letter Book, 26 February 1866–31 July 1869', Mitchell Library, State Library of New South Wales, Tasmanian Papers 315, 231.

157 'Port Arthur – Tickets-of-Leave Report of the Select Committee', *House of Assembly Papers Tasmania,* No. 98, 1860, 5.

158 'Tickets-of-Leave Report of the Select Committee', *House of Assembly*, 16.

159 'Port Arthur Report of the Select Committee, with Minutes of the Proceedings, and Evidence', *House of Assembly Papers,* No. 127, 1871, 6.

160 *The Australasian*, 22 April 1865, 14.

161 Bowring iv. 71–6.

Bibliography

Primary Sources

Archival sources

Mitchell Library, State Library of New South Wales, Sydney Tasmanian Papers, 315, Port Arthur Convict Establishment.

National Archives UK, PCOM 2/86, Minutes of the Commissioners of Pentonville Prison, 1846–7.

Tasmanian Archives and Heritage Office, Hobart, GO 33, Governor's Duplicate Despatches received by the Colonial Office, 1825–55.

University of Tasmania Library Special and Rare Materials Collection, Hobart, RS 16/1, Letter from Elizabeth Fry to Lady Jane Franklin, Royal Society of Tasmania Collections, 1841–2.

Newspapers
The Australasian.
The Austral-Asiatic Review, Tasmanian and Australian Advertiser.
Launceston Examiner.
The True Colonist.

Parliamentary papers

Commons Sessional Papers (1837–8), vol. xxii. 1–424: 'Report from the Select Committee on Transportation; together with the Minutes of Evidence, Appendix, and Index', 3 August 1838.

Commons Sessional Papers (1844), vol. xxviii. 127–99: 'Report of the Surveyor-General of Prisons on the Construction, Ventilation and Details of Pentonville Prison, 1844', 1844.

Commons Sessional Papers (1846), vol. xx. 97–143: 'Fourth Report of The Commissioners for the government of the Pentonville Prison', 1846.

Commons Sessional Papers (1846), vol. xxix. 291–361: 'Copies or Extracts of any Correspondence between the Secretary of State for the Colonies and the Governor of Van Diemen's Land, on the Subject of Convict Discipline', 9 February 1846.

Commons Sessional Papers (1846), vol. xxix. 363–444: 'Copies or Extracts of an Correspondence between the Secretary of State for the Colonies and the Lieutenant-governor of Van Diemen's Land, on the subject of Convict Discipline; and of any Reports from the Comptroller-general of Convicts in Van Diemen's Land', 17 June 1846.

Commons Sessional Papers (1847), vol. xxxviii. 513–37: 'Copies of Correspondence between the Secretary of State and Sir Eardley Wilmot, Bart., relative to the Recall of the latter from the Government of Van Diemen's Land', 30 March 1847.

Commons Sessional Papers (1847), vol. xlviii. 93–192: 'Correspondence on the subject of Convict Discipline and Transportation', 16 February 1847.

Commons Sessional Papers (1849), vol. xlviii. 63–622: 'Further Correspondence on the subject of Convict Discipline and Transportation', February 1849.

Commons Sessional Papers (1850), vol. xlv. 11–170: 'Further Correspondence on the subject of Convict Discipline and Transportation', 31 January 1850.

Commons Sessional Papers (1852–3), vol. lxxxii. 1–505: 'Further Correspondence on the subject of Convict Discipline and Transportation', 13 December 1852.

Commons Sessional Papers (1854), vol. xxxiii. 1–103: 'Report on the Discipline and Management of the Convict Prisons, and Disposal of Convicts, 1853. By Lieut.-Col. Jebb, C.B. Surveyor-General of Prisons, Chairman of the Directors, &c', 1854.

Commons Sessional Papers (1854), vol. liv. 303–599: 'Further Correspondence on the subject of Convict Discipline and Transportation', May 1854.

Commons Sessional Papers (1854–5), vol. xxxix. 267–376: 'Further Correspondence on the subject of Convict Discipline and Transportation', February 1855.

Printed sources

Backhouse, J. *A Narrative of a Visit to the Australian Colonies.* London: Hamilton, Adams, 1843.

Bentham, J. *The Works of Jeremy Bentham, published under the superintendence of … John Bowring,* 11 vols. Edinburgh: William Tait, 1838–43.

Bobbin, T. *The Revelations of P.A.; or, News from our penal settlement.* Hobart Town: J.C. Hall, 1868.

Bonwick, J. *The Bushrangers: Illustrating the Early Days of Van Diemen's Land.* Melbourne: George Roberton, 1856.

Castieau, J.B. *The Difficulties of My Position: The Diaries of Prison Governor John Buckley Castieau, 1855–1884,* ed. M. Finnane. Canberra: National Library of Australia, 2004.

Frost, J. *The Horrors of Convict Life.* Hobart: Sullivan's Cove, 1856.

Fry, H.P. *A Letter to the Householders of Hobarton, on the Effects of Transportation, and on the Moral Condition of the Colony.* Hobart: John Moore, 1847.

Fry, H.P. *A System of Penal Discipline: With a Report on the Treatment of Prisoners in Great Britain and Van Dieman's Land*. London: Longman, Brown, Green and Longmans, 1850.

Jeffrey, M. *A Burglar's Life: Or, the Stirring Adventures of the Great English Burglar Mark Jeffrey; a Thrilling History of the Dark Days of Convictism in Australia*. Sydney: Angus and Robertson, 1968.

Maconochie, A. *Australiana: Thoughts on Convict Management and Other Subjects Connected with the Australian Penal Colonies*. London: J.W. Parker, 1839.

Mayhew, H. and Binny, J. *The Criminal Prisons of London: And Scenes of Prison Life*. Cambridge: Cambridge University Press, 2011 [1862].

Nicholls, M. *Traveller under Concern: The Quaker Journals of Frederick Mackie on His Tour of the Australasian Colonies, 1852–1855*. Hobart: University of Tasmania, 1973.

Syme, J. *Nine Years in Van Diemen's Land*. Dundee: J. Syme, 1848.

Ullathorne, W.B. *The Catholic Mission in Australasia*. Liverpool: Rockliff and Duckworth, 1837.

Secondary Sources

Abruzzo, M. *Polemical Pain: Slavery, Cruelty, and the Rise of Humanitarianism*. Baltimore: Johns Hopkins University Press, 2011.

Anderson, C. 'The Genealogy of the Modern Subject Indian Convicts in Mauritius, 1814–53'. In *Representing Convicts: New Perspectives on Convict Forced Labour Migration*, ed. I. Duffield and J. Bradley, 164–82. London: Leicester University Press, 1997.

Anderson, C. *A Global History of Convicts and Penal Colonies*. London: Bloomsbury Publishing, 2018.

Anderson, S. *A History of Capital Punishment in the Australian Colonies, 1788–1900*. London: Palgrave Macmillan, 2021.

Baldry, E., Carlton, B., and Cunneen, C. 'Abolition and the Paradox of Penal Reform in Australia: Indigenous Women, Colonial Patriarchy, and Co-option', *Social Justice* 41: 3 (2015): 168–89.

Barclay, K. 'Falling in Love with the Dead', *Rethinking History* 22: 4 (2018): 459–73.

Barnes, J. '"More Beautiful than Port Phillip": The La Trobe Family in Van Diemen's Land', *The La Trobe Journal* 80 (2007): 65–75.

Battye, J.S. *The History of the North West of Australia: Embracing Kimberley, Gascoyne and Murchison Districts*. Victoria Park: Hesperian Press, 1985.

Bennett, R. '"Bad for the Health of the Body, Worse for the Health of the Mind": Female Responses to Imprisonment in England, 1853–1869', *Social History of Medicine* (2020): 532–52.

Bevan, J.G. and Forster, J. *Extracts from the Letters and Other Writings of the Late Joseph Gurney Bevan: Preceded by a Short Memoir of His Life*. London: William Phillips, 1821.

Brand, I. *Port Arthur, 1830–1877: A Compelling History of Australia's Most Infamous Convict Settlement*. Hobart: Jason Publications, 1980.

Brand, I. 'Charles Joseph La Trobe and the Van Diemen's Land Probation System', *Bulletin of the Centre for Tasmanian Historical Studies* 2: 1 (1988): 49–67.

Brand, I. *The 'Separate' or 'Model' Prison, Port Arthur*. Launceston: Regal Publications, 1990a.

Brand, I. *Penal Peninsula: Port Arthur and Its Outstations, 1827–1898*. Launceston: Regal Publications, 1998.

Brand, I., La Trobe, C.J., Sprod, M.N., and Boyd, J. *The Convict Probation System, Van Diemen's Land 1839–1854: A Study of the Probation System of Convict Discipline, Together with C.J. La Trobe's 1847 Report on Its Operation and the 1845 Report of James Boyd on the Probation Station at Darlington, Maria Island*. Hobart: Blubber Head Press, 1990b.

Brand, I. and Staniforth, M. 'Care and Control: Female Convict Transportation Voyages to Van Diemen's Land, 1818–1853', *The Great Circle* 16: 1 (1994): 23–42.

Burt, J.T. *Results of the System of Separate Confinement: As Administered at the Pentonville Prison*. London: Longman, Brown, Green, and Longmans, 1852.

Carey, H.M. *Empire of Hell: Religion and the Campaign to End Convict Transportation in the British Empire, 1788–1875*. Cambridge: Cambridge University Press, 2019.

Casella, E.C. 'Bulldaggers and Gentle Ladies: Archaeological Approaches to Female Homosexuality in Convict-Era Australia'. In *Archaeologies of Sexuality*, ed. R. Schmidt and B. Voss, 143–68. London: Routledge, 2005.

Causer, T. 'Anti-Transportation, "Unnatural Crime", and the "Horrors" of Norfolk Island', *Journal of Australian Colonial History* 14 (2012): 230–40.

Clark, M. *A History of Australia (Volumes 3 and 4): From 1824 to 1888*. Melbourne: Melbourne University Publishing, 1999.

Coad, D. *Gender Trouble Down Under: Australian Masculinities*. Valenciennes: Presses Universitaires de Valenciennes, 2002.

Davie, N. *The Penitentiary Ten: The Transformation of the English Prison, 1770–1850*. Oxford: Bardwell Press, 2016.

Davis, R.P. *The Tasmanian Gallows: A Study of Capital Punishment*. Hobart: Cat & Fiddle Press, 1974.

Dwyer, P. and Nettelbeck, A. *Violence, Colonialism and Empire in the Modern World*. Springer International Publishing, 2017.

Edmonds, P. 'Travelling "under Concern": Quakers James Backhouse and George Washington Walker Tour the Antipodean Colonies, 1832–41', *Journal of Imperial and Commonwealth History* 40: 5 (2012): 769–88.

Edmonds, P. and Maxwell-Stewart, H. '"The Whip is a Very Contagious Kind of Thing": Flogging and Humanitarian Reform in Penal Australia', *Journal of Colonialism & Colonial History* 17: 1 (2016), https://doi.org/10.1353/cch.2016.0006.

Epstein, J. *Scandal of Colonial Rule: Power and Subversion in the British Atlantic during the Age of Revolution*. Cambridge: Cambridge University Press, 2012.

Evans, R. and Thorpe, B. 'Commanding Men: Masculinities and the Convict System', *Journal of Australian Studies* 22: 56 (1998): 17–34.

Foucault, M. *Discipline and Punishment*. London: Allen Lane, 1977.

Foxhall, K. 'From Convicts to Colonists: The Health of Prisoners and the Voyage to Australia, 1823–53', *Journal of Imperial and Commonwealth History* 39: 1 (2011): 1–19.

Foxhall, K. *Health, Medicine, and the Sea: Australian Voyages, c. 1815–1860*. Manchester: Manchester University Press, 2018.

Gatrell, V.A.C. *The Hanging Tree: Execution and the English People 1770–1868*. Oxford: Oxford University Press, 1994.

Gibson, M. 'Global Perspectives on the Birth of the Prison', *American Historical Review* 116: 4 (2011): 1040–63.

Gilchrist, C. '"The Victim of His Own Temerity"? Silence, Scandal and the Recall of Sir John Eardley-Wilmot', *Journal of Australian Studies* 28: 84 (2005): 151–61.

Gilchrist, C. '"This Relic of the Cities of the Plain": Penal Flogging, Convict Morality and the Colonial Imagination', *Journal of Australian Colonial History* 9 (2007): 1–28.

Godfrey, B. and Lawrence, P. *Crime and Justice 1750–1950*. Cullompton: Willan Publishing, 2013.

Graeme-Evans, A. and Ross, M. *A Short History Guide to Port Arthur 1830–1877*. Launceston: Regal Publications, Tasmania, 1993.

Harling, P. 'The Trouble with Convicts: From Transportation to Penal Servitude, 1840–67', *Journal of British Studies* 53: 1 (2014), https://doi.org/10.1017/jbr.2013.213, 80–110.

Heath, D. *Purifying Empire: Obscenity and the Politics of Moral Regulation in Britain, India and Australia*. Cambridge: Cambridge University Press, 2010.

Hughes, R. *The Fatal Shore: A History of Transportation of Convicts to Australia, 1797–1868*. London: Collins Harville, 1987.

Ignatieff, M. *A Just Measure of Pain: The Penitentiary in the Industrial Revolution, 1750–1850*. London: Macmillan, 1978.

Inda, J.X. *Anthropologies of Modernity: Foucault, Governmentality, and Life Politics*. Oxford: Blackwell Publishing, 2008.

Ludwig, M. 'Murder in the Andamans: A Colonial Narrative of Sodomy, Jealousy and Violence', *South Asia Multidisciplinary Academic Journal* (2013), https://doi.org/10.4000/samaj.3633.

McKenzie, K. 'Discourses of Scandal: Bourgeois Respectability and the End of Slavery and Transportation at the Cape and New South Wales', *Journal of Colonialism and Colonial History* 4: 3 (2003), https://doi.org/10.1353/cch.2004.0011.

McKenzie, K. *Scandal in the Colonies*. Melbourne: Melbourne University Publishing, 2013.

McLaren, A. and McLaren, T. *The Trials of Masculinity: Policing Sexual Boundaries, 1870–1930*. Chicago: University of Chicago Press, 1997.

Menis, S. *A History of Women's Prisons in England: The Myth of Prisoner Reformation*. Cambridge Scholars Publishing, 2019.

Milton, A., Gregory, J., Strong, R., Morris, J.N., and Sachs, W.L. *The Oxford History of Anglicanism*. Oxford: Oxford University Press, 2017.

Morin, K. and Moran, D. *Historical Geographies of Prisons: Unlocking the Usable Carceral Past*. Abingdon: Routledge, 2015.

Nolan, B. 'Up Close and Personal: Lesbian Sub-Culture in the Female Factories of Van Diemen's Land', *Journal of Lesbian Studies* 17: 3–4 (2013): 291–304.

Ogborn, M. 'Discipline, Government and Law: Separate Confinement in the Prisons of England and Wales, 1830–1877', *Transactions of the Institute of British Geographers* 20: 3 (1995): 295–311.

Pateman, C. *The Sexual Contract*. Stanford: Stanford University Press, 1988.

Peart, M. 'Sodom Island: Pandæmonium and the Botany Bay of Botany Bay', *Journal of the History of Sexuality* 28: 2 (2019): 263–96.

Petrow, S. 'After Arthur: Policing in Van Diemen's Land, 1837–46'. In *Policing the Lucky Country*, ed. M. Enders and B. Dupont, 176–99. Sydney: Hawkins Press, 2001.

Pratt, J. *A Punitive Society: Falling Crime and Rising Imprisonment in New Zealand*. Wellington: Bridget Williams Books, 2013.

Preston, K. 'Prison Treadmills in Van Diemen's Land: Design, Construction and Operation, 1828 to 1856', Paper presented at the Tasmanian Historical Research Association conference, 2013.

Reid, K. 'The Horrors of Convict Life: British Radical Visions of the Australian Penal Colonies', *Cultural and Social History* 5: 4 (2008): 481–95.

Reid, K. *Gender, Crime and Empire: Convicts, Settlers and the State in Early Colonial Australia*. Manchester: Manchester University Press, 2017.

Ritchie, J.M. 'Charles Joseph La Trobe in Van Diemen's Land, 1846', Paper presented at the Tasmanian Historical Research Association conference, 1976.

Schofield, P. 'The Legal and Political Legacy of Jeremy Bentham', *Annual Review of Law and Social Science* 9 (2013): 51–70.

Semple-Kerr, J. and Torrance, J. *Out of Sight, out of Mind: Australia's Places of Confinement, 1788–1988*. Sydney: S.H. Ervin Gallery, 1988.

Smith, P.S. 'A Religious Technology of the Self: Rationality and Religion in the Rise of the Modern Penitentiary', *Punishment & Society* 6: 2 (2004): 195–220.

Stoler, A.L. *Race and the Education of Desire: Foucault's History of Sexuality and the Colonial Order of Things*. Durham, NC: Duke University Press, 1995.

Taylor, L. 'Speaking the Unspeakable: Buggery, Law, and Community Surveillance in New South Wales, 1788–1838', *Law and History Review* (2020): 1–39, https://doi.org/10.1017/S0738248019000774.

Tuffin, R. 'The Evolution of Convict Labour Management in Van Diemen's Land: Placing the "Penal Peninsula" in a Colonial Context', Paper presented at the Tasmanian Historical Research Association conference, 2007.

Weidenhofer, M. *Port Arthur, a Place of Misery*. Oxford: Oxford University Press, 1981.

Wiener, M.J. *Reconstructing the Criminal: Culture, Law, and Policy in England, 1830–1914*. Cambridge: Cambridge University Press, 1994.

Unpublished theses

Causer, T. '"Only a Place Fit for Angels and Eagles": The Norfolk Island Penal Settlement, 1825–1855', PhD thesis, King's College London, 2009.

Cave, E.C. 'Flora Tasmaniae: Tasmanian Naturalists and Imperial Botany, 1829–1860', PhD thesis, University of Tasmania, 2012.

Gilchrist, C. 'Male Convict Sexuality in the Penal Colonies of Australia, 1820–1850', PhD thesis, University of Sydney, 2004.

Hilton, P. 'Separately Treated: An Assessment of the Effectiveness of Port Arthur's Separate Prison, in the Crushing of Convict Resistance, 1849–1877', PhD thesis, University of Tasmania, 1999.

Kamphuis, A.R. 'Bleeding, Blistering and Observations of the Bowel: A Comparative Analysis of Hospital Treatment in the Mid-Nineteenth Century', PhD thesis, University of Tasmania, 2012.

Mickleborough, L.C. 'Victim of an "Extraordinary Conspiracy"?: Sir John Eardley Eardley-Wilmot Lieutenant-Governor of Van Diemen's Land 1843–46', PhD thesis, University of Tasmania, 2011.

Upward, F. 'The Dismissal of Sir John Eardley-Wilmot, Lt. Governor of Tasmania, 1843–1846', PhD thesis, University of Tasmania, 1974.

Wood, C. 'Great Britain's Exiles Sent to Port Phillip, Australia, 1844–1849: Lord Stanley's Experiment', PhD thesis, University of Melbourne, 2014.

11

The panopticon archetype and the Swan River Colony

establishing Fremantle Gaol, 1831–41[1]

Emily Lanman

Introduction

The European history of Australia is intertwined with narratives of crime and punishment, beginning with the invasion of the east coast to establish two penal colonies, New South Wales (1788) and Van Diemen's Land (1803).[2] The Swan River Colony (1829) was the third Australian colony established by the British, but unlike its predecessors, it was to be free from convicts.[3] This did not negate the need for imprisonment, with the colony's first prison, Fremantle Gaol,[4] which opened in 1831, being based on the principles of Bentham's panopticon penitentiary. It came to symbolize British power and dominance through its status as the first permanent public structure in the colony.[5] The construction of the gaol was particularly important as tensions surrounding settlement agitated less privileged settlers. It was also compounded by a resentful Indigenous population who rejected the British occupation of their country.

This chapter will centre on the panoptic structures of the Fremantle Gaol, the punishments utilized by the local government and the institution, and will explain where the gaol deviates from the panopticon model. Whilst Fremantle Gaol is not an exact replica of Bentham's panopticon, it can be argued that it is a colonial reinterpretation of the design. The utilization of the panoptic archetype for the Fremantle Gaol is often overlooked by the literature surrounding the colony's early penal history. To establish that Fremantle Gaol was a panoptic institution, several factors need to be considered. First, the formation of the Swan River Colony itself, including the struggles that occurred in founding it, and the factors that led to the establishment of a penal system, must be examined; from this, the gaol itself can be considered, namely, its location, architecture and maintenance, as well as its role in colonial society. Second, the operation of the prison can be compared to the panopticon to determine how Bentham's plan was amended to ensure its success in a colonial setting. Third, the methods of punishment utilized in the gaol against colonial and indigenous prisoners will be highlighted, with particular reference to the differences in the way the two groups were punished. It will also discuss where the punishments used deviated from Bentham's innovative ideas in favour of harsher methods.

The formative years of the Swan River Colony

To understand the Fremantle Gaol's role in the colony, the formative events in the colony's history must first be examined. The coast of the land that would become Western Australia was most likely first sighted and reported by the Portuguese in the early sixteenth century, and it was the Dutch who first charted the coast during the seventeenth century.[6] It was not until the eighteenth century that significant interest was taken in the region, and only in 1826 when King George's Sound, in the southern part of the territory, was claimed by the British.[7] However, this was not a formal claim but rather a way of establishing prior occupation out of concern that the French were looking to colonize the area; the British did not want the security of the eastern penal colonies to be compromised.[8]

Captain James Stirling,[9] along with Charles Frazer, the Colonial Botanist of New South Wales, had spent three weeks in February and March 1827 exploring the western coast of the Australian continent for a site for a potential settlement.[10] Stirling was already convinced of the location's suitability, despite earlier, less favourable reports; as he argued, it would be advantageous to British interests to have a colony on the opposite side of the continent for purposes of trade. The environment of the region, he further suggested, would not only be well-suited for agriculture, but there was also potential to mine rich seams of iron and coal.[11] Stirling's report was not well received in London, with the Colonial Office finding no justification for a settlement.[12] Initial objections were based on the vast cost associated with establishing a new settlement, but as concerns around population size in Britain and urbanization grew, and amidst reports of French interest in the region, opinions about the potential utility of a proposed colony at Swan River began to change.[13] Interest was further advanced when a group of four investors known as The Peel Associates backed the new colony. These investors requested 4 million acres of land in the new colony in return for a £100,000 investment, but out of reluctance to allow a small, private group such a monopoly of influence, the British government rejected the proposal, perhaps owing to their prior experience of dealing with the East India Company.[14] Instead, the 'Conditions of Settlement' finalized by the Colonial Office between December 1828 and February 1829 stated that land would be granted to settlers based on their capital as a way of minimizing expense to the British government.[15] Stirling, who was to be the colony's first governor, along with the first settlers, departed from Plymouth in the *Parmelia* on 5 February 1829, with Swan River having been claimed for the British by Captain Charles Howe Fremantle on 2 May 1829.[16] The Swan River Colony was officially established on 1 June 1829, the first non-penal colony in Australia (although convicts were present in the King George's Sound military outpost until 1831), as well as the first new free British settlement since the loss of the American colonies in 1783.[17]

Stirling's confidence in Swan River did not falter on the voyage, which possibly helped contribute to high expectations among the new settlers.[18] However, the settlers soon came to consider that Swan River's potential had been grossly oversold.[19] Contrary to Stirling's anticipation of successful agricultural production, the colony's poor soil meant that European methods of agriculture were unsuited for the land and thus required adaptation in order to succeed.[20] Life overall was tough for the new settlers, with a precarious supply of food and a high degree of sickness – so much so that by 1832, 12 per cent of the first arrivals had died.[21] Reports from settlers regarding the abysmal conditions at the colony reached family and friends back in Britain, leading many to reconsider plans to settle at Swan River. There followed a stark drop in rates of immigration, with the colony struggling to reach a population of 5,000 two decades after establishment.[22] In addition, the colony greatly suffered with limited cash flow, prompting Stirling to return to England in 1832 to petition, without success, for financial support from the Colonial Office.[23] The economic crisis was exacerbated by the limited amounts of cash brought out by settlers, since assets and not money

Figure 11.1: The entrance to Fremantle Gaol. Photograph by the author.

would qualify them for land, and therefore precedence was given to investing in equipment and livestock.[24] The absence of cash quickly became such a concern that influential settlers considered creating a bank to allow farmers to borrow against their predicted harvests, thus placing the colony in a precarious state in that it depended on its small group of wealthy settlers – a situation the British government had sought to avoid.[25] This stunted the growth of the colony, a problem that continued into the 1840s, much of which was spent in depression.[26]

Despite its status as a non-penal colony, incarceration was resorted to almost immediately at Swan River, initially in response to drunkenness and assumed indiscipline of indentured servants.[27] Like Britain, the colony briefly utilized a prison hulk, the *Marquis of Anglesea*, which housed 27 prisoners between December 1829 and July 1830 off the coast of Fremantle. However, the hulk proved impractical owing to a scarcity of boats, making the transportation of prisoners to and from the hulk difficult.[28] By April 1830, the need for a permanent prison was felt by the local government to be pressing, with Governor Stirling suggesting to the magistrates that a gaol should be built at Perth. In addition, a further prison was proposed for Fremantle, which was thought to be a better location for the colony's primary place of incarceration,[29] largely due to the issues of drunkenness among settlers, but also because, as a port town, Fremantle was often 'plagued by undesirable strangers'.[30]

Following further lobbying by the Chairman at the Quarter Sessions for a prison at Fremantle, at the colony's first Quarter Session in July 1830, Fremantle was confirmed as the site for the prison. Subsequently a location at Arthur Head was chosen, and plans were drawn up and tenders were called.[31] Responsible for the design and oversight of the construction work was the colony's Civil Engineer, Henry Willey Reveley, who utilized the panoptic archetype for the prison.[32] This was no coincidence: his father, Willey Reveley, had worked alongside Jeremy and Samuel Bentham to refine the panopticon model in 1791 and had been commissioned by Jeremy Bentham to draw up plans for the building.[33] Though Reveley senior died whilst his son was young, his architectural preferences appear to have influenced Henry, as evidenced through his works in the colony such as the Perth Court House, which was modelled on Greek-Doric architecture.[34] Richard Lewis was selected as contractor for the erection of the gaol for the sum of £1,840. However, the unsuccessful bidders John Duffield and William Manning also maintained involvement in the construction and maintenance of the prison.[35] The building of the gaol progressed rapidly between August and December 1830, an impressive feat given the infant state of the colony.[36]

The Fremantle Gaol and its panoptic infrastructure

An exploration of the Fremantle Gaol from an architectural standpoint highlights the panoptic features of the colony's principal penal institution. This is first demonstrable through an examination of the location chosen for the prison and a description of the building's structure. Second, issues that concerned the maintenance of Fremantle Gaol must also be investigated, as the institution deviates from Bentham's scheme, and negatively impacted upon the well-being of the incarcerated prisoners.

Location

Two possible locations for the Fremantle Gaol were considered: Arthur Head or the surrounding flats.[37] The former location, sitting 10 metres above sea level, was chosen though the precise reasoning behind the decision remains unclear.[38] The gaol dominated the local landscape as it was the first permanent public structure, not only in Fremantle, but

Figure 11.2: Overlooking present-day Fremantle from the steps of
Fremantle Gaol. Photograph by the author.

in the entire colony. Its position on the coastline meant it was the first
visible object to ships approaching the shore, serving both as a reminder
of home to those arriving in the foreign land as well as a symbol of
British control.[39] This symbolism was strengthened through settlers
referring to the building as resembling a castle – though admittedly
the gaol was not frequently mentioned in surviving letters from settlers
back to England, most likely owing to the Swan River Colony being
non-penal at the time of foundation, and thus an aversion to tarnishing
the overall impression of the settlement by drawing attention to its
system of incarceration.[40] Arthur Head was also a significant location
for the local Whadjuk Noongar people as it was utilized for a number
of social and cultural purposes. This area, known as Manjaree to the
Indigenous population, was where meetings between different language
groups would take place and goods traded, facilitated by the abundance
of food and access to fresh water. The juxtaposition between the area's
use by colonial and Indigenous inhabitants, as John Litchfield suggests,
'makes a perverse mimicry of the traditional use of the area', as in
both instances people were brought together but for vastly different
purposes.[41] It can be suggested that the location of the Fremantle Gaol

has echoes of Bentham's scheme, as he believed the panopticon needed to be visible to wider society in order to have a deterrent effect on future offending, as well as in saying 'This is the dwelling-place of crime'.[42]

Architecture

The architecture of the Fremantle Gaol essentially conforms to the design of the panopticon model, and embodies the importance placed on the management of prisoners by means of supervision and control.[43] Henry Reveley, the architect, sought to give the prison an appearance worthy of its status in the colony. The Fremantle Gaol was built on a dodecagon plan, with centrally placed quarters for the gaoler.[44] It should be noted that Bentham did not define the panopticon by its shape but rather stated that central inspection, in other words that the prisoners could be observed by an unseen inspector at any time, was the most important factor.[45] The layout of Fremantle Gaol was divided into 12 compartments: one was used as an entrance, one for the gaoler's accommodation, one as a kitchen, two for privies, and seven for prison cells. There was also a separate bakehouse under the steps that led to the prison's entrance.[46] Each of the compartments measured 4 by 1.9 metres, with no windows overlooking the outside world.[47] The lack of windows on the prisoner cells does create some conflict with its panoptic archetype, as while prisoners would have had some privacy, the cells in the panopticon were to have windows for daylight. This was not afforded to prisoners in Fremantle Gaol as very little natural light infiltrated the cell when it was locked; however, most prisoners would not be in their cells during the day. Instances where prisoners in the panopticon would be given privacy from inspection was when they were naked, for example, when washing or changing. However, this was with the caveat that prisoners would have to come back into the sight of the inspector at his request.[48] All the compartments of Fremantle Gaol opened into a common courtyard – spanning 12 metres – for exercise and ablutions.[49] The gaoler was housed on the outer wall, with the majority of the prisoners being held along the opposite wall, allowing for constant observation with a degree of anonymity. Incarcerated women and children, however, were kept in accommodation adjacent to the gaoler, separate from the male prisoners but also allowing for observation.[50] The small size of the gaol meant that any further classification by age, gender and offence was practically impossible.[51] Whilst prisoners of all races, ages and gender were confined within the gaol, the building was much smaller than Bentham's proposed panopticon. His prison was initially designed to span six storeys and accommodate a thousand prisoners, whereas Fremantle Gaol only had seven cells, with a maximum population of 21 prisoners.[52] Although Bentham had originally intended to keep prisoners in solitude, he later deemed it proper to house between two and four inmates per cell, since he came to consider solitary confinement as 'a degree of barbarous perfection never yet given', with damaging effects on the mental health of prisoners.[53] Congregate confinement would also allow for the diversification in the labour that prisoners could do within their cell and allow for more profitable prison labour.[54] The limited size of Fremantle Gaol can be attributed not only to the available resources at the time of construction but, most importantly, to the size of the colony, which by 1839 only had 2,154 settler inhabitants.[55]

Maintenance

Fremantle Gaol regularly required maintenance and repairs, which negatively impacted the prisoners and at times left the prison insecure. Concerns about its state of repair were expressed soon after it opened in 1831, when a coroner's report on the death of an inmate strongly recommended improvement not only to the structure of the building but to the interior comforts as well.[56] Further inconvenience occurred in 1837 when, during a period of heavy rain, water penetrated the roof, flooding the prisoners' cells as well as two compartments used by the gaoler. The gaol was rendered uninhabitable and the inmates were moved into the neighbouring courthouse at three o'clock in the morning.[57] Bentham designed the panopticon to prevent inflicting the sorts of pains endured by Fremantle Gaol's inmates: in addition to plentiful food in order to provide adequate sustenance to work, the building was to have had central heating, piped hot water, bathing and medical facilities, and be light and airy.[58]

Maintenance issues with fireplaces and chimneys also caused problems within Fremantle Gaol, especially in relation to the preparation of food for inmates. A letter from Henry Reveley to Peter Broun, the Colonial Secretary, in 1836 stated that as a result of ongoing issues a cell had to be utilized as a kitchen, otherwise the prison population would be 'compelled to put up with cold makeshift dinners for the impossibility of cooking'.[59] This would cause the inmates to experience the pain of hunger, as they lacked access to adequate nourishment.[60] Shortcomings in the gaol's structure also contributed to prisoner escape, such as when, in 1835, an Indigenous man named

Figure 11.3: The gaoler's quarters (centre) and two cells (far left and far right) at Fremantle Gaol. Photograph by the author.

Boogaberry was able to take advantage of a fault in the iron work to wriggle his cell door loose, and then use a nail to scrape holes into the limestone wall as a means to support himself whilst he climbed over the gaol wall.[61] The use of soft limestone greatly undermined the gaol's security, and successful and failed escape attempts were commonplace, also highlighting the faults with the system of inspection.[62] Weaknesses in the structure and design of the Fremantle Gaol could be attributed to the rapid construction of the building and the limited resources in the colony.[63] However, the weaknesses of the gaol's roof can be attributed to Reveley's design, which was widely recognized as defective in contemporary reports.[64]

Uses of the Fremantle Gaol

Fremantle Gaol's primary purpose was the incarceration of criminals, but it also served as a comprehensive institution for a local government lacking the infrastructure available in England. Other functions of the Fremantle Gaol included acting as a 'lunatic' asylum, a hospital, and a poorhouse. The construction of a gaol early in the colony's history highlights the colonial, and British, desire for the control and confinement of the 'criminal citizens of British colonies'.[65] The diversity in the gaol's function aligns, moreover, with Bentham's panopticon as an institutional design capable of being adapted to serve multiple purposes.[66]

Asylum

Fremantle Gaol functioned as an asylum during the early years of its operation, before the erection of dedicated institutions; Bentham had also envisioned his panopticon model being applicable to this purpose.[67] The gaol's role as an asylum began not long after its completion in 1831, with its first patient being Doctor Nicholas Langley, a medical professional, who was admitted in February of that year.[68] Correspondence from Reveley to Peter Broun[69] in May 1831 indicates that the preparation of a suitable strong cell had been delayed, and Reveley instead recommended the use of 'strait waist coat and trousers ... which will effectually prevent any further damage'.[70] The panopticon would have featured adapted cells set aside for patients such as Langley.[71] By September 1831, Langley was said to be greatly improved, with the superintendent wishing to move him from the gaol.[72] There is no apparent record for Langley's discharge from the gaol, though by the end of 1832 he was sufficiently recovered to be back practicing medicine.[73]

It is difficult to gauge how many inmates were confined in the gaol as asylum patients since few admissions records exist. However, there is a record of the admission for George Hagstaff in 1835 on the recommendation of the colonial surgeon, although no further details are to be found.[74] It can be assumed that no patients were admitted to the gaol from 1837–41, or rather there is no evidence of any admissions in the Blue Book Statistical Returns for the Swan River Colony.[75]

Hospital

Alongside the gaol's function as an asylum, it was also utilized as a hospital for those unable to afford medical care, prisoner and free settler alike. Similarly, Bentham's panopticon would have included a hospital, although he also expected the panoptic model to be applicable to a stand-alone hospital.[76] To maintain prisoner health, sick inmates would be kept apart from the rest of the prison population.[77] The gaol's annual return in 1835, under the heading of 'Lunatics or Other Extraordinary Prisoners', lists two sick people residing in the gaol.[78]

One of these individuals was the aforementioned George Hagstaff who had been confined as an asylum patient.[79] The annual return of 1837 tells a similar story, with two sick men temporarily residing in the institution, one of whom was Charles Spyers, who was possibly admitted in late September or early October on account of his 'melancholy state'.[80] The second patient admitted in 1837 can be assumed to be a servant who had similar symptoms to Spyers. However, no further evidence beyond a letter from the Colonial Secretary regarding Spyers's condition appears to have survived.[81] According to the Blue Book for 1839, an Indigenous man had been admitted into the gaol for assistance after being involved in a physical altercation with another Indigenous man, although he did not recover from his injuries.[82] There were a further two cases of sick persons entering the gaol in 1840. The first appears in the Quarterly Return for January, which indicates that a pauper by the name of Samuel Thomas had been in the institution for several months on account of his poor health.[83] Not long after this return had been lodged, a boy named only as Stanley had appeared at the gaol 'in a most destitute state' and 'suffering great agony', though it was later recommended that he be removed to the colonial hospital, as the gaol already held 12 inmates and had not enough cells to house him.[84] Removal of the sick to another building was something Bentham also thought necessary in some cases, particularly when it involved infectious disease.[85]

Poor house

Bentham had, separate from the panopticon prison, developed plans for a network of workhouses throughout England built according to panoptic architecture.[86] Similarly, the Fremantle Gaol functioned as the Swan River Colony's house for the destitute, and did so with some frequency as evidenced by the surviving correspondence. The first recorded instance was in December 1835 when William Snippard was admitted to take up residence in the gaol on account of his ailing health and destitution.[87] It was further utilized in early 1836 for Simon Johnson, and though it is unclear when he was first admitted, communication from the Colonial Secretary to the Government Resident in Fremantle stated Johnson could remain 'on the destitute list, but he must not be continued in the jail'.[88] It is unclear how paupers were accommodated in the gaol; they were most likely housed in one of the cells due to it being used seemingly for people in dire circumstances. Poor relief in the colony relied predominantly on outdoor relief, a practice which had in principle been done away with in England through the Poor Law Amendment Act of 1834, which saw relief being given solely through the workhouse – a method Bentham endorsed.[89] Whilst the workhouse method applied in the colony deviated somewhat from Bentham's scheme, this can largely be explained by the colony being unable to sustain a stand-alone pauper institution, and the limited capacity of Fremantle Gaol to house large numbers of paupers.[90] There was, however, a push from the colonial government for certain departments to employ paupers as labourers, which circumnavigated the need to sustain them solely out of the government pocket or house them in government-funded institutions.[91]

Operations of the Fremantle Gaol

Key aspects of the operation of the Fremantle Gaol highlight strong links between the prison and the panopticon archetype. Evidence of this connection can be found in the rules and regulations promulgated by the Colonial Secretary's Office from 1831 and 1835, as well as reports produced in the colony for the Secretary of State for the Colonies, and in the Blue Book Statistical Returns for 1837–41. The gaol rules established in 1835 were published in the *Perth Gazette*, reflecting Bentham's view that such rules had to be known in the community on which the deterrent effect of punishment was intended to operate, and in order to remind society of the consequences of disobedience.[92] Both the 1831 and 1835 editions of the Fremantle Gaol's rules and regulations show conformity to Bentham's panoptic philosophy, and are split into two overarching categories, namely 'Duties of the Keepers and Officers' and 'Treatment of Prisoners'. For the sake of clarity, the following discussion will focus upon the latter category, and include the following sub-divisions: health and cleanliness; prison provisions; inmate diet; separation and communication; labour; and the reformation of prisoner morality. Throughout this discussion, any significant deviations in the operation of Fremantle Gaol from the panoptic model will be mentioned where appropriate, with suggestions as to the possible reasons for such deviations.

Health and cleanliness

Health and cleanliness were essential in the routine of both the panopticon and Fremantle Gaol.[93] The preservation of health and cleanliness was something Bentham saw as integral to a penal institution, and essential to the maintenance of a healthy convict workforce.[94] Upon arrival at Fremantle Gaol a prisoner would be bathed prior to being admitted, according to rules 17 and 25 (1835), he would then be given a prison uniform. His own clothes would be taken to be fumigated, if necessary, and stored until his release.[95] The panopticon's inmates would similarly have been cleaned prior to admission, a practice which, Bentham believed, constituted a symbolic ritual where the prisoner became integrated with the institution.[96] Each day Fremantle Gaol's prisoners would be expected to air their bedclothes and sweep the prison yard, privies and cells, a routine Bentham had incorporated into the panopticon plan, and which would be undertaken at the cessation of work.[97] At Fremantle, prisoners were also expected to wash their bodies and prison uniforms on a weekly basis, usually on a Saturday afternoon, for which they would be provided with towels, combs and a quarter-pound of soap.[98] In Bentham's plan thorough cleaning would also occur on a Saturday, although there were some differences as to the regularity of washing: first, in the panopticon, prisoners would be expected to wash their hands, face and feet multiple times a day, something that was not stipulated in the rules at Fremantle; second, in the gaol prisoners would wash themselves once a week, whereas in the panopticon the frequency of bathing was weekly during summer, monthly during winter, fortnightly during spring and autumn. Finally, Bentham stipulated how frequently different items of clothing and bedding should be cleaned; for example, shirts would be cleaned twice a week, trousers once a week, with sheets to be washed once a month and the blankets once in summer. Regulations for Fremantle Gaol did not elaborate on a set routine for the cleaning of apparel, only to suggest this should occur weekly.[99] The rules of 1835 also stated that the prison would be scrubbed and whitewashed regularly. Although a specific timeframe was not mentioned, it appears that it did occur as a matter of routine as evidenced by communication in the Colonial Secretary's correspondence.[100]

Also built into the daily routine of Fremantle Gaol, as laid out by the 1835 regulations, was the allowance for exercise and access to fresh air, as also mandated in Bentham's scheme. According to the 36th rule all prisoners, including those in solitary confinement, were to receive adequate access to air and exercise.[101] Bentham had seen regular exercise as an important means of preserving health, and the panopticon's cells were designed to allow for adequate ventilation, as such exercise had to take place under, as Bentham put it, the 'inviolable law' of inspection.[102]

Maintaining the health of the panopticon's inmates was of great importance to Bentham, as evidenced by, amongst other things, the inclusion in the design of an on-site infirmary.[103] In the event of Fremantle Gaol prisoners falling ill or being injured, either the superintendent (1831) or gaoler (1835) would notify the resident magistrate that medical assistance was required so that the Colonial Surgeon could be sent for.[104] In addition, the Colonial Surgeon was to make weekly visits, although these were abandoned in 1836, reinstated in 1837, and abandoned again in 1841 over concerns that they were an unnecessary expense when treatment was infrequently needed.[105] The methods of reporting prisoner health were enshrined in the regulations in 1835, and included notifying the relevant authorities in the event of the death of an inmate.[106] In the 1831 rules, the death of a prisoner was to be reported to the coroner via the superintendent, though not in the 1835 regulations as the office of coroner appears to have been abandoned by the local government.[107]

Gaol provisions

Provisions and the prison diet were closely considered both by Bentham and in regulations for Fremantle Gaol.[108] In the latter, the gaoler was to keep a sufficient quantity of water in the gaol at all times for both consumption and maintaining hygiene.[109] A list of material provisions was not provided in the 1831 regulations, with the exception of stated allowances of soap to maintain cleanliness.[110] The regulations of 1835 were, however, more detailed as to allowances for each prisoner, who were to be provided with a bedstead, a mattress, one blanket, one rug or coverlet, two shirts and trousers, a jacket, and a pair of shoes, in addition to the aforementioned allowance of soap.[111] Bentham insisted on sufficient clothing to protect against the weather, and thought it best left to the discretion of the prison authorities to determine what mode of bedding was cheapest and most suitable.[112] Provisions for Fremantle Gaol, including prison uniforms and other required equipment such as handcuffs and leg irons, were usually sourced from government stores in Van Diemen's Land. At times when these items were urgently needed, or could not be sourced from the eastern colonies, local tenders would be called for and this was often the case for prison bedding.[113] Those in the gaol on remand were treated with more leniency, as they were permitted to purchase items by which to supplement the prison ration, with the exception of alcohol, which was prohibited in the regulations for both the gaol and the panopticon.[114] Admitting alcohol into the Fremantle Gaol was a punishable offence, while Bentham viewed consumption of alcohol as a vice that could corrupt individuals.[115] This corruption, Bentham argued in his first 'Letter to Lord Pelham', was prevalent in New South Wales where productivity was extremely low, with a contributory factor being the prevalence of drunkenness.[116]

The food, and its quantity, provided to prisoners in the panopticon and the Fremantle Gaol show significant differences. Bentham paid great attention to the diet to be provided to the panopticon's inmates, going so far as to collect a series of recipes for dishes, capable of being cooked at scale.[117] Bentham stipulated that, according to the rules of lenity and economy, inmates should have access to as much cheap, nourishing food as they wished in order to sustain them at work, though according to the rule of severity such food must not be palatable and not superior to that enjoyed by a free, honest worker.[118] Along with the food provided in the panopticon, Bentham would grant permission to prisoners to purchase food from their earnings although this would mean they would have less money upon release.[119] Although the basic diet of the prisoners was outlined in the rules for Fremantle Gaol, it is unclear what considerations were made when they were being drawn up.[120] That prescribed for 1831 was the same regardless of gender or employment status; each prisoner would receive '1½lb of bread and a pint of gruel for breakfast', or 2lb of bread with ½lb of meat on Sundays, provided the prisoner had displayed good behaviour.[121] In the 1835 edition of the regulations, the diet prisoners were given depended upon the class to which they belonged. The general prison population, that is, those awaiting trial or not sentenced to labour, were given 1½lb of bread with ½lb of meat each day, or 1lb of fish on Sundays, contingent upon good behaviour. Prisoners employed in hard labour, either compelled to it following conviction or voluntarily engaged in it, would have their daily ration increased by ½lb of meat or 1lb of fish. Convicted female prisoners at labour would receive daily 1lb of bread and ¼lb of meat.[122] Prison diet, according to Bentham, should provide sufficient nourishment whilst being economical, which was largely conformed to within Fremantle Gaol namely through Bentham's rules of lenity, economy and severity.[123] However, it does deviate from the panopticon in terms of quantity, as otherwise prisoners would have had a diet superior to that of free labourers.[124]

Figure 11.4: The well which would provide Fremantle Gaol with water. Photograph by the author.

Separation

Separation was a critical method of control in the Fremantle Gaol and was arranged by both gender and age. Children were to be kept away from adult offenders as much as possible. The segregation of inmates also occurred according to offence, as prisoners convicted of felony were not to share a cell or socialize with prisoners convicted of misdemeanour, to prevent the spread of moral corruption.[125] This is mirrored in Bentham's panopticon scheme, as he did not wish felons to have the opportunity to corrupt individuals who had committed lesser crimes, which would defeat the reforming goal of the institution.[126] Separation by gender was also considered to be of great importance to Bentham, either by housing female prisoners in a separate building or within a different ward.[127] In cases where solitary confinement was inflicted upon Fremantle Gaol prisoners for part of their sentence, it would be strictly adhered to in order to be effective.[128] Bentham, though rejecting general use of solitary confinement, considered it as a potentially effective short-term punishment to break the spirit of an inmate or to control the disobedient and allow the process of reformation to begin.[129]

There were strict regulations regarding the circumstances in which visitors could enter Fremantle Gaol, and only with the written permission of a magistrate.[130] Though Fremantle Gaol's inmates were excluded from society, allowing visitors to see the prisoner undergoing punishment was a method of making their fate an example and deterrent to future offending in the community.[131] One example of an occasion where prisoners were put on public display, possibly for the purpose of example, was in 1836 when they were included in a public celebration of the wedding of Stephen George Henty; while details are not apparent, this could have been used as a way of highlighting the consequences of offending to the free settlers.[132] Whilst the gaol authorities sought to keep prisoners separate from each other and from wider society, it was not always successful as prisoners could call through the walls to people outside, or have brief exchanges with people whilst they were labouring outside the gaol walls.[133] However, as these interactions with free settlers were limited, it would not severely undermine the separation of prisoners from the rest of the colony. While public access to Fremantle Gaol was greatly restricted, Bentham envisaged that the public would be allowed access to the panopticon as he thought public scrutiny would regulate the conduct of the prison's officials and ensure the prisoners were not being mistreated.[134]

Labour

Key to reformation of prisoners in both Bentham's panopticon and the Fremantle Gaol was engaging inmates in labour. The tasks at which prisoners would be employed at Fremantle depended on their gender: men laboured on public works, such as building jetties and stone walls, or on maintaining the gaol, while women were employed under the supervision of the gaoler's wife in the domestic duties associated with prison life, such as washing and cooking.[135] Neither the panopticon nor the Fremantle Gaol regimes would compel inmates awaiting trial to labour, though at Fremantle they could volunteer their labour in exchange for an increase in their rations.[136] The length of time prisoners would be kept at work differed in the two editions of Fremantle Gaol's rules and regulations. In 1831 prisoners were to work for ten hours a day all year round.[137] However, this changed in 1835, with labouring hours differing depending on the season, so that in summer prisoners worked for eight hours, and for nine hours in winter.[138] This is also reflected in Bentham's scheme which would keep prisoners in physical labour for eight hours per day in winter, but up to 14 hours in sedentary labour in the summer months with longer periods of daylight.[139] The arrangement of work in both Fremantle Gaol and the panopticon, though rigorous, appears to have sought to avoid causing injury to the health of the prisoners.[140]

Labour at Fremantle Gaol was enforced by the threat of punishment. According to the 1831 regulations, if a prisoner sentenced to labour refused to work he would be reported to the next Petty Session by the Superintendent, whereas according to the 1835 regulations he would be locked in his cell and immediately reported to a magistrate.[141] Bentham had outlined a similar punishment: if a prisoner refused to work, he would be confined alone to his cell in the expectation that boredom would compel him back to labour.[142] Whilst Bentham outlined a scheme in which the panopticon inspector and the prisoners would share the profits of their labour, the prisoners of Fremantle Gaol typically laboured on account of the local government.[143] However, in one instance prisoners were employed in erecting a jetty on a private account and did receive payment for their work – though not until their release in order to help them readjust to life outside of confinement.[144] The employment and training received by inmates in the panopticon would help them transition into gainful employment at the completion of their sentence. Bentham envisioned that this would occur if a prisoner could secure a responsible person who could provide a £50 bond to ensure their good behaviour, subsequently they could also join the military. If the prisoner was unable or unwilling to meet either of those requirements, they were to enter a 'subsidiary panopticon', a kind of factory for former offenders.[145]

Morality

Reforming inmates was a core aim of both the panopticon and Fremantle Gaol. This was to be achieved at Fremantle through labour, the prohibition of gaming, and religious teaching.[146] Gaming was prohibited by rule 40 (1835), which stated that any 'instruments of gaming', typically 'dice and cards', would be taken by the gaoler and destroyed.[147] Bentham believed that gambling was particularly corrosive, promoting the abandonment of labour and recidivism.[148] Despite his own agnostic beliefs, Bentham was willing to acknowledge the benefit of utilizing religious teachings in penal institutions.[149] This included the provision of divine service and chaplains being made available to the inmates, with having a chapel incorporated within the building, which, he noted, was 'a point to be assumed [rather] than argued'.[150] Bentham's sincerity about the utility of religious instruction is questionable, and it could be argued that he expected the government might be more inclined to adopt the panopticon if it included such provisions – as was the expectation at the time to facilitate prisoner reform. It can be further argued that Bentham did not consider the government to be sincere in their promotion of religious instruction as insufficient provisions had been made for convicts at New South Wales.[151]

However, at Swan River, owing to the limited number of Church of England clergy in the colony, divine service was not regular, but concessions were made for religious education. Whilst not mentioned in 1831, the 1835 regulations stated that anyone who wished should have access to a Bible and a prayer book.[152] The Blue Books for 1837–9 indicate that a magistrate would occasionally provide instruction to the prisoners of the gaol, while from 1840 the Government Resident at Fremantle performed divine service for the prisoners in the neighbouring courthouse.[153] It can be demonstrated, then, that at Fremantle, the stress on hard work and religious instruction constituted a method of 'moral management' in an attempt to modify 'all aspects of inmate behaviour', and thus rehabilitate the prisoners, and help them transition back into society.[154]

Punishments utilized in the Fremantle Gaol

While the operation of Fremantle Gaol demonstrates a strong, general correlation with the panopticon archetype, punishments inflicted upon its prisoners demonstrate significant deviation. Such deviation was all the more evident where the prisoner was Indigenous: Indigenous prisoners tended to be subjected to corporal punishment more frequently than European prisoners. The deviations in this regard from the panopticon archetype can largely be explained by viewing Fremantle Gaol as a modification of Bentham's scheme, and by the perceived need to maintain control over a restless and resentful population, in an attempt to deter future offenders. In order to assess the infliction of punishment at Fremantle Gaol in relation to the panoptic archetype, the following elements will be discussed: the management of punishment; auxiliary punishments; forfeiture of property; transportation; and the death penalty.

The management of punishments was detailed in both the 1831 and the 1835 regulations for Fremantle Gaol, which stated that for a prisoner to be placed in solitary confinement, to be placed in handcuffs or leg irons, or to have their diet reduced, required the written authority of a magistrate.[155] According to the 1831 regulations, the infliction of corporal punishment had to be reported to the next Fremantle Petty Sessions by the superintendent of the gaol,[156] while the 1835 regulations required that if prior approval from a magistrate to inflict a whipping could not be obtained, then the gaoler was to alert a magistrate at the first opportunity afterwards.[157] However, there were concerns raised about the power this granted to the gaoler, with a piece published in the *Swan River Guardian* in 1837 which claimed that 'The jailer inflicts summary punishment, without any order of a magistrate'. Bentham, meanwhile, had expected that the constant surveillance of prisoners in the panopticon would render the use of irons and corporal punishment unnecessary.[158] Moreover, inflicting corporal punishment upon the prisoners would have harmed their wellbeing, reduced their capacity to work and thereby harmed the economy of the prison, and, in cases where an inmate may have died after corporal punishment, made the panopticon inspector liable for a heavy fine.[159]

Auxiliary punishments

Several different auxiliary punishments were utilized within Fremantle Gaol. A reduction in a prisoner's ration was thought by Bentham to be the most effective auxiliary punishment as it would invoke the pain of hunger and, since its infliction required the approval of a magistrate, would eliminate the risk of it being abused by the gaoler.[160] However, there is no surviving record that indicates a reduction in rations was used in Fremantle Gaol, despite it being allowed by the gaol's rules.[161] European prisoners could also be prohibited from labouring out of the gaol for dissent: John Pingelly, for instance, had been employed by a settler, but upon returning to the gaol drunk had this privilege rescinded.[162]

In terms of physical restraint Bentham noted that the use of a gag to subdue inmates might be useful, though he did remark that the prospect alone of being gagged might be enough of a deterrent.[163] At Fremantle, both European and Indigenous prisoners were placed in irons, and an examination of the requests sent by the Government Resident at Fremantle for more irons to be acquired from Van Diemen's Land suggests that ironing occurred with some frequency.[164] Bentham, on the other hand, did not condone the use of irons within the panopticon, as he considered that they would be unnecessary owing to the prisoners being under constant observation.[165] There were occasions at Fremantle when Indigenous prisoners were chained together in multiple pairs by leg irons, although the public use of irons may not have been popular: one report in the *Swan River Guardian* of a Quarter Session hearing in 1837 noted that when an Indigenous prisoner was brought into the court in irons it 'excited the indignation of many of the spectators'.[166] The need to punish exemplarily Indigenous prisoners was generally assumed by colonists, yet the local government had great difficulty in finding suitable punishments, though solitary confinement was found to be a useful method of control.[167] This is because, as one report stated, congregate confinement and whipping did not always have the desired results.[168] Whipping, meanwhile, was not reserved solely as a punishment for Indigenous prisoners, but was inflicted upon soldiers and, in some cases, colonial prisoners: between July 1830 and January 1836, 13 prisoners had been whipped.[169] Indigenous prisoners would usually receive two separate whippings, one at the scene of the crime and another at the gaol.[170] The greater resort to corporal punishments against Indigenous, as opposed to European prisoners, most probably stems from their perceived inferiority by settler society.[171]

Fremantle Gaol prisoners could also be subjected to forced sale of their property, with the funds raised retained by the government, although it is unclear if this was a colonial law or related English laws of forfeiture.[172] Such a measure threatened hardship to prisoners upon their release as they might, for instance, have to repurchase the tools of their trade in order to assimilate back into society. Petitions against forfeiture were drawn up by prisoners who argued that their ability to support their families would be greatly compromised, and that their families would greatly suffer as a result. Such pleas were, however, rarely successful.[173] Bentham would have strongly opposed such a method of forfeiture, as he sought to prepare prisoners for reintegration into society upon their release from the panopticon, as evidenced by investing their prison earnings in a savings account.[174] The policy of forfeiture at Fremantle Gaol was most probably owing to the local government seeking to recoup the cost of imprisonment.[175] It should be noted, however, that surviving evidence indicates that the forced sale of property only occurred in 1835–6, and it remains unclear as to whether this was a sustained mode of punishment.

Transportation was utilized as a criminal punishment within the colony for both colonial and Indigenous prisoners, though the way in which it was carried out differed between them. Bentham was vehemently opposed to transportation, which, he argued, was inferior to the panopticon in every way: he believed that transportation did not prevent crime nor reform the criminal, and pointed to the great and unjustifiable expense that the government would incur through the removal of criminals, having estimated that in a panopticon the upkeep of an inmate would be £13.10s a year, compared to £37 per year per transported convict.[176] In respect to reformation of the offender, Bentham argued that this was simply impossible in New South Wales, owing to the absence of close inspection. He was also concerned that the free settlers of New South Wales would be exposed to corruption, living in a society where industry suffered due to the prevalence of idleness and drunkenness.

Despite Bentham's concerns, transportation was used as a mode of punishment between Swan River and the other Australian penal colonies. European prisoners would be transported to Van Diemen's Land, or on occasion New South Wales, for offences such as theft, receiving stolen goods, escaping from prison, or for military desertion, whereas Indigenous offenders were not sent to Van Diemen's Land, since it was thought 'no Aboriginal inhabitants exist on the island' as reported in the *Swan River Guardian* – an allusion to the supposed wiping out of the Indigenous Tasmanians.[177] Instead, Indigenous men sentenced to transportation did not leave the colony's jurisdiction, but rather were sent to Rottnest Island, known as Wadjemup to the Whadjuk Noongar population.[178] Use of Rottnest Island in this way had been suggested as early as 1830, as settlers began to fear reprisals for encroaching further into Indigenous territory, although it was not adopted for this purpose until 1838.[179] Indigenous offenders were sent to Rottnest for killing livestock, theft, assault and 'tribal murder', though such 'crimes' stemmed from the displacement of Aboriginal people from their traditional land and lives, and their criminalization under British law.[180] While transportation was condemned by Bentham, its utilization at the Swan River Colony highlighted the absence of sufficient infrastructure to deal with criminals locally, as the main penal institution – Fremantle Gaol – after all only had the capacity for 21 prisoners, with Perth Gaol predominantly serving as a lock-up.[181]

The use of Wadjemup as a prison for Aboriginal prisoners was strategic, forming a tactic of frontier warfare which removed men from their community, and drastically reduced the ability of Indigenous peoples to resist the invasion of their territory.[182] In addition, Wadjemup had deep cultural meaning to the Whadjuk people, and was considered to be forbidden, as it held 'bad spirits'.[183] Thus, deterrence was at the forefront of the decision to establish the Rottnest Island prison, as the deep fear that could be elicited by the mere threat of being sent there was difficult to replicate in other ways, and escape was thought to be difficult.[184] The colonizers insisted that confinement to Rottnest would be the mildest form of punishing Indigenous people, as imprisonment in gaol had been 'found to operate most prejudicially to their health'. On the island, the prisoners were to be instructed in white agricultural practices (as well as working in construction and in the salt works), while on Sundays, they would be allowed to practice their traditions.[185] This form of internal transportation exhibits a conformity of sorts to Benthamite principles, in that Indigenous prisoners remained under colonial observation, were housed on an island within sight of the shore and, it was supposed, confinement there would have a deterrent effect upon the rest of the community.[186] Moreover, Wadjemup's regime appeared to adhere to similar aims and intentions, with its stated outcomes being the 'reformation' of Indigenous prisoners, preservation of their health, their education, and the promotion of industry.[187] While this was the apparently progressive intent behind the Wadjemup establishment, in reality, these principles were not implemented.[188]

Only Indigenous people suffered capital punishment during the period under consideration, though such executions were not included in the colony's criminal statistics. For instance, an 1836 report stated that the penalty of death 'had not yet been passed or recorded in the colony' – but this was not true. Although no white person had been sentenced to death for a criminal offence, Indigenous people had been executed by the government since as early as 1833.[189] However, on occasion, Indigenous criminal statistics would be published in the colony's newspapers; for example, in the *Inquirer* in March 1841 a report stated that the death sentence had been inflicted twice and recorded once between 1838 and 1840 (in other words, commuted to transportation for life) on Indigenous men.[190]

The death penalty may not have been a popular solution in the early years of the Swan River Colony, as intimated by *The Western Australian Journal*, which stated in April 1834 in relation to criminal punishments: 'let the punishment be severe – anything short of taking a life'.[191] This sentiment appears to have shifted by 1841 when the same newspaper stated that 'we are no advocate for the shedding of blood, but this we do confidently expect ... the government will continue ... to exact the full penalty for the offence' of the murder of settlers by Indigenous people, despite the outrage of the British public.[192] The use of the death penalty in the Swan River Colony put it in direct opposition to Bentham. Punishment by death, Bentham argued, should be abolished due to its embodying four 'bad properties': first, it was inefficient; second, it was irreversible; third, it did not deter offending; and fourth, caused injustice through 'ill-applied pardons', that is, pardoning introduced uncertainty and the evil of influence into the criminal justice system.[193] The first execution of an Indigenous man in 1833 was not well received in other colonies. For instance, an article first published in the *Hobart Town Review*, and subsequently commented on in the *Perth Gazette,* condemned the hanging as 'a cruel murder' and hoped that it was done only as 'a case of absolute necessity'.[194] Later executions sought to deter by leaving the bodies hanging as a 'salutary memorial to the Aborigines of our determination to carry out a system of retributive justice'.[195] This avowedly retributive punishment deviated from Bentham's view, and can be attributed to the frontier warfare of the 1830s, leading to the British settler administration seeking to protect its interests against a population who sought to defend its homeland.[196]

Conclusion

Whilst the Swan River Colony was established as a non-penal colony, its own penal system was quickly required, with Fremantle Gaol opening in 1831.[197] The gaol, much like the panoptic archetype, fulfilled a plethora of institutional uses, functioning as an asylum, hospital, and a poor house for the destitute. The prominent location of the gaol aligned with Bentham's belief that prisons needed to be visible to a free population to deter crime. Perhaps the most notable parallel between the panoptic model and the Fremantle Gaol is in the architecture of the institutions: while Fremantle Gaol was necessarily constructed on a much smaller scale than Bentham's planned building, it encompassed a circular floor plan with the gaoler's quarters being prominently placed, with the prisoners' cells predominately occupying the opposite wall to ensure unobstructed visibility.[198] In addition, both institutions were intended to pay considerable attention to the health and cleanliness of their inmates, to provisions and the prison diet, as well as the separation of prisoners into classes, their work, and their reformation.

A key difference between the panopticon and the Fremantle Gaol was in the methods of punishing inmates, as in the latter corporal punishment, transportation, and the forfeiture of property were all resorted to. Though such punishments conflicted with Bentham's views on punishment and reformation, that they were used might be attributed to the isolated location of the colony and out of a perceived need to deter the Indigenous peoples of the territory from seeking to protect their homeland from foreign invaders – in other words, maintaining at least a perception of control became paramount to the local government.[199] As a result, Indigenous prisoners were often subjected to harsher forms of punishment when compared to their settler counterparts: they were more likely to endure corporal and capital punishment, and to be sentenced to transportation. Whilst Fremantle Gaol can thus be said to conform with the core principles of Bentham's panopticon, it does deviate in some respects, but this can be attributed to the Fremantle Gaol being a colonial response to the archetype.

Notes

1   This research has been made possible through an Australian Government Research Training Program Scholarship.
2   Hussey 1971, 134; Peel and Twomey 2018, 49.
3   Convict transportation was introduced in Western Australia in 1850 and discontinued in 1868.
4   Fremantle Gaol was later known as Fremantle Round House; however, the former has been used throughout this chapter as it was the contemporaneous name.
5   Bavin-Steding 1996, 55.
6   Bolton 2008, 5; Appleyard and Manford 1979, 21, 18; O'Brien and Statham-Drew 2009, 5.
7   Petchell 2017, 4; Appleyard and Manford 1979, 21; Bolton 2008, 5; Garis 1979, 3.
8   Bolton 2008, 5; Garis 1979, 3.
9   Stirling (1791–1865) served in the Royal Navy and was involved in conflicts with France, Spain and the United States before retiring on half pay before becoming a key figure in the foundation of the Swan River Colony and was governor between 1829–39. Staples 1994, 593; Statham Drew 2002, 117; Garis 1979, 4.
10 Fletcher 1989, 98.
11 Garis 1979, 4.
12 Cameron 1997, 324; Fletcher 1989, 98.
13 Cameron 1997, 2; Bolton 2008, 5.
14 Statham 1996, 41.
15 Statham 1996, 41; Haast 2015, 138.
16 Cameron 1997, 332; Barteaux 2016, 22.
17 Maude 2013, 397; Pitt Morison 1979, 11; Statham 1996, 34; Fletcher 1989, 99; Gare 2016, 9.
18 Appleyard and Manford 1979, 133.
19 Peel and Twomey 2018, 52; Bolton 2008, 9.
20 Peel and Twomey 2018, 52; Gascoigne 2002, 71.
21 Reece 2010, 463; Gare 2016, 17.
22 Vanden Driesen 1986, 14; Hussey 1971, 135.
23 Appleyard and Manford 1979, 199.
24 Vanden Driesen 1986, 14; Haast 2015, 138-9.
25 White 2000, 7; Statham 1996, 41.
26 Strong 2010, 518, 531; Godfrey 2019, 1140-1.

27 Bavin-Steding 1996, 54; Mazzarol 1978, 30; M.M.C. 1832, in Berryman ed. 2002, 243–4; Reece 2010, 463.
28 Maude 2013, 398.
29 Bavin-Steding 1996, 55.
30 Pitt Morrison 1979, 11.
31 Maude 2013, 398.
32 Pitt Morrison and White 1983, 517.
33 Steadman 2007, 9.
34 Nicholson 1994, 635; Martens 2011, 38.
35 Henry Reveley to Peter Broun, 10 May 1831; 29 February 1832, State Records Office of Western Australia (hereafter AU WA) AU WA S2941, CSR/15/73; CSR/20/168.
36 Richard Lewis to Peter Broun, 6 August 1830; 31 December 1830, AU WA S2941, CSR/8/64; CSR/11/128.
37 Richard Lewis to Peter Broun, 6 August 1830, AU WA S2941, CSR/8/64.
38 Barteaux 2016, 27; Pitt Morrison 1979, 11.
39 Bavin-Steding 1996, 58–9; Adams 2012, 88.
40 Stirling, 16 December 1830, in Berryman ed. 2002, 207; Bosworth 2009, 3.
41 Litchfield 1998, 34.
42 'Rationale of Punishment' in Bentham, ed. Bowring 1838–43, i. 424.
43 Bavin 1993, 127; Dinwiddy 1989, 7.
44 Bavin-Steding 1996, 55.
45 Bentham, ed. Božovič 1995, 43.
46 Blue Book 1837, 172.
47 Maude 2013, 400.
48 Bentham, ed. Božovič 1995, 38.
49 Maude 2013, 400.
50 Bavin-Steding 1996, 55.
51 Blue Book 1837, 173.
52 Bavin-Steding 1996, 65; Bentham 1843, 209; Blue Book 1838, 170.
53 'Postscript I' in Bentham, ed. Bowring 1838–43, iv. 73.
54 'Postscript I' in Bentham, ed. Bowring 1838–43, iv. 73–4.
55 White 2000, 14.
56 Broun, 'Regulations of 1831', AU WA S2755, CSF/4/37, 125–6.
57 Richard Broun to Peter Broun, 10 October 1837, AU WA S2941, CSR/54/84.
58 'Rationale of Punishment' in Bentham, ed. Bowring 1838–43, i. 422–3.
59 Henry Reveley to Peter Broun, 24 October 1836, AU+ WA S2941, CSR/48/197.
60 'Rationale of Punishment' in Bentham, ed. Bowring 1838–43, i. 422; Bentham, ed. Harrison 1960, 159–60.
61 *Perth Gazette and Western Australian Journal*, 7 November 1845, 594.
62 *Perth Gazette and Western Australian Journal*, 25 May 1833, 62; *Perth Gazette and Western Australian Journal*, 2 November 1833, 173; *Perth Gazette and Western Australian Journal*, 1 July 1837, 928; *Inquirer*, 20 October 1841, 2.
63 Barteaux 2016, 29; Richard Lewis to Peter Broun, 6 August 1830; 31 December 1830, AU WA S2941, CSR/8/64; CSR/11/128.
64 Peter Broun to Henry Reveley, 8 June 1831; 26 June 1834; 9 April 1838, AU WA S2755, CSF/4/107; CSF/6/359–60; CSF/8/332–3; Henry Reveley to Peter Broun, 29 February 1832, AU WA S2941, CSR/20/168. White 1979, 81–2.
65 Maude 2013, 399.
66 Bentham, ed. Božovič 1995, 76, 80–2, 86.
67 Bentham, ed. Božovič 1995, 81–2.
68 Peter Broun to Charles Simmonds, 9 September 1831, AU WA S2755, CSF/5/20; Daniel Scott to the Harbour Master's Office, Fremantle, 2 February 1831, AU WA S2941, CSR/12/140.
69 Whilst Peter Broun later adopted the anglicized name 'Brown', the original spelling is utilized throughout the chapter.
70 Henry Reveley to Peter Broun, 10 May 1831, AU WA S2941, CSR/15/73.
71 Bentham, ed. Božovič 1995, 82.
72 Peter Broun to Richard Lewis, 5 September 1831, AU WA S2755, CSF/5/19.
73 Peter Broun to Doctor Langley, 3 October 1832, AU WA S2755, CSF/5/181.

74   Peter Broun to Richard Broun, 9 December 1835, AU WA S2755, CSF/7/339–40.
75   Blue Book 1837, 174; Blue Book 1838, 174; Blue Book 1839, 174; Blue Book 1840, 201; Blue Book 1841, 194.
76   Bentham, ed. Božovič 1995, 82, 85.
77   Bentham, ed. Božovič 1995, 83.
78   Henry Vincent, 'Annual Return of the State of His Majesty's Jail at Fremantle Western Australia During the Year 1835', AU WA S2941, CSR/44/6.
79   Peter Broun to Richard Broun, 9 December 1835, AU WA S2755, CSF/7/339–40.
80   'Annual Return of the State of Her Majesty's Jail at Fremantle Western Australia for the Year 1837', AU WA S2941, CSR/58/36.
81   Peter Broun to Richard Broun, 8 October 1837, AU WA S2755, CSF/8/226–7.
82   Blue Book 1839, 171.
83   Thomas Hunt, 'Quarterly Return of Prisoners', January 1840, AU WA S2941, CSR/83/6.
84   Richard M.B. Brown to Peter Broun, 3 January 1840; 12 September 1840, AU WA S2941, CSR/85/1–2; CSR/85/43.
85   Bentham, ed. Božovič 1995, 85.
86   Bentham, ed. Quinn 2010, 104.
87   Peter Broun to Richard Broun, 9 December 1835, AU WA S2755, CSF/7/339–40.
88   Peter Broun to Richard Broun, 2 March 1836, AU WA S2755, CSF/7/387–8.
89   *Swan River Guardian*, 20 October 1836, 10; Hetherington 2009, 6, 9–11; Crowther 1983, 27–8; Bentham, ed Quinn 2010, 104.
90   Appleyard and Manford 1979, 199; Blue Book 1837, 173.
91   Peter Broun to Henry Reveley, 20 June 1834; 10 June 1834, AU WA S2755, CSF/6/351–2; CSF/6/345–6; Hetherington 2009, 7, 9.
92   Broun, 1835, 454; 'Rationale of Punishment' in Bentham, ed. Bowring 1838–43, i. 422.
93   Peter Broun, 'Rules and Regulations for the Management of the Common Jail at Fremantle Established by the Magistrates in General Quarter Sessions Assembled at Fremantle Aforesaid on the 4th Day of April', AU WA S2755, CSF/4/37, 39; Peter Broun, 'Regulations for the Management of the Common Jail at Fremantle in the Colony of Western Australia Recommended by His Majesty's Justices of the Peace for the Said Colony and Approved by His Excellency the Governor', 26 February 1835, AU WA S2755, CSF/41/42–3.
94   'Postscript II' in Bentham, ed. Bowring 1838–43, iv. 153–6.
95   Broun, 'Regulations of 1835', AU WA S2755, CSF/41/43–4, rules 17 and 25.
96   'Postscript II' in Bentham, ed. Bowring 1838–43, iv. 158.
97   Broun, 'Regulations of 1831', AU WA S2755, CSF/4/37, 39; Broun, 'Regulations of 1835', AU WA S2755, CSF/41/45; 'Postscript II' in Bentham, ed. Bowring 1838–43, iv. 162–3.
98   Broun, 'Regulations of 1831', AU WA S2755, CSF/4/37, 39; William H. Mackie, 'A Report on the State of the Prisons in Western Australia as called for by His Majesty's Secretary of State for the Colonies in a Circular Dated 18 September 1835', 25 September 1836, AU WA S2941, CSR/48/125.
99   'Postscript II' in Bentham, ed. Bowring 1838–43, iv. 157–8; Broun, 'Regulations of 1831', AU WA S2755, CSF/4/37, 39; Broun, 'Regulations of 1835', AU WA S2755, CSF/41/45.
100 Broun, 'Regulations of 1835', AU WA S2755, CSF/41/45; Broun to Henry Reveley, 13 April 1832, AU WA S2755, CSF/5/108; Reveley to Broun, 24 October 1836, AU WA S2941, CSR/48/197; J. Birch to Broun, 1 August 1837, 1 August 1837, AU WA S2941, CSR/52/136.
101 Broun, 'Regulations of 1835', AU WA S2755, CSF/41/46, rule 36; Bentham, ed. Bowring 1838–43, iv. 156.
102 'Postscript II' in Bentham, ed. Bowring 1838–43, iv. 158–60; Mackie, 'Report on the State of the Prisons in Western Australia', 25 September 1836, AU WA S2941, CSR/48/128.
103 Blue Book 1837, 174; Blue Book 1838, 174; Blue Book 1839, 174; Mackie, 'Report on the State of the Prisons in Western Australia', 25 September 1836, AU WA S2941, CSR/48/126; Blue Book 1840, 200; Blue Book 1841, 193.
104 Broun, 'Regulations of 1831', AU WA S2755, CSF/4/36; Broun, 'Regulations of 1835', AU WA S2755, CSF/41/42–3.
105 Blue Book 1837, 174; Blue Book 1838, 174; Blue Book 1839, 174; Mackie, 'Report on the State of the Prisons in Western Australia', 25 September 1836, AU WA S2941, CSR/48/126; Blue Book 1840, 200; Blue Book 1841, 193.
106 Broun, 'Regulations of 1835', AU WA S2755, CSF/41/43, rules 11 and 12.

107 Broun, 'Regulations of 1831', AU WA S2755, CSF/4/39; Broun, 'Regulations of 1835', AU WA S2755, CSF/41/43.

108 Broun, 'Regulations of 1831', AU WA S2755, CSF/4/38; Broun, 'Regulations of 1835', AU WA S2755, CSF/41/45–6; Bentham, ed. Bowring 1838–43, iv. 156.

109 Broun, 'Regulations of 1831', AU WA S2755, CSF/4/39; Broun, 'Regulations of 1835', AU WA S2755, CSF/41/45.

110 Broun, 'Regulations of 1831', AU WA S2755, CSF/4/39.

111 Broun, 'Regulations of 1835', AU WA S2755, CSF/41/44–5.

112 'Postscript II' and 'Rationale of Punishment' in Bentham, ed. Bowring 1838–43, iv. 157–8, i. 422, respectively.

113 Mackie, 'Report on the State of the Prisons in Western Australia', 25 September 1836, AU WA S2941, CSR/48/125–6.

114 Broun, 'Regulations of 1831', AU WA S2755, CSF/4/39; Broun, 'Regulations of 1835', AU WA S2755, CSF/41/45.

115 Broun, 'Regulations of 1831', AU WA S2755, CSF/4/39; Broun, 'Regulations of 1835', AU WA S2755, CSF/41/45; Bentham, ed. Bowring 1838–43, 131–2.

116 'Letter to Lord Pelham' in Bentham, ed. Causer and Schofield 2019, 77, 101.

117 See Owen *et al.* 2015.

118 'Postscript II' in Bentham, ed. Bowring 1838–43, iv. 153–4; Reece 2010, 462–3; Hetherington 2009, 5–6, 8–9; 'Postscript I' in Bentham, ed. Bowring 1838–43, iv. 76–7.

119 'Postscript I' in Bentham, ed. Bowring 1838–43, iv. 85–6.

120 Broun, 'Regulations of 1831', AU WA S2755, CSF/4/38, rule 13; Broun, 'Regulations of 1835', AU WA S2755, CSF/41/45–6, rule 33.

121 Broun, 'Regulations of 1831', AU WA S2755, CSF/4/38.

122 Broun, 'Regulations of 1835', AU WA S2755, CSF/41/45–6.

123 'Panopticon; or, The Inspection House' in Bentham, ed. Bowring 1838–43, iv. 45–6.

124 Reece 2010, 462–3; Hetherington 2009, 5–6, 8–9.

125 Broun, 'Regulations of 1831', AU WA S2755, CSF/4/38; Broun, 'Regulations of 1835', AU WA S2755, CSF/41/44.

126 'Postscript II' in Bentham, ed. Bowring 1838–43, iv. 137–8.

127 'Postscript II' in Bentham, ed. Bowring 1838–43, iv. 134.

128 Broun, 'Regulations of 1831', AU WA S2755, CSF/4/38; Broun, 'Regulations of 1835', AU WA S2755, CSF/41/44, rule 20.

129 'Postscript I' in Bentham, ed. Bowring 1838–43, iv. 71–2.

130 Broun, 'Regulations of 1831', AU WA S2755, CSF/4/37, rule 5; Broun, 'Regulations of 1835', AU WA S2755, CSF/41/44, rules 20 and 21.

131 Broun, 'Regulations of 1831', AU WA S2755, CSF/4/38; Broun, 'Regulations of 1835', AU WA S2755, CSF/41/44; 'Postscript II' in Bentham, ed. Bowring 1838–43, iv. 122.

132 *Perth Gazette and Western Australian Journal*, 16 April 1836, 686.

133 Green 1983, 93.

134 Bentham, ed. Božovič 1995, 63–4.

135 Mackie, 'Report on the State of the Prisons in Western Australia', 25 September 1836, AU WA S2941, CSR/48/127.

136 Broun, 'Regulations of 1831', AU WA S2755, CSF/4/38; Broun, 'Regulations of 1835', AU WA S2755, CSF/41/46; Bentham, ed. Božovič 1995, 78.

137 Broun, 'Regulations of 1831', AU WA S2755, CSF/4/38.

138 Broun, 'Regulations of 1835', AU WA S2755, CSF/41/46.

139 'Postscript II' in Bentham, ed. Bowring 1838–43, iv. 141–2.

140 'Postscript II' in Bentham, ed. Bowring 1838–43, iv. 141–2.

141 Broun, 'Regulations of 1831', AU WA S2755, CSF/4/38, rule 8; Broun, 'Regulations of 1835', AU WA S2755, CSF/41/46, rule 39.

142 Bentham, ed. Božovič 1995, 66.

143 'Postscript II' in Bentham, ed. Bowring 1838–43, iv. 144, 152–4; Mackie, 'Report on the State of the Prisons in Western Australia', 25 September 1836, AU WA S2941, CSR/48/125.

144 Mackie, 'Report on the State of the Prisons in Western Australia', 25 September 1836, AU WA S2941, CSR/48/125.

145 Bentham, ed. Božovič 1995, 55–6, 68–9; Bentham, ed. Bowring 1838–43, iv. 165–9.

146 Broun, 'Regulations of 1831', AU WA S2755, CSF/4/38–9; Broun, 'Regulations of 1835', AU WA S2755, CSF/41/46.
147 Broun, 'Regulations of 1835', AU WA S2755, CSF/41/46.
148 'Postscript II' in Bentham, ed. Bowring 1838–43, iv. 130–2; 'Letter to Lord Pelham' in Bentham, ed. Causer and Schofield 2019, 77, 85.
149 For more on the intersection of Bentham's views on religion, penal reform, and New South Wales, see Carey's chapter in this volume.
150 'Postscript I' and 'Postscript II' in Bentham, ed. Bowring 1838–43, iv. 78–9, 121–2 respectively.
151 'Letter to Lord Pelham' in Bentham, ed. Causer and Schofield 2022, 78–80.
152 Broun, 'Regulations of 1835', AU WA S2755, CSF/41/46, rule 41.
153 Blue Book 1837, 174; Blue Book 1838, 174; Blue Book 1839, 174; Blue Book 1840, 201; Blue Book 1841, 194.
154 Bavin-Steding 1996, 58–9.
155 Broun, 'Regulations of 1831', AU WA S2755, CSF/4/37, rule 1; Broun, 'Regulations of 1835', AU WA S2755, CSF/41/43, rules 14 and 16.
156 Broun, 'Regulations of 1831', AU WA S2755, CSF/4/37.
157 Broun, 'Regulations of 1835', AU WA S2755, CSF/41/43.
158 Bentham, ed. Božovič 1995, 81–2.
159 *Swan River Guardian*, 23 November 1837, 253; Bentham, ed. Bowring 1838–43, iv. 121–2, 127–8.
160 Bentham, ed. Božovič 1995, 137.
161 Broun, 'Regulations of 1835', AU WA S2755, CSF/41/43.
162 Henry Vincent to Peter Broun, 14 June 1832, AU WA S2941, CSR/22/141; Broun to the Jailer at Fremantle, 21 June 1832, AU WA S2755, CSF/5/130.
163 'Postscript II' in Bentham, ed. Bowring 1838–43, iv. 164; Bentham, ed. Božovič 1995, 49.
164 Richard M.B. Brown to Peter Broun, 21 October 1839, AU WA S2941, CSR/73/162–4.
165 Bentham, ed. Božovič 1995, 49.
166 *Swan River Guardian*, 5 January 1837, 56.
167 *Perth Gazette and Western Australian Journal*, 11 March 1837, 864; 26 April 1834, 274.
168 *Perth Gazette and Western Australian Journal*, 11 March 1837, 864.
169 *Perth Gazette and Western Australian Journal*, 11 April 1835, 475; W.H. Mackie to Peter Broun, 10 October 1832, AU WA S2941, CSR/24/142–4; *Perth Gazette and Western Australian Journal*, 18 June 1836, 712.
170 Green 1983, 83; *Perth Gazette and Western Australian Journal*, 6 September 1834, 351.
171 R.M. Lyon, 'A Glance at the Manners, and Language of the Aboriginal Inhabitants of Western Australia', *Perth Gazette and Western Australian Journal*, 30 March 1833, 51; *Perth Gazette and Western Australian Journal*, 11 March 1837, 864.
172 George Stone to Peter Broun, 11 January 1836, AU WA S2941, CSR/44/47.
173 John Thomas to Peter Broun, March 1835, AU WA S2941, CSR/38/151–2.
174 Bentham, ed. Božovič 1995, 68–9; 'Postscript II' in Bentham, ed. Bowring 1838–43, iv. 169.
175 *Perth Gazette and Western Australian Journal*, 16 April 1835; Amy Keates to James Stirling, 28 July 1835, AU WA S2941, CSR/37/234–5; 'Government Notice' in *Perth Gazette and Western Australian Journal*, 16 January 1836, 633.
176 'Rationale of Punishment' in Bentham 1843, i. 491–2, 501.
177 Peter Broun to Edward Deas Thomson, 20 January 1836, AU WA S2755, CSF/7/361; Thomson to Broun, 23 December 1841, AU WA S2941, CSR/96/98; *Swan River Guardian*, 5 October 1837, 229.
178 Kwaymullina 2001, 109; Roscoe 2018, 61; Roscoe 2016, 43.
179 Roscoe 2018, 61; Whitely 2015, 126.
180 Mackie 1841, 61; 'Quarter Sessions' 1840, 3; 'Quarter Sessions' 1834, 365; Vincent 1834, 168; Kwaymullina, 2001, 113.
181 'Rationale of Punishment' in Bentham, ed. Bowring 1838–43, i. 491; Blue Book 1838, 170.
182 Roscoe 2018, 48, 62–3.
183 Kwaymullina 2001, 109; Roscoe 2018, 61.
184 Roscoe 2018, 61–2; Kwaymullina 2001, 110.
185 Roscoe 2018, 61; Roscoe 2016, 44.
186 Bentham 1843, 491; Kwaymullina 2001, 113.

187 Bentham, ed. Božovič 1995, 31; *Perth Gazette and Western Australian Journal*, 25 July 1840, 4; Roscoe 2018, 61. This alleged 'civilising' process is also discussed in Roscoe and Godfrey's chapter in this volume.

188 Roscoe 2018, 61; Roscoe 2016, 44; Kwaymullina 2001, 109–10.

189 'Report of the Committee of Correspondence, appointed at a General Meeting of the Inhabitants of the Colony of Western Australia, on the present State of the Settlement up to 1835' in *Perth Gazette and Western Australian Journal*, 18 June 1836, 712; 'Execution' in ibid., 25 May 1833, 83.

190 'VIII State of Crime', in *Inquirer*, 31 March 1841, 5.

191 'The Western Australian Journal' in *Perth Gazette and Western Australian Journal*, 26 April 1834, 274.

192 'The Western Australian Journal' in *Perth Gazette and Western Australian Journal*, 16 October 1841, 2.

193 Bentham 1838, 526.

194 'Execution' in *Perth Gazette and Western Australian Journal*, 25 May 1833, 83; 'The Western Australian Journal' in ibid., 11 January 1834, 214.

195 *Inquirer*, 20 October 1841, 2.

196 Roscoe 2018, 48; Gare 2016, 16, 18.

197 Bavin-Steding 1996, 55.

198 Bavin-Steding 1996, 55, 65; 'Postscript II' in Bentham, ed. Bowring 1838– 43, iv. 118; Blue Book 1838, 170.

199 Roscoe 2018, 48; Gare 2016, 16, 18.

Bibliography

Primary Sources

Archival sources: State Records Office of Western Australia, Perth

AU WA S2755, Colonial Secretary's Correspondence Outward, 1829–1900.
AU WA S2941, Colonial Secretary's Correspondence Received, 1828–78.
AU WA S4148-cons 1855 01 Blue Book (Statistical Returns for the Swan River Colony), 1837.
AU WA S4148-cons 1855 02 Blue Book (Statistical Returns for the Swan River Colony), 1838.
AU WA S4148-cons 1855 03 Blue Book (Statistical Returns for the Swan River Colony), 1839.
AU WA S4148-cons 1855 04 Blue Book (Statistical Returns for the Swan River Colony), 1840.
AU WA S4148-cons 1855 05 Blue Book (Statistical Returns for the Swan River Colony), 1841.

Newspapers
Inquirer.
Perth Gazette and Western Australian Journal.
Swan River Guardian.

Printed sources

Bentham, J. *The Works of Jeremy Bentham, published under the superintendence of … John Bowring*, 11 vols. Edinburgh: William Tait, 1838–43.

Bentham, J. *Principles of Penal Law*. London: Simpkin, Marshall & Co., 1843.

Bentham, J. 'An Introduction to Principles of Morals and Legislation'. In *A Fragment on Government and An Introduction to the Principles of Morals and Legislation*, ed. W. Harrison, 113–435. Oxford: Basil Blackwell, 1960.

Bentham, J. *The Panopticon Writings*, ed. Miran Božovič. London: Verso, 1995.

Bentham, J. *Writings on the Poor Laws: Volume II (CW)*, ed. M. Quinn. Oxford: Clarendon Press, 2010.

Bentham, J. *Panopticon versus New South Wales and other writings on Australia*. London: UCL Press, 2022.

Berryman, I., ed. *Swan River Letters, Vol. 1*. Glengarry: Swan River Press, 2002.

Secondary Sources

Adams, S. 'Capital Punishment and the Spectacle of Death in Colonial Fremantle'. In *Voice from the West End: Stories, People and Events that Shaped Fremantle*, ed. P.L. Arthur and G. Bolton, 87–8. Welshpool: Western Australia Museum, 2012.

Appleyard, R.T. and Manford, T. *The Beginning: European Discovery and Early Settlement of Swan River, Western Australia*. Nedlands: University of Western Australia Press, 1979.

Barteaux, J. 'Urban Planning as Colonial Marketing Strategy for the Swan River Settlement, Western Australia', *Australasian Society for Historical Archaeology* 34 (2016): 22–32.

Bavin, L.J. 'Punishment, Prisons and Reform: Incarceration in Western Australia in the Nineteenth Century', *Studies in Western Australian History* 14: 1 (1993): 121–48.

Bavin-Steding, L.J. *Crime and Confinement: The Origins of Prisons in Western Australia*. Perth: Stone's Publishing, 1996.

Bolton, G. *Land of Vision and Mirage: Western Australia since 1826*. Crawley: University of Western Australia Press, 2008.

Bosworth, M. *Convict Fremantle: A Place of Promise and Punishment*. Crawley: University of Western Australia Press, 2009.

Cameron, J. 'Thomas Moody, James Stirling and Swan River', *Early Days* 3: 11 (1997): 320–37.

Dinwiddy, J.R. *Bentham*. Oxford: Oxford University Press, 1989.

Fletcher, B. *Colonial Australia before 1850*. Melbourne: Thomas Nelson Australia, 1989.

Gare, D. 'In the Beginning: Empire, Faith and Conflict in Fremantle', *Studies in Western Australian History* 31 (2016): 7–24.

Garis, B.K. de. 'Settling on the Sand: The Colonisation of Western Australia'. In *European Impact on the West Australian Environment 1829–1979 – Octagon Lecture*, 1–16. Nedlands: University of Western Australia Press, 1979.

Gascoigne, J. *The Enlightenment and the Origins of European Australia*. New York: Cambridge University Press, 2002.

Godfrey, B. 'Prison versus Western Australia: Which Worked Best, the Australian Penal Colony or the English Convict Prison System?', *British Journal of Criminology* 59 (2019): 1139–60.

Green, N. 'Aboriginal and White Settlers in the Nineteenth Century'. In *The Foucault Effect: Studies in Governmentality with Two Lectures by and an Interview with Michel Foucault*, ed. G. Burchell, C. Gordon, and P. Miller, 72–124. Nedlands: University of Western Australia Press, 1983.

Haast, A. 'Convicts and Commodities: An Archaeological Approach to the Economic Value of the Western Australian Penal System', *Archaeology in Oceania* 50: 3 (2015): 138–44.

Hetherington, P. *Paupers, Poor Relief and Poor Houses in Western Australia 1829–1910*. Crawley: UWA Publishing, 2009.

Hitchcock, J.K. *The History of Fremantle: The Front Gate of Australia 1829–1929*. Fremantle: The S.H. Lamb Printing House, 1929.

Hussey, W.D. *British History 1815–1939*. London: Syndics of the Cambridge University Press, 1971.

Litchfield, J. 'The Round House and Its Questions about Community in Fremantle'. In *Imagined Places: The Politics of Making Space*, ed. C. Houston, F. Kurasawa, and A. Watson, 31–8. Bundoora: School of Sociology, Politics and Anthropology, La Trobe University, 1998.

Martens, J. *Government House and Western Australian Society 1829–2010*. Crawley: UWA Publishing, 2011.

Maude, P. 'Treatment of Western Australia's Mentally Ill during the Early Colonial Period, 1826–1865', *Australasian Psychiatry* 21: 4 (2013): 397–401.

Mazzarol, T.W. 'Tradition, Environment and the Indentured Labourer in Early Western Australia', *Studies in Western Australian History* 3 (1978): 30–7.

Nicholson, R.D. 'Seats of Justice – Courthouses as Places of History', *Early Days* 10: 6 (1994): 629–46.

O'Brien, J., and Statham-Drew, P. *On We Go, the Wittenoom Way: The Legacy of a Colonial Chaplain*. Fremantle: Fremantle Press, 2009.

Owen, A., Lupu, D., Timmins, J., O'Neill, J., Gambus, K., and Ogundipe, T. *Jeremy Bentham's Prison Cooking: A Collection of Utilitarian Prison Recipes*. London: UCL Centre for Publishing and the Bentham Project, 2015.

Peel, M. and Twomey, C. *A History of Australia*. London: Palgrave, 2018.

Petchell, B. *The Swan River Colony: Did the British Government Want It to Survive?* Rivervale: Stone's Publishing, 2017.

Pitt Morison, M. 'Settlement and Development: The Historical Context'. In *Western Towns and Building*, ed. M.P. Morison and J. White, 1–74. Nedlands: University of Western Australia Press, 1979.

Pitt Morison, M. and White, J. 'Builders and Buildings'. In *A New History of Western Australia*, ed. C.T. Stannage, 511–51. Nedlands: University of Western Australia Press, 1983.

Reece, B. 'Eating and Drinking at Early Swan River Colony', *Royal Western Australian Historical Society* 13: 4 (2010): 462–77.

Staples, A.C. 'Spanish Colonial Influence on Sir James Stirling', *Early Days* 10: 6 (1994): 592–604.

Statham, P. 'Contrasting Colonies, or a Tale of Three Colonies'. In *Beyond Convict Colonies*, ed. B. Dyster, 34–54. Sydney: Department of Economic History, University of New South Wales, 1996.

Statham-Drew, P. *James Stirling: Admiral and Founding Governor of Western Australia.* Crawley: University of Western Australia Press, 2003.

Steadman, P. 'The Contradictions of Jeremy Bentham's Panopticon Penitentiary', *Journal of Bentham Studies* 9 (2007): 1–31.

Strong, R. 'Church and State in Western Australia: Implementing New Imperial Paradigms in the Swan River Colony, 1827–1857', *Journal of Ecclesiastical History* 61: 3 (2010): 517–40.

Thomas, J.E. and Stewart, A. *Imprisonment in Western Australia: Evolution, Theory and Practice.* Nedlands: University of Western Australia Press, 1978.

Vanden Driesen, I.H. *Essays on Immigration Population in Western Australia 1850–1901.* Nedlands: University of Western Australia Press, 1986.

White, J. 'Building in Western Australia 1829–1850'. In *Western Towns and Building*, ed. M. Pitt Morison and J. White, 74–90. Nedlands: University of Western Australia Press, 1979.

White, M. 'Agricultural Societies in Colonial Western Australia 1831–1870', *History of Education* 29: 1 (2000): 3–28.

Whitely, T.G. 'Permeability and Persistence of Physical and Social Boundaries in the Context of Incarceration in Nineteenth Century Western Australia', *Archaeology in Oceania* 50: 1 (2015): 123–9.

Winter, S. 'Coerced Labour in Western Australia during the Nineteenth Century', *Australasian Historical Archaeology* 34 (2016): 3–12.

12

Religion and penal reform in the Australian writings of Jeremy Bentham

Hilary M. Carey

This chapter examines Bentham's views on religion as a means of penal reformation and their relation to the panopticon penitentiary, as well as the anti-transportation campaigns in which he was an early and leading advocate. It argues that Bentham found it convenient to ally with penal reformers, including Quakers and other Rational Dissenters and practical Christian humanitarians such as William Wilberforce. Australia was useful to him as an intellectual and physical laboratory in which he could test his theories of the efficacy of utilitarian as opposed to religiously inspired penal systems.

The problem of religion

Prior to the constitutional revolution of 1828–31, the United Kingdom of Great Britain and Ireland was not a secular state, and its institutions reflected the overt and extensive discretionary power of the two estab-lished churches. While subject to considerable recent revisionism, there is some truth in Leslie Stephen's claim that, in the eighteenth century, the Church of England was 'simply a part of the ruling class told off to perform divine services: to maintain order and respectability and the traditional morality'.[1] By the 1820s in England, the established Church was losing members to the rising bands of Methodists and other forms of evangelical dissent as church goers voted with their feet to abandon an institution which did not serve their needs, and was tarnished by its association with the old regime.[2] To study or practice law, to serve as a judge or a magistrate, to be engaged as a chaplain in a prison, workhouse, penal colony, entailed a legal obligation, under the terms of the Test Acts (1672), to comply to the confessional demands of the Church of England.[3] Originally applied to holders of civil office, the Test Acts were progressively extended to all beneficed clergy, students and academics, lawyers, schoolteachers, and preachers. While the Test Acts were repealed in 1828, the universities were the last bastion of resistance, and it was not until 1871 that the passing of the Universities Test Act made it legal for non-Anglicans to take up academic appointments at Oxford, Cambridge and Durham.

Jeremy Bentham was the leader of those secular utilitarians who wished to reform penal institutions and do away with the malign influence of religion on criminal law and punishment. There would appear to be a fundamental division between his views and those of Christian advocates for terror and retribution, or humanitarian comforts, for the guilty. But this is not entirely the case. The Bentham Project has uncovered a number of ways in which Bentham collaborated with religious reformers of the prison. What divided Christian and utilitarian penal reformers was Bentham's belief that transportation was a fatally defective system when compared with the utilitarian advantages of his prison machine, the panopticon. In contrast, Christians argued that moral reformation was a possible and necessary aspiration for any proposed alternative to capital or secondary punishment, including transportation. This does not imply that Bentham was without influence on penal reformers from across the denominational spectrum.

Despite the many objections that could be made to the mischiefs of an established church, Bentham's systematic writing on religion was focused on two questions: first, was it useful? and second, was it true? In relation to penal reform where he seems to have assumed institutional religion had a part to play, his questions were equally pragmatic. If chaplains are necessary to prisons, how many are sufficient and, secondarily, can religious instruction work to discourage prisoners from reoffending? The next section will consider how Bentham's solutions to these problems are reflected a) in his mostly unpublished writing on religion; and b) in his more public Australian writings on penal reform.

Bentham and religion

Bentham's religious doubts began early. Some of his earliest published *pensées* (written 1773–4) stress the value of reason over religion: 'There is no pestilence in a state like a zeal for religion, independent of (as contradistinguished from) morality.'[4] He was equally disgusted with the cupidity of the established Church, even if admitting the English variety was less virulent that elsewhere: 'In England the clergy are scorpions which sting us. On the continent they are dragons which devour us'.[5] His scorn for the Church, especially what he called 'priestcraft' softened little over time. In 'Auto-Icon; or, Farther Uses of the Dead to the Living', left unpublished but completed by about May 1832, he gleefully proposed alternatives to the tedious religious decorum associated with the disposal of the dead, including his own body: 'Has religion anything to do with the matter? Nothing at all. Free as air does religion leave the disposal of the dead'.[6] It was 'priestcraft' that demanded control of the dead, for what Bentham considered the basest of financial motives: 'From its birth to its death, the priest keeps his fixed predatory eye on the prey he covets, and this prey is everything human that either breathes or has breathed'.[7] Bentham consistently favoured a moral secularism even as he drifted further away from acceptance of any of the formal tenets of confessional Anglicanism. Indeed, James Crimmins suggests his aim was nothing less than that of 'extirpating religious beliefs, even the idea of religion itself, from the minds of men'.[8]

In its initial formulation, Bentham's panopticon was partly a response to the Penitentiary Act of 1779, drafted by the Rational Dissenter John Howard (1726–90), whose ideas Bentham freely adapted.[9] The final, painful rejection of the panopticon after 1813 helped to confirm Bentham's distaste for governing elites in both church and state. In the wake of the panopticon scheme, Bentham published a series of studies attacking both 'natural' and institutional religion.[10] By 'natural' religion Bentham was using the language of William Paley's *Natural Theology* (1802), which offered an attempt to provide logical demonstrations of the existence of a beneficent deity.[11] At much the same time, between 1811 and 1821, Bentham prepared a series of unpublished studies of the utility and veracity of religion known collectively as the 'Juggernaut', 'Jug.', or 'Jug. util.' manuscripts, his disparaging shorthand for institutional religion.[12] Bentham's work on religion can therefore be divided into three classes: (i) published works on religious themes; (ii) more adventurous pieces which were either left unpublished or published pseudonymously; and (iii) pieces written in connection with the panopticon project. The programme was not so much comprehensive, as riddled with nodes of obsession, including the mendacity involved in compulsory oaths of allegiance, objections to the claims of the established church over persons of other religions or none, and the evident (to him) failure of internal or external religious precepts to reform prisoners, prevent crime or make people happy. What has not been recognized is the extent to which all three bodies of religious writing were evoked by Bentham's opposition to convict transportation and the penal colony of New South Wales.

Published works

In *Swear Not At All* (1817) Bentham lambasted the caprice that required him to sign the Thirty-nine Articles as a condition for receiving his degree after studying at Queen's College, Oxford. At both Oxford and Cambridge, he suggested, oath taking in the absence of belief promoted the corruption of national morals.[13] His most thorough debunking of religious establishment is his *Church-of-Englandism and its Catechism Examined* (1818), which demolished the intellectual foundations of the Anglican code with particular attention to its claims in regard to education. Bentham opposed the principles of the 'National Schools for the Education of the Poor' that required children to learn the Anglican catechism, defining this as an attempt to indoctrinate children with the pabulum of the state church.[14] He argued that the National Schools Society (founded 1811) represented a fraudulent imposition by the state, which he calls 'purposely deceptious [sic]'.[15] In its place he promoted the claims of the rival, Dissenting, British and Foreign School Society (formed 1808), which was based on the principles of the Quaker Joseph Lancaster (1778–1838).[16]

A few years after *Church-of-Englandism*, certain of Bentham's 'Juggernaut' manuscripts were edited for publication by the radical historian and crypto-atheist George Grote (1794–1871), and published under the pseudonym of Philip Beauchamp as *Analysis of the Influence of Natural Religion on the Temporal Happiness of Mankind* (1822). 'Beauchamp' sought to debunk theological reasoning and demonstrate the failure of religion, through the mechanism of internalized guilt and penance, to keep society safe.[17] Where Paley argued that religion provided the foundation for morality, civic duty and respect for the law, 'Beauchamp' vigorously disagreed. Natural religion, he argued, among other mischiefs inflicted 'unprofitable suffering', 'useless privations' and 'undefined terrors' that were a burden not only to the individual but to the whole of society.[18] Whether 'Beauchamp' reflects Bentham's considered view or that of his editor is not clear. *An Analysis of the Influence of Natural Religion* certainly accords with Grote's strident, but privately held, objections to the existence of God: 'there cannot be a benevolent God who suffers evil and pain to exist'.[19] It is less clear, though, that Bentham followed Grote all the way to militant rejection of Christian precepts, even as he lambasted the pretensions of the 'Juggernaut' in the manuscripts written between 1811 and 1821.[20] Bentham's target was consistently the utility and logical veracity of religion; indeed, these appear to be the only religious questions that sparked his attention.[21] As Fuller notes, Bentham showed no interest in questions of transcendence or the metaphysics of the sacred and it is pointless to seek his views on these points.[22] Regardless of whether or not God existed, Bentham was firmly convinced that institutional religion should be displaced from its functional role within law and society. This was because religion was neither useful nor true and, in some instances, including the Sermon on the Mount, caused outright mischief.[23]

Unpublished works

While unafraid of controversy, Bentham chose either to leave his most radical critique of religion unpublished, or to be published pseudonymously. Among this unpublished material, there are about 1,000 manuscript pages which were intended to form Parts II and III of 'Not Paul, but Jesus', the first part of which was published in 1823 under the pseudonym Gamaliel Smith. These unpublished sections, as Philip Schofield notes, formed part of Bentham's attack on the asceticism of St Paul, which promoted pain as a necessary part of Christian virtue, including abstinence from all sexual activity except that within the confines of marriage.[24] In 'Not Paul, but Jesus', Bentham argued that engaging in homosexual activity was a personal choice, that Jesus himself had enjoyed homosexual relationships, and that the state should play no role in governing a personal preference and one, moreover, that accorded with the utilitarian principle of maximizing pleasure and happiness. Unsurprisingly, most of these radical religious writings, along with any promoting sexual liberty, were not included as part of John Bowring's edition of Bentham's writings, completed in 1843.[25] There is increasing interest in Bentham's evolving religious and sexual radicalism as his full unpublished corpus is being made available by the Bentham Project.[26]

While Bentham made trenchant criticisms of religion as a rival to his own brand of secular utilitarianism, it is less clear the extent to which Bentham was prepared to reject openly the role of Christian religion altogether. Avowed atheism or rejection of Christian principles in the conduct of human institutions only begins to make an appearance in the late eighteenth century. There are practical reasons for this, including the blasphemy laws which ensured that those who might privately have rejected all divine causes did so with discretion, either on their deathbeds like Hume, or pseudonymously like George Grote and Bentham.[27] While he is sometimes claimed as a prophet of humanism, secularism, or, with more justice, as an advocate for the separation of church and state, Bentham's views are more nuanced than might appear from his published work on the subject. Undoubtedly, he believed that religion was corrupting and a vehicle for generating unhappiness, duplicity and terror instead of 'the greatest happiness of the whole community'.[28] However his position was less radical than that of the Church's most vehement critics among enlightened philosophes, such as Voltaire (1694–1778), as reflected in Bentham's translation of *The White Bull* (*Le taureau blanc*), published in 1774, a satire of Biblical exegesis.[29] As de Champs notes, Bentham appropriated Voltaire's views while acclimatizing his biblical critique to the British context.[30] Only those parts of religion that were useful were worth preserving; the useless parts of Christian dogma should be abandoned. At the same time, he felt the Church had outlived its usefulness. In *Church-of-Englandism* Bentham confidently called for the 'euthanasia' of the Church.[31] This was partly a failure of sympathy; Bentham could not conceive why anyone would choose to believe the – to him – preposterous tenets of the Anglican catechism. Religion, like other aspects of human emotional psychology was, for Bentham, a closed book.[32] This does not imply, though, that his attack on the Church – an integral part of Old Corruption – lacked integrity or rational coherence.

Religion and the panopticon

Despite his evident and well justified reservations about state supported religion, Bentham appeared to make a significant utilitarian exception in the case of penal institutions. In the Preface to his first printed work on penal reform, 'A View of the Hard-Labour Bill' (1778),[33] Bentham explained how his reading of Howard inspired him to create a 'plan of punishment' which would incorporate solitary confinement and labour.[34] He had no quarrel with arrangements for the appointment of a chaplain as one of the senior officers of a gaol, or for the central place of religious duties. In discussion of section 45 of the Bill, Bentham approved of the requirement that inmates attend services on all Sundays, as well as Christmas and Good Friday, that the sexes be separated, that officers and servants be present and that a chaplain be available to visit prisoners. His only quibble, which was in any case too expensive to be enacted, was that these requirements were an imposition on Dissenters, Catholics and Jews, who should be allowed to have visitors of their own persuasion, or, in the case of Jews, that if a single labour house was set up for them that it might be possible to arrange for them to have their own rabbis, cooks and butchers.[35] Bentham was concerned that too much time was set aside for leisure on Sunday, and provided suggestions to lengthen the time devoted to religion by extending services with sermons, prayers, moral exhortations and music.[36] He saw benefits in reading the Bible and religious books, but since few inmates would be able to read, most would in effect do nothing. Idleness was the enemy, and, in the absence of work, he could tolerate time set aside for devotion.

Bentham developed his ideas on the role of religion in penal institutions when devising the panopticon, as well as in the many years spent polishing and improving his scheme. The 21 letters he wrote on this subject in 1787, in the course of which he learned of the plan to send convicts to New South Wales, admittedly say little if anything about the appointment of chaplains or any religious activities.[37] This was remedied in the two lengthy postscripts first printed in 1791.[38] The first 'Postscript' proposed placing a chapel within the 'dead' part of the cylinder, separate from the cells.[39] The role and function of the chapel is 'introduced' in section VII:

> The necessity of a chapel to a penitentiary-house, is a point rather to be assumed than argued. Under an established church of any persuasion, a system of penitence without the means of regular devotion, would be a downright solecism. If religious instruction and exercise be not necessary to the worst, and generally the most ignorant of sinners, to whom else can they be other than superfluous?[40]

Bentham never suggested that penal institutions should be entirely secular and appeared comfortable with conceding the moral regulation of the panopticon to a Christian chaplain. In section XI of the second 'Postscript' Bentham goes on to discuss Sunday employment, suggesting that the vacant time created by the obligation of a day of rest be taken up with Sunday Schools, devotions and music. With rather less than his usual cynicism, he suggests that these activities would not only fill the time but provide an aesthetic and spiritual benefit: 'The great object of this consecrated day is to keep alive the sentiment of religion in men's minds'.[41]

The religious element within the panopticon was the subject of considerable revision as the Bentham brothers worked with successive architects to perfect their design. According to John Howard, a chapel was 'necessary' to a gaol, and his designs for local prisons incorporated galleries for female prisoners and debtors to enable them to remain separate from other offenders.[42] Following Howard's model and that of like-minded Christian penal reformers, Bentham recognized that religious elements were necessary in gaols if only to secure government approval. Bentham's sketch for the cover of a projected book on the 'Panopticon or the Inspection House' is accompanied by a quotation from Psalm 139 in the Miles Coverdale translation from the *Book of Common Prayer*: 'Thou art about my path, and above my bed: and spiest out all my ways' (Figure 12.1). Bentham accordingly gave a central role to the chapel and chaplain within the panopticon well before the Gaol Act of 1823 legislated for visiting chaplains, magistrates, and medical officers in English gaols.[43]

Despite his pragmatic arrangements for religious services, which Bentham may well have regarded as a suitable part of the punishment merited by those who had been found guilty of offences against the law, the location of the chapel and chaplain within the panopticon was a challenge for its designers. A cross-section of the 1791 iteration of the panopticon drawn by architect Willey Reveley (1760–99) shows the chaplain at a chapel placed between arches within the central well of the building, theoretically enabling prisoners to receive religious instruction without leaving their cells (Figure 12.2). As Steadman points out, this arrangement would have blocked access and oversight of prisoners and ensured that the chaplain and prison officers were more visible than their charges.[44] Possibly for this reason the chaplain was not featured in the earliest printed illustrations of the panopticon.[45]

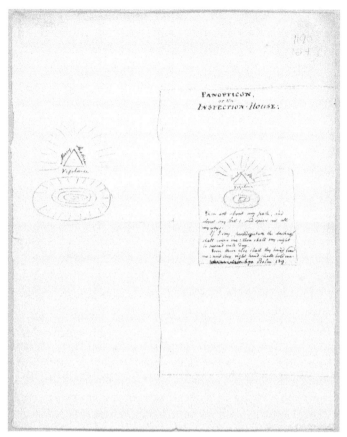

Figure 12.1: Jeremy Bentham, hand-drawn, but unused, frontispiece for 'Panopticon, or the Inspection-House', c. 1791. Bentham Papers, Special Collections, University College London Library xix. 124
(hereafter UC. Roman numerals refer to the boxes in which the papers are placed, Arabic to the leaves within each box)

The placement of the chapel was also a problem in versions of the panopticon which, unlike the plans of the Bentham brothers, were actually constructed. When Reveley's son, Henry Willey Reveley (1788–1875), designed the 12-sided Fremantle Gaol (1831) now known as the Round House in Fremantle, Western Australia, he adapted his father's design for the panopticon, though on a smaller scale.[46] Among other modifications, Fremantle Gaol had no provision for a chapel or chaplain in the central courtyard, which suggests this was always an optional element. Lanman argues, on the other hand, that Fremantle Gaol included all the religious elements that Bentham aspired for in the

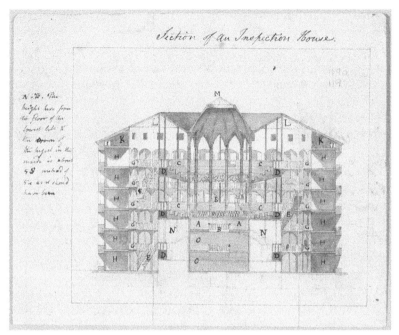

Figure 12.2: Willey Reveley (1760–99), 'Section of an Inspection House', *c.* 1791, UC xix. 119.

panopticon.[47] In practice, this amounted to little more than occasional visits by overburdened colonial chaplains.[48]

Bentham and religion in Australia

The next section will consider how Bentham's views on religion and penal reform impacted on his Australian writings, especially those in relation to transportation. Thanks to the work of Tim Causer and Philip Schofield, we now have fresh editions, from the manuscripts, of his output on this topic, an advance on the cautious printed and published versions which appeared in his lifetime or, having been carefully curated, after his death.[49]

New Wales (1791)

Bentham provided some reflection on the religious uses of convict colonization in his earliest, though ultimately unpublished, intervention on the plans for the penal colony of New South Wales.[50] Indeed, in the very first line of 'New Wales' (1791), Bentham ironically refers to the supposed religious claims of the colony or, at least, 'the making use of convicts as the instruments under God' to accomplish benefits which ranged, improbably, from transforming 'vice of all kinds into virtue', to extending the empire, increasing trade, and preventing prisoners from becoming a permanent charge on the public purse. Bentham regarded these claims, including hopes for the 'propagation of true religion', as illusory.[51] At this early date, Bentham's sources for information about the colony were scanty. However, he may have known that at least one minister of religion had been sent to the colony with hopes that they might convert both the convicts and the peoples of the surrounding seas. He refers to 'a Right Reverend Divine' who might, with other missionaries, contribute to the propagation of the gospel, though typically he undercuts this by going on to observe that success would be short-lived without a proper plan of colonization, including the provision of sufficient women to sustain the population.

Though possibly unknown to Bentham, the Rev. Richard Johnson (c. 1756–1827) was appointed 'chaplain to the settlement' of New South Wales in October 1784. The Rev. James Bain also served as chaplain to the New South Wales Corps from 1791 to 1794 and he was not without support from the major Anglican missionary societies. Before his departure for the colony, Bain corresponded with the Society for the Propagation of the Gospel (SPG) with a view to appointing schoolmasters for the 'whole of New South Wales', which implied teaching the children of convicts as well as the Corps.[52] When Bain was posted from New South Wales to Norfolk Island, it was left to Johnson to devise rules for a School, the first of which was an inclusive one: 'That the School is to be considered for the Benefit of the Children of all descriptions of persons, whether Soldiers, Settlers, or Convicts'.[53] However, it was not until March 1794, with the arrival of the Rev. Samuel Marsden (1765–1838), that Johnson had an assistant chaplain, as well as a commitment from the SPG to pay salaries to schoolmasters and provide students with books, enabling him to be chaplain to the penal colony in more than name only.[54]

Johnson did little to merit Bentham's deprecation of the utility and sincerity of the established clergy. Being given very little support from the secular establishment, he used his own funds to print religious literature and even build the colony's first church. In 1792, he wrote a moral address to his spiritual charges which was printed in 1794 and sold by several London booksellers.[55] Despite Bentham's strictures about the limited capacity of the colony for expansion, Johnson observed that the colony had grown so rapidly that he was unable to preach to all his charges without the benefit of the printed word.[56] Death was nevertheless more in evidence than births, and in five years Johnson had conducted 854 burials as opposed to 220 marriages and 226 baptisms. Johnson urged his people to read his 'plain, affectionate Address' seriously, preferably many times, and to live better lives, observe the Sabbath and think of the day of Judgement.[57] Significantly, Johnson made no distinction between readers who came free to the colony and those who came out under sentence, and concluded by signing himself 'your affectionate Friend and Servant in the Gospel of Christ'.[58] The same spirit of Christian welcome is reflected in the church he designed, which was capacious enough to include the whole community. Regrettably, Johnson's church was destroyed by fire, probably arson, though the culprit was never identified.

Bentham is unlikely to have read either Johnson's *Address* of 1792, or his letters and journals which were read out to the Eclectic Society,[59] but he might have realized the bare fact of his appointment through Stockdale's unauthorized publication of Governor Arthur Philip's letters from the colony in 1789, and the sequel based on those of Governor John Hunter.[60] Of the 20 contemporary accounts of the First Fleet, Bentham seems to have relied almost entirely on that of Judge Advocate, David Collins (1756–1810) in producing his later writings on New South Wales.[61] Collins laced his *Account* with vivid details of crime and daily life in Botany Bay's community of felons and exiles. The first volume appeared in 1798, during Collins's return to London, with a second, based on the reports by Governor Hunter, appearing in 1802. Assisted by his wife, Maria, Collins published a single-volume abridgement in 1804.

Unlike earlier accounts of the colony, Collins did not ignore Johnson, but from the point of view of his reputation as an effective shepherd of the penal colony it might have been better if he had. Inadvertently, or simply because it provided a rhetorical backdrop to the founding drama of the colony, Collins reported with wry indifference on Johnson's ineffectual efforts to preach morality, save life and do good.[62] Collins appreciated the moral tone of Johnson's sermons, such as that, following the death of two convict lads struck dead by lightning, which took its text from Samuel 20: 3: 'There is but a step between me and death'.[63] On Christmas Day 1793, however, he reported that Johnson preached to no more than 40 people, though up to 500 were hovering around the storehouse doors hoping for alcohol. So little respect was shown to Johnson by reason of his office that his own house was broken into.[64] Collins's attitude toward religion in general is reflected in the Appendix which provides an account of Indigenous government and religion. Collins states that, based on his inquiries, he could find no trace of any religious sentiment among the Aborigines: 'I am certain that they do not worship either sun, moon, or star, that, however necessary fire may be to them, it is not an object of adoration; neither have they respect for any particular beast, bird, or fish'.[65] This is far from the truth as we now understand it, but it is revealing about Collins's reservations about established religion which appear to have accorded with Bentham's own views. Collins also found it amusing that 'the young [Aboriginal] people who resided in our houses' wanted to go to church on Sundays, without appreciating what purpose this served: 'I have often seen them take a book, and with much success imitate the clergyman in his manner (for better and readier mimics can no where be found)'. It may be relevant that Collins did not find it incompatible with his respect and affection for his wife that he co-habited in the colony with convict women who bore him several children.

Bentham evidently shared Collins's insouciant disregard for the quality of Johnson's sermons, but happily plundered his *Account* in his later writings on the penal colony for evidence of the failure of religious props to produce either a change in character of the convicts or a reduction in crime. Drawing on Collins, Bentham found ample evidence to suggest the moral failings of the penal colony and Johnson's ineffectualness. Bentham had argued in 1791 that the absence of suitable marriage partners ensured the colony could not prosper without 'promiscuous intercourse' contrary to the 'Xtianity as professed by the Church of England'.[66] This naturally compared unfavourably with what Bentham presented as the superior prospects for religious and moral reformation within the panopticon.[67] Reflecting on the reasons for the disparity, he tartly suggested that 'Priests, if useful' should be provided in numbers sufficient to have an impact, noting that there was no provision for the 887 convicts on Norfolk Island.[68] In contrast, and no doubt as he had assured William Wilber-force, in the panopticon, 'religious exercise [would be] constant' and therefore enhanced the prospects of reformation.[69]

Whatever his views on the efficacy of religious instruction on the morals of prisoners, Bentham was prepared to compromise the security and potentially the effectiveness of the panopticon to demonstrate its compatibility with the strictest religious compliance. In correspondence with government officials, Bentham could point to the compulsory, central and visible role of the chaplain in the panopticon and compare it favourably with the easily evaded and optional provision of religion in the penal colony. In 1802, he hastened to do so in the form of three letters, two printed, and one unprinted, addressed to the Home Secretary, Lord Pelham (1756–1826).

Letter to Lord Pelham (1802)

Bentham made a more detailed critique of the religious failings of the convict colony in his first 'Letter to Lord Pelham', which was mostly written between May and August 1802.[70] In relation to the potential reformation of the prisoner, defined as 'curing him of the will to do the like in future', Bentham applied himself with withering sarcasm to admonishing the penal colony and advancing the panopticon. Unlike the panopticon, he argued that the colony provided inadequate inspection, 'the only effective instrument of reformative management'. In its place, other tools had to be deployed, namely the civil and military officers (dressed in red) or ministers of religion (dressed in black), along with chaplains and chapels and good books. Yet the means were inadequate to the task: 'Thus far the head-reformers saw: farther it was not given them to see. Would the books be read? The chapels visited? The chaplains heard?'[71] He then went on to enumerate the clergy despatched to serve the convicts and the troopers in the penal colony, including the unfortunate James Harold (1744–1830), a Catholic priest transported for his involvement in the United Irishmen revolt, whom he refers to as a 'seditionist' who inflamed the convicts to further rebellion.

Second Letter to Lord Pelham (1802)

Bentham's 'Second Letter to Lord Pelham', completed by the end of December 1802, continued his campaign (one cannot help but feel sympathy for the government officers who were obliged to read and respond to it – and he enumerates every encounter so no one could escape). This is the longest component of the composite work republished 10 years later as *Panopticon versus New South Wales* (1812) and incorporates his research into American penitentiaries. Bentham's account draws on four historians and two exemplary prisons: Walnut Street in Philadelphia, begun in 1790, and Newgate, New York, begun in 1796 and completed in 1797.[72] Both institutions were influenced by Quaker principles of silence, contemplation, humane and sanitary conditions and industry to cover the costs of confinement. In the 1820s, Newgate was superseded by Auburn, which embraced a more puritan work ethic and implemented harsher, industrial conditions of labour. Referring to the prime movers behind the prisons, Caleb Lownes (1754–1828) in Philadelphia and Thomas Eddy (1758–1827) in New York, Bentham praised them for displaying 'under the garb of a quaker, the head of a statesman'.[73] In comparing the penitentiaries with convict transportation, Bentham extols the evidence of reformation and industry in the former, with the sloth, drunkenness, and immorality of the latter.

Drawing once again on David Collins's *Account* to sustain his claims about irreligion in the colony, Bentham refers to the arson attack on Richard Johnson's church, the murder of the missionary Samuel Clode in 1799, and the immorality of the people where, from 14 marriages there had been 87 births, in effect 'the morals of Otaheite introduced into New Holland by the medium of Old England'.[74] His longest analysis of the religious deficiencies of the penal colony come in section VII, describing how spiritual remedies had been 'unavailing'. Despite Bentham's disdain for established religion, he nevertheless professed to lament the absence of religious commitment on the part of the authorities: for instance, a church clock was delivered to the colony – and a tower erected to hold it – with a church to be added at a future date. Bentham took this as failure of engagement with anything but the 'externals of religion': 'Better no church than to be burnt down; better no service than to be scoffed at'.[75] Even such externals were neglected until repeated orders were made to compel the attendance of convicts at church, the Governor attempting, so Bentham maintained, to fight the 'Daemon of irreligion' with the same straws he attempted to fight the 'hydra of drunkenness'.[76] Against this, though, Bentham has very little to say about the advantages of the penitentiary system.[77] In fact, at this date neither Philadelphia nor Auburn had resident, full-time salaried chaplains, permitted prisoners to assemble for religious worship or provided schools or formal training.[78] Such reforms were part of the later development of the evangelical prison, but the Quaker experiments were important and well-known Christian alternatives to the panopticon. Bentham goes on to compare the supposed industry, sobriety, reformation and cleanliness of the American penitentiaries, their absence of opportunities for escape, impact on the rate of crime, and overall economy with their opposite in the supposed 'improved' colony of New South Wales.

Third Letter to Pelham (written 1802–3; unpublished)

In Bentham's third and final letter to Lord Pelham, unpublished until the new edition by Tim Causer and Philip Schofield, he again made use of religious sources, this time the report on prison visitation by the Quaker philanthropist James Neild (1744–1814).[79] Neild is not so well known as either John Howard in England or the Quaker reformers influential in the design of the American penitentiaries reviewed in Bentham's 'Second Letter to Lord Pelham'. This is regrettable because Neild was as assiduous as Howard in his chosen field of prisons for debtors and his testimony makes just as grim reading.[80] Bentham called him 'the indefatigable Agent of the Charity for the relief of debtors', who preceded Howard in the field of prison visiting: 'I called Neild a second Howard: with more propriety I might have called Howard a second Neild'.[81] They also corresponded and met, with Bentham making use of Neild's data to argue that the recidivism rate in Philadelphia (five in 100 over five years) was substantially better than rates in the supposedly reformed British prisons.[82] Both Neild and his friend, Sir Henry St. John Mildmay (1764–1808),[83] were significant in Bentham's analysis of English penal institutions, as examples of authorities who should have been sought out in relation to the appointment of an inspector of prisons and the hulks – but who were overlooked because of the corruption of the ruling elite.[84]

The theme of this 'Third Letter' is nominally the hulk system, but Bentham's analysis also discusses 'improved' local prisons. Concerning the hulks, his initial analysis did not extend beyond a three-column table comparing the penitentiary, hulks and 'N.S. Wales' system', after which he came to the surprising conclusion that even the hulks, 'pernicious as they are', were better than New South Wales. On consulting a report of March 1802 on conditions in the hulks by Neild and St. John Mildmay, Bentham was able to add a new section to this work. Having been authorized to do so by the Home Secretary, Neild and St. John Mildmay visited the hulks in March 1802, and their report was published in Neild's *Account of the Society for the Discharge and Relief of Persons Imprisoned for Small Debts*. It provided a terrible indictment of conditions where, despite attempts on the part of authorities rapidly to prepare for their arrival, they reported on rampant famine and disease among the convicts.[85] At more or less the same time, Parliament passed the Hulks Act of 1802, which appointed an Inspector of Hulks with obligations to make quarterly reports to Parliament. Bentham objected to the cronyism which ensured that neither Neild nor St. John Mildmay was considered for the post – but rather a friend of an official and patron in the Home Office: 'A new screen is bought for the abuse and the public pay for it.'[86]

Bentham and Christian Utilitarianism

Having reviewed Bentham's published and unpublished writings on religion, and the religious aspects of his writings on the panopticon, New South Wales and penal reform, there would seem little reason to question his uncompromising scepticism about the function of religion in society. Two matters suggest his position was more nuanced than has been assumed. In the first place, there is Bentham's unwavering respect for Christian penal reformers, especially James Neild and John Howard. He praised Howard unreservedly, 'to whose merits, as a zealous and intelligent friend of human kind, it is difficult for language to do justice'.[87] He was even more effusive on the merits of James Neild, of whom he notes: 'year after year his active beneficence had embraced and covered the whole island'.[88] Bentham admired, respected and emulated Christian utilitarians who shared his commitment to evidence-based reasoning and the promotion of human wellbeing.

Secondly, there is Bentham's collaboration with the anti-slavery campaigner William Wilberforce (1759–1833). This was not a casual relationship: Bentham refers to Wilberforce as 'my pious and benevolent friend', 'one of the most distinguished, zealous, and influential patrons of the [panopticon] measure'.[89] Having been well received in Republican France, in 1796 (after the Terror and during Napoleon's rise to power) Bentham wrote a remarkable letter to Wilberforce suggesting that, since both he and Wilberforce had been honoured with the title of 'French citizen', that they head to Paris to 'bring peace to it', taking along a sketch of the panopticon plan and letters of introduction from Talleyrand and others to smooth the way.[90] For his part, Wilberforce frequently had Bentham to dine, and assured him: 'I will never forsake you; but the Minister is not with you' – something Wilberforce appreciated long before Bentham finally accepted defeat. They seem to have found each other mutually useful – the practical Christian and the secular reformer.[91] Bentham excused Wilberforce from the general conspiracy which he believed had caused the collapse of his panopticon plans: 'From the first to last, his wishes for the melioration, temporal and spiritual, as well as comfort of these peccant members of society, had been sincere: his labours towards the effectuation of those objects correspondent: so long as my share in the promised institutions for that purpose afforded a ray of hope, he had stood by me.'[92] That being said, even Wilberforce was at times not seen as beyond suspicion. On one occasion, writing to Sir Charles Bunbury, Bentham asked of Wilberforce and another supposed ally, 'are they good Samaritans, or are they Priest and Levite?'[93] That is, if Bentham was the man assailed by robbers in the parable (Luke 10:25), would Wilberforce come to his aid or, like the Priest and Levite, would he pass by on the other side of the road?

Despite its anti-clerical edge, Bentham's secular vision was not incompatible with that of the Quakers, Unitarians and Congregationalists who adhered to Rational Dissent. It is evident that secular and Christian utilitarians made common cause on issues such as anti-slavery, non-sectarian access to education, amelioration of poverty and, of course, penal reform. As is well known, Rational Dissent was transformed in the nineteenth century with significant numbers moving to Unitarianism and embracing philanthropic causes.[94] Bentham numbered Unitarians among his disciples and beneficiaries from his will, including the linguist Sarah Austin (1793–1867) and John Bowring (1792–1872), his unfortunate and not very competent literary executor.[95] Less is said about the reformism of Orthodox Anglicans, notably William Paley (1743–1805) and other Scottish moral philosophers who also contributed to the Enlightened reform of institutions. Bentham attacked Paley's claims for the utility of religious principles embodied in the latter's *Natural Theology* (1802) in his 'Juggernaut' manuscripts, but their views were not entirely divergent.[96] Paley's influence is clear on the post-Napoleonic 'Evangelical turn' in penal reform embodied in the work of the Prison Discipline Society (1818), led by the former Quaker Samuel Hoare III (Elizabeth Fry's brother-in-law) and other Evangelicals. Anthony Page has described the significance of Rational Dissenters for the abolition of the slave trade; in relation to anti-convict transportation, the lead was taken by the Liberal Anglican, Richard Whately, whose theological opposition to convict transportation owes a significant debt to Paley.[97] The real enemies of both secular and Rational Dissent were, after all, 'Old Corruption', the malign allegiance of church and state which assumed a licence to terrorize and impoverish the poor. They both opposed the irrational and malign penal and justice system justified by Romans 13:4 ('For he beareth not the sword in vain: for he is the minister of God, an avenger to execute wrath upon him that doeth evil').[98]

We should not be surprised that Bentham found tacit backing among enlightened Christians. Indeed, a remarkable degree of forbearance was shown to Bentham's particular brand of radical, anti-clerical rationalism, not least by his Unitarian friends. When Samuel Romilly read the draft of *Church-of-Englandism* he immediately warned Bentham that it was libellous and that he was opening himself up to legal attack. As he did on other occasions when Romilly or his other friends warned of libel,[99] Bentham published regardless – and remained remarkably untroubled by libel actions. In relation to 'Letter to Lord Pelham', Aaron Burr jokingly remarked that Bentham was likely soon to make a practical experiment on the project by making an involuntary voyage to Botany Bay. Although a good deal of his more adventurous work lay in manuscript, and more was printed but remained in manuscript until a publisher dared to test the laws of libel, Bentham never spent a day in prison or paid a penny in defamation. A note in Bentham's Memorandum Book for 1820 read: 'Under libel law, whatever I have done for the safety, for the liberty, for the morality of the people, depends for its efficacy on the weakness of the law'.[100]

Conclusion

Despite their iconic status as leaders of penal reform, neither Bentham nor his friends among the Rational Dissenters were particularly influential in the direction taken by prison reform in the 1820s.[101] These reformers looked back to an earlier generation, which included John Howard and William Blackstone (another of Bentham's *bêtes noires*), who were influential in the passing of the Penitentiary Act (1779),[102] as well as James Neild and Samuel Romilly. Before Bentham invented the term 'utilitarian', both Christian and Secular utilitarians were distinguished by their active visitation, including the veteran Neild (1744–1814) on behalf of the Society for the Discharge and Relief of Small Debtors, and later Joseph John Gurney (1788–1847) and Elizabeth Fry, whose work with female prisoners in Newgate began in 1813 on the urging of the American Quaker Stephen Grellet. This reforming alliance supported classification, healthy prison conditions, supervision, and opportunities for industry. Unlike Quakers and Evangelicals, Christian utilitarians were opposed to solitary confinement. They recommended prisoners associate by day while at work, and be kept separate at night. Having originally favoured solitary cells for the panopticon, Bentham agreed, recommending cells that accommodated three or four.[103] The key point of distinction between Bentham and Quaker reformers was that the latter supported amelioration of home prisons, convict transportation, and penal colonies, whereas Bentham advocated abolition of transportation and the erection of the panopticon.

As a product of the Evangelical revival, soon to capture a significant number of quietist Quakers, William Wilberforce had little compuncton in supporting Bentham's panopticon in preference to Botany Bay, because it was centrally concerned with the moral salvation of the prisoner. As we have seen, Bentham was not opposed to the deployment of religious agents in prisons, seeing them as psychological officers providing necessary reinforcement to the military, the black coats marching to the same drum as the redcoats. In condemning the religious provision made at Botany Bay, his main argument was not that when tested on the ground – as testified by David Collins – it made no difference to prospects for reformation in the absence of any effective form of surveillance: 'the truth is, that so far as the convicts were concerned, the real service which it was in the power of any ministers of religion, of any persuasion, or in any number, to render to these wretches, was in all places alike: presence or absence made no sort of difference'.[104] Despite the religious cynicism, Bentham's views were compatible at many points with his Rational Christian collaborators.

Bentham's outrage at the failure of his plans for the panopticon resound in his voluminous writings on the theme of penal reform. Plans for a model penitentiary were taken up again in the 1830s, but by this stage both the secular and the Christian utilitarians had shifted their ground. It is arguable that the passion for American-style separation and classification embodied in the original plans for Millbank and – even more so – in Pentonville, are radically different from either the panopticon or even Howard's penitentiary. I think Bentham would have been dismayed by the direction that the Benthamites eventually took in relation to both prison reform and transportation, since the utilitarian prisons such as Pentonville and its colonial counterpart, the probation system, attempted to legislate for morality and education as part of the price paid for reformatory sentencing.

But let us leave the last words to Bentham. To quote the *pensée* which Bowring says he found 'scattered over fragment of blotting paper':

When will men cease beholding in Almighty Benevolence a cruel tyrant, who (to no assignable end) commands them to be wretched?

And

Men ought to be cautious ere they represent Religion to be that noxious thing which magistrates should proscribe.[105]

Notes

1 Stephen 1900, 48.
2 For statistical evidence of a shift from established church to Arminian Methodist affiliation between 1800–40, see Field 2012, fig. 2.
3 For the complexities of the legal and civil disabilities created by the Test Acts across the four kingdoms, see Brown 2001, 1–92.
4 Bentham, ed. Bowring 1838–43, x. 70.
5 Bentham, ed. Bowring 1838–43, x. 74.
6 Bentham, ed. Crimmins 2002, 16. For commentary, see lxii. I thank Tim Causer for providing me with this and other references for this chapter.
7 Bentham, ed. Crimmins 2002, 16.
8 Crimmins 1986, 95. For another view, Schofield 1999. For a reply to Schofield, see Crimmins 2001.
9 For Bentham's indebtedness to John Howard's Penitentiary Act for the Panopticon, see Semple 1993, ch. 4.
10 Crimmins 1990a; Crimmins 1990b; McKown 2004.
11 Paley 1802, p. vii.
12 Schofield 2012. For the 'jug' manuscripts, see Fuller 2010.
13 Bentham 1817, sections 11 & 12.
14 Bentham, ed. Crimmins and Fuller, 2011. The full version of *Church of Englandism*, complete with its five appendices, comes to 656 published pages.
15 Bentham, ed. Crimmins and Fuller 2011, part iv.
16 Taylor 1978.
17 Beauchamp 1822.
18 Beauchamp 1822. The quoted phrases are section titles in Part II, chapter 1.
19 George Grote, Letter of 23 February 1823, cited by Berman 2013, 193.
20 Berman 1988, 193.
21 Schofield 2015.
22 Fuller 2010, 4.
23 Schofield 2015. For the mischiefs arising from the Sermon on the Mount, see Fuller 2010, 25, discussing Bentham's 'History of Jesus', written in 1815 (BL Add. MS 29,806 and 29,807).
24 Schofield 2012.
25 Bentham, ed. Bowring, 1838–43.
26 For Bentham's unpublished writings on religion, including the 'Juggernaut' manuscripts (1811 to 1821), see Fuller, 2008; Fuller, 2010. For Bentham's sexual philosophy and the clash between 'Paulism' (i.e. religious asceticism) and his own brand of sexual Epicureanism, see Schofield 2020, 6; Sandford 2020.
27 Berman 2013, 116–17 suggests Grote and Bentham's *Analysis of the influence of natural religion* (1822) argued strategically in favour of Christian precepts in order to impugn belief in God. On the basis of the surviving manuscripts, Berman suggests (ibid. 192) that Grote was the major and Bentham the minor partner in the production of this work and that the atheistic elements are most likely Grote's contribution.
28 Bentham, *Introduction to the Constitutional Code*, cited by Bowring.
29 de Champs 2012.
30 de Champs 2012, 8.
31 Bentham, ed. Crimmins and Fuller, 2011, Appendix No. IV, 2.
32 Here I sympathize with the analysis of Lucas and Sheridan 2006.
33 'A View of the Hard-Labour Bill' in Bentham, ed. Bowring 1838–43, iv. 1–36.
34 'A View of the Hard-Labour Bill' in Bentham, ed. Bowring 1838–43, iv. 2.
35 'A View of the Hard-Labour Bill' in Bentham, ed. Bowring 1838–43, iv. 25.
36 'A View of the Hard-Labour Bill' in Bentham, ed. Bowring 1838–43, iv. 18.
37 'Panopticon Letters' in Bentham, ed. Bowring 1838–43, iv. 37–66.
38 'Panopticon: Postscript I', and 'Panopticon: Postscript II' in Bentham, ed. Bowring 1838–43, iv. 67–121, 121–72.
39 'Panopticon: Postscript I' in Bentham, ed. Bowring 1838–43, iv. 67. For the need to provide accommodation for a chaplain and a matron, see ibid. 76.

40 'Panopticon Letters' in Bentham, ed. Bowring 1838–43, iv. 37–66.
41 'Panopticon: Postscript II' in Bentham, ed. Bowring 1838–43, iv. 161.
42 Howard 1777, 48.
43 4 Geo IV c. 64. The Gaols Act of 1823 followed Reports to the House of Commons in 1819 and 1823 recommended the appointment of resident or visiting prison chaplains to every gaol: see *Commons Sessional Papers* (1819), vol. xvii. 1–4; *Commons Sessional Papers* (1819), vol. vii. 1–571. For religious aspects of prison reform and the penitentiary movement, see Carey 2019, 42–5; McConville 1981, 129–30. For the rise of the evangelical prison, see Follett 2000, 9.
44 Steadman 2007.
45 'Panopticon Letters' in Bentham, ed. Bowring 1838–43, iv. 172–3.
46 Heritage Council of Western Australia 2013.
47 Lanman 2021. See also Lanman's discussion of Fremantle Gaol and its panoptic features in this volume.
48 Carey 2019, 283–94.
49 Bentham 1812, reproduced in Bentham, ed. Bowring 1838–43, vi. 212–48.
50 'New Wales' in Bentham, ed. Causer and Schofield 2022, 3–22.
51 'New Wales' in Bentham, ed. Causer and Schofield 2022, 3.
52 Rev. James Bain to the Rev. William Morice, on Board the *Gorgon*, Portsmouth Harbour, 13 February 1790, Bodleian Libraries (hereafter BodL), USPG C/Aus/Syd 4, 1790.
53 Richard Johnson, 'Rules & Articles to Be Observed Respecting Schools at Sydney, New South Wales', BodL, USPG C/Aus/Syd 4, 1798.
54 Rev. Samuel Marsden to the Society for the Propagation of the Gospel, 19 March 1821, BodL, USPG C/Aus/Syd 4, 1821.
55 Johnson 1894.
56 Johnson 1894, iv.
57 Johnson 1894, 72.
58 Johnson 1894, 74.
59 For Johnson's account of the arrival of the Second Fleet, see Johnson, ed. Mackaness 1954, No. 9; The Rev. Richard Johnson to Mr S. Thornton, [July 1790] in Britton and Bladen eds. 1892–1901, i. part 2, 386.
60 Phillip 1789; Hunter 1793. Neither volume has any information about Johnson other than his name. Divine Service, though regularly mentioned, for example by Lieutenant King, was conducted by the commanding officer, not by the resident chaplain. On his journey to Norfolk Island, February 1789 to March 1790, King's orders required convict attendance at Divine Service, unless prevented by illness, on pain of extra work, stopping a day's provisions or, for a repeated offence, corporal punishment.
61 Collins i. 1798.
62 Collins i. 1798.
63 Collins i. 1798, ch. 23.
64 Collins i. 1798, ch. 26.
65 Collins i. 1798, Appendix 1.
66 'New Wales' in Bentham, ed. Causer and Schofield 2022, 22.
67 Enacted by the Penitentiary for Convicts Act of 1794 (34 Geo. III, c. 84), but never realized in practice.
68 'Correspondence, sent to William Wilberforce, of Jeremy Bentham with Sir Charles Bunbury' in Bentham, ed. Causer and Schofield 2022, 49.
69 'Correspondence, sent to William Wilberforce, of Jeremy Bentham with Sir Charles Bunbury' in Bentham, ed. Causer and Schofield 2022, 53.
70 'Letter to Lord Pelham' in Bentham, ed. Causer and Schofield 2022, 74.
71 'Letter to Lord Pelham' in Bentham, ed. Causer and Schofield 2022, 77.
72 Note that the 'Auburn system', with its characteristic communal work and strictly enforced code of silence, was not instituted until the 1820s.
73 'Second Letter to Lord Pelham' in Bentham, ed. Causer and Schofield 2022, 169. Caleb Lownes was an iron founder. See Teeters 1963.
74 'Second Letter to Lord Pelham' in Bentham, ed. Causer and Schofield 2022, 184. On the burning of Johnson's church, see 189, 194–5; for Clode, see 182–3.
75 'Second Letter to Lord Pelham' in Bentham, ed. Causer and Schofield 2022, 193.
76 'Second Letter to Lord Pelham' in Bentham, ed. Causer and Schofield 2022, 195.

77 'Second Letter to Lord Pelham' in Bentham, ed. Causer and Schofield 2022, 196.
78 Graber, 93–6, notes that the Rev. Jared Curtis, the first resident, salaried chaplain at Auburn, took up his post in 1825. He was appointed by the Prison Discipline Society of Boston.
79 'Third Letter to Lord Pelham' in Bentham, ed. Causer and Schofield 2022, 262. Bentham notes that Neild's prison visiting began before Howard's and continued longer. See ibid., 290–1. The major focus of Neild's philanthropy were debtors. He was Treasurer of the Society for the Relief and Discharge of Persons Imprisoned for Small Debts from 1774 until his death. With his friend, Dr John Coakley Lettsom, he published accounts of his prison visitation in a series of letters to the *Gentleman's Magazine* published between 1803 and 1813: (1803) 73(2) to (1813) 93(2), 437. Neild's major work was his edited report, *The State of the Prisons in England, Scotland, and Wales* of 1812, 2011.
80 For studies of Neild, see Condon 1964; Neild 1981.
81 'Third Letter to Lord Pelham' in Bentham, ed. Causer and Schofield 2022, 290.
82 'Third Letter to Lord Pelham' in Bentham, ed. Causer and Schofield 2022, 262. These rates of recidivism are much lower than those for modern cities, but this says more about the modern rise of policing and reporting crime.
83 See Thorne, for St. John Mildmay's 1803 visitations to London prisons with Neild.
84 'Third Letter to Lord Pelham' in Bentham, ed. Causer and Schofield 2022, 291–2 for the various appointees derided by Bentham for corrupt incompetence.
85 'Third Letter to Lord Pelham' in Bentham, ed. Causer and Schofield 2022, 285 n., citing Neild 1802, 312.
86 'Third Letter to Lord Pelham' in Bentham, ed. Causer and Schofield 2022, 292.
87 'A View of the Hard-Labour Bill' in Bentham, ed. Bowring 1838–43, iv. 9.
88 Bentham cites Howard several times in his 'Second Letter to Pelham', which was printed in December 1802.
89 'Memoirs and Correspondence', in Bentham, ed. Bowring 1838–43, xi. 105.
90 Bentham received this honour in September 1792: see Jeremy Bentham to William Wilberforce, 1 September 1796 in Wilberforce and Wilberforce eds. 1840, vol. 1, 139; *Life of Wilberforce*, xliii. 171.
91 For the relationship between Bentham and Wilberforce, see Hirst 2008, 10.
92 'Memoirs and Correspondence', in Bentham, ed. Bowring 1838–43, xi. 106.
93 Bentham to Sir Charles Bunbury, n.d., 'Memoirs and Correspondence', in Bentham, ed. Bowring 1838–43, xi. 121.
94 Ditchfield 1998, 193.
95 Bentham's 'Last Will and Testament', 30 May 1832, refers to Bowring as 'my most intimate and confidential friend': see Bentham, ed. Crimmins 2002, 7.
96 Fuller 2010, 28.
97 Page 2011.
98 McGowen 1987.
99 For example, Romilly to Bentham, 1 November 1802; Aaron Burr to Bentham, 22 August 1808 (in relation to the 'Letters to Lord Pelham' and 'A Plea for the Constitution'); Romilly to Bentham, 31 January 1810, in relation to the 'Element of Packing': 'I do most sincerely and anxiously entreat you not to publish it', in 'Memoirs and Correspondence' in Bentham, ed. Bowring 1838–43, x. 450.
100 'Memoirs and Correspondence' in Bentham, ed. Bowring 1838–43, x. 518.
101 Cooper 1981.
102 Throness 2008.
103 Bowring, iv. 45–9, cited by Condon 1964, 247.
104 'Letter to Lord Pelham' in Bentham, ed. Causer and Schofield 2022, 79.
105 'Memoirs and Correspondence' in Bentham, ed. Bowring 1838–43, x. 10. Possibly 'prescribe' rather than 'proscribe' is intended here.

Bibliography

Primary Sources

Archival sources

Bodleian Libraries, Oxford, USPG, Papers of the United Society for the Propagation of the Gospel, 1701–1982.

Parliamentary papers

Commons Sessional Papers (1819), vol. vii. 1–571: 'Report from the Select Committee on the State of Gaols, &c', 12 July 1819.

Commons Sessional Papers (1819), vol. xvii. 1–4: 'Report of the Committee of the General Penitentiary at Millbank', 3 March 1819.

Printed sources

Beauchamp, P. *Analysis of the Influence of Natural Religion on the Temporal Happiness of Mankind*. London: R. Carlile, 1822.

Bentham, J. *Panopticon versus New South Wales: Or, the Panopticon Penitentiary System, and the Penal Colonization System, Compared*. London: R. Baldwin, 1812.

Bentham, J. *"Swear Not At All": Containing an Exposure of the Needlessness and Mischievousness, as well as Antichristianity, of the Cermony of an Oath*. London: sold by Hunter, 1817.

Bentham, J. *Church-of-Englandism and Its Catechism Examined*. [S.l.]: Effingham Wilson, 1818.

Bentham, J. *The Works of Jeremy Bentham, published under the superintendence of … John Bowring*, 11 vols. Edinburgh: William Tait, 1838–43.

Bentham, J. 'Auto-Icon; or, Farther Uses of the Dead to the Living. A Fragment [completed 1831–1832]'. In *Bentham's Auto-Icon and Related Writings*, ed. J.E. Crimmins, [41–63]. Bristol: Thoemmes Press, 2002.

Bentham, J. *Church-of-Englandism and Its Catechism Examined (CW)*, ed. J.E. Crimmins and C. Fuller. Oxford: Oxford University Press, 2011.

Bentham, J. *Not Paul, but Jesus, Vol. III: Doctrine*. London: The Bentham Project, UCL, 2013 [http://discovery.ucl.ac.uk/1392179/3/npbj.pdf].

Bentham, J. *Panopticon versus New South Wales and other writings on Australia*. London: UCL Press, 2022.

Collins, D. *An Account of the English Colony in New South Wales: With Remarks on the Dispositions, Customs, Manners, &C., of the Native Inhabitants of That Country; to Which Are Added, Some Particulars of New Zealand*, 2 vols. London: T. Cadell, 1798 and 1802.

Historical Records of New South Wales, ed. A. Britton and F.M. Bladen, 7 vols.. Sydney: Charles Potter, Government Printer, 1892–1901.

Howard, J. *The State of the Prisons in England and Wales, with Preliminary Observations, and an Account of Some Foreign Prisons*. London: Warrington, 1777.

Hunter, J. *An Historical Journal of the Transactions at Port Jackson and Norfolk Island*. London: J. Stockdale, 1793.

Johnson, R. *An Address to the Inhabitants of the Colonies, Established in New South Wales and Norfolk Island*. London: Printed for the author and sold by Mathews, Strand; Deighton, Holborn; Trap, Paternoster-Row; and Goff and Amey, No. 8, Ivy-Lane, 1894.

Johnson, R. *Some Letters of Rev. Richard Johnson, BA First Chaplain of New South Wales*, ed. G. Mackaness, 2 parts. Sydney: Ford, 1954.

Neild, J., ed. *An Account of the Rise, Progress, and Present State, of the Society for the Discharge and Relief of Persons Imprisoned for Small Debts Throughout England and Wales*. London: Nichols and Son, 1802.

Neild, J., ed. *The State of Prisons of England, Scotland and Wales: … Not for the Debtor Only, but for Felons Also, and Other Less Criminal Offenders*, first pub.1812. Cambridge: Cambridge University Press, 2011.

Paley, W. *Natural Theology: or, Evidences of the Existence and Attributes of The Deity*. London: Faulder, 1802.

Phillip, A. *The Voyage of Governor Phillip to Botany Bay*. London: pr. John Stockdale, 1789. https://www.gutenberg.org/files/15100/15100-h/15100-h.htm.

Secondary Sources

Berman, D. *A History of Atheism in Britain: From Hobbes to Russell*. London: Croom Helm, 1988.

Brown, S.J. *The National Churches of England, Ireland, and Scotland 1801–46*. Oxford: Oxford University Press, 2001.

Carey, H.M. *Empire of Hell: Religion and the Campaign to End Convict Transportation in the British Empire, 1788–1875*. Cambridge: Cambridge University Press, 2019.

Condon, R.H. 'James Neild, Forgotten Reformer', *Studies in Romanticism* 3 (1964): 240–51.

Cooper, R.A. 'Jeremy Bentham, Elizabeth Fry, and English Prison Reform', *Journal of the History of Ideas* 42: 4 (1981): 675–90.

Crimmins, J.E. 'Bentham on Religion: Atheism and the Secular Society', *Journal of the History of Ideas* 47: 1 (1986): 95–110.

Crimmins, J.E. *Secular Utilitarianism: Social Science and the Critique of Religion in the Thought of Jeremy Bentham*. Oxford: Clarendon, 1990a.

Crimmins, J.E. *Religion, Secularization and Political Thought: From Locke to Mill*. London: Routledge, 1990b.

Crimmins, J.E. 'Bentham's Religious Radicalism Revisited: A Response to Schofield', *History of Political Thought* 22: 3 (2001): 494–500.

De Champs, E. 'Bentham, Voltaire, and Biblical Exegesis'. Paper Presented at the Isus Conference, New York, 8–11 August 2012.

Ditchfield, G.M. 'English Rational Dissent and Philanthropy, c. 1760–c. 1810'. In *Charity, Philanthropy and Reform*, ed. J. Cunningham and J. Innes, 193–207. London: Palgrave Macmillan, 1998.

Field, C. 'Counting Religion in England and Wales: The Long Eighteenth Century, c. 1680–c. 1840', *Journal of Ecclesiastical History* 63: 4 (2012): 693–720.

Follett, R.R. *Evangelicalism, Penal Theory, and the Politics of Criminal Law Reform in England, 1808–30*. New York: St Martin's Press, 2000.

Fuller, C. 'Bentham, Mill, Grote, and an Analysis of the Influence of Natural Religion on the Temporal Happiness of Mankind', *Journal of Bentham Studies* 10 (2008): 1–15.

Fuller, C. '"Utility of Religion a Subject Little as yet Examined": A Survey of Bentham's Writings on the Utility of Religion', *Revue d'études benthamiennes* 6 (2010).

Graber, J. *The Furnace of Affliction: Prisons and Religion in Antebellum America*. Chapel Hill: University of North Carolina Press, 2011.

Heritage Council of Western Australia. 'Round House and Arthur Head Reserve (1830–31)', *Register of Heritage Places*, Data Base No. 0896 (2013). http://inherit.stateheritage.wa.gov.au/Public/Content/PdfLoader.aspx?id=5b9ff660-4ea3-4f6f-a831-75cfafa5c12b.

Hirst, J. *Freeedom on the Fatal Shore: Australia's First Colony*. Melbourne: Black Inc., 2008.

Lanman, E. 'Establishing a Panoptic Prison: An Examination of Fremantle Gaol, 1831–1841', *Revue d'études benthamiennes* 19 (2021).

Lucas, P. and Sheridan, A. 'Asperger's Syndrome and the Eccentricity and Genius of Jeremy Bentham', *Journal of Bentham Studies* 8 (2006): n.p. https://discovery.ucl.ac.uk/id/eprint/1322989/1/008_Lucas_and_Sheeran__2006_.pdf.

McConville, S. *A History of English Prison Administration*. Vol. I *1750–1877*. London: Routledge & Kegan Paul, 1981.

McGowen, R. '"He Beareth Not the Sword in Vain": Religion and the Criminal Law in Eighteenth-Century England', *Eighteenth-Century Studies* 21: 2 (1987): 192–211.

McKown, D.B. *Behold the Antichrist: Bentham on Religion*. Amherst, NY: Prometheus Books, 2004.

Neild, F.G. 'James Neild (1744–1814) and Prison Reform', *Journal of the Royal Society of Medicine* 74 (1981): 834–40.

Page, A. 'Rational Dissent, Enlightenment and Abolition of the British Slave Trade', *The Historical Journal* 54: 3 (2011): 741–72.

Sandford, S. '"Envy Accompanied with Antipathy": Bentham on the Psychology of Sexual Ressentiment'. In *Bentham and the Arts*, ed. A. Julius, M. Quinn, and P. Schofield, 71–90. London: UCL Press, 2020.

Schofield, P. 'Political and Religious Radicalism in the Thought of Jeremy Bentham', *History of Political Thought* 20 (1999): 272–91.

Schofield, P. *Jeremy Bentham: Prophet of Secularism,* London: South Place Ethical Society, 2012. https://discovery.ucl.ac.uk/id/eprint/1370228/.

Schofield, P. 'Jeremy Bentham on Utility and Truth', *History of European Ideas* 41: 8 (2015): 1125–42.

Schofield, P. 'Introduction'. In *Bentham and the Arts*, ed. A. Julius, M. Quinn, and P. Schofield, 1–20. London: UCL Press, 2020.

Semple, J. *Bentham's Prison: A Study of the Panopticon Penitentiary.* Oxford: Oxford University Press, 1993.

Steadman, P. 'The Contradictions of Jeremy Bentham's Panopticon Penitentiary', *Journal of Bentham Studies* 9 (2007). https://www.scienceopen.com/document/read?vid=d52d76d1-3263-4ed8-83d9-0123ea18545f.

Stephen, L. *The English Utilitarians*, 3 vols. London: Duckworth, 1900.

Taylor, B.W. 'Jeremy Bentham, the Church of England, and the Fraudulent Activities of the National Schools Society', *Paedagogica Historica* 18 (1978): 373–85.

Teeters, N.K. 'Caleb Lownes of Philadelphia: 1754–1828: Administrator of the First Penitentiary in the World – the Walnut Street Jail', *The Prison Journal* 43: 2 (1963): 34–45.

Thorne, R., ed. 'St John Mildmay, Sir Henry Paulet, 3rd Bt (1764–1808)'. In *The House of Commons 1790–1820*, vol. 4. London: Secker and Warburg, 1986. https://www.historyofparliamentonline.org/volume/1790-1820/member/st-john-mildmay-sir-henry-paulet-1764-1808.

Throness, L. *A Protestant Purgatory: Theological Origins of the Penitentiary Act, 1779.* Aldershot: Ashgate, 2008.

Wilberforce, R.I. and Wilberforce, S., eds. *The Correspondence of William Wilberforce*, 2 vols. London: John Murray, 1840.

13

The panopticon penitentiary, the convict hulks, and political corruption

Jeremy Bentham's 'Third Letter to Lord Pelham'

Tim Causer

Jeremy Bentham's position as a major critic of criminal transportation to New South Wales is well established, as is the role that transportation played in the failure of his panopticon penitentiary scheme.[1] However, Bentham's criticism of the convict hulks is less well appreciated, as is the fact that he devised his prison in significant part as a response to their failings. For instance on 23 January 1791, when he first offered the panopticon to the Pitt administration, Bentham had promised that he could deliver a national penitentiary, as provided for by the Penitentiary Act of 1779,[2] 'at about half the annual expence of that [system] pursued on board the Hulks'. He hoped that Pitt would respond quickly for two reasons. First, he feared that recent 'bad tidings' from New South Wales might have already prompted Pitt to seek an alternative to transportation, but the second, more urgent reason 'for not losing time', was that hulk convicts were then 'perishing at the rate of ⅕ and ⅙ of them in a year'.[3]

The importance of the hulks to the genesis of the panopticon penitentiary scheme is made clearer by the second of two documents accompanying his offer, in which he outlined the principles by which the panopticon would be managed.[4] Pre-empting a theme of his later writings, Bentham contrasted the opacity of the hulks with his panopticon, a transparent institution which would constantly be open to the general public, so that its officials, like its prisoners, would be constantly surveilled. As Bentham pointed out,

The hulks are and must be impenetrable to the public eye: they need more than human goodness to ensure them from abuse. My prison is transparent: my management no less so ... The best friend to innocence I know of is open and speedy Justice.

Moreover, in an unpublished manuscript draft of 1798, Bentham stated that he had set out to devise his new 'chronical punishment' having on one hand intended to reckon with the 'acknowledged incompetency of the Hulk system in a moral point of view', and on the other with the 'unpromising aspect of the original Penitentiary plan in an economical point of view'. By adopting the panopticon, the 'disadvantages of both might be avoided and the advantages of both combined in a superior degree'.[5] Bentham's promise in 1791 that the panopticon would be cheaper than the hulks was a recognition that they would be a major obstacle, and that he would have to make a strong case for government to consider surrendering an established, convenient, and cheap mode of punishment in favour of his novel form of penitentiary imprisonment. His experience during the following 12 years, however, demonstrated that the hulks were remarkably resilient to criticism, and that resilience, Bentham came to believe, owed to corruption and patronage in the Home Office.

Bentham's views on the hulks, an enduring part of the British penal estate, have attracted relatively little attention.[6] This neglect is understandable, given that most of these views are to be found in the essentially unknown 'Third Letter to Lord Pelham'[7] which Bentham had drafted in 1802–3 as part of his attempt to force the government to proceed with the panopticon scheme.[8] By drawing upon this work, discarded drafts Bentham drew up in its preparation, as well as other unpublished official and private manuscript material, this chapter will examine Bentham's views on the hulks, and how he regarded their operation as symptomatic of the corruption and patronage exercised by ministers which had repeatedly thwarted the realization of the panopticon. In so doing it will demonstrate that the hulks played an important role not only in the origins of the panopticon scheme but also in the story of its failure. The focus of the chapter will be upon the hitherto unpublished 'Third Letter to Lord Pelham', but it will first examine Bentham's earliest written remarks on the hulks, dating from 1778, as well as his 1798 proposal that he be awarded the contract to manage the hulks as compensation for the delays in bringing the panopticon to fruition.

Bentham, the origins of the panopticon, and the hulks, 1778–92

From the passage of the Transportation Act of 1718[9] until the outbreak of the American Revolutionary War in 1775, an estimated 50,000 men, women, and children were transported from the British Isles to the North American colonies.[10] The shipping of convicts had been contracted out to merchants – including the slave-owner and slave-trader Duncan Campbell – who in return were granted 'Property and Interest in the Service of such Offenders',[11] thereby permitting them to sell to colonists the indentures of transportees for the duration of their sentences. As Simon Devereaux notes, the British government's early confidence that the American rebels would quickly be defeated had given way, by November 1775, to a realization that 'some intervention in the interrupted process of transporting convicts might be required'.[12] In January 1776 Campbell had provided his vessel *Tayloe* as a stop-gap hulk to alleviate pressure on London's gaols,[13] but it was not until later that year that their use was formalized by a Hulks Act.[14] Campbell, whose business had suffered at the cessation of transportation to America, was awarded the hulk contract and on 12 July 1776 was appointed Overseer of Convicts on the Thames.[15] The *Justitia* began operating at Woolwich around this time, and was joined there in June 1777 by the *Censor*. Though the Hulks Act was intended as a temporary measure, operating during what had been envisaged as a two-year moratorium on transportation while the American revolt was put down, hulks remained in use in Britain until 1857, in imperial naval dockyards at Bermuda until 1863, and at Gibraltar until 1875.[16]

On a 'very cold' Thursday 8 January 1778 Bentham visited the Woolwich hulks for himself. What prompted his visit is unknown, though later that year he would begin work on his 'Plan of a Penal Code', intended to replace criminal codes reliant upon corporal and capital punishments with milder punishments, such as imprisonment with hard labour, but which were certain to be inflicted and could be calibrated in accordance with the magnitude of the individual offence. Accounts of the hulks had appeared in the London press and Campbell seems to have welcomed a degree of public scrutiny. In August 1777, for instance, the *Morning Chronicle* sought to correct recent reports that the public were forbidden from visiting Woolwich Warren 'without an order from the Board of Ordnance'; on the contrary, the *Chronicle* noted, 'the public are permitted, as usual, to see the warren; and every

Figure 13.1: Bowles and Carver, *View near Woolwich in Kent, shewing the Employment of the Convicts from the Hulks, c.* 1779 (National Library of Australia PIC Drawer 3856 #PIC/7488).

person who has an inclination to view the unhappy convicts at work is soon convinced that the punishment is most exemplary, and it is to be hoped will have the best effect on the minds of every spectator'.[17] In this respect, Campbell's permitting of such visits preceded the surveillance by the public to which the panopticon's inspector was to have been exposed.

Bentham recorded his visit in five pages of notes[18] which are, as Janet Semple suggests, a 'straightforward description very much in the Howard mode'.[19] Nevertheless, it is possible to discern similarities between Campbell's hulk establishment and aspects of the panopticon scheme. For instance, hulk prisoners were supposed to receive filtered water and three meals per day, while the panopticon's convicts would have received as much nourishing, though cheap and unpalatable food, as they required to sustain their work.[20] Bentham found the *Censor* 'abundantly warm' and its hospital section 'tolerably sweet and clean',[21] while the panopticon would have had central heating and a separate infirmary. Campbell refused to recommend any prisoner be liberated until he had interviewed their friends to satisfy 'himself that some feasible plan is fixed on for the man's subsistence',[22] while Bentham would not have discharged a prisoner from the panopticon until they had agreed to join the army or navy, or had found a 'responsible householder' willing to guarantee an annually-renewable £50 behaviour bond.[23]

Bentham's notes were headed 'Accounts of the Working Convicts', suggesting that his interest was less in the hulks as an institution and more in their being an experiment in imprisonment with hard labour[24] – he may therefore have considered visiting them to be an ideal opportunity to assess the arrangement and value of convict labour. Bentham found the convicts 'remarkably silent', most of whom worked on building a wharf, while the remainder dredged ballast from the Thames.[25] Semple speculated that the 'memory of these convicts, their good behaviour under the eye of authority, and the value of their labour may have persuaded Bentham that his panopticon would be both practicable and profitable'.[26] Campbell estimated that though a hulk convict did around half the work of a common workman, during the previous six months the overall accommodation and subsistence of the convicts had 'not cost the public £500 more than the value of their labour'. Campbell had found, though, that his efforts to organize work had been hampered by having received 'Improper objects', such as an elderly man convicted of stealing a cock, who died soon after having been sent all the way from Cornwall, as well as another man 'who had lost one arm, and several who from other causes are unable to work'.[27] While Campbell thus oversaw prisoners of varying degrees of physical strength and capability, the Hulks Act of 1776 offered him little discretion and apart from a limited number of posts in the *Censor*'s hospital for the less able, he had no option than to put convicts to hard, servile work, or else leave them idle. (Bentham noted that Campbell was thinking about how to diversify the available work, though Campbell's idea of establishing a brewery aboard the *Censor* was surely unwise.[28])

When in 1791 Bentham refined the details of the panopticon scheme, he commented that the hard labour inflicted on the hulks had mistakenly been '*made* hard, that it may be *called hard*; and it is called *hard*, that it may be frightful', thereby granting a 'bad name to industry, the parent of wealth and population' and causing economy to be 'sacrificed in a thousand shapes'. The panopticon's '*Mixture of employments*' would correct this perversion of the reformative power of hard work, and allow differing forms of labour to be profitably done by prisoners of differing ages, capabilities, and dispositions, without risk to their well-being and thereby constituting 'one great improvement in the economy of a prison'.[29] Bentham's visit to the hulks may therefore not only have convinced him that the panopticon might work, as Semple suggested, but also to fundamentally shape his view of how to arrange a proportionate, reformative, and profitable prison labour regime.

Bentham's notes indicated, though, that not all aboard the hulks was well. Anticipating his allegations of 1802–3 that their reality was hidden from the public, Bentham found 'very considerable sickness and mortality' at Woolwich, which Campbell told him was 'concealed as much as possible'. When Bentham visited the hospital on the *Censor*, Campbell 'declined going down with us ... and before we had been there long he called us out'.[30] Campbell had good reason to be nervous about visitors lingering below deck: he later told a House of Commons committee that of the 632 prisoners he had received from August 1776 to 26 March 1778, 176 (8 per cent) had died during their imprisonment, largely of diseases such as smallpox and typhus.[31] By 1791 Bentham had come to conclude that Campbell's concealment of significant convict deaths aboard the hulks had become absurd, observing in the second panopticon 'Postscript':

> I look at Mr. Campbell's *hulks*, and to my utter astonishment I see that nobody dies there. In these receptacles of crowded wretchedness, deaths should naturally be more copious than elsewhere. Instead of that, they are beyond comparison less so ... Now and then, indeed, there comes a sad mortality—Why?—because where pestilence has been imported, hulks neither do nor can afford the means of stopping it. But, bating pestilences, men are immortal there. Among 200, 300, quarter after quarter, I look for deaths, and I find none—Why?—because Mr Campbell is intelligent and careful.[32]

Bentham referred to his notes of 1778 when he discussed the hulks in print for the first time in 'A View of the Hard-Labour Bill', written in late February to mid-March 1778.[33] This work was Bentham's commentary on a bill[34] which intended to introduce a network of hard-labour houses across England and Wales, and which would also 'extend and perpetuate' the hulk establishment.[35] Bentham's chief concern in this work in regard to the hulks was the absence of fixed regulations or provisions for regular inspection which, however strong a testament to the 'extraordinary confidence' of the Government in Duncan Campbell, Bentham was hesitant to 'see the merit of this individual officer made an argument for entailing powers so unlimited upon that person [who] soever may chance at any time hereafter to bear his office'.[36] Bentham praised, though, the provision that the superintendent of the hulks was required to make quarterly returns to the Court of King's Bench, thereby providing '*data* for the legislator to go to work upon', and forming a 'kind of *political barometer*' by which to measure the 'moral health of the community'.[37]

Bentham's view of the hulks, and of Campbell, had – as noted above – hardened by 1791 when he first offered the panopticon to Pitt.[38] Bentham had received no reply by the time he wrote again on 10 December 1792, where, in continued recognition of the need to surmount the hulks, he claimed to be able to execute his plan 'at an expence per man less by 25 per cent than that of the Hulk system'.[39] In light of a continued lack of response from Pitt, in May 1792 Bentham discussed with his ally, Charles Bunbury MP, how the latter might raise the subject of the panopticon for debate in the House of Commons. Alluding to the fact that the panopticon would be run by contract management, and that as contractor he would share with the convicts the profits of their labour, Bentham feared being represented as someone 'who for the sake of making the same money that Mr Campbel [sic] has made wants to do the same sort of work that Mr Campbel has done, only at a less price'. Bentham hoped that the panopticon scheme would be discussed in Parliament only after receiving the 'countenance of Administration' and when 'shewn in its proper colours: which it could hardly be said to be if mentioned in so general a way that all the good points' were indistinguishable from the 'tag rag and bobtail of White-Negro drivers' like Duncan Campbell.[40] In other words, the proverbial awfulness of Campbell's regime had so damaged the principle of contract management that Bentham feared the panopticon being associated, however remotely, with the hulks – which were themselves, Bentham seemed to infer, thanks to Campbell's business interests, tainted by association with the slave trade.

In addition to profiting from human misery, Bentham suspected that Campbell exercised an improper influence to protect his commercial interests – a decade later, Bentham's key claim in 'Third Letter to Lord Pelham' was that the manner in which the hulks were conducted was facilitated by patronage and corruption at the highest level.[41] In 1792 Bentham expressed his suspicion that the government's failure to respond to his panopticon offer owed to a 'connection betwixt' Campbell and the Home Secretary, Henry Dundas. He recounted a conversation between Campbell and Bunbury in which the former had lamented that Bunbury 'should be so much my enemy etc.', alluding to Bunbury's attempts to have the hulks replaced with penitentiary imprisonment. Campbell seemed unable to comprehend that Bunbury could be motivated by reformatory intentions, rather than simply seeking to '[set] up a hungry jailor [i.e. Bentham] in the room of an overgrown one [i.e. Campbell]', indicative to Bentham of Campbell's narrowness of mind in only conceiving of convict discipline from the 'mercantile point of view'.[42]

The 'temporary panopticon' plan, 1798

During July 1793 Pitt and Dundas visited Bentham's home where they viewed models of the panopticon and afterwards, as Semple notes, Pitt 'casually signified his approval' and told Bentham to begin preparing to bring the panopticon to fruition.[43] Bentham was subsequently granted £2,000 of public money by the Penitentiary Act of 1794 to fund these preparations, but despite a contract being prepared in 1796,[44] by February 1798 little further progress had been made, largely owing to difficulty in securing an appropriate site on which the government would commit to building a panopticon. To summarize a long story, Earl Spencer objected to the panopticon being built at Battersea Rise, the Wilson family refused to sell a piece of land known as Hanging Wood near Woolwich for the same purpose, and when Bentham subsequently identified an alternative site at Tothill Fields he was opposed by Earl Grosvenor and his son, Viscount Belgrave, the neighbouring landholders. Bentham drafted two bills to legislate for the acquisition of the Tothill Fields site, but in February 1798 was informed that it would need to be an enclosure bill, and therefore required certain conditions to be met before it could be introduced in Parliament – namely the display, for three consecutive weeks in August and September, of notices on church doors announcing the bill.[45] This arcane procedure led Bentham to conclude that ministers had, rather than promoted the universal interest, acted in the private interest of their noble friends by manufacturing this scenario with the intent of ultimately causing the abandonment of the panopticon scheme.

During February 1798, Bentham told William Wilberforce that, in relation to the panopticon, 'every thing centers with me' in the 'sink of perdition – the Hulks'.[46] He sought to force the issue with a plan in which the required notices for the Tothill Fields Bill would be issued and, despite his earlier condemnation of the hulks and their operators, he would himself be awarded the hulk contract. Bentham had in fact first hinted at running the hulks in June 1797[47] but only seriously broached the idea on 23 February 1798 when he complained to George Rose, secretary to the Treasury, that the delays to the panopticon had caused him such financial difficulties that he had been forced to 'shut up my house'. Awarding Bentham the hulk contract would have collateral benefits: it would grant 'present relief', initiate him in convict management, and ensure that the post-panopticon abolition of the hulks would be 'attended with less hazard'. Recognizing that the government would be reluctant to cancel its long-standing relationship with Campbell in favour of a neophyte, Bentham tartly noted that 'no uncommon qualities have hitherto been regarded as requisite' to manage the hulks. Moreover, Campbell's system was 'too radically vitious to admit of much improvement', whereas Bentham would give 'birth to a new and better plan'[48] – an implicit criticism of the administration for having allowed the hulks to fester. Accordingly, during July 1798 he submitted to Rose a proposal, with a request for an advance of £15,000 on the panopticon contract, to build a 'Temporary Penitentiary House of Wood or other slight Materials'[49] capable of holding 2,000 prisoners and managed on the 'same principle and effect' as the permanent panopticon. In addition, he requested the 'present hulk price', £22.1s. to maintain each convict each year, until six months after the land at Tothill Fields had been purchased, whereafter the price would reduce to £13.10s.5d., as agreed in the panopticon contract.[50]

Outwardly, the temporary panopticon sounded hulk-like: a wooden structure on the banks of, or on a mud flat on, the Thames, providing 'Insulation ... as compleat as that of the Hulks' and which would be akin to 'a *Ship at moorings*' since it was 'accessible only by water'.[51] Ministers might reasonably have wondered why this expensive, makeshift prison, which sounded like a hulk, was needed when the hulks existed. While it might seem counter-productive for Bentham to have portrayed the temporary panopticon in this manner, it could also be suggested that Bentham was playing a longer game. Convinced that the government was in no rush to realize his prison, Bentham here proposed a measure that outwardly looked incremental and transitional, yet within its wooden walls his radically different mode of convict management would be implemented, the success of which could stir the government into proceeding with the panopticon proper. That said, even the most developed version of the proposal – which could equally be characterized as a desperate attempt to push the panopticon scheme forward – was spare on detail. Bentham did not, for instance, explain how a sufficiently large wooden structure could be arranged to facilitate the central inspection principle, nor, since it would be situated in a similarly unhealthy locale on the Thames and filled with 2,000 prisoners, how he would have avoided outbreaks of disease that had so assailed the hulks.

Nevertheless, Bentham believed that the temporary panopticon plan would mark a 'decisive' step towards establishing the permanent one, and that the initial reception the idea had received was 'not altogether a discouraging one'.[52] His optimism was misplaced: the proposal was peremptorily rejected in August 1798 when George Rose refused point-blank to 'hear either of Temporary Panopticon – or of the Hulks', and in so doing called over a Mr Lowndes who 'joined with him most cordially in his admiration of the absurdity of the idea'. Rose also observed that Bentham had, in asking for more public money, attempted to take 'very good care of [himself] indeed', realizing Bentham's fear that the panopticon might be characterized as an endeavour in rent-seeking.[53] The manner of the rejection was merely another insult on top of the many Bentham had already endured, and he had to settle only for an order that the notices for a Tothill Fields Bill would be issued – and the land had still not been acquired by the end of 1798.

Around the same time Bentham had attempted to gain control of the hulks, during the summer of 1798, he had also written in more detail about their shortcomings. This arose from his dealings with the Select Committee on Finance which was then examining the expense of the police and convict establishments for its 28th report. George Rose had, in February 1798, encouraged Bentham to consider approaching the Committee on the ground that its authority could force the government to commit to a site for the panopticon,[54] and its report did indeed recommend that the panopticon contract be executed without further delay. (Bentham in fact contributed unofficially to the drafting of the report, being, as R.V. Jackson noted, 'directly responsible for preparing most of the material on New South Wales'.[55]) Bentham's discussion of the hulks did not appear in the Committee's report, but rather in what Semple described as a 'shadow report' of his own.[56] Though there is no complete manuscript of this work and it does not seem possible to entirely separate it from his contributions to the official report, an apparently more-or-less complete section of the shadow report contains an important but little-known discussion of the five 'chronical punishments' in the British penal armoury: i) *Simple* imprisonment'; ii) '*transportation* to an *existing colony*'; iii) confinement with hard labour in a hulk; iv) penitentiary imprisonment; and v) 'transportation for the purpose of hard-labour to a *new Colony* founded for the purpose'.[57]

Regarding the hulks, Bentham sought to undermine the arguments in support of their retention. On the one hand, he admitted that an economic case could be made for the hulks, since the annual cost per convict had been reduced to £22.1s.½d. from £38 in 1776, and the value of the convicts' labour was likely 'more than equivalent' to the overall expense of the hulks.[58] On the other hand, there was a 'point of view superior to economy … out of all doubt with every body', namely 'promiscuous association' among hulk convicts where 'out of the reach of every inspecting eye' they were 'encouraged in guilt by one another'. When released, these unreformed individuals would inevitably reoffend, resulting in great expense through crime as well as in prosecuting, re-imprisoning, and transporting recidivists.[59] In addition, Bentham had recently discovered that the Board of Ordnance provided hulk convicts at Woolwich with '5 pints of Beer' per day, at a cost of nine pence per man. Assuming the tone of a disapproving patrician parliamentarian, Bentham suggested that the 'notion that labour is not to be extracted without the materials of intoxication administered in large quantities is a prejudice that appears … unfriendly to good morals and true economy'.[60] In short, even if the hulks cost nothing to run, not only would the 'ends of punishment remain unattained', but in the long-run they would prove 'of all engines of punishment that were ever invented the most expensive'.[61]

Panopticon versus the south coast hulks: the 'Third Letter to Lord Pelham'

Ultimately the land at Tothill Fields was never acquired and Bentham settled, in November 1799 – after £36,000 was voted to him by the Appropriation Act of that year[62] – for the purchase of a site at Millbank. As was customary in the history of the panopticon scheme, nothing was straightforward: the land was encumbered with leases and Bentham retained designs on Tothill Fields.[63] As he set about making preparations his concerns focused upon how many inmates the panopticon would hold. In August 1799 Bentham had told Charles Long, junior secretary at the Treasury – having been forbidden from contacting Rose, Long's superior – that he required certainty on the matter and suggested he could accommodate 2,000 inmates, double the number in the contract.[64] Long took eight months to respond, confirming on 25 March 1800 that Bentham should indeed prepare to house 2,000 prisoners. Bentham subsequently revised his estimated costings to reflect this change, as well as a recent increase in prices, and accordingly requested more money and a larger site.[65]

This 'increase in terms' was one factor which led to Treasury officials, in August 1800, having suggested to their Home Office counterparts that it 'would not be expedient to carry into Effect this Plan to the whole Extent proposed by Mr. Bentham', and left it to the Home Secretary, the Duke of Portland, to decide 'whether by way of Experiment, it may be fit to carry it into Effect on a more limited Scale' or to 'relinquish the Plan altogether'.[66] Bentham officially only became aware of this decision seven months later in March 1801, when Long requested that he state either the terms on which he would contract for 500 convicts or, if he did not wish to proceed, the compensation he believed he was owed.[67] Bentham concluded that the Treasury and Home Office had, since August 1799, thus spent time concocting a ruse by which to reduce the scale of the panopticon to unviability, with the deliberate failure to communicate that excuse to Bentham until the last moment being a measure of 'sophistry and equivocation' that 'might have commanded a premium from the Academy of Ignatius Loyola'.[68] Bentham might well have cursed himself, though, for being engineered into this position. It was he who had proposed doubling the scale of the original panopticon plan which, by having agreed to it, the government had essentially forced him into asking for more public money to deliver it, making Bentham appear unreasonable and grasping in straitened times. Having then rejected the superficially reasonable – but in reality financially unfeasible – alternative of a panopticon for 500 prisoners, Bentham had allowed the government room in which to raise the possibility of abandoning the scheme altogether. Bentham poured his frustration into writing, from early 1802, 'A Picture of the Treasury', his bitterly amusing 200,000-word history of the panopticon scheme. Part of this project led him to investigate the state of New South Wales and to produce his two 'Letters to Lord Pelham' and 'A Plea for the Constitution'.[69]

The hulks merited only a brief mention in these works, such as where Bentham derisorily noted that the colonial government had, in August 1801, decided to convert its vessel *Supply* into a hulk, thereby confirming the 'complete inefficacy and inutility of everything that is peculiar to the penal colonization system'. As he put it,

> To avoid employing *prisons* and *hulks* at home, expeditions upon expeditions are fitted out, to employ convicts in farming at the antipodes. In the course of a few years a discovery is made ... that nothing is to be done without *hulks* and *prisons* even *there*, though in a situation in which profitable labour under

confinement is impossible; and it is this combination of particular forced idleness, with universal unbridled drunkenness ... that would have been carried on at home at a fraction of the expence.[70]

The hulks were also at the heart of one of Bentham's six legal objections to transportation, namely that people had been sent to New South Wales despite having served, in English gaols and hulks, upwards of five years of their seven-year sentences of transportation. In other words, after a voyage to Port Jackson of five to eight months such individuals became free in little over a year – but since no provision was made to return expirees to Britain, every fixed term of transportation had in effect been illegally converted into banishment for life from the British Isles.[71] (Bentham had himself in 1791 interceded with government to prevent the transportation of William Chapman, who was to be sent to New South Wales despite having served four years of a seven-year sentence on the *Stanislaus* at Woolwich.)[72]

Bentham had originally planned to have 'Third Letter to Lord Pelham' printed around the same time as his works on New South Wales, having closed 'Second Letter to Lord Pelham' with a promise to shortly thereafter provide a 'supplement of very moderate length' examining the '*Hulks* and "*Improved Prisons*"', and completing thereby his 'review of the several modifications of *chronical* punishment ... exemplified or proposed, among Britons and men of British race'.[73] Ostensibly, 'Third Letter to Lord Pelham' is a discussion of the shortcomings of local gaols and hulks in comparison to the panopticon, with the first section seeking to demonstrate that the hulks sat on the 'scale of utility in the *midway* between that of *penitentiary* imprisonment taken without the benefit of the *panopticon* improvements, and that of *penal colonization* taken on the footing on which it stands in New South Wales'.[74] Bentham's essential message was that the hulks were 'pernicious', though 'a *less* pernicious' receptacle for convicts than New South Wales[75] – and yet the panopticon had been sacrificed to persist with the latter, the worst of all forms of punishment. (Only a short time after writing this passage, Bentham gave a contrary opinion to Benjamin Hobhouse MP, that 'the penal Colonization system is, in every point of view, so bad ... as to be absolutely *untenable*', yet the hulks were 'if possible still worse'.)[76]

Yet 'Third Letter to Lord Pelham' is considerably more than a comparison of modes of punishment. It constituted not only part of Bentham's assault of 1802–3 on the utility and legality of British penal policy but was also an exposé of the corruption and patronage exercised in a clandestine plot to cancel the panopticon, thereby illegally setting aside the will of Parliament. To appreciate the work in its full context, though, it should be read alongside 'On the Dispensing power exercised by the Duke of Portland and his confederates', essentially a companion piece which similarly exists only in manuscript.[77] 'On the Dispensing power'[78] is the longest section of 'A Picture of the Treasury' and is chiefly concerned with an 'extra-financial and super-parliamentary' letter,[79] dated 14 October 1799, from the Duke of Portland to the Lords Commissioners of the Treasury.

In this letter, Portland claimed that the national penitentiaries provided for by the Penitentiary Acts of 1779 and 1794 were intended to house convicts who could not be accommodated in English local prisons until such time as they were to be transported, and that the panopticon, if it was to be built, should also be a holding depot. Semple rightly suggests that this was a 'perverse' reading of the legislation, since neither Act could 'reasonably be read as setting up a temporary receptacle' for convicts.[80] In addition, Portland stated that it would be 'very inexpedient' to remove convicts from

> the Country Gaols [to the panopticon], unless the crowded state of these Gaols should render it absolutely necessary, for it would naturally tend not only to check that spirit of improvement which now so universally prevails … but would be the means of the Gaols themselves being neglected by which the greater part of the Prisoners who are now, or may be hereafter, confined in them, would necessarily be sent to the Panopticon where the Expences attending their custody must be borne by Government instead of being defrayed by the respective Counties.[81]

In other words, Portland also sought to ensure that the financial burden of imprisonment was paid for locally, rather than by Westminster. The letter was Bentham's proof that Portland, his Under Secretary John King, and the Home Office's criminal counsel William Baldwin had illegally obstructed and prevented the establishment of the panopticon, not owing to any philosophical or practical conviction about how criminals should be treated, but rather to a wish to ensure that criminals could be cheaply accommodated in England and subsequently transported, and as a favour to noble landowners who did not, for their own selfish reasons, wish to see the panopticon built near their estates. Meanwhile, the clandestine nature of this conspiracy had been revealed to Bentham in October 1800, when in somewhat strange circumstances, he first saw Portland's letter.[82]

Bentham contended that the letter revealed that Portland had committed three 'impeachable Heresies'. First, Portland had sought to 'prevent the execution of an imperative Act of Parliament', i.e. the Penitentiary Act of 1794. Second, he had professed 'for the same purpose an intention of crowding' local gaols who should, by rights, have been sent to the panopticon, 'in contempt' of the Penitentiary Act of 1779. Third, Portland had assumed the 'power of taxation' by 'throwing the expence of such Convicts upon the contributors to the Poor Rates, instead of the general Fund assigned by Parliament'. (Bentham's lawyer friend – and future Solicitor General – Samuel Romilly agreed with his interpretation.[83]) It should be noted, though, that Bentham believed that the letter was really the work of the two 'Ex Lawyers', King and Baldwin, and that Portland merely 'had the unnecessary folly' to have signed it 'with his own hand'.[84]

Bentham expressed astonishment that 'in the reign of George the third – a dispensing power', emblematic of Stuart tyranny, 'should not only have been assumed but exercised'. He considered it impossible for Portland and King to have misconstrued the Penitentiary Acts – besides, allowing the defence of misinterpretation might, Bentham feared, set a precedent for any official with responsibility 'for the execution of any branch of the law – to unmake or even to make whatever laws he please'.[85] Portland was thus 'an usurper ... of the authority of Parliament' and his conduct constituted a 'state crime'.[86] Bentham sought to demonstrate that Portland was conscious of having acted criminally, though did concede that the Home Secretary had not acted out of personal malice but had instead sought to 'pay a compliment to some very Noble and Right Honourable persons', only to find himself 'embar[r]assed that there was a foolish law in their way'.[87] It was merely Bentham's rotten luck that he, 'a worm', had incidentally been 'crushed' with the panopticon.[88] The only person to whom Bentham showed 'On the Dispensing power' was Romilly who, though in agreement that Portland could not have innocently misinterpreted the Penitentiary Acts, did not see sufficient evidence of a conspiracy 'to assume a legislative power, etc' and warned Bentham that the work was 'in point of law, a libel on the duke, and the more a libel for being true, cannot, I think, be doubted'.[89] What Romilly would have thought of the vituperative 'Third Letter to Lord Pelham' can only be speculated upon.

If 'On the Dispensing power' explored Portland's motives for and methods of relinquishing the panopticon, 'Third Letter to Lord Pelham' turned to the effects wrought upon the hulks in consequence, as well as the subsequent attempt by Pelham, after he succeeded Portland as Home Secretary in July 1801, to cover up those effects. Bentham summarized the policy of the Home Office as one of

> emaciating his Majesty's subjects by "long confinement" in illegally and purposely crowded Jails, for producing Jail-Fevers in them or whatever other miseries might be the result of their being "crowded" ... for exercising over his fellow subjects, by the secret will of this servant of the Crown out of sight of his royal master, that authority which, if attempted to be exercised by the master, a Hampden would have resisted with his blood.[90]

As for the hulks, they too had been crowded with 'Convicts designed for the Penitentiary House by Parliament', an action that had 'not been without its fruit ... sweet, I suppose, to the taste of those who cultivate it, bitter I should have supposed, to the taste of every man who has any sense remaining either of humanity or justice'.[91]

The 'fruit' in question was the appalling disease and mortality aboard the hulks at Portsmouth and Langstone harbours, which had been revealed in a report by the philanthropist James Neild and the local MP Sir Henry Mildmay.[92] Neild and Mildmay had found that during 1801 there had been an average of 500 convicts aboard *La Fortuneé*, 120 (24 per cent) of whom had died that year, while from 1 January 1802 to 16 March 1802 a further 34 convicts had died, even though, as Bentham noted, 'the number alive was by that time reduced to 300'.[93] Bentham calculated that if that rate were maintained throughout 1802, another 165 of *La Fortuneé*'s men would be dead by the end of the year. In an especially vicious passage in which he sarcastically quoted from Portland's letter of 14 October 1799, Bentham pointed out that the Home Office's surreptitious attempt to cancel the panopticon had directly caused the deaths of dozens of convicts: 'Nobly done, Duke of Portland and Lord Pelham! how convenient to Mr Addington[94] in his accounts! What a relief to the only grand grievance that presses upon most Noble minds, *"the expences attending the custody"* of these wretches *"borne by Government"*'.[95] At least, Bentham drily remarked, sickness aboard *La Fortuneé* was 'not without its consolations' since convict discipline had improved: 'Among the dying, insurrection difficult: – among the dead, impossible'.[96]

In a discarded draft Bentham had been even more direct, enquiring 'to whom do so many departed wretches owe their deaths? ...

to the Duke who chalked out the plan, and to the Lord who follows it'. Was this a charge of murder, Bentham asked?

> Oh no, my Lord! no such thing! Homicide in retail – destruction of a single life … homicide in private life – homicide by low people – homicide for a few pounds or shillings – such homicide may indeed be murder: homicide by wholesale – destruction of lives by hundreds – destruction contemplated for months or years – homicide in high life – homicide in such high office – homicide to oblige a friend or so … such homicide, if it were homicide, would be without punishment – without delinquency – without danger – without blame! Oh no, my Lord! so far from murder, I charge not so much as *homicide* – not so much as excusable homicide – certainly not justifiable homicide – upon the author of all these Deaths.[97]

The key question for Bentham was why, since convicts had died at an alarming rate for some time, no official investigation had been mounted. Neild and Mildmay were private citizens who had only been alerted to conditions on the hulks by a letter from James Chapple, Keeper of the New Prisons at Bodmin who, when delivering 11 prisoners to *La Fortuneé*, had been shocked at the sight of the hulk's 'half-starved' convicts.[98] After Neild had shown Chapple's letter to Pelham, orders were sent to the south coast requiring those in charge of the hulks to provide Neild and Mildmay with 'every information [they] should require'.[99] It was telling, Bentham remarked, that no Home Office official, 'so well paid for looking after these things', had hitherto investigated and he expected that the convicts would have been 'rotten … before any of these Under Omrahs would have thought of disturbing the slumbers of the Subahdar by so much of a whisper [of] what was passing in the *Black-Hole*'.[100] Of course, an official investigation would become public knowledge, exposing what the Home Office preferred to be hidden, and it was thus a 'happy opportunity' that the harmless Neild and Mildmay had offered to visit. That advance notice of the visit had been sent to the south coast was proof to Bentham of the Home Office's mendacity, since it gave time for temporary improvements: the 'filth might be shoveled away: – that eatable food might for the moment take place of the uneatable … that every mouth might have a padlock put to it'.[101]

Bentham expected that the alarming details of Neild and Mildmay's report would have caused Pelham to 'start out of his sleep' and he imagined how the Home Secretary would respond:

Does he change the system? Does he bethink himself of law? of engagements? of a system of unintermitted inspection? of appropriate separation and aggregation? of universal industry? Does [it] occur to him to transfer the undistroyed remnant from the clutches of their distroyers to the hand of a guardian already named by Parliament? of a keeper acting under thousands of eyes? … In this way, or in any other way, does he make, or for a moment think of making, any the smallest change in the system … of destruction carried on under a pretence of management?[102]

In other words, Bentham found, not even the death of dozens of his fellow men, with the prospect of many more to come, could stir Pelham into following the law and proceeding with the panopticon. Instead, to continue with his illegal course and hide reality from public view 'he employs a gentleman … he creates a place',[103] discussion of which constitutes the main topic of the latter part of 'Third Letter to Lord Pelham'.

That 'gentleman' was the Bow Street magistrate Aaron Graham, who on 25 March 1802 had been appointed Inspector of the Temporary Places of Confinement of Felons, the 'place' created by the Hulks Act of 1802.[104] For an annual salary of £350 Graham was required to make four inspections of the hulks each year and a full report to Parliament at the start of each session, though in instances of 'extreme or pressing Necessity' he could at any time report to the Court of King's Bench.[105] Bentham lamented that the new office had not been filled by an individual with the 'will to fulfil the duties of it', remarking that 'under Lord Pelham, such requisites are not required'.[106] Had Pelham sincerely wished to reform the hulks then the job would have been offered to the 'indefatigable' James Neild – 'I have called Neild a second Howard', eulogized Bentham, 'but with more propriety I might have called Howard a second Neild' – yet Pelham had not even consulted Neild about potential candidates.[107] Bentham was even willing to do the job himself without taking 'a single penny' though suspected that he 'would not have been to your Lordship's taste'.[108] Appointing Graham also appears to have rendered superfluous the services of Sir Jeremiah Fitzpatrick, Inspector of Health for Land Forces, who since September 1797 had, without remuneration, examined the health of the hulk convicts at Portsmouth prior to their embarkation for New South Wales. Aware of Graham's appointment, in June 1802 Fitzpatrick asked Pelham whether, since he had not been called upon since the convict ships *Coromandel* and *Perseus* had sailed four months previously, his attendance at the hulks was still required. If not, he requested back-pay 'as such Services had merited'.[109] Had Bentham been aware that the Home Office had discarded Fitzpatrick's free, expert service in favour of their placeman, it would surely have confirmed his view that the new Inspectorship had been created with sinister intent.

Bentham's criticism of Graham's appointment had two key features. First, it was an exercise of patronage for a friend and client, and second, the job was a sinecure by which the Home Office had purchased a 'screen' for the abuses it had itself created, in order to fool the public that matters were being addressed 'while the public pays for it'.[110] As Bentham put it, 'Put in a sure man and give it him in charge to cover it up: [and] the pretence for meddling will thus be taken from all such busy-bodies' like Neild and Mildmay, thereby ensuring that 'abuse contains concealment; favourites provision; Ministers patronage'.[111] In short, for Bentham the hulks had by 1802 become a nexus of the corruptive practices which, in preparing his later programme of democratic reform, he sought to eliminate from the British establishment.

Though the patronage was exercised by Pelham, Bentham claimed that it was done at the behest of John King – when Pelham tapped 'the wainscot as usual for the gentleman by whom every thing is done', in came King 'with a friend in his pocket for the place'.[112] (Bentham considered King to be the real power in the Home Office, the puppet master who pulled Pelham's 'wires'.)[113] Graham had, Bentham alleged, done well from his friendship with King. Since becoming a police magistrate in 1791 Graham had subsisted on a salary of £400, which had been increased to £500 by the Metropolitan Police Magistrates Act of 1802.[114] 'God knows why' that augmentation had been necessary, Bentham wondered, but to mask the patronizing of Graham, the raise had been granted to every London magistrate and the public purse imposed upon. The Magistrates and Hulks Acts (sardonically referred to elsewhere by Bentham as the *'Police-Magistrate super-pensioning'* and the *'Blind-Inspectorship'* Acts)[115] had thus been 'made *uno flatu* for one gentleman' and Graham's compliance purchased by increasing his salary by £450.[116]

Admitting that he had only 'rumour – notoriety' as evidence of these charges, Bentham presented four 'antecedent features' as proof. First, the evils of the hulks had long endured 'under the very *noses* ... of such a pyramid of official personages whose duty it was to prevent it'. Second, nothing but 'neglect' had been shown to those who sought to remedy those evils. Third, 'no signs of displeasure' had been directed at the hulk contractors by the 'silent and motionless' officials of the Home Office. Fourth, Portland and Pelham, the 'very patrons and protectors of the abuse', had turned to King for a remedy despite it being King's responsibility to have prevented it in the first place. The inspectorship was thus a '*douceur*' for King's friend Graham, though it required 'more than a hecatomb' to grant it.[117]

Bentham then turned to assess how well Graham had performed the duties of the Inspector of Hulks. Though the requirement to produce four reports per year was but a 'beggarly account of empty duty' Bentham found that the 'sleepy guardian' of the hulks had yet fallen short of this low bar.[118] The most recent session of Parliament had begun on 16 November 1802, and Graham had failed to present his report before it adjourned six weeks later. Having made private enquiries about Graham's exertions on the south coast, Bentham had been told that Graham had not visited for 'near six months; he was at Portsmouth about three months since but did not come on board the Hulk'.[119] Bentham alleged that Graham, a native of nearby Gosport with 'connections at Portsmouth', had found 'inspection enough for Portsmouth, but there was none left for the Hulks'.[120] Even though the hulks were so close to where Graham was staying 'humanity, official duty … the positive injunction of an Act of Parliament – all together could not prevail upon the gentleman for these few hundred yards'.[121] That the apparently idle and uncaring Graham had not been reprimanded led Bentham to conclude that 'every thing *almost* is as it should be', and that the 'place either ought never to have been created, or ought now to be abolished'.[122] It was a place, after all, which relied upon the 'non-existence' of the panopticon.[123]

Despite the attempted cover-up, information nevertheless leaked from the '*Black Holes*' of the south coast.[124] Whereas in the two preceding 'Letters to Lord Pelham' Bentham had discussed only in general terms the impact of government policy upon the lives of transported convicts, in 'Third Letter to Lord Pelham' he gave a serving hulk convict a voice. He reproduced sections of a letter, dated 11 October 1802, by Samuel Hadfield, who on 8 July 1801 had been sentenced at the Chester assizes to seven years' transportation for petty larceny, and who had been received aboard the *Captivity* on 18 February 1802.[125] (Such was Bentham's distrust of Home Office officials he refused to name Hadfield in 'Third Letter to Lord Pelham' for fear that the 'scourge of the tyrant' would be brought down upon the convict. Though willing to name Hadfield to a House of Commons committee, he would not while Pelham and 'least of all' John King were in post.)[126]

Having been *'double ironed'* and put to hard labour, Hadfield complained that when not at work he and his fellows were *'so close shut down betwixt decks'* that we *cannot keep ourselves clean'*, were *'raw with lice'* and *'break out all over sores, and look so bad and so yellow, that you would not take them to be Englishmen at all'*. Food was plentiful, but the 'quality is so bad, and cooking so nasty, that nothing but clemming [i.e. starving one's self] can force a man to eat it'. Hadfield longed to have been one of those who in September 1802 were embarked upon the *Glatton* for New South Wales, since the hulk was 'a very bad place ... it is impossible to live here long'.[127] Here was a first-hand account of the evils which should have been eliminated by a capable Inspector and further evidence for Bentham's conclusion, in June 1803, that 'In design – conduct – result – in every thing', Graham's appointment was 'as scandalous a job as a corrupt or weak man or both need wish to organize, or an honest man expose'.[128] Had Bentham proceeded to have 'Third Letter to Lord Pelham' printed it may have constituted his attempt to do just that.

Graham's appointment would have made an ideal case-study for Bentham's 1822 work 'Economy as applied to Office', in which he established the necessary requirements for good government, summarized by the motto 'Aptitude maximized, Expence minimized'. Good government required of its officials three types of 'appropriate official aptitude': 'moral aptitude', which required a functionary to promote the universal interest, regardless of their own particular interest or that of their superiors; 'intellectual aptitude', which required a functionary to have the requisite knowledge and judgement; and 'active aptitude', that the functionary will do the task required of them.[129] On this standard, Graham was entirely unsuitable for office.

Can Bentham's criticism of Aaron Graham's inspectorship, and of government policy with regard to the hulks, be sustained? Though somewhat obscure, Graham had powerful connections. Having served in the Royal Navy from 1779 to 1791, he was secretary to four successive governors of Newfoundland, in 1789 and 1790 was a judge of the Newfoundland civil court, and according to a modern biographer was 'incomparably the greatest civil servant in the history of Newfoundland'.[130] Upon returning to England and being appointed a police magistrate in 1791, Graham was, according to his obituary, 'employed in various confidential situations by government',[131] working on behalf of John King and the Home Office. Such clandestine work included having been sent in 1797 to investigate the mutinies at Spithead and the Nore,[132] and in reporting on the state of the peace in Staffordshire during the dearth of winter 1800–1.[133] In addition Graham had spent some time working at the south coast hulks during 1801, prior to being appointed Inspector. According to Graham's obituary, the mortality at the Portsmouth hulks had caused Portland 'to pay attention ... and, luckily for the sake of humanity', Graham was sent to investigate.[134] Having accordingly prepared a report on the hulks during February 1801[135] Graham considered himself 'compleat in the History of Convicts and Convict Contracts' and justified in concluding the 'present mode' of conducting the hulks to be 'disgraceful to the Nation', claiming that he had 'the strongest proof' that 'iniquitous practices' had endured 'for several years'.[136]

Graham and the Home Office were, then, aware of the problems on the hulks and their management required change. On 17 June 1801 Portland presented to the Treasury a proposal, probably drawn up by Graham, 'for the better care and management' of the convicts at the Portsmouth and Langstone Harbour hulks. The proposal recommended that the existing hulk contract be cancelled and that the government take direct control and oversight of the system, with the only role for contractors being to supply clothing and victuals. The proposal was approved by the Treasury on 24 August 1801[137] and two days later, at the request of Pelham, the new Home Secretary, Graham provided estimates for 'my proposed Establishment for the Convict Hulks at Portsmouth and Langston'.[138] Graham was thus at the heart of the shift in policy, in which the existing hulks *Lion* and *La Fortunée*, along with the hospital ship *Laurel*, were replaced by the *Captivity* and *Portland*. (Bentham may have appreciated the irony of a hulk being named after one of the panopticon's nemeses.) During late 1801 and early 1802 Graham personally oversaw the implementation of the new system,[139] which came into force on 1 April 1802.[140] His correspondence with the Home Office during this period demonstrates apparent engagement with the task at hand as well as concern for convict welfare. For instance, he was particularly exercised when told that the new Langstone Harbour hulk would be smaller than expected, warning that this would perpetuate the 'old improper mode' of 'crowding so many people into so small a space' and risking a repeat of the disease the new system was introduced to prevent. In addition, it would be impossible to incorporate a chapel – 'the most material point of reform' – in a smaller vessel.[141]

Graham was even more forthright about conditions on the soon to be replaced *La Fortunée*, observing in December 1801 – and anticipating Bentham's interpretation of Neild and Mildmay's report – that to embark convicts on the vessel was 'actually to send one fourth of them out of the world'.[142] Much of Graham's work during early 1802 was, until the transfer to the new hulk was completed, directed towards preventing sickness. He had *La Fortunée* fumigated, ensured that new and clean bedding was provided, and that convalescent convicts received a full ration, of which they had been deprived by the contractor who Graham, 'if it were not for fear of creating an alarm ... would not hesitate to indict'.[143] In other words, for several months prior to being appointed Inspector in March 1802, Graham had essentially acted in that capacity – even referring to himself as 'the Inspector' in his December 1801 report.[144] While such presumption might support Bentham's contention that Graham's appointment was an inside job, Graham's knowledge of policing, connections on the south coast, prior work at the hulks, and having shaped the new regulations suggest that he was at least qualified for the post. Moreover, Graham's apparently genuine concern for convict welfare is at odds with Bentham's portrayal of him as a feckless tool of his patrons, and that he had been sent to the hulks during 1801 indicates that the Home Office was concerned enough about reports from there to have investigated.

Bentham was correct in his claim that, by the end of 1802, Graham had not attended the hulks for some time and had failed to submit a report to Parliament. Yet there were extenuating circumstances, of which Bentham does not appear to have been aware until at least 4 February 1803, when Graham finally submitted a short report.[145] Graham explained that, after being appointed Inspector on 25 March 1802, he went immediately to oversee the fitting out of the *Captivity* and *Portland* and the transfer of the convicts to them in preparation for the institution of the new system. Around this time, Graham issued detailed regulations for running the hulks, including requiring their captains to keep detailed records of each convict, to carry out daily inspections, and to publicly proclaim rations so that convicts knew what they were due to receive – measures which Bentham would surely have approved.[146] Once the new system was in effect Graham sent a private report to Pelham.[147] He made 'another very full Report' of a visit at the end of June 1802, before visiting once more during September 1802. Graham acknowledged that he should 'have made my next visit of enquiry' by the end of 1802 but had been 'prevented by indisposition, which, for several months past, has ... confined me to my room'. Graham was 'convalescent' by February 1803 and hoped soon to be able 'to attend again to this material part of my duty'.[148] In these circumstances, Bentham's allegations of idleness seem a little unfair.

Graham's report painted a rather rosier picture than had Neild and Mildmay on their visit a year earlier. The new hulks were 'comfortably and well fitted out' and the officers of the *Captivity* 'humane and attentive', though he admitted to unspecified 'irregularities' aboard the *Portland*. The convicts' health had improved, with but a few sick prisoners on each vessel, which Graham found remarkable considering the 'dreadful sickness which prevailed in the old Hulks'. Though the convicts were well behaved, Graham conceded that they had been less productive than the men of the Woolwich hulks, largely owing to the sickness aboard the old vessels, which had delayed the transfer of the men to the new hulks.[149]

Though Bentham did no further work on 'Third Letter to Lord Pelham' after mid-January 1803, he does appear to have contemplated further lines of attack on the hulks. During February 1803 James Neild had forwarded him a letter by the *Portland* convict George Lee, who made several allegations about conditions on the hulk.[150] Confined to the *Portland*, Lee found himself ironed among the 'degrading ranks', and a 'mute ... witness of the sordid, corrupting and oppressive measures of the ignorant and mercenary Guardians of the offenders of the law'. Half of the *Portland*'s convicts were 'Johnny Raws, i.e. country Bumpkins in whose composition there is more of the fool than rogue', but the remainder were 'irrecoverable by long habits' who, when released, would 'return to their vomit like the dog in Scripture'. Lee closed by claiming that 'Sodomy rages so shamefully ... that the Surgeon & myself were more than once threatened with assassination for striving to put a stop to it'.[151] Sir John Carter, the mayor of Portsmouth, believed Lee's allegations were true and been transmitted 'to Lord Pelham & to many others'.[152]

It was to Lee and Carter's letters that Bentham referred when he suggested to Romilly in early March 1803 that he had 'distinct evidence' from both Portsmouth and Woolwich,[153] 'and – what is more – equally distinct evidence of Lord Pelham's having notice of it' that 'Crimes, distinguished by the name of unnatural, are endemical not to say universal', and as the hulks were 'emptied of their contents these crimes flow out with them'. Bentham also claimed that, based upon 'indubitable evidence', an 'initiation of this sort stands in the place of garnish' – that is, instead of being robbed or extorted upon arriving at the hulks (the 'garnish'), they were sexually assaulted.[154] These, Bentham claimed, were the 'abominations which Lord Grosvenor has *obtained*' by preventing the building of the panopticon at Tothill Fields, and which Pelham and Addington[155] had '*decreed*' by persisting with Portland's setting aside of Bentham's prison.

In a draft of a letter to William Wilberforce, dated March 1803 but which went unsent, Bentham indicated that he had wished to submit 'to the public' a question in regard to these claims about the hulks: who was 'most guilty', the individual prisoner who committed such 'crimes' or the Home Secretary who oversaw the hulk establishment?[156] The question went unposed since, as he explained to Romilly in March 1803, 'These things I would not put into the ostensible [Third] Letter, because in that place they would have been threats'.[157] But by June 1803, as time ran out on the panopticon scheme, Bentham appears to have contemplated resorting to such threats when he sent to Charles Bunbury a copy of the unsent letter to Wilberforce by way of 'shewing what I meant to do and mean to do if forced'.[158] What Bentham meant to do, in addition to publishing his writings on New South Wales to force the government to proceed with the panopticon, may have included a scare campaign about the hulks. Ultimately, this thought was never acted upon, as in June 1803 Bentham was informed that the government did not wish to proceed with the panopticon scheme.

Conclusion

Almost a decade after drafting 'Third Letter to Lord Pelham' Bentham retained both his anger that the government had preferred the hulks to his panopticon, as well as his conviction that their continuance had been secured by corruption and patronage. When in 1810 fresh moves were made to finally erect a national penitentiary, Wilberforce had encouraged Bentham to believe that the panopticon might now be favourably received.[159] Ultimately the three reports of 1811–12 of the Penitentiary Committee[160] chaired by George Holford signalled a decisive rejection of both the panopticon and Bentham's philosophy of convict management, and paved the way for the construction of Millbank Penitentiary.[161] The rejection was officially confirmed, despite Bentham's efforts, in February 1813 by Viscount Sidmouth, the Home Secretary.[162]

During September 1812 Bentham had attempted to prevent that rejection by countering the Holford Committee's objections to the panopticon.[163] As Semple notes, Bentham was 'particularly incensed' by one of the Committee's criticisms,[164] namely that in the panopticon 'by night as well as by day, several males will co-exist in the same apartment' and that 'irregularities of the sexual appetite will ... unavoidably take place'.[165] This, Bentham seethed, was the 'grand argument relied upon' and he wondered how this objection could be raised against 'an unremittingly inspected prison' as opposed to 'an uninspected apartment in a ship'. 'Two measures', he continued, had been 'predetermined *upon* – viz. the *suppression* of *Panopticon*, and ... the *preservation* of the *Hulks*', on board which the 'prevalence of these practices was a matter of *notoriety*'. Setting aside for the moment that Bentham appeared to have himself briefly contemplated in 1803 capitalizing upon reports of sexual assault on the hulks, in 1812 he concluded that the panopticon was thus to be *'blackened'* in the eyes of the public. He also considered the Holford Committee's discussion of the hulks in its third report a *'whitewash'*, since sufficient mental gymnastics were performed to on one hand find the hulks fundamentally 'defective', but on the other to suggest that they were 'not so bad as to be *incorrigible*' and so *'ought to be preserved'* – going so far as to propose measures 'to *lessen, if not altogether remove the evil'*.[166]

During 1802–3 Bentham had argued that the government's persistence with the hulks over the panopticon, and the appointment of Aaron Graham as Inspector, was indicative of corruption and jobbery. Little had changed by 1812: the panopticon was to be set aside again despite the wretched state of the hulks, and the Holford Committee had proposed that this be remedied by replacing the Inspector with an 'Overseer' to take 'superintendence and control of every part of the Hulk Establishment' and have responsibility for 'a subordinate officer' at each site.[167] Bentham bemoaned the creation of *'Offices! offices!* ... the nests of offices promised, with the expences attached to them, innumerable. To begin with, a few thousands a year in offices ... Reformation is it still tardy? a few thousands more to quicken it; and so on till the cure is perfected'. It was, therefore, 'among the *maxims* of Honourable Gentlemen' motivated by *'sinister interest'*, that if 'in an establishment of this sort any thing is amiss, it is for want of offices', and 'upon the ruins' of the panopticon was to be built an 'accumulation of job, profusion, and arbitrary power'. Worst of all, who had made this possible? None other than Aaron Graham, whose long reign as Inspector had been 'so *efficient*' and 'so *well approved*' of by the Home Office that a 'building, of which *universal*, and *simultaneous*, and *perpetual inspectability* is the undeniable characteristic' could be readily discarded.[168] Graham eventually resigned and retired at the end of 1814, and in July 1815 John Henry Capper was appointed Superintendent of the Hulks;

Capper was then a clerk in the Home Office which, had he commented upon it, would surely have seemed to Bentham like the appointment of another trusty.[169]

While Bentham's frustrations at the failure of the panopticon scheme were, in 1802–3, most famously directed towards the New South Wales penal colony, they spilled over into a wider critique of British penal policy – including of the hulks, as this chapter has sought to demonstrate – as well as of the corruptive, sinister interest at the heart of government at the turn of the nineteenth century. 'Third Letter to Lord Pelham' is thus at once an integral part of Bentham's writings on Australia as well as an important text in Bentham's thinking on wider matters. Taken together, Bentham's three 'Letters to Lord Pelham' are fundamental to the story of the failure of the panopticon, though the full story of the scheme can only be truly told with the production of a complete edition of all of Bentham's many published and unpublished panopticon writings.

Notes

1 For Bentham's attempt to use his writings on Australia to salvage the ailing panopticon scheme see 'Editorial Introduction' in Bentham, ed. Causer and Schofield 2022, xxxiii–lxi, lxxi–lxxxix; Causer 2019.

2 19 Geo. III, c. 74 provided for the construction of two national penitentiaries, one for men and one for women. Ultimately, it was not until 1816 when the national penitentiary opened at Millbank.

3 Bentham to Pitt, 23 January 1791, in Bentham, ed. Milne 1981a, 223–4.

4 These were 'No. 1. Outline of the Plan of Construction of a Panoptican [sic] Penitentiary House, as designed by Jeremy Bentham of Lincoln's Inn Esqr.' in Bentham, ed. Milne 1981a, 225–6, which outlined the architectural arrangement of the building, and 'No. 2. Outline of a Plan of Management for a Panopticon Penitentiary House' in ibid, 226–9.

5 Bentham Papers, University College London Library Special Collections (hereafter UC), cl. 363. Roman numerals refer to the boxes in which the papers are placed, Arabic to the leaves within each box.

6 Brief mentions of Bentham's views on the hulks can be found in Semple 1993, 48–51, 55–6, 202–12, 250–1; Hume 1973, 703–21. The most widely available popular histories of the hulks are Branch Johnston 1970 [1957], and Campbell 2001. Scholarly accounts of the early hulks can be found in Oldham 1990, 33–64; Frost 2012, 55–81; and Devereaux 1999, 405–33. James 2017, 3–24 discusses the fates of some of the hulks' early prisoners; McKay 2020 and her forthcoming monograph promise to considerably widen our understanding of the hulks and the lives of their prisoners.

7 Bentham, ed. Causer and Schofield 2022, 249–302.

8 For more detail see Causer 2019.

9 4 Geo. III, c. 11.

10 Maxwell-Stewart 2018, 192. See also Ekirch 1990; Morgan and Rushton 2004.

11 4 Geo. III, c. 11, § 1.

12 Devereaux 1999, 413.

13 By December 1776 all of the convicts housed on the *Tayloe* had either enlisted in the military, left England or been pardoned, and the ship was closed down: see Frost 2012, 58.

14 16 Geo. III, c. 43.

15 Frost 2012, 61.
16 Carey 2019, 257–81.
17 *Morning Chronicle*, 6 August 1777.
18 UC cxvii. 1–2. These manuscripts are headed 'CRIT. JUR. CRIM.', that is 'Critical Jurisprudence Criminal', and consist of 400 pages of short discussions from which Bentham drew upon as notes: see Schofield 2019, 65–74, at 67 n. A (not completely accurate) transcript of Bentham's notes on his visit to the hulks appears as 'Appendix 3. Conditions on the Hulks, 1778' in Oldham 1990, 201–2.
19 Semple 1993, 55. That is, John Howard, the philanthropist and prison reformer.
20 Bentham, ed. Bowring 1838–43, iv. 153.
21 UC cxvii. 1–2. The *Censor*'s hospital was supervised by the notorious pickpocket George Barrington (c. 1755–1804), with whom Bentham spoke. Barrington, transported in 1791, is best known for his name having been attached to the allonymous Barrington 1795 which was followed by numerous derivatives, translations, and pirated works: see Garvey 2008.
22 UC cxvii. 2.
23 Bentham, ed. Bowring 1838–43, iv. 165–6.
24 Devereaux 1999, 416.
25 UC cxvii. 1; 16 Geo. III, c. 43, § 1.
26 Semple 1993, 108.
27 UC cxvii. 2.
28 UC cxvii. 2.
29 Bentham, ed. Bowring 1838–43, iv. 144, 141.
30 UC cxvii. 2.
31 *Journals of the House of Commons* (1777–8), vol. xxxvi. 927.
32 Bentham, ed. Bowring 1838–43, iv. 120–1.
33 Bentham to Reverend John Foster, April/May 1778, Bentham, ed. Sprigge 1968, 100.
34 The bill was presented to the Commons on 11 May 1778 but did not pass. A revised bill, presented in April 1779, subsequently passed into law as that year's Penitentiary Act.
35 Bentham 1778, 1, 3.
36 Bentham 1778, 96–7.
37 Bentham 1778, 99.
38 A factor in this hardening may have been the critical report, of 15 April 1778, of the committee inquiring into the operation of the Hulks Act of 1776: see *Journals of the House of Commons* (1777–8), vol. xxxvi. 926–32.
39 Bentham to Pitt, 10 February 1792, Bentham, ed. Milne 1981a, 359.
40 Bentham to Bunbury, 30 May 1792, Bentham, ed. Milne 1981a, 366–7.
41 Campbell certainly had powerful connections: he was consulted by William Eden in the drawing up of a new hulks bill in January 1788, while in early 1797 he successfully appealed to Sir Evan Nepean, First Secretary to the Admiralty, and George Rose, Secretary to the Treasury, to have his son John added to the hulks contract: see Campbell 2005, reel 4, 12, 18–19.
42 Bentham to Francis Burton, 2–3 July 1792, Bentham, ed. Milne 1981a, 371.
43 Semple 1993, 95. See also Bentham to Earl Spencer, 13 August 1793, in Bentham, ed. Milne 1981a, 446.
44 See 'Draft of a Contract between the Lords Commissioners of the Treasury and Jeremy Bentham Esquire', Appendix F. 3 in 'Twenty-Eighth Report from the Select Committee on Finance, &c. Police, including Convict Establishments', 26 June 1798, in Lambert ed. 1975, vol. cxii. 64–77.
45 Semple 1993, 192–217; Hume 1973, 708–21.
46 Bentham to Wilberforce, 27 February 1798, in Bentham, ed. Dinwiddy 1984, 15.
47 Bentham to Rose, 22 June 1797, in Bentham, ed. Milne 1981b, 368–9.
48 Bentham to Rose, 23 February 1798, in Bentham, ed. Dinwiddy 1984, 7–8.
49 Bentham to Rose, 30 July 1798, in Bentham, ed. Dinwiddy 1984, 5. Bentham also described his plan to Sir John William Anderson, MP for London, in mid-June 1798: Bentham, ed. Dinwiddy 1984, 41–4. A draft of the full proposal, in Bentham's hand, is at UC cxvii. 85–9, with a fair copy at UC cxvii. 90–3.
50 UC cxvii. 90–1.
51 UC cxvii. 91; Bentham to Rose, 2–3 April 1798, Bentham, ed. Dinwiddy 1984, 20–1.

52 'June 23d, 1798. – Examination of Jeremy Bentham, Esquire', Appendix G. in 'Twenty-Eighth Report', in Lambert ed. 1975, vol. cxii. 79–80.

53 Bentham to Abbot, *c.* 10 August 1798, in Bentham, ed. Dinwiddy 1984, 62.

54 At the same time, Rose indicated that the Committee would be 'competent to consider of your Proposal for taking Care of the Convicts in the Hulks': Rose to Bentham, 24 February 1798, in Bentham, ed. Dinwiddy 1984, 9–10.

55 Jackson 1988, 42–59. See also Semple 1993, 203–17; Hume 1973, 717–19. Bentham had a direct line to the Committee: his friend Reginald Pole Carew was responsible for drawing up the report, and the Committee's chair was Bentham's step-brother Charles Abbot.

56 Semple 1993, 208.

57 UC cl. 336.

58 UC cl. 343–4.

59 UC cl. 345.

60 UC cl. 348.

61 UC cl. 346.

62 39 Geo. III, c. 114, § 23.

63 Semple 1993, 192–217.

64 Bentham to Long, 17 August 1799, in Bentham, ed. Dinwiddy 1984, 188–9. Bentham arrived at this figure by examining the number of convicts then confined to English gaols and hulks.

65 Long to Bentham, 25 March 1800, in Bentham, ed. Dinwiddy 1984, 279.

66 'Copy of a Treasury Minute, of the 13th August 1800', in Lambert ed. 1975, vol. cxviii. 585 reasoned that 'the Number of Years which have elapsed since the first Steps were taken … the improved State of the Colony of New South Wales … the various Improvements which have taken place in the different Gaols of this Kingdom; and the great Increase of Terms which Mr. Bentham now proposes' meant the panopticon could potentially be set aside.

67 Long to Bentham, 24 March 1801, in Bentham, ed. Dinwiddy 1984, 382–3. Bentham had unofficially learned in September 1800 of the reduction in the scale of the panopticon when 'by accident' he met John King, who told him it 'was as good as settled that I was to have but 500' convicts: Bentham to Nepean, 10 September 1800, in ibid. 352.

68 UC cxxi. 165 (7 January 1802).

69 Causer 2019.

70 'Letter to Lord Pelham' in Bentham, ed. Causer and Schofield 2022, 92. See also where Bentham refers to 'imported blessings – idle hulks and equally idle gaols – the foundation, of a sort of *national debt*, appears thus to be laying, if not already laid' in New South Wales at ibid, 155.

71 Bentham to Étienne Dumont, 29 August 1802, and Bentham to Charles Abbot, 4 September 1802, in Bentham, ed. Dinwiddy 1988, 94–5, 102–3. See also Causer 2019, 10–11.

72 See Bentham to Evan Nepean, 22 February 1791; Nepean to Bentham, 28 February 1791; and Bentham to Nepean, 14 February 1793, in Bentham, ed. Milne 1981a, 239–41, 257–8, 420.

73 'Second Letter to Lord Pelham' in Bentham, ed. Causer and Schofield 2022, 247.

74 'Third Letter to Lord Pelham' in Bentham, ed. Causer and Schofield 2022, 251.

75 'Third Letter to Lord Pelham' in Bentham, ed. Causer and Schofield 2022, 254.

76 Bentham to Hobhouse, 15 January 1803, Bentham, ed. Dinwiddy 1988, 189.

77 I am grateful to Philip Schofield, who transcribed the 'Dispensing Power' manuscripts, and to Chris Riley, who assembled the transcripts into a tentative order.

78 By a 'dispensing power' Bentham referred to the prerogative or discretionary power of the Crown to allow exemptions from the provisions of statutes. In the Bill of Rights of 1688 (1 Will. and Mar., Sess. 2, c. 2), the first complaint about the conduct of James VII of Scotland and II of England was of his having assumed and exercised 'a Power of dispensing with and suspending of Laws, and the Execution of Laws, without Consent of Parliament', such as when he had allowed Catholics to take command of army regiments without having to swear the oath provided for by the English Test Act of 1673 (25 Car. II, c. 2) or the Scottish Test Act of 1681. According to Bentham the establishment of New South Wales had violated, amongst other things, the Bill of Rights: see 'A Plea for the Constitution' in Bentham, ed. Causer and Schofield 2022, 384–8. I am grateful to Ian Williams for making this connection.

79 UC cxvi. 502.

80 Semple 1993, 225.

81 Portland to the Lords Commissioners of the Treasury, 14 October 1799, The National Archives, Kew (hereafter TNA), HO 42/48, fos. 182–3.

82 According to UC cxxi. 52–3, during an audience at the Home Office in October 1800, John King entered with 'a Manuscript book in folio in his hand. What I am doing (says he) is not usual, nor quite regular: here in this page you will find a copy of the letter: I leave the book with you, while I go about other business. Pen ink and paper was on the table. It is every thing to me (says I) I hope I am at liberty to take notes of it. Notes? Yes: says he: – as you please: only but not a copy. – Accordingly what I have taken, is not a copy. It is no more than what I have intitled it an Extract.' This 'Extract', in Bentham's hand, is at British Library (hereafter BL) Add. MS 33,543, fos. 143–4. Copies are at UC cxvi. 387 (in Bentham's hand), and at UC cxvi. 400 and UC cxxi. 220 (in the hands of copyists).

83 Bentham to Dumont, 29 August 1802, in Bentham, ed. Dinwiddy 1988, 97–8.

84 Bentham, ed. Dinwiddy 1988, 97.

85 UC cxx. 416–18.

86 UC cxxi. 384; UC cxx. 473.

87 UC cxxi. 419. Bentham alludes to his allegation that Portland had sabotaged his efforts to establish the panopticon, on the grounds of a secret promise he had made to Robert Grosvenor (1767–1845), styled Viscount Belgrave, who on 5 August 1802 had succeeded as second Earl Grosvenor, that the prison would not be built on land adjacent to his estate. See, for instance, UC cxx. 46–56.

88 UC cxxi. 541.

89 Romilly to Bentham, 1 November 1802, in Bentham, ed. Dinwiddy 1988, 154–5. See also Bentham to Dumont, 29 August 1802, in ibid., 97–8, where Bentham conceded that 'Romilly, though agreeing with me so completely on all the points of law, yet has no hope of success from any of them' (ibid., 98).

90 'Third Letter to Lord Pelham' in Bentham, ed. Causer and Schofield 2022, 273–4.

91 'Third Letter to Lord Pelham' in Bentham, ed. Causer and Schofield 2022, 275.

92 'Third Letter to Lord Pelham' in Bentham, ed. Causer and Schofield 2022, 283.

93 The reports were published in Neild 1802, 307–19, where the date of both visits is given as 16 March 1802. The manuscript of their report on the Portsmouth hulks is dated 16 March 1802, and that on the Langstone Harbour hulks 18 March 1802: see Mildmay to Pelham, 23 March 1802, TNA, HO 42/65, fos. 85–6.

94 Henry Addington (1757–1844), later Viscount Sidmouth, leader of the administration as First Lord of the Treasury and Chancellor of the Exchequer 1801–4, Home Secretary 1812–22.

95 'Third Letter to Lord Pelham' in Bentham, ed. Causer and Schofield 2022, 284.

96 'Third Letter to Lord Pelham' in Bentham, ed. Causer and Schofield 2022, 285.

97 UC cxvi. 518.

98 'Third Letter to Lord Pelham' in Bentham, ed. Causer and Schofield 2022, 286. For Chapple's letter, dated 24 February 1802, see Neild 1802, 321.

99 Neild 1802, 321.

100 'Third Letter to Lord Pelham' in Bentham, ed. Causer and Schofield 2022, 285.

101 'Third Letter to Lord Pelham' in Bentham, ed. Causer and Schofield 2022, 287.

102 'Third Letter to Lord Pelham' in Bentham, ed. Causer and Schofield 2022, 287–8.

103 'Third Letter to Lord Pelham' in Bentham, ed. Causer and Schofield 2022, 288.

104 42 Geo. III, c. 28.

105 The appointment of an inspector of the hulks had first been recommended at the end of 1778: see 'Report from the Committee who were Appointed to Consider the Several Returns, Which Have Been Made to the Order of the House of Commons, Of the 16th Day of December 1778, "That there be laid before this House, an Account of the Persons convicted of Felonies or Misdemeanors, and now under Sentence of Imprisonment, in the Gaols and Houses of Correction in the City of London etc', in Lambert ed. 1975, vol. xxxi. 388.

106 'Third Letter to Lord Pelham' in Bentham, ed. Causer and Schofield 2022, 289.

107 'Third Letter to Lord Pelham' in Bentham, ed. Causer and Schofield 2022, 290.

108 UC cxvi. 511–12.

109 Fitzpatrick to Pelham, 9 June 1802, TNA, HO 42/65, fos. 185–7. Graham had clashed with Fitzpatrick in January 1802, having 'been obliged to talk very seriously' with him 'in consequence of his haranguing people at Taverns upon the State of Convicts – whose

Friend he styles himself': see Graham to King, 17 January 1802, TNA, HO 42/65, fo. 174. For Fitzpatrick's career, see Blanco 1976, 402–21.

110 'Third Letter to Lord Pelham' in Bentham, ed. Causer and Schofield 2022, 292.

111 'Third Letter to Lord Pelham' in Bentham, ed. Causer and Schofield 2022, 291.

112 'Third Letter to Lord Pelham' in Bentham, ed. Causer and Schofield 2022, 292.

113 UC cxvi. 526.

114 42 Geo. III, c. 76, § 9.

115 UC cxvi. 505.

116 'Third Letter to Lord Pelham' in Bentham, ed. Causer and Schofield 2022, 293, 311.

117 'Third Letter to Lord Pelham' in Bentham, ed. Causer and Schofield 2022, 295.

118 'Third Letter to Lord Pelham' in Bentham, ed. Causer and Schofield 2022, 296; UC cxvi. 504.

119 'Third Letter to Lord Pelham' in Bentham, ed. Causer and Schofield 2022, 296, 299. See Joseph Helby, foreman at Portsmouth Dockyard, to Bentham, 26 December 1802, which is reproduced at ibid., 298 n. The original, with Bentham's pencil emendations, is at UC cxvi. 397.

120 'Third Letter to Lord Pelham' in Bentham, ed. Causer and Schofield 2022, 297. For a biography of Graham, see *The Annual Biography and Obituary, for the Year 1820*, iv. 402–22.

121 'Third Letter to Lord Pelham' in Bentham, ed. Causer and Schofield 2022, 298.

122 'Third Letter to Lord Pelham' in Bentham, ed. Causer and Schofield 2022, 299.

123 UC cxvi. 511.

124 'Third Letter to Lord Pelham' in Bentham, ed. Causer and Schofield 2022, 299.

125 Hadfield was discharged from the *Captivity* to his freedom on 14 July 1808. A copy of his letter 'directed to Bagot Ball' at Chester Castle, perhaps a fellow convict, is at BL Add. MS 33,543, fos. 644–5.

126 'Third Letter to Lord Pelham' in Bentham, ed. Causer and Schofield 2022, 301.

127 'Third Letter to Lord Pelham' in Bentham, ed. Causer and Schofield 2022, 300–1.

128 Bentham to Bunbury, 10 June 1803, Bentham, ed. Dinwiddy 1988, 238.

129 'Economy as applied to Office' in Bentham, ed. Schofield 1989, 4, 16, 79, 87–8.

130 Evans 1983.

131 *The Annual Biography and Obituary, for the Year 1820*, iv. 403. According to Wilkinson 2003, 131, Graham had done 'secret service' work for the Home Office.

132 Wells 1983, 92–6.

133 See Graham to King, 29 December 1800, TNA, HO 42/55, fos. 233–4.

134 *The Annual Biography and Obituary, for the Year 1820*, iv. 404.

135 See, for instance, Graham's report on the *Lion*, 17 February 1801, TNA, HO 42/61, fos. 156–7.

136 Graham to King (Private), *c*. February 1802, TNA, HO 42/61, fo. 137.

137 See Nicholas Vansittart to John King, 24 August 1801, TNA, HO 42/57, fo. 197.

138 Graham to King, 26 August 1801, TNA, HO 42/62, fos. 430–2.

139 See, for instance, Graham to King, 30 November 1801, TNA, HO 42/62, fo. 562.

140 'The Report of Aaron Graham, Esq. Inspector of Convicts in the River Thames and at Portsmouth', 4 February 1803, *Journals of the House of Commons* (1802–3), vol. lviii. 790–1.

141 Graham to King, 10 December 1801, TNA, HO 42/62, fo. 584.

142 Graham to King[?], 11 December 1801, TNA, HO 42/62, fos. 590–2.

143 Graham to King, 19 January 1802, 23 January 1802, and 17 January 1802, TNA, HO 42/65, fos. 166, 171, 173.

144 Graham to King[?], 19 December 1801, TNA, HO 42/62, fos. 619–20.

145 See *Journals of the House of Commons* (1802–3), vol. lviii. 124, 790–1. Bentham seems to have been kept apprised of Graham's activities, having received on 4 February 1803 a note from James Mitchell, Assistant Deliverer of the Vote at the House of Commons, informing him of the report's appearance: see Bentham, ed. Dinwiddy 1988, 197.

146 See Graham's regulations in 'Third Report from the Committee on the Laws Relating to Penitentiary Houses', *Commons Sessional Papers* (1812), vol. ii. 383–2, as well as the slightly different version reproduced at *The Annual Biography and Obituary, for the Year 1820*, iv. 411–19.

147 For what was probably the report alluded to, as well as for detailed returns for the south coast hulks for 1 April 1802 to 30 June 1802, see TNA, HO 42/65, fos. 78–9, and 2–58.

148 *Journals of the House of Commons* (1802–3), vol. lviii. 790.

149 *Journals of the House of Commons* (1802–3), vol. lviii. 790–1.

150 Neild to Bentham, 17 February 1803, in Bentham, ed. Dinwiddy 1988, 203–4. The original letter, addressed to Sir Henry Mildmay and dated 24 January 1803, is at UC cxvii. 252, with a partial copy at BL Add. MS 33,544, fos. 14–15. Lee had been convicted of forgery at Worcester on 6 March 1802 and sentenced to 14 years' transportation. He was received aboard the *Portland* in June 1802, where he remained until embarked upon the *Calcutta* which sailed for Port Phillip on 24 April 1803: see Convict hulks moored at Portsmouth: Portland, Captivity, Leviathan. Register of Prisoners, TNA, HO 9/8, fo. 34.

151 Lee to Mildmay, 24 January 1803, UC cxvii. 252.

152 Carter to Mildmay, 13 February 1803, BL Add. MS 33,544, fo. 32. Neild had also forwarded this letter to Bentham.

153 Bentham to Romilly, Bentham, ed. Dinwiddy 1988, 208. Bentham's source for the Woolwich hulks was the Reverend Dr Thomas Brownlow Forde, the ordinary of Newgate, with whom Bentham corresponded during late 1802 and early 1803 (see Bentham, ed. Dinwiddy 1988, 171, 173, 176–7, 181–2, and 182–5). When Bentham wrote to Bunbury on 10 June 1803 (ibid., 237–8), forwarding an unsent draft of a letter to Wilberforce (ibid, 212–14), the former was docketed 'Dr Ford's intelligence of sexual irregularities in the Hulks'. The 'intelligence' itself has not been located.

   Similar allegations about the Thames hulks had been made in 'The Hulks at Woolwich', a paper apparently written by a Joseph Macoul, which on 19 March 1802 had been forwarded to Pelham by Robert Albion Cox, Sheriff of London: see TNA, HO 42/65, fos. 91–102. In his paper Macoul condemned the hulks as a 'Seminary of Vice, starvation, and destruction', and made allegations about convicts' bodies being dumped in shallow graves in the mud of the Thames, about disease and mortality, 'unnatural proceedings', and about prisoners who had become hardened and in 'contempt of Death'. Sheriff Cox, in his forwarding letter, suggested that the paper contained 'a great deal of Truth'.

154 Bentham, ed. Dinwiddy 1988, 208, 212.

155 i.e. Henry Addington, the leader of the administration.

156 Bentham to Wilberforce, *c.* 7 March 1803, Bentham, ed. Dinwiddy 1988, 212.

157 Bentham to Romilly, Bentham, ed. Dinwiddy 1988, 208.

158 Bentham to Bunbury, 10 June 1803, Bentham, ed. Dinwiddy 1988, 237.

159 Wilberforce to Bentham, 7 May 1810, Bentham, ed. Conway 1988, 64.

160 *Journals of the House of Commons* (1810–11), vol. lxvi. 144.

161 For Bentham's dealings with the Penitentiary Committee, see Semple 1993, 263–78. For the Committee's reports, see *Commons Sessional Papers* (1810–11), vol. iii. 567–689, iii. 691–702, and (1812) ii. 363–422.

162 Bentham to Dumont, 22 February 1813, Bentham, ed. Conway 1988, 308.

163 Bentham to Sidmouth, 17 September 1812, Bentham, ed. Conway 1988, 263–82.

164 Semple 1993, 278.

165 Bentham to Sidmouth, 17 September 1812, Bentham, ed. Conway 1988, 277.

166 Bentham to Sidmouth, 17 September 1812, Bentham, ed. Conway 1988, 277–9; *Commons Sessional Papers* (1812), vol. ii. 374–5.

167 *Commons Sessional Papers* (1812), vol. ii. 381.

168 Bentham to Sidmouth, 17 September 1812, Bentham, ed. Conway 1988, 279–80.

169 In 1823 Capper was allowed to employ his nephew Robert as his clerk, and together they ran the hulks until 1847 when both resigned following a critical report: see 'Inquiry into the state of the convict establishment at Woolwich. Report and Minutes of Evidence taken upon an inquiry into the general treatment and condition of the convicts in the Hulks at Woolwich', 28 May 1847, *Commons Sessional Papers* (1847), vol. xviii. 1–649.

Bibliography

Primary Sources

Archival sources

British Library Add. MS 33,543, Correspondence and papers of the family of Bentham ... 1651–1847, vol. vii. 1799–1802.

British Library Add. MS 33,544, Correspondence and papers of the family of Bentham ... 1651–1847, vol. viii. 1803–12.

National Archives UK, HO 9, Home Office: Convict Prison Hulks: Registers and Letter Books, 1802–49.

National Archives UK, HO 42, Home Office: Domestic Correspondence, 1782–1820.

UCL Library Special Collections, Bentham Papers.

Newspapers

Morning Chronicle.

Parliamentary papers

Commons Sessional Papers (1810), vol. iii.

Commons Sessional Papers (1812), vol. ii.

Commons Sessional Papers (1847), vol. xviii.

House of Commons Sessional Papers of the Eighteenth Century, ed. Sheila Lambert, 145 vols. Wilmington, DE: Scholarly Resources Inc., 1975.

Journals of the House of Commons (1777–8), vol. xxxvi.

Journals of the House of Commons (1802–3), vol. lviii.

Journals of the House of Commons (1810–11), vol. lxvi.

Printed sources

The Annual Biography and Obituary, for the Year 1820, vol. iv. London: Longman, Hurst, Rees, Orme, and Brown, 1820.

Barrington, G. *A Voyage to New South Wales*. London: George Barrington, 1795.

Bentham, J. 'A View of the Hard-Labour Bill'. London: T. Payne and Son, T. Cadell and P. Elmsley, and E. Brooke, 1778.

Bentham, J. *Panopticon versus New South Wales: or, The Panopticon Penitentiary System, and the Penal Colonization system, Compared*. London: Robert Baldwin, 1812.

Bentham, J. *The Works of Jeremy Bentham, published under the superintendence of ... John Bowring*, 11 vols. Edinburgh: William Tait, 1838–43.

Bentham, J. *The Correspondence of Jeremy Bentham, Volume 2: 1752–76*, ed. T.L.S. Sprigge. London: The Athlone Press, 1968.

Bentham, J. *The Correspondence of Jeremy Bentham, Volume 4: October 1788 to December 1793*, ed. A.T. Milne. London: The Athlone Press, 1981a.

Bentham, J. *The Correspondence of Jeremy Bentham, Volume 5: January 1794 to December 1797*, ed. A.T. Milne. London: The Athlone Press, 1981b.

Bentham, J. *The Correspondence of Jeremy Bentham, Volume 6: January 1798 to December 1801*, ed. J.R. Dinwiddy. Oxford: Clarendon Press, 1984.

Bentham, J. *The Correspondence of Jeremy Bentham, Volume 7: January 1802 to December 1808*, ed. J.R. Dinwiddy. Oxford: Clarendon Press, 1988a.

Bentham, J. *The Correspondence of Jeremy Bentham, Volume 8: January 1809 to December 1816*, ed. S. Conway. Oxford: Clarendon Press, 1988b.

Bentham, J. *First Principles Preparatory to Constitutional Code*, ed. P. Schofield. Oxford: Clarendon Press, 1989.

Bentham, J. *Panopticon versus New South Wales and other writings on Australia*, ed. T. Causer and P. Schofield. London: UCL Press, 2022.

Campbell, D. *Convict Transportation and the Metropolis: Letterbooks and Papers of Duncan Campbell, 1726–1803*. Marlborough: Adam Matthew Publications, 2005.

Neild, J. *An Account of the rise, progress, and present state, of the society for the discharge and relief of persons imprisoned for small debts throughout England and Wales.* London: Nichols and Son, 1802.

Secondary Sources

Blanco, R.L. 'The Soldier's Friend – Sir Jeremiah Fitzpatrick, Inspector for Health of Land Forces', *Medical History* 20 (1976): 402–21.

Branch Johnston, W. *The English Prison Hulks.* London: Phillimore & Co., 1970 [1957].

Campbell, C. *The Intolerable Hulks: British Shipboard Confinement, 1776–1857,* 3rd ed. Tucson, AZ: Fenestra Books, 2001.

Carey, H.M. *Empire of Hell: Religion and the Campaign to End Convict Transportation in the British Empire, 1788–1875.* Cambridge: Cambridge University Press, 2019.

Causer, T. '"The Evacuation of That Scene of Wickedness and Wretchedness": Jeremy Bentham, the Panopticon, and New South Wales, 1802-3', *Journal of Australian Colonial History* 21 (2019): 1–24.

Devereaux, S. 'The Making of the Penitentiary Act, 1775–1779', *The Historical Journal* 42 (1999): 405–33.

Ekirch, A.R. *Bound for America: The Transportation of British Convicts to the Colonies, 1718–1775.* Oxford: Clarendon Press, 1990.

Evans, C.D. 'Aaron Graham', *Dictionary of Canadian Biography,* vol. v., 1983. http://www.biographi.ca/en/bio/graham_aaron_5E.html. [accessed 12 June 2021].

Frost, A. *Botany Bay: The Real Story.* Collingwood: Black Inc., 2012.

Garvey, N. *The Celebrated George Barrington: A Spurious Author, the Book Trade, and Botany Bay.* Sydney: Hordern House, 2008.

Hume, L.J. 'Bentham's Panopticon: An Administrative History – I', *Historical Studies* 15 (1973): 703–21.

Jackson, R.V. 'Luxury in Punishment', *Australian Historical Studies* 23: 90 (1988): 42–59.

James, J. '"Raising Sand, Soil and Gravel": Pardon Refusers On-Board Prison Hulks (1776–1815)', *Family & Community History* 20 (2017): 3–24.

Maxwell-Stewart, H. 'Transportation from Britain and Ireland, 1615–1875'. In *A Global History of Convicts and Penal Colonies,* ed. C. Anderson, 183–210. London: Bloomsbury Academic, 2018.

McKay, A.L. 'The History of the British Prison Hulks, 1776–1864', PhD thesis, University of Leicester, 2020.

Morgan, G. and Rushton, P. *Eighteenth-Century Criminal Transportation: The Formation of the Criminal Atlantic.* Basingstoke: Palgrave Macmillan, 2004.

Oldham, W. *Britain's Convicts to the Colonies.* Sydney: Library of Australian History, 1990.

Schofield, P. '"The First Steps Rightly Directed in the Track of Legislation": Jeremy Bentham on Cesare Beccaria's *Essay on Crimes and Punishments*', *Diciottesimo secolo* 4 (2019): 65–74.

Semple, J. *Bentham's Prison: A Study of the Panopticon Penitentiary.* Oxford: Clarendon Press, 1993.

Wells, R. *Insurrection: The British Experience 1795–1803.* Gloucester: Sutton Publishing, 1983.

Wilkinson, D. *The Duke of Portland: Politics and Party in the Age of George III.* Basingstoke: Palgrave Macmillan, 2003.

Index

Note. The following is an index of names of persons and places, and subjects, appearing in the text and notes of the chapters in this volume; the last are indicated by 'n'. Under Bentham's name, only references to his other works are indicated. 'Britain', 'England', 'Australia', 'New South Wales' are referred to so frequently throughout the volume they do not appear in the index.

Lightning Source UK Ltd.
Milton Keynes UK
UKHW021453040522
402466UK00002B/8